The Tropics of Empire

Transformations: Studies in the History of Science and Technology

Jed Z. Buchwald, general editor

The Tropics of Empire

WHY COLUMBUS
SAILED SOUTH
TO THE INDIES

Nicolás Wey Gómez

THE MIT PRESS   Cambridge, Massachusetts   London, England

Publication of this work was supported in part by the 2007 Premio Grinzane Editoria, awarded to the MIT Press in May 2007 by Premio Grinzane Cavour.

For information about special quantity discounts, please email special_sales@mitpress.mit.edu

This book was set in Scala and Scala Sans by Graphic Composition, Inc., Bogart, Georgia. Printed and bound in China.

Library of Congress Cataloging-in-Publication Data

Wey Gómez, Nicolás.
    The tropics of empire : why Columbus sailed south to the Indies / by Nicolás Wey Gómez.
      p. cm. — (Transformations: studies in the history of science and technology)
    Includes bibliographical references and index.
    ISBN 978-0-262-23264-7 (hardcover : alk. paper)
    1. Columbus, Christopher—Knowledge—Geography. 2. America—Discovery and exploration—Spanish. 3. Tropics—Geography. 4. Geography, Medieval. 5. Discoveries in geography—15th century. 6. Navigation—History. 7. Europe—Intellectual life—15th century. 8. Albertus, Magnus, Saint, 1193?–1280—Knowledge—Geography. 9. Ailly, Pierre d', 1350–1420?—Knowledge—Geography. 10. Casas, Bartolomé de las, 1474–1566—Knowledge—Geography. I. Title.

E112.W48 2008
980'.013092—dc22

                                                                              2007020947

10 9 8 7 6 5 4 3 2 1

For María Eugenia, Marcelo, and Luis; and other travelers seized with wonder.

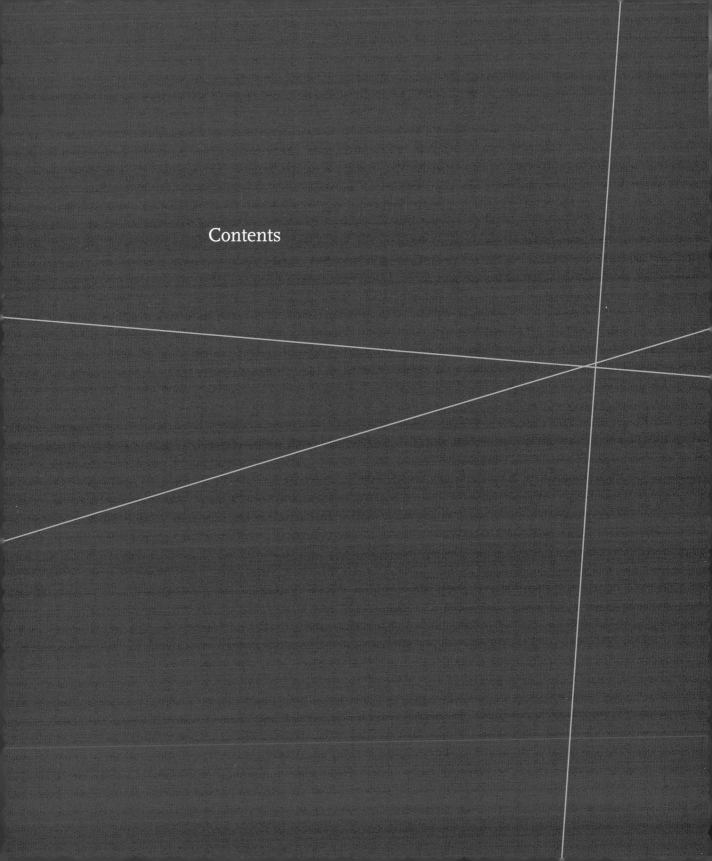

Contents

Figures

Preface

Everyone knows that in 1492 Christopher Columbus confounded learned opinion by seeking a western route to the East across the Atlantic. Almost nobody seems to notice that Columbus also intended to sail *south* to a tropical part of the globe that he and his contemporaries had some reason to identify initially as legendary India. Indeed, the early transatlantic encounter was not just meant to be a rendezvous between east and west. It was also meant to be a rendezvous between north and south. The present book attempts to explain why Columbus also sailed south to the Indies and how his doing so ultimately contributed to the process of European expansion we know as the Age of Exploration.

Columbus's turn to the south obeyed complex assumptions concerning the relation between the concept of latitude and the nature of places. And, although the Discoverer himself may not have been the schooled individual his early biographers once led us to believe, he did share these assumptions with a learned scientific and technical tradition that conceived of place as the basis for explaining and predicting the constitution and behavior of all creatures in the "machine" of the cosmos. The assumptions Columbus carried with him as he sailed south concerning the nature of the lands and peoples he

sought to find were of pivotal importance for the development of the complex ideas and practices we associate with early modern colonialism.

Columbus drew a fundamental distinction between the lands and peoples in the higher, and traditionally cooler, latitudes of Mediterranean Europe and those he intended to find as he sailed south into the lower, and traditionally hotter, latitudes of the globe. This geographical distinction enabled him to believe not only that he was about to venture into the most sizable and wealthiest lands of the globe but also that the peoples he would encounter in those latitudes were bound to possess a nature—ranging from "childish" to "monstrous"—that seemed to justify rendering them Europe's subjects or slaves. The political lessons he drew from the geographical distinction between a "temperate" north (Europe) and a "hot" south (the Bahamas and Caribbean basin) provided critical legitimacy to the process of territorial expansion that his contemporaries were consciously coming to construe as the "invention" or discovery of the immensely productive region of the globe then known as the "torrid zone." This book studies the complex nexus between place and colonialism in Columbus's invention of the American tropics.

Such a task requires an important shift in our understanding of the cosmographical ideas that Columbus is supposed to have culled at one time or another from his reading of ancient and medieval geographers. I examine those ideas believed by Americanists to underlie his claim that he was bound to reach habitable lands somewhere in the high Atlantic, whether they were part of Asia or not. The present book draws new attention to the nature of the official debate that Columbus's proposal to the Spanish Crown precipitated in the years preceding the discovery. We shall move from existing testimony of this debate, to Columbus's annotations on the books now counted as part of his "library," to his *Diario,* letters, and other documents, and to the seminal intellectual portraits of Columbus contained in the biography attributed to his son Ferdinand and in the account of the discovery and colonization of the Indies rendered by the humanitarian friar Bartolomé de las Casas. Columbus's project is best understood in the context of a confrontation between two divergent but equally complex ways of interpreting one and the same body of scientific and technical knowledge, geographical literature, and fresh information afforded by the exploration of Atlantic Africa. These two inimical modes of interpretation—equally concerned with theological and philosophical correctness in the assessment of old and new geographical facts—provide a crucial roadmap for reading Columbus's most famous postils to the works he read, his own statements

as a cosmographer, and the early intellectual portraits that have largely shaped our understanding of his enterprise.

Columbus's project was forged between two diametrically opposed explanations about how earth and water had come to be lodged at the center of the cosmos and about how life had come to be allocated in the region of the four elements. First, his opponents in the royal council appointed to evaluate his proposal argued that the sphere of water was eccentric with respect to the sphere of earth, which meant that the continental masses formed an unrepeatable "island" surrounded by the abyss of an otherwise watery globe. But Columbus and his supporters argued that water was concentric with respect to earth, which meant that Africa, Asia, and Europe were the result of imperfections in the earth's sphere that, for the sake of physical and geometrical balance, were bound to occur elsewhere around the globe. In other words, either the traditional *oikoumenē* extended far beyond the limits conventionally assigned by geographers, or Africa, Asia, and Europe did not necessarily account for all land around the globe. Second, Columbus's opponents, citing the theory of the so-called five zones today attributed to Parmenides, argued that the lonely island of the earth was besieged to the north and to the south by the inhospitable cold and heat of the arctic and equatorial zones. Columbus and his supporters contended, however, not only that the inhabited world extended farther east and west than many believed, but that it also extended north and south into the allegedly uninhabitable regions of the globe. Third, advocating the theory of the five zones, Columbus's opponents construed all geographical information old and new concerning inhabited places outside the temperate bounds of what they saw as the totality of the inhabited world as an example of nature's immoderacies and accidents. Columbus and his supporters, on the contrary, construed this same information as an indication that the terraqueous globe was far more universally fertile and hospitable than suspected. Finally, while Columbus's opponents represented an intellectual trend that had long construed the "marvels" and "monsters" of sub-Saharan Africa and the extended basin of the Indian Ocean as the antithesis of everything that accorded Mediterranean Europe a central place among nations, Columbus and his supporters represented an intellectual trend that, certainly still construing "Ethiopia" and "India" as exotic, was still willing to concede the fact that Mediterranean Europe might actually be geographically liminal to a vast inhabited world extending south into the tropics.

It is as part of an intellectual and material culture that was beginning to reimagine sub-Saharan Africa and the extended basin of the Indian Ocean as a herculean

landscape, brimming with natural and human resources, that one can properly explain why Columbus thought of sailing west and *south* to a region of the world that he and his contemporaries labeled "the parts of India." And, as we shall see, it is in the rift between two opposing perceptions of the belt of the tropics that one can more fully explain Columbus's often paradoxical certainties concerning the lands and peoples he had set out to encounter. His are the certainties of a culture intent on remaining the moral center of an expanding geography that was slowly relegating Europe to the northern fringes of the orb.

Acknowledgments

Last spring, a friend summed up fifteen years of conversation about Columbus by pointing to a line spoken by Captain Barbossa, the pirate lord in Disney's film sequel *Pirates of the Caribbean: At World's End* (2007): "'For certain, you have to be lost to find a place that can't be found, elseways everyone would know where it was.'" This bit of roguish wisdom, uttered as Barbossa steers ship and friends over the ocean's edge to survey the Land of the Dead, speaks directly to the saga of Christopher Columbus, whose tenacious disorientation definitively reacquainted the Old World with the Americas. But it also speaks more generally to the surrender of self required by all truly exploratory journeys, personal or collective: we must be willing to lose track of ourselves if we really wish to discover something new about us or about the world. This book has been that sort of journey for me. And the key to finding my way to that new place in myself and the world has been largely to learn to stop for directions from those who happened already to know where they were standing at the time our paths crossed. So it is that fifteen years of being lost to Columbus—since I began grasping for a dissertation topic in graduate school—have earned me many marvelous debts.

This book could simply not have been written without my series editor, Jed Z. Buchwald. A writer's dream, Jed took on this project long before I understood the story it was asking to tell, taught me how to think as a historian, and then freed me to write that story down as it had to be written. His wife, Diana L. Kormos-Buchwald, and his parents, Evie and Bernie Buchwald, wholeheartedly signed up for the ride. Jed's colleagues at the California Institute of Technology have made my summers writing in Pasadena the happiest of my career, especially Mordechai Feingold, whose kindness and serenity are unshakable, and Kristine Haugen and George Pigman III, who devoted eons of precious time to rewriting my barbarous Latin and nonexistent Greek and who answered many a question about the ancient works mentioned here. I am also grateful to Susan Davis, John B. Geasland, the late Sanja Ilic, Dominic Murphy, Carol W. Readhead, and Robert S. Rosenstone for making me feel so welcome at the Institute. Other members of Caltech's community provided precious logistical support for this book, including Robin M. Bonitz, the late Michael Butler, Ginevra Crosignani, Orlando Dungca, Barbara Estrada, Lisa Keppel, Victoria Mason, and Gail Nash.

Learning one's field means, to my mind, growing to observe at least the major constraints that govern any statement one might bring to bear upon it. From this admittedly vague viewpoint, interdisciplinarity entails learning to steer one's course between sets of constraints one can at best come to observe from a somewhat skewed perspective. Without providential coaching from scholars in diverse fields, I could hardly have pieced together a study purporting to outline the complex knowledge system that informed the early transatlantic encounter. Peter Hulme, who wrote one of my favorite books on Caribbean history and literature, encouraged me from the start to think about Columbus's conspicuous southing in terms of that Western malaise we have come to know as tropicality. The late Lily E. Kay rallied for me to work as a historian of science, and she urged me to apply for a fellowship at the Dibner Institute for the History of Science and Technology in Cambridge, Massachusetts—a turning point in my career as a scholar. A fine reader for Stanford University Press thoughtfully impressed upon me at the time I worked at the Dibner Institute that my journey with Columbus was not quite over, but that it was well worth faithfully trailing to the end. Helen S. Lang offered priceless insight into Aristotle's philosophy and its assimilation to the Latin West, particularly where his ideas about nature and place are concerned. The late Richard Lemay urged me to think about place at the intersection between Aristotle and astrology. James Muldoon offered invaluable feedback on the legal framework surrounding the relationship between the papacy and infidels. The late Helen Rand

Parish, whose dedication to Bartolomé de las Casas and humanitarianism was maximally contagious, understood long before I did that a learned Las Casas was the treasure map to Columbus's thought. Alison Sandman, for her part, taught me to visualize space as a geographer and cartographer. At the risk of heresy, I should also confess that the author who first opened my eyes to the myriad possibilities of interdisciplinary research was the late Lynn Thorndike, who passed away years before I even learned the alphabet, but whose *History of Magic and Experimental Science* (Columbia University Press, 1923) devoured many hours of guilt-ridden wandering for my doctoral dissertation on Columbus and Pierre d'Ailly.

A number of scholars have kindly read drafts of this book, offering their suggestions and heartiest encouragement: Mario Biagioli, who rooted for my work on scholastic cosmology long before this book was conceived; Jorge Cañizares Esguerra, whose unconventional historiography has shed unprecedented light on the early transatlantic world; Anthony Grafton, who generously blessed this book for publication; Katharine Park, who, understanding more than anyone my mania for Albertus Magnus and the wonders of his world, invited me last spring to conduct new research in the Department of the History of Science at Harvard University; Consuelo Varela, whose rigor as an editor and scholar of the discovery continues to inspire an entire generation of early Americanists; and Margarita Zamora, whose work on the corporate authorship of the *Diario* was fundamental to my own meditation on the dialogue between Las Casas and Columbus. Other colleagues were equally benevolent to various chapters of this book, including Carol Delaney, Felipe Fernández-Armesto, Snait Gissis, Arne Hessenbruch, Frederick Luciani, Victoria Morse, Rosario Ramos, and Benjamin Weiss. In addition, Betsey Barker-Price, Jeffrey E. Brower, Alfonso Gómez-Lobo, David C. Lindberg, John McGinnis, and the late David Woodward answered vital questions in the course of this research. And who could ever find the words to thank this book's godparents among the Hispanists? I shall remain forever grateful to Roberto González Echevarría, E. Michael Gerli, Eduardo González, and Diana de Armas Wilson for voicing their fiercest support for this book at every stage of its production.

Numerous people at the institutions where I have worked since graduate school provided unimaginable support toward the completion of this book. It was at MIT that I came into my own as a scholar. Anyone who has worked at the Institute will understand what a natural playground it is for someone willing to venture beyond the boundaries of his or her field of training. Administrators, colleagues, and friends alike encouraged me from the start to engage in such a miraculous venture, and they have continued their unflagging support long after my years at the Institute. In the Foreign Languages and Literatures Section, I am particularly grateful to Margery Resnick for so generously sharing her dreams and family with me; to Isabelle de Courtivron and Edward Baron Turk for their loving mentorship and friendship; to Jane Dunphy, Nancy Lowe, and Monica Totten for always listening with their hearts; to Jing Wang for her wise encouragement; to Ellen Crocker, Kurt Fendt, Adriana Gutiérrez, Margarita Groeger, Douglas Morgenstern, and Emma Teng for their warm trust in me as a colleague; and to all staff members of FL&L, who made me proud to work in the section, mainly Cara Cheyette, Pamela Grimes, Lili Kepuska, Shannon McCord, and Andrew Roberts. A number of other colleagues and friends in the School of the Humanities, Arts, and Social Sciences have continued to rally the cause of this book throughout the years, most especially Suzanne Flynn, Mary Fuller, Jean Jackson, Louis Kampf, and Harriet Ritvo. I hope that the seeds of confidence that MIT planted in me will have borne some fruit with this finished work.

Brown University, and the Department of Hispanic Studies in particular, also helped me bring this work to its conclusion. Within the department, I am uniquely indebted to Antonio Carreño and Stephanie Merrim for their rigor as scholars, for their upright generosity as colleagues, for their dedication as teachers, and for their unfaltering faith in my work. Their example will always remind me that I have much to strive for as an educator. I also thank Beth Bauer, Nidia Schuhmacher, Victoria Smith, and Silvia Sobral, whose discipline, collegiality, and optimism remind me every day that our first and last duty as a department is service to our students. I have also been fortunate to come across two mentors I do not deserve, José Amor y Vázquez and Geoffrey Ribbans, who have never ceased looking out for Hispanic Studies. Needless to say, I shall always miss working with Christopher Conway, whose beatific generosity made my transition to Brown far easier than I could have anticipated. Without exception, our students in Hispanic Studies remind me daily of why I would be willing to embark again a thousand times over on a jittery journey with Columbus. A number of graduates and undergraduates have invited me to come along as they abandon themselves to their own journeys—among them, Dánisa Bonacic, Brian Brewer, Isis Burgos, Noah Gardiner, Chad Leahy, Arturo Márquez, Natalia Matta, Carmen Saucedo, Geoffrey Shullenberger, Jennifer Silverman, Jorge Terukina-Yamauchi, Charlotte Whittle, and Daniella Wittern. Our curator Patricia Figueroa played a crucial role in affording rare materials for my research. And no scholarly work would ever get done without the invisible machinations of those who ensure that departmental life runs smoothly: thank you, Marie Roderick and John O'Malley! Colleagues and friends across the Brown campus also lent special support and encouragement in the final, anguished phases of this project: Onésimo Almeida, Réda Bensmaia, Michel-André Bossy, Douglas Cope, Anne Fausto-Sterling, Norman Fiering, James Green, Susan Hirsch, Virginia Krause, Evelyn Lincoln, Catherine Lutz, Tara Nummedal, Amy Remensnyder, Joan Richards, Pierre Saint-Amand, Moshe Sluhovsky, Samuel Streit, Mark Swislocki, Esther Whitfield, and Edward Widmer. Finally, I thank Lynn Carlson in Geological Sciences for her meticulous work as a cartographer retracing Columbus's routes and reconstructing Eratosthenes' globe.

This book was written with financial and logistical support from numerous sources. A Senior Fellowship at the Dibner Institute for the History of Science and Technology (1998–1999) enabled me to change the course of this and future research. An Old Dominion Fellowship at the Massachusetts Institute of Technology allowed me to take the necessary time to conduct my work at the Dibner Institute. A Post-doctoral Fellowship of the National Endowment for the Humanities granted in that same year would have allowed me to acquaint myself much earlier than I did with the riches of the John Carter Brown Library at Brown University. The Class of 1954 Career Development Professorship I received at MIT (1999–2002) provided extraordinary funds that allowed me to travel and acquire the materials for this and future research. Funds in FL&L at MIT and in Hispanic Studies at Brown covered miscellaneous expenses for this book, including translations of Latin sources rendered by Robert Mac Donald and proofreading by Chad Leahy. A Kenyon Humanities Fellowship at Brown (Spring 2004) enabled one of our graduate students, Joanne Kedzierski, to format work in progress and to gather bibliography for future research. An Undergraduate Teaching and Research Award (UTRA) at Brown also afforded me the opportunity to collaborate with Brian Lee, who doctored numerous figures in this book and created stunning illustrations, some of which, alas, could not be included here. A leave granted by Brown last spring gave me the breathing space to meet production deadlines with the MIT Press while proceeding with new research. Lastly, the production of this work was supported in part by the 2007 Premio Grinzane Editoria, awarded to the MIT Press in May 2007 by Premio Grinzane Cavour.

I am most grateful to the Department of the History of Science at Harvard for my time there as a Visiting Researcher, particularly to Mario Biagioli, Janet Browne, Anne Harrington, and Katharine Park, whose conversation is lighting up new horizons for me; to Carole Broadbent, Signe Castro, Judith Lajoie, Dennis Olofson, and Richard Wright for making my daily work a true joy; to Michael Kelley for his technical help with last-minute illustrations; and to Temitope Oluwaseun Charlton and Justin Merrill Grosslight for sharing with me the excitement of their own projects. I also thank Ann Blair, Galen Brokaw, Joyce Chaplin, Tom Conley, and Diana Sorensen for the faith they have placed in my work.

Most recently, this book has found safe harbor with my colleagues in the Department of Spanish and Portuguese Languages and Cultures at Princeton University. I particularly thank Marina S. Brownlee and Angel G. Loureiro for their wisdom and encouragement.

In the span of over a decade, I enjoyed the great privilege of working in numerous libraries in Spain and the United States, some of which supplied various figures in this book. I wish to thank the following institutions and individuals: in Madrid, the Archivo de la Casa de Alba (especially José Manuel Calderón), the Biblioteca Nacional de España, the Museo Naval de Madrid (especially María Luisa Martín-Merás), and the Biblioteca de la Real Academia de la Historia. In Seville, the Archivo General de Indias and the Biblioteca Capitular y Colombina (especially Nuria Casquete de Prado Sagrera, director of the Institución Colombina). At Brown University, the John Carter Brown Library (especially Susan Danforth, Lynne A. Harrell, Richard Hurley, Heather Jespersen, Leslie Tobias Olsen, and Richard Ring), the John Hay Library (especially Ann Dodge, William S. Monroe, J. Andrew Moul, and Patricia Sirois), the John D. Rockefeller, Jr. Library, and the Sciences Library. At the California Institute of Technology, Dabney Humanities Library (especially Judith Nollar and Ruth A. Sustaita), the Institute Archives, and Millikan Library (especially Sandy Garstang, Shadye Peyvan, and John Wade). At the Dibner Institute, the Burndy Library. At Harvard University, the Andover-Harvard Theological Library, the Map Collection in Pusey Library, Houghton Library, and Widener Library. At MIT, Rotch Library and Hayden Library (especially Marie Cloutier, Michael Pavelecky, Andrew Thompson, and Theresa A. Tobin). In San Marino, California, the Huntington Library. Other libraries in Europe and the United States facilitated rare materials, granted permission to use other figures in this book, or provided crucial copyright information, including the Biblioteca Nazionale Centrale in Florence (special thanks to Paola Pirolo), the Biblioteca Nacional de Portugal in Lisbon, the British Library in London, the Germanisches Nationalmuseum in Nuremberg (special thanks to Ingrid Kassel), the Bibliothèque Nationale de France in Paris, and the Map Collection at the Library of Congress in Washington, D.C. A few publishers have also granted permission to use copyrighted materials for this book: the University of

Chicago Press; M. Moleiro Editor, S.A. in Barcelona (special thanks to Mónica Miró); Testimonio Compañía Editorial in Madrid (special thanks to Enrique Olmos); and Urs Graf Publishing Company in Dietikon-Zurich.

The MIT Press enthusiastically embraced the publication of this book. No effort was spared to give my work its best fighting chance, and I particularly cherish the support given by my acquisitions editor, Marguerite Avery, by the director of marketing and promotions, Gita Manaktala, by my production editor, Matthew Abbate, by my designer, Erin Hasley, and by Cristina Sanmartín, who appreciates the many detours it has taken to complete this journey. I also thank Thomas Kozachek for taming this book's prose.

Apologies are also due readers who may be insiders in fields with which I can claim at most a nodding acquaintance. I hope that the honest urgency with which I have written this story will somewhat attenuate the sins of fact and method often incurred by work between disciplines. I also apologize to the contributing authors of the splendid third volume of the History of Cartography, *Cartography in the European Renaissance* (University of Chicago Press, 2007), edited by the late David Woodward, which only reached my hands as this book was being sent to the typesetter. This has prevented me from doing full justice to studies that will take years to assimilate properly and that will remain a standard reference for all readers concerned with the Age of Exploration. Publication schedules have also prevented me from supplying one of the authors in that volume, Victoria Morse, with the title of the present book, which she thoughtfully cites by its provisional title, *The Machine of the World: Scholastic Cosmography and the Place of Native Peoples in the Early Caribbean Colonial Encounter.*

Needless to say, I also owe this book to more distant mentors whose lessons I have never forgotten. They include Jay Cantor, John T. Irwin, Patricia Khoury, Richard Macksey, Teresa Méndez-Faith, Nancy J. Peláez, Juan Manuel Pombo, John Russell-Wood, Harry Sieber, Robert Szulkin, Francis Wehri, O.S.B., Geoffrey Wolff, and Luis E. Yglesias.

Without my friends, this book's journey would have been intolerable. Livia Polanyi knows everything there is to know about total surrender not only to one's dreams but also to the dreams of one's friends. She knew that my soul rode on this book, and she never once stopped talking to Columbus on the trail for that soul. I am grateful to Martin van den Berg, my godson Mishka Kornai, and Ellen Zweig for joining us through the years in this conversation. In deed and in word, Silvia Unzueta has reminded me every day for twenty-five years that true courage is always heeding your conscience, no matter your fear and no matter the consequences. From María Antonia Garcés, I learned early on in graduate school that one's vocation is a marvelous palliative for travel's solitude.

And from Verónica Salles-Reese, the muse and sister who first suggested that I work on Columbus, I learned that unswerving loyalty to one's family and friends can be that solitude's actual cure. I owe the completion of my doctoral dissertation to Verónica and to our mutual friend Jorge Olivares. Jane Rabb, who urged on me the importance of following work routines, has provided plenty of chocolate and sympathy at her house in Cambridge to last us a lifetime. Brenda and Tanya Athanus, for their part, taught me along the way that hard traveling does not preclude good living. And my friend Maureen Costello blesses me every day with the constancy of a love that reaches far beyond life and loving. John P. Manis patiently endured a decade of foundering and discovery on my part. Sam Schweber, who has frequently advanced the cause of this book, is finally persuading me that there is some justice in the world, if only we care to look for it in the right places. And I shall never forget that Urmila Seshagiri was willing to shower endless love and intelligence on the most difficult pages of this book. I am also grateful to friends who have shared, at one time or another, the joys and sadnesses of this process: Rolena Adorno, the late David Adorno, Inés Alcalde, Ignacio Atienza, Nicolás Bermúdez, Catalina Berti, Michael A. Carver and his daughter Ellie, Peter Dunn, Ricardo Gaviria, Peter Halstad, James Iffland, Juan Carlos Isaza, Aldo Mazzucchelli, Sarita Nori, Helena Otero, Alan Reese, María V. Rivera, María Helena Rueda, Juanita Sanz de Santamaría, Libby Schweber, Yvonne Senouf, Mallikarjun Shankar, Amy Storrow, Edwin Tait, Angela Uribe, Maureen Whalen, and Felipe Zuleta.

And, finally, what would become of us travelers if we did not have those back home to count the days since we embarked on life's adventure? This book is dedicated to my family back in the tropics of our beloved Colombia, especially to my mother Tatiana Gómez Durán, who has always known to follow her dreams to the end of the world; to my stepfather Alvaro Cabrera Galvis, who has made room in his own dreams to ride with us all to world's end; to my brother Santiago Cabrera Gómez, who is bravely testing the waters of his own magical musing; to my clairvoyant sister Natalia, who has taught me that one need not leave one's home to have traveled the world or invented new ones; and to my brother-in-law José Matiz Filella, who shares my sister's wisdom. I also thank my father, Nicolás Wey Vall-Serra, his wife Florencia, and my siblings Paul, Jack, and Helen Christine for waiting at the other end of this journey. Last but never least, I offer this book in gratitude to my grandmother Lucía Durán Bravo. Without her liberating understanding of comedy's marriage to tragedy, life itself would be unthinkable.

Acknowledgments

Introduction:

Why Columbus Sailed South to the Indies

Latitudes, however, are more significant for the diversity of lands than longitudes.

Averroës, on Aristotle's *Meteorologica*

A centuries-old tradition on the discovery of the Americas maintains that Columbus sailed *west* across the Atlantic Ocean to lands that Europeans initially identified as part of Asia. This habit of mind concerning the geographical direction of the most celebrated navigational feat in recorded memory is by no means unjustified: Columbus himself foresaw, even as he poised himself to cross the ocean, that his fame would come to rest with having sought to reach the East "by way of the West."[1] His plan rested—so reads the classic account derived from the biography of Columbus attributed to his son Ferdinand and from Columbus's own writings—on the equivocal claim that the ocean was narrow between the westernmost and easternmost ends of the known inhabited world. And, insofar as Columbus would have relied on scientific and technical arguments, he arrived at this claim by underestimating the equatorial circumference of the globe and by overestimating the horizontal length of the known inhabited world.[2] These are certainly not the sole cosmographical praecognita traditionally ascribed to the Discoverer, but they do constitute the defining assumptions without which our reading of the documentary corpus today associated with the discovery would seem suddenly rendered meaningless. Terrestrial longitude—the east-west separation in degrees between any given point on the globe and a prime meridian, such as is Greenwich today—has long shaped our grasp of this most consequential transatlantic event. Nevertheless, the notion that Columbus's goal was to reach the East "by way of the West" has significantly skewed our understanding of the plan he developed preceding the discovery, of his subsequent achievements and mistakes, and of the general orientation of the age of European expansion he helped to forge.

Columbus did not merely sail west across the Atlantic. Had he only wested from the Atlantic coast of Spain to the Americas (an insurmountable physical challenge for sails, given the slant of the trade winds in the North Atlantic), the residents of today's Virginia and North Carolina in the United States—not Cubans or Dominicans—might have traced their European heritage to the Spain of the *reconquista*. Readers of Columbus who have paused to consider his choice to cross the ocean from the Canary Islands instead, or his half-baked attempts in Cuba to locate the legendary ruler of the Mongols once depicted by the Venetian merchant Marco Polo, or the puzzling latitude measurements recorded in the only surviving sample of his *Diario,* or his keen intuition that the huge torrent of the Orinoco River in modern-day Venezuela issued from a southern continent unbeknownst to Europe, will surely have noticed that Columbus also sailed a long way *south* to lands and waters that he and his contemporaries would variously identify as "India," "the parts of India," or "the Indies."

Indeed, Columbus also sailed *south* to the Indies. But this aspect of Columbus's geography continues to play a negligible role in standard treatments of his celebrated enterprise. A blind spot of this magnitude in the Columbian tradition is all the more perplexing when one considers that Columbus's biographers since the late fifteenth century (not to mention Americanists who have studied the discovery since the Enlightenment) have not failed to notice that Columbus's exploration took place both to the west *and* to the south of Mediterranean Europe. Testimonies of Columbus's southing date back to the earliest days of European presence in the Americas, beginning with the first known chronicler and geographer of the so-called New World, the Italian humanist Peter Martyr d'Anghiera, who knew Columbus personally and who wrote his famous epistolary "decades" on the very heels of the discovery (first collected as *De orbe novo* in 1530). Peter Martyr, who claimed to have extracted his information from original documents facilitated by Columbus, carefully recorded that on his first three voyages, Columbus had followed ever-steeper routes to the south. On his first voyage, Columbus navigated westward from the Canaries "always following the sun, though slightly to the left."[3] On his second voyage, he steered "far more to the left than on the first voyage." And on his third voyage, "he pursued a journey toward the southern region, seeking the equatorial line."

So too the crucial sixteenth- and early-seventeenth-century histories that recounted the discovery indicate in one way or another that Columbus had labored westward *and* southward in pursuit of the Indies.[4] Among these foundational works are *Historia de los*

Reyes Católicos Don Fernando y Doña Isabel (completed 1513), by the palace curate Andrés Bernáldez, who hosted Columbus upon his return from the second voyage; *Historia de la inuencion de las yndias* (completed 1528), by the rector of the University of Salamanca Hernán Pérez de Oliva, who relied almost exclusively on Peter Martyr's first "decade"; the first part of *Historia general y natural de las Indias* (1535), by the first known official "chronicler of the Indies," Gonzalo Fernández de Oviedo y Valdés; the so-called life of Christopher Columbus attributed to his son Ferdinand, which was completed around 1539 and is known to us only in an Italian translation as *Historie del S. D. Fernando Colombo* (1571); *Historia general de las Indias y conquista de México* (1552), by Hernán Cortés's so-called chaplain Francisco López de Gómara; *Historia de las Indias* (completed about 1561), by the humanitarian friar Bartolomé de las Casas; and the voluminous *Historia general de los hechos de los castellanos en las islas y tierrafirme del mar océano* (1601–1615), by the "chronicler general of the Indies" Antonio de Herrera y Tordesillas.

Columbus's southing was not just known to the early chroniclers and historians who retold the story of his voyages. The fact that the inhabited lands he found lay not only to the west but also *to the south* of Mediterranean Europe was acknowledged by the most diverse (and crucial) documents drafted in the wake of his discoveries—from the papal bulls immediately issued by Alexander VI granting the Crowns of Aragon and Castile exclusive right of access to the lands and peoples newly discovered by Columbus *versus occidentem et meridiem* (literally "to the west and to the south"), to the works of various cartographers and cosmographers who since the turn of the sixteenth century celebrated the fact that Portuguese and Spanish explorers had discovered vast inhabited territories within the seemingly forbidden domain of the "torrid zone," or the belt of the tropics,[5] and to the philosophical arguments wielded by learned scholars who in the course of the same century set out to establish or to contest Spain's legal titles to its occupation of the tropical Americas, foremost among them the jurist Juan Ginés de Sepúlveda and, of course, Sepúlveda's sworn enemy, the justly famous humanitarian friar Bartolomé de las Casas.

On his first voyage (1492–1493), so reads the abstract of Columbus's *Diario* rendered by Las Casas, Columbus sailed mostly "to the south by southwest" (*al sur quarta del sudueste*) from the port of Palos de la Frontera in Spain's Atlantic coast to the Canary Islands off of Saharan Africa's western shoreline (**fig. I.1**).[6] Peter Martyr, explaining that Columbus had stopped at the Canaries to gather water and careen his ships, mindfully notes that these islands already stood at significantly lower, and therefore warmer,

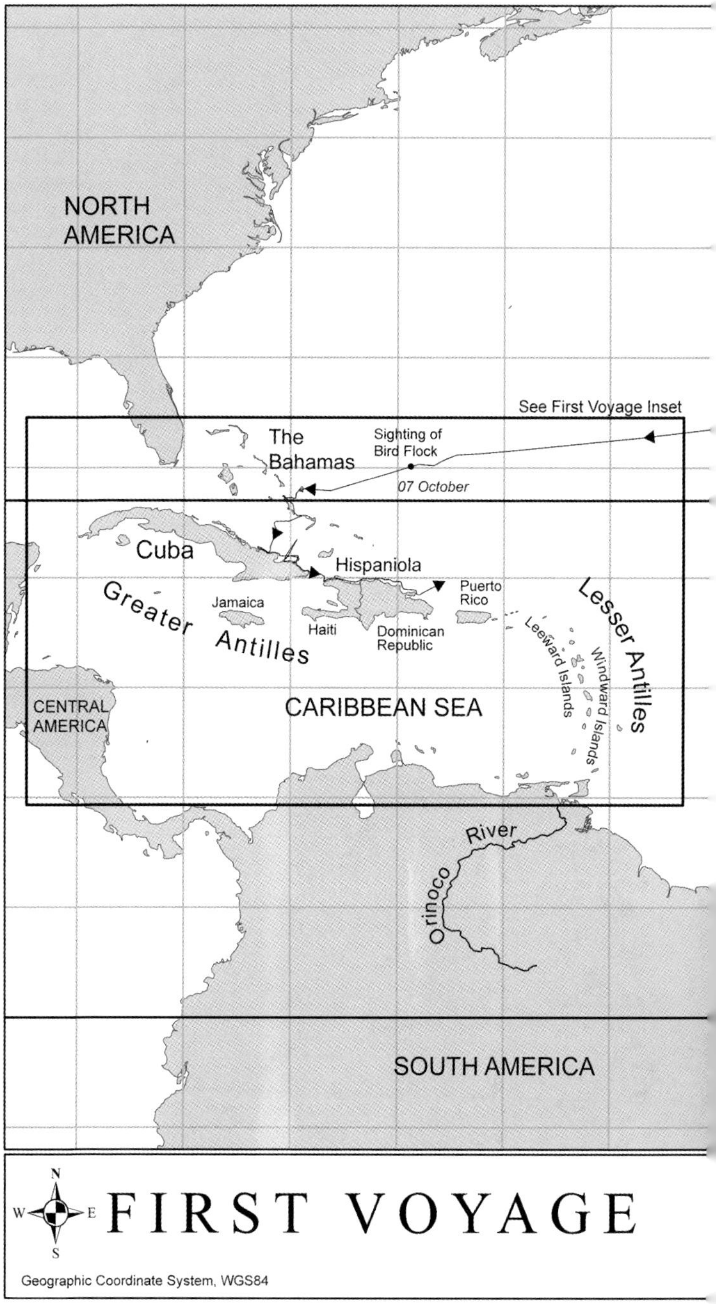

I.1 Columbus's first voyage, 1492–1493. After Samuel Eliot Morison, *Admiral of the Ocean Sea: A Life of Christopher Columbus*, 2 vols. (Boston, 1942). Prepared by Lynn Carlson, Geological Sciences, Brown University, Providence, Rhode Island.

NORTH AMERICA

See First Voyage Inset

The Bahamas

Sighting of Bird Flock

07 October

Cuba

Hispaniola

Puerto Rico

Jamaica

Haiti

Dominican Republic

Greater Antilles

Lesser Antilles

Leeward Islands

Windward Islands

CENTRAL AMERICA

CARIBBEAN SEA

Orinoco River

SOUTH AMERICA

N
W E
S

FIRST VOYAGE

Geographic Coordinate System, WGS84

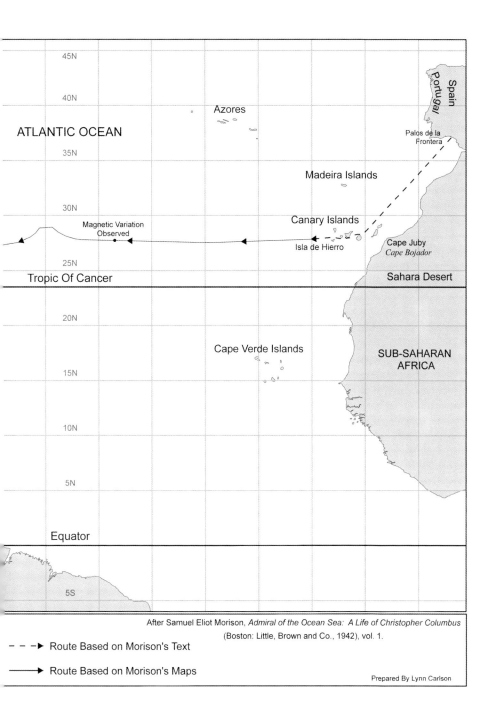

45N

40N

Azores

ATLANTIC OCEAN

35N

Portugal

Spain

Palos de la
Frontera

Madeira Islands

30N

Magnetic Variation
Observed

Canary Islands

Cape Juby
Cape Bojador

Isla de Hierro

25N

Tropic Of Cancer

Sahara Desert

20N

Cape Verde Islands

SUB-SAHARAN
AFRICA

15N

10N

5N

Equator

5S

After Samuel Eliot Morison, *Admiral of the Ocean Sea: A Life of Christopher Columbus*
(Boston: Little, Brown and Co., 1942), vol. 1.

– – –▶ Route Based on Morison's Text

——▶ Route Based on Morison's Maps

Prepared By Lynn Carlson

7

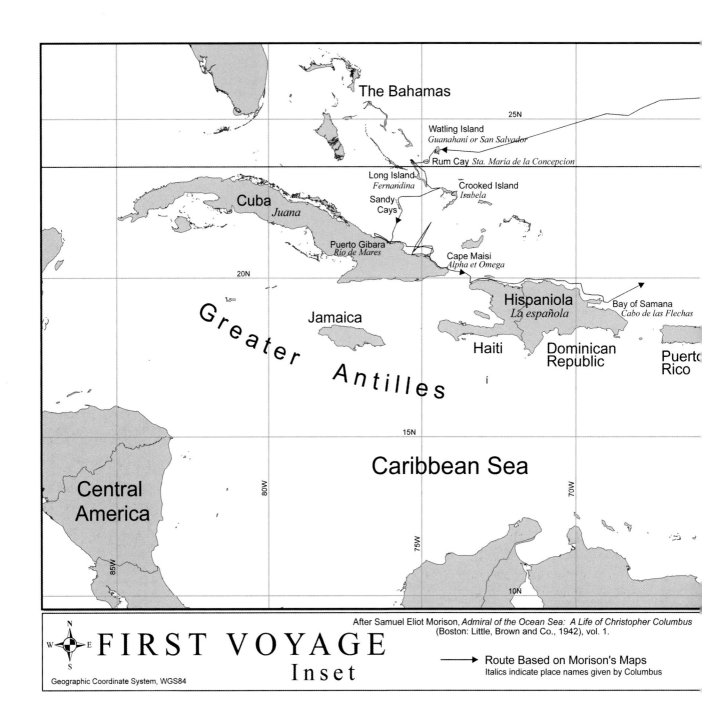

The Bahamas

25N

Watling Island
Guanahaní or San Salvador

Rum Cay *Sta. María de la Concepción*

Long Island
Fernandina

Sandy
Cays

Crooked Island
Isabela

Cuba
Juana

Puerto Gibara
Río de Mares

Cape Maisi
Alpha et Omega

20N

Jamaica

Greater Antilles

Hispaniola
La española

Bay of Samana
Cabo de las Flechas

Haiti

Dominican
Republic

Puerto
Rico

15N

Caribbean Sea

80W

75W

70W

Central
America

85W

10N

N
W—E
S

FIRST VOYAGE
Inset

After Samuel Eliot Morison, *Admiral of the Ocean Sea: A Life of Christopher Columbus*
(Boston: Little, Brown and Co., 1942), vol. 1.

Route Based on Morison's Maps
Italics indicate place names given by Columbus

Geographic Coordinate System, WGS84

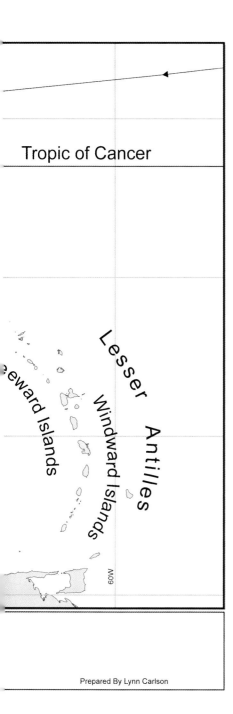

Tropic of Cancer

Lesser Antilles

Windward Islands

eward Islands

60W

Prepared By Lynn Carlson

I.2 Detail of Columbus's first voyage, 1492–1493. After Samuel Eliot Morison, *Admiral of the Ocean Sea: A Life of Christopher Columbus,* 2 vols. (Boston, 1942). Prepared by Lynn Carlson, Geological Sciences, Brown University, Rhode Island.

latitudes than continental Europe. In Peter Martyr's words, the Canaries were "outside of every European climate, to the south," although, as he and other authors since antiquity tended to qualify with admiration, local conditions had spared the so-called Fortunate Isles from the excessive heat that was known to desolate the nearby African mainland around those latitudes.[7] Since the opening decades of the fifteenth century, when the Portuguese prince Henry the Navigator began sending exploration parties to Atlantic Africa, the Canaries and the mainland African cape then known as Bojador (Cape Juby, modern 28° N) had marked for Christian Europeans the very threshold to the hotter, and seemingly more perilous, latitudes of the tropics.[8] (Not in vain has Columbus's biographer Paolo Emilio Taviani observed, referring to the intensely formative role that traveling to the equatorial coast of Guinea played for Columbus, that Henry the Navigator's greatest achievement had been "the discovery of fertile lands beyond the desert, [into] the torrid zone.")[9] Now in 1492 the Canarian archipelago—specifically, the southernmost island of El Hierro (27° 44′ N)—was to serve Columbus as a crucial reference point, both for westing across the Atlantic and for proceeding to south his way through the Bahamas toward the Caribbean basin.

In preparation for this voyage, Columbus had been strictly forbidden by King Fernando of Aragon and Queen Isabel of Castile from treading below the Canaries and toward Atlantic Africa. In a peace accord signed years before between Castile and Portugal, known as the Treaty of Alcáçovas (Toledo, 1479–1480), Castile had recognized Portugal's sovereignty over that meridional expanse in exchange for Portugal's recognition of Castilian sovereignty over the Canaries.[10] It may well have been evident to Columbus and his royal patrons, even before Columbus put out to sea, that King Dom João II was poised to interpret the terms of that pact to mean that *everything* below the parallel of the Canaries belonged to Portugal, not just what extended below the Canaries and toward Atlantic Africa. Setting aside the much-debated question of Columbus's technical competence at establishing accurate latitudes, Columbus's fear of Portugal's Atlantic agenda certainly serves to explain his later reluctance to admit that the lands he had discovered on the first voyage—the Bahamas, Cuba, and Hispaniola—were anything but directly across from the Canarian archipelago.

On this first voyage, Columbus appears to have followed an old custom with dead-reckoning sailors—first to reach the approximate latitude on which one expected to meet one's goal and then to set course along this latitude toward that goal.[11] On the authority of the extant *Diario*, Columbus tried to pursue a largely westerly course across the Atlantic, briefly distracted from this goal by the need to skirt mid-ocean calms, by variable winds, by false alarms of land, and even, as the great navigator complains, by the clumsy steering of his own pilots, who failed properly to compensate for lateral drag on his ships.[12] But, as Peter Martyr was already reporting just months after Columbus's return to Europe, the Discoverer had in fact declined slightly toward the south across the Atlantic ("slightly to the left"). The *Diario* further records that in the final moments of the outward passage (7 October 1492), Columbus decided to steer due "west by southwest" (*guesudueste*) in pursuit of a bird flock that he thought was seeking dry shelter before sunset. This new rhumb soon led his fleet to an island in the Bahamas presumably known to its inhabitants as Guanahaní. Columbus renamed this island San Salvador, and it is often identified today as Watling Island (**fig. I.2**).[13]

Upon landing on San Salvador on 12 October, the Discoverer appears to have believed that he had reached the uppermost and easternmost reaches of legendary India—a vast geographical system that he and his European contemporaries, largely following Marco Polo's cues, imagined to be organized around the distinctly tropical accident still known today as the Indian Ocean. For Marco Polo and his followers, the Indian Ocean covered an even broader area than what we think of today as its basin proper—pouring eastward well beyond what would be the Bay of Bengal today, to include not only Indochina and the Malaysian Peninsula but even the continental shores and islands of the South China Sea and Indonesia. Perhaps the most complex surviving depiction of this vast geographical system as it was understood on the eve of the discovery is the famous "earth apple," or globe, that Martin Behaim presented to the town of Nuremberg in 1492 (**fig. I.3**). Like Columbus, Behaim was familiar with the cartographic tradition flourishing in Portugal at the time, and his globe provides our best approximation of Columbus's picture of the Far East. By Columbus's calculations, the island of San Salvador would have stood in the midst of the "Indian" mega-archipelago Marco Polo had described off of the mainland province of Mangi that today would be southern China (**fig. I.4**).

Columbus evidently meant to reassure his royal patrons that he had never steered below the Canarian latitudes on the outward passage: as an explanation for his claim that the "Indians" he had just found displayed the same skin color as the inhabitants of the Canaries, "neither black nor white," Columbus underscored that the island of San Salvador stood on the very same parallel as the Canarian island of El Hierro, that is, somewhere above the twenty-seventh parallel. (In today's terms, Watling Island stands

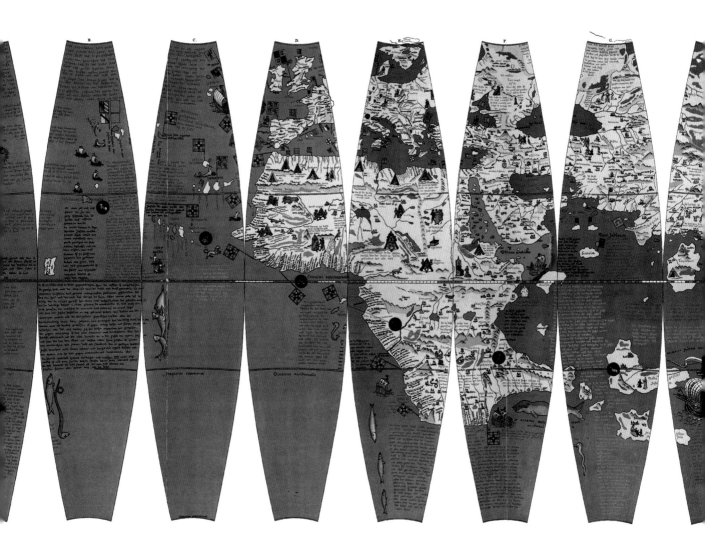

I.3 Martin Behaim's globe, 1492.
From E. G. Ravenstein, FRGS,
*Martin Behaim: His Life and His
Globe* (London, 1908). Courtesy
of the John Carter Brown Library
at Brown University. Original
globe at the Germanisches
Nationalmuseum, Nuremberg,
Germany.

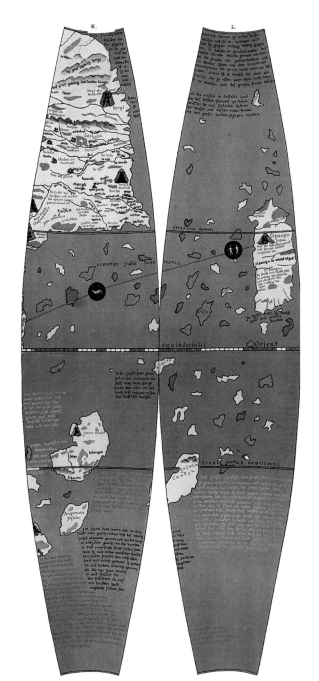

I.4 Detail of Martin Behaim's globe, 1492, and outline prepared by the author. From E. G. Ravenstein, FRGS, *Martin Behaim: His Life and His Globe* (London, 1908). Courtesy of the John Carter Brown Library at Brown University, Providence, Rhode Island. Original globe at the Germanisches Nationalmuseum, Nuremberg, Germany.

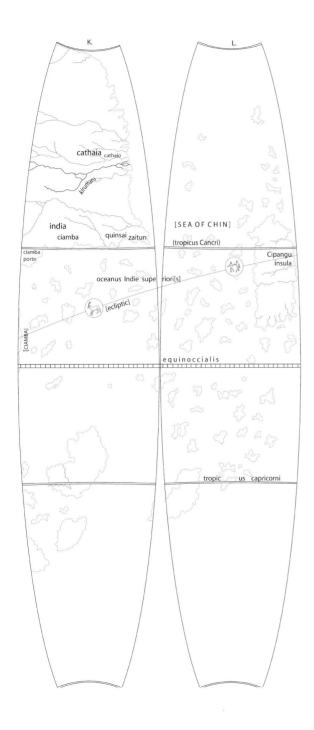

K.

L.

cathaia cathaio

kirumaru

india

ciamba   quinsai zaitun

[SEA OF CHIN]

(tropicus Cancri)

ciamba
porte

oceanus Indie supe rior[s]

Cipangu
insula

[ecliptic]

[CIAMBA]

equinoccialis

tropic us capricorni

at a latitude of 24° N and El Hierro at 27° 44′ N.)[14] Columbus must have known that he had ended up declining slightly to the south across the Atlantic, for this fact would even be reported by Peter Martyr on the basis of Columbus's documents as early as November 1493. But caution must have played some role in Columbus's official stance that the lands discovered on this first voyage—the Bahamas, Cuba, and Hispaniola—were not south of the Canaries. Yet experts on Columbus's navigation might reasonably argue that Columbus possessed neither the expertise nor the means to measure latitudes across the ocean to such an accurate degree. Indeed, it would have been difficult for Columbus to estimate the extent to which leeway had put him off course or to account for the effects of magnetic variation on the reading of the compass.[15] Therefore, with these reservations in mind, one should also be content to state that Columbus simply overestimated by nearly four degrees the latitude of the island he reached on 12 October, and that in the early moments of the first voyage he did truly believe that San Salvador stood neck to neck with El Hierro.

The fact is that, having situated San Salvador on the parallel of El Hierro, Columbus now deliberately steered an itinerary generally to the south of the latitude he had tried to follow out of the Canaries—perhaps from today's Watling Island to Rum Cay, to Long Island, and to Crooked Island (successively named by Columbus San Salvador, Santa María de la Concepción, Fernandina, and Isabela). This generally southbound course led Columbus from the Bahamas to the outer shores of the Caribbean basin, where he proceeded to explore the northeastern coast of Cuba (Juana) and the northern coast of Hispaniola, that is, Haiti and the Dominican Republic. He had thus descended from San Salvador, which stands on the twenty-fourth parallel, crossing the Tropic of Cancer as he coasted the Bahamian Long Island, and southing all the way to the Bay of Samaná, or Cabo de las Flechas, on northern Haiti, which stands at a latitude of merely 19° N. This implies a drop of over seventeen degrees from the Atlantic port of Palos de Moguer on his first voyage alone.

Columbus may well not have known exactly how far he had southed from Palos, and indeed the *Diario* and other documents by him underestimate the extent of his southing from the twenty-seventh parallel he assigned to San Salvador and El Hierro. But he sure was explicit about having generally southed his way from the site of the landfall through the Bahamas and along the outer shores of the Caribbean basin. And to judge from the *Diario,* by the end of the first voyage, Columbus seems to have believed that somewhere along the coasts of Cuba and Hispaniola, he had approached, maybe

even crossed, the Tropic of Cancer, which he and other sources of the period tended to place at 24° N. On the *Diario*'s authority, Cuba, which Columbus at first had identified as Marco Polo's fabulously wealthy "Indian" island of Çipango, or Japan, was now the mainland province of Mangi, in today's southern China. His coasting due southwest toward Cuba's easternmost point, Cape Maisi, which he baptized Alpha et Omega, had allegedly brought him to the very end of mainland Asia, within a stone's throw of the "Indian" port city of Zaiton, in Marco Polo's mainland province of Mangi. And the island of Hispaniola, which Columbus had heard the "Indians" call Çibao, now appeared to be nothing less than the legendary Çipango.

Early chroniclers of the discovery, namely, Hernán Pérez de Oliva and Francisco López de Gómara, claim that Columbus was drawing nautical charts from the moment he arrived in Portugal.[16] No independent evidence exists to confirm this claim. Nevertheless, prior to crossing the Atlantic, Columbus must have at the very least come across world maps reflecting Portuguese discoveries in Atlantic Africa and such influential "new" works as Ptolemy's second-century *Geography* and Marco Polo's thirteenth-century *Il milione,* and he could not have failed to notice that modern cartography plotted the toponyms he was now using for Cuba and Hispaniola—Mangi, Zaiton, and Çipango—along the Tropic of Cancer. But fear that the Portuguese or other foreigners to Castile should lay hands on Columbus's precious *Diario,* may have led the Discoverer, or the royal chancellery in charge of duplicating his *Diario* back in Castile, to inflate the latitudes recorded in this document beyond recognition: 42° N for Puerto Gibara (Columbus's Río de Mares) in northeastern Cuba, placing Columbus's fleet directly to the west of Portugal and Castile; and 34° N for Moustique Bay (Columbus's Puerto de la Concepción) on northern Haiti, placing his fleet on the approximate latitude of the Portuguese Madeiras—well above the latitude of the Canary Islands.[17]

Whatever the cause for such exaggerated readings, Columbus's official stance also was to prove disorienting vis-à-vis the location of the lands discovered on the first voyage. Such is the case with the instantly famous letter to Luis de Santángel of 15 February 1493, which the Crown ordered to be printed upon Columbus's victorious return in order to spread the news of the discovery. In a letter that in every other way extolled the lush tropicality of the lands newly discovered in the high Atlantic, Columbus (or perhaps other hands in charge of editing this letter) declared not that Cuba was part of the province of Mangi in southern mainland China but rather that it was the mainland province of Catayo, where Marco Polo and other travelers to the Far East had located

the seat of the Mongols, in northern China. Maps of the period, including Behaim's globe, distinctly located Cathay to the north of Mangi, across from Mediterranean Europe rather than verging on the Tropic of Cancer. Unfortunately, this geographical distinction between the two Far Eastern provinces has eluded many an Americanist who has wrestled with the question of why the Columbus of the *Diario* so easily gives up the explicit quest for the Great Khān of the Mongols. But the distinction between a Cathay in the cooler latitudes of the globe and a Mangi verging on the hotter latitudes of Marco Polo's India had long been established in the cartographic tradition informed by his *Il milione* and other sources; and to an attentive reader of the famous letter to Luis de Santángel, Columbus would have been sending the signal that he had not dared venture into the coveted tropics so jealously guarded by Portugal in the latitudes below the Canaries.

Elsewhere in the same letter announcing the discovery, Columbus underscored the fact that the lands he had just discovered stood directly across from the Canaries, by linking latitude, as he had in the *Diario,* with the skin color of local people. As Columbus put it, his "Indians" were not "monstrous men," as many believed were to be found in the farthest reaches of the inhabited world; nor were they "black as in Guinea"; nor did they seem to be born "where the aspect of the solar rays is too strong," *although,* the author readily admits, "it is true that the sun is very strong there, as [those lands] stand twenty-six degrees from the equinoctial line."[18] The figure of 26° N for the lands discovered on the first voyage was probably wrought up not by Castile's royal chancellery to fool foreign powers but by Columbus himself. Admittedly, Columbus could have simply been in error, but out of fear of Portugal or of his present royal patrons, he also must have hesitated to disclose how far he had southed below the parallel of the Canaries. Indeed, in a letter written to the Catholic Monarchs only a year later (20 January 1494) from the newly founded town of La Ysabela, on the northern coast of today's Dominican Republic, Columbus pointed his addressees to a Ptolemaic map he was supposed to have drafted locating their new overseas possessions by latitude and longitude. He insisted that La Ysabela itself was twenty-six degrees from the equator, and that it all was parallel with the Canaries "save for thirty minutes" (*salvo treinta minutos*).[19] Taking La Ysabela to approximate the lowest boundary for the lands discovered on the first voyage, we can see that Columbus had by 1494 pushed the Bahamas, Cuba, and Hispaniola even farther to the north of the position he had initially assigned to them: whereas upon landing on San Salvador, he had set the upper limit for his exploration on

the twenty-seventh parallel corresponding to El Hierro, now in La Ysabela, which would have stood nearly five degrees due south of San Salvador, Columbus was setting the lower limit of the first voyage barely thirty minutes to the south of the same parallel.

We may never know whether Columbus's insistence in placing the newfound lands directly across from the Canaries was due to cartographic imprecision or political expediency. But this official stance did have a tangible effect on the early cartography of the Bahamas and the Caribbean. Consider the justly celebrated portolan supposed to have been drawn around 1500 by Juan de la Cosa, Columbus's trusted cartographer on the first and second voyages (**fig. I.5**). On this world map attesting to the transatlantic exploration conducted by Columbus and others, including Juan de la Cosa himself, Cuba and Hispaniola appear to the north of the Tropic of Cancer, stretching all the way to the approximate latitude of the Strait of Gibraltar, whereas modern cartography depicts them inside the belt of the tropics.[20]

Whatever we make of Columbus's latitudes, even by the official figure divulged in the letter to Santángel, Columbus was known to have dropped from the Atlantic port of Palos in Spain to Cabo de las Flechas in Hispaniola more than ten degrees in latitude, enough to have taken him to a place whose nature was tangibly different from Mediterranean Europe's. This was a place where the sun's rays were "very strong" because they tended to strike at steeper angles than they did in the higher latitudes of the globe from which Columbus had come. Indeed, Columbus understood that in the course of his first voyage he had, at the very least, come to knock at the doors of the tropics, and this is the story followed in the present book.

Columbus's southing proved even bolder on the three voyages he carried out between 1493 and 1504 to the Caribbean basin. Upon Columbus's first return to Europe, Fernando and Isabel had persuaded Alexander VI to issue a series of papal bulls granting Castile exclusive right of access to the newly discovered lands. One of these bulls, known as *Inter cetera* [II] (antedated 4 May 1493), drew a vertical line of demarcation 100 leagues due west of the Portuguese Azores and Cape Verde Islands, dividing the entire Atlantic into an eastern half for Portugal and a western half for Castile. (This demarcation line was of course the predecessor to the line drawn a year later by the Treaty of Tordesillas [7 June 1494] 370 leagues to the west of the Cape Verde Islands.) Columbus was no longer officially bound to pursue a largely westerly course out of the Canaries to the newly discovered lands in the high Atlantic. Moreover, in a letter to Columbus of 5 September 1495 Fernando and Isabel urged their "Admiral of the Ocean Sea" not to

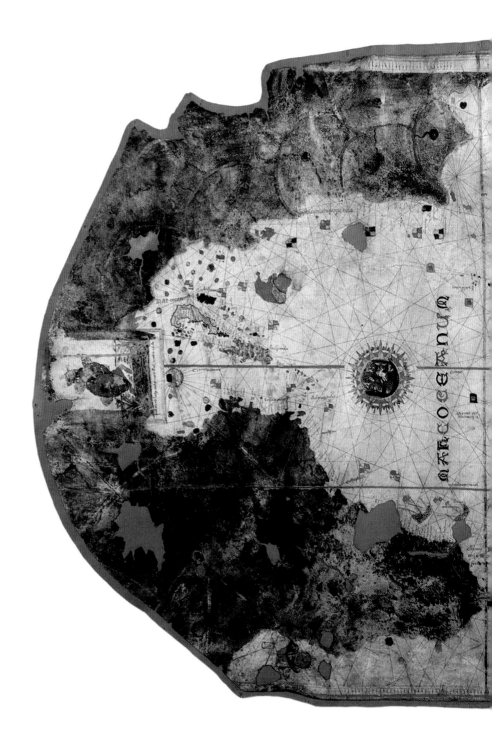

I.5   Map attributed to Juan de
la Cosa, 1500. Courtesy of Museo
Naval de Madrid, Spain.

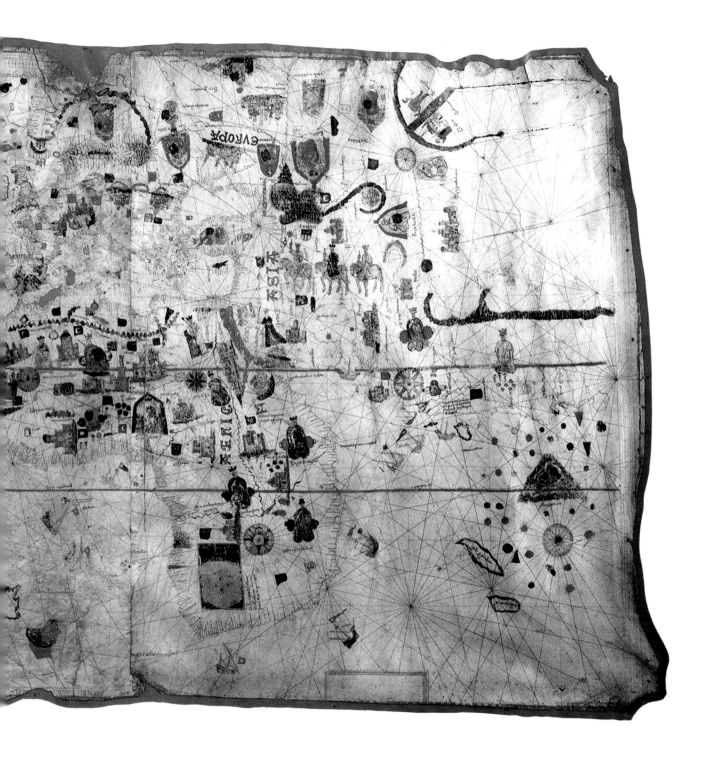

delay his second departure for the Indies for fear that Portugal might be on the warpath over the newly discovered territories. The Catholic Monarchs noted that during their conversations with the Portuguese ambassadors sent to negotiate with Castile the possibility had been mentioned that the Atlantic space now divided between Portugal and Castile might harbor numerous islands—or even a continent—all of which might be richer and more profitable than the ones Columbus had discovered on the first voyage, precisely *because* they were "in the part of the sun" (*en la parte del sol*).[21] Naturally, Fernando and Isabel were referring to the tropical belt. Columbus needed little encouragement to south his way even deeper across the Atlantic, and this letter from his royal patrons must have read like a direct order to do so.

Thus on the second voyage (1493–1496) Columbus descended from the Canary Islands to the Windward island of Dominica in today's Lesser Antilles (15° 20′ N) (**fig. I.6**). For centuries to come, the itinerary Columbus followed out of the Canaries to the Lesser Antilles ("west by southwest") would be fairly standard with Spanish vessels taking part in what was known as the *carrera de Indias.* By later calculation of Crown historian Gonzalo Fernández de Oviedo in the first part of his *Historia general y natural de las Indias* (1535), the route from the Canaries to the Lesser Antilles, specifically to the tiny Leeward island of Deseada, today's La Désirade off of Guadeloupe, entailed a drop in latitude from 27° N to 14° N.[22] The historian rightly deemed this route to be the "straighter and narrower . . . route" (*más derecha y justa . . . derrota*) to the Indies.[23] It is by this route that Columbus dropped across the Atlantic on his second voyage in search of lands "in the part of the sun," reaching the southeastern quarter of the Caribbean basin. The previous year's "Indian" informants along northeastern Cuba and northern Hispaniola had indicated that in this quarter of the Caribbean, Columbus was bound to find the islands of the "monstrous" *caniba* or *caribe*—an allegedly warlike people who raided the islands of the Indies, feeding on the flesh of the islanders they took as captives. The Caribes, as they are still called today, perfectly seemed to match the profile of the "monstrous men" Columbus and his contemporaries had expected to chance upon in the farthest reaches of the inhabited world, namely, in the colder and hotter latitudes of the globe. Columbus had not just dropped across the Atlantic in search of lands "in the part of the sun." He appears to have been poised to descend toward these lower latitudes in order to harvest his first slaves on the "Indian" side of the tropical Atlantic.

From Dominica, Columbus was to follow the rosary of the Antilles toward the northwest—from the Leeward Islands, to the Virgin Islands, and to the southern coast of Puerto Rico, which he named San Juan Bautista, on his way back to Navidad, the fort he had built the previous Christmas on northern Hispaniola following the shipwreck of the caravel *Santa María* (**fig. I.7**). Columbus would return to find that the natives of Hispaniola, outraged by the looting, extortion, and rapes committed by the garrison of men Columbus had left in charge of Navidad, had massacred all thirty-nine of the colonists and leveled the fort to the ground. As we know, this was only the beginning of Columbus's disastrously short career as a colonial ruler and administrator for the Crown. Months later, probably eager to take a rest from the rising discontent among his colonists, Columbus launched the second stage of this voyage. Setting out from the recently founded town of La Ysabela on northern Hispaniola, he was to survey the inner shores of the Greater Antilles beyond Cape Maisi, his Alpha et Omega—the cape on the tip of eastern Cuba that he believed marked the eastern end of continental Asia. Rounding Cape Maisi by south, Columbus coasted all of the Oriente Province in southern Cuba, and from there he southed his way to Jamaica. He then returned to Cape Cruz in southern Cuba, from where he proceeded to coast Cuba's southwestern shores all the way to today's Bahía Cortés. On his way back to La Ysabela, Columbus would round Jamaica by south and then survey the southern and eastern shores of Hispaniola.

Columbus's exploration of Cuba's southwestern coast may strike us today as a Quixotic attempt to prove to those back in Castile who already doubted that Columbus had wested far enough to reach Asia that this was Marco Polo's mainland province of Mangi, where he would have expected to find the port city of Zaiton and the great inland city of Quinsay. Having reached the southward trending coast of today's Bahía Cortés, which he believed led to the continental province of Ciamba in what today would be Indochina, Columbus drafted an official report on 12 June 1494, in which he forced his men to declare—under threat of having their tongues sliced out if they were ever to state otherwise—that Cuba was not an island.[24] The *carta-relación* Columbus wrote to Fernando and Isabel reporting his exploration of the inner shores of the Caribbean basin (26 February 1495) tells us that, as Columbus had coasted southern Cuba, he had imagined himself cruising along *Cancro,* or the Tropic of Cancer, and looking south onto a vast oceanic expanse he imagined to be dotted with islands that reached all the way to the *trópico del Capricornio.*[25] By Columbus's account, had he thought of carrying enough provisions on this voyage and had he continued to follow Cuba's southward trending coast, he could have attempted "to reach Spain by way of the East, coming to the Ganges, from there to the Arabic Gulf, and then by way of Ethiopia [i.e., sub-Saharan Africa]."[26]

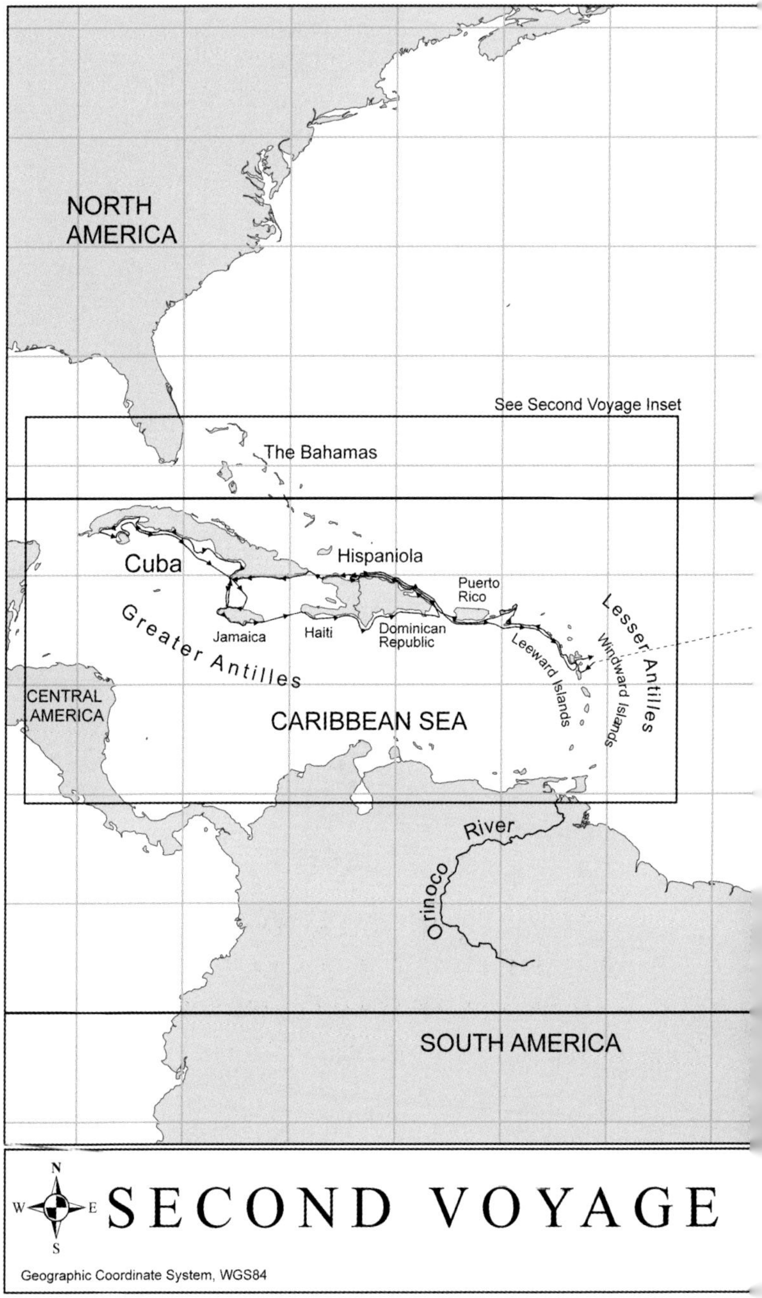

NORTH
AMERICA

See Second Voyage Inset

The Bahamas

Cuba

Hispaniola

Puerto
Rico

Greater Antilles

Jamaica   Haiti   Dominican
Republic

Leeward Islands

Lesser Antilles

Windward Islands

CENTRAL
AMERICA

CARIBBEAN SEA

Orinoco River

SOUTH AMERICA

N
W ✦ E
S

SECOND VOYAGE

Geographic Coordinate System, WGS84

I.6   Columbus's second voyage,
1493–1496. After Samuel Eliot
Morison, *Admiral of the Ocean Sea:
A Life of Christopher Columbus*, 2
vols. (Boston, 1942). Prepared by
Lynn Carlson, Geological Sciences,
Brown University, Providence,
Rhode Island.

After Samuel Eliot Morison, *Admiral of the Ocean Sea: A Life of Christopher Columbus*
(Boston: Little, Brown and Co., 1942), vol. 2.

- - -▶ Route Based on Morison's Text

——▶ Route Based on Morison's Maps

Prepared By Lynn Carlson

The

Cuba
Juana

Bahía Cortés

20N

Cabo Cruz

Greater Antilles

Jamaic

15N

80W

CENTRAL
AMERICA

85W

N
W E
S

SECOND VOYA
Inset

Geographic Coordinate System, WGS84

I.7 Detail of Columbus's second voyage, 1493–1496. After Samuel Eliot Morison, *Admiral of the Ocean Sea: A Life of Christopher Columbus,* 2 vols. (Boston, 1942). Prepared by Lynn Carlson, Geological Sciences, Brown University, Providence, Rhode Island.

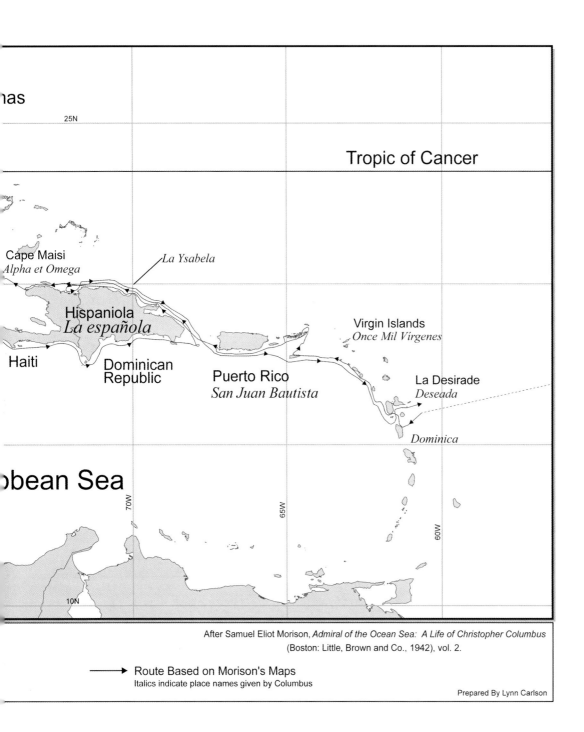

Tropic of Cancer

Cape Maisi
Alpha et Omega

La Ysabela

Virgin Islands
Once Mil Virgenes

Hispaniola
La española

La Desirade
Deseada

Haiti

Dominican
Republic

Puerto Rico
San Juan Bautista

Dominica

bean Sea

70W

65W

60W

10N

After Samuel Eliot Morison, *Admiral of the Ocean Sea: A Life of Christopher Columbus*
(Boston: Little, Brown and Co., 1942), vol. 2.

Route Based on Morison's Maps
Italics indicate place names given by Columbus

Prepared By Lynn Carlson

27

On Cuba's southern coast, Columbus had found himself contemplating a herculean landscape extending all around the globe under the belt of the tropics.

On his third voyage (1498–1500), Columbus once again found himself scouting out the hypothetical islands and continent that the Crown had previously urged him to find "in the part of the sun," so he dipped his way from the Canaries to the Cape Verde Islands, which stand off of West Africa's coast at a latitude of 16° N (**fig. I.8**). His intention was "to reach the equinoctial line and from there head to the west until I had the island of Hispaniola to the north."[27] Thus from the Cape Verdean island of São Tiago, Columbus sailed "due southwest" until he calculated that he had "the North Star at five degrees." But hitting the Doldrums between the North and South Atlantic, he and his men found themselves suffering such unbearable heat, that Columbus, invoking the scorching temperatures that had long earned the belt of the tropics its epithet as "torrid zone," came to fear "that my vessels and crew would burst into flames."[28] Columbus dared not tread farther south toward the equator; instead, he stayed the course along the fifth parallel, calculating that he was directly to the west of *sierra lioa* in Guinea (Sierra Leone, today 9° N). Past the Doldrums, Columbus soon began to pick up evidence of nearby land, but failing to sight any, and finding himself short of fresh water, he steered north by northwest, making for where he thought he would meet the islands of the "man-eating" Caribes in the Lesser Antilles.[29] This rhumb almost instantly brought his fleet within sight of the island of Trinidad, across from the Orinoco River in today's Venezuela (like Sierra Leone, approximately 9° N) (**fig. I.9**).

Bartolomé de las Casas, who had at his disposal the documents kept by the Columbus family, tells us in *Historia de las Indias* that in the now-lost diary of the third voyage Columbus declared that it was "a miracle that so close to the equinoctial line—at about six degrees north—the monarchs of Castile [should have come to possess] lands, considering that La Ysabela measured twenty-four degrees from the said line."[30] Setting aside the fact that Columbus had by now subtracted two degrees from his original official measurement of 26° N for the latitude of La Ysabela on northern Hispaniola, we should note that Columbus, like other geographers before him, including Ptolemy, equated the twenty-fourth parallel with the Tropic of Cancer. It may be no coincidence that, by this late reckoning, the first town Columbus had founded in the Indies, La Ysabela, should have stood precisely at the threshold of the tropics. In any case, Columbus was telling his royal patrons nothing less than that his explorations across the Atlantic had already won

for the Crown a vast territory that extended into the belt of the tropics almost all the way to the equator.[31]

From the sound between Trinidad and the Orinoco delta, Columbus entered the Gulf of Paria (his Golfo de las Ballenas) through what he called Mouth of the Serpent (Boca de la Sierpe). Having explored the Gulf of Paria, Columbus exited through, as he called it, the Mouth of the Dragon (Boca del Drago), rounding the Paria Peninsula, which he thought was an island (Isla de Gracia), and he followed the Venezuelan coastline to the island of Margarita, from where he set course across the Caribbean for Hispaniola. On this voyage to the equatorial region, Columbus had spawned an intuition that, if anything, ought to have earned *him,* rather than his friend Amerigo Vespucci, the honor of having the lands Columbus had discovered bear his name. Marveling at the voluminous torrent of fresh water that issued from the mouth of the Orinoco River, Columbus inferred that he had discovered "infinite land that is to the south" (*tierra infinita q'es al austro*) and that the waters of the Orinoco River flowed from no less noble a place than "earthly Paradise" itself (*parayso terrenal*).[32] It is precisely the pronounced verticality of this voyage to the equatorial region that Columbus was to index upon his return to Castile in 1500, when he wrote a now-famous letter to the former nanny of the young Prince Don Juan, the heir to the thrones of Aragon and Castile who had met a premature death in 1497. Alluding to the change in the configuration of the skies that accompanies changes in latitude, Columbus explained that the glorious third voyage, which he claimed he had launched in part to distract Queen Isabel from the sorrow she felt for the death of her son, had been carried out "to the new heaven and earth that had until then remained hidden" (*al nuevo çielo y mundo que fasta entonces estaua oculto*).[33]

Finally, on the haphazard fourth voyage (1502–1504), Columbus, who had been forbidden by the crown from setting foot on Hispaniola on account of his disastrous colonial policies, made his way across the Atlantic once again to the Windward Islands and followed the inner shores of the Antilles all the way to southeastern Cuba (**fig. I.10**). He wished to continue the exploration beyond the Cuban coastline he had surveyed on his second voyage, this time with the aim of finding a passage into the basin proper of the Indian Ocean. He reasoned that this passage must lie somewhere between the Asian "terra firma" he still believed Cuba to be and the southern continent he had discovered on his third voyage. The letter of 14 March 1502 written to Columbus by the Catholic Monarchs, forbidding him from visiting Hispaniola on the outward passage, suggests that Columbus may have contemplated satisfying his fancy of rounding the globe by

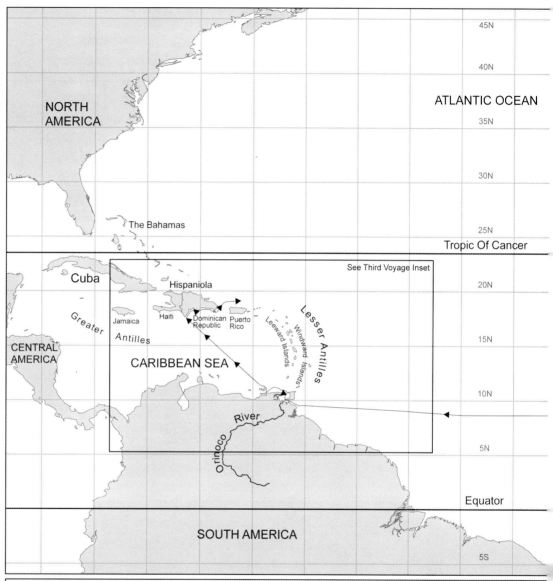

45N

40N

ATLANTIC OCEAN

35N

NORTH
AMERICA

30N

25N

The Bahamas

Tropic Of Cancer

See Third Voyage Inset

Cuba

20N

Hispaniola

Greater

Jamaica   Haiti   Dominican   Puerto
Republic   Rico

Lesser Antilles

Windward Islands

Leeward Islands

15N

CENTRAL
AMERICA

Antilles

CARIBBEAN SEA

10N

Orinoco River

5N

Equator

SOUTH AMERICA

5S

After Samuel Eliot Morison, *Admiral of the Ocean Sea: A Life of Christopher Columbus*
(Boston: Little, Brown and Co., 1942), vol. 2.

N
W   E
S

THIRD VOYAGE ⟶ Route Based on Morison's Maps

Geographic Coordinate System, WGS84

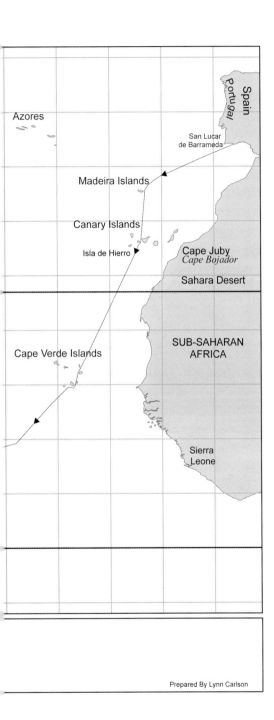

Azores

Spain

Portugal

San Lucar
de Barrameda

Madeira Islands

Canary Islands

Isla de Hierro

Cape Juby
Cape Bojador

Sahara Desert

SUB-SAHARAN
AFRICA

Cape Verde Islands

Sierra
Leone

Prepared By Lynn Carlson

I.8   Columbus's third voyage,
1498–1500. After Samuel Eliot
Morison, *Admiral of the Ocean Sea:
A Life of Christopher Columbus*, 2
vols. (Boston, 1942). Prepared by
Lynn Carlson, Geological Sciences,
Brown University, Providence,
Rhode Island.

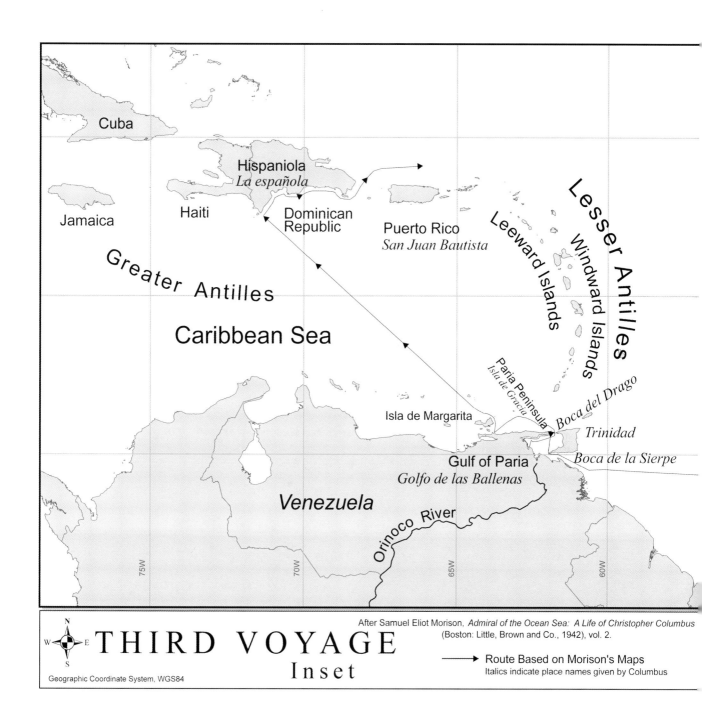

Cuba

Hispaniola
La española

Haiti

Dominican
Republic

Jamaica

Puerto Rico
San Juan Bautista

Greater Antilles

Lesser Antilles

Windward Islands

Leeward Islands

Caribbean Sea

Paria Peninsula
Isla de Gracia

Boca del Drago

Isla de Margarita

Trinidad

Gulf of Paria
Golfo de las Ballenas

Boca de la Sierpe

Venezuela

Orinoco River

75W

70W

65W

60W

N
W E
S

THIRD VOYAGE
Inset

Geographic Coordinate System, WGS84

After Samuel Eliot Morison, *Admiral of the Ocean Sea: A Life of Christopher Columbus*
(Boston: Little, Brown and Co., 1942), vol. 2.

→ Route Based on Morison's Maps
Italics indicate place names given by Columbus

50W

Prepared By Lynn Carlson

I.9 Detail of Columbus's third voyage, 1498–1500. After Samuel Eliot Morison, *Admiral of the Ocean Sea: A Life of Christopher Columbus,* 2 vols. (Boston, 1942). Prepared by Lynn Carlson, Geological Sciences, Brown University, Providence, Rhode Island.

I.10 Columbus's fourth voyage, 1502–1504. After Samuel Eliot Morison, *Admiral of the Ocean Sea: A Life of Christopher Columbus*, 2 vols. (Boston, 1942). Prepared by Lynn Carlson, Geological Sciences, Brown University, Providence, Rhode Island.

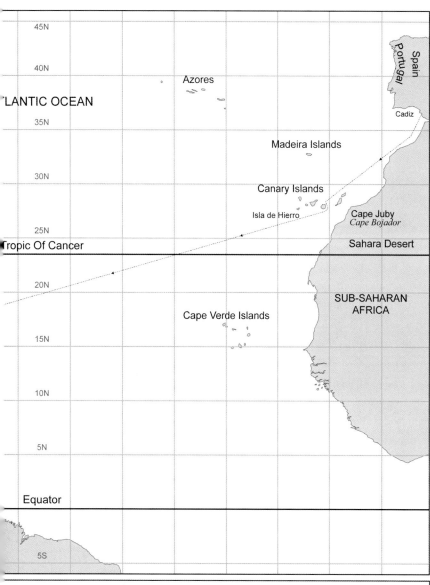

45N

40N

35N

30N

25N

20N

15N

10N

5N

ATLANTIC OCEAN

Azores

Spain

Portugal

Cadiz

Madeira Islands

Canary Islands

Isla de Hierro

Cape Juby
Cape Bojador

Tropic Of Cancer

Sahara Desert

SUB-SAHARAN
AFRICA

Cape Verde Islands

Equator

5S

After Samuel Eliot Morison, *Admiral of the Ocean Sea: A Life of Christopher Columbus*
(Boston: Little, Brown and Co., 1942), vol. 2.

– – –▶ Route Based on Morison's Text

———▶ Route Based on Morison's Maps

Prepared By Lynn Carlson

crossing the Indian Ocean and circumnavigating Africa all the way back to Spain. Fernando and Isabel explained in this letter to Columbus that they had honored his wish to have the Portuguese navigator Vasco da Gama, who was readying his second armada to the actual India, alerted to the fact that he might come across Columbus and that, should their paths cross, they should treat each other "as friends."[34] Thus, from Cuban waters, Columbus set course to the southwest for what he clearly wanted to believe was the province of Ciamba in today's Indochina. This rhumb led him to Cape Honduras (his Punta Caxinas), from where he proceeded to follow the Central American coastline, along Nicaragua, Costa Rica, and Panamá, all the way to a cape he named Marmoro, which could be anywhere from Punta de Mosquito in today's Panama to Cape Tiburón on the western tip of Colombia's Gulf of Urabá (**fig. I.11**).[35] By Columbus's estimates, his coasting along the province of Mangi had brought him within a "ten day's journey" to the mouth of the Ganges River.[36]

Columbus's failure to find a passage to the Indian Ocean must have been the most vexing disappointment of his long career at sea. And, as we know, the honor of returning to Spain by way of the West, was reserved for Juan Sebastián del Cano of the galleon *Victoria* in 1522, whose circumnavigation of the globe, Francisco López de Gómara insists in *Historia general de las Indias,* had been carried out "under the equinoctial line."[37] Yet, no matter how much doubt the failure to find a passage to the "Indian" ocean that his contemporaries were to call Mar del Sur, or Southern Sea, may have instilled in Columbus regarding the "true" identity of the lands he had discovered, the Discoverer was never to admit anything other than that he had wested across the Atlantic and also southed his way to a tropical expanse he paradoxically called "west Yndies unbeknownst to all the world" (*Yndias oçidentales a todo el mundo ignotas*).[38]

Numerous practical explanations have been forwarded in the course of five centuries to explain the Discoverer's southing.[39] Considering Columbus's first voyage, for instance, everyone knows that the Canary Islands were Spain's outermost territories in the Atlantic on the eve of the discovery, and this location made them a most suitable stop for repairing and restocking ships for an ocean crossing. However, overwrought emphasis on the horizontality of the early transatlantic encounter has all too often prevented Americanists from noticing that the Canaries were not just Spain's farthest territories to the west, but also its farthest territories to the south—meaning that these islands also represented an ideal launching pad for descending into the tropics, and

this is indeed the role they had been meant to play in the history of Atlantic Africa's exploration by the Portuguese.

It is also known that wind patterns and water currents in the Atlantic were crucial factors for launching an outward passage from the Canaries: Columbus understood that his chance of crossing the ocean was significantly greater just beyond the Canary calms, where he expected to catch the northeastern trade winds—although, as some authors have pointed out, simply "westing" from the Canaries, instead of dipping farther south, was hardly an optimal sailing choice, since Columbus's fleet was bound to lose, as soon it did, the northeasterlies in the mid-Atlantic.[40]

As we now know, political factors also determined Columbus's choice to launch his first voyage from the Canaries: he was under strict orders not to venture below the Canaries and toward Atlantic Africa, so it made sense for him to first descend to the archipelago and from there to try his luck across the ocean along the latitude of the boundary recognized by Castile and Portugal in the peace treaty of Alcáçovas.

And of course there is the dream of Asia traditionally imputed to Columbus: following Marco Polo's account of India in *Il milione,* cartography of the period plotted the huge gilded island of Çipango, or Japan, along the same general parallel as the Canaries, and it would have made sense for Columbus to aim for the largest island in the mega-archipelago that presumably extended to the east of the mainland province of Mangi.[41]

As for Columbus's last-minute turn due "southwest" on the outward passage, we know that Columbus also counted on years of experience at sea reading nature's slightest symptoms, and he had learned that one could often detect approaching land by watching the direction of bird flocks at sundown. Columbus also meant to shy away from higher latitudes, given that winter was approaching in the northern hemisphere. And, finally, the topography of the Bahamas and the Antilles presents rosaries and clusters of islands often within close range of one another, a factor that played no minor role in the general routes Columbus would follow south of San Salvador and in the course of his subsequent surveys of the Caribbean basin.

But the Discoverer's southing involved more than geographical accidents such as the location and conditions of the Canaries, Bahamas, and Caribbean, or political contingencies such as Castile's success in wresting the Canaries away from Portugal, or cartographic conventions such as Çipango's being placed across from the Canaries. Columbus tended to state very explicitly his reasons for wanting to steer south, and

Cape Honduras
Punta Caxinas

15N

Cape Gracias a Dios

Honduras

Nicaragua

Costa Rica
Cariai

10N

Panama
Veragua

N
W ✦ E
S

FOURTH VOYAGE
Inset

Geographic Coordinate System, WGS84

I.11   Detail of Columbus's fourth voyage, 1502–1504. After Samuel Eliot Morison, *Admiral of the Ocean Sea: A Life of Christopher Columbus,* 2 vols. (Boston, 1942). Prepared by Lynn Carlson, Geological Sciences, Brown University, Providence, Rhode Island.

Caribbean Sea

Punta de Mosquito
Marmoro

Cape Tiburón
Marmoro

Colombia

Gulf of Urabá

75W

After Samuel Eliot Morison, *Admiral of the Ocean Sea: A Life of Christopher Columbus*
(Boston: Little, Brown and Co., 1942), vol. 2.

Route Based on Morison's Map

Route Suggested by Taviani

Italics indicate place names given by Columbus

Prepared By Lynn Carlson

he acted on these reasons rather consistently. Many such instances in his writings afford us a snapshot of the beliefs that informed his southing. Readers of his famous *Diario* will surely have noticed Columbus's attempt to explain the medium skin color of the inhabitants of San Salvador by noting that the island of the landfall stood on the same parallel as the Canaries. Readers may have also noticed Columbus's understated perplexity, as he ventured beyond San Salvador, at finding that the pigmentation of Bahamian and Caribbean peoples failed to darken to the "blackness" he had sighted in sub-Saharan Africans, and his expectation that, farther down, on the southeastern end of the coasts he was surveying, he was also bound to encounter nations of physically deformed humans who regularly practiced the most abject cruelties and depravities. Readers may also have wondered how the Discoverer would have gathered from the speech and gestures of the islanders he found along the way from the Bahamas to Cuba—with whom he must have shared few if any linguistic or gestural codes at all—the whereabouts of precious minerals like gold and coveted spices like cinnamon. As the *Diario* insists, "informants" from different islands invariably pointed Columbus in directions that entailed displacing himself due generally south—"south," "southwest," or "southeast"—of wherever he happened to find himself interrogating locals.

But a casual assertion in an entry of the *Diario* recounting the instance in which Columbus is supposed to have used his quadrant to establish the latitude of Puerto Gibara in northeastern Cuba (21 November 1492) suggests that his interpretation of the "directions" provided by locals on the way from San Salvador obeyed a deeply held preconception: Columbus believed that he was bound to find ever-greater quantities of coveted resources as he sailed farther south. Disputing the gross misreading shown by his quadrant (42° N), Columbus reasoned that the great "heat" he was suffering here proved that he could not be as far from the equator as the instrument read.[42] From this heat, he also concluded that he was venturing into one of the richest gold-bearing regions of the globe. As Las Casas reports in *Historia de las Indias,* Columbus, upon striking the Doldrums near the equator on his third voyage, and suffering the heat that he thought was in danger of setting his crew and ships ablaze, observed about the equator in his now-lost diary that "under that parallel of the world more gold and things of value are found."[43] And as Columbus reasoned years later, in his *carta-relación* of the fourth voyage (7 July 1503), "gold is generated in sterile lands *and wherever the sun is strong.*"[44]

Geographical certainties of this sort pervade Columbus's writings, and the fact that he should have seen many treasured certainties shattered in the course of his voyages (not to mention the fact that he never did reach Asia's periphery) should not lead us to conclude that Columbus's expectations obeyed, as sometimes claimed, the fancies of a feverish mind or the devious tendency to indulge in hyperbole. It is not surprising that five additional centuries of discovery and invention by individuals as bent on transforming human thought as Columbus was on redrawing the face of the globe should have rendered his logic flawed or recondite for us.

Since the early nineteenth century, when crucial documents from the early decades of Spanish exploration were first edited and published by Martín Fernández de Navarrete in his *Colección de los viages y descubrimientos, que hicieron por mar los españoles desde fines del siglo XV* (1825), Columbus's biographers and other scholars have often noted that the steep course that led Columbus to discover South America on his third voyage was urged on the Discoverer by one of Spain's foremost cosmographers at the time, the Catalan Jaume Ferrer de Blanes.[45] Ferrer is known today for having suggested to the Spanish Crown an ingenious method for establishing the longitude of the meridian that the famous Treaty of Tordesillas (1494) drew in mid-ocean to settle Castile and Portugal's dispute over the Atlantic. Incidentally, one of the few early tributes on record paid to Columbus as a navigator comes from Ferrer himself, who declared in his report to the Catholic Monarchs (1495) that he was more than willing to stand corrected in his calculation of the site of the line of demarcation "by those who know and understand more than myself, especially by the Admiral of the Indies, who is more learned in these matters than anyone in our time, for he is a great theoretician and an admirable practitioner, as his memorable achievements manifest."[46]

But Ferrer also happened to be an expert on precious stones (he wrote a brief treatise on mineralogy posthumously printed in Barcelona in 1545), and he had successfully engaged in the gem trade on the eastern shores of the Mediterranean.[47] In 1495, as Columbus labored to establish a colony in Haiti, the Crown was evidently growing anxious to realize the elusive profits of a dubious enterprise, and by request of Queen Isabel, Ferrer addressed a letter to Columbus in which he explained how the Discoverer might find those things which he had glaringly failed to find so far. In this most curious letter (5 August 1495), Ferrer expressed his opinion that it was "at the turn of the equator" that one was sure to find "great and valuable things like precious stones and gold and spices and medicines."[48] Ferrer assured Columbus that, while conducting business in the Levant, Ferrer had taken care to determine the climates and regions from which goods were brought. And what Ferrer had been able to gather in the course of many conversations with "Indians and Arabs and Ethiopians" was that "all good things come from very hot regions whose inhabitants are black or dark brown; and therefore, in my judgment, until Your Lordship meets such peoples, You shall fail to find an abundance of such things." Ferrer's advice to Columbus was written at a time when Mediterranean Europe was only just beginning to set eyes again on the vast world that extended beyond the forbidding deserts and semideserts of Saharan Africa and Arabia Deserta now largely controlled by Muslims. Ferrer's letter speaks to the profound ambivalence with which Mediterranean geographers reaching back to classical antiquity had regarded the regions of Africa and Asia that extended into the lower—and, by some accounts, intolerably hot, sterile, and inhospitable—latitudes of the globe.

Naturally, Columbus's most noted biographers in the last two centuries—among them, Washington Irving, Alexander von Humboldt, Samuel Eliot Morison, Antonio Ballesteros Beretta, Paolo Emilio Taviani, and Felipe Fernández-Armesto—have credited the cosmographer and lapidarian Ferrer with planting in Columbus's mind the goal of overtaking the equator in 1498.[49] Taviani, one of Columbus's most accomplished biographers in the twentieth century, in *I viaggi di Colombo: La grande scoperta* (1984) justly calls attention to Ferrer's larger role in the events unfolding from the discovery, not just in the steep exploration conducted by Columbus on the third voyage.[50] It is also hardly a surprise that the indelible connection that Ferrer seemed to establish in his letter to Columbus between heat, an abundance of precious goods, and the complexion of peoples in equatorial regions should have elicited different remarks from Columbus's post-Enlightenment biographers. In *A History of the Life and Voyages of Christopher Columbus* (1828), the romantic Irving already regarded such logic as little more than a historical curiosity. Much more recently, other Americanists have also taken note of the logic communicated by Ferrer's letter to Columbus: the distinguished editors of the recent *Colección documental del Descubrimiento (1470–1506)* (1994)—one of the most valuable compendia of Columbiana to have appeared since the publication of the massive *Raccolta* (1892–1896)—venture to say that the "meridional inflexion" presented by Columbus's itinerary on his third voyage appears to obey an ancient commonplace they term a "cosmography of riches."[51] And in some cases Ferrer's letter has played a role in developing important insights concerning Columbus's enterprise: thus Emiliano Jos in his succinct studies of Columbian cosmography, collected as *El plan y la génesis del descubrimiento colombino* (1979–1980), argues that Columbus's choice of the Canaries as a point of departure across the Atlantic had less to do with wind patterns out of the archipelago than with the fact that the Canaries stood on the way to the lower latitudes of the globe, for "to travel south was to approach the hottest regions of the globe and, thus, the richest in gold, as Columbus believed, and as was generally believed in his time."[52] And yet this important insight into Columbus's way of thinking, remains ancillary to Jos's general definition of the enterprise Columbus had in mind to undertake—as is the case with most references to Columbus's southing in the literature on the discovery.

Indeed, references to Columbus's southing are relatively common in the vast corpus on the discovery—in the documents drafted by Columbus himself, in the invaluable testimonies by his contemporaries and quasi contemporaries, and in subsequent studies of the period. But it is remarkable that no one in the last two centuries should appear to have taken Ferrer's advice to Columbus as an open invitation to explore the *systemic* role that terrestrial latitude may have played in both the planning and the execution of the Indies enterprise. As I argue here, our understanding of Columbus's enterprise can be greatly enhanced by according *latitude*—the north-south separation in degrees between any given place on the globe and the equator—the same importance we have accorded his idea of reaching the East "by way of the West." This is not to say that Americanists have failed to examine the concept of latitude itself in Columbus's works. On the contrary, numerous works on the protocols he followed to establish his location at sea and on land have touched upon this specific problem.[53] Did Columbus really know how to "shoot" the heavens? This was once suggested by Fernández de Oviedo, who claimed that Columbus was the first to teach Spanish pilots how to sail by the "altitudes" of the north pole and the sun. Or did Columbus only really know how to "chart" his way at sea, as the great nautical biographer Samuel Eliot Morison tried to show, concluding in his *Admiral of the Ocean Sea* (1942) that Columbus was a very poor celestial navigator but a great dead-reckoning sailor?[54] To be sure, studies of Columbus's latitudes have meticulously considered problems ranging from the egregious readings recorded in the extant *Diario* to Columbus's understanding of the relation of temperature to latitude in his later elaboration of the peculiar claim, following his exploration of the South American mainland, that the terraqueous globe was not really spherical but rather a pear-shaped spheroid. But precious little has been done to relate Columbus's latitudes to the whole of his thought or of his actions.

The problem, to my mind, is in part that we tend to construe the problem of Columbus's latitudes as a technical one involving the *art* of navigation rather than as a philosophical problem involving the *sciences* that came to surround the concept of latitude during the late medieval and early modern periods. This philosophical approach to the question of Columbus's southing is extremely rare in the literature on the discovery. For obvious reasons, those of Columbus's contemporaries and quasi contemporaries who documented the discovery tended to take for granted the theoretical knowledge behind Columbus's certainties. In fact, the only early historian to have made explicit this theoretical knowledge was the humanitarian friar Bartolomé de las Casas, whose monumental *Historia de las Indias* contains not only one of the fullest and ablest intellectual portraits we have of the Discoverer, but also the most thoroughly devastating indictment on record of European colonialism in the African and American tropics. Fully aware of the *verticality* of the early transatlantic encounter, Las Casas may be counted as the only biographer of Columbus in five centuries to have fully grasped the urgency of understanding both the deep assumptions behind Columbus's southing and the strong implications that his southing carried for the world order that followed in his wake. To my knowledge, the only post-Enlightenment author to have studied Columbus's southing from a philosophical perspective is the eminent cosmologist and explorer Alexander von Humboldt, whose *Examen critique de l'histoire de la géographie du nouveau continent et des progrès de l'astronomie nautique aux 15me et 16me siècles* (1836–1839) also offers one of the most lucid accounts of the intellectual origins of the discovery. A careful observer of the phenomena that accompanied latitudinal changes, Humboldt justly saw a systematic mind at work in everything Columbus cared to observe in his exploration of the Bahamas and Caribbean basin: "Nothing escaped Columbus's sagacity upon his arrival to a new heaven and a new world . . . neither the configuration of lands, nor the aspect of vegetation, nor the habits of animals, nor the distribution of heat along different longitudes, nor the island currents, nor magnetic variation. . . . Columbus did not content himself with just collecting isolated facts: he weighed them against each other, he looked for the connections between them, he applied himself, sometimes audaciously, to the discovery of the general laws governing the physical world."[55]

Some Americanists have seen in Columbus's southing reason to doubt the objectives traditionally ascribed to his enterprise. They have interpreted that element of his exploration as a distraction from the alleged goal of reaching the East "by way of the West"—in some cases as evidence that Columbus intended not to reach Asia at all but lands whose existence had been disclosed to him by means that remain at present only conjectural. Such is the role implicitly or explicitly assigned to latitude since the turn of the twentieth century by authors such as Henry Vignaud, Juan Ulloa, Rómulo D. Carbia, Cecil Jane, Juan Manzano Manzano, and Juan Pérez de Tudela y Bueso, most of whom favor arguments that a "pre-discovery" of one sort or another, whether by Columbus himself or by someone else who eventually confided in Columbus, inspired him to undertake his first voyage.[56] The unsuspecting instigator of this modern thesis—which tends to deny Columbus any true intellectual merit in the conception of his enterprise—was Fernández de Oviedo himself, who recorded in 1535 the rumor that a dying pilot in Columbus's care had confided to him a chance landfall in mid-ocean.[57] Fernández de Oviedo himself lent no credit to this rumor, but the notion that Columbus was the bearer of a "secret" has proved irresistible to a number of scholars since the turn of the twentieth century.

Henry Vignaud, the bad cop of Columbus studies, responsible for creating what has been dubbed "the schism among Americanists," famously revived the legend of the anonymous pilot in the course of three major studies, *Toscanelli and Columbus* (1902), *Études critiques sur la vie de Colomb avant ses découvertes* (1905), *Histoire critique de la grande entreprise de Christophe Colomb* (1911). He applied himself vigorously to demonstrating that those documents suggesting Asia as Columbus's original goal (particularly the famous correspondence attributed to the Florentine Paolo dal Pozzo Toscanelli) were either spurious or adulterated early on by a party interested in representing the Indies enterprise as the result of erudite reading on Columbus's part. (Vignaud's suspects included Columbus's seminal biographers, his son Ferdinand Columbus and Bartolomé de las Casas as well as Columbus's bon vivant grandson Luis Colón.) In Columbus's choice of the Canaries as a point of departure across the Atlantic—and in Columbus's famous supposition that the inhabited world extended into the arctic and tropical regions previously thought to be uninhabitable—Vignaud read a secret design that undermined the classical thesis established by Ferdinand and Las Casas (and followed by influential nineteenth-century historians like Henry Harrisse [1871] and Cesare de Lollis [1892]) that Columbus intended to reach the region once described by Marco Polo. If Columbus had really intended to sail "to the Indies or to Cathay," Vignaud argues, he would have simply wested from Spain's Atlantic coast across the ocean rather than venture out along the Canarian parallel.[58] Ignoring the fact that Columbus had been under strict orders not to sail directly south of the Canarian archipelago into Portuguese waters, Vignaud even claimed that had Columbus really wished to reach the Spice Islands, he would have chosen an even lower parallel for the outward passage. Vignaud's attempt to demolish the documentary edifice of the discovery prompted outraged rebuttals from a number of his contemporaries, and his thesis that Columbus was solely looking for the mid-ocean shores described by the unknown pilot has been judged by many a respected Americanist since as a highly erudite aberration. Vignaud's argument, however, is still important to understand for this reason: Vignaud tended to use interchangeably the toponyms *Cathay* and *India* mentioned in primary sources, an error one tends to find in the works of many an Americanist to this day. Vignaud failed to grasp that Cathay, the northern Chinese province once identified by Marco Polo as the seat of the Mongols on the Asian mainland, was not at all the India that Marco Polo had distinctly associated with those territories south of Cathay. Marco Polo's India faced *south* toward a vast geographical system that included the basin of the Indian Ocean, Indochina, and the islands of Indonesia (so did the Chinese port city of Zaiton and the island of Çipango). Failing to make this crucial geographical distinction between continental and maritime Asia, Vignaud also failed to understand the extent to which, in the eyes of Columbus and his contemporaries, sailing across the ocean "to the parts of India" (*ad partes Indie*) would have entailed sailing to the west *and* to the south of Mediterranean Europe. In other words, sailing "to the parts of India" also meant sailing south *away* from the higher latitudes of Cathay. And Vignaud mistakenly read this north-south opposition between Cathay and India in Columbus's writing as an east-west opposition between Asia and an embryonic America.

Some Americanists, including Vignaud and his heirs, have tended to underestimate Columbus's theoretical knowledge as a fundamental component of his enterprise. Consider the crucial insight forwarded in the 1920s by Cecil Jane, one of Columbus's best-known translators and editors in the English-speaking world today. In his *Select Documents Illustrating the Four Voyages of Christopher Columbus,* published by the Hakluyt Society between 1930 and 1933 and reprinted in 1988 on occasion of the recent quincentenary, Jane argued emphatically that Columbus's most pressing goal may have been to sail south in search of considerable landmasses, peoples, and resources previously unknown to Europeans and that this goal may even have been motivated by a generalized view that the richest lands lay to the south.[59] But this was a goal that in Jane's view disenfranchised the prevailing thesis that Columbus had meant to reach Asia, or even the mid-Atlantic islands depicted on *mappaemundi* like Behaim's; moreover, Jane thought, this was also a goal whose unorthodox geography Columbus would have guarded most jealously, even from his royal benefactors, for fear that he should never see it realized. Jane, however, refused to identify the means, intellectual or otherwise, that Columbus might have had at his disposal to conclude that he would find considerable lands unrelated to mainland Asia or its immediate periphery. We are left to assume that Columbus arrived at this conviction by means other than intellectual, since Jane stubbornly maintains that Columbus lacked significant scientific and technical information prior to crossing the ocean, and that he only came to dabble in pseudo-learned theories when he was later forced to defend himself from those who doubted the merits of his accomplishments.[60] In deference to Jane's claims about Columbus's learning, we do know that Columbus was hardly the erudite figure that he and his early biographers Ferdinand and Las Casas wished to portray. Columbus himself was painfully aware that he had always been scorned in learned circles as someone "not learned in letters, an ignorant sailor, a vulgar man."[61] But Jane's view of Columbus as a crass, superstitious sailor on a lucky streak is demonstrably wrong. This position on Columbus's learning prevented Jane from bringing to fruition the wonderful, raw insight that Columbus desperately wished to sail south: Jane failed to appreciate the degree to which Columbus's southing had obeyed a coherent, intricate worldview—a view that hardly obligated Columbus or his contemporaries to instantly recognize that the lands and peoples found in the Caribbean basin were geographically or, even more important, *ontologically* unrelated to those of legendary India.

The present book argues that latitude was an integral and explicit organizing principle in the Indies enterprise. The great Strabo, whose *Geography* has taught us nearly everything we know about Greek theoretical geography and cartography into the first century before the common era, mentions two different methods for observing differences in latitude. The first method, used for calculating greater differences in latitude, relied "on the evidence of the eye itself, or of the crops or of the temperature of the atmosphere."[62] The second method, used for calculating lesser differences in latitude, relied on measurements afforded by sundials and dioptrical instruments. This book does not delve into Columbus's aptitude at measuring latitude by technical means—an issue that has caused much ink to be spilled among Americanists. Instead, it focuses attention on Columbus's ability to correlate, by means of his bare senses, latitude, temperature, and the nature of places on the globe.

Columbus's geographical certainties obeyed a complex set of assumptions that were shared, no matter how imperfectly, with the most learned minds in the Latin West concerning what one may properly call the nature of places. Place was a crucial cosmological concept in the intellectual tradition that witnessed the encounter between Europeans and the native peoples of the Americas. In their involved discussions of the structure and workings of the cosmos, the "schooled" heirs of Plato's and Aristotle's physics considered place to be one of the principles of the universe. The elements and their compounds tended to occupy places in the geocentric cosmos in accordance with their own particular natures. Heavenly bodies in this cosmos were God's intermediaries, responsible for generating and destroying all physical creatures—whether humans, beasts, plants, or minerals. And place was the key for understanding the celestial causes that acted upon bodies as well as for predicting much of their behavior. This cosmological tradition, primarily rooted in classical antiquity, had come of age in the Latin West with the momentous translation of Greek and Arabic works in the twelfth and thirteenth centuries. Writers in this tradition, who pictured a relation of cause and effect that bound the heavenly and elemental regions, often referred to this cosmos as a working artifact, or *machina*. And in a universe so conceived, any consideration of place stood at the intersection of a broad, logical array of knowledge domains, many of which no longer bear to each other the connections that were once obvious to schoolmen or even to informally educated individuals like the Discoverer.

Not surprisingly, geography was hardly just a tool for locating, describing, or reaching the various parts of the inhabited world. As an art concerned with places, geography fully participated in the philosophical quest to apprehend the nature of all things placed; and as a discipline geography was closely tied to a range of other fields whose connections to one another were thought to obey the structure and functioning of an artifactual universe. Briefly stated, geography also deeply concerned the nature of places. And only by considering the epistemic system underlying the practice of geography in the late medieval cosmological tradition can we more fully explain crucial aspects of Columbus's thought—from his concept of the ratio and distribution of earth and water at the center of the cosmos to his notion of the extent to which the globe was habitable, his ideas concerning the nature of the lands and peoples he was setting out to find, and even what he believed he ought to accomplish in the course of his wanderings.

Columbus shared with the great geographers before him—especially theoretical thinkers like Eratosthenes, Strabo, and Ptolemy—the fundamental premises that every place had its own unique nature, that similar places gave way to similar natures, and that different places gave way to different natures. And when it came to describing the similarities and differences between places on the surface of the globe, it was *latitude,* not longitude, that geographers had most closely associated with the nature of places. In the words of one of Aristotle's most able and influential commentators, the Cordoban philosopher Averroës (Ibn Rushd, 1126–1198), "Latitudes . . . are more significant for the diversity of lands than longitudes."[63] We need only recall Ptolemy's famous sentence in his own influential *Geography* (2nd century CE) that "all animals and plants that are on the same parallels or [parallels] equidistant from either pole ought to exist in similar combinations in accordance with the similarity of their environments."[64] It was with latitude in mind that Mediterranean geographers had long established meaningful connections between sub-Saharan Africa, or "Ethiopia," and the extended basin of the Indian Ocean, or "India." Latitude explains why, for instance, geographers thought it natural that gold, cinnamon, crocodiles, elephants, and dragons should flourish in both Ethiopia and India, and why they marveled at the fact that the Ganges River should not have had hippopotamuses, like the Nile. Latitude also explains why Ptolemy, the most influential geographer of antiquity, should have assumed that "black" peoples equally flourished in sub-Saharan Africa, the Arabian Peninsula, and the very confines of the Indian Ocean, and why many centuries later Columbus should have been perturbed not to find them in the Caribbean basin. In short, while longitude may have initially represented for Columbus the nightmare of crossing an unknown ocean, it was latitude that would tell Columbus again and again—when he admired the gold ornaments on indigenous bodies and when he gazed overhead at parrot flocks so dense they obscured the sun—that he had indeed arrived in the Indies, or at least in a place that shared the same nature with the old Ethiopia and India.

Most unfortunately, while longitude may speak to a technical feat that many of Columbus's contemporaries deemed impossible, latitude speaks to a geopolitical process that Bartolomé de las Casas called the "destruction of the Indies" (*destruyçion delas yndias*).[65] The history of Columbus's westing has been, and will remain, largely a chapter in the history of the technical challenges that long involved attempts to measure longitude. As such, Columbus's ideas concerning the value of an equatorial degree, the horizontal extension of the inhabited world, and the narrowness of an intervening ocean will continue to be cited as idiosyncratic precepts that gave way to what Europeans only gradually realized was a "mistake"—what Taviani aptly calls a "productive error."[66]

Columbus's southing is another matter. His conscious distinction between the higher and traditionally "cooler" latitudes of Mediterranean Europe and the lower and traditionally hotter latitudes of the Indies irrefragably points to an intellectual and material culture that in the course of a little more than a century—from Portugal's taking control of the North African port of Ceuta in 1415 to Elcano's completing the first circumnavigation of the globe in 1522—reached the problematic realization that Europe was only the northern neighbor to a vast and immensely rich and populous world to the south. The fact is that the bulk of discoveries carried out by European explorers in this early phase of exploration and colonization—first in Atlantic Africa, then in the Americas and the greater basin of the Indian Ocean, and finally in the Pacific Ocean—took place within the region of the globe we know today as the belt of the tropics. And, as Ferrer's memorable letter to Columbus seems to suggest, this process was fraught with changing certainties concerning the nature of that belt and of its peoples.

Indeed, Columbus's project was conceived and executed between two antithetical perceptions of the tropics. One need only browse Pierre d'Ailly's *Ymago mundi* (1410), one of Columbus's favorite treatises, to come across the view that had long prevailed in the Latin West concerning the distribution of land and life around the globe: the three known continents—Europe, Africa, and Asia—were supposed to configure a single landmass stranded on an upper quarter of a globe otherwise covered by water, and the inhabited world itself was supposed to form a narrow "temperate" and, thereby, "civilized" corridor of this geographical system, besieged to the north and to the south by the extreme cold and heat of the "wild" arctic and tropics.[67] Sub-Saharan Africa, or "Ethiopia," and the lands that verged on the extended basin of the Indian Ocean, or "India," were thus imagined as the hot, infertile, and uninhabitable fringes of the world, where a merciless heat forged the precious metals and stones so coveted in Europe, and where only geographical accidents such as the Nile or the Ganges occasionally invited nature to come back with a vengeance, spawning the myriad living "marvels" and "monsters" that had gripped the imagination of Mediterranean geographers since antiquity. This narrow definition of the "normal" limits of habitation had its ground in a cosmological paradigm today attributed to the Eleatic philosopher Parmenides (early 5th century BCE)—the theory of the five zones. This theory had gained great acceptance in the Latin West thanks to works as diverse as Virgil's *Georgica* (1st century BCE), Ovid's

Metamorphoses (1st century CE), Pomponius Mela's *De chorographia* (1st century CE), Pliny's *Naturalis historia* (1st century CE), and Lucan's *De bello civili* (1st century CE).[68]

But a rather different view of the geographical extent of life on the globe contended that the tropics were *not* the desolate fringes of the inhabited world. The great modern proponents of this view—Henry the Navigator and Columbus himself—had met fierce opposition for their willingness to breach the forbidding gates of the torrid zone. In the opening decades of the fifteenth century, Prince Henry had literally wasted years attempting to persuade the sailors in his service on the coast of Morocco to cross the threshold of the Canaries and Cape Bojador into what even the learned in Portugal expected to be a hellish wasteland from which no one would return alive. Columbus and his supporters in Castile, for their part, would fail to persuade the council in charge of evaluating his project that he could find any land, much less productive or inhabited land, in the tropical latitudes of the high Atlantic.

Nevertheless, in the wake of Columbus's momentous discovery, the view appears to have gained some ground that the belt of the tropics might harbor a truly vast geographical system, and that it might constitute a hugely productive and populous region of the globe. Indeed, this is the tenor of the letter that the Catholic Monarchs had already written to Columbus in 1493, urging him to return to the high Atlantic in search of possible lands that would be even wealthier than those he had discovered on his first voyage, precisely because they stood "in the part of the sun." The Savonese Michele Cuneo, who wrote a famous letter (15 and 18 October 1495) to his compatriot Girolamo Annari describing the events of the second voyage, recounted that his great friend Columbus had sailed from the recently founded town of La Ysabela on northern Hispaniola back to Alpha et Omega, on Cuba's eastern tip, with the intention of resuming his exploration of the Indies. According to Cuneo, Columbus had held council with his men at Cape Maisi in order to determine whether they should now retrace last year's footsteps along northeastern Cuba in the direction of the northwest (where Columbus would have expected eventually to run into Cathay), or whether they should explore Cuba's inner coasts to the south (further into Columbus's India), and "all agreed that it was better to take the route of the south, because if something good was to be found, it would more likely be toward the south than toward the north."[69]

By the time of Columbus's death, the tide appears to have turned on the traditional theory of the five zones. Thus in 1507 the renowned cosmographer Martin Waldseemüller had slightly revised its tenets. In his *Cosmographiae introductio*,

Waldseemüller dared to claim that the so-called "torrid zone" was not absolutely desolate; rather, it was "habitable with difficulty."[70] And in the main caption of the extraordinary *mappamundi* that accompanied the *Cosmographiae introductio,* the map that gave America its name, Waldseemüller even celebrated the fact that the "land discovered by great and exceedingly worthy men, Columbus, Captain of the King of Castile, and Amerigo Vespucci," stood squarely "under the circuit and path of the sun between the tropics" (**fig. I.12**).[71] Indeed, the America known to Waldseemüller was nothing less, and nothing more, than the southern landmass discovered by Columbus and later explored by his friend Amerigo. And in Waldseemüller's mind this landmass now formed part of a vast and almost equally novel geographical system comprehended by the belt of the tropics—the newly explored sub-Saharan Africa and extended basin of the Indian Ocean.

In 1519 the Spanish explorer and colonial officer Martín Fernández de Enciso, celebrating the recent exploration of a tropical expanse Columbus had insisted on calling the "West Indies," marveled in his *Suma de geographia* at the fact that the ancients should have ever thought that the lands Enciso's contemporaries had by now reached in "Ethiopia," "Arabia Felix," "Calicut," and "Melacca" were uninhabitable.[72] In *De orbe novo* (1530) Peter Martyr would even scorn the attempts of a certain *oidor* of Hispaniola by the name of Lucas Vázquez de Ayllón to explore the continental mass to the north of Greater Antilles then known as "Florida" (1521). What need was there, Martyr asked, to return to the higher latitudes where one was sure to find similar products to those already found in Europe? "To the south, to the south!" he urged his reader, for it was in that direction that anyone with any sense whatsoever could have expected to harvest the treasures of the globe.[73]

By 1552 Hernán Cortés's "chaplain," Francisco López de Gómara, frankly celebrated in his *Historia general de las Indias* the exploits of imperial Spain in the belt of the tropics, referring to his fellow Spaniards as the "scarecrows of the ancients."[74] And by the turn of the seventeenth century, in *Historia general de los hechos de los castellanos en las islas y tierrafirme del mar océano* (1600–1615), the official historian and cosmographer Antonio de Herrera y Tordesillas had defined once and for all Columbus's place in the "glorious" history of territorial expansion begun by the Spanish nation by stating that the Discoverer had never let himself be "shooed away by the equinoctial line, or by the torrid zone."[75] In sum, without an understanding that Columbus's Indies enterprise actively contributed to a colonial awakening that fundamentally involved the "invention" of the tropics, the geographical history of the discovery will, to my mind, remain sorely incomplete.[76]

The transition from a view of the tropics as forbidding inferno to one of the tropics as prodigal paradise was slow to dawn on the Age of Exploration. In fact, the work of scholars who in recent years have sought to examine the cultural syndrome aptly called "tropicality" is showing again and again that both perceptions have remained paradoxically ensconced in the Western imagination.[77] Indeed, Columbus's exploration of the Bahamas and Caribbean basin simultaneously invoked these inimical views of the tropics. Columbus was keenly aware that all lands and waters he proceeded to explore beyond San Salvador (the island he mindfully located on the same parallel as the Canaries) fell toward or south of the Tropic of Cancer. And he seems to have been bent on proving that, contrary to the conventional wisdom about the torrid zone, the territories he had found in the high Atlantic were not only admirably productive and populous but also more generally temperate than even *he* had dared anticipate—not at all the desolate hinterlands predicted by the theory of the five zones. Yet, even as he marveled at the ever more sublime temperateness, fertility, and inhabitability of the Indies, Columbus also refused to relinquish the view that its peoples were the barbarians whom Mediterranean antiquity had tended to locate in the freezing and scorching regions of the arctic and the tropics. Indeed, while Columbus's India was proving to be a superlatively temperate, fertile, and inhabitable Eden, Columbus's Indians remained, by his testimony, childish or monstrous creatures of the globe's infernal fringes whose liminal nature seemed to justify rendering them Europe's subjects or slaves. In effect, even as the belt of the tropics seemed to be gradually displacing Mediterranean Europe as the uniquely temperate and, thereby, civilized center of the inhabited world, Columbus and his ideological heirs would insist on construing tropical peoples as Europe's moral periphery. This, to my mind, was and remains a fundamental paradox of imperial geopolitics.

The geographical distinction between the higher latitudes of Mediterranean Europe and the lower latitudes of the Bahamas and Caribbean basin was to prove of enormous political consequence for the peoples Columbus invented. Columbus certainly regarded this distinction as crucial grounds for subjecting and enslaving the peoples of the Indies. Such a distinction also crucially anticipated imperial Spain's efforts to establish the lawfulness to its occupation of the Americas. One needs only read the work of eminent historians like Lewis Hanke and Anthony Pagden to realize that Columbus's inaugural

54

55

geopolitics soon found a "learned" voice in the seminal philosophical debate in the sixteenth century between the apologists of empire who sought to establish Spain's legal titles to its overseas colonies, and humanitarian figures like Bartolomé de las Casas, who sought to discredit every title Spain had claimed to its lording rights in the Indies. While apologists like Juan Ginés de Sepúlveda continued to construe Spain's Indians as the natural subjects or slaves whom Aristotle and his cohorts had believed to be generated in the hot margins of the inhabited world, Las Casas's strategy to deprive the conquest of all legitimacy was precisely to subvert the geopolitical paradigm that he saw at work in Columbus's life and works: if Columbus's exploits in the Bahamas and Caribbean basin had proved that the Indies formed an unimaginably vast and unbeatably fertile, populous, and, of all things, *temperate* part of the globe, how could anyone in good conscience continue to identify Indians with barbarians on the scorched edges of a narrow world? As Las Casas ultimately argued, if experience had shown that nature was even more "perfect" in the American tropics than anywhere else on the globe—not excepting Mediterranean Europe—why should Indians be treated as Europe's "natural" subordinates? Indeed, it is largely Las Casas's attack on the contradiction attendant to Columbian geopolitics that lends significance to his monumental *Historia de las Indias,* undoubtedly the most conscientious and fearless treatment ever written of early modern Europe's devastation of the tropics.

The distinction that accompanied Columbus's southing between the higher latitudes of Mediterranean Europe and the lower latitudes of the Indies carries broader implications. To mention only a few of relevance to the intellectual and literary history of the Americas, it was in conversation with this geopolitics that such masterpieces of American ethnology as Las Casas's own *Apologética historia sumaria* (completed around 1561), Jesuit cleric Joseph de Acosta's *Historia natural y moral de las Indias* (1590), and "mestizo" historian Garcilaso de la Vega's *Comentarios reales de los incas* (1609) sought to forge a "place" for the Indians within the "natural" and "moral" orders acknowledged by European theologians and philosophers across the Atlantic.[78] And, as recent work on "creole" thought in the Americas by a younger generation of distinguished scholars like Jorge Cañizares Esguerra is beginning to suggest, "novel" interpretations of the very geopolitics inaugurated by Columbus between Europe and the American tropics were conceptually significant to emerging local elites who began to imagine themselves politically autonomous from the Old World.[79] It is no coincidence that we should later find independence hero Simón Bolívar portraying himself in his best-known manifesto,

Carta de Jamaica (1815), as the future guardian of his beloved *América meridional,* by which Bolívar meant everything from Mexico and the Caribbean to Patagonia; nor that his illustrious contemporary, the influential lawyer and philologist Andrés Bello, should have bequeathed to later generations of Latin Americans a patriotic ode we know as "Silva a la agricultura en la zona tórrida" (1826).[80]

I would go so far as to insist that the geopolitical paradigm that Columbus and his contemporaries inherited from classical antiquity remains alive and well in the West. To the extent that five hundred years after Columbus's death we continue to wrestle with the divide between the "developed" nations of the north and the "developing" nations of the south, we too are heirs to an intellectual tradition whose ancient notions of place paved the way for recent colonialism.

Machina Mundi

THE MORAL AUTHORITY OF PLACE
IN THE EARLY TRANSATLANTIC ENCOUNTER

Geography and politics were closely allied disciplines in a cosmological tradition that imagined the orderly workings of the geocentric universe as the *machina mundi,* or "machine of the world." This book describes the knowledge system that connected concepts of *place*—a subject of philosophical commentary among the ancient and medieval heirs of Plato's and Aristotle's physics—to what eventually became *colonialism*—a set of beliefs and practices associated with Christian Europe's great territorial expansion in the latter half of the fifteenth century.[1] Scholars have typically studied the transition from late medieval to early modern geography in relative isolation from this broad intellectual context. The strongest ancient model for this finite approach to the history of the field continues to be Claudius Ptolemy's *Geography* (2nd century CE), which was imported from the besieged Byzantine Empire and translated into Latin at the turn of the fifteenth century. Ptolemy's remarkable treatise defined geography as a general description of the known inhabited world and provided the technical knowledge that helped transform map making in the Age of Exploration (**fig. 1.1**). But well into the seventeenth century, many generations of Christian writers were also deeply influenced by the Greek and Arabic works first rendered into Latin during the twelfth and thirteenth centuries, most importantly, the Aristotelian corpus. And for many of these writers, geography fully participated in the search for an explanation of the *nature* of all physical creatures in the cosmos. It is this philosophical aspect of scholastic geography that informs our discussion of geography's ties to ideologies of empire during the early years of Spanish presence in the Americas. What follows is an attempt to further explain the epistemology by which Christian Europe began to articulate its lordship over the horizontal belt of the globe we know as the tropics.

1.1 Ptolemy's first projection.
From his *Cosmographia* (Bologna,
1477). Courtesy of the John Carter
Brown Library at Brown University,
Providence, Rhode Island.

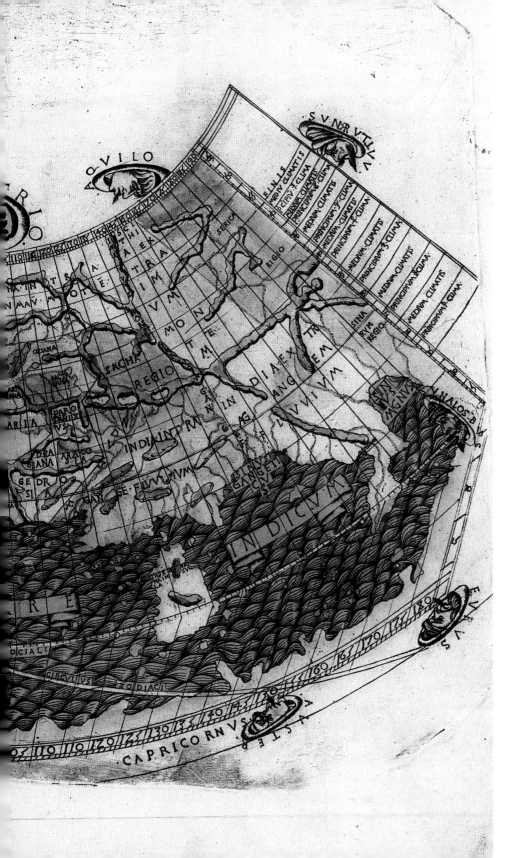

63

The main figures considered here—Albertus Magnus (about 1200–1280), Pierre d'Ailly (1350–1420), Christopher Columbus (about 1451–1506), and Bartolomé de las Casas (1484–1566)—uniquely shape the geographical history of the early Euro-Caribbean encounter. The Dominican priest Bartolomé de las Casas is best known for his unabating defense of American native peoples' rights under the Spanish Empire, but he also remains Columbus's most influential early editor and biographer.[2] Las Casas produced the only extant summary copy of Columbus's now-lost *Diario* of the first voyage (1492–1493) as well as the fullest early intellectual portrait of the Discoverer in a work that challenged the legality of Spain's occupation of the Americas, *Historia de las Indias* (written between 1527 and 1561 but not printed until 1875).[3] In the opening chapters, Las Casas mindfully indexed Albertus Magnus's *De natura loci* (On the Nature of Place; about 1251–1254) as one of the scholastic sources that anticipated the discovery. In Albertus, Columbus would have found confirmation for his belief that the belt of the tropics was, contrary to geographical lore, a generally temperate and vastly fertile and inhabitable region of the globe. Albertus's *De natura loci* is of vital importance for understanding the relation that Christian Aristotelianism established early on between "nature" and "culture," and it crucially informed Las Casas's explanation of Columbus's geography and its sources. In the opening chapters of his *Historia,* Las Casas also identified Pierre d'Ailly's *Ymago mundi* (Image of the World, 1410) as the most important scholastic source behind the Discoverer's plan to cross the Atlantic to the end of the Orient. While Las Casas could claim only that Columbus was well acquainted with such geographical theories as were forwarded in Albertus's *De natura loci,* Las Casas did have at hand Columbus's annotated copy of a collection of treatises by Pierre d'Ailly and Jean Gerson, *Tractatus de ymagine mundi et varia ejusdem auctoris et Joannis Gersonis opuscula,* which was published in Louvain between 1480 and 1483.[4]

Albertus and d'Ailly are cited today among the numerous authorities whose geography informed the Indies enterprise, although Albertus has failed to draw due attention from scholars.[5] Columbus's annotated copy of d'Ailly's and Gerson's *Tractatus*—containing hundreds of postils by him, his brother Bartholomew, and his son Ferdinand—has secured d'Ailly's prominence among students of the discovery.[6] D'Ailly is widely believed to have played a significant role in the planning stages of the ocean crossing, despite occasional claims that Columbus's reliance on his work was only retrospective.[7] In contrast, Albertus remains virtually unexamined in relation to the origins of the Indies enterprise. We have no direct evidence that Columbus ever read

Albertus's *De natura loci,* though the argument was forwarded in the nineteenth century that Columbus would have been introduced to Albertus's treatise in 1486 by Dominicans at the University of Salamanca.[8] This book does not attempt to demonstrate that Columbus was directly acquainted with Albertus's *De natura loci,* although Columbus was by no means a stranger to the fundamentals and particular claims this treatise shared with other ancient and medieval works. Instead, it treats Las Casas's inclusion of Albertus as Columbus's forebear as an open invitation to revisit the question of Columbus's geography along a far broader front than has been previously considered. Albertus provided Las Casas the "schooled" foundation to explain the epistemology that fueled Columbus's discoveries and that justified his colonial policies in the Bahamas and Caribbean basin. Moreover, Albertus's presence in Las Casas's intellectual biography of Columbus speaks as profoundly to Columbus's geography as it does to the anticolonialist argument of Las Casas's monumental *Historia de las Indias.*

Our present understanding of the intellectual origins of the discovery has largely followed the leads of Columbus's most important early biographers: Las Casas himself and the Discoverer's son Ferdinand. In its Spanish manuscript version (about 1537–1539), Ferdinand's biography of his father constituted one of Las Casas's main sources for *Historia de las Indias.*[9] Despite its manifest blunders, and despite some suspicion that other hands intervened in its composition, the work we now know only in Alfonso Ulloa's 1571 Italian translation as *Historie del S. D. Fernando Colombo* remains a vital source on Columbus's life.[10] Ferdinand—and Las Casas after him—laid out the geographical fundamentals that Columbus is generally agreed to have culled from his readings of ancient and medieval authors: his ideas about the globe's sphericity, which, incidentally, were common currency in his day;[11] his underestimation of the value of an equatorial degree and thus of the globe's circumference; his overestimation of the eastward extension of Asia, which reduced the distance separating the Canary Islands from the end of the Orient; his contention that the torrid zone and the antipodes were inhabitable; and—one of the most debated aspects of Columbus's geography—the identity of the lands he intended to find.[12] These geographical particulars, crucial though they are, continue to overpower our understanding of d'Ailly's role as Columbus's forebear in the formulation of an ocean crossing.[13] Nevertheless, a growing body of scholarship has begun to examine the question of Columbus's geography—and, with it, the question of d'Ailly's legacy to Columbus—in connection with other aspects of the Discoverer's thought, such as his militant religiosity.[14] In contrast, Albertus receives only

perfunctory citation in catalogs of Columbus's sources. While Ferdinand's biography of his father does not mention Albertus among Columbus's forebears, Las Casas's *Historia de las Indias* strategically introduces Albertus's *De natura loci* in preparation for repudiating the colonialist project begun by Columbus and subsequently defended by apologists of the Spanish Crown.

This book revisits the question of Columbus's geography by establishing geography's complex philosophical grounding in Albertus's *De natura loci* and in d'Ailly's and Gerson's *Tractatus* and by illuminating the logic that led Las Casas to catalog Albertus, along with d'Ailly, as Columbus's forebear. Columbus was certainly not as schooled or well read as Ferdinand and Las Casas claimed. On this matter, one must unfortunately agree with sixteenth-century historian Francisco López de Gómara's ill-blooded but succinct portrayal of the Admiral as one less "learned" than "savvy."[15] However, if we fail to consider Las Casas's *learned* interpretation of Columbus's geography, we shall never fully understand either the powerful intellectual capital that links Columbus to Albertus and d'Ailly or, for that matter, the full status of geography in the history of the early transatlantic encounter.

Geography played an exceedingly complex role in the intellectual culture that witnessed Columbus's exploration and colonization of the Bahamas and Caribbean basin (1492–1503). For writers in the high scholastic tradition, the quantitative measuring and naming of Euclidean extension on the globe was but one component of spatial theory and practice. Place was a key cosmological concept, no matter how diverse or irreconcilable its treatments in this tradition. As one sees in Albertus's *De natura loci,* Aristotle's definitions of place coexisted uneasily with those of Albertus's Neoplatonic sources.[16] Aristotle posited that every physical body tended to occupy a place in the spherical cosmos in accordance with its own particular "nature," that is, its intrinsic ability to be moved or changed.[17] But for Albertus and many who followed in the high scholastic tradition, motion and change were actively communicated to physical creatures from without, so that place was largely the medium through which celestial bodies imparted form to sublunary creatures.[18] In a cosmos conceived as a working artifact, place was a fundamental category for understanding the behavior of *all* physical bodies, including the besouled bodies of humans, beasts, and plants.[19] For the writers considered here, concepts of place—no matter how implicitly—pervaded *and* joined seemingly remote fields of knowledge, such as physics and politics.

Because place was a key cosmological concept, geography was part of a broad network of interrelated sciences and arts that reflected the harmony and internal workings of the world-machine. Even as geographical exploration in the fifteenth and sixteenth centuries imported data that greatly advanced imperial cartography's precision in Europe, geography retained its logical ties to a broad range of interrelated disciplines.[20] Well into the seventeenth century, in the numerous cosmographies, chronographies, geographies, hydrographies, and navigational manuals produced in the Spanish Empire, writers continued to practice geography in relation to what Lorenzo Ferrer Maldonado, in his highly technical manual *Imagen del mundo sobre la esfera, cosmografía y geografía, teórica de planetas y arte de navegar* (1626), called the *universal máquina del mundo*.[21] Titles from the period attest to geography's connections to a broad range of fields. Consider, for instance, Jerónimo de Chaves's well-known *Chronographia o Repertorio delos tiempos* (1548), which declared its subject to be "Philosophy, Astrology, Cosmography, and Medicine, and a Few Brief Histories of the World's Ages"; Juan Pérez de Moya's *Fragmentos mathemáticos* (1567), which treated "Matters of Astronomy, Geography, Natural Philosophy, the Sphere, the Astrolabe, Navigation, and the Clock"; or Francisco Vicente Tornamira's own *Chronographia, y Repertorio de los tiempos* (1585), which treated "Cosmography, the Sphere, Planetary Theory, Philosophy, Computation [Time-Reckoning], and Astronomy," as well as the connection of "Medicine with Astrology."[22]

During the thirteenth century, Albertus had been one of geography's founding theorists in this cosmological tradition. His *De natura loci* repositioned ancient and medieval geography within a philosophical and technical system of disciplines that explicitly connected concepts of place with political theory. Not without justification has this treatise been called "the most important and the more elaborate discussion of geographical theory with relation to human cultures since the Hippocratic *Airs, Waters, and Places*."[23] In his treatment of geography's ties to this epistemic system, Albertus was rivaled perhaps only by his illustrious contemporary, the Franciscan Roger Bacon (born about 1214–1220; died about 1292), whose celebrated *Opus maius* (about 1266–1267) ghosts lengthy and highly significant passages of d'Ailly's *Ymago mundi* (1410).[24]

Although d'Ailly himself was not nearly as "original" as his two predecessors, he was one of the earliest scholars to use Jacopo d'Angelo's 1406 translation of Ptolemy's *Geography*, the work that established the methods and data of a field we now understand as "cartography."[25] D'Ailly's work bears witness to the fact that the introduction of

Ptolemy's technical treatise, which Jacopo had deliberately christened *Cosmographia*, did not automatically redefine spatiality or divorce geographical practice from its broad intellectual context.[26] D'Ailly's primary interest in Ptolemy's terrestrial coordinates was astrological, not cartographic.[27] The recent schism, splitting papal power between the sees of Rome and Avignon, had caused members of the clergy to believe that the advent of the Antichrist was imminent.[28] The theological question posed by this troubled geopolitics led d'Ailly to pair up historical events since the time of Creation with the major planetary conjunctions that the ninth-century Arabic astrologer Albumasar (Abū Ma'shar) and his successors had associated with the rise and fall of religious sects.[29] In this context, Ptolemy's geographical coordinates promised to render operative a complex philosophical and technical system that explained cause and effect in the physical world in terms of celestial influence. Columbus's annotated copy of d'Ailly's and Gerson's *Tractatus* was, among other things, a "practical" application of the cosmological framework that connected geography and politics in this tradition.

It is precisely in this light that Las Casas would come to understand Albertus's, d'Ailly's, and other authors' parentage of Columbus's geography. The "savvy" Columbus and the erudite Las Casas would deploy a reasoning identical to Albertus's and d'Ailly's in order to map the Bahamas and Caribbean basin. But, whereas Columbus used this cosmological framework to justify the subjection of native peoples, Las Casas was to use it a generation later to challenge Spain's titles to the occupation of the New World.

Las Casas's assertion of Albertus and d'Ailly as Columbus's geographical sources took place in the context of a political battle over the fates of American peoples. Las Casas produced his summary of Columbus's *Diario* in preparation for his fiercely anticolonial *Historia de las Indias* and its companion volume, *Apologética historia sumaria*. The *Apologética*—a most thorough "natural" and "moral" history of the New World—argued that the geography of the Americas, contrary to the traditional view that the tropics were a hot and inhospitable part of the globe, fostered instead ideal temperate conditions for the development of highly complex civilizations capable of self-government.[30] Like many of his Spanish contemporaries, Las Casas viewed the discovery as a thoroughgoing theological event that had opened the doors for American peoples to embrace Christianity. Unlike many of his contemporaries, however, Las Casas also believed that the Indians should be free to choose whether or not to be treated to Christian doctrine or to European customs, and he came to consider the Spanish occupation of the Americas sinful and illegal.[31] For Las Casas, Columbus was God's pious "apostle and minister of these Indies,"[32] but Las Casas bitterly condemned Columbus's transatlantic policy, which had introduced slavery, compulsory tribute, and the *repartimiento*—the system of forced peonage that supported agriculture and mining in Spain's overseas colonies.[33]

The fact that Las Casas made the *Diario* an accessory to his polemical writings invites us to revisit the question of Columbus's geography in the wider context of the cosmology that Las Casas explicitly formalized in *Historia de las Indias* and the *Apologética*.[34] Las Casas's histories provide us with a model for understanding geography in the Age of Discovery as part of a broad scientific and technical enterprise rather than as a mere a tool for navigation and surveillance. Remarkably, in Las Casas's summary copy of the *Diario,* two antithetical views on the rights of New World peoples—Columbus's colonialism and Las Casas's anticolonialism—lay claim to one and the same cosmology. Together, Albertus, d'Ailly, Columbus, and Las Casas offer a rich picture of the intellectual framework that steered Spain's early exploration of the Indies and the ensuing legal controversy in Crown circles over the rights of the newly colonized peoples.

Writers in the high scholastic tradition accorded great moral authority to places.[35] And it is in this sense that scholastic concepts of place anticipated European colonialism.[36] It was widely believed that nations (political entities that were thought to occupy spatially discrete territories) owed their unique physiologies, characters, and *mores* (customs) to their natural locations in the world-machine.[37] The great diversity of nations—as Las Casas and many sixteenth- and seventeenth-century writers argued—could be traced in part to the postdiluvian diaspora that had forced Noah's descendants, as well as beasts and plants, to adapt in specific ways to their new locations under the heavens.[38] More to the point of the present argument, natural places were thought to assign nations their unique positions in a hierarchy of polities as well as their roles in a teleological history.[39]

The idea that nations possessed or lacked political sovereignty by virtue of their locations had its models in such diverse authorities as Hippocrates (about 460–about 377 BCE), Aristotle (384–322 BCE), Vitruvius (1st century BCE), Pliny the Elder (23–79 CE), Ptolemy (about 100–178 CE), Albumasar (about 786–886 CE), Avicenna (Ibn Sīnā, 980–1037 CE), and Averroës (1126–1198 CE). Pliny's encyclopedic *Naturalis historia* (about 77 CE), which circulated widely since its composition and inspired many scientific works in the Latin West, offered one of the most popular theses in this geopolitical tradition,[40] namely, that the earth's cold region fostered fair-skinned people who were fierce but unwise—and therefore unable to govern. The earth's hot region fostered dark-skinned people who were wise but tame—and therefore also unable to govern. In contrast, the earth's temperate region fostered people of medium complexion whose "moderate customs, keen senses, [and] fertile intellects" enabled them to wield the political authority that eluded their neighbors in the earth's cold and hot regions.[41]

Aristotle assigned the privileged temperate location to the Greeks, who stood between other "Europeans" to the northwest and "Asians" to the southeast;[42] Pliny assigned it to the Romans, who stood between the light-skinned Europeans to the north and the dark-skinned "Ethiopians" to the south. Christian writers, who often conceived of Christendom as the divinely appointed territorial and political heir to the Roman *imperium*, privileged the temperate location of their immediate pagan predecessors.[43] Albertus, for instance, adopted the variant of this model found in Vitruvius's *De architectura*.[44] According to Albertus, northern nations are "wolfish," whereas "southern nations . . . are capricious beyond measure."[45] Middle nations, however, "easily cultivate justice, keep their word, embrace peace, and prize the society of men." And for this reason Roman rule had endured longer than other rules.

This tripartite geopolitics was hardly a mere relic from the Greco-Roman period empty of meaning for readers of scripture who invoked it all the way to the Age of Exploration. At least since the first century CE, an important hermeneutic tradition had actively assimilated the political lessons of Greco-Roman geography in seeking to justify the enslavement of "black" Africans based on the Mosaic account of what we know today as the "curse of Ham."[46] According to Genesis 9:18–25, Noah awoke from his bout of drinking to learn that his son Ham had "seen" his father's "nakedness" and punished Ham by cursing Ham's own son: "Cursed be Chanaan, a servant of servants shall he be unto his brethren" (Genesis 9:25).[47] This enduring hermeneutic tradition had taken an important turn in the decades following Mohammed's death (632 CE), when the Muslim occupation of the Nile basin and Cyrenaica (Lybia) precipitated a veritable boom in the importation of slaves from sub-Saharan Africa, greatly reinforcing the somatic association between physical "blackness" and the political condition of slavery.[48] At the same time, Christian and Muslim exegetes in the Near East had built the infamous case that Noah's curse on his grandson extended back a generation to Noah's own "accountable" son Ham. And this curse on Ham was supposed to carry with it the physical branding of blackness that doomed sub-Saharan Africans, the "progeny" of Ham's son Kush, to slavery.[49] The earliest intimations of this enduring adaptation of

Greco-Roman geopolitics to the interpretation of scripture have been usefully traced as far back as the greatly influential Jewish exegete Philo of Alexandria (1st century CE). Philo's allegorical reading of Genesis interpreted Ham's name to mean "hot," an acceptation that was later literalized to indicate that Ham's progeny would inhabit the hotter parts of the world and that also became interchangeable with "dark" or "black."[50] Like so many schools across the ages that have interpreted physical darkness as a privation of spiritual or intellectual light, Philo had seen Ethiopian blackness as evil.[51] More to the point, however, Philo had laboriously traced the etymology of the term *Ethiopia* to the Greek word for "lowness" (*tapeinōsis*), which the author significantly decoded as "cowardice."[52]

While many centuries later, scholastic authors like Albertus would write in the context of a Christian Europe that had lost immediate contact with sub-Saharan peoples, it was only a matter of time before the political lessons of Greco-Roman geography would germinate in new ground. So one finds them in one of Las Casas's most despised sources for *Historia de las Indias,* a chronicle by Gomes Eanes de Zurara, who had recorded the Portuguese exploration of Atlantic Africa under the crusading scholar-prince Henry the Navigator (1394–1460 CE).[53] In his *Crónica dos feitos notáveis que se passaram na conquista da Guiné por mandato do Infante D. Henrique* (written about 1457–about 1465), Zurara included an account of Antão Gonçalvez's abduction of the very first black slaves to have been taken under the Portuguese flag in 1441, near today's Bay de Río de Oro in Western Sahara.[54] Recounting the alleged efforts by one of these captives to persuade Antão Gonçalvez back in Portugal to return him to his land in exchange for other "five or six black Moors," Zurara added that "these blacks, although they were Moors [i.e., dark] like the others, were nonetheless slaves to them, in accordance with ancient custom, which I believe must be on account of the curse that, following the Deluge, Noah cast on his son Cham, by which curse Noah damned Ham's progeny to be subject to all other lineages. . . ."[55]

The tripartite geography of nations would assert itself again well into the era of European colonialism in the Americas, starting perhaps with Columbus's very plan to cross the ocean in search of the Indies. Whether one considers Greco-Latin sources like Pliny and Ptolemy or scholastic authors like Albertus and d'Ailly, this geopolitical model was unmistakably tied to the theory of the five zones, the most fundamental cosmological paradigm available to Western geography since its formulation by the Eleatic philosopher Parmenides (5th century BCE).[56]

Its iconography in the Latin West, well into the Age of Exploration, derived largely from Macrobius's early-fifth-century epitome of Neoplatonism, *Commentarium in somnium Scipionis,* which interpreted Scipio's dream in Cicero's *De re publica* (1st century BCE) **(fig. 1.2)**.[57] Macrobius had continued the geographical tradition that followed Homer's description of Achilles' shield in the *Iliad* in its conception of the continental landmass that included Europe, Asia, and Africa as an "island" surrounded by an "Ocean River."[58] Macrobius's model of the globe, which showed the correspondence between the heavens and the earth, synthesized earlier contributions to the field of cartography, including those of Eudoxus of Cnidus (about 408–355 BCE), who introduced the cosmographic convention of depicting the geocentric universe from the perspective

1.2 Macrobius's zonal *mappamundi* (Brescia, 1483). From Ambrosius Aurelius Theodosius Macrobius, *In somnium Scipionis expositio: Saturnalia,* viii v. Courtesy of the John Hay Library, Providence, Rhode Island.

of an outside observer looking in and who determined the position of the equator, the tropics, the arctic circles, the ecliptic, and the zodiac; Eratosthenes (about 275–194 BCE), who first calculated the location and dimensions of the known inhabited world on the northern hemisphere; and, most significantly, Crates of Mallos (2nd century BCE), who first theorized the existence of inhabited landmasses in the temperate zones of the remaining three horizontal quadrants of the globe separated by vast stretches of ocean (*antoikoi, antichthones,* or antipodes, and *perioikoi*) **(fig. 1.3)**.[59]

The theory of the five zones, as explained and illustrated in d'Ailly's celebrated *Ymago mundi,* divided both the heavens and the earth in accordance with the sun's yearly transit under the slanted belt of the zodiac. The tropics of Cancer and Capricorn marked the sun's maximal declination north and south of the equatorial circle (as recorded by d'Ailly, 23° 51′ from the equator). Since the slanted zodiac, like the equatorial circle,

1.3   Reconstruction of the globe by Crates of Mallos, about 150 BCE. From Germaine Aujac, "Greek Cartography in the Early Roman World," chapter 10 in *Cartography in Prehistoric, Ancient, and Medieval Europe and the Mediterranean,* vol. 1 of *The History of Cartography,* ed. J. B. Harley and David Woodward (Chicago, 1987), 141. After Edward Luther Stevenson, *Terrestrial and Celestial Globes: Their History and Construction, Including a consideration of Their Value as Aids in the Study of Geography and Astronomy,* vol. 1, Publications of the Hispanic Society of America, no. 86 (New Haven, 1921; reprint, New York, 1971), fig. 5. Prepared by Brian Lee, Brown University, Providence, Rhode Island.

revolved around a pole, the Arctic and Antarctic circles marked the zodiacal pole's corresponding declination with respect to the equatorial pole (23° 51′ from the pole) (**fig. 1.4**). The theory of the five zones stated that the two cold zones that lay beyond the Arctic and Antarctic circles were uninhabitable due to the relative absence of the sun's heat. The hot, or torrid, zone that lay between the tropics of Cancer and Capricorn was likewise uninhabitable due to the relative excess of the sun's heat. Only the two temperate zones, which lay north and south of the tropics of Cancer and Capricorn and which extended toward the Arctic and Antarctic circles, were theoretically inhabitable. The sun's yearly motion along the zodiac alternately heated and cooled these two intermediate zones, rendering them relatively temperate.[60]

D'Ailly's "zonal" *mappamundi*—as indebted to Ptolemy and his Arabic successors as it is to Macrobius—followed the long-established convention of placing the *orbis terrarum* on one-half of the northern hemisphere (**fig. 1.5**).[61] D'Ailly's world map perfectly illustrates how Greco-Roman sources like Pliny and Ptolemy, or scholastic authors like Albertus, would have plotted the tripartite geography of nations onto the continental landmass. Invoking Aristotle's tripartite model, d'Ailly divided the known inhabited landmass into cold nations "toward the north," hot nations "toward the south," and temperate nations in the middle. This geopolitical model was thus applied to the northern temperate zone and to its northern and southern fringes, which extended into the zones thought to be uninhabitable: the northern cold zone and the northern portion of the torrid zone. Southern Europe (Greece, Italy, Spain, Portugal) was known in the Latin West to stand squarely in the middle of the northern temperate zone, while Africa began on the southern fringe of this temperate zone and extended south into the torrid zone toward the equator.

Significantly, the Ethiopians or "burnt-faces" (*aithiopes*)—as the black inhabitants of Africa, specifically beyond the arid regions of northern Africa, were termed in ancient Greece—shared their lot in the hottest fringes of the inhabitable world with the peoples of an otherwise geographically elusive "India."[62] Long before the extended basin of the Indian Ocean was imagined by the Greeks as an entity of its own, this geopolitical equation had been invited by Homer when he referred to Ethiopians in his *Odyssey* as "a people split in two, one part where the Sungod sets/and part where the Sungod rises," that is, to the west and east.[63] And it was later explicitly established by Greek and Roman Indographers, among them the historian and geographer Herodotus (about 489–about 425 BCE), whose influential *History* mentioned the earliest reconnaissance of Asia by

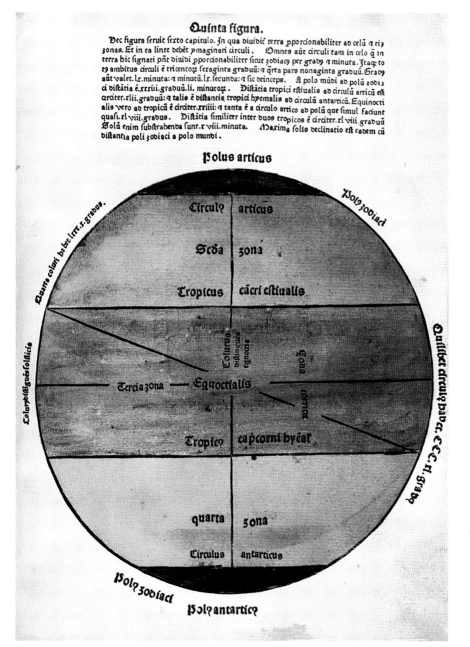

1.4   Zonal *mappamundi*. From "Quinta figura" in Pierre d'Ailly and Jean Gerson, *Tractatus de ymagine mundi et varia ejusdem auctoris et Joannis Gersonis opuscula* (1480–1483), Tabula Americae, facs. no. 852 (Madrid, 1990), 3r. Courtesy of the Institución Colombina, Biblioteca Colombina, Seville, Spain; and Testimonio Compañía Editorial, Madrid, Spain.

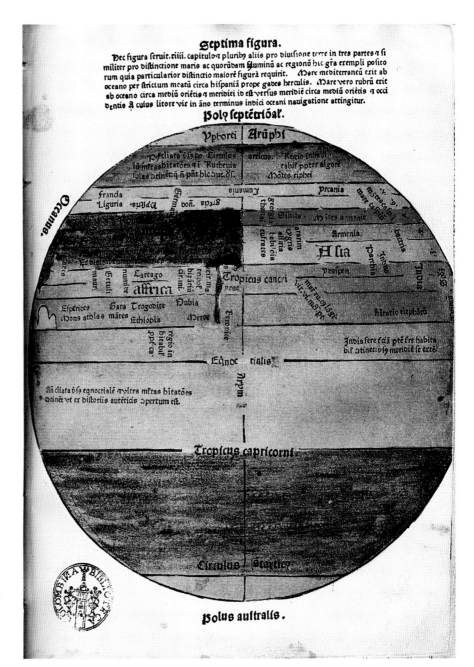

1.5 *Mappamundi,* with outline prepared by Brian Lee, Brown University, Providence, Rhode Island. From "Septima figura" in Pierre d'Ailly and Jean Gerson, *Tractatus de ymagine mundi et varia ejusdem auctoris et Joannis Gersonis opuscula* (1480–1483), Tabula Americae, facs. no. 852 (Madrid, 1990), 4r. Courtesy of the Institución Colombina, Biblioteca Colombina, Seville, Spain; and Testimonio Compañía Editorial, Madrid, Spain.

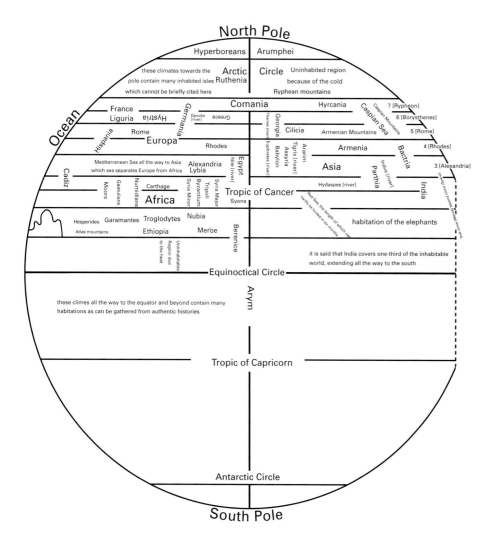

North Pole

Hyperboreans | Arumphei

these climates towards the pole contain many inhabited isles which cannot be briefly cited here

Arctic **Ruthenia** Circle

Uninhabited region because of the cold

Ryphean mountains

Ocean

France
Liguria

Hystria

Germania

Danube [river]

Greece

Comania

Tanais [river]

Hyrcania

Caspian Mountains

Caspian Sea

7 [Rypheon]
6 [Borysthenes]

Georgia

Hispania

Rome

Europa

Rhodes

Euphrates [river]

Cilicia

Armenian Mountains

5 [Rome]

Armenia

Bactria

4 [Rhodes]

Mediterranean Sea all the way to Asia which sea separates Europe from Africa

Alexandria
Lybia

Egypt

Nile [river]

Ararim
Tigris [river]
Assyria
Babylon

Asia

Parthia

Indus [river]

3 [Alexandria]

Cadiz

Moors

Gaetulians

Numidians

Carthage

Syria Minor

Byzantium

Tripoli

Syria Major

Tropic of Cancer

Syene

Hydaspes [river]

India

Hesperides

Atlas mountains

Garamantes

Africa

Troglodytes

Ethiopia

Nubia

Meröe

Berenice

Red Sea, the length of which can hardly be forded in six months

habitation of the elephants

Uninhabitable Region due to the heat

it is said that India covers one-third of the inhabitable world, extending all the way to the south

Equinoctical Circle

Arym

these climes all the way to the equator and beyond contain many habitations as can be gathered from authentic histories

Tropic of Capricorn

Antarctic Circle

South Pole

Scylax of Caryanda, who had been ordered by the Persian King Darius I to sail down the Indus River in search of its outlet to the ocean.[64] Herodotus stated that the skin of the Indians was "as black as that of Ethiopians," and located them in a hot region "furthest from the Persians, to the south."[65] The historian and geographer Strabo (64/63 BCE–about 25 CE), our most crucial source on the achievements of Greek theoretical cartography, included in his *Geography* Indian material partly gathered from the lost *Indica* by the Greek historian and diplomat Megasthenes (about 350–about 290 BCE) and from the lost testimonies of Nearchus and Onesicritus, members of Alexander the Great's military flotilla that sailed down the Indus River (326 BCE). Strabo employed the same equation as Herodotus in his description of "southern" Indians as well as in his peculiarly involved explanation for why the hair of Indians did not "curl" like that of Ethiopians.[66] Pliny, for his part, would borrow his own description of the inhabitants "south" of the Ganges from Pomponius Mela's *De chorographia*, the earliest surviving Latin geography (44 CE), which reported that Ethiopians, or black peoples, flourished along the entire coastline between the Ganges River and Cape Colis (i.e., Cape Comorin, the southernmost point on the Indian subcontinent).[67] The crucial works known as *Anabasis of Alexander* and *Indica*, by the later Greek historian Arrian (died about 180 CE), whose detailed information about India heavily drew on Megasthenes and Nearchus, similarly equated Ethiopians and Indians.[68] Ptolemy himself, whose *Geography* would add an entirely novel genre to fifteenth-century cartography, readily showed the extent to which hot latitudes were thought to impart the same complexion to Ethiopians and Indians. He imagined the Indian Ocean as a tropical accident "locked in" by sub-Saharan Africa directly to the west, continental Asia to the north, and unknown land to the east and to the south (**fig. 1.6**).[69] And he located the race of "Icthiophagi Ethiopes," or Fish-Eating Ethiopians, adjacent to the equatorial Sinarum Sinus (Bay of the Chinese), along the remote eastern littoral that presumably extended beyond the Aurea Chersonesus (Malaysian Peninsula) and that eventually curved south toward the farthest point known to Ptolemy on the landlocked sea of India, "Cattigara Sinarum Statio," or the port of Kattigara (perhaps today's Hanoi) (**fig. 1.7**).[70]

Among the early Christian geographers who echoed Greco-Roman comparisons between Ethiopians and Indians, the Visigothic saint Isidore of Seville (about 560–636), deserves special notice, for his widely influential *Etymologiae* itself foreshadowed the hermeneutic tradition that was about to cast the curse of Ham on sub-Saharan peoples. Influenced by Philo of Alexandria, Isidore claimed that the Hebrew name "Cham"

meant "hot," as a sign that Ham's progeny would inhabit that part of the earth which on account of the sun's proximity was hotter.[71] According to Isidore, Ethiopians were the progeny of Ham's son "Chus" or "Kush," the term by which early readers of Genesis had known the region that Greeks called Ethiopia. These Ethiopians had originally settled the basin of the Indus River and later migrated to the region between the Nile and the Indian Ocean, "in the south in the very vicinity of the sun," eventually giving rise to the Hesperians "on the west" (on sub-Saharan Africa's Atlantic coast), the Garamantes in Tripolitana (a "province" in the heart of Africa), and the "Indians" themselves "on the east."[72] But, of the Christian sources who continued to associate Ethiopians and Indians, none is more pertinent here than Pierre d'Ailly, who, incidentally, borrowed his own geographical genealogy of Ethiopians directly from Isidore. D'Ailly bluntly stated that India was the eastern part of Ethiopia.[73] In a postil to d'Ailly's *Ymago mundi* that suggests the extent to which Columbus had in mind Africa as a starting point in the *east* for a western crossing to *India,* Columbus would carefully record that "the *eastern* part of India is Ethiopia . . . and note that all authors call Ethiopians all people who are black."[74] It should come as no surprise that the subordinate political status that Mediterranean geography had long accorded to nations in the hottest fringes of the world should come to haunt the Discoverer's conception of the peoples he found in lands he insisted unto his death were part of "the Indies"—despite the fact that Columbus failed to find Ethiopians in the Bahamas or Caribbean basin.[75]

The theory of the five zones denoted the most general causal correlation between the heavens and the earth. And the concomitant classification of nations according to the northern hemisphere's cold, hot, and temperate zones constituted the most general cosmological explanation for a political world order. Pliny had considered the five zones to be the "heavenly causes" underlying this hierarchical division of the known inhabited landmass.[76] For d'Ailly, whose immediate sources were Aristotle's *Politics* and the eighth-century Jewish astrologer Māshā'allāh's *De revolutione annorum mundi,* the geopolitical partition of the northern hemisphere in relation to the five zones was the first (and most basic) corollary to an intricate knowledge system that attributed political hierarchies and historical change to celestial influence.[77] D'Ailly's variant of Aristotle's model in *Ymago mundi* bears quoting fully for the clues it offers to Columbus's own geopolitics:

> For, as Aristotle teaches in his book on politics, those who are farther toward the
> south are greater in intellect and prudence but weaker and less spirited and

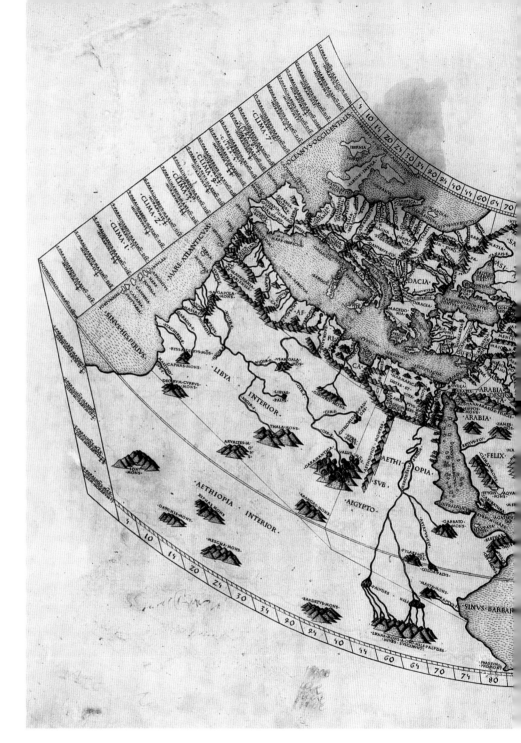

1.6 Ptolemy's first projection in the edition known to Columbus. From Ptolemy's *Cosmographia* (Rome, 1478). Courtesy of the John Carter Brown Library at Brown University, Providence, Rhode Island.

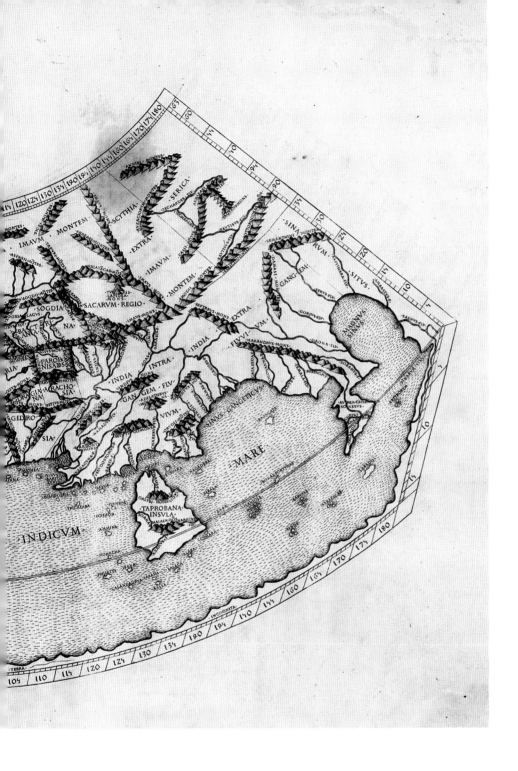

81

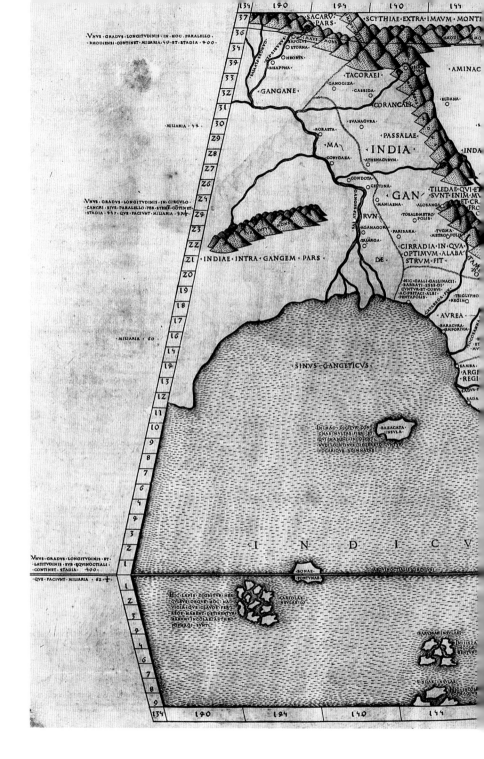

1.7 Regional map of India in the edition known to Columbus. From Ptolemy's *Cosmographia* (Rome, 1478). Courtesy of the John Carter Library at Brown University, Providence, Rhode Island.

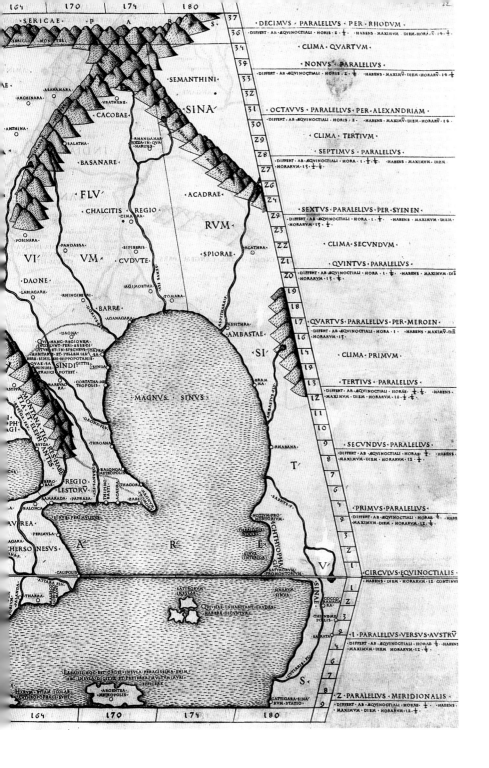

164 · 170 · 174 · 180 · 37

SERICAE · P · A · R · S · 36

· DECIMVS · PARALELLVS · PER · RHODVM ·
· DIFFERT · AB · AEQVINOCTIALI · HORIS · 2 · 1/2 · HABENS · MAXIMVM · DIEM · HORA · 14 · 1/2 ·

34

· CLIMA · QVARTVM ·

32

SEMANTHINI 33

· NONVS · PARALELLVS ·
· DIFFERT · AB · AEQVINOCTIALI · HORIS · 2 · 1/4 · HABENS · MAXIMVM · DIEM · HORARV · 14 · 1/4 ·

ARCHINARA ASANAMARA 32

VRATHENE 31

SINA · OCTAVVS · PARALELLVS · PER · ALEXANDRIAM ·
· DIFFERT · AB · AEQVINOCTIALI · HORIS · 2 · HABENS · MAXIMVM · DIEM · HORARV · 14 ·

CACOBAE 30

ANTHINA · CLIMA · TERTIVM ·

SALATHA 29

· SEPTIMVS · PARALELLVS ·

RHANDAMAR 28

· DIFFERT · AB · AEQVINOCTIALI · HORA · 1 · 3/4 · HABENS · MAXIMVM · DIEM ·
· HORARVM · 13 · 3/4 ·

TOFZA · IN · QVA · NARDVS · 27

BASANARE 26

ACADRAE · SEXTVS · PARALELLVS · PER · SYENEN ·
· DIFFERT · AB · AEQVINOCTIALI · HORA · 1 · 1/2 · HABENS · MAXIMVM · DIEM ·
· HORARVM · 13 · 1/2 ·

FLV · 24

CHALCITIS · REGIO 24

CIMARA 23

RVM · 22

· CLIMA · SECVNDVM ·

POSINARA 21

PANDASSA SIPIBERIS 20

· QVINTVS · PARALELLVS ·
· DIFFERT · AB · AEQVINOCTIALI · HORA · 1 · 1/4 · HABENS · MAXIMVM · DIE ·
· HORARVM · 13 · 1/4 ·

VI · VM · CVDVTE SPIORAE 19

DAONE 18

LARIAGARA 17

· QVARTVS · PARALELLVS · PER · MEROEN ·
· DIFFERT · AB · AEQVINOCTIALI · HORA · 1 · HABENS · MAXIMV · DIE ·
· HORARVM · 13 ·

RHINGIBERRI 16

BARRAE 14

AGANAGARA 13

AMBASTAE · CLIMA · PRIMVM ·

DAONA SI · 12

· TERTIVS · PARALELLVS ·
· DIFFERT · AB · AEQVINOCTIALI · HORAE · 3/4 · HABENS ·
· MAXIMVM · DIEM · HORARVM · 12 · 3/4 ·

SINDI 11

CORTATHA · METROPOLIS 10

MAGNVS · SINVS · 9

· SECVNDVS · PARALELLVS ·
· DIFFERT · AB · AEQVINOCTIALI · HORAE · 1/2 · HABENS ·
· MAXIMVM · DIEM · HORARVM · 12 · 1/2 ·

MONTANA · TIGRES · HABE 8

THROANA RHABANA 7

PH · AGI · 6

REGIO BALONGA · METROPOLIS 5

· PRIMVS · PARALELLVS ·
· DIFFERT · AB · AEQVINOCTIALI · HORAE · 1/4 · HABENS ·
· MAXIMVM · DIEM · HORARVM · 12 · 1/4 ·

LESTORV · ACADRA 4

SAMARADA PAPRASA 3

AVREA · 2

CHERSONESVS 1

· CIRCVLVS · AEQVINOCTIALIS ·
· HABENS · DIEM · HORARVM · 12 · CONTINVA ·

CALIPOLIS 1

ATTARA · FLV 2

SINARVM · SINVA 3

· I · PARALELLVS · VERSVS · AVSTRV ·
· DIFFERT · AB · AEQVINOCTIALI · HORAE · 1/4 · HABENS ·
· MAXIMVM · DIEM · HORARVM · 12 · 1/4 ·

4

5

S · 6

7

ARGENTEA · METROPOLIS 8

· Z · PARALELLVS · MERIDIONALIS ·
· DIFFERT · AB · AEQVINOCTIALI · HORAE · 1/2 · HABENS ·
· MAXIMVM · DIEM · HORARVM · 12 · 1/2 ·

CATTIGARA · SINARVM · STATIO 9

164 170 174 180

audacious. For this reason they were subject to others in antiquity. And conversely, those who live farther toward the north are more audacious and of lesser prudence, and they fiercely defend their liberties. And he says that the Greeks are in the middle, and they possess sufficient strength as well as prudence; from which he concludes that they are suited by nature to rule the others toward the north and toward the north. Even so, as experience has shown, they did not exercise this rule for long, for it was transferred to the Romans.[78]

Of particular significance here is the manner in which d'Ailly tied the concept of *dominium* inherited from the Romans to Aristotle's concept of nature: temperate nations held *natural rule* over hot and cold nations. During the sixteenth century, the notion of natural lordship—discussed largely in the context of the Aristotelian corpus—would come to play a crucial role in the thought of scholastic writers who, like Las Casas, examined the question of Spain's titles to its newly acquired domains.[79]

A more extreme version of this tripartite geopolitics had also come to be found in the widely read version of Ptolemy's astrological second-century *Tetrabiblos* accompanied by the commentary of Egyptian physician and astrologer Haly ('Alī ibn Ridwān, about 998–about 1061). D'Ailly's version of Haly's commentary to the model offered by Ptolemy claims that

the four extremes of the world, even within the limits of the climates, are not easily habitable, and especially the two extremes of which one is toward the south and the other toward the north. And this is why Ptolemy and Haly and other ancient authors say that in these two extremes there are forest-dwelling men who eat human flesh and whose faces are deformed and horrible. And the cause for this, according to Haly, is the intemperance of those regions in terms of heat and cold, as a result of which their bodies are disorderly in their temperaments and poor and ugly in their arrangement. For this reason they have wicked customs and savage manners, so that the people, or the beasts and monsters, are of such horrible appearance that one can hardly discern whether they are men or beasts, as Saint Augustine relates. Haly also cites Hermes, who states that in the two extremes [i.e., to the north and to the south] there live evil spirits and devils, as well as malicious beasts that harm men. It is well to know, however, that the other two extremes, namely, the one toward the east and the one toward the west, are not so inhospitable to life, for they are not so intemperate except insofar as they meet the other two at the four corners of the inhabited world. In their other parts [i.e., in the middle parts], these are sufficiently temperate and at a convenient distance from the sun.[80]

Needless to say, the notion that extreme latitudes, hot or cold, gave rise to extreme natures had played no menial role in Mediterranean geography's perception that Ethiopia and India were veritable factories of marvels and monsters.[81] To speak of a memorable sentence to be found in Pliny's *Naturalis historia,* Ethiopia and India were the places where the monstrous races "have been made by the ingenuity of nature as toys for herself and marvels for us."[82] Or, as Haly would later argue in his commentary on Ptolemy's *Tetrabiblos,* the extreme heat and cold altered the bodily temperaments of tropical and nordic peoples, thus hampering the nature of their sperm, so that their progeny were born with deformed and horrible faces.[83] Or consider Aristotle's most prolific commentator among the Arabs, Averroës, who in one of his commentaries on the *Meteorologica* carefully drew a most perfect link between latitude, temperature, and the nature of places. Against a dissident tradition attended by the likes of Ptolemy and Avicenna that claimed that the equatorial region was universally temperate, fertile, and hospitable, Averroës countered that life in that region *could* happen, but only in the manner one could expect in a latitude where the sun came directly overhead, for its inhabitants were, by necessity, short-lived, which meant that "many of them are not natural."[84] Strong evidence that the equatorial region was largely uninhabitable could be found in those people who lived near the Tropic of Cancer, namely, Ethiopians, "for their life is non-natural, and their temperaments deviate greatly from human temperaments. And they live in that place only by accident, that is, when there is a cave where they dwell, just as other animals make their dwellings in the hollows of mountains or in the waters. And moreover, in their way of life in these matters which are beyond nature, they are found to resemble those who live at the limit of the inhabitable world, to the north."[85] In other words, evidence that the lower latitudes of the globe were largely hot, infertile, and uninhabitable rested with the exotic physiologies and customs of its black inhabitants, who flourished only where geographical accidents counteracted the sun's lethal heat—whose bodies and lives were non-natural or beyond nature. Indeed, even if one were to have admitted that there was such a thing as nature in extreme places, tropical nature itself could have been nothing short of a tyrannical mother whose sporadic bouts of benevolence spawned every sort of physical and moral aberration in her children.

The tripartite geography of nations was ripe for use in the context of a nascent European colonialism in the second half of the fifteenth century. Certainly, writers had long disagreed regarding the world map's "specifications," such as the measurement of the earth's circumference, the eastward and southward reach of the continental landmass, the possibility of landmasses outside of Europe, Africa, and Asia, and the possibility of inhabited places beyond the so-called hospitable limits of the known inhabited world. And it was in dialectical relation to such disagreements that Columbus formulated his plan to navigate to "the Indies." Columbus's most famous postils to d'Ailly's *Ymago mundi*—first documented in Ferdinand's biography of his father— reveal the Discoverer's preference for those opinions cited by d'Ailly that exaggerated the longitudinal and latitudinal dimensions of the *orbis terrarum* and diminished the distance between the westernmost lands in the Atlantic and the end of the Orient.[86] But a great many of Columbus's postils were also written as frank endorsements of the canonical geography contained in the celebrated copy of d'Ailly's and Gerson's *Tractatus*. Columbus's, in effect, *commentary* on this work alternately disputed and corroborated the geographical ideas available in Europe prior to the discovery, and this commentary occasionally also took the form of a studious dialogue between Columbus and his "right hand," his brother Bartholomew. This store of marginalia holds capital importance for understanding the geopolitics of Columbus's exploration of the Bahamas and Caribbean basin—an area of the globe which, just like Atlantic Africa below the Canaries, turned out to be near and within the ostensibly "uninhabitable" bounds of the torrid zone.

Prior to 1492 Columbus had good reason to believe that the torrid zone was *not* uniformly inhospitable. What is more, it harbored the promise of incalculable wealth. During his years in Portugal (?1478–1485), Columbus visited the recently founded fort of São Jorge da Mina (1482), on the equatorial coast of Guinea, where the Portuguese had established a prosperous trade in slaves, gold, ivory, and Malagueta pepper.[87] (Incidentally, the toponym *Guinea* denoted for the Portuguese, just as *Ethiopia* had for the ancient Greeks, an Africa distinctly occupied by "black" peoples below the Sahara.[88] This is why we have seen Columbus marvel in the letter to Luis de Santángel of 15 February 1493 at the fact that his own "Indians," who by his admission lived in a latitude where "the sun is very strong," nevertheless should have failed to be, as he put it, "black as in Guinea.")[89] The Fernandine *Historie* tells us that Columbus was the author of a "memorandum or note" on the five zones in which he drew on his Atlantic experiences to argue that both the northern cold zone and the torrid zone were indeed navigable and inhabitable. This memorandum, if it did exist and if Ferdinand is not referring to Columbus's postils to the incunabula in the Biblioteca Colombina, is regrettably lost.[90] What we do have—apart from numerous allusions in the *Diario* to the Guinean experience—are Columbus's and his brother Bartholomew's better-known postils to d'Ailly's *Ymago mundi,* which disputed the geographical commonplace that the torrid zone was everywhere uninhabitable and which erroneously located São Jorge da Mina directly under the equator.[91]

One of these postils, on the margins of d'Ailly's exposition of the theory of the five zones, reads that the torrid zone "is not uninhabitable, because it is navigated today by the Portuguese. Indeed, it is densely populated, and under the equatorial line lies the Very Serene King of Portugal's mining fortress, which we saw."[92] A subsequent postil, which calls attention to the relative temperateness of São Jorge da Mina, despite its centrality in the torrid zone, explains that "Africa is twice the size of Europe; and even though in its midst lies a sandy region [i.e., Saharan Africa], it is inhabited in some places. In its northern and southern regions live innumerable peoples, nor does this prevent it from being extremely hot. And under the equatorial line, where the days are always twelve hours long, the Very Serene King of Portugal owns a fortress that I visited, and I found the place to be temperate."[93]

A great number of the postils contained in this and other incunabula of the Biblioteca Colombina consistently single out information to the effect that considerable populations and abundant goods were to be found within the infamous limits of the tropics.[94] And it was partially against the thesis that the torrid zone generally sustained little or no human life that Columbus would carry out his exploration due south through the Bahamas toward the Caribbean basin after finding the island of San Salvador in 1492. By Columbus's account, the site of the landfall lay on the same latitude as the southernmost colony in Spain's recently acquired Canary Islands, El Hierro (modern 27° 44′ N). Columbus was certainly compelled to make this observation for diplomatic reasons: following the famous Treaty of Alcáçovas (Toledo 1479–1480), and in exchange for recognition of Castile's sovereignty in the Canaries, the Crowns of Aragon and Castile had vowed to recognize Portugal's hold on the sea routes and territories below the

Canaries and toward the African mainland; Columbus was now under strict orders to respect the terms of this treaty.[95]

But Columbus's observation is significant for another reason: barely four degrees north of the Tropic of Cancer, the Canary Islands and the neighboring mainland accident known as Cape Bojador had for generations marked the ominous doorway to the belt of the tropics.[96] The Discoverer's soon-to-be subjection and enslavement of the peoples newly discovered near and within the torrid zone were deliberately intended to reenact Portugal's own monstrous harvesting of human labor and natural resources along sub-Saharan Africa's western coast. It is no accident that Las Casas himself should later consider the presence of European Christians on the Canary Islands and in western Africa a prelude to what he famously condemned as the "destruction of the Indies" (*destruyçion delas yndias*).[97]

Columbus's exploration of the Bahamas and Caribbean basin certainly helped overturn the belief that the torrid zone was generally uninhabitable. For many decades the geographers of the Spanish Empire—bypassing the feats of their Portuguese rivals in Africa—were to boast that Spaniards had shown the ancients wrong by subduing unexpectedly vast and temperate territories inhabited by countless peoples.[98] Nevertheless, Columbus's discoveries did not prevent him or his ideological successors in the bourgeoning empire from adopting the Europe-centered political theory contained in this tripartite geography. Columbus's copy of d'Ailly's and Gerson's *Tractatus* bears witness to the fact that Columbus found this geopolitical model worthy of attention. In a postil to d'Ailly's *Ymago mundi*, Columbus paraphrased d'Ailly's variant of Aristotle's model: "The inhabitants toward the south [*versus meridiem*] are greater in intellect and prudence, but they are less strong, audacious, and spirited; and those toward the north [*versus septentrionem*] are more audacious and of lesser prudence and strength. The Greeks were in the middle, and they possess sufficient strength and prudence."[99] In interrelated postils to a subsequent treatise by d'Ailly entitled *De concordia discordantium astronomorum* (On the Agreement of Discordant Astronomers, 1414), Columbus or Bartholomew again wrote that "the northerners are deficient in intellect but full of spiritedness. In southerners everything is the opposite."[100] The political lesson to be drawn from this was, according to Columbus, that "the inhabitants of the north and of the south are unfit to hold empire. This [middle] region has both [i.e., spiritedness and intellect]."[101] And in yet another postil to d'Ailly's *Ymago mundi,* Columbus would diligently note what Ptolemy's commentator Haly had to say regarding the peoples who inhabited the coldest and hottest extremes of the world: "In these two extremities live forest-dwelling men who eat human flesh. They have deformed and horrible faces. The cause for this is the intemperance of those regions, for which reason they are of evil habits and savage. There, the peoples, or beasts and monsters, are of such horrendous shape, that it is hardly possible to tell whether they are men or beasts. In that place there are evil spirits and devils, as well as malicious beasts."[102]

We cannot be sure *when* these postils were written, that is, whether they anticipated or ratified the political terms of a geographic endeavor. But consider, to cite a most famous instance, Columbus's notorious verdict upon landing on the island of Guanahaní, the site of the landfall thereafter known as San Salvador (12 October 1492): its inhabitants—whose speech he admitted was incomprehensible to him—"must be *good servants and of great ingenuity* [*buenos seruidores y de buen ingenio*], because I see that they instantly repeat everything I said to them."[103] Columbus's insistence on the docility, or "servility," and great "ingenuity" of San Salvador's inhabitants does not merely exemplify the wishful thinking that often motivates the highly suspect "dialogues" between Europeans and Indians recounted in the *Diario*. Columbus also came to believe in the course of his first voyage that as he southed further away from the Bahamas and toward the lower, more extreme latitudes of the Caribbean, he was bound to find the *caniba* or *caribe*—a physically and morally deformed people "with dog's snouts who ate men, and who, upon capturing one, would disembowel him and drink his blood and slice off his genitals."[104] Columbus owes his insistence on the childish docility and intelligence of San Salvador's inhabitants, today known as Taínos, and on the monstrosity and cruelty of the peoples he later thought he had found in the Lesser Antilles, today known as Caribes, to the tripartite geography of nations. This political scheme fundamentally influenced the geography deployed by Columbus as he explored the Bahamas and Caribbean basin.

Throughout the sixteenth century, as Spain expanded its effective control of the Americas north to contemporary Arizona and New Mexico and south to Santiago and Buenos Aires, imperial geographers invoked this ancient geopolitical model to justify Spain's colonization of the tropics. Consider the navigational manual by royal cosmographer Francisco Falero, *Tratado del Esphera y del arte del marear* (1535), which was published in the same year that the viceroyalty of New Spain was being established in Mexico and that Francisco Pizarro founded the city of Lima as the new capital of Peru. Falero claimed that the temperate zone harbored "people more reasonable and of better understanding and more skill, and meant for greater purposes, than the other people who inhabit other zones."[105] The author's claims for Spanish superiority included the remarkable thesis that any and all theologically significant events had taken place—and would continue to take place—in the temperate zone until the end of the world:

> All the notable things that have been witnessed in this world have happened in this temperate zone; for in it the first man was born, and in it he fell; and in it the ark was built and preserved in which the human lineage was protected and spared from the Great Flood. . . . In it, Christ ordered the teaching of the Gospel, and in it, for the most part, stand all Christians and the militant Church. And in this zone was born He who created it and all other things. And in it He performed all the other miracles and prodigies that He has performed in this century for the salvation of fallen man. In this zone was built and destroyed that most illustrious city in the world, Jerusalem, in which He who created all sinners suffered on their behalf. And in this zone He shall come at the end of the century to preside on Judgment Day.[106]

Falero's mention of the "miracles and prodigies" performed by God "in this very century for the salvation of fallen man" undoubtedly referred to celebrated events like the discovery and the defeats of the Aztecs and the Incas. Like many apologists of the Spanish Empire, Falero cast these events as part of a long-standing militancy against infidels, which had fueled not only the Christian *reconquista* of Islamic Spain and Iberian expansionism in Atlantic Africa but also Columbus's own understanding of the significance of his discovery.[107] Falero, incidentally, published his *Tratado* in the same year that royal historian Gonzalo Fernández de Oviedo brought to light the first part of his major apology for the conquest, *Historia general y natural de las Indias* (1535), one of the works that would instigate an indignant Las Casas to forge on with the writing of his own *Historia de las Indias*. Oviedo claimed that Spaniards had been the scourge visited by God on the Indians for "the great and ugly and ominous sins and abominations of these savage and bestial peoples."[108] Like Oviedo's apology for the conquest, Falero's thesis that God had bestowed his divine geography solely on the inhabitants of the temperate zone undoubtedly stemmed from the need in official circles to defend the legitimacy of empire against dissidents like Las Casas who denounced Spain's misdeeds in the Americas.

Fifty years later, in line with previous Crown apologists, Francisco Vicente Tornamira would invoke the tripartite geography of nations to claim that the cultivation of the sciences had been an exclusive privilege of those nations that lay in the temperate zone. In his *Chronographia, y Repertorio de los tiempos* (1585), Tornamira traced this privilege to the dispersion of Noah's descendants, who had gradually forgotten the religious, moral, and scientific legacy they had received from Noah and his three sons. The degeneration of this legacy, which explained the diversity of nations, was most visible among

> those peoples who, because of the disposition of their regions, were unable to reach an understanding of the sciences, as were those who inhabited intemperate regions due to excessive cold, or excessive heat, which cause people to have uneven temperaments and a rough and beastlike understanding. But there were some in the temperate parts [of the globe] who were always eager to investigate and discover nature's admirable secrets, as well as the order and concerted motion of the celestial orbs and their stars. As these men investigated and discovered things, the sciences gradually grew, each man adding to what he had been taught what he himself had invented and learned. And thus by this means the sciences have come to reach the degree of perfection that they now possess, and very learned men are flourishing in different parts of the world.[109]

Tornamira's claim that the sciences had been perfected only in the temperate zone and had eventually spread around the globe offers an eloquent connection between geography and politics. His use of the tripartite scheme explained colonial power as the natural right of the inhabitants of the temperate zone. But it also self-consciously linked the exercise of this power to the cultivation of knowledge and to the use of philosophical and technical tools like the *Chronographia* itself.[110]

A later geographical manual, Pedro de Syria's *Arte de la verdadera navegación* (1602), addressed to Philip III, likewise found in the tripartite geopolitics inherited from Greco-Latin culture a suitable model for praising the achievements of the inhabitants of the temperate zone. Europe was, according to Syria, "the most noble, the most noted, and the most named throughout the world, as Strabo writes, on account of the empire and power that the Romans in it once lorded. . . . It is a land agreeable to human nature, and thus densely populated, with many and great cities, as well as peoples more vigorous than anywhere elsewhere in the world."[111] Tornamira's and Syria's works—like so many Spanish works that mentioned the Indies in the sixteenth and seventeenth centuries—formed part of a broad indictment of the religious, moral, scientific, and technical systems that flourished in the Americas prior to the civilizing work of empire.

The tripartite geography of nations described above is deceptively simplistic. Like all reductive models, it appears to reflect only the trite prejudices by which advocates of empire inevitably visualize their relationship to colonized peoples. But as Las Casas well understood when he embarked on the writing of *Historia de las Indias* and the *Apologética,* this model only served as a shorthand for an explanatory system that reached all the way back to formative propositions on the relationship between soul and body in the works of Plato and Aristotle. It is no coincidence that Plato's terms to describe the soul's descent into the body were *dioikein,* or the act of managing a household, and—more to the argument at hand—*katoikizein,* or the act of settling a colony.[112] As Albertus and d'Ailly illustrate, the connection between geography and politics in the high scholastic cosmological tradition has its roots in Western culture's preoccupation with the problematic interface of soul and body. And as both Columbus and Las Casas illustrate, these were precisely the terms in which imperial Spain would come to think of the legal status of the Indians within the colonial order.[113]

The theory of celestial influence lent at least nominal coherence to the knowledge system that connected geography and politics in the high scholastic tradition.[114] In the cosmology inherited most directly from the Greeks and the Arabs, celestial bodies governed a chain of causation that, through the four elements and their compounds, affected the humors in the human body and influenced behavior. Celestial bodies predisposed—though they did not compel—humans to act in accordance with their natures.[115] Knowledge of place beneath the heavens thus revealed the causes not only for the motion and change of all physical bodies but also for the complex conduct of rational creatures. To the extent that humans—as individuals and collectivities—might yield to the nature induced in them by the heavens, their behavior was a function of place. Albertus's contribution to geography in this cosmological tradition was to treat place as a crucial concept for understanding—even predicting—the nature of all things. As a philosophical treatise, *De natura loci* set forth the logic that connected geography to a network of interrelated domains of knowledge. These domains included Christian theology, metaphysics, physics, mathematics, geometry, astronomy, astrology, optics, the psychology and physiology of humans, beasts, and plants, and, as we shall see, those subdivisions of moral philosophy we know today as ethics and politics.

One must qualify the sense in which this knowledge system was coherent, as well as the manner in which Albertus's ideas formalized geography's status in the high scholastic cosmological tradition.[116] The very need for "commentary" in this tradition stemmed from the fact that individual propositions belonging to disparate arguments, intellectual schools, or cultures had to be located within an ostensibly universal knowledge system that reflected the harmonious workings of a created cosmos. Albertus's *De natura loci* illustrates the paradoxes that could result from forced marriages between systems: Christian theology and pagan philosophy; Aristotle's cosmology and the Alexandrian and Arabic astrological sources; or Aristotle's physics, in which the nature of things was their inherent ability to be moved to their own places, and the physics of the Neoplatonists, in which place was the medium by which superior bodies imparted form and motion to inferior ones. Albertus's use of contrary teleologies to understand physical causality shows how Aristotle's Christian commentators profoundly altered his philosophy in the very process of incorporating it.

These complexities in Albertus's work and elsewhere serve to remind us that the cosmological tradition available in the works of d'Ailly, Columbus, and Las Casas was heterogeneous and inconsistent. Scholastic thinkers disagreed, for instance, on the manner in which celestial bodies communicated motion and change to sublunary creatures.[117] While generations of writers used the term *machina* to describe the harmonious operations of a created whole, this term must not be understood to reflect an equally harmonious system of knowledge. Nevertheless, this metaphor did evoke the pervasive hierarchical causality that gave the cosmos its working coherence, and it also implied concomitant links between knowledge domains concerned with individual aspects of this created whole. It was the relatively stable assumptions of this epistemic system that authorized geographers to connect concepts of place—with different degrees of explicitness and detail—to the political ideas that came to underwrite colonial practices in the second half of the fifteenth century.

The term *machina mundi* was originally coined by the Epicurean poet Lucretius (about 99–about 55 BCE) in *De rerum natura* to refer to the random vibration of minima out of which, over the span of eons, the cosmos had emerged.[118] But Lucretius's "godless" version of universal harmony would not have appealed to Christian writers had his work circulated extensively before the early fifteenth century. Instead, early Christian writers probably culled the term from Chalcidius's fourth-century translation and commentary of Plato's *Timaeus*, the single most influential cosmology in the Latin West until the momentous introduction of Aristotle's *libri naturales* in the twelfth and thirteenth centuries.[119] In the works of Chalcidius and his successors in the Latin West, the term "machine" clearly retained its ties to the slippery Doric term *māchānā*, which had stood for a medium of sorts, or in the physical sense, an apparatus.[120]

The concept of world-as-God's-machine enjoyed wide currency during the twelfth and thirteenth centuries, no doubt in the context of growing interest in nature as "second cause" to the Creator, and also in the context of a technological revolution that sought to mechanize a wide range of human activities.[121] One of Albertus's most surprising and crucial sources, a twelfth-century Latin version of the Arab philosopher al-Kindī's magical treatise *De radiis stellarum* (9th century), referred to celestial bodies as having unique places in the *mundana machina* from which they imparted distinct forms to inferior bodies in their locations.[122] The anonymous twelfth-century Neoplatonic cosmology *De sex rerum principiis* defined the *machina mundi* as the composite motion of all of the heavens—a "harmonious" and "moderate" motion that gently permeated the entire universe with its life-generating heat.[123] And a memorable use of the concept of the world-as-God's-machine appeared in thirteenth-century Latin translations of the eclectic pseudo-Aristotelian handbook *De mundo* (about 40–140 CE), which compared God to a master machinist enthroned on the periphery of the cosmos, dispensing his power throughout the whole, moving the heavens, and causing all elementary bodies to come into being. All this, God accomplished "with ease and by simple movement, even as machine-operators [*megalotechnoi*] by one turn on a machine accomplish many different operations."[124]

But the treatise that gave widest currency to the term *machina mundi* in the high scholastic tradition was John of Sacrobosco's early-thirteenth-century *De sphaera*, a handbook used well into the seventeenth century to teach the basic qualitative and quantitative specifications of the world-machine. Ostensibly following Aristotle's cosmology, Sacrobosco (and his many commentators) taught that the *universalis machina mundi* was composed of the celestial region, which was incorruptible, and the region of the elements, which was constantly subject to change.[125] The *machina mundi* was governed by predictable principles that could be suspended only by miracles, that is, through God's direct intervention in nature.[126] As d'Ailly's disciple Jean Gerson would later write in a treatise included in the widely noted copy of their *Tractatus*, "Heaven is like an instrument of the glorious Lord by which the corruptible machine is governed according to rules."[127]

The use of the term *machina mundi* varied, of course, across arguments in the many centuries after it was coined. But in the geographical works of the sixteenth and seventeenth century (many of which contained direct paraphrases or commentaries of Sacrobosco's *De sphaera*) the term consistently denoted the Christian cosmos as a working artifact in which celestial bodies—God's intermediaries—regulated motion and change in the elements and their compounds.[128] And in this world-machine, every physical body occupied a place according to its nature. As Pedro de Syria wrote in his *Arte de la verdadera navegación* (1602), asserting the pervasive emplacement of all physical creatures in Aristotle's voidless cosmos, "No sooner would a body be without a place, than the machine of the world be destroyed."[129] Syria's memorable epithet is a reminder of the universalizing and paradoxical impulses of a monotheistic tradition that had for centuries invoked Aristotle's authority concerning such crucial concepts in the natural sciences as place and void; whereas Aristotle's own view of nature as an inherent ability in physical bodies hardly rested on the notion of the cosmos as someone's artifact, or machine.

In the mid-sixteenth century, Las Casas, the "apostle of the Indies," freighted the term *machina mundi* with polemical significance. In the scathing prologue he wrote in 1552 for *Historia de las Indias,* denouncing Spanish atrocities in the Americas, Las Casas declared that one of his goals was "to offer readers of many ancient things clarity and certainty concerning the principles upon which this world-machine was discovered."[130] This was, of course, a reference to the conceptual origins of the discovery, the subject of Las Casas's intellectual biography of Columbus in the opening chapters of *Historia de las Indias.* Las Casas's reference to a newly discovered "machine" pointed to the equivocal neologism *mundus novus,* or "new world," by which many Europeans since Peter Martyr had marveled at the discovery of a vast and seemingly alien orb populated by nations whose cultural practices appeared inscrutable, if not demonic. Las Casas was here stating the obvious: the New World was merely the newly discovered province of one and the same world-machine, and its discovery had some bearing on concepts available in a written tradition that had long pondered this *machina mundi.* But, by thus wielding the term *máquina mundial* against the falsely dichotomous term New World, Las Casas was also reminding his learned readers that the orb subjected by Spain since 1492 was governed by the same nature that governed the Old World and that its native peoples could be vindicated by the very knowledge system that had accorded Europeans their own privileged place in the cosmos.

It was by deploying the epistemic system encoded in the term *machina mundi* against itself that Las Casas would work to dismantle the connections between geography and politics established by Columbus and his ideological heirs in the Spanish Empire. This is why Las Casas's treatment of Columbus's *Diario*—like his recognition of Albertus and d'Ailly as Columbus's forebears—must be understood in the context of an intellectual culture that regarded political life as a direct consequence of the operations of the world-machine.

It took Las Casas over three decades to mount his attack in *Historia de las Indias* against Spain's legal titles to the conquest and settlement of the Americas.[131] During this period, Las Casas handled an impressive array of documents and sources to build the case that Amerindians, by virtue of their geography, were naturally predisposed to exercise substantial political autonomy.[132] Las Casas's case was largely built on a philosophical alternative to the theory of the five zones that was originally formulated by the Hellenistic thinkers and later revived in the Latin West by figures like Gerard of Cremona (about 1114–1178), Michael Scot (about 1175–about 1235), Robert Grosseteste (about 1175–1253), Robertus Anglicus (13th century), and, of course, Albertus Magnus and Roger Bacon. According to this ancient cosmological variant of the theory of the five zones, the belt of the tropics was not at all the scorched, barren, and empty expanse once imagined by Parmenides; rather, it was a generally temperate, fertile, and most hospitable region of the globe. The case that the Americas conquered by Spain was part of such a place would constitute the object of a compendious section of *Historia de las Indias* announced by Las Casas in the prologue of 1552 and excised by him in 1555 to compose his natural and moral history of the Americas, the *Apologética historia sumaria*.[133] Significantly marking the place of the Spanish Americas (not just to the west but also to the *south* of Mediterranean Europe), Las Casas would accord this companion volume to *Historia de las Indias* the following title: "Apologetic Summary History, Concerned with the Qualities, Disposition, Description, Heaven, and Earth of these Lands, as well as with the Natural Dispositions, Polities, Republics, Manners of Life, and Customs of the peoples *of these Western and Meridional Indies,* Whose Sovereign Domain Belongs to the Monarchs of Castile."[134] In this natural and moral history, Las Casas would set out to prove that "the Indies" were more universally temperate than even the most temperate places in the Old World. But the move to establish this controversial case in favor of Amerindians had been made well before Las Casas began his final revision of his *Historia* in 1552. The argument of the *Apologética* already announces its presence in the first four chapters of Las Casas's earliest completed work, the pacifist evangelical doctrine *De unico vocationis modo omnium gentium ad veram religionem,* which Las Casas may have drafted on the island of Hispaniola (Haiti and Dominican Republic) between 1522 and 1527.[135] Las Casas appears to have excised these opening chapters from *De unico vocationis modo,* used them briefly in *Historia de las Indias* in 1551, and finally incorporated them in 1555 as the nucleus of the subversive geopolitics in his *Apologética.*[136]

Columbus's *Diario* would come to play a critical role in Las Casas's geopolitical defense of Amerindian peoples. Las Casas may have copied the *Diario* between 1523 and 1526, when he first consulted the Columbus family archives in Hispaniola.[137] The *Diario* structured Las Casas's nearly exhaustive account of the first voyage in *Historia de las Indias,* begun perhaps as early as 1527.[138] But more importantly, Columbus's *Diario* also offered Las Casas firsthand testimony of the nature and cultures of the Bahamas and Caribbean basin.[139] On this score, the extant summary copy of the *Diario* presents a dual perspective on the discovery. As Columbus's own work, the *Diario* documents the coercive geopolitics Columbus had practiced in the reaches of the newly discovered torrid zone. But paradoxically, as an accessory to *Historia de las Indias,* the *Diario* offered Las Casas incontrovertible evidence of the temperate Bahamian and Caribbean conditions that Europeans had long associated with their own privileged location in the world-machine. Columbus's stubborn insistence on the relative temperateness of the Bahamas and Caribbean basin unwittingly yielded a political lesson Las Casas may have fully intended to deploy in defense of Amerindians when he began to draft *Historia de las Indias.*[140] Needless to say, this dual interpretation of the *Diario*'s geopolitics is also patent in Las Casas's finished account of the first voyage in *Historia de las Indias.*

The urge to mount a geopolitical case in favor of Amerindian peoples also pervades Las Casas's intellectual biography of the Discoverer in the opening chapters of *Historia de las Indias.* In 1552, after years of intermittent writing, Las Casas was prepared to thoroughly document, revise, and complete his *Historia de las Indias.*[141] In that same year, Las Casas wrote the prologue announcing the subject matter of the *Apologética* and also revised an earlier intellectual portrait of Columbus to reflect a number of significant sources newly at his disposal in Seville.[142] Apart from the documentation Las Casas had collected over a long career in the Americas and Spain, he now had full access to Ferdinand's monumental library, which had been entrusted temporarily to the Dominican convent of San Pablo after Ferdinand's death in 1539, and which was permanently deposited in the chapter of the cathedral of Seville as Las Casas began the final stage in the writing of *Historia de las Indias*.[143] In Ferdinand's library, which at over 15,000 volumes dwarfed almost any other private collection in Europe, Las Casas had ample opportunity to consider Columbus's sources for the discovery.

It was in the Biblioteca Colombina that Las Casas undertook a detailed examination of not only Ferdinand's biography of his father in the Spanish original but also of Columbus's celebrated copy of d'Ailly's and Gerson's *Tractatus*. In the Biblioteca Colombina, Las Casas may well have also consulted a printed copy of Albertus's *De natura loci* that Ferdinand had personally registered in his bibliographical inventories. We may never know whether Columbus—whose death in 1506 preceded the 1514 *princeps* edition of *De natura loci*—had ever read or owned a manuscript version of this work, which Las Casas himself came to know most thoroughly.[144] We can be sure that Las Casas would not have failed to document the existence of such a manuscript copy in Ferdinand's library. The fact is that *De natura loci* became instrumental for Las Casas, both to explain Columbus's geography and its sources and to develop the anticolonialist argument of the *Apologética*.

Las Casas was a meticulous—some would say fastidious—scholar who cultivated the habit of protractedly citing or paraphrasing his sources.[145] He explicitly deferred to Ferdinand's authority in *Historie* on multiple counts, including Ferdinand's intellectual biography of his father.[146] And like Ferdinand, Las Casas certainly relied heavily on Columbus's postils to d'Ailly's *Ymago mundi* for his own version of the intellectual origins of the discovery in *Historia de las Indias*. But while both biographers agreed on d'Ailly's paramount importance to Columbus, they did so with different degrees of thoroughness. The Fernandine *Historie* acknowledged Columbus's debt to d'Ailly only implicitly, by lifting its list of the *auctores* Columbus may have known straight from the Discoverer's postils to *Ymago mundi,* if not from the peculiar *carta-relación* of the third voyage that Columbus had addressed to the Catholic Monarchs from Santo Domingo in 1498. Las Casas, on the other hand, provided careful commentary on d'Ailly as Columbus's source. Of d'Ailly's and Gerson's *Tractatus,* Las Casas would write in *Historia de las Indias* that

> it was so familiar to the said Christopher Columbus, that he had, in his own hand and in Latin, annotated and rubricated its margins all over, writing there many

things that he had read in other books and that he had gathered from them. I held this very old book in my own hands many times, from which I abstracted things written in Latin by the said Admiral Christopher Columbus—or, rather, who later became admiral—in order to clarify certain points pertinent to this my history that I had previously regarded with doubt.[147]

By identifying his own sources consistently and often commenting on them, Las Casas elaborated substantially on Ferdinand's version of the intellectual origins of the discovery. Indeed, Las Casas's *Historia* partly constitutes a "commentary" of Ferdinand's *Historie*. Las Casas's own discussion of Columbus's forebears supplied information and analysis that he found to be latent or conspicuously lacking in Ferdinand's *Historie*.[148] Nowhere is this more evident than in Las Casas's inclusion of Albertus as Columbus's source.

The Fernandine *Historie* does not name Albertus among Columbus's forebears. Ferdinand did claim that, while in Portugal, Columbus "began to study again the cosmographers whom he had read before" in search of ideas that confirmed the feasibility of his plan.[149] According to Ferdinand, his father, upon rereading these writers, "grew convinced beyond the shadow of a doubt that *to the west* of the Canary and Cape Verde Islands lay many lands, and that it was possible to sail to them and to discover them." (The Cape Verde Islands were known to stand well inside the limits of the torrid zone.) Las Casas conjectured that Albertus was one of the geographers from whose works Columbus "might have reasonably moved himself to believe—and indeed to hold for certain—that he would find [these lands and peoples] on the ocean sea, *to the west and to the south*" (*al poniente y al mediodia*).[150]

Las Casas's conjecture was fully justified. Albertus was one of the first and few Christian writers to have theorized at length that the torrid zone (where Columbus had indeed carried out most of his exploration) was neither hot nor uninhabitable—as most geographical literature declared—but rather remarkably temperate and most fertile.[151] As Las Casas saw it, while Columbus had discovered a vast, temperate, fecund, and inhabited belt of the tropics, Albertus had been one of its learned "inventors," proving by philosophical means that its nature was neither radically different nor inferior to that of Mediterranean Europe. Las Casas's motion to list Albertus among Columbus's predecessors bears the mark of an expert strategist by now feared in Crown circles for fastidiously long *argumenta* in which he out-documented the very sources he cited. This trait causes one very meticulous reader of sources on the discovery, the schismatic Americanist Henry Vignaud, to call Las Casas's introduction of Albertus a "chapitre curieux" of *Historia de las Indias*.[152]

In fact Las Casas devoted two full chapters of his intellectual biography of Columbus in *Historia de las Indias* to the arguments of Albertus, d'Ailly, and the ancient authors who had speculated that the torrid zone and the southern temperate zone—previously thought to be uninhabitable—enjoyed temperate and abundant habitation.[153]

What is at stake in Las Casas's treatment of Albertus's *De natura loci* and d'Ailly's *Ymago mundi* as two of Columbus's capital readings is a disagreement with the deceased Columbus regarding the political status of the inhabitants of the Bahamas and Caribbean basin. While the Columbus of the *Diario* had proved that the torrid zone in the Indies was unimaginably temperate, he had failed to reject the tripartite geography of nations that accorded temperate polities the natural right to govern themselves and others. *De natura loci* and *Ymago mundi* were more than two of the most complete treatises in theoretical geography ever written in the high scholastic tradition: both treatises—Albertus's in particular—offered Las Casas detailed philosophical and technical models for confirming *and* opposing a geopolitics that was slowly consigning the peoples of the Americas to perpetual subjection.

Las Casas knew well that Columbus was only the first in a line of writers to invoke the moral authority of place to justify Spain's territorial voracity in the Americas. In an empire obsessed with legal minutiae, the most potentially effective appeals to the tripartite geography of nations were to be found in the speciously crafted philosophical arguments of other schoolmen who had, since the opening years of the sixteenth century, sought to establish once and for all the legal framework of an imperial enterprise. The story of these efforts has been made most familiar in the English-speaking world by scholars like Lewis Hanke and Anthony Pagden.[154]

In 1504, following the death of Queen Isabel, King Fernando of Aragon, now regent of Castile, had summoned what was perhaps the first official *junta* of theologians and jurists ever to consider the legality of Spain's occupation of the Americas.[155] Far less sympathetic to the cause of the newly discovered peoples than his late wife, Fernando may have been prompted to summon this *junta* by the need to find a loophole to bypass the terms that Isabel had laid down in her last will and codicil for future treatment of the Indians.[156] In her will (23 November 1504), Isabel cited the papal bulls Alexander VI had issued in 1493 granting the Catholic Monarchs, as the pope had famously called Fernando and his wife, exclusive access to the territories just discovered by Columbus in the high Atlantic.[157] According to Isabel, the purpose of this concession had been to attempt the conversion of the peoples of the "Isles and Terra Firma of the Ocean Sea" and to send members of the church to instruct them in the faith and to teach them "lofty customs."[158] With this in mind, Isabel begged her husband and ordered her heirs to the Crown of Castile, Juana and her husband, Philip I (the Handsome), "to pursue this goal with great diligence, and not to allow the Indians—neighbors and inhabitants of the said Indies and Terra Firma, won and to be won—to suffer any harm whatsoever to their persons or to their possessions; and, instead, to order that they be treated well and justly, and, should they have been harmed in any way, to seek proper remedy and to ensure that what we have been sworn and ordered to do by virtue of the said Apostolic letters of concession not be exceeded in any manner whatsoever."[159]

Isabel's final bout of good conscience seemed to suggest that the character of Alexander VI's concessions to the Catholic Monarchs was spiritual and not temporal. In other words, it could be read to suggest that these concessions constituted a right of way for evangelization but not a charter for possession or occupation of the new orb, much less for disposing at will of its inhabitants. Since the opening years of the fifteenth century, papal bulls had served to legitimize Castile's and Portugal's claims to Atlantic Africa; both the (mostly Portuguese) monarchs who had petitioned for them and the popes who had issued them assumed that the goal of converting non-Christians did *not* preclude—to use the jargon often deployed in such documents—"invading," "conquering," "dispossessing," "subjugating," or otherwise "enslaving" them.[160]

It was only a matter of time, however, before someone would come to question the reach of such broad concessions, for, at least since the thirteenth century, learned figures in Europe had already hotly debated whether the pope could wield any temporal authority whatsoever and, if he did, whether such authority extended to infidels.[161] Any shadow of admission by the Crown of Castile that the nature of such concessions as popes had granted in Atlantic Africa and the Indies might be purely spiritual could invite a resurgence of this debate in Castile. We know little about the *junta* called by King Fernando in 1504, except that the Crown wished to believe it had been granted the right to wield spiritual and temporal sovereignty in the Indies.[162] But the very fact that Fernando had felt compelled to call such a *junta* was itself tacit acknowledgment that the title that the papal bulls of 1493 had conferred on Fernando and Isabel might not suffice to justify Spain's occupation of the Americas.

The solution to this problem, especially as it applied to the use and traffic of forced labor inaugurated by Columbus in the Indies, would soon suggest itself to

Crown apologists, most likely in a set of commentaries printed in 1510 on Peter Lombard's widely taught theological *Sententiae* (mid-12th century). The author of these commentaries, John Mair, a Scottish theologian and philosopher at the University of Paris, is the first schoolman we know who applied himself to the question of the legality of empire in the new orb by turning away from the thorny debate about the extent of papal authority, instead to invoke the *nature* of the Indians as a title for subjecting or enslaving them.[163] Mair reframed the question in terms of Aristotle's discussion of slavery in the *Politics;* not surprisingly, the commentator's conclusion that Indians were "by nature" slaves hinged on first indexing their *place* in the world-machine.[164] Mair's *In secundum librum sententiarum* cited the geopolitical model found in Ptolemy's *Tetrabiblos* to explain why the newly discovered peoples were Aristotle's natural slaves:

> These people live like beasts on this and that side of the equator; and beneath the poles wild men live, as Ptolemy says in his *Quadripartitum*. And this has now been demonstrated by experience, wherefore the first person to conquer them, rules over them because they are by nature, clearly, slaves. As the Philosopher says in the third and fourth chapters of the first book of the *Politics,* it is clear that some men are by nature slaves, others by nature free; and in some men it is determined that there be such a thing [as to be enslaved or free], and that they should profit from it. And it is fair that one man should be a slave and another free, and it is fitting that one man should rule and another obey, for the mark of leadership is also inherent in the natural master. On this account the Philosopher says in the first chapter of the said book that this is the reason why the Greeks should be masters over the barbarians because, by nature, barbarians and slaves are the same.[165]

The logic of place that governed Mair's case against the Indians must have seemed self-evident and, indeed, infallible to Mair's readers—infallible, that is, as long as one continued to believe that the newly discovered peoples in the high Atlantic, like the inhabitants of sub-Saharan Africa and of the Arctic circle, were the unnatural tenants of the unnatural margins of an inhabited world whose geographical and moral center had always been and would remain Mediterranean Europe. And this is precisely what Crown apologists continued to assume in the decades to come, despite increasingly copious evidence that the globe was vastly more hospitable, abundant, diverse, and temperate than even the boldest geographers among the ancients had suspected.

In 1511, only a year after Mair published his commentaries, Fray Pedro de Córdoba, vicar general of the Indies, and his fellow Dominicans at Santo Domingo launched a momentous round of public sermons against the unspeakable abuses visited by Christian colonists on the native population of Hispaniola.[166] The story of these protests is well known today thanks to Las Casas, who writes that on the fourth Sunday of Advent (21 December), the most eloquent member of the convent, Fray Antonio de Montesinos, having enumerated the *crueldades exquisitas* committed against the Indians, informed the stunned members of his audience, who included the governor of Hispaniola, Columbus's legitimate son Diego, that, as things stood, they could "no more expect salvation than the Moors or Turks who lack the Faith of Christ and do not wish to seek it."[167] The outraged colonists sent a Franciscan emissary to the city of Burgos, where Fernando's court was stationed, to protest what they mindfully construed as an attempt to deprive the king of his sovereignty and revenues in the Indies.[168] An outraged Fernando, whose growing concern with maximizing the royal revenues from gold extraction in Hispaniola implied the use of ever-greater quantities of forced labor, replied to Don Diego and officials with a warrant to silence the Dominican friars of Santo Domingo (20 March 1512). Fray Pedro de Córdoba and his colleagues were to be allowed to remain in Hispaniola only under strict condition that they never mention another word on the subject, from the pulpit, or in public or private, "lest it be to say that, if they once held that opinion, it was only because they were not informed concerning the right we have to these islands, and also because they were not familiar with the justification we had not only to force those Indians to serve as they do already, but also to hold them in even greater servitude."[169]

But the Dominican friars of Santo Domingo also managed—and barely—to be heard by the king, who, somewhat alarmed by the atrocities described to him in person by Antonio de Montesinos, also promised to seek a solution to the problem.[170] As Pagden has observed, by construing Montesino's sermons as an attack on the king's sovereignty, Hispaniola's colonists had obliged Fernando to reassert his titles to the new orb.[171] Thus in 1512 a new *junta* of theologians, jurists, and members of Fernando's council met in Burgos to discuss how best to deal with the question of the Indies.[172] Much to the dismay of those in court who believed in the right of colonists to dispose of Indians as little more than beasts of burden, the Burgos *junta* concluded that the Indians should be treated as free vassals of the Crown; that they could be ordered to work, as long as their labor did not interfere with their proper indoctrination and education and as long as this was tolerable labor that included regular intervals of recreation; that they could own property and take the necessary time off from their other obligations in order to tend to it; and, finally, that they had a right to remuneration in kind (clothes, food, etc.) for their work.[173]

Not content with the findings of the council, Fernando himself, or others acting on the Crown's behalf, asked for a second diagnosis from two of the king's in-house preachers, a certain Bachelor Gregorio, who had already participated in the Burgos *junta,* and a Dominican friar known as Bernardo Mesa, whose *parecer,* or opinion, speaks directly to our argument.[174] In his *parecer,* which evidently sought to answer a loaded question regarding the legal status of the Indians—could they be enslaved?—Mesa stated that the Indians were not slaves *de iure* since they had not been won in a holy war against infidels (because they were ignorant of the Faith, Indians could not be considered infidels). Nor were they slaves bought in the market, slaves born of other slaves, or slaves in the eyes of either Fernando or the late Isabel, "who always called them free, and this is a manifest sign of their freedom." The only reason Mesa could see to hold the Indians as slaves was their "lack of understanding and capacity, and the absence of will to persevere in the practice of the Faith and of lofty customs, for that is the condition of natural slavery, as the philosopher says. *Or perhaps they are, he says, slaves on account of the nature of the land, because there are certain lands that the aspect of the heavens renders subject to others, and [they could not be properly governed] if there were not some sort of slavery in them. . . ."*[175] This is not the first time that the theory of natural slavery was cited in the Spanish Empire to refer to the Indians.[176] Columbus had long endorsed Aristotle's concept of natural slavery on the margins of d'Ailly and in the very terminology with which he characterized the native peoples of the Indies. But with Mesa's "opinion," the official debate was certainly on in schooled circles concerning the *nature* of the newly discovered peoples. And this debate would implicitly or explicitly assume that whatever the nature of the Indians, it had been conferred on them by *place.*[177]

But among the apologists of empire who came to consider the question of the Indies in the following decades, few would prove to be as skilled or as vocal as the distinguished translator of Aristotle, Juan Ginés de Sepúlveda.[178] Las Casas had recently faced his foe Sepúlveda in the dramatic Juntas de Valladolid (1550–1551) summoned by Charles V to debate the legality and future of Spain's ventures in the New World.[179] And while Las Casas's *Historia* and *Apologética* were being broadly aimed against a coercive geopolitics already at work in Columbus's *Diario,* Las Casas's most immediate target in the years following the juntas was Sepúlveda.[180] This Crown jurist had authored a short treatise entitled *Apologia pro libro de iustis belli* (Rome, 1550), which cited the tripartite geography of nations to claim that Indians failed to meet the natural preconditions for preserving political autonomy from Christians. Lifting directly from Thomas Aquinas's own commentary on Aristotle's *Politics*, Sepúlveda defined the Indians as "barbarians" (*barbari*), that is, as "those who are deficient in reason, whether because of the region of the heavens, which makes them weak, for the most part; or because of some evil custom, which makes men almost like beasts."[181]

Sepúlveda's *Apologia* was itself a fugitive summary of his work best known today among Americanists, *Democrates secundus* (written between 1544 and 1545). Las Casas had successfully lobbied to suppress publication of *Democrates secundus* upon his final return to Spain in 1547, though Las Casas himself appears to have been prevented from inspecting its contents firsthand.[182] As Las Casas rightly feared, Sepúlveda's work constitutes a most comprehensive and detailed philosophical blueprint of colonial imperialism. Indeed, Sepúlveda was highly qualified to articulate the knowledge system that connected geography and politics in the high scholastic tradition. *Democrates secundus* opens with a question that foreshadowed Sepúlveda's general indictment of Amerindians by pointing to a geography (to the west *and* to the south) that confirmed native peoples' subordination in the political world order: "Is it by a just war, or unjustly, that the kings of Spain and our countrymen have brought and work to bring into subjection those barbarous peoples who inhabit the western and southern region and who are commonly called Indians in Spanish? And what is a just way of ruling these mortals? This is a matter of great dispute."[183] Sepúlveda's use of the term *plaga* or "region" was not accidental. This Latin term had long been used in geographical literature to refer to the horizontal belts of the five zones.[184]

Neither was Sepúlveda's use of the locator "western and southern region" accidental. For Sepúlveda, as for Las Casas, this locator constituted *legal* terminology established in the papal bulls that Alexander VI had issued to Fernando and Isabel upon Columbus's return from the first voyage in 1493, specifically the *Inter cetera* [II] (antedated 4 May 1493) and *Dudum siquidem* (26 September 1493). These bulls had "donated" to the Crowns of Aragon and Castile "all islands and terrae firmae discovered and to be discovered . . . *to the west and to the south*" that did not already lie within the dominion of the Portuguese or of any other Christians.[185] Alexander's concessions themselves had been drafted with an eye to the Treaty of Alcáçovas, which had officially ended the war that King Alfonso V of Portugal had waged since 1464 against the Catholic Monarchs to contest Isabel's succession to the throne. With Alcáçovas, Portugal had, after decades of conflict, recognized Spain's control of the Canaries, and Spain Portugal's monopoly over Guinea and over all islands discovered or to be discovered "from the Canary Islands down and toward Guinea" (*de las yslas de Canaria para yuso contra Guinea*)—conceivably, *to the south* and *to the east* of the Canaries.[186] Alexander VI's papal bulls of 1493 were largely meant to prevent Portugal from interpreting its rights "below" the Canaries to include any territories *to the south* and *to the west* of the Spanish archipelago. The pope's abominable "donations" were destined to become during the first half of the sixteenth century—thanks to a number of schoolmen including Las Casas—the most contentious legal documents in the protracted debate over the legitimacy of the Spanish conquest of the Americas.

Sepúlveda's learned deployment of the tripartite geopolitics by which Greeks, Romans, and their Christian heirs had rationalized their rule over "barbarians" demanded equally learned replies. Las Casas recognized the great hold of such geopolitical models, and he knew that any argument against them required deploying the knowledge system in which they flourished against itself. This is perhaps the most urgent task at hand in Las Casas's *Historia de las Indias* and its companion volume, the *Apologética*. The "apostle of the Indians" was fully cognizant of the complex assumptions behind the concept of the world-as-God's-machine. And he devoted nearly a lifetime to overturning an imperialist geopolitics that confined Amerindians to a lesser place in this cosmos. The present book attempts to honor his efforts.

Columbus and the Open Geography of the Ancients

. . . But now
Poseidon had gone to visit the Ethiopians worlds away,
Ethiopians off at the farthest limits of mankind,
a people split in two, one part where the Sungod sets
and part where the Sungod rises.

Homer, *The Odyssey* 1.22–24 (trans. Fagles)

In 1486, the year following Columbus's arrival in Castile from Portugal, King Fernando of Aragon and Queen Isabel of Castile appointed a special commission to evaluate Columbus's plan to sail across the ocean. This royal *junta*, presided by the eminent Jeromite friar Hernando de Talavera and honored by some of the finest minds in the realm, appears to have assembled on at least two occasions to discuss Columbus's proposal—first in 1486 and again nearly six years later, in January of 1492, at a pivotal moment in the history of Christian Spain.[1] At the war encampment of Santa Fe, where Christians were celebrating the defeat of Muslim Granada, the royal commission dealt what seemed to be a death blow to Columbus's dreams, issuing irrevocable judgment to the effect that his project was preposterous. In the end, Columbus and his supporters could not persuade the Santa Fe assembly that his plan was feasible, and it appears to have been last-minute intervention by individuals with personal influence on Fernando (and the queen) that led the Crown to override the royal *junta*'s pronouncement. An embittered Columbus was to complain to the Catholic Monarchs years after the discovery (1501) that "neither reason, nor mathematics, nor *mappaemundi* proved of any use to me toward the execution of the enterprise of the Indies."[2]

No official record has survived of the commission's deliberations or of the specific plan that Columbus laid before the Crown. In the arduous years that followed the discovery, Columbus alluded to his troubled interactions with the royal commission when he mentioned the scorn that his detractors had shown for his proposal: even in the closing statements of his *Diario* (15 March 1493), as he anticipated a hero's welcome on his way back to Europe from the Caribbean, Columbus did not miss the opportunity to complain to his royal benefactors of years spent "in Your Highnesses' court, facing opposition, and against the better judgment of so many principals in Your household, all of whom were against me, making jest of what has now been accomplished."[3] But Columbus himself appears not to have left behind any formal record of the proposal or proposals that he and his supporters had presented in Castile. And it was only years later, as he contemplated the erosion of the rights and privileges conferred upon him prior to his first voyage, as he found himself defending the merits of an enterprise that had failed to yield the fabulous spoils he had promised, and as he fended off those who questioned whether he had made it all the way to Asia, that Columbus felt compelled to spell out some of his geographical ideas in writing. But we may never know for sure whether the specific ideas Columbus espoused this late in the game precisely reflect the ideas he had once presented to Fernando and Isabel. Columbus's most seminal biographers, his son Ferdinand and Las Casas, largely reconstructed the geographical *praecognita* now associated with Columbus's project from key passages in the letters Columbus had written *after* the discovery (particularly from his famous *carta-relación* of the third voyage [30 May–31 August 1498]), and from related postils in the margins of the works now preserved in the Biblioteca Colombina, which the two biographers perhaps all too easily assumed could only have been written during the years Columbus had elaborated his plan.

Fortunately, the scarce testimony we do have concerning the official debate that preceded the discovery sheds crucial light on fundamental aspects of the project Columbus presented to Fernando and Isabel. And, insofar as today's Americanists fail to see in this testimony—or in the evidence used by Ferdinand and Las Casas for their accounts of Columbus's geography—any more than Columbus's plan to reach the East "by way of the West," this testimony and that evidence deserve further consideration.

In revisiting the conceptual parameters that governed the official debate prompted by Columbus's proposal, I wish to show that *southing*, not merely westing, played a systemic role in the very planning stages of Columbus's enterprise. Columbus's project was forged between two irreconcilable explanations for how earth and water had come to be lodged at the center of the cosmos in the beginning of time and how life had come to be allocated in the region of the four elements.[4] Columbus's detractors in Castile argued that the sphere of water was eccentric with respect to the sphere of earth—the continental masses formed a lonely island surrounded by the abyss of an otherwise watery globe. Columbus and his supporters, more faithful to Aristotle's cosmology, argued that water was concentric with respect to earth—Europe, Africa, and Asia were the result of imperfections in the earth's sphere that were bound to occur elsewhere around the globe. This is the only meaning we should ascribe to Ferdinand's famous, and so often misread, claim in *Historie del S. D. Fernando Colombo* that his father had believed "that all the water and the earth in the universe constituted and formed a sphere that could be rounded from east to west, men being able to walk all around it until they came to stand feet to feet, the ones opposite the others, wherever they wished to be that stood on the opposite side."[5] The debate between Columbus and his detractors never rested on the roundness or flatness of humankind's abode; rather, it was a matter of whether the spheres of earth and water configured an *open* or *closed* geographical system. Columbus's detractors also cited the theory of the five zones in arguing that the lonely island of the earth was itself besieged to the north and south by the intolerable cold and heat of the frigid and torrid zones. By contrast, Columbus and his supporters argued that the inhabited world generally extended not just farther east and west than some believed but also farther north and south, into the allegedly inhospitable regions of the globe. And what ultimately lay at stake in this second disagreement between Columbus and his detractors was the *nature* of the lower latitudes of the globe we know today as the belt of the tropics.

Ferdinand and Las Casas record a few highly significant details about the objections raised against Columbus's uncertain geography by the royal council headed by Fray Hernando de Talavera. According to Las Casas, who followed the Fernandine *Historie* almost to the letter, some members of the council "better versed in mathematical doctrine, touching on the subject of astrology and cosmography, claimed that of this lower sphere of water and earth, only a small part was left uncovered, because everything else was covered by water and, therefore, that it was not possible to navigate, were it not along the shores or rivieras like the Portuguese did in Guinea."[6] Las Casas, who shared Ferdinand's disdain for the paucity of geographical knowledge in Castile prior to the discovery, adds that other council members "cited Saint Augustine, who . . . denied the existence of antipodes, those whom we say walk opposite to our feet; and so they invoked the saying: 'Saint Augustine doubts it.' There were still some who brought up the question of the five zones, of which three are—according to many—entirely uninhabitable, and the other two inhabitable, which was the common opinion of the ancients, who in the end knew very little."[7] Las Casas's and Ferdinand's accounts of these objections unequivocally indicate that even at this early stage, Columbus banked on the possibility of finding hospitable and inhabited land in the belt of the tropics, perhaps even as far down as the southern temperate zone, where, some had theorized, one would find the antipodes.

These accounts of the royal council's proceedings are usefully supplemented by an earlier (and, in all likelihood, unrelated) source, the Umbrian humanist Alessandro Geraldini (1455–1524), who served as papal legate for Leo X. Geraldini had enjoyed a long career at court by the time Columbus came to lobby for his project in Santa Fe. He was, among other things, the tutor of Fernando and Isabel's younger children as well as Great Chaplain of *infanta* Catalina; in later years (in 1516) he was presented by the young Charles V for the bishopric of Santo Domingo.[8] Geraldini's brother Antonio had endorsed Columbus's cause at court, and, after Antonio's death in 1489, Geraldini himself participated as a member of the last assembly to review Columbus's proposal in Santa Fe. In fact, the only extant witness account we have of the proceedings of the Santa Fe assembly appears in Geraldini's *Itinerarium ad regiones sub aequinoctiali plaga constitutas,* completed in 1522 as a petition to Pope Leo X for funds to build the present Cathedral of Santa María de la Encarnación in Santo Domingo.[9] The *Itinerarium* was never sent to Leo X, because the pontiff died a few months before its completion. Geraldini instead deposited it with his family in Italy, where an Italian translation and only a handful of Latin copies would be produced in the latter half of the sixteenth century. The *Itinerarium* was finally published in 1631 by one of Geraldini's grandnephews.[10]

Incidentally, Geraldini's petition to the pope, which recorded Geraldini's endorsement of Columbus's plan, also explicitly corroborated the tripartite geopolitics that had guided Columbus's exploration of the Bahamas and Caribbean basin. The *Itinerarium* not only described Geraldini's passage through western Africa and the minor Antilles on his way to the new bishopric of Hispaniola; it also described the "irrational" practices of the many peoples in the torrid zone, whose geographical proximity to the equator—Geraldini argued—impaired their ability to govern themselves spiritually or politically.[11] Geraldini described the royal council's proceedings in the encampment of Santa Fe as follows:

> When a council of important men had assembled, there were various opinions because many Spanish bishops plainly alleged that he [Columbus] was manifestly guilty of heresy, because Nicholas of Lyra states that the whole fabric of the

inhabited earth extending above the sea from the Fortunate Isles [i.e., Canary Islands] to the Orient does not have borders turned toward the sphere's lower side. And Saint Aurelius Augustine holds that there are no antipodes. Then I, who happened to be young, was sitting behind Cardinal Diego de Mendoza . . . and suggested to him that Nicholas of Lyra was indeed a remarkable expounder of sacred theology and Aurelius Augustine a great man by virtue of his doctrine and saintliness, but that they had lacked any knowledge of cosmography, since the Portuguese had already traveled to the farthest parts of the lower hemisphere, in such a way that—leaving behind our own arctic circle—they had discovered the anctarctic circle under another pole, and they had found a densely populated torrid zone; and they had contemplated new stars under the axis of the antipodes.[12]

Columbus's biographers cite Geraldini as an irreproachable eyewitness, although we should treat his testimony with some caution.[13] The task of persuading Leo X to finance the Santo Domingo cathedral undoubtedly informed Geraldini's recollection of the council's objections to Columbus's plan. Geraldini's memory of the Santa Fe assembly, where he claims that he registered his endorsement of Columbus's plan with the influential cardinal Diego de Mendoza, confers legitimacy on a petition to the pope that attested to the existence of a densely populated equatorial region in need of clergy and churches. But Geraldini's motives aside, his recollection of that intervention with Cardinal Mendoza speaks clearly to the learned polemics engaged by the royal council in Santa Fe. His *Itinerarium* supplies crucial information for qualifying Las Casas's and Ferdinand's renditions of the debate in the assemblies that preceded the discovery.

The royal council's mention of Nicholas of Lyra (1270–1349) has been shown to be a reference to the "Additions" written by the convert rabbi-bishop Paul of Burgos (Pablo de Santa María, about 1351–1435) to Nicholas's popular glosses on the Latin Vulgate, Saint Jerome's translation of the Old and New Testaments.[14] Specifically, Columbus's opponents in Santa Fe were citing Burgos's philosophical proof of the Mosaic account of God's works on the third day of Creation in Genesis 1:9–10:

God also said: Let the waters that are under the heaven, be gathered together into one place: and let the dry land appear. And it was so done.

And God called the dry land, Earth: and the gathering together of the waters, he called Seas. And God saw that it was good.[15]

Burgos's *additio* to these verses reflects the rigor that schoolmen tended to apply to the task of reconciling pagan and Arab philosophies with Christian theology—particularly the thought of Aristotle and his commentators. The problem posed by these verses was how the separation of earth from water had been achieved during Creation and, particularly, what the gathering of the waters "in one place" (*in locum unum*) meant. Burgos's solution spoke directly to the key *incognitae* of Columbus's plan—the earth-to-water surface ratio and distribution of both on the globe, which facts depended largely on the answer to a cosmological debate that had occupied Aristotle's commentators since antiquity, namely, the manner in which earth and water were lodged together as the heaviest components of a universe assembled in a series of concentric spheres. Aristotle's contention that earth and water were concentric spheres—and its mathematical proof by Archimedes (about 287–212 BCE)—had posed an insurmountable paradox for proponents of geocentricity: if earth's tendency as the heavier element of the two was to be moved down to the absolute center of the cosmos, immediately below water (that is, with the sphere of the earth being entirely contained by the sphere of water), what explained the presence of land on the globe's surface?[16]

Columbus's opponents in Santa Fe viewed the presence of the *orbis terrarum* as a divinely sanctioned exception to water's tendency to move down and to thus entirely surround the sphere of the earth. It was through God's direct suspension of nature's works that the *orbis terrarum* had come into being as a shelter for animated land creatures. As John of Sacrobosco stated in his popular *De sphaera*, each of the three elements surrounded the earth on all sides, "except in so far as the dryness of the earth stays water's humor in order to protect the life of living creatures."[17]

In the Christian imagination, the Mosaic view of Adam and Eve as the sole progenitors of a geographically dispersed human race coexisted uneasily with the Homeric view of the known inhabited world as an island surrounded by the "Ocean River" in a northern quadrant of the globe. Homer's *Iliad* thus came to inform much Christian iconography of the *orbis terrarum*, most starkly, perhaps, in the celebrated T-O *mappaemundi*, which depicted a disk-shaped island divided into the three known continents by the T-shaped arrangement of the Mediterranean Sea and the rivers Nile and Tanais (Don) (**fig. 2.1**).[18] But Homer's geographical heirs in the Greco-Roman tradition had by no means ruled out the existence of inhabited landmasses outside this known inhabited world. And it is ultimately against this aspect of the Homeric geographical tradition that Paul of Burgos would direct his learned interpretation of

Genesis 1:9–10. Certainly this is how Columbus's opponents at the royal council read Burgos's *additio:* Burgos's philosophical and technical elucidation of Mosaic cosmogony methodically confirmed a geographical canon that—reaching back to Saint Augustine—had attempted to absolve itself of its pagan foundations.

Prominent Greco-Roman thinkers posited an open geography, despite Homer's influential depiction of the known inhabited world. Unquestionably, the idea that land distribution on the globe's surface might exceed Europe, Africa, and Asia was already latent in the theory of the five zones attributed to Parmenides, which posited a second temperate zone in the southern hemisphere. The first explicit challenge to Homeric geography was the *History* of Herodotus, which scorned Homer's invention of the circumambient Ocean River as a poetic device that poorly masked a lack of information

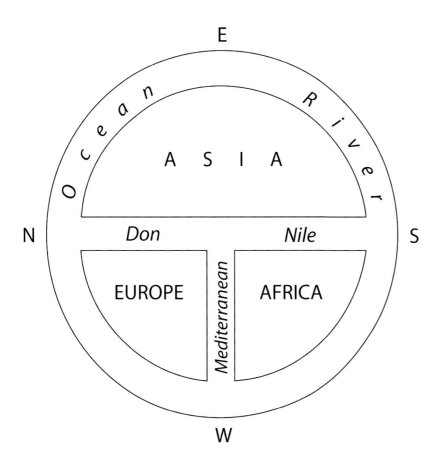

2.1   The tripartite structure of T-O maps. After David Woodward, "Medieval *Mappaemundi,*" chapter 18 in *Cartography in Prehistoric, Ancient, and Medieval Europe and the Mediterranean*, vol. 1 of *The History of Cartography*, ed. J. B. Harley and David Woodward (Chicago, 1987), 297. Prepared by the author.

about the inhabited world's furthest reaches. Herodotus referred to unreported land instead as "empty space" (*erēmos*), much the way uncharted territory would often come to be depicted in maps.[19] But the philosophical argument for an open geography emerged from the earliest speculations about the dynamics between fresh and salt water. Homer had described the Ocean River in the *Iliad* as "the source of all rivers and all the seas on earth and all springs and all deep wells"; and Hesiod referred to the rivers in his *Theogony* (7th century BCE) as "Slender-ankled Ocean nymphs scattered everywhere / Haunting earth and deep waters. . . ."[20] Such views survived in the joint propositions in Plato's *Phaedo* (4th century BCE) that water, mist, and air were condensates of ether that "everywhere" filled the "hollows" of the earth, and that all rivers (including the Ocean River) alternately fed one another through channels and reservoirs deep in the earth.[21] Plato's theory seemed to imply that these subterranean channels and reservoirs held water that would have otherwise covered land—perhaps all land—on the globe's surface.

This theory of water circulation would spawn intriguing metaphors for the terraqueous globe. In his *Naturales quaestiones* (about 62–65 CE), for instance, the philosopher Lucius Annaeus Seneca, following the Stoic concept of the cosmos as an animated whole, likened the earth and its hollows to a human body with veins and arteries: "Nature fashioned these routes [subterranean channels] so like human bodies that our ancestors also called them 'veins' of water."[22] And in a passage of *Naturalis historia,* Seneca's contemporary Pliny the Elder recorded a related and highly illustrative argument for the manner in which earth and water were lodged at the center of the cosmos. He ventured that the "Artificer of nature" had wanted "to unite earth and water in a mutual embrace, earth opening her bosom and water penetrating her entire frame by means of a network of veins radiating within and without, above and below, the water bursting out even at the tops of mountain ridges. . . ."[23] In the argument collected by Pliny, the earth "at every point of its globe is encircled and engirdled by the sea flowing round it. . . ."[24] Significantly, it was this passage in Pliny that Columbus would come to cite in his *carta-relación* of the third voyage, when he intuited that the huge water flow at the mouth of the Orinoco River in present-day Venezuela indicated the presence of a continent extending toward the southern hemisphere, or, as he called it, "infinite land that is toward the south."[25] According to Columbus, earth and water were mixed together "like the bitter core of the walnut with a thick membrane girdling the whole."[26] Columbus's remarkable metaphor invoked a cosmology that ultimately explained the extrusion of land above water as the result of significant irregularities in the earth's sphere.

Aristotle, for his part, forwarded an important alternative to the theories of water circulation endorsed by Plato and other earlier thinkers, but his cosmology also implied an open geography. In his *Meteorologica,* Aristotle objected that the earth could not house the great volume and flow of water by which previous explanations of water circulation explained the presence of bare land: "A receptacle that is to contain all the water that flows in the year would be larger than the earth, or, at any rate, not much smaller."[27] His alternative to the subterranean hydraulics theorized by Plato and others obeyed the postulates set forth in *On Generation and Corruption* concerning the cyclical exchange between the four elements and their compounds. Aristotle there subscribes to the view (derived from Empedocles' concept of *roots*) that the four elements result from the various couplings of four fundamental qualities organized in pairs of contraries: the hot and the cold, the dry and the wet.[28] (Earth is supposed to be primarily cold and somewhat dry; water, mostly cold and somewhat moist; air, mostly moist and somewhat hot; and fire, mostly hot and somewhat dry.)[29] The elements and their compounds are generated out of one another as the primary qualities in them give way to their contraries. Water, for instance, is generated as the dry gives way to the moist in earth; air, as the cold gives way to the hot in water, and so on.[30] Change in the elements and their compounds is thus an unending, reciprocal "change into contraries and out of contraries."[31]

In a section of *On Generation and Corruption* that Christian writers into the seventeenth century were to invoke repeatedly in favor of the theory of celestial influence, Aristotle claimed that the main generator of contraries in the elements and their compounds was the sun. The unending approach and retreat in the sun's daily and yearly motion along the slanted, ecliptic circle was supposed to cause the respective coming-to-be and passing-away observed in the elements and their compounds.[32] Aristotle's theory of water circulation in *Meteorologica* predictably assumed that the heat and cold generated by the sun's unending motion caused the cyclical rarefaction and condensation of water around the globe, uncovering lands over the span of eons where the waters had once been and vice versa.[33] In fact, Aristotle understood the ancient concept of the Ocean River as a metaphor for the immense circular exchange between water and air caused by the sun's motion.[34] Aristotle's cosmology was thus profoundly implicated in the articulation of an open geography in which land-water distribution on the globe's surface underwent constant, cyclical permutation.[35]

The most explicit endorsement of an open geography in the Greco-Roman tradition, however, was offered in the second century BCE by Crates of Mallos, who, in part to illustrate Homer's account of "Ethiopians" in the *Odyssey*, developed his concept of inhabited landmasses in the temperate zones of the three remaining quarters of the globe (*antoikoi, antichthones,* or antipodes, and *perioikoi*)(**fig. 1.3**, p. 73).[36] For Crates, two groups of Ethiopians, isolated from each other by the portion of the Ocean River that ran through the hot equatorial region, respectively bordered the northern and southern temperate zones—one group as part of the *oikoumenē*, or known inhabited world, to the north, and the other group as part of the *antoikoi* directly to the south of the *oikoumenē*. Crates' concept was very influential, even though his invention of two races of Ethiopians was an evident misreading of Homer's orientation in these lines of the *Odyssey* as north-south rather than southwest-southeast ("where the Sungod sets . . . where the Sungod rises").[37] Even the methodical Strabo, who would note this misreading in his own exegesis of Homer in the *Geography,* recommended Crates' concept of the globe for visualizing the location of the *oikoumenē* (i.e., *orbis terrarum*) and readily admitted the plausibility of other inhabited worlds on the globe.[38] Another notable corroboration of this model came from Ptolemy himself, who corrected his predecessor Marinos of Tyre's overestimate of the longitudinal and latitudinal extent of the known inhabited world.[39] Major technical works like the *Almagest* and the *Geography* certainly bounded the known inhabited world largely within a horizontal quadrant of the northern hemisphere that measured 180 degrees in longitude and 90 degrees in latitude.[40] But these works make it abundantly clear that Ptolemy considered the known inhabited world to be only part of a hypothetically larger inhabited world. In the *Almagest,* Ptolemy registered his debt to Cratesian geography with the phrase "our portion of the inhabited world" (*hē kath' hēmas oikoumenē*) in order to describe the quadrant occupying the half of the northern hemisphere in which the tricontinental landmass stood. And he later referred to inhabited zones in different parts of the globe as distinct from "our portion of the inhabited world," among which he named the "so called 'Antichthones'" (*hoi antichthonoi kaloumenoi*).[41] Similarly, the *Geography* hypothesized an *antoikoumenē* directly south of the *oikoumenē,* in a quarter occupying one-half of the lower hemisphere and mirroring the conditions for habitation that applied to the known inhabited world in the north.[42] This unknown world in the southern hemisphere (the location of Crates' *antoikoi*) would have enclosed the Indian Ocean, connecting Cape Prason in Africa's southeasternmost hinterlands (perhaps Cape Delgado on Mozambique's northern border, today 10° 45′ S) with the elusive port of Kattigara, the farthest point known to Ptolemy in southeast Asia (see, respectively, "Rhaptum promonturium" and "Cattigara" on **fig. 2.2**).[43] In the early fifth century it was Crates' concept of inhabited landmasses centered on the temperate zones beyond the known inhabited world that Macrobius would incorporate into his zonal *mappamundi* as "the temperate [zone] of the antipodes unknown to us" (*temperata antipodum nobis incognita*) (**fig. 1.2**, p. 72).[44] And many centuries after Macrobius, medieval *mappaemundi* sometimes reflected Crates' concept as a *fourth* continental landmass incommunicated from the *orbis terrarum* by the equatorial portion of the Ocean River (**fig. 2.3**).[45] In sum, the Homeric geographical legacy did not preclude the possibility of landmasses—inhabited or uninhabited—beyond Europe, Asia, and Africa.

In contrast, the Christian tradition followed by Columbus's opponents in the royal council favored a closed geography. In the years following the sack of Rome (410), Macrobius's Christian contemporary Saint Augustine had explicitly rejected the open geography of his Greco-Roman predecessors, at least insofar as pagan geography hypothesized the existence of *humans* outside the known inhabited world. Augustine's formidable attack on pagan theology and philosophy, *De civitate Dei* (413–426), would command great authority not only in the official deliberations preceding Columbus's historic voyage but also in later attempts by ethnographers like the Jcsuit cleric Joseph de Acosta, who in *Historia natural y moral de las Indias* (1590) posited the existence of a land bridge to explain how the Americas had come to be populated by humans, beasts, and plants.[46] Augustine's polemical departure from Greco-Roman geography is best understood in relation to Crates' concept of inhabited landmasses in the temperate zones of the remaining three quadrants of the globe, particularly in relation to Crates' invention of two races of Ethiopians *isolated* from each other by a vast ocean running through the inhospitable torrid zone. Greco-Roman mythology espoused multiple origins for humankind, including instances of autochthonous generation (such as the birth of Erichthonius, the mythical first king of Athens) and population by preternatural migration (such as the mass exodus of the Phaeacians led by their god-king Nausithous to the land of Scheria, an island that Homer's *Odyssey* situates "off at the world's end").[47] It is because this mythology imagined multiple lineages for the human species that the concept of races entirely incommunicated from the known inhabited world seems to have posed no conflict for pagan geographers like Strabo or Macrobius. If anything tells us that Macrobius was not a Christian, as some have believed, it is his frank endorsement of Cratesian geography. And as Strabo had reasoned, if indeed there

2.2 Ptolemy's second projection.
From *Cosmographia* (Ulm, 1482).
Courtesy of the John Carter Brown
Library at Brown University,
Providence, Rhode Island.

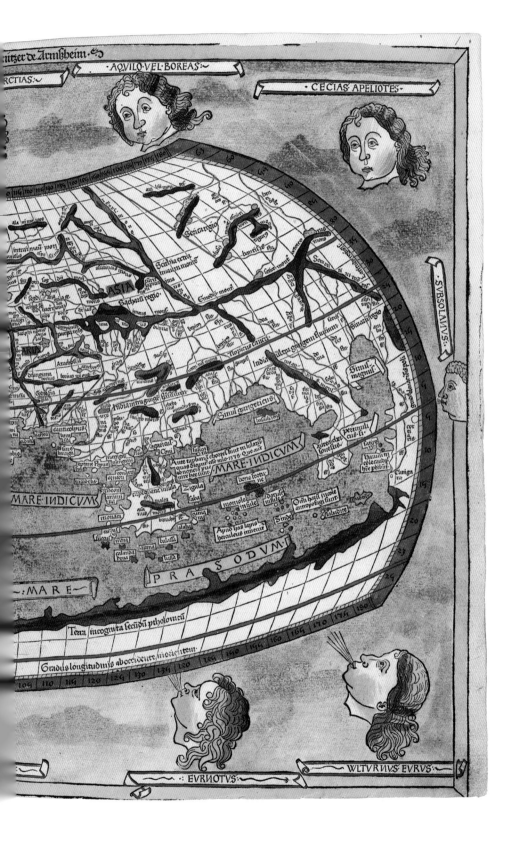

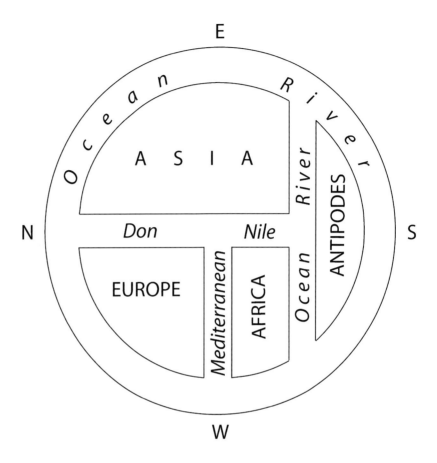

2.3 The structure of T-O maps showing a fourth continent in the southern hemisphere. After David Woodward, "Medieval *Mappaemundi*," chapter 18 in *Cartography in Prehistoric, Ancient, and Medieval Europe and the Mediterranean*, vol. 1 of *The History of Cartography*, ed. J. B. Harley and David Woodward (Chicago, 1987), 297. Prepared by the author.

were other inhabited quarters on the globe, these were "not inhabited by men such as exist in our fourth."[48]

But for Saint Augustine this concept amounted to heresy. Augustine and other church fathers lacked the philosophical and technical framework that Burgos would come to deploy in the fifteenth century to refute Cratesian geography. Reading Genesis 1:9–10 in his *De genesi ad litteram* (completed in 415), Augustine admitted bewilderment over God's motion to separate earth from water by ordering the waters to gather *in locum unum*. And, appropriating the pagan idea that water was a "condensate" that filled the "hollows" of the earth, he wondered, "Could it be that water in a rarefied state, like a cloud, had covered the earth, and that it was brought together and became dense, thus disclosing some of the many regions of the world and making it possible for dry land to appear?"[49] Augustine's literal interpretation of the "gathering" of the waters as "condensation" nominally and only briefly followed the open geography of his pagan predecessors.

But Augustine's influential *De civitate Dei* soon dismissed those pagan authors who had endorsed Crates' invention of the antipodes, breaking significantly with the Greco-Roman tradition that offered the possibility of *inhabited* landmasses incommunicated from Europe, Africa, and Asia. Those pagan authors had speculated "that the other half of the earth, which lies beneath our portion [i.e., in the southern hemisphere], cannot lack human occupants." Such authors met with Augustine's contempt because "they fail to observe that even if the world is held to be global or rounded in shape, or if some process of reasoning should prove this to be the case, it would still not necessarily follow that the land on the opposite side is not covered by masses of water. Furthermore, even if the land there be exposed, we must not jump to the conclusion that it has human inhabitants."[50] Augustine believed that humankind had a unique origin in Adam and Eve, whose progeny—after the Great Flood and the destruction of the Tower of Babel—had geographically and linguistically dispersed.[51] And if his conception of humanity included even the monstrous races that had long populated the margins of Greco-Roman geography, Augustine argued that a single humanity descended from Adam and Eve could not possibly have traversed the vast ocean separating the northern from the southern hemispheres: "The idea is too absurd to mention that some men might have sailed from our part of the earth to the other and have arrived there by crossing the boundless tracts of ocean, so that the human race might be established there also by descent from the one first man."[52] An entire lineage of writers who touched upon the subject of the inhabited world—all the way to chroniclers of the newly discovered "Indies" like Acosta—would feel obligated to tip their hat at Augustine's invective against pagan geography. Augustine's negation of the antipodes may also explain why the "insular" model of the *orbis terrarum* derived from Homer's *Iliad* would tend to find resonance with Christian cartographers all the way to the end of the fifteenth century.[53]

Of course, not all Christian works fell prey to the ecumenical angst that had led Augustine to deny the existence of land and life around the globe. Early enthusiasts of the open geography promised by Aristotle's cosmology, mainly Albertus Magnus and Roger Bacon, found remarkably intricate loopholes around Augustinian doctrine.[54] But perhaps the best-known and most striking example in medieval literature comes from

John Mandeville's *Travels.* The palace curate Andrés Bernáldez, who hosted Columbus upon his return from the second voyage in 1496, suggests in *Historia de los Reyes Católicos Don Fernando y Doña Isabel* (completed 1513) that Mandeville was one of the authors from whom Columbus may have persuaded himself that the earth was round, meaning, that there was land all around the globe.[55] Indeed, in a remarkably technical chapter of his *Travels,* Mandeville assured his readers that he had journeyed all the way from a latitude of 62° 10′ N to a latitude of 33° 16′ S, and that having found land so far to the south, he could guarantee that anyone setting out to round the globe could be sure always to find "men, lands, and isles" all the way back to his point of departure.[56] Further, no doubt replying to Saint Augustine, Mandeville insisted that the antipodes were "habitable and reachable," and that the islands of India, where the legendary Christian king "Prester John" was supposed to have ruled, were located down "under us."[57] Nevertheless, Augustinian geography continued to wield unmistakable authority well into the Age of Exploration, and it was Augustine who would still rule the day in the minds of Columbus's opponents in the Santa Fe assembly when they chose to cite Paul of Burgos's schooled interpretation of Genesis 1:9–10 against Columbus's proposal.

In order to explain how the separation of earth and water had been achieved on the third day of Creation, Burgos minimally—and implicitly—resorted to certain fundamentals of Aristotle's cosmology. First, to speak of the "nature" of physical bodies was, in part, to speak of their inherent ability to be moved or changed.[58] Second, physical bodies had "according to nature" the tendency to be moved to and rest in their respective places.[59] Third, by virtue of their heaviness or lightness, the four elements and their compounds tended to be moved toward their proper places: fire, which was absolutely light, tended to be moved upward toward the extremity of the cosmos; earth, which was absolutely heavy, tended to be moved downward toward the center of the cosmos; and air and water, which combined varying measures of lightness and heaviness, tended to be moved upward toward the surface, or down toward the bottom, of other elements.[60] Burgos thus began his explanation of Genesis 1:9–10 by positing that earth, in accordance with its tendency to be carried to the center of the universe, should have been completely covered by water, but it was not.[61] He then rejected as an explanation for the extrusion of land on the globe the views we have found in Plato and Augustine that water filled the earth's hollows.[62] Like Aristotle in *Meteorologica,* Burgos considered that the water volume to be contained underground would have been significantly greater than the earth's volume. But Aristotle's cosmology seemed to assume a volume ratio

among the four elements that precluded the very possibility that land could surface from the waters.[63]

Burgos cites the volume ratio between earth and water to be a formidable one to ten.[64] This cosmic ratio was indebted to a passage in Aristotle's *On Generation and Corruption* that discussed the manner in which the four elements were comparable.[65] Aristotle argued that a comparison between elements could only be made if they shared "an identical something." In the example he used—one pint of water yielded ten pints of air—the comparison in volume units assumed an identical quantity between a given amount of water and the total amount of air that could be generated from it. While the quantity remained constant in the permutation between these two elements, volume increased tenfold from water to air, and by implication, decreased tenfold from air to water; that is, volume increased or decreased between water and air in inverse relation to their density or rarity.[66] In a separate argument in *Meteorologica*, Aristotle further claimed that "the proportion between any given quantity however small of water and the air that is generated from it ought to hold good between the total amount of air and the total amount of water."[67] If we read Aristotle to be consistent with his previous claim in *On Generation and Corruption*, the volume ratio between the spheres of water and air was supposed to be one to ten.

In *On Generation and Corruption* and *Meteorologica*, Aristotle's claims regarding the proportion between the spheres of water and air did not extend to the proportions between other contiguous spheres. However, Aristotle did seem to imply that the "identical something" shared by the four spheres of the elements might be quantity. In a cosmology that posited that the four elements and their compounds were cyclically generated out of one another, the total quantities of each of these elements could, at least *potentially*, equal one another. More significantly, Aristotle's cosmos supposed that every physical body was emplaced, with no possibility of just emptiness around it, and the permutation between one element and another had to be compensated by reverse permutation elsewhere; otherwise, either a void would have been created, or the universe would have constantly changed magnitudes.[68] Aristotle's claims regarding the proportion between the spheres of water and air said little, however, about the volume ratio between contiguous spheres other than water and air.

Plato's cosmology, on the other hand, would have certainly inclined Aristotle's commentators to surmise that the one-to-ten volume ratio between the spheres of water and air stood in some relation to the volume ratios between other contiguous spheres.

According to Plato's *Timaeus,* the Artificer had made the four elements "as proportionate to one another as was possible, so that what fire is to air, air is to water, and what air is to water, water is to earth. He then bound them together and thus he constructed the visible and tangible universe."[69] Macrobius's *Commentarium in somnium Scipionis* relayed Plato's views regarding the proportion among the four spheres of the elements:

> A similar difference of density and weight exists between water and air as between air and fire, and again, the difference in lightness and rarity between air and water is the same as the difference between water and earth. Likewise, the difference in density and weight between earth and water is the same as between water and air, and the difference between water and air the same as between air and fire. Moreover, the difference of rarity and lightness between fire and air is the same as between air and water, and the difference between air and water is the same as between water and earth.[70]

If the density ratios between contiguous elements were the same, and if volume increased or decreased between elements in inverse relation to their density or rarity, then the volume ratio between contiguous spheres remained one to ten: water's volume was ten times earth's, air's volume ten times water's, and fire's volume ten times air's.

Plato's concept of proportion among the elements possibly underlies Paul of Burgos's claim regarding the volume ratio between the spheres of earth and water. According to Burgos, just as air was much more rarefied than its immediate element water, so was water much more rarefied than its immediate element earth.[71] Sensible proof was to be found in the fact that a given quantity of water "dispersed," that is, heated and turned into water vapor, yielded a far greater volume of air.[72] Therefore, bearing in mind that the elements had their "proper" places, Burgos explained that the farther the place of each from the center of the cosmos, the greater their "holding" capacity. To conclude this part of his argument, he invoked Ptolemy's claim in the *Almagest* that the known inhabited world was "approximately bounded" by one of the two horizontal quadrants in the northern hemisphere: given that the *orbis terrarum* occupied almost one-fourth of the globe's surface, the earth clearly lacked the capacity to receive in itself the water volume that would have previously covered the known inhabited world.[73] Like many schoolmen who had yet not read the *Geography* in the early years

of the fifteenth century, Burgos seemed oblivious to the fact that Ptolemy himself had advocated an open geography.

Burgos's reading of Genesis 1:9–10 also rejected Saint Augustine's suggestion in *De genesi ad litteram* that the gathering of the waters *ad locum unum* on the third day of Creation could mean their significant reduction through condensation: scripture explicitly stated not that God had ordered the waters to "be condensed" but, rather, that he had ordered them to "be gathered."[74] Burgos equally rejected a possibility offered by Saint Basil (about 329–379) in his own *Hexameron,* namely, that God had ordered the sea waters to recede from the shores and to accumulate in such a way that they towered high above the land without flooding it (as evidence, Basil cited the fact that the Red Sea had long been found to stand higher than the land surrounding it).[75] Against Basil's explanation for the emergence of land from the waters, Burgos claimed that one "descended" rather than "ascended" to the ocean, citing as evidence Psalms 106 [107]:23 ("They that go down to the sea in ships, doing business in the great waters . . .") and Jonah 1.3 ("[Jonah] went down to Joppe, and found a ship going to Tharsis . . ."). Because the sphere of water was fluid, Burgos explained, it could not form uneven bulges or "mountains," for all of its parts possessed the very same tendency to be carried down or gravitate toward the center. Further, Burgos explained, the experience of sailors in the Mediterranean showed that, in calm waters, the sea appeared as flat as featureless land.

Burgos belonged to an ancient line of commentators of Aristotle's *Meteorologica* who assumed that the total volume of water significantly exceeded the total volume of earth and some of whom proposed solutions of great relevance to the question that the Spanish *junta* would face prior to 1492. Consider only two among the late ancient commentators who preserved in Alexandria the teachings of the Neoplatonist school of Athens suppressed in 529 by Justinian. The influential Christian philosopher John Philoponus (6th century)—true to Aristotle's metaphor of the Ocean River as the great circular exchange between water and air caused by the sun's motion—proposed that water filled the hollows of the earth but that a considerable amount of water was also suspended in the air in the form of clouds.[76] By contrast, his pagan contemporary Olympiodorus the Younger argued that, just as water poured on a flat surface tended to bulge around its own center, so did the sphere of water naturally tend toward its own center.[77] It was this latter line of thought, perhaps derived from the theory of tides attributed to the Stoic philosopher Posidonius (about 135–about 51 BCE)—who appears to have invoked the sphericity of water droplets in order to argue that water tended

2.4 Paul of Burgos's diagram
for the gathering of the waters on
the third day of Creation. From
his *additio* to *Genesis*, in vol. 1,
chap. 1 of Nicholas of Lyra, *Postilla
super totam Bibliam* (Cologne,
about 1485), iiiiv. Courtesy of The
Huntington Library, San Marino,
California. The explanation for this
figure in Burgos's *additio* reads: "In
this figure, let *a* be the centre of
the earth, which is also the centre
of the universe, and let the sphere
of the earth be *bdge*, with *a* as its
center. And let the sphere of water
before its gathering be *mno*, with
the aforementioned *a* as its centre,
which is the center of the universe.
For water, by virtue of its primordial
nature evenly surrounded the earth,
for any given part of that water
had an equal tendency toward the
earth's center, which is the center
of the universe. However, God
ordained that this sphere of water
be gathered in one place, so that the
dry land might appear. Therefore let
the second sphere of water—that
is, the water gathered together
where it now is following God's
command—be *fcde*. And this sphere
is equal in size to the first sphere of
water, namely *mno*. Further, let the
centre of the sphere of water after

toward its own center—that found its way into Burgos's explanation of the manner in which the spheres of earth and water were lodged together at the center of the cosmos.[78] But in Burgos's work it was not nature that accounted for water's eccentricity with respect to earth. Rather, this gathering of the waters had been achieved by God "by means of a firm law or ordinance that God put into effect."[79]

According to nature, Burgos reasoned, all parts of the spheres of earth and water would have "equally" tended to be carried down toward the absolute center of the cosmos (that is, its geometrical center *and* its center of gravity).[80] But on the third day of Creation, with the purpose of providing shelter for animals, God had ordered water to be gathered around its own center, preserving its own sphericity. In other words, God had effected a permanent bypass on nature to make room for animated land creatures. As evidence for this foundational miracle, Burgos invoked Ptolemy's discussion of the moon's apparent motion in the *Almagest*, which argued that the moon's orb had a different center than that of the earth and cosmos.[81] Despite the fact that Ptolemy had maintained (like Aristotle) that earth and water were concentric, his concept of planetary "eccentricity" here lent authority to the Posidonian claim that water tended toward its own center. What Genesis meant by the words "Let the waters . . . be gathered together in one place" was, on Burgos's authority, "let all waters under the heavens tend toward one place or one center, which is different from the earth's, and to this center let the waters be gathered like the parts of the earth to the earth's center" (**fig. 2.4**).[82] Burgos's method of proof surely met with contradictions: we have seen (to cite only the most relevant instances) that he used Ptolemy's planetary theory in favor of a terraqueous model that Ptolemy himself would have disavowed and that he cited Ptolemy's measurement for the limits of known inhabited world in isolation from Ptolemy's otherwise open geographical model. But these were, to some extent, the necessary predicaments of an intellectual tradition that merged disparate propositions in its quest to construct an epistemic system mirroring God's machine. From this standpoint, Burgos's "schooled" interpretation of Genesis 1:9–10 *authoritatively* wielded available philosophical and technical tools against the explanation by hexameral authors that dry land had emerged when water was made to condense and settle in the earth's hollows.

Here, in sum, is the pressing cosmological problem behind the debate in the Santa Fe assembly on the eve of the discovery: the fundamental proposition in Aristotle's physics that earth was by nature carried down toward the center (to its proper place below water) complicated the task of explaining the substantial presence of dry land

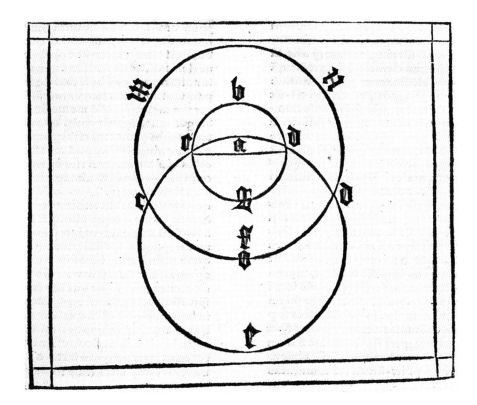

its gathering be *f*, which is excentric, as has been said, since it is distant or discrepant from the center *a*, which is the center of the universe. Therefore let this sphere of water intersect the sphere of earth at two points, or places, namely *d* and *e*."

above water. This problem remained particularly vexing if one assumed—as Aristotle and many of his commentators, into the fifteenth century, seemed to—that earth's total volume was smaller than water's total volume. Aristotle solved this problem by suggesting that the great circular exchange between water and air (of water vapor generated by the sun's heat) diverted the water volume not contained by the earth's hollows from entirely surrounding the earth. But his explanation for the presence of dry land became less plausible the smaller the volume of earth one assumed existed in relation to the volume of water. And while Aristotle had suggested that the four elements could exist in equal quantities, he specified only the volume ratio of water to air. Indeed, his claim that "all the water that flows in the year would be larger than the earth, or, at any rate, not much smaller," identified the upper limit of the volume ratio of earth to water as not much more than one to one. But the lower limit of this ratio was anybody's guess—unless one extended Aristotle's one-to-ten volume ratio for water and air, as Burgos did, to all pairs of contiguous elements.

In adopting and extending Aristotle's lower limit for this ratio, Burgos could no longer explain the presence of dry land without qualifying Aristotle's claims regarding the natural places of earth and water. Burgos modified Aristotle's cosmology by subsuming the Posidonian claim that water tended toward its own center, under Ptolemy's theory of planetary eccentricity. This strategy ostensibly rendered a literal interpretation of God's separation of the waters from the earth as the miraculous displacement of water *ad locum unum*. More importantly, Burgos's proof that dry land had resulted from water's displacement to its own center was predicated *against* a cosmology that explained the presence of dry land primarily as a function of significant irregularities in the earth's sphere. And in the context of the Santa Fe assembly, these competing versions of geocentricity yielded antithetical solutions to the geographical problem at the heart of Columbus's plan to sail across the ocean: the surface ratio and distribution of earth and water on the globe.

Burgos's inflection of Aristotle's cosmology minimized the proportion of land to water and confined all land to a northern quadrant of the globe. As Burgos stated in the conclusions to his argument, the dry land "according to cosmographers [i.e, Ptolemy], is approximately one fourth of the earth, while the other parts of the earth itself remain covered by water."[83] Burgos's version of geocentricity is correctly said to have furnished Columbus's opponents in the royal council with proof against his plan to bridge the distance between Spain and "the Indies."[84] (This model implied that the intervening ocean measured at least 180 degrees in longitude.) But this reading of Burgos's contribution to the Santa Fe assembly yields only a partial picture of the geographical risks weighed out by the members of the royal council; we must also bear in mind that *latitude* mattered to Columbus as much as—if not more than—longitude. For by refuting a cosmology that explained the presence of dry land in terms of earth's irregularities, Burgos also discredited the open geography theorized by Homer's Greco-Roman successors, including, of course, the Cratesian model that posited inhabited worlds centered on the temperate zones in the globe's three remaining quadrants.

Columbus's opponents in the royal council certainly appear to have invoked Burgos to this effect. By Geraldini's testimony, Columbus's opponents invoked Nicholas of Lyra's glosses on the Vulgate (i.e., Burgos's *Additiones*) in rebutting Columbus's proposal to search for inhabited territories inside the torrid zone, perhaps reaching the southern temperate zone, just as the Portuguese had done in Atlantic Africa. Columbus's opponents, according to Geraldini, reformulated Burgos's conclusion that dry land accounted for about one-quarter of the globe: "The whole fabric of the inhabited earth extending above the sea from the Fortunate Isles to the Orient does not have borders turned toward the sphere's lower side." Columbus's opponents cited Burgos's refutation of pagan geography in order to prove that the tricontinental landmass did not extend *down* into the southern hemisphere ("the sphere's lower side"). And it was clearly Columbus's intention to sail to the *south*—not solely to the west—that compelled members of the royal council to connect Burgos's reading of Genesis 1:9–10 with Augustine's attack in *De civitate Dei* on pagan belief in the antipodes. As Geraldini testifies, the royal council's invocation of Nicholas of Lyra and Augustine prompted Geraldini to remind Cardinal Diego de Mendoza that "the Portuguese had already traveled to the farthest parts of the lower hemisphere, in such a way that—leaving behind our own arctic circle—they had discovered the antarctic circle under another pole, and they had found a densely populated torrid zone; and they had contemplated new stars under the axis of the antipodes."[85]

Geraldini's testimony of the Santa Fe assembly thus illuminates the meaning behind Las Casas's and Ferdinand's records of the objections against the Indies enterprise. Las Casas justifiably asserted that it was Columbus's more "learned" opponents, those "better versed in mathematical doctrine," who relied on the theory that "of this lower sphere of water and earth, only a small part was left uncovered, because everything else was covered by water" in order to argue that "it was not possible to navigate [the ocean], were it not along the shores or *rivieras* as the Portuguese did in Guinea."[86] Columbus's detractors rightly understood that Burgos's thesis that dry land was confined to a small part of an otherwise aqueous globe not only was aimed against the idea that land might surface *anywhere* but also automatically discounted the Cratesian model that had imagined four *orbes terrarum* on the globe. This is why, as Las Casas and Ferdinand report, the skeptics in the royal *junta* also cited Augustine's attack on the pagan invention of the antipodes and why they also cited the theory of the five zones, which in this instance specifically served Columbus's detractors both to deny that the torrid zone was either inhabitable or traversable.

In short, the geographical canon that Columbus's opponents invoked against his enterprise rendered the *orbis terrarum* as an unrepeatable island besieged by the watery abyss. The tricontinental landmass was confined within a single northern quarter measuring 180 degrees in longitude and 90 degrees in latitude. And the inhabitable world itself was a narrow horizontal corridor flanked toward the north pole and the equator by the inhospitable northern cold and the torrid zones. The sun's heat within the torrid zone supposedly desolated the parts of the *orbis terrarum* that extended toward the equator (sub-Saharan Africa and the extended basin of the Indian Ocean), and it rendered the equatorial waters of the Ocean River unassailable.

One might be tempted to believe that Columbus's opponents cited this closed geographical model of the globe not out of true conviction but merely as a way to deny Columbus what he wanted, much as state bureaucracies cite obsolete but still active codes in order to disarm law-abiding petitioners. Yet although Ferdinand and Las Casas might want us to share their disdain for the state of cosmography in Castile on the eve of the discovery, it was clearly more than possible at the time to advocate a closed geographical model without embarrassing oneself and to use it legitimately to disenfranchise seemingly novel geographical ideas as heretical—like sailing south into the lower latitudes of the globe. It was also not the first time that someone in Christian Europe had objected to the prospect of exploring the tropics. The notion that the tropics were unbearably hot, infertile, and desolate had, in the early decades of the fifteenth century, made the prospect of exploring Africa's western shores—let alone of circumnavigating Africa—almost as daunting to the Portuguese as the prospect now of venturing west across the Atlantic. The physical obstacle apparently posed by the torrid zone to navigation along Atlantic Africa is graphically recorded by two key Portuguese sources, Gomes Eanes de Zurara and João de Barros, whom Las Casas scornfully cites in *Historia de las Indias* for celebrating the African "prelude" to the "destruction of the Indies."

In his *Crónica dos feitos notáveis que se passaram na conquista da Guiné por mandado do Infante D. Henrique* (written about 1457–about 1465), Zurara records the intense trepidation with which navigators had regarded the expanse beyond the African landmark known as Cape Bojador before it was rounded for the first time in 1434 by order of Henry the Navigator, the scholar-prince who pioneered Portugal's imperial expansion on the African side of the Atlantic.[87] Cape Bojador stood on the mainland directly across from Grand Canary Island, which Henry had tried to conquer in 1424. In Henry's mind, Bojador and the Canaries stood together as a threshold to what no one other than Henry and his close associates appear to have anticipated to be invaluable.

Indeed, until 1434, Bojador and the Canaries had tended to mark in the Atlantic the southernmost boundary of the inhabited world known to Christian Europe—a fact of no little consequence for Columbus's choice to cross the ocean along the lower parallel of the Canaries. According to Henry's chronicler Zurara, Henry's sailors, when faced with Henry's plans to round Cape Bojador, had been in the habit of exclaiming: "'How shall we trespass . . . the boundaries set by our fathers? Or how can the perdition of our souls together with our bodies benefit the prince? For we surely shall be our very own murderers.'"[88] By Zurara's authority, the sun's heat in this latitude had been thought by navigators to desolate the land and to turn the surrounding ocean into a treacherous brew of shallow waters and sandbanks: "Sailors said that beyond this cape there were neither people nor towns of any sort. The land is no less sandy than Lybia's deserts, where there is no water, nor trees, nor pasture. And the sea is so shallow that, at a league's distance from land, the bottom lies no more than a fathom's deep. The currents are so strong, that no ship that sails beyond it would ever be able to turn back."[89]

In the first part, or "decade," of the work known as *Ásia de João de Barros: Dos feitos que os portugueses fizeram no descobrimento e conquista dos mares e terras do oriente* (1552–1615), Barros explained in similar terms why the first ships sent by Prince Henry down the west African coast dared not sail beyond Cape Bojador:

> In front of this cape there was a current that pulled in the same westerly direction for about six leagues, where, because of the waters within that expanse, the shallows shake them in such a way that they seem to jump and boil, which sight so frightened everyone, that no one dared to take on those waters, much less so upon sighting those shallows. The said fear blinded everyone, because they failed to understand that sailing away from the said cape to the distance of six leagues covered by the shallows, they would have been able to pass. For, since they were used to navigating as they had before from east to west, always keeping the coast close at hand, they knew not how to tack away from the coast for the distance needed to avoid this current's reach, [and] at the mere sight of the boiling of these waters and of the shallows in them, they believed that the sea from then on was all parceled out and unassailable, and that this was why the inhabitants of this part of Europe did not care to navigate in those regions.[90]

Barros's account of Henry the Navigator's men's breakthrough passage clearly stated that the expanse south of Cape Bojador had posed as great an obstacle to the navigators as it did to the learned who considered this problem back in Portugal: "Some who had an understanding of natural things ventured that the sea in those hot regions was not as deep as that in the cold regions, adding that the sun so much burned the lands under its course, that all philosophers had justly deemed those lands to be uninhabitable by reason of the sun's heat; and that this heat was what consumed the fresh waters that generally emanate from the earth."[91] In other words, to Henry's critics, Cape Bojador represented the ominous toll to an even deadlier tropics. And even though another of Henry's fleets rounded Cape Bojador in 1435 to find the first traces of human habitation south of the known inhabited world's expected limits, the myth of uninhabitability in the latitudes below this cape of no return and the Canaries would be slow to dissipate.

Indeed, the idea that the torrid zone was generally uninhabitable *and* unnavigable continued to hold sway with Columbus's opponents in the royal council nearly six decades later. It persisted despite the fact that the Portuguese had continued to establish imperial outposts along sub-Saharan Africa's western coast, such as the fort of São Jorge da Mina, and despite the fact that Bartholomeu Dias had already captained three Portuguese vessels around the Cape of Good Hope in 1488. As the most famous postils to d'Ailly's *Ymago mundi* (1410) suggest, Columbus would have not have missed the occasion to inform the members of the Santa Fe assembly that he himself had found the "equatorial" São Jorge da Mina to be a "temperate" and densely populated place and perhaps even that he or his brother had been present in Lisbon when Bartholomeu Dias returned to inform Dom João that he had rounded the Cape of Good Hope.[92] In fact, what Geraldini presents as his own original contribution to the debate in Santa Fe—that the Portuguese had already explored the entire breadth of the torrid zone and had found it to be densely populated—must have been perfectly known to the members of the royal commission.

But Portugal's exploits along the entire width of the torrid zone did not lead Columbus's opponents in the royal *junta* to the symmetrical conclusion that land, inhabitable or otherwise, extended or could be reached due south of the *orbis terrarum* at the end of the Orient, as now was proved to be the case in Africa. Columbus's opponents were committed to interpreting any geographical information, old or new, in terms of the closed geographical model we have described, and for them the ongoing saga in Atlantic Africa merely counted among the exceptions to the theory of the five zones long

cataloged by geographers—along with such famous tales as those about the rounding of Africa during the Greco-Roman period, or those about Taprobane (Sri Lanka), which Indography described as an inordinately bountiful, inhabited island, to use Pomponius Mela's words, "relegated by Nature beyond the orb."[93] Indeed, Columbus's opponents represented an intellectual trend that had long construed the hyperproductivity of the tropics as the marvelous or monstrous outcome of nature's accidents and immoderacies. One cannot blame Columbus's opponents in the royal commission for taking such a hard-line view about the distribution of land and life around the globe. Columbus's proposal was, after all, utterly speculative, relying on unorthodox theories, circumstantial evidence, or the tall tales that already circulated about sightings of land in the Atlantic. The testimonies we have from Las Casas, Ferdinand, and Geraldini unequivocally indicate that Columbus's opponents did not merely object to the technical feasibility of a westward crossing; they objected to the possibility of finding more dry land—much less inhabited land—in the direction of the torrid and southern temperate zones. We have then a rather definite, if general, picture of the nature of the debate that preceded the discovery and of what Columbus proposed to do: Columbus intended to find inhabited land by sailing to the west across the ocean, but also to the south into the belt of the tropics, perhaps as far south as the southern temperate zone.

Regrettably, the objections raised against Columbus's proposal do not point us to the specific arguments and sources that Columbus and his supporters presented to the royal *junta*. We do not know, for example, what earth-to-water volume ratio—and thus what land-to-water surface ratio—was originally cited in favor of Columbus's enterprise. We can only infer that this ratio would have been significantly higher than the lower limit of one to ten that Burgos had extrapolated from Aristotle's discussion of the proportions among the elements: the greater the volume of earth one assumed existed in relation to water, the more persuasively one might argue for a greater *surface* ratio and/or distribution of earth and water around the globe. In other words, by assuming a greater volume-ratio of earth to water than Burgos's followers did, Columbus and his supporters would have had greater cause to argue that both in longitude and latitude the *orbis terrarum* extended well beyond the northern quadrant assigned to it by canonical geographers. And they would also have had greater cause to argue that the *orbis terrarum*—contrary to Augustine's claims—did not necessarily account for all the world's dry land. This all certainly matches what we know about Columbus's geographical preferences: that he privileged Marinos of Tyre's generous estimate for the

known inhabited world to Ptolemy's conservative one; that, mindful of those who had branded his geography as less than orthodox, he preferred the company of hexameral writers who saw the congregation of the waters on the third day of Creation as a condensation of water vapor to those who saw it as a displacement of the watery sphere; and that, attempting to outbid the proclaimed orthodoxy of his enemies, he would go so far as to cite the apocryphal prophet Esdras (Ezra), who in his own hexameron had claimed that of seven parts of the world, only one had remained covered by water, and six had remained dry land.

Finally, the objections raised against Columbus's proposal do not tell us whether he ultimately fancied himself southing all the way to antipodal lands centered on the southern temperate zone or lingering in the torrid zone. The earliest known chronicler of the Indies, Peter Martyr, who instantly doubted whether Columbus had sailed far enough to have reached the Indies and who believed that Columbus had instead only reached the legendary island of Antilia—may all too soon have encouraged his correspondents in Italy to believe that a "certain" Ligurian had just returned from the "western" antipodes, a notion that even came to be consigned in early portraiture of Columbus.[94] I contend that Columbus was ultimately interested in reaching the belt of the tropics. Consider merely the fact that, even years after the discovery, in 1498, when Columbus came to the understanding that he had found "infinite land that is to the south," he chose *not* to continue his exploration due south of the Orinoco River toward the southern temperate zone. (It was rather his friend Amerigo Vespucci who soon undertook the task of exploring the coastline beyond the Orinoco.) Columbus instead returned to Hispaniola and devoted later exploratory efforts to finding a passageway along the coast of Central America into the distinctly tropical accident we know today as the Indian Ocean. Indeed, Columbus's long-declared intention of reaching "the parts of India" encoded nothing if not the notion of reaching a vast geographical system that he and his contemporaries understood as extending near and within the belt of the tropics.

Testimony of Columbus's attempts to sell his ideas to other crowns in Europe is nearly as sparing in detail as the sources concerned with the *junta* appointed by Fernando and Isabel to evaluate the feasibility of an Atlantic crossing. But this testimony must be mentioned, because it strongly supports the case we have made concerning the nature of the debate that preceded the discovery. The Portuguese chronicler João de Barros has left

us the following account of Columbus's lobbying efforts with King João II of Portugal, which took place in 1483 or 1484, after Columbus had visited Guinea:

> Seeing that Dom Joam ordinarily dispatched his men to discover Africa's coast with the intention of reaching India by this route; and because [Columbus] was versed in Latin and curious about geographical matters; and because he read in Marco Polo that he spoke so modernly of the Oriental things of the kingdom of Cathay [i.e., northern China] as well as of the great island of Çipango [i.e., Japan], *he began to fathom that by way of this western ocean one could navigate so far as to come upon this island of Çipango and other terrae incognitae.* Since the Third Islands [i.e., Cape Verde Islands] were discovered during the time of Prince Henry, as well as so much of Africa's territory never known or tended to by Spaniards, [Columbus reasoned that] more islands and lands could be had to the west, because Nature should not have been so disorderly in the composition of the universal orb that it should have accorded a greater part to the element of water than to dry land for the sheltering of animals.[95]

Barros unequivocally tells us that Columbus had offered to bring to fruition Dom João's intention of reaching India, not by rounding Africa, but by way of the Atlantic. Having read Marco Polo's account of Cathay and Çipango, Columbus would have come to imagine that it was possible to reach "Çipango and other terrae incognitae," meaning, the region that Marco Polo had broadly defined as India. Marco Polo's India did not include Cathay—a fact that Americanists sometimes fail to consider when discussing references to Asia in the Columbian corpus.[96] This oversight has misled more than one distinguished scholar, beginning with Henry Vignaud at the turn of the twentieth century, to reason thus concerning the first voyage: if Columbus so quickly lost interest in searching for the Great Khān of the Mongols, whose seat was supposed to be Cathay, his true objective must not have been Asia. But early readers of Marco Polo and of other travelers to Asia made a clear distinction between Cathay and India. And for these readers, Cathay was part of a continental Asia to the north, in the midst of the "temperate" zone, while India was part of a maritime Asia to the south, an Asia organized around that vast and decidedly tropical accident we know today as the Indian Ocean.[97] Thus Cathay and India are not interchangeable terms, and this is why Barros, having made reference to both places, says only that Columbus fathomed reaching

"Çipango and other terrae incognitae," meaning the India already known to have been coveted by Dom João.

Columbus would have found support for this fancy in the fact that the Portuguese had already discovered the Cape Verde Islands and "so much of Africa's territory never known or tended to by Spaniards." Barros was here alluding specifically to the territories that had been discovered south of the Canary Islands and Cape Bojador thanks to Henry the Navigator and which by the Treaty of Alcáçovas (1479–1480) had been granted to the Portuguese "from the Canary Islands down and toward Guinea" (*de las yslas de Canaria para yuso contra Guinea*).[98] As for Barros's reference to the Cape Verde Islands, we know that they stand at a considerable distance off of Africa's western coast—approximately 400 miles due west of continental Africa's westernmost tip, today's Dakar in Senegal. The Cape Verdes also stand well within the belt of the tropics—approximately between 14° N and 17° N. The fact that so much land had been discovered due south and east of the Canaries, in territory now recognized by Castile as belonging to Portugal, plus the fact that this territory included islands that were so distant from the known continental landmass, had persuaded Columbus that he would find, as Barros puts it, "more islands and lands . . . to the west." But, again, these new lands would not be found just anywhere in the Atlantic; they extended to the west of the vast territory presumably controlled by Portugal below the Canaries, reaching all the way to the maritime India described by Marco Polo. And Columbus's hope of extending Portugal's African monopoly to the west all the way to India would have been founded in opposition to a geographical canon that accorded the *orbis terrarum* a minimal one-quarter of the globe's surface, denied the existence of any dry land beyond the immediate confines of this tricontinental landmass, and presumed that the belt of the tropics was just a marginal wasteland of deserts besieged by unfordable oceanic waters.

If we are to believe Barros, Columbus would have not just relied on Marco Polo nor on the fresh evidence furnished by Portuguese discoveries in Atlantic Africa. He would have also brought to bear a speculative argument that may well have its learned origins in the so-called "principle of plenitude" of Plato.[99] Contrary to hexameral writers, who saw the appearance of dry land from the gathering of the waters as merely a divine concession for the sake of providing shelter for terrestrial life, Columbus would have argued that "Nature"—God's handmaiden—would have been better served by making as much room as possible for the purpose of harboring as many land creatures as could be generated. Significantly, in the substitution of God for nature, the words that Barros attributes to Columbus bespeak the conflict between the closed geographical model communicated by Augustine to Christian geographers and the open one posited by Greco-Roman sources. At this stage, Columbus would well have advocated the generous geographical model that his enemies in Castile later branded as heretical.

No less significant to our understanding of the proposal that Columbus would present years later to the Crowns of Aragon and Castile is Barros's mention of Marco Polo. Marco Polo had rendered the most complete and influential account of Cathay and India available by a European. Whether Columbus had indeed read Marco Polo this early on, we shall never know. Yet some Americanists, observing that Columbus did not purchase his copy of Francesco Pipino's translation of *Il milione, De consuetudinibus et conditionibus orientalium regionum* (Antwerp, 1485), until 1497, would have us believe the unbelievable—that Columbus did not "know" his Marco Polo until the later years of a plummeting transatlantic career, that Columbus did not do his reading "homework" until he found himself in need of regaining credibility with the Crown for his disastrous colonial policy in Hispaniola, and that, by faking learning in the form of Pliny, Ptolemy, d'Ailly, Marco Polo, Piccolomini, and company, Columbus attempted to persuade the skeptics that he had in fact delivered the "Indian" lands and riches he had originally promised to Aragon and Castile.[100] No doubt Columbus liked to think of himself as more learned than he was. But, as we well know, acquaintance with the contents of books does not proceed only from having purchased and read them—especially when books were still precious commodities that few could afford. Columbus had at least indirectly become acquainted with Polian geography long before the discovery—if not by dint of being a native to Venice's great commercial rival, Genoa, where Marco Polo himself had been imprisoned and dictated his work to Rustichello of Pisa, then most certainly by virtue of later imbibing the culture of expansion that flourished in the Portugal of King João II. Marco Polo's work was known to the Portuguese in manuscript form long before the 1485 printing of Pipino's Latin abridgment. It is also in Portugal that, perhaps as early as 1481, Columbus had requested from the famous Florentine humanist and physician Paolo dal Pozzo Toscanelli, the copy of a letter that Toscanelli had written in 1474 to the canon of Lisbon Fernão Martins with the aim of coaxing Dom João's father, King Afonso V of Portugal, to ford the Atlantic to Asia.[101] Marco Polo thoroughly informed Toscanelli's letter, and, many years later, Columbus would almost certainly have the humanist's letter at hand when he wrote the controversial prologue to the *Diario*, outlining the character of his enterprise.[102] Moreover, Marco Polo, along with

Ptolemy, played a critical role for modern cartographers, who were newly concerning themselves with the easternmost reaches of the inhabited world, and Columbus (like the famous Martin Behaim) would have certainly assimilated Polian geography from the cartographic works being produced in Portugal at the time.

What in Marco Polo might have inspired Columbus to believe that he could reach "Çipango and other *terrae incognitae*"? Marco Polo's account of the vast geographical system he calls India opens with an account of the failed naval campaign mounted by the lord of Cathay, Khubilai Khān, against Çipango, or Japan, around 1269.[103] In this account, Marco Polo explained that Çipango was a huge island rich in gold, pearls, and precious stones 1,400 miles off the coast of the Indian province of Mangi (southern China); that the sea containing Japan was really part of the ocean; that the few pilots and sailors who had ventured into the ocean had counted the exhorbitant number of 7,378 islands; and that most of those islands were populated and also yielded innumerable spices. From Marco Polo, Columbus would have learned that the mainland Chinese province of Mangi, in southern China, and the island of Çipango were part of India; that Çipango was an extremely wealthy island in the midst of a huge, remarkably fertile, and generally populated archipelago conceptualized by Marco Polo as part of India; that the outer limits of this archipelago were unknown—at least to Marco Polo and his informants; that Cathay was *not* the same place as Mangi or Çipango; and that Khubilai Khān had failed miserably to conquer Çipango (although, as Marco Polo has previously explained in his work, Khubilai Khān succeeded in unifying China by annexing Mangi to Cathay in 1279).

Columbus could have effortlessly extrapolated, as he did eventually, a number of working hypotheses from this section of Marco Polo's work. First, while the mainland province of Mangi might still be subject to the province of Cathay, the Mongols had never gotten around to conquering Çipango or, for that matter, any of the myriad and for all intents and purposes unknown islands in the ocean around Çipango. Second, Çipango and these other islands were, both by nature of their marvelous profligacy and by association with the rest of India described by Marco Polo, largely tropical. We return to this point below in considering a work that has long been associated with the worldview that informed Columbus's first voyage, the globe presented by Martin Behaim to the town of Nuremberg in 1492 (**fig. I.3**, pp. 12–13): cartography of the period, following Marco Polo's cues, appears to have located Çipango and its cohorts much farther south than modern maps do Japan today—on the very Tropic of Cancer, as part of a geographical system that, including all the shores bathed by the Indian Ocean, extended all the way south to and across the Tropic of Capricorn.[104] Third, Columbus would have assumed that the Indian mega-archipelago associated with Çipango could easily extend sufficiently eastward to make it possible, from a convenient outpost such as the Cape Verde Islands, to "hop" one's way across the ocean to "Çipango and other terrae incognitae."

This would have been, to follow Barros's account, the plan Columbus presented to Dom João. Las Casas's later account of Columbus's attempt to entice Dom João to cross the Atlantic, partly based on Barros himself, speaks even more loudly than Barros's to the openness of the geographical model espoused by Columbus, to its tropical inflection, and to the communicability between the lands Columbus intended to reach by this route and the mainland territories of Mongol Asia. According to Las Casas, "What [Columbus] offered to do was the following: that by way of the West, *toward the south or midday,* he would discover great lands, islands, and terra firma, the happiest of all, the richest in gold, silver, pearls, and precious stones and infinite peoples; and that in that direction he expected to reach land belonging to India, and the great island of Çipango and the domains of the Great Khān, which in our language means 'King of Great Kings.'"[105]

Columbus must have left Portugal for Spain in 1485 on rather bristly terms with Dom João, or at the very least with the members of his council. Not only had the king's council scorned the proposed Atlantic crossing, but Columbus now also felt duped by the king: he suspected Dom João of secretly dispatching his own men to search for land west of the Cape Verde Islands even as the king egged Columbus on to think that he would be taken up on his offer.[106] It took seven more years of lobbying in Castile for Columbus finally to persuade Fernando and Isabel to take a chance on his project, ultimately against the better judgment of their own *junta.* During those seven years, Columbus must have often despaired that he would never see his project realized. But he certainly did not sit idly waiting for Fernando and Isabel to make up their mind. In 1487, following the first rejection of his plan by the royal commission, Columbus entrusted his brother Bartholomew with the task of persuading King Henry VII of England to finance his project. In the meantime, Columbus wrote to Dom João, asking for safe conduct back to Portugal. Dom João, who by now really had chartered a westbound expedition out of the Cape Verde Islands that returned empty-handed, replied to Columbus. Welcoming his proposal once again, the king reassured him that, should he return to Portugal, he would not be imprisoned, retained, accused, summoned, or sued by Dom

João's authorities on any civil or criminal count. (We are not sure what Columbus might have said or done before leaving Portugal for Spain to fear any of these actions.)[107] In fact, Columbus may have visited Portugal once again between 1488 and 1489 (some scholars claim that it was not he but Bartholomew, after his return from England), and that the renewed dealings with Dom João came to a halting crash following Bartholomeu Dias's celebrated return to Lisbon from the Cape of Good Hope.[108] The rounding of this cape meant that India could now be reached "simply" by circumnavigating Africa, and this rendered Columbus's plan to reach the East "by way of the West" utterly superfluous in the eyes of the Portuguese.

But of Bartholomew's business in England we do have one last piece of useful information.[109] According to Ferdinand and Las Casas, when Bartholomew presented himself at the English court in 1488, he showed Henry VII a *mappamundi* of his own making (signed on 13 February of the same year), which bore the following inscription in Latin: "Whosoever wishes successfully to know about all the shores of the lands, this attractive and erudite picture will teach you everything. This picture is affirmed by Strabo, as well as Ptolemy, Pliny, and Isidore, who nevertheless are not all of one mind. *Also painted here is that torrid zone recently furrowed by Spanish keels, formerly hidden to people, which now at last is very well known to many.*"[110] Regrettably lost, this *mappamundi* might have told us at a glance what so much controversy on the nature of the Columbus's enterprise in the course of the past century or so has not. Bartholomew had left Castile for England before Columbus reopened negotiations with Portugal, and he must have wished to portray the Spanish, with whom negotiations only seemed stalled for the moment, as the client who already had an edge over the English: the inscription on the *mappamundi* Bartholomew showed King Henry cleverly erased the Portuguese from the picture by misattributing the exploration they had already conducted within the infamous torrid zone to Castile, whose ships were in fact forbidden from treading freely south of the Canaries. Whatever world picture this *mappamundi* might have portrayed, Ferdinand's and Las Casas's brief accounts of the negotiations conducted by Bartholomew in England give pride of place not to the prospect of a westward crossing but to the beckoning call of the tropics.

Bartholomew soon returned to Castile to inform his brother that their business with England had failed. Columbus must then have sent Bartholomew to France—at the very latest, in the early days of January 1492, when the Santa Fe assembly newly rejected Columbus's plan. Bartholomew's charge was to persuade King Charles VIII to finance the enterprise.[III] We know nothing about the nature of the plan presented to King Charles; only that, stationed in France under protection of the king's older sister, Anne de Beaujeu, Bartholomew would come to receive the news that Columbus had already found land in the name of Aragon and Castile. The proposed enterprise had seemingly borne its fruit, and this fruit was sweet with the promise of a vast, fecund, and populated torrid zone.

Having considered the available testimony of Columbus's proposals to Portugal, Spain, and England, we turn our attention to the geographical *praecognita* now generally credited to Columbus, thanks largely to the intellectual biographies contained in the Fernandine *Historie* and Las Casas's *Historia de las Indias:* Columbus's understanding of the globe as a sphere; his underestimation of the value of an equatorial degree and therefore of the globe's circumference; his overestimation of the eastward extension of Asia, which reduced the distance between the Canaries and the end of the East; his belief that the torrid zone and the antipodes were inhabitable; and his identification of the lands he intended to find as the Indies. These particulars emerged in Ferdinand's and Las Casas's seminal works from information offered by Columbus only *after* the discovery—most particularly, it would seem, from Columbus's conspicuously pedagogical *carta-relación* of the third voyage (30 May–31 August 1498). These particulars also emerged from related postils on the margins of the few incunabula now preserved as part of his library—particularly those postils on the margins of d'Ailly's and Gerson's *Tractatus.* Debate has often raged among Americanists as to *when* Columbus came to espouse these particulars, a debate attended by sharp disagreement over the dating and authorship of the postils in Columbus's library. This debate has taught us something, learned perhaps more from battle exhaustion than from solid argumentation: Ferdinand, and Las Casas after him, too easily assumed that the geographical notions espoused by Columbus in late documents, like his letter of the third voyage, were the very same notions that would have persuaded him of the affordability of the Atlantic. These early biographers also too easily assumed that the postils on Columbus's books predated the discovery. In other words, the particulars that stand foremost in our minds today as the core of Columbus's world map were granted prominence by Ferdinand and Las Casas on the basis of Columbus's later writing and on the basis of postils of uncertain dating and, in many cases, uncertain authorship. Thus one can no longer assert as conclusively as Ferdinand and Las Casas did that these exact particulars played the seminal role of persuading Columbus that he ought to seek royal patronage for his enterprise, at least not as early on as the Fernandine *Historie* implies in its introductory chapters. Nevertheless, such particulars are widely cited as having attended Columbus's plan to ford the Atlantic, and we ought to revisit at least those which loom large in the geographical history of the discovery.

For present purposes, we need go no farther than the famous eighth chapter in d'Ailly's *Ymago mundi,* "De quantitate terre habitabilis," which was identified by Alexander von Humboldt in the nineteenth century as having been directly lifted from the geographical section of Roger Bacon's *Opus maius.*[112] The information from this chapter, heavily annotated by Columbus, is repeatedly cited in the vast literature on the discovery. This information has molded more than anything else in Columbus's library our understanding of Columbus's plan as that of reaching the East "by way of the West." And to the extent that we have failed to consider the importance of *latitude* in d'Ailly's discussion of the quantity of inhabited land on the globe, we have also failed fully to understand what Columbus may have seen at stake in this celebrated chapter of d'Ailly's *Ymago mundi* (**fig. 2.5**).

Ferdinand claims that, having moved with his young wife Dona Felipa Moniz Perestrello to the Madeiran island of Porto Santo, Columbus found a chance to study the writings and nautical charts left behind by Bartolomeo Perestrello, his father-in-law and former governor of Porto Santo. On this island, Columbus would also have learned about the voyages of the Portuguese down to São Jorge da Mina and all along the coast of Guinea. From the information he gathered, Columbus "began to conjecture that, just as the Portuguese had traveled so far to the south, it should be equally possible to travel by way of the west, and that with reason one could find land in that direction."[113] In search of assurance for this conjecture, a Columbus admittedly portrayed by Ferdinand as the "schooled" individual he was not, "began to study again the cosmographers whom he had read before." And upon rereading these writers, he "grew convinced beyond the shadow of a doubt that to the west of the Canary and Cape Verde Islands lay many lands, and that it was possible to sail to them, and to discover them." On Ferdinand's account, one of three capital reasons "that encouraged the Admiral to launch this enterprise, and by virtue of which he could reasonably call India the land he should discover, were the many authoritative claims of learned men who had said that from the western end of Africa, and of Spain, it was possible to navigate by west to the eastern end of India, and that it was no great sea that stood between them."[114]

2.5 Columbus's annotations to chapter 8 of d'Ailly's *Ymago mundi*. From Pierre d'Ailly and Jean Gerson, *Tractatus de ymagine mundi et varia ejusdem auctoris et Joannis Gersonis opuscula* (1480–1483), Tabula Americae, facs. no. 852 (Madrid, 1990), 13r. Courtesy of the Institución Colombina, Biblioteca Colombina, Seville, Spain; and Testimonio Compañía Editorial, Madrid, Spain.

At this point the Fernandine *Historie* silently quotes the specifics contained in "De quantitate terre habitabilis" that Las Casas, later reading Ferdinand for his own intellectual portrait of Columbus, would cite to justify his claim that d'Ailly's and Gerson's *Tractatus* had been Columbus's most treasured book of all. One might reasonably contest the chronological priority that Ferdinand implicitly ascribes to Columbus's reading of Pierre d'Ailly. If, as Ferdinand claims, Columbus had formulated his plan to reach lands due west of Atlantic Africa around the time he resided with Felipa in Porto Santo, sometime between late 1479 and late 1481, then it is unlikely that Columbus would have persuaded himself that these lands were part of India from the copy of d'Ailly's and Gerson's *Tractatus* now held in the Colombina, which was only published in Louvain some time between 1480 and 1483.[115]

Now, Ferdinand (assuming that Ferdinand *is* the unadulterated author of these controverted chapters in the *Historie*) may not have known that he could not altogether credibly date Columbus's earliest acquaintance with d'Ailly to the period between 1479 and 1481; or the biographer may have known this, and that is why he quoted silently from d'Ailly's chapter. At any rate, it is clear that the biographer was eager to excuse Columbus for the by-now-demonstrated mistake of having called the lands he should discover the Indies. For this reason, he attributed such a mistake to the authoritative writers Columbus would have consulted in order to justify his conjecture that lands could be reached due west of Atlantic Africa. Ferdinand also insists that Columbus "did not call them the Indies because they had been seen or discovered by others [i.e., Europeans], but because they were the eastern part of India beyond the Ganges, to which no cosmographer set limits [i.e., to the east], nor boundaries with another land or province to the east, save with the ocean."[116] In order to illustrate his claim that authoritative writers had persuaded Columbus to call those lands he intended to discover the Indies, the biographer reached for the obvious choice in Columbus's annotated library, d'Ailly's "De quantitate terre habitabilis." Apart from its thematic pertinence, this chapter of *Ymago mundi* displayed the most involved annotations of any section in Columbus's library, and it thoroughly informed the *carta-relación* Columbus addressed to Fernando and Isabel recounting the extraordinary events of the third voyage.

Whatever we make of Ferdinand's sleight of hand as a historian and panegyrist, d'Ailly's "De quantitate terre habitabilis" remains central to the geographical history of the discovery, even for those Americanists who have suggested that Columbus did no significant reading until years after his momentous achievement. Before turning to the

particulars that Columbus is sure to have gleaned from "De quantitate terre habitabilis," let us briefly interpret Ferdinand's definition of the plan formulated by Columbus in Portugal. On Ferdinand's authority, Columbus espoused an open geographical model that greatly expanded the narrow limits traditionally assigned to the distribution of land and life around the globe. The lands Columbus intended to find were largely within the the belt of the tropics, or, more correctly, in the latitudes of and below the Canaries ("to the west of the Canaries and Cape Verde Islands"). And because the lands he imagined finding stood in the same general latitudes as the parts of Africa newly discovered by the Portuguese, Columbus was somewhat justified in calling those "easternmost" lands due west of Portuguese Africa the Indies—just as Mediterranean geographers had long referred to India as the eastern part of Ethiopia. The next chapter considers the question of where Columbus and his contemporaries imagined India to be and what its nature was. First let us consider what d'Ailly can tell us anew about Columbus's own understanding of his enterprise.

We cannot be certain when Columbus first read and annotated d'Ailly's "De quantitate terre habitabilis" in the exemplar now held at the Biblioteca Colombina, although few Americanists today would credibly deny that Columbus had already done so when he first crossed the Atlantic.[117] What we do know is that Columbus turned to this text sometime in 1498 as the result of inferring that the torrential surge of fresh water from the Orinoco River could only mean that he had stumbled upon "infinite land that is to the south." In other words, in the context of having sailed south nearly all the way to the equator as he crossed the Atlantic and of finding a huge landmass that he correctly surmised extended a long way into the southern hemisphere, Columbus found himself rereading and quoting almost verbatim from his favorite passage in *Ymago mundi*. What Americanists tend to read as a passage that speaks to Columbus's intention of reaching the East "by way of the West," Columbus himself came to revisit years after the discovery as a result of his conspicuous southing.

Columbus paraphrased "De quantitate terre habitabilis" in his *carta-relación* of the third voyage as follows:

> Pliny writes that the sea and the earth all form a sphere; and he writes that this ocean sea is the greatest body of water and stands toward heaven; and that the earth's place is under the waters holding them up; and that the one is mixed together with the other like the bitter core of the walnut with a thick membrane

girdling the whole. The master of the *Scholastic History* [Peter Comestor], in his reading of *Genesis,* states that the waters are very few; and that when they were first created to cover the earth, they were vaporous like fog; and that once they were made to solidify and to gather together, they occupied very little room. And with this agrees Nicholas of Lyra [i.e., Lyra's own *Postilla,* not Burgos's *Additiones*]. Aristotle says that the globe is small and the amount of water small, and that one can easily cross from Spain to the Indies; and this is confirmed by Averroës [commentaries to *De caelo*]; and the same argues Pierre d'Ailly [*Ymago mundi*], lending authority to this claim; and also that book by Seneca [*Naturales quaestiones*], which agrees with the others, adding that Aristotle could have known many of the world's secrets thanks to Alexander the Great, and Seneca thanks to Cesar Nero, and Pliny thanks to the Romans—all of whom invested moneys and peoples, and were very diligent in unveiling the world's secrets and making them known to other peoples. The said Cardinal [d'Ailly] ascribes to these authors [i.e., Aristotle, Seneca, and Averroës] far more authority than to Ptolemy or to any other Greeks or Arabs. And, as confirmation of the claim that the amount of water is small, and that it covers little of the world, against what was said on the authority of Ptolemy and his associates, [d'Ailly] brings to bear an authoritative claim from the *Book of Esdras* that is, from his Third Book [i.e., *Fourth Ezra*], where it says that out of seven parts of the world, six of them remain uncovered, and one is covered up by water.[118]

Needless to say, Columbus's return to d'Ailly's "De quantitate terre habitabilis" is in part a reply to the learned arguments wielded years before against the plan he had submitted to Fernando and Isabel. According to Ferdinand and Las Casas, Columbus's detractors in Castile had countered Columbus's proposal by citing Augustine's belief that there were no antipodes and by invoking the theory of the five zones to deny that the torrid zone was inhabitable. And, according to Geraldini, Columbus's detractors in the Santa Fe assembly had branded his proposal as heretical, citing Paul of Burgos, via Nicholas of Lyra, to the effect that "the whole fabric of the inhabited earth extending above the sea from the Fortunate Isles to the Orient does not have borders turned toward the sphere's lower side."

Columbus's appeal to Pliny's depiction of how earth and water were lodged together at the center of the cosmos constituted an appeal to a geocentric model that explained the presence of dry land as the result of irregularities in and around the earth's sphere.

Indeed, Columbus's elucidation of Pliny—that earth and water were mixed together "like the bitter core of the walnut with a thick membrane girdling the whole"—endorsed the open geography espoused by pagan writers. Mindful that Pliny was a pagan and that his own plan to ford the ocean had long been branded, and might continue to be branded, heretical by his enemies in Castile, Columbus next appealed to hexameral authors who interpreted the gathering of the waters on the third day of Creation as a condensation of water vapor that rendered land bare all around the globe. This is the purpose of his reference to Peter Comestor (died 1178), author of the influential *Historia scholastica*. Columbus had already extensively cited and glossed Comestor in his postils to d'Ailly's "De quantitate terre habitabilis."[119] And still attempting to fight off the ghosts of his enemies at the Santa Fe assembly, Columbus next cited one of his favorite authors, the genuine Nicholas of Lyra, who could be counted among the Christian readers of Genesis 1:9–10 who still explained the gathering of the waters as a condensation of water vapor rather than as the displacement of the sphere of water away from the center of the universe. Indeed, Lyra himself endorsed the open geography of the pagans, if not with the philosophical and technical elegance that Burgos would use to defend the closed geography espoused by Augustine.

Columbus's invocation of Comestor and Lyra served Columbus to argue that, in the process of condensing to water in the beginning of time, the water vapor that covered the earth had come to occupy "very little room." In other words, the gathering of the waters had significantly reduced the total volume of water in the world, which implied a significantly larger surface ratio of land to water than his opponents in Castile had been ready to admit prior to the discovery. And just as this "schooled" reading of Genesis 1:9–10 would have previously furnished legitimacy to the prospect of fording the Atlantic, it now did so to Columbus's insight that he had stumbled upon a landmass that may have long been intuited by, but had ultimately remained unknown to, the ancients.

Next, in his paraphrase to "De quantitate terre habitabilis," Columbus was ready to argue both in favor of the claim that he had truly breached the distance between the ends of East and West, and that vast amounts of inhabited land ought to be found precisely in the region where he had just found "infinite land that is to the south." It is at this point in Columbus's argument that *latitude* can be said to have played a crucial role in his understanding of all that he had accomplished, both by first having forded a "narrow" ocean to the Indies and now by discovering terra firma in the very midst of the torrid zone. Always faithful to d'Ailly, Columbus next appealed to the greatest authority among

the pagans, Aristotle, who speculates in *On the Heavens* that the Pillars of Hercules (i.e., Strait of Gibraltar) and India stood at a communicable distance from each other.[120] As Columbus himself had previously noted about Aristotle in the margins of the eighth chapter of *Ymago mundi,* "Between the end of Spain and the beginning of India there is a sea, small and navigable in a few days."[121] D'Ailly, following Bacon's lead in the *Opus maius* IV, had endorsed Aristotle's claim about India's proximity to Spain by appealing to the very logic underlying the open geographical model Aristotle had espoused in *Meteorologica* and *On Generation and Corruption.* Being the main generator of contraries in the world of the elements, the sun, as it approached any given zenith relative to the observer, caused air to be generated out of water (i.e., evaporation), whereas, as the sun receded from that observer's zenith, it caused water to be generated out of air (i.e., condensation). The implications of this simple principle were clear: evaporation of water was greater toward the equator, where it was hotter because the sun tended to reach directly overhead; and condensation was greater toward the poles, where it was colder because the sun never reached overhead and instead tended to approach any given observer's horizon. In other words, one could expect to find more dry land in the belt of the tropics, and more water in the arctic regions.[122] This schooled argument—diligently annotated by the Discoverer in yet another chapter of *Ymago mundi* concerned with the different bodies of water—would have been of crucial importance to Columbus's plan to ford the Atlantic, whether out of the Cape Verde Islands, as he had proposed to Portugal, or out of the Canaries, as he had finally done in the name of Aragon and Castile in 1492. And this argument was equally pressing now that Columbus suspected he had found terra firma near the equator.

Even more significant is the fact that Columbus's immediate source, d'Ailly, should have carefully qualified what he meant by Spain, or Hispania. As d'Ailly explains it, his claim that the ends of Spain and India were separated by a small sea did not apply to Hispania Citerior, or "Hither Spain," which was the country now commonly referred to as Spain, but rather to Hispania Ulterior, or "Thither Spain," which was now called Africa.[123] This clarification was invited by Aristotle himself, who in *On the Heavens* offers the following evidence for his claim that the Pillars of Hercules and India were close together: elephants were generated "in each of these two extreme regions, suggesting that the common characteristic of these extremes is explained by their continuity."[124] Evidently, Aristotle was referring to Africa, not to the Iberian peninsula. And his claim

rested on the basic principle that places close to each other, or that stood along the same latitude, possessed a similar nature.

Elsewhere in a section of *Ymago mundi* concerned with Spain and annotated by either Columbus or Bartholomew, d'Ailly further justified his substitution of the term Hispania for Africa, by explaining that in ancient times, Hispania had formed continuous land with Africa, but that they had eventually come to be divided by the Mediterranean.[125] Anyone who has observed the geographical affinities between southern Spain and northern Morocco might understand how d'Ailly and other followers of Aristotle could have claimed that the two had once formed one body of land. Moreover, d'Ailly was truly justified in qualifying the term Hispania as Africa on one very crucial political count. At the turn of the fourth century, when the Christian emperor Diocletian reorganized the Roman Empire, nearly all Iberian provinces—including Lusitania but excluding Galicia—had been brought together under one single diocese, along with the northwest African province then known as Mauretania Tingitana, which would run today due west of the Moulouya River all the way through Morocco. In the thirteenth century, the Christian kingdoms of the *reconquista* had breathed new life into the notion that northwest Africa was a territorial and political extension of the Iberian peninsula.[126] Arguing that the late Roman diocese of Hispania and the Visigothic kingdom fallen to the Moors in 711 had originally extended into Mauretania, Aragon and Castile would come to draft a pact between them, known as the Accord of Monteagudo (1291), which assigned to Aragon the future conquest of Mauretania Caesarensis, to the east of River Molouya toward Egypt, and to Castile the future conquest of Mauretania Tingitana itself. Not surprisingly, in the fourteenth century, Castile would cite its ancestral right to northwest Africa when it began to wrestle with Portugal for control over both the Marinid sultanate of Fez and the Canary Islands. D'Ailly's claim that it was *Africa* that was close to India, including Aristotle's bit about the elephants, certainly did not escape a reader who had declared his intention to Dom João of finding lands due west of the Cape Verde Islands and who would later launch his first transatlantic voyage from the African Hispania, that is, from the Spanish-held Canaries. Indeed, in the chapter of d'Ailly's *Ymago mundi* entitled "De aquarum varietate et primo de Oceano," Columbus had written: "Near Mount Atlas, elephants are abundant, and similarly in India. Therefore, one place is not very distant from the other."[127]

In sum, Columbus's return to "De quantitate terre habitabilis" strongly suggests that while Columbus may have indeed once made use of d'Ailly to persuade himself or others that he could reach the East "by way of the West," that plan had banked on the prospect of finding vast amounts of dry land, even inhabited land, in the region of the tropics. And it was precisely in the traditionally infamous torrid zone that in 1498 Columbus appeared to have found a fertile, inhabited—and to his evident surprise, inordinately *temperate*—landmass reaching south toward the antipodes. Here we must draw a distinction between, on the one hand, Columbus's insight that he had reached a landmass that extended south indefinitely as a counterpart for the tricontinental landmass formed by Europe, Africa, and Asia and, on the other hand, the intention sometimes attributed to Columbus of overreaching the tropics to the antipodes, meaning to the region opposite the *orbis terrarum,* in the southern temperate zone. Peter Martyr accidentally introduced this intention to the historiography of the discovery when, abandoned to epistolary fervor, he called the lands Columbus had just reached on his first voyage the "western antipodes"—an unfortunate turn of phrase that Martyr actually nowhere uses in the account of the discovery he included in *De orbe novo*—or a turn of phrase that Martyr only chose to mean that Columbus had discovered inhabited lands long incommunicated from the known inhabited world. But, once again, not only would Columbus choose *not* to explore the coastline south of the Orinoco River, he also never appears to have wanted to return to what he had called the land of Paria. The obsession that instead would claim his mind on his next and last voyage was to find a gateway along the coast of Central America that would lead him even farther into his precious Indies, a region of the globe that for Columbus, as it had been for Marco Polo, was organized around that huge *tropical* accident known then and today as the Indian Ocean.

Columbus wrote his paraphrase of d'Ailly's "De quantitate terrre habitabilis" to counter those who had originally derided his intention of fording the Atlantic and those who presently doubted whether he had in fact traveled far enough to reach the India described by Marco Polo and others. He had not forgotten that his early detractors followed the strategy of citing Christian authors like Burgos, who tried to purge pagan authors of elements at odds with Christian doctrine. Thus, as noted above, Burgos incorporated Ptolemy's conservative measurement for the known inhabited world—approximately one-fourth of the globe—into a *closed* geographical model of the globe. (Ptolemy had only meant to account for the extent of the inhabited world so far measured in his time.) Columbus came to read Ptolemy's *Geography* very differently: Ptolemy had set out to correct the estimates of his predecessor Marinos of Tyre, who not only granted the known inhabited world 225° in longitude but also claimed that it extended all the way south to the Winter Tropic, that is, the Tropic of Capricorn.[128] As we might imagine, Columbus greatly preferred Marinos's figures to Ptolemy's. And this is why, in his paraphrase of "De quantitate terre habitabilis," Columbus reminded his royal addresses that d'Ailly—an irreproachable author in Columbus's estimation—had lent Aristotle, Seneca, Averroës and all other authors who claimed that the sea was small between Spain and India "far more authority than to Ptolemy or to any other Greeks or Arabs."

Like d'Ailly and Bacon before him, Columbus was anxious to realign his "novel" ideas about the distribution of lands and life on the globe with Christian doctrine. He thus cited a geographical blunder that he had culled from d'Ailly's "De quantitate terre habitabilis"—perhaps the Discoverer's best-known blunder. Columbus reminded Fernando and Isabel that d'Ailly, against those who believed that there was scarcely any land on the globe's surface, had also invoked the authority of the prophet Esdras. Indeed, in the pseudoepigraphical apocalypse known as *Fourth Book of Ezra* (1st century CE), we find the following interpretation of Genesis 1:9–10: "On the third day thou didst command the waters to be gathered together in the seventh part of the earth; six parts thou didst dry up and keep so that some of them might be planted and cultivated and be of service before thee."[129] On the margins of "De quantitate terre habitabilis" Columbus glossed d'Ailly's reference to Ezra rather more boldly than we have seen in his *carta-relación* of 1498: "Ezra: Six parts [of the earth] *are inhabited* and the seventh is covered by water."[130]

Though the *Fourth Book of Ezra* had often been included in copies of the Vulgate since the time of Saint Jerome, it was classified as one of the Apocrypha.[131] Aware of this, Columbus had devoted much energy on the margins of "De quantitate terre habitabilis" to explaining that early fathers like Jerome and Saint Augustine had approved of Ezra as a true prophet and that his prophecies, though not "canonical," could still be considered authentic.[132] Referring to Ezra's doctrine about the proportion of dry land to water, Columbus also appealed to the great authority of fresh experience in Atlantic Africa: "And Petrus Comestor agrees with that dictum about the water; concerning it, to judge by what we have seen until now from navigations, that [claim] is found to be true."[133] Again, in his *carta-relación* of the third voyage, Columbus would conclude by underscoring the role of experience in tempering the excesses of written authority, although, as we know, Columbus himself was not exempt from cultivating those excesses: "And with regard to the dryness of land, it has been amply shown by experience that it is much greater than the vulgar believed; and this is no wonder, for the more one goes, the more one knows."[134] Columbus's strategy is clear: prompted by the natural phenomenon he witnessed at the mouth of the Orinoco River, Columbus hypothesized that he had found "infinite land to the south." With this hypothesis in hand, he proceeded to reclaim those pagan, or Arabic, authors whose works confirmed this hypothesis, in some cases radically reinterpreting works that Columbus's enemies in Castile had read, or continued to read, more restrictively than him. Having reclaimed those works, Columbus proceeded to find endorsement for them in texts written by authors approved by the Church, like the prophet Ezra, or by the schoolmen Peter Comestor and Nicholas of Lyra. Having found this endorsement, Columbus returned full circle in his argument to the authority of experience—illustrating by this means not the power that experience had to discredit written authority but the power that experience had to transfer legitimacy from one set of authoritative texts to another.

As I have stated, the *carta-relación* of the third voyage is a late paraphrase of the eighth chapter in d'Ailly's *Ymago mundi*. Together, this chapter and Columbus's remarkable marginal annotations have been read as the most compelling evidence that the Discoverer intended to reach the East "by way of the West." But this evidence also speaks to the imperative of southing into the belt of the tropics in search of vast tracts of fertile and inhabitable land—whether or not such land formed part of the *orbis terrarum* and whether or not, by standing to the west of Guinea and toward the Indian Ocean, such land could be reasonably said to constitute the easternmost part of legendary India. Southing, then, not merely westing, would have been a crucial and explicit element of the plan Columbus had submitted to the royal commission in the years preceding the discovery.

This and no other is the explicit meaning of the most famous postil Columbus—some say, his brother Bartholomew—ever wrote, in the margins of *Ymago mundi*:

> Note that in this year 1488, in the month of December, arrived in Lisbon Bartholomeu Dias, captain of three caravels, whom the Most Serene King of Portugal had sent to Guinea to survey the land. And he reported to the said Most Serene King that he had navigated beyond Yan 600 leagues—that is, 450 to the south and 250 to the north, up to a promontory he called "Cape of Good Hope" [modern 34° 24′ S], which we believe to be in Agysimba [i.e., an uncharted southern region that Ptolemy had placed in the farthest southern reaches of Aethiopia

Interior]. And in that place he found by the astrolabe that he was 45° beyond the equator [i.e., in the middle of the southern temperate zone], which latter place is 3,100 leagues distant from Lisbon. He drew this voyage and recorded it league-by-league on a nautical chart in order to present it to the view of the Most Serene King, and I was present in all of this.

This agrees with what Marinos says, whom Ptolemy corrects with regard to the journey to the Garamantes. [Marinos] says that a journey had been made 27,500 stades beyond the equinoctial line, which Ptolemy denies and corrects. [Marinos] agrees with Pierre d'Ailly that water does not cover three-fourths of the earth.

He agrees that the sea is completely navigable; nor does this prevent extreme heat.[135]

What could be the purpose of this famous postil to "De quantitate terre habitabilis" if not to endorse an open geographical model that anticipated the discovery of considerable lands by navigating south into the regions of the world previously thought to be universally unnavigable and uninhabitable? True, this postil invites the inference now familiar to us: if land had been found by navigating so far south into the lower hemisphere, then land might also be found by navigating to the west. Canonical geographers must have been wrong to assume that dry land was the result of water's displacement to a center other than the earth's. And if one assumed instead, as Aristotle had done, that earth and water were concentric spheres—meaning, that they shared the same geometrical center and that they both uniformly tended toward that center—then dry land to one side of the globe probably found its countervalent somewhere else. This would have been precisely the logic informing the inference drawn by Columbus in Madeira on the basis of recent discoveries along Atlantic Africa's shores. And Columbus would not have been alone in drawing this inference. The same inference was drawn years later by Columbus's contemporary, Martin Behaim, for his globe of 1492, which not only pushed the southern limits of the inhabited world beyond the Tropic of Capricorn all the way to the Cape of Good Hope just rounded by Bartholomeu Dias but also pushed its eastern reach far beyond the 180 degrees assigned it by Ptolemy. Just after Columbus returned victorious to Europe, a similar inference would compel the famous cosmographer Hieronymus Münzer to extend to King João II of Portugal an invitation without future: the Holy Roman Emperor Maximilian I invited Dom João to engage in a joint venture across the Atlantic from Portugal to *Cathay* (29 May 1493).[136] In short, Columbus's famous postil to d'Ailly does speak to Columbus's intended westing across the Atlantic.

But this postil speaks even more directly and urgently to Columbus's intended southing to the belt of the tropics. Bartholomeu Dias's rounding of the Cape of Good Hope evidently prompted Columbus or Bartholomew to effect a few significant corrections on long-established geographical claims, even though some of the figures provided by the annotator are suspect or incorrect: the figure of 45° S for Dias's farthest latitude nowhere appears on Portuguese records; the figure of 27,500 stades for the voyage reported by Marinos of the military campaign of the Garamē to the country of Agysimba in Aethiopia Interior, should read 27,800 stades; and this last figure, which would have placed the southernmost limit of the inhabited world at nearly 56° S, was in fact ultimately rejected by Marinos in favor of the Tropic of Capricorn (23° 51′ S, or about 24° S).[137] The figures Columbus cites in this postil obviously inflated both the southern reach of Portuguese discoveries in Africa and Marinos's own final estimate for the southernmost limits of the inhabited world. But these figures aside, Columbus or his brother obviously saw in Dias's voyage an occasion to express their geographical preferences in detriment of Ptolemy's narrow measurements for the inhabited world: Dias's descent to 45° S proved that Marinos's figure of 27,500 ought to be preferred over Ptolemy's (Ptolemy, by the way, had located this southernmost boundary at 16° 25′ S);[138] Ptolemy had erred on the side of caution by stating that the known inhabited world occupied less than one-fourth of the globe's surface, whereas Marinos served to confirm d'Ailly's contention that "water does not cover three fourths of the earth." Marinos's figures also spoke against those who contended that it was impossible to navigate, or to inhabit, the torrid zone; " . . . the sea is completely navigable; nor does this prevent extreme heat." In sum, every component of this famous postil to d'Ailly's "De quantitate terre habitabilis" was written with latitude, not longitude, in mind.

Testimony of the plan submitted to the royal commission appointed by Fernando and Isabel to evaluate the feasibility of Columbus's enterprise points to a learned debate engaged by two parties equally concerned with theological and philosophical correctness in their assessments of old and new geographical information.

According to the testimony provided by Ferdinand, Las Casas, and Geraldini, Columbus's project was forged between antithetical views about how land and life had come to be distributed around the globe. While Columbus's opponents in Castile espoused a closed geographical model of the globe, Columbus and his supporters espoused an open one. Columbus's opponents maintained that, in the beginning of time, the sphere of water, ten times greater in volume than the sphere of the earth, had come to be displaced with respect to the sphere of earth. This meant that the continental masses known as Europe, Africa, and Asia would have configured an irreplicable island that covered less than a quarter of an otherwise watery globe. Columbus and his supporters, on the contrary, maintained that the sphere of water had remained concentric with the sphere of the earth, meaning that both spheres had retained the same center of symmetry, and that each uniformly tended toward that center. Assuming this to be the case, the three known continents would have been the result of protrusions and depressions on the earth's surface that were bound to occur elsewhere around the globe. By Aristotle's reckoning, the sphere of water was at the very most barely greater in volume than the sphere of the earth. By Columbus's own inflated reckoning, the condensation of water vapor into water at the beginning of time had rendered the surface ratio of earth to water six to one. Whatever the volume or surface ratio of earth to water cited by Columbus and his supporters before the royal commission, they clearly believed that dry land significantly exceeded the boundaries traditionally ascribed to the known inhabited world—whether because the tricontinental mass reached farther east and west, and north and south, than canonical geography conceded or because this known landmass did not constitute the only body of land on the terraqueous globe.

Columbus's opponents in Castile also maintained that the *orbis terrarum* did not generally extend into the southern hemisphere, that there were no antipodes, and that the torrid zone itself was generally unnavigable and uninhabitable. But Columbus and his supporters maintained that the inhabited world generally extended farther north and south than canonical geography conceded, that there could be antipodes, and that the torrid zone was itself generally navigable and inhabitable. No matter how we read this testimony, Columbus intended to sail south of the traditional boundaries ascribed to the inhabited world, into the torrid zone, and nominally at least as far as the southern temperate zone.

Testimony of the plans Columbus submitted to other crowns in Europe lets us create an even more detailed account of Columbus's intentions. In Portugal, Columbus would have argued that the proportion of dry land to water was significantly greater than was normally assumed, and he would have proposed to find inhabited lands due west of Portuguese Africa all the way to the legendary India. Similarly, the plan submitted to

England appears to have called attention to the fact that the torrid zone could no longer be considered the unrelenting wasteland it had been famed to be. Indeed, we may well consider the globe presented by Bartholomew Columbus to Henry VII to be the first brochure on record enticing the apprehensive bystander to come and visit the friendly tropics: "Also painted here is that torrid zone recently furrowed by Spanish keels, formerly hidden to people, which now at last is very well known to many."

Lastly, Columbus's interpretation of the eighth chapter of d'Ailly's *Ymago mundi*—whether in his marginal postils or in the *carta-relación* of the third voyage—points to his intention of bridging the distance, not just generally between the East and the West, but specifically between Africa and India. And this plan would have rested on the prospect of finding ever-greater tracts of land, perhaps vastly fertile and inhabited, within the very belt of the tropics.

Thus the infamous torrid zone appears to have played a significant role—I would argue, a central role—in the drama leading to the discovery. And if we fail to understand that Columbus's intention was, in great part, to extend the discoveries made by the Portuguese in Africa along the belt of the tropics to the west, perhaps all the way to legendary India, we truly fail to understand the dire geopolitics that informed Columbus's descent from a "temperate" Europe to the American tropics.

The Meaning of India in Pre-Columbian Europe

In 1517, twenty-five years after the discovery, the Spanish explorer and colonial officer Martín Fernández de Enciso (about 1469–1530) completed a *Suma de geographia* worthy of some reflection. This "geographical summation" was printed two years later with a dedication to the young Holy Roman emperor Charles V, and it was the first work in Spain to have attempted a systematic description of the new expanse that, thanks to Columbus, had come to be called Indias Occidentales, or West Indies. The *Suma* was written under the aegis of the Casa de Contratación de Sevilla, the agency created by the Castilian Crown in 1503 with the purpose of overseeing all commercial ventures to and from Spain's overseas territories.[1] Given the official character of this work, it is no surprise that Fernández de Enciso's use of the term Indias Occidentales should have meticulously observed the geopolitical terms of the Treaty of Alcáçovas (1479–1480) and of the documents issued by Pope Alexander VI in 1493 that granted the Catholic Monarchs exclusive right of access to the territories just discovered by Columbus in the high Atlantic. The *Suma* explicitly wrote off those territories newly discovered by other Europeans to the north in the direction of the land then known as Labrador, defining Indias Occidentales instead solely as those territories newly acquired by Spain to the west *and* to the south of El Hierro Island. As we already know, the phrase *versus occidentem et meridiem* had served as the locator deployed by Alexander VI to demarcate the newly discovered territories; and El Hierro was the island in the Canaries that had crucially informed Columbus's sense of latitude upon his arrival in the Bahamas.[2] Enciso's geographical demarcation for the West Indies thus bears its immediate political antecedent in a decades-old dispute between Castile and Portugal for control over Atlantic Africa's shores and waters. But its intellectual ancestry falls with a geographical tradition that had long tended to associate legendary India with the lower latitudes of the globe we know today as the belt of the tropics.

Fernández de Enciso's *Suma* indelibly linked the term *Indias occidentales* to the *latitudinal* axis of the enterprise famously sponsored by Aragon and Castile "to the parts of India." In his introductory treatment on the theory of the five zones, the geographer patriotically noted that Fernando and Isabel's discovery of "the Indies, Terra Firma, and Western Isles" had revealed vastly inhabited territories within the torrid zone, to the discredit of "astrologers" who had claimed that the belt of the tropics was uninhabitable. The geographer marveled at the fact that the ancient experts on "the sphere" should have erred so grossly in their characterization of the torrid zone, knowing as they must have known that the entire region of Ethiopia, Arabia Felix, Calicut, and Melaka was "densely populated, and lies directly under the torrid zone and within the tropics."[3] In other words, the theory of the five zones had prevailed among Greco-Roman geographers despite the fact that the very authors who espoused the claim that the tropics were intolerably hot, and therefore infertile and inhospitable, simultaneously supplied information about sub-Saharan Africa, the Arabian Peninsula, the Indian subcontinent, and the Malaysian peninsula. Such information, insists Enciso, should have compelled those authors to revise the theory of the five zones—or even to dispense with it altogether.

Fernández de Enciso's invective against the ancients may reveal less about the state of the field among Greco-Roman geographers than about an intellectual and material culture that was gradually reawakening to the call of the tropics and, in this process, beginning to read the old geographical corpus on a new register. Indeed, the theory of the five zones had long coexisted with plenty of references to land and life in the belt of the tropics—in the case of sub-Saharan Africa, at least since Homer had mythified the Ethiopians in the *Odyssey,* and in the case of the Indian Ocean basin, at least since Hecataeus of Miletus had counted the inhabitants of the Indus River basin in his long-lost description of the world (6th century BCE). But Greco-Roman writers had been under no obligation to detect the contradiction that now appeared so obvious to Fernández de Enciso. Because the theory of the five zones entailed universal claims, evidence of inhabited places outside the so-called temperate zone could be considered as the exception that proved the rule: while the torrid zone might be *universally* uninhabitable on account of the sun's heat, it could nonetheless be *accidentally* inhabited on account of local conditions—like the presence of rivers that provided enough water to

defeat drought or of cool winds that tempered the sun's searing heat. So the notion that the cold or hot regions of the world could harbor life *per accidens* had dispensed with the need to revise the claim that the torrid zone was inhospitable. And this notion went hand in hand with the perception that tropical nature was intemperate—an unnatural mother that, when it *did* generate life, exceeded itself in every way, bringing about the myriad marvels and monsters that were supposed to thrive in places like Ethiopia and India.

Unbeknownst to Fernández de Enciso, the cosmological paradigm invented by Parmenides had, in fact, been contested long before Christian Europe's discovery of the tropics: Strabo's conscientious analysis of the state of the field in the opening years of the first century BCE attests to a number of models that Greek philosophers had already voiced as alternatives to the theory of the five zones—precisely because they intuited that nature's hyperactivity in the tropics might obey causes more universal than mere accidents of geography. It is ultimately a variant of this established paradigm, attributed by Strabo to the great theoretical geographer Eratosthenes (about 275–194 BCE), that Arabic and Latin writers, including Albertus Magnus and Pierre d'Ailly, would invoke in favor of the argument that the region between the tropics was, contrary to the established belief, *generally* fertile, inhabitable, and even remarkably temperate.

But the theory of the five zones had ultimately prevailed in the Latin West, and it had taken many decades of Iberian exploration in the belt of the tropics for the illogic of this paradigm to begin to become plain. With the weight of experience at hand, Fernández de Enciso had returned to the reading of his classics, and they now read as they never had before. For Fernández de Enciso, the discovery of the Indias Occidentales was part of a larger process of imperial expansion in sub-Saharan Africa and the extended basin of the Indian Ocean, and this process of expansion in the places the author calls Ethiopia, Arabia Felix, Calicut, Malacca, *and* the Indias Occidentales had begun to reveal to Christian Europeans a vast habitat that in no way reflected the sweltering desolation the ancients had imputed to the torrid zone. Fernández de Enciso published his *Suma de geographia* in 1519—in retrospect, a significant year for the geographical history of the Americas. At this time, a friend of Columbus, Ferdinand Magellan (about 1480–1521) would come to round the South American strait named after him today (52° 30′ S) on a mission to demonstrate that the coveted Moluccas (Maluku Islands in Indonesia, 1° S) extended on the Spanish side of the "ante-meridian" that would have lain opposite the Atlantic demarcation of Tordesillas. Since the conquest of the Malaysian port of Melaka in 1511, the Portuguese had wielded control over the trade

route through the strait of Melaka all the way to the spice-bearing Moluccas and had opened the door to the South China Sea. Now Castile wanted its share of the action. Magellan was killed in the Philippines before reaching the Moluccas, and the only ship from his fleet to return to Spain safely was the galleon *Victoria,* captained by Juan Sebastián del Cano (about 1476–1526). Nevertheless, Magellan and del Cano's perilous crossing of the Pacific Ocean to the Philippines (1519–1521) did confirm what many in the Spanish Empire had suspected since Columbus's victorious return to Europe in 1493: the Indies discovered by Columbus were not geographically contiguous with the vast territories earliest documented by Greek Indographers. Columbus had been "wrong" to think that he could cross the Atlantic *ad partes Indie.* The longitudinal tie between East and West Indies had finally been severed; not so, however, the tie that had bound them together by reason of latitude.

In the *Suma de geographia,* the West Indies remains firmly an extension of the traditional India. Not just because Europeans had yet to confirm that a vast ocean intervened between the Americas and Asia. But also because the bulk of the territories newly claimed by Spain in the Americas shared in the hottest latitudes of the globe with sub-Saharan Africa and the extended basin of the Indian ocean. In this sense, the term so precisely used by Fernández de Enciso hardly represents the charitable accommodation that history had allowed for Columbus's stated goal of reaching the Indies. The term Indias Occidentales appropriately designated a geographical region that had instantly claimed its share in Mediterranean culture's long-lived and ambivalent fascination with the tropics. By virtue of sharing its general latitude with the traditional India of legend, the West Indies formed part of a continuous belt that had long given Mediterranean geographers—from Herodotus to Columbus—cause to draw profound analogies between sub-Saharan Africa and the basin of the Indian Ocean. And it is as a relatively coherent entity that Ethiopia and India had figured in the geographical corpus that preceded the discovery. As Fernández de Enciso implicitly records, Columbus explored to the west and to the south of El Hierro. And the Discoverer always insisted that the lands he had discovered in the high Atlantic were a part of the Indies. What follows is an attempt to identify information in the foundational record left behind by the earliest authors to have written about India's *place* and, thereby, about its *nature,* that could have ultimately etched in Columbus's mind an indelible tie between the prospect of sailing west across the Atlantic and south toward the belt of the tropics and the dream of reaching legendary India.

The earliest extant mention of the toponym *India* in Mediterranean literature appears in the *Periodos ges* by the Ionian author Hecataeus of Miletus (5th–6th century BCE), the first detailed description of the earth known to us and one of the earliest works to have brought into practice the cartographic convention allegedly invented by Homer, and followed by medieval *mappaemundi,* of drawing the inhabited world as a circular island surrounded by a circumfluent ocean.[4] The surviving fragments of this geographical work suggest that "India" was first known to the Greeks, via the invading Persians, as the territories on or just west of the basin of the Indus River (*Indon*).[5] However, in the considerable geographical corpus leading to Columbus's discovery of the Americas, India came to evoke, often rather vaguely, a far greater range of territories not part of this river basin. For instance, in his lost but influential *Indica,* the Greek historian and diplomat Megasthenes (about 350–about 290 BCE) referred to India as the "quadrilateral," or rhomboidal, shape bounded by the Indus River on the northwest, the Himalayan mountain range on the northeast, and the ocean on the southwestern and southeastern flanks of the Asian subcontinent we know today as India.[6] Diodorus Siculus (1st century BCE), whose *Bibliotheca historica* preserved some of Megasthenes' work and inspired many a line in Pliny's *Naturalis historia,* illustrates why the convention of thinking about Africa as a separate continental mass from India may not always apply for interpreting pre-Columbian geographies. According to Diodorus, India was separated from Scythia (the northern portion of Asia) by Mount Hemodes (the Himalayan mountain range), and it was bounded to the west by the Nile River. India was, in effect, all the lands facing, or within, the basin of the Indian Ocean, including those African territories to the east of the Nile.[7] Slightly more restrained, but equally suggestive, definitions for India appeared in Strabo's *Geography* and Pomponius Mela's *Chorographia* (44 CE). According to Strabo and Mela, who adopted a skewed version of the quadrilateral suggested by earlier writers like Megasthenes, India was bound on the north by the Taurus Range (a horizontal mountain range that, according to Strabo, ran horizontally east from the shores of the Mediterranean, through Mount Hemodes, and ended on Asia's eastern shores) and on the west by the Indus River. From these boundaries, it extended all the way to the eastern and southern portions of the circumambient ocean.[8]

In his second-century *Geography,* Ptolemy used the toponym *India* to denote not only the territories that stood *intra Gangem,* or "on this side of the Ganges," that is, the Indian subcontinent, but also those territories that stood *extra Gangem,* or "beyond the Ganges"—bounded on the north by the Seres, or Silk People, as the Chinese had come

to be known by way of the north along the inland routes of the silk trade, and on the east by the open-ended region of the Sinai, as the Chinese had come to be known from the south, along the trade routes of the Indian Ocean (**fig. 1.6**, pp. 80–81).[9] The use of the plural form of the term *las yndias,* brought into vogue by Columbus in the widely printed and translated letter to Luis de Santángel announcing the discovery (dated 15 February 1493), in all likelihood most directly derived from Ptolemy's "novel" distinction between an intra-Gangetic and an ultra-Gangetic India, although Arabic and Christian writers in the intervening centuries had also introduced threefold divisions that included Africa east of the Nile as a "third" India.[10] It is to India *extra Gangem* that Ferdinand Columbus is referring when, excusing his father, he explains that Columbus "[had] not call[ed] them the Indies because they had been seen or discovered by others [i.e., Europeans], but because they were the eastern part of India beyond the Ganges, to which no cosmographer set limits [i.e., to the east], nor boundaries with another land or province to the east, save with the ocean."[11]

The most comprehensive use of the term *India,* however, may have been offered by the Venetian merchant Marco Polo, whose thirteenth-century *Il milione,* like Ptolemy's *Geography,* wielded a determining influence on fourteenth- and fifteenth-century iconography of the farthest confines of Asia. Columbus himself was already conversant with Marco Polo's geography when he embarked on his first transatlantic voyage. He had perhaps even read *Il milione* as early as 1483 or 1484, when he first submitted his plan to Dom João of Portugal. In the Latin translation of *Il milione* (Antwerp, 1485) now preserved in the Biblioteca Colombina, leaving behind his description of the trans-Asian caravan routes to the Mongol empire and of the territories directly within the Great Khān's sphere of influence, Marco Polo focused on the geographically and politically separate regions of India. His geography of India opens with an account of Khubilai Khān's failed attempts to conquer Çipango (Japan), which he located 1,400 miles off the coast of Mangi—the Chinese mainland south of the Huang He, or the Yellow River, conquered by Khubilai Khān in 1279. Its waters were the Sea of Chin—perhaps the waters now jointly comprehended by the Yellow, East China, and South China seas—and it lay in the midst of a vast, populated archipelago of more than seven thousand islands. From Çipango, Marco Polo's account of India followed innumerable sites of commercial value, all the way from the port of Zaiton (Quanzhou, 24° 55′ N, in southwestern China's Fujian province across from Taiwan) to the farthest confines of the "Sea of India" with its more than 1,378 islands. Marco Polo's route through India included the province of

Ciamba (today's North and South Vietnam on the Malaysian peninsula); the Indonesian islands of Java Maior (Java) and Java Minor (Sumatra); the island of Ceylon (Sri Lanka); and numerous coastal provinces on India Maior (the Indian subcontinent). This route also included the east African islands of Scoiran (Socotra, on the Horn of Africa); the island of Madagascar, which Marco Polo placed 1,000 miles south of Scoiran (in front of today's Mozambique, 20° S); and, supposedly farther than Madagascar, the remote island of Zanzibar (actually, off of today's Tanzania, 6° 12′ S).

Such remarkable range in the uses of the term India prior to the discovery begins to explain why Columbus on his first transatlantic voyage would carry an official *Carta comendaticia,* or passport, in Latin introducing him as a royal envoy on his way "to the parts of India" (*ad partes Indie*).[12] India's extension to the *east* of the Nile and to the *south* of the horizontal mountain range that included the Himalayas had remained, so to speak, anybody's guess. Ptolemy and Marco Polo—the two sources that most immediately served to rehaul the iconography of Asia's confines before Columbus—had expressed India's geographical indeterminacy in ways that could equally have invited the Discoverer to dream of an Atlantic crossing.

Ptolemy had encoded the limits of his knowledge regarding the eastern and western reaches of the Sea of India by drawing an enormous littoral between the two farthest points known to him on the coasts of southeast Asia and east Africa. This littoral joined the remote port of Kattigara in the open-ended region of the Sinai (Cattigara Sinarum Statio) with the east African Cape Prason (Rhaptum Promonturium).[13] Ptolemy thus rendered the Indian Ocean as a landlocked sea, and he visualized the blank extensions to the east of the Sinai and to the south of Africa and the Indian Ocean as unknown land (**figs. 1.1**, pp. 62–63; **1.6**, pp. 80–81; and **2.2**, pp. 120–121).[14] Columbus did not fail to notice the open geographical model proposed by Ptolemy. A postil to the *Compendium cosmographie I,* in Columbus's copy of d'Ailly and Gerson's *Tractatus,* reads: "One part of our entire inhabited world is bounded on the east by a terra incognita, on the south by a terra incognita," and, as Columbus slyly adds to Ptolemy's scheme, "on the west by terra incognita."[15] Marco Polo, for his part, had granted India indefinite elbow room to the east and to the south by adding to the place names he already knew the formidable number of 7,378 islands on the Sea of Chin and 1,378 islands on the Sea of India. Such is the meaning, for instance, of the myriad gem-shaped isles with which the celebrated mapmaker Abraham Cresques dotted the southwestern margins of the hybrid portolan world map known as the Catalan Atlas of 1375 (last panel of **fig. 3.1**).

3.1 (*next six pages*) Catalan Atlas, 1375. From Georges Grosjean, ed., *Mappamundi: The Catalan Atlas of the Year 1375* (Dietikon-Zurich, 1978). Courtesy of the Bibliothèque Nationale, Paris, France; and Urs Graf Publishing Company, Dietikon-Zurich, Switzerland.

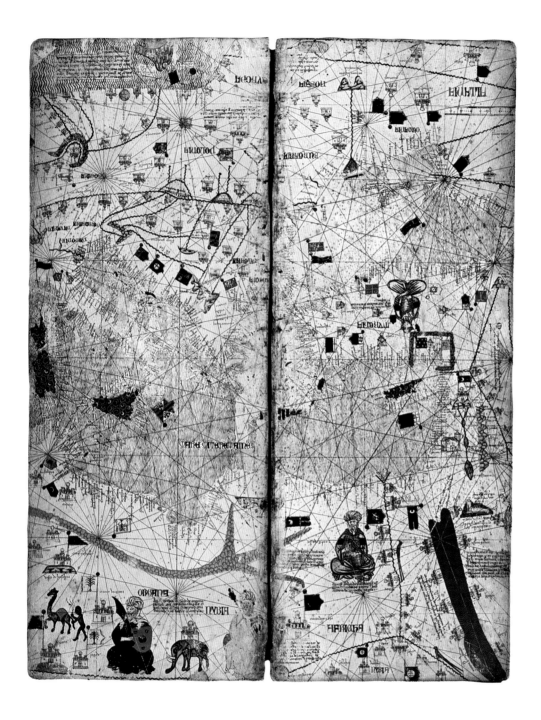

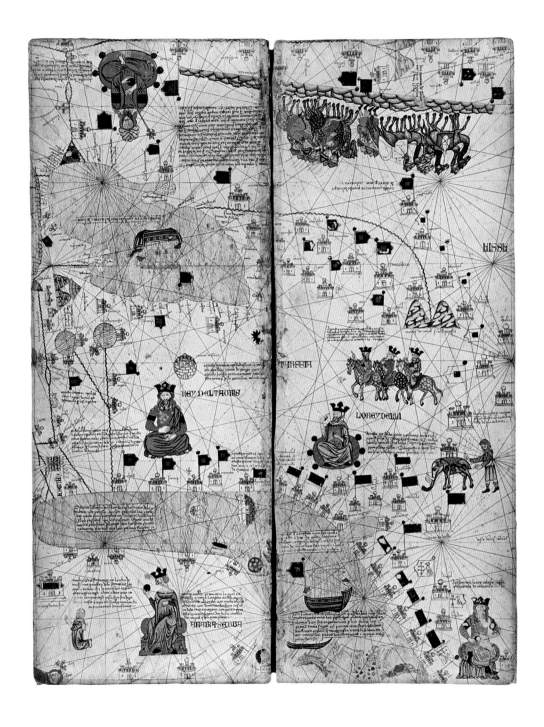

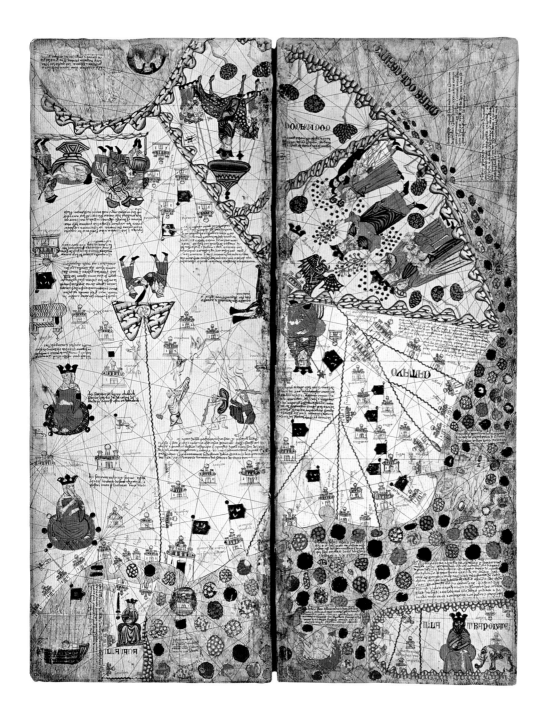

Ptolemy's and Marco Polo's methods of encoding India's geographical indeterminacy were, so to speak, negatives of each other: Ptolemy's India was organized around a distinctly *tropical* landlocked sea whose eastern and southern littorals opened on terra incognita. Marco Polo's India was organized around a seemingly open sea whose waters and islands extended indefinitely to the east and to the south. But both methods would have equally suggested that the territories within the radius of the Indian Ocean might include land that extended indefinitely to the east and to the south—"islands and terrae firmae" (*islas e tierras firmes*), as one finds in the open-ended legal terminology specifying the rights and privileges that the Crown conditionally granted Columbus just before his first voyage.[16] India's geographical indeterminacy is the wild card that allowed Columbus and his few supporters to argue for the feasibility of crossing the ocean "to the parts of India," and it is this same indeterminacy that allowed his detractors in Castile to dismiss his project as little more than a shot in the dark.

India's great geographical elasticity to the east and to the south also explains Columbus's *always* insisting that the lands he had discovered were part of "the Indies," even after he had rightly concluded, during his survey of modern-day Venezuela in 1498, that the overpowering flow of fresh water from the delta of the Orinoco River indicated the presence of a previously "unknown" landmass "infinitely" extending toward the southern hemisphere.[17] This conclusion did compel Columbus to inform the Catholic Monarchs that he had found "another world" (*otro mundo*), and this terminology unequivocally points to the fact that Columbus had in mind the ancient model that posited alternative inhabited landmasses like the antipodes.[18] But the closest Columbus ever came to granting the newly discovered islands a toponym that might distinguish them from the Asia previously "familiar" to Europeans occurs in a legal document Columbus dictated in 1501 or 1502, reasserting his right to preside as a judge in all legal suits arising from commerce in the Bahamas and Caribbean basin. At the time, Columbus was desperately trying to persuade the Crown to restore him to the gubernatorial duties he had lost on account of his disastrous colonial policy in Hispaniola and to turn the tide of opinion on those who doubted the merits of an enterprise that had so far failed to summon the great spoils expected of the Indies.[19] To make matters worse for the Discoverer, King João II's successor, Dom Manuel, had recently informed the Spanish Crown of the successful returns of Vasco da Gama's and Pedro Àlvares Cabral's armadas from India's wealthy Malabar Coast.[20] Columbus could no longer credibly claim that his India was the India just reached by da Gama

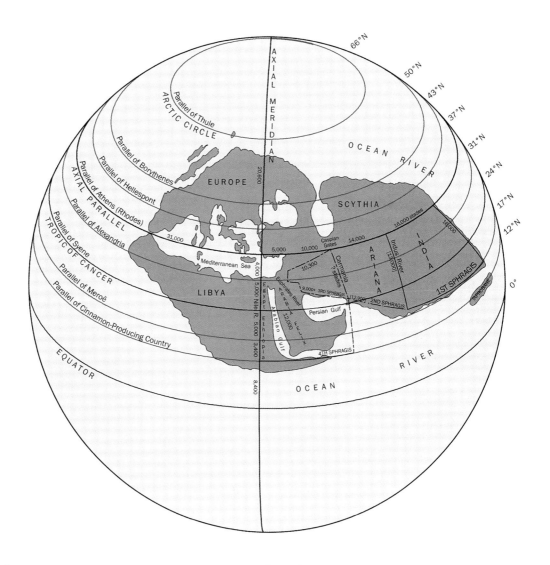

3.2   Reconstruction of
Eratosthenes' world map. After
Strabo's *Geography* (1917–1932).
Prepared by Lynn Carlson, Brown
University, Providence, Rhode
Island.

— Determinate boundaries for Eratosthenes' sphragides
-- Indeterminate boundaries for Eratosthenes' sphragides
[ ] Boundary measurements supplied by Strabo

had subscribed to the Homeric view that the inhabited world was an "island" entirely surrounded by ocean. But his world map parted ways with the cartographic tradition previously established by geographers like Hecataeus, who depicted the inhabited world as a disk-shaped island. Because the inhabited world was in some sense shorn flat on the north and on the south by intemperate latitudes, Eratosthenes and other geographers assumed that the width, or longitude, of this "island" was at least twice its breadth, or latitude, save for the fact that the world map also tapered in toward the poles. As Strabo explains, the inhabited world was contained within one of the two horizontal quadrants that resulted on the northern hemisphere from drawing a perpendicular circle to intercept the equatorial circle and the poles. Assuming that the inhabited world was bound on the east and west by this meridian, as well as on the north and south by the inhospitable cold and heat, Eratosthenes had likened the inhabited world to a Macedonian chlamys, or a near-trapezoidal cloak.[49]

Having built this chlamys, Eratosthenes proceeded to locate the known inhabited world and its regions according to a matrix composed of one parallel and one meridian (**fig. 3.2**). As we have mentioned, Eratosthenes assumed that the Egyptian city of "Syene"—the "door" to Ethiopia—stood on the Tropic of Cancer, which, by his measurement in stades (16,800) rendered a latitude of approximately twenty-four degrees north of the equator. He also assumed (mistakenly) that Syene stood along a single meridian that ran vertically from the frontier African region known as cinnamon-producing country (3,400 stades south of Meroë, or about 12° N); through the Ethiopian capital Meroë (5,000 stades south of Syene or 17° N); through Syene itself (24° N); through the city of Alexandria (5,000 stades north of Syene or 31° N [actually 31° 13′ N]); through the island of Rhodes (about 4,000 stades from Alexandria or 37° N [modern 36° 15′ N]); through the Hellespont or Dardanelles (about 8,100 stades from Alexandria or about 43° N [modern 40° 17′]), through the mouth of the Borysthenes River (5,000 stades from Hellespont or about 50° N [Dnieper River, actually 46° 30′ N]); and, finally, through the island of Thule, or Iceland (11,500 stades north of Borysthenes or about 66° N [modern 64° 45′ N]).[50] By these numbers, the breadth of the known inhabited world would have covered 38,000 stades, or about fifty-four degrees—from about half the distance between the equator and the Tropic of Cancer nearly all the way north to the Arctic circle.[51]

Eratosthenes had also estimated the width of the inhabited world along the parallel of Rhodes (approximately 37° N), which ran through the Pillars of Hercules (Strait

How far south Alexander's explorers situated the lands of the Indian Ocean we know only from hearsay gathered by Onesicritus, one of the captains on Nearchus's flotilla and the earliest Mediterranean geographer known to have described the legendary island of Taprobane (Sri Lanka). According to Strabo, Onesicritus reported that this inordinately fertile island stood "twenty days' voyage from the mainland," the "farthest south" of all the islands extending beyond continental India.[43] And according to Pliny, Taprobane had been considered part of the *antichthones* until Alexander's campaign to India (undoubtedly, Nearchus and Onesicritus's outing on the Indian Ocean) revealed that it was an island.[44] (Actually, Pliny's *antichthones* was Crates of Mallos's *antoikoi*, directly south of the *oikoumenē*, not the true *antichthones*, or antipodes.) Needless to say, Taprobane was to become one of ancient and medieval geography's most ubiquitous *topoi*, pictured again and again as an inordinately bountiful, inhabited region at a great distance from the Indian mainland, or, as Pliny handsomely stated, an island "relegated by Nature beyond the orb."[45]

Once early Indographic materials such as these were assimilated by the great theoretical geographers of the Hellenistic period, India emerged far more explicitly as a substantial portion of the inhabited world reaching well into the torrid zone. As Strabo's *Geography* explicitly indicates, theoretical geographers heavily relied on the comparison of reports carried back to the Mediterranean by travelers who had noted climatic conditions and celestial phenomena in that region and others.[46] The earliest known theorist who conceived of India as an integral part of a larger geographical area extending into the tropics was Eratosthenes (about 275–174). His now-lost works in the fields of geodesy, geography, and cartography—*Measurement of the Earth* and *Geography*—are largely known to us through Strabo. Eratosthenes is most famous for devising a simple method to calculate the globe's circumference, a method that, despite its flaws, produced what some consider to have been a remarkably accurate figure (252,000 stades).[47] But Eratosthenes is also widely considered today to have been the first Greek thinker to systematize the field of geography. He located and measured the known inhabited world and its individual regions according to a basic matrix that anticipated the use of parallels and meridians in later cartography.[48]

In his *Geography,* Strabo would construct his own world map largely following Eratosthenes' method, and although Strabo disagreed with Eratosthenes concerning the latitudinal and longitudinal extent of the known inhabited world, his picture of the Afro-Indian tropics was nearly identical to that of his predecessor. Eratosthenes

Arrian's *Indica* (2nd century) expressed in yet other ways the general latitudes explored by Onesicritus and Nearchus, who accompanied Alexander on his military campaign to the greater basin of the Indus River (326 BCE). Alexander had appointed Nearchus as commander of a flotilla that, retracing Scylax of Caryanda's journey, surveyed the Indus all the way to its outlet on the ocean, crossed the Arabian Sea and the Persian Gulf, and soon reached the Euphrates River (326–325 BCE). Nearchus would encode the tropicality of the region he had explored by stating that he and his men had often noticed at sea that their shadows "did not always cast in the same way" and that when they sailed long distances due south, their shadows also fell in that direction. Although we have no clue as to how far Nearchus's fleet sailed into the Indian Ocean, he and his men had clearly left the temperate zone, where shadows at noon invariably fall to the north; and they had entered the torrid zone, where, except when the sun casts no shadow at noon, shadows at noon will fall either to the north or to the south, depending on the sun's location along the ecliptic.

Arrian's interpretation of Nearchus's testimony also bears recalling, for like so many other Mediterranean Indographers, Arrian used his knowledge of Africa—in this case of the frontier cities of Syene and Meroë—as points of reference to discuss India. Syene and Meroë had played an important role in Greek cartography, particularly since the great theoretical geographer Eratosthenes had used their latitudes to construct his world map.[39] Egyptian Syene, famous for its stone quarrying, had long been known to stand directly under the Tropic of Cancer (modern-day Aswan in Egypt, 24° 4′ N). As Strabo would put it, the noon sunlight shining into one of Syene's "wells" during the summer solstice failed to cast any shadows at all.[40] Significantly, Syene marked the frontier between Egypt to the north and Ethiopia to the south (sub-Saharan Africa). The remote "island" metropolis of Meroë, for its part, had been known to Herodotus as the capital of Ethiopia, and Eratosthenes would place it 5,000 stades south of Syene, at an approximate latitude of 17° N (Meroë is now known to have stood south of today's Sudanese capital Khartoum [15° 31′ N], near the confluence of the White and Blue Niles).[41] Arrian reasoned that Nearchus's report concerning the general latitude of his fleet's whereabouts was perfectly credible. If it was possible for the sun to cast no shadow at noon on the summer solstice in Syene and during the summer months in Meroë, it followed that the same phenomena should be observed "among the Indians, too, since they are far south, and especially in the Indian Ocean, since the sea falls still further south."[42]

region we know as Saharan Africa, whereas Ethiopia extended south of the parallel of Syene (i.e., Tropic of Cancer), occupying what we know as sub-Saharan Africa on either bank of the Nile River. Strabo's north-south division of the African continent along the Tropic of Cancer unmistakably associates black Africa with the hotter latitudes of the globe. And, as we have already seen, Strabo extended this connection to those parts of India that reached as far south as Ethiopia.[64] We need only revisit the advice that cosmographer Jaume Ferrer de Blanes offered Columbus in the wake of the discovery to appreciate the hold that the connection between tropicality, heat, and blackness would continue to exert on Mediterranean perceptions of sub-Saharan Africa and the basin of the Indian Ocean: by Ferrer's account, years of conversation with "Indians and Arabs and Ethiopians" had persuaded him that "all good things come from very hot regions whose inhabitants are black or dark brown; and therefore, in my judgment, until Your Lordship meets such peoples, you shall fail to find an abundance of such things."[65]

Strabo also carried Eratosthenes' protocol for map building well beyond the use of an axial parallel and an axial meridian to locate separate regions: he proposed drawing a set of parallels and meridians to either side of each of these two "elements" in order to divide land and sea.[66] In a now-lost treatise entitled *Against Eratosthenes,* the astronomer Hipparchus (flourished 161–126 BCE) had derided Eratosthenes for failing to use astronomically observed latitudes as the primary criteria for situating individual regions on the world map.[67] Hipparchus had divided the globe into 360 degrees (700 stades each), with the intention of describing individual places degree by degree of latitude from the equator to the pole.[68] While Strabo agreed that Hipparchus's use of *climata* would produce a more precise world map than Eratosthenes', he did excuse himself from the tedious task of providing a description of the known inhabited world degree by degree. Based on Hipparchus's table of latitudes, however, Strabo reverted to an older division of the world according to seven parallels, precisely the seven *climata* later specified by Ptolemy in his *Almagest* and widely adopted from him by Arabic cartographers for their own *mappaemundi.*[69]

The system of parallels implemented by Strabo for his world map observed more or less regular intervals determined by the duration in "equinoctial hours" of the longest day of the year for each of the seven parallels.[70] (This appears to have been one of the technical means used by Columbus in the Caribbean in order to establish specific latitudes, including the egregious latitudes recorded in his *Diario*.)[71] According to Strabo, each "clime" was separated from the one before it by "half an equinoctial hour": the inhabited world still began with cinnamon-producing country (3,000 stades south of Meroë, or 13° N), but the first clime ran through Meroë, where the longest day measured thirteen equinoctial hours (17° N). The second clime ran through Syene, where the day measured thirteen and a half equinoctial hours (24° N, that is, the Tropic of Cancer). The third clime ran 400 stades south of Alexandria, where the day measured fourteen hours (about 30° 20′ N). The fourth clime ran through the island of Rhodes, where the longest day was fourteen and a half hours (37° N). The fifth parallel ran "south of Rome but north of Neapolis," where the longest day was fifteen hours (3,400 stades from the parallel of Rhodes, or about 42° N). The sixth parallel ran through the Pontus, or the Black Sea, where the longest day was fifteen and a half hours (1,400 stades north of Byzantium, itself 4,900 stades north of Rhodes, or about 46° N). And the seventh clime ran through the Borysthenes River, where the longest day was sixteen equinoctial hours (3,800 stades north of Byzantium, or about 50° N).[72]

According to Strabo's system, the parallel of Rhodes still divided the known inhabited world along the Mediterranean and the Taurus Range all the way from the Pillars of Hercules to the farthest capes of India. Nearly everything below this parallel was supposed to fall in either Africa or India. Thus the parallel 400 stades south of Alexandria ran west of Egypt "through Cyrene and the regions 900 stadia south of Carthage and central Marurusia [Mauretania]," and due east of Egypt through "Coelesyria, Upper Syria, Babylonia, Susiana, Persia, Carmania, Upper Gedrosia, and India."[73] The parallel of Syene (Tropic of Cancer), ran due west "almost five thousand stadia south of Cyrene" and due east "through the country of the Fish-Eaters in Gedrosia [first identified by Nearchus and Onesicritus], and through India."[74] The parallel of Meroë ran due west through the "unknown regions" of Lybia and due east through the "capes of India."[75] And, finally, the parallel through cinnamon-producing country ran due west through "the most southerly regions of Lybia [here the toponym stands for Africa west of the Nile, including Ethiopia]," and due east through the mouth of the Arabian Gulf [Red Sea], and "to the south of Taprobane."[76] Such is the system by which India assumed its place on Strabo's world map, on which a vast portion of the inhabited world extended a long way south of the Tropic of Cancer. More important, the "diaphragm" by which both Eratosthenes and Strabo divided the world map—which placed Europe in the northwest, Africa in the southwest, Scythia in the northeast, and India in the southeast—should make it clear why geographers continued to make a distinction between the higher and supposedly cooler latitudes of Asia, that is, Scythia, and the hotter southerly regions of Asia, that is, India. We return to this crucial latitudinal distinction in chapter 6. For now, note that it is precisely this latitudinal distinction that motivated Columbus to theorize in the margins of one of his favorite books, the *Historia rerum ubique gestarum* (Cologne, 1477) by Aeneas Sylvius Piccolomini (Pope Pius II, 1405–1464), that the "beginning" of India stood directly across from Hispania and toward the south.[77] In its most generous sense, India was for Columbus that southeastern quarter of the world that extended indefinitely to the east of the Nile River and indefinitely to the south of the parallel of Rhodes.

Perhaps Strabo's most important reservation with regard to Eratosthenes' world map concerns the insularity of the inhabited world suggested by his chlamys-shaped model. Strabo's objection to representing the known inhabited world as an island is of crucial importance when we consider the terms of the project presented by Columbus in Castile: as Strabo argued, because the geographer was concerned with describing only those places that were known to him, it mattered little whether he rendered the known inhabited world as an island—drawing a hypothetical littoral to join the farthest points known along its outer edges—or as an open geographical system—drawing nothing between such endpoints. (This means, for instance, that Ptolemy's later decision to enclose the Indian Ocean—by first "drawing" a Great Bay [Magnus Sinus] to join the Malayan Peninsula [Aurea Chersonesus] to the port of Kattigara [Cattigara Sinarum Statio], and by then drawing a littoral around the Indian Ocean between Kattigara and the African Cape Prason [Rhaptum Promonturium]—constitutes a cartographic convention by which ancient geographers conveyed the absence of geographical data.) Strabo's world map, unlike that of Eratosthenes, was indeed open-ended. By the time Strabo composed his *Geography*, Crates of Mallos had in the meantime constructed a globe that posited alternative inhabited landmasses centered on the temperate zones in the three remaining quadrants of the globe and separated from one another by vast stretches of ocean (*antoikoi, antichthones* [or antipodes], and *perioikoi*).[78] For Strabo, the proper construction of the world map would have plotted the known inhabited world on a globe constructed after Crates' model.[79] Like littorals drawn between known frontier points, the existence of such landmasses was only hypothetical—that is, inferred by means of philosophical reasoning. So too was their habitability, which—given that Crates' landmasses were completely incommunicated from one another by vast stretches of ocean and, in the case of the northern and southern hemispheres perhaps also by the intolerable heat of the torrid zone—meant for Strabo that those other landmasses were "not inhabited by men such as exist in our fourth."[80]

The fact that India was part of a larger geographical system extending into the tropics was by no means lost in the transition from the great theoretical works written by Hellenistic cartographers like Strabo and Ptolemy to early encyclopedic works in Latin like Pliny the Elder's first-century *Naturalis historia* and Macrobius's fifth-century *Commentarium in somnium Scipionis*. Pliny, for instance, adopted a system of parallels similar to the sevenfold system once designed by Eratosthenes to divide the inhabited world. By way of Megasthenes, Pliny also situated the farthest points of India on or well beyond the Tropic of Capricorn itself. It was also in the influential work of Macrobius that the Latin West primarily came to visualize India's participation in a larger geographical system that extended into the torrid zone (**fig. 1.2**, p. 72). Simple as the sketch of the continental masses appears in Macrobius's map, it crisply depicted significant portions of Africa, Arabia, and India reaching well into the area of the map marked by Macrobius as uninhabitable on account of the sun's heat. (Our particular version of Macrobius includes the labels "aethiopia," "mare rubrum," and "taprobana" within this "burnt" region of the *orbis terrarum*.) No less than 150 maps traced upon Macrobius's specification have survived today in manuscripts of his *Commentarium* produced between the ninth and fifteenth centuries, attesting to the relative popularity of Macrobian iconography in the Latin West.[81]

But of the world maps that may have been known to Columbus in the tradition that preceded the introduction of the graticular format prescribed by Ptolemy's *Geography*, the most significant for our purpose is the hybrid *mappamundi* contained in the opening folios of d'Ailly's *Ymago mundi* (**fig. 1.5**, pp. 76–77). D'Ailly's *mappamundi* incorporated the chlamys-shaped model of theoretical geographers like Eratosthenes and Strabo; the division of the globe into five zones of Macrobius; and the division of the known inhabited world into seven *climata*, which d'Ailly's most immediate sources, Albumasar's *Introductorium in astronomiam* and al-Farghānī's *Liber aggregationum stellarum*, owed to Ptolemy's *Almagest*. D'Ailly most certainly made good use of Jacopo d'Angelo's 1406 translation of Ptolemy's *Geography*, as is shown by the two compendia of the *Cosmographia* included in d'Ailly and Gerson's *Tractatus*. But at the time he composed *Ymago mundi* (1410), d'Ailly probably remained unfamiliar with the maps that had been constructed by Maximus Planudes around 1300 on the basis of Ptolemy's instructions. The maps we know today as distinctly Ptolemaic only appeared with Francesco Lapacino and Domenico Buoninsegni's 1415 translation of the *Geography*, too late for d'Ailly to have used them in his treatise.[82]

A number of features on d'Ailly's *mappamundi* alert us to crucial concepts for apprehending Columbus's understanding of the world map. First, this *mappamundi* constituted an explicit rejection of the cartographic model offered by tripartite *mappaemundi* produced in the aftermath of the Crusades, which sometimes located Jerusalem at the center of a disklike inhabited world and which ascribed axial importance to the relation between this center and its periphery rather than to differences in latitude among places. The best-known example of such *mappaemundi* is perhaps the map held today in Hereford Cathedral (about 1290), which shows Jerusalem's walls as a crenellated circle at the center of the map (with the figure of the Crucifixion hovering just above it) and the monstrous races along the right-hand edge of the map, presumably, in the southernmost hinterlands of the *orbis terrarum* (**fig. 3.3**). As d'Ailly explains in his consideration of the *ante-climata* that, by Ptolemy's *Almagest*, were supposed to mirror the canonical *climata* from the southern hemisphere, Jerusalem was no more the center of the inhabited world than had been Rome or Greece. Christian geographers had claimed, on the basis of the famous passages in Psalm 73 [74]:12 and Ezekiel 5:5, that Jerusalem stood at the center of all nations. D'Ailly carefully qualified this claim, explaining that Jerusalem only stood at the center of the seven *climata*, that is, in the middle of the northern hemisphere. For d'Ailly, and for his Arab predecessors, the true geographical center of the world map was a city that the Arabs had called Arym. This city was supposed to stand on the very equator, equally separating the northern from the southern hemisphere as well as the eastern from the western portions of the inhabited world.[83] In fact, Jerusalem figures not at all in the version of d'Ailly's *mappamundi* annotated by Columbus! And Columbus did not fail to draw the same distinction between Jerusalem as the spiritual center of all nations, which he *did* firmly believe, and Jerusalem as the geographical center depicted by tripartite *mappaemundi*. On the margins of this passage in d'Ailly's *Ymago mundi*, Columbus dutifully noted "the error of locating Jerusalem at the center of the earth."[84] Indeed, it may not be far-fetched to suggest that in d'Ailly's motion to displace the geographical center from Jerusalem to Arym, we are already witnessing the transition from a geographical imaginary that regarded the Mediterranean basin as the absolute, temperate middle between a cold periphery to the north and a hot periphery to the south, to an imaginary that was beginning to regard the Mediterranean as merely the northern fringe of a far broader geographical system, the middle of which was now the equator itself.

3.3 Hereford *mappamundi*, about 1290. From a facsimile by Schuler-Verlag, Stuttgart, Germany. Courtesy of the Dean and Chapter of Hereford Cathedral, Hereford, United Kingdom.

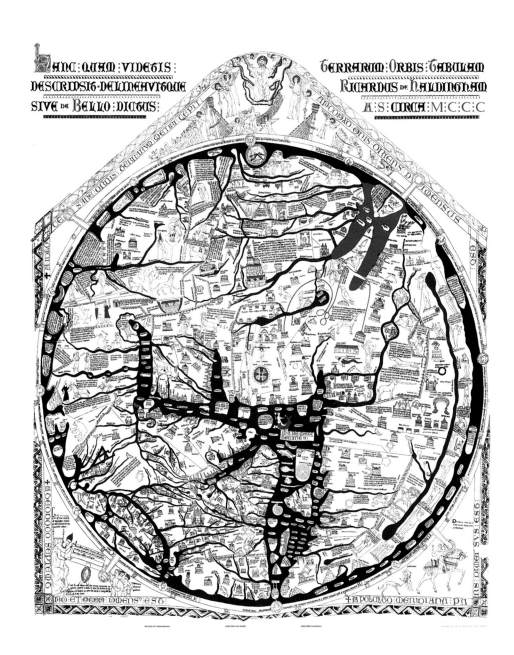

It is also of great significance that d'Ailly should have considered India as extending all the way to the Tropic of Capricorn, a notion that he explicitly borrowed from the passages we have mentioned in Pliny's *Naturalis historia*. On the margins of d'Ailly's assertion regarding the latitudinal reach of India, we find a crucial postil by Columbus that reads: "It should be understood that the side of India that is toward us, that is, toward Spain, extends from the north all the way to the Tropic of Capricorn."[85] Again, d'Ailly's *mappamundi,* which is meant to illustrate the above information, unequivocally depicted India as part of a larger geographical system extending far into the tropics. India's tropicality is signified on this map by the vertical direction of the letters spelling out its name, to the east of an equally vertical Red Sea and of sub-Saharan Africa. A legend located between the First Clime (Meroë) and the equator, reads thus: "It is said that India covers one-third of the world, extending all the way to the south." And on the left hand side of the map, below the equator, another legend reads: "These climes all the way to the equator and beyond contain many habitations, as can be gathered from authentic histories."

The momentous arrival of Ptolemy's *Geography* (about 1400) in the Latin West and the discoveries conducted by the Portuguese beyond Cape Bojador undoubtedly enabled European cartographers in the second half of the fifteenth century to begin to visualize a vast and rich and populous world in the torrid zone (**figs. 1.1**, pp. 62–63; **1.6**, pp. 80–81; and **2.2**, pp. 120–121). Ptolemy's influential work specifically placed the northernmost and southernmost limits of the known inhabited world at 63° N and 16° 25′ S (approximately eighty degrees in latitude), and its easternmost and westernmost limits at 119° 30′ E and 60° 30′ W of the meridian of Alexandria (approximately 180 degrees in longitude).[86] Ptolemy corrected the estimates of his predecessor Marinos of Tyre regarding the latitude and longitude of the known inhabited world. Marinos had placed the northernmost and southernmost limits of the known world at 63° N and at the Winter Tropic, or Tropic of Capricorn (23° 51′ S), and its easternmost and westernmost limits—the mainland port of Kattigara (in Southeast Asia) and the Isles of the Blest (Canary Islands)—fifteen one-hour intervals apart. This made the known inhabited world 86.5 degrees in latitude and 225 degrees in longitude.[87] Columbus was thoroughly acquainted with Ptolemy's *Geography,* and he of course preferred Marinos's measurement for the known inhabited world because it would have greatly extended Asia's easternmost reach and narrowed down the ocean between the Canaries and the end of the Orient from 180 degrees to merely 135 degrees in longitude.

Significantly, both Ptolemy and Marinos located a major portion of the known inhabited world within the belt of the tropics. Ptolemy's southernmost latitude of 16° 25′ S mirrored the latitude of the parallel of Meroë on the northern hemisphere (16° 25′ N).[88] In the heart of Africa, just beyond this parallel, Ptolemy pointed to an uncharted region of Aethiopia Interior that he called Agysimba, the region later mentioned by Columbus in his postil to d'Ailly's "De quantitate terre habitabilis," which was meant to emphasize the latitudinal extent of Portugal's discoveries into the southern hemisphere (**fig. 3.4**).[89] According to Ptolemy, Marinos of Tyre had located Aethiopia Interior's Agysimba and "Indian" Africa's Cape Prason considerably farther south, along the Tropic of Capricorn (23° 51′ S). In Atlantic Africa, Ptolemy charted the inhabited world to an otherwise unidentified coastal location called Hypodromus Aethiopiae that he placed at 5° 15′ N.[90]

On Africa's eastern shores, Ptolemy's southernmost outpost was Cape Prason at 8° 25′ S, perhaps Cape Delgado on Mozambique's northern border (modern 10° 45′ S). And the farthest location known to Ptolemy in southeast Asia was Kattigara at 8° 30′ S, today disputably identified with Hanoi (see, respectively, "Rhaptum promonturium" and "Cattigara" on **fig. 2.2**, pp. 120–121).[91] Nearly the entire African and Asian coastline connecting Cape Prason and Kattigara converged on a landlocked sea that Ptolemy had explicitly encased between the tropics of Cancer and Capricorn. As we know, Ptolemy had enclosed this "tropical" sea by drawing a hypothetical littoral joining Cape Prason and Kattigara, so that the eastern and southern rims of what we know today as the Indian Ocean opened toward terra incognita to the east and to the south. Thus Ptolemy's terra incognita to the east suggests that while he may have measured the longitude of his *oikoumenē* at 180°, he was accounting only for the *known* part of the inhabited world and conceded that it might extend well beyond the easternmost boundary marked by Kattigara. More important, the uncharted African region of Agysimba and the southern rim of the Indian Ocean gestured in Ptolemy's world map toward what one can only interpret as the Cratesian *antoikoumenē,* which was supposed to mirror the known inhabited world from the southern hemisphere.

One can only imagine the skepticism with which Christian geographers who preferred the closed geographical model of the inhabited world proposed by Augustine would have regarded the convention of showing the confines of Africa and the Indian Ocean as terra incognita. The world map included in the 1482 Ulm edition of Ptolemy's *Geography* may well have registered this theological scruple in the form of a disclaimer that reads not simply "Terra incognita," as did the earlier printed editions of 1477 (Bologna) and 1478 (Rome), but rather "Terra incognita secundum Ptholomeum" (unknown land according to Ptolemy) (**fig. 2.2**, pp. 120–121; compare to **figs. 1.1**, pp. 62–63, and **1.6**, pp. 80–81).[92] But Ptolemy's picture of sub-Saharan Africa and the Indian Ocean basin as a herculean geographical system that could hardly be construed as the outer fringes of a world revolving around the Mediterranean was meant to win ground in the end. Indeed, the belt of the tropics gradually usurped center stage on world maps, acquiring ever-greater specificity and weight as cartographers began to correct and augment Ptolemy's projections in order to reflect the discoveries conducted by Portugal and Castile in the course of the fifteenth and early sixteenth centuries.

For the period immediately preceding Columbus's discoveries, our prime example is Martin Behaim's globe of 1492 (**fig. I.3**, pp. 12–13). Behaim's globe unequivocally illustrates why anyone thinking of sailing "by way of the West" to the so-called Indies, might have anticipated sailing west across the Atlantic *and* south into the lower latitudes of the globe then known as the torrid zone. Behaim probably resided in Portugal at the same time as Columbus, although it is not clear that they ever met.[93] But, like Columbus, Behaim may have seen the tropics firsthand, for it appears that he traveled with the Portuguese to Guinea between 1484 and 1485. And, like Columbus, Behaim came to inform himself very thoroughly concerning the discoveries of the Portuguese in Atlantic Africa: the globe he constructed upon his return to Nuremberg is widely considered today the state of the art on the eve of the discovery. Behaim's principal sources were the Ulm edition of Ptolemy's *Geography* (1482), Isidore of Seville's *Etymologiae,* a German edition of Marco Polo's *Il milione* (Nuremberg, 1477), and, most likely, a number of portolan charts afforded by the new discoveries in Atlantic Africa.[94] His globe traced the trajectory of the Portuguese just beyond the Cape of Good Hope, rounded by Bartholomeu Dias in 1488, to a place labeled Cabo Ledo (Joyful Cape).

Behaim's globe amended the Ptolemaic view of the inhabited world in crucial ways. First, owing to the recent experience of the Portuguese, this globe no longer portrayed the Indian Ocean as a *mare clausum,* or a landlocked sea. Second, it showed rather matter-of-factly what the young Alessandro Geraldini would have dared to voice earlier that year at the assembly that had gathered in Santa Fe to discuss Columbus's project: that the Portuguese had already crossed the entire span of a perfectly navigable and inhabitable torrid zone along Atlantic Africa, reaching beyond the Tropic of Capricorn into the southern temperate zone. In other words, the Portuguese had charted inhabited land well beyond the modest limits of Ptolemy's *oikoumenē* (16° 25′ S), and even beyond the more generous limits of Marinos's inhabited world—the Tropic of Capricorn.

3.4 Regional map of Africa in the edition known to Columbus. From Ptolemy's *Cosmographia* (Rome, 1478). Courtesy of The John Carter Brown Library, Providence, Rhode Island.

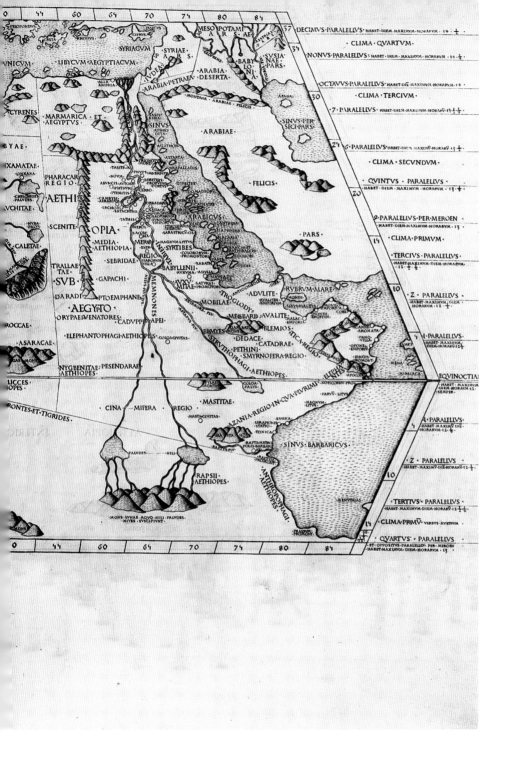

And this realization concerning the latitude of the *orbis terrarum* appears to have been of immediate consequence for Behaim's portrayal of its longitude: since Ptolemy's predecessor, Marinos, had more closely approximated the extent of the inhabited world reaching into the southern hemisphere (all the way down to the Tropic of Capricorn), why not assume that Marinos's generous measurement for the longitude of the inhabited world was also closer to the truth? This may well be why Behaim was willing to assign a longitude of 234 degrees to the *orbis terrarum,* significantly greater than the 180 degrees assigned to it by Ptolemy. And this does not count the innumerable islands that Behaim was willing to portray extending far to the east of the Asian landmass. Columbus, it seems, was not a lone voice crying out in the wilderness when he claimed that the ocean was narrow between the ends of East and West. This inference evidently floated around already in the minds of those who had considered the extent of Portugal's incursions into the southern hemisphere. Thus, beyond the eastern shores of the Indian Ocean, where Ptolemy had pointed to terra incognita extending indefinitely to the east, Behaim now took license to plot an entire geographical system largely derived from Marco Polo's description of the Far East, specifically, from Marco Polo's own account of India.

Marco Polo's India did not concern itself, at least in the Latin edition of *Il milione* known to Columbus, with the continental inlands reaching toward the northern latitudes of Asia. Marco Polo described instead a *maritime* system, largely concerned with water routes and coastal regions, which is not at all surprising for a merchant, who would have envisioned himself trading through India by boat from one port to another. This maritime India extended all the way from an oceanic archipelago that included the island of Çipango to the coast of Mangi, to the coast of Ciamba, to Indonesian islands like Java Maior and Java Minor, to the inner shores and islands of the Indian Ocean itself, and to the African islands of Madagascar and Zanzibar. Behaim chose to plot this huge maritime system, like Ptolemy's Indian Ocean, squarely under the torrid zone: the island of Çipango and the port of Zaiton, on the southern Chinese mainland, stand directly on the Tropic of Cancer; while Madagascar and Zanzibar—the other bookend to Marco Polo's India—stand on, and just beyond, the Tropic of Capricorn, just off the eastern coast of Africa. Significantly, Behaim still conceived of the ocean waters bathing the shores of Japan, southern China, Malaysia, and Indonesia as an eastern extension of that vast tropical accident we know today as the Indian Ocean. And if Columbus's world picture looked anything like Behaim's, it would have been this eastern extension of India that Columbus may have imagined himself reaching when he thought of sailing out of the lower latitudes of the Canaries with the intention of reaching the East "by way of the West."

It is unfortunate that the *mappamundi* presented by Bartholomew Columbus to King Henry VII of England does not survive. Neither does the nautical chart that Columbus is supposed to have carried with him on his first navigation to the Indies, which according to the *Diario,* displayed "certain isles" that Columbus had drawn on the region of the mysterious sea he thought he was traversing in the final stages of the outward passage (25 September 1492).[95] Nor do any of the other cartographic works that Columbus promised to draft for King Fernando and Queen Isabel.[96] Had these works survived, and if they did provide significant geographical information other than that contained by works like Behaim's globe, we might have more conclusively answered where Columbus believed he was heading.

It does appear that Columbus, who may have learned the craft from his own brother Bartholomew, was an able cartographer. Some scholars have even fancied the two brothers making a living drawing and selling nautical charts since their earliest days in Portugal, although this claim cannot be substantiated, given the dearth of information surrounding Columbus's early career.[97] It is also true that one ought to read the Discoverer's own claims about the early Columbus with caution, since the late Columbus did develop a penchant for aggrandizing himself in the face of mounting opposition for his failed policies in Hispaniola and of deepening skepticism concerning the nature of his enterprise. And yet he may not have been bragging altogether when he famously recounted for Fernando and Isabel what he had sought to learn in the arts of navigation and cosmography early on in his career.

In the cover letter he wrote for the celebrated *Libro de las profecías* in 1501 or 1502 urging the Catholic Monarchs to take on the task of reconquering Jerusalem, Columbus provided an intriguing account of the relationship between the art of navigation, which for him would have involved an understanding of all the *artes* involved in establishing one's location on the globe, and scientific knowledge itself, suggestively encoded in this letter as "knowledge of the secrets of this world":

Very High Majesties: at a very young age, I began sailing the sea, and have continued to do so until today. *The very art of navigation predisposes he who practices it to want to know the secrets of this world*. I have been trying to do so now for over forty years.

I have dealt and conversed with learned men, ecclesiastical and secular, Latins and Greeks, Jews and Moors, and many others of other sects. I found Our Lord to be well disposed toward this my wish, and I received from Him the spirit of intelligence to carry it out. *In the marine arts, He made me knowledgeable, and gave me enough understanding of astrology, as well as of geometry and arithmetic, and also the ingenuity of soul and the manual skills to draw spheres and, on them, cities, rivers and mountains, islands and ports, each in its proper place.* In this time I have come upon and have sought all manners of writings on cosmography, histories, chronicles, and philosophy and other arts, to which Our Lord palpably opened my understanding with His hand, so that I should see it possible to navigate from here to the Indies, and He imparted in me the necessary strength of will to do so. With this fire I came to Your Highnesses.[98]

However we judge Columbus's assertions about the divine origin and girth of his interests, this passage does speak to a sensible understanding of the skills involved in drawing things in their "proper place" on the world map. And it is not just the Discoverer who paid the early Columbus the compliment of having crafted himself as an able cartographer. This may well have been part of the impetus behind the tribute paid to Columbus by Jaume Ferrer de Blanes when, in 1495, the preeminent cosmographer stated that he was happy to stand corrected in his method for placing the meridian of Tordesillas "by those who know and understand more than myself, especially by the Admiral of the Indies, who is more learned in these matters than anyone in our time, *for he is a great theoretician and an admirable practitioner,* as his memorable achievements manifest."[99]

Other early sources attest to Columbus's abilities as a cartographer: Andrés Bernáldez, a close acquaintance of Columbus, soberly asserted in *Historia de los Reyes Católicos Don Fernando y Doña Isabel* (completed 1513) that Columbus was "a man of very great ingenuity, not very well read, [but] very well versed in the art of Cosmography and of dividing up the world."[100] Hernán Pérez de Oliva, who in *Historia de la inuencion de las yndias* (completed in 1528) described Columbus as "barely trained in letters but very greatly trained in the art of navigation," also believed that, upon Columbus's arrival in Portugal, "where a certain brother of his [i.e., Bartholomew] painted the images of the world used by mariners," Columbus had "learned from him all that can be learned by means of painting [i.e., by means of drafting maps]."[101] Gonzalo Fernández de Oviedo, who hailed Columbus as "the first inventor and discoverer and admiral of these Indies," claimed in the first part of *Historia general y natural de las Indias* (1535) that Columbus was "well read and learned" in what the official chronicler of the Indies calls the "science" of "navigation and cosmography."[102] Columbus's son Ferdinand, who boasts a distinct preference for tying Columbus's abilities to studious reading, asserted for his part that, "because Ptolemy says at the opening of his *Geography* that no one can be a good cosmographer unless he also knows how to draw, [Columbus] learned how to draw the earth and configure geographical bodies plane and round."[103] Francisco López de Gómara even believed in *Historia general de las Indias y conquista de México* (1552) that Columbus had long displayed a talent as a master or teacher in the art of drawing nautical charts, and that his primary reason for moving to Portugal in the first place had been to inform himself of Portugal's discoveries in Atlantic Africa, "so that he might better draft and sell his charts."[104] And Bartolomé de las Casas assures us in *Historia de las Indias* that during the years of penury that accompanied Columbus's lobbying in the court of Castile, he had been reduced to supporting himself by recourse to "the industriousness of his great ingenuity and the labor of his hands, making or drawing nautical charts, which he knew very well how to make . . . [and] selling them to navigators."[105]

The few surviving sketches thought to be in his hand do bear out such laudatory assessments of Columbus's draftsmanship: the reticular arrangement of the northern hemisphere attached to the opening folios of d'Ailly and Gerson's *Tractatus,* the reticulated planisphere drafted on the blank folios of Piccolomini's *Historia rerum ubique gestarum,* and the devastatingly simple sketch of the island of Hispaniola (Haiti) preserved today in the Palacio de Liria in Madrid—the only fragment to have survived of the original *Diario* (**figs. 3.5, 3.6,** and **3.7**).[106] Some still believe that the extraordinary calfskin in the Bibliothèque Nationale in Paris bearing a portolan chart and an island-shaped *mappamundi* once attributed to Columbus may at least have indirectly inherited some of its cartographic peculiarities from Columbus on the brink of the discovery; however, apart from displaying the huge southward reach of Portugal's discoveries in Atlantic Africa (all the way down to *Cabo Redondo* in the case of the portolan, and to *Cabo de Buena Esperanza* in that of the *mappamundi*) these maps betray no traces of transatlantic ambition (**fig. 3.8**).[107]

Of the few cartographic works that have been associated with Columbus, one more set of maps deserves mention, even though the maps date from the end of Columbus's

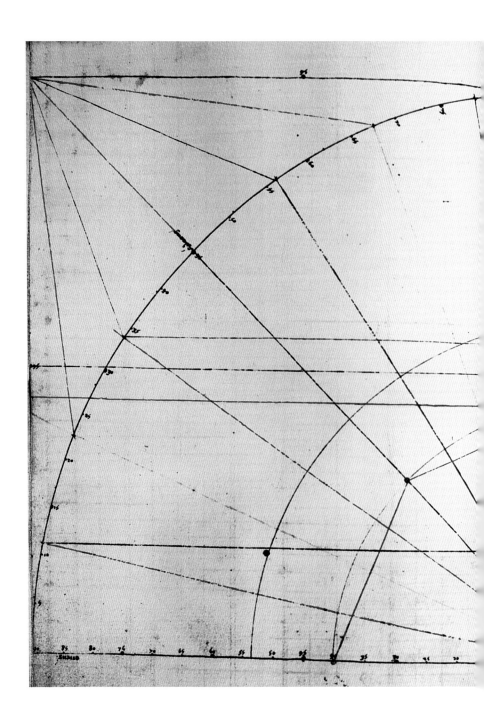

3.5   Columbus's reticular
arrangement for the northern
hemisphere. From Pierre d'Ailly and
Jean Gerson, *Tractatus de ymagine
mundi et varia ejusdem auctoris et
Joannis Gersonis opuscula* (1480–
1483), Tabula Americae, facs. no.
852 (Madrid, 1990), 5v–6r. Courtesy
of the Institución Colombina,
Biblioteca Colombina, Seville, Spain;
and Testimonio Compañía Editorial,
Madrid, Spain.

3.6 Columbus's reticulated planisphere. From Aeneas Sylvius Piccolomini, *Historia rerum ubique gestarum: Cum locorum descriptione non finita Asia Minor incipit* (1477), Tabula Americae, facs. no. 186 (Madrid, 1991), appended booklet, 5r. Courtesy of the Institución Colombina, Seville, Spain; and Testimonio Compañia Editorial, Madrid, Spain.

career, about 1506, and even though the originals appear to have been drafted by Bartholomew in his brother's name. Upon Columbus's return from his fourth voyage in 1504, having failed to find a passageway from the Caribbean basin into what he believed would be the inner sanctum of the Indian Ocean, and aware that he could never again return to full grace with the Crown, Columbus appears to have sent his brother Bartholomew to Italy with the aim of enlisting the pope's assistance in future ventures. It is from this final period of Columbus's life that we have a copy of the so-called *Lettera*

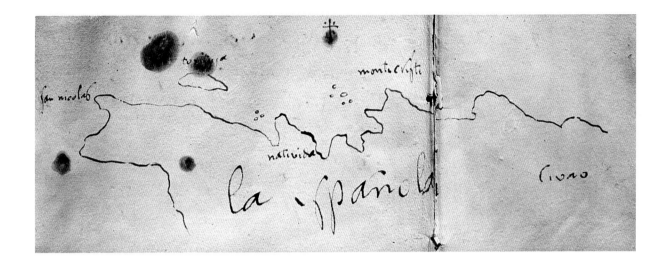

rarissima (7 July 1503), which recounts the disastrous events of the fourth voyage, as well as three geographical sketches derived from Bartholomew's documents, in Alessandro Zorzi's *Informazione di Bartolomeo Colombo della Navegazione di ponente et di garbin di Beragua nel Mondo Novo.*[108]

The first two sketches, which should be read in horizontal contiguity with each other, draw on a graduated matrix provided by Ptolemy's *Geography* and are distinctly localized on the band comprehended by the Tropic of Cancer (24° N) and the "Linea Capricornii" (24° S) (**figs. 3.9** and **3.10**; and see **fig. 3.11**). In line with Columbus's preference for Marinos of Tyre's measurements for the breadth and width of the inhabited world over Ptolemy's, the author of these two sketches portrays the newly discovered landmass of Santa Crose and the Antipodi (South America), as well as Aethiopia Interior (sub-Saharan Africa) and the eastern continental coastline on which Ptolemy had once located the port of Kattigara (marked on the second map by the legends "Catticara sinarum statio" and "Sinarum situs"), as extending all the way to and just beyond Marinos's limit for the inhabited world—the Tropic of Capricorn. And warning us that, "according to Marinos and Columbus, [the distance] from Cape Saint Vincent to Kattigara measures 225 degrees [or] 15 hours," the cartographer makes room beyond the terra incognita originally located by Ptolemy to the east of Kattigara for the continental coastline recently explored by Columbus during his fourth voyage

3.7 Columbus's sketch of northern Hispaniola (Haiti), 1493. Courtesy of the Archive of the House of Alba, Palacio de Liria, Madrid, Spain.

3.8 Portolan chart and *mappamundi* once attributed to Columbus, about 1492. Courtesy of the Bibliothèque Nationale, Paris, France.

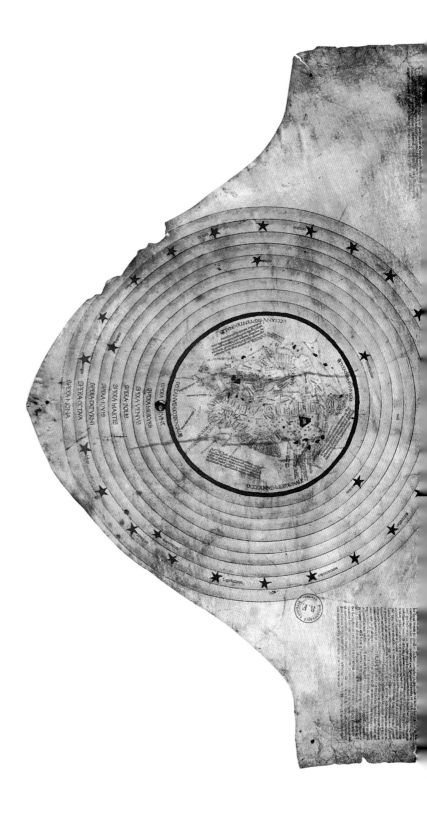

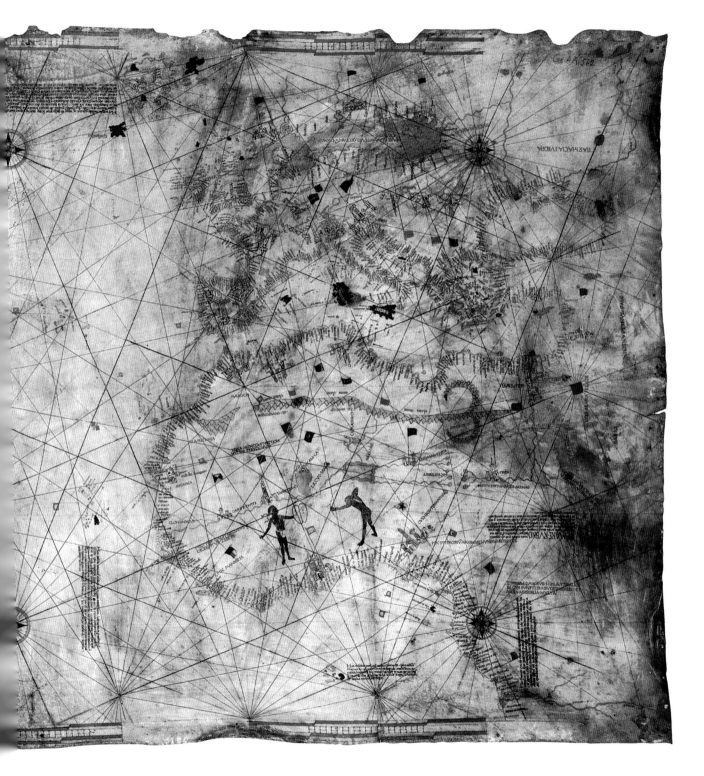

3.9 Sketch of Africa and of the land of Santa Crose and the antipodes, based on a design by Bartholomew Columbus. From Alessandro Zorzi, *Informazione di Bartolomeo Colombo della Navegazione di ponente et garbin di Beragua nel Mondo Novo* (about 1506), Collezione Alberico, no. 81, 56v. Courtesy of the Biblioteca Nazionale Centrale, Florence, Italy.

3.10   Sketch of the extended basin of the Indian Ocean with the coastline presumably explored by Columbus on his fourth voyage, based on a design by Bartholomew Columbus. From Alessandro Zorzi, *Informazione di Bartolomeo Colombo della Navegazione di ponente et garbin di Beragua nel Mondo Novo* (about 1506), Collezione Alberico, no. 81, 57r. Courtesy of the Biblioteca Nazionale Centrale, Florence, Italy.

3.11 Outlines after figs. 3.9
and 3.10, prepared by the author.

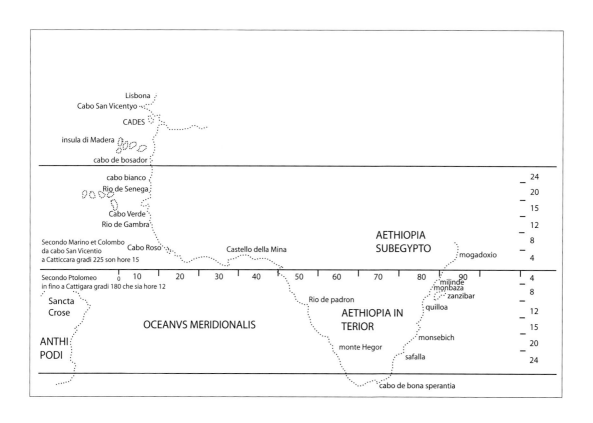

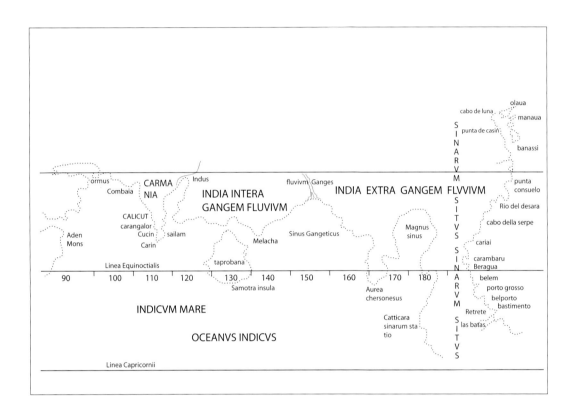

Aden
Mons

ormus
Combaia

CARMA
NIA

Indus

CALICUT
carangalor
Cucin
Carin   sailam

INDIA INTERA
GANGEM FLUVIVM

fluvivm Ganges

INDIA EXTRA GANGEM FLVVIVM

taprobana

Samotra insula

Melacha

Sinus Gangeticus

Magnus
sinus

Linea Equinoctialis

90   100   110   120   130   140   150   160   170   180

Aurea
chersonesus

Catticara
sinarum sta
tio

INDICVM MARE

OCEANVS INDICVS

Linea Capricornii

S
I
N
A
R
V
M

olaua

cabo de luna
manaua

punta de casiñ

banassi

S
I
T
V
S

punta
consuelo

Rio del desara

cabo della serpe

cariai

S
I
N
A
R
V
M

carambaru
Beragua

belem

porto grosso

belporto
bastimento

S
I
T
V
S

Retrete
las batas

(i.e., Central America). This easternmost coastline is unequivocally construed as part of India beyond the Ganges ("India extra Gangem fluvium") and as the region of the Sinai ("Sinarum Situs"), which is how the Chinese had come to be known from the south, along the trade routes of the Indian Ocean. And it runs all the way from a cape designated "Cabo de Luna"—which may signal Columbus's stubborn conviction that Cuba's inner shores connected beyond the Bay of Cortés with the coast of Central America—down to a bay or a truncated sea inlet incorrectly labeled "Las Barbas"—which appears to signal Columbus's frustrated search for a passage to the Indian Ocean's inner sanctum through the Mulatas archipelago, today near the Panamanian Gulf of San Blas. The question is also left open on these two sketches as to whether the coastline explored by Columbus on his fourth voyage is continuous with the newly discovered landmass of Santa Crose or the Antipodi, that is, with South America as known to the Portuguese in Brazil (on the southwesternmost corner of the first sketch). What does remain exceedingly clear on these two sketches is that Columbus's exploration of the coast of Central America is construed by their author as part of a broader process of exploration that had largely taken place under the belt of the tropics, all the way from the Canaries and Cape Bojador to the easternmost reaches of India *extra Gangem*.

The third sketch represents the newly emerging Atlantic world between the ends of the East and the West (**fig. 3.12**). Predicated once again on a graduated matrix of Ptolemaic provenance, this sketch is now distinctly centered on the half-band comprehended by the Tropic of Cancer ("Linea cancri") and the equator ("Linea equinoctialis"). It incorporates the discoveries conducted by the Portuguese in Atlantic Africa all the way from Cape Bojador to São Jorge da Mina ("Cabo Bosador" and "Mina San Gorge," respectively), as well as those in Brazil ("Santa Crose"), with the discoveries conducted under the Castilian banner across the Atlantic—mainly those places found by Columbus in the course of his four voyages. Insofar as it may be thought to reflect Columbus's composite understanding of the territories he had discovered, this sketch gestures toward Cuba, encoded here by "Cabo de luna" in today's Bay of Cortés, as part of an Asiatic mainland reaching toward the northwest in the direction of the Seres or Silk People ("Serica"), the name by which the Chinese had come to be known by way of the north, along the inland routes of the silk. The Cuban "mainland," along with the islands of the Greater and Lesser Antilles discovered during the first and second voyages (marked here as "Jamaicha," "Spagnola," "Carucura," "Guadalupa," "Dominica," and "Canibali") stand directly across from the "Canaria," just outside or across from the Tropic of Cancer—perhaps still echoing Columbus's original fear of disclosing to the Crowns of Castile and Portugal that he had ventured below the latitude of the Canary Islands on his first voyage. In the middle of the Atlantic, toward the equator, stands a distinctly antipodal mainland designated "New World" ("Mondo novo"), which includes the "Sea of Fresh Water" found by Columbus at the mouth of the Orinoco River, as well as the Gulf of Paria on today's Venezuela and the "Mouth of the Dragon" between the Paria Peninsula and the island of Trinidad ("Mar de agua dolce," "Paria," and "Boca dil dragon," respectively). This antipodal mainland no doubt corresponds to what Columbus had imagined as "infinite land that is to the south"—what he had hailed, when speaking of his third voyage to the equatorial region, as a near-miraculous find in "the new heaven and earth that had until then remained hidden."[109] On the western margin in this sketch, the cartographer also tried to reconcile the Central American coastline explored by Columbus on his fourth voyage with the easternmost reaches of Ptolemy's Asia: a sea inlet or strait labeled "Retrete" (perhaps Puerto Escribanos in today's Panama) gestures toward the Ptolemaic Kattigara ("Bahia cattigara"), signaling once again Columbus's belief that somewhere between the Cuban "mainland" and the land of Paria a passage would be found into the Indian Ocean. We may never know the extent to which the author of this sketch altered the contents of the documents that Bartholomew is supposed to have brought with him to Rome.[110] Were Bartholomew's own sketches copied straight onto the folios of Zorzi's *Informazione,* or did they merely supply raw information used in creating a substantially different set of maps? And if these sketches do faithfully represent Columbus and his brother's picture of the region Columbus had explored in the course of his transatlantic career, to what extent do they reflect his identification of the place he was originally aiming for? Nonetheless, whoever the author of this sketch might have been, he clearly conceived of the new Atlantic as a world weighted toward the precious belt of the tropics.

A final word is in order on the subject of India's nature in the geographical tradition preceding the discovery—much of which was established by the earliest known Greek and Latin Indographers. Among these early authors, Herodotus appears to have been the first to speak of India as a fabulously wealthy gold-bearing region whose vast scorching deserts were guarded by gold-digging ants bigger than foxes.[111] According to Herodotus, India's inhabitants harvested the gold away from these giant ants by waiting for the high noon sun to drive them underground. India's mountains and rivers were also

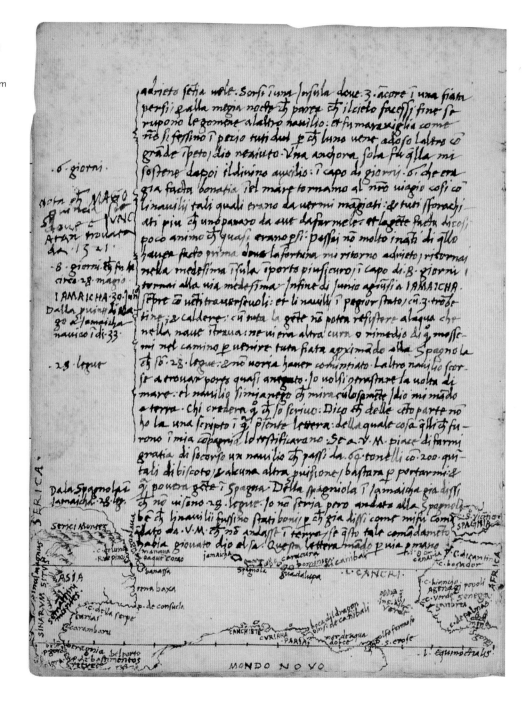

3.12 Sketch of Asia, Africa, and the *Mondo novo*, based on a design by Bartholomew Columbus, with outline prepared by the author. From Alessandro Zorzi, *Informazione di Bartolomeo Colombo della Navegazione di ponente et garbin di Beragua nel Mondo Novo* (about 1506), Collezione Alberico, no. 81, 60v. Courtesy of the Biblioteca Nazionale Centrale, Florence, Italy.

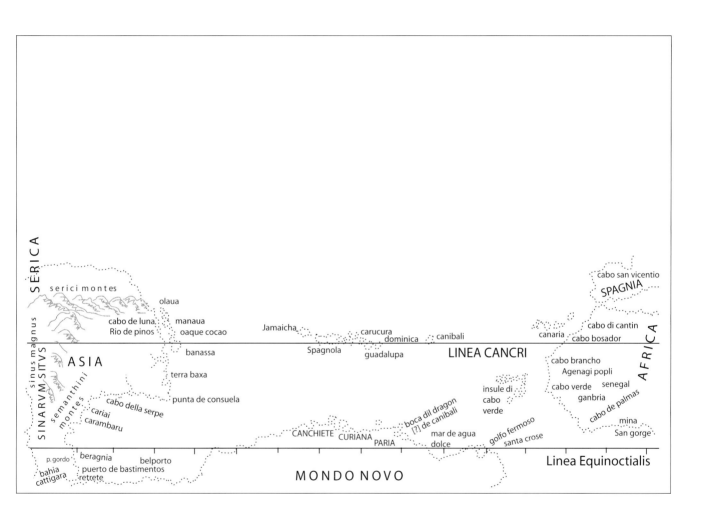

SERICA

serici montes

olaua

cabo de luna   manaua

Rio de pinos   oaque cocao

sinus magnus

ASIA

banassa

terra baxa

SINARVM SITVS

semanthini montes

cariai

carambaru

cabo della serpe

punta de consuela

p. gordo   beragnia   belporto

bahia   puerto de bastimentos

cattigara   retrete

Jamaicha

Spagnola

carucura

dominica   canibali

guadalupa

LINEA CANCRI

CANCHIETE   CURIANA

PARIA

boca dil dragon

[?] de canibali

mar de agua

dolce

MONDO NOVO

insule di

cabo

verde

golfo fermoso

santa crose

cabo san vicentio

SPAGNIA

canaria

cabo di cantin

cabo bosador

cabo brancho

Agenagi popli

AFRICA

cabo verde   senegal

ganbria

cabo de palmas

mina

San gorge

Linea Equinoctialis

213

great sources of gold.[112] According to Photios's *Library*, Ctesias additionally described gold-bearing Indian wonders such as a "fountain that filled every year with liquid gold from which a hundred pitcherfuls [were] drawn,"[113] as well as very tall silver- and gold-bearing mountains guarded by griffins.[114] Ctesias's account of these and other marvels, Photios warns us, omitted "many far more marvellous things, for fear that those who had not seen them might think that his account was utterly untrustworthy."[115] Isidore would later add dragons and oversized human monsters to the list of treasure guardians, an association one later sees in Columbus's claims that various gold-bearing quarters of his Indies were inhabited by ferocious man-eaters.[116] Like Ctesias, the Indographers Megasthenes and Diodorus Siculus imagined India's soil rife with most numerous veins bursting with gold, silver, copper, iron, and tin.[117] Strabo, for his part, whose distaste for exaggeration led him to speak ill of Herodotus's and Ctesias's ants, could not help but cite Megasthenes' description of precious stones "dug up of the color of frankincense and sweeter than figs or honey."[118] And Pliny, who spoke of Sri Lanka as an island far away, "relegated from the orb," said that it was even more abundant in gold and pearls than the mainland and that its great prodigality in gold, silver, pearls, and precious stones made it a place where luxury was carried "to a far higher pitch than ours."[119] On the abundance of pearls, Arrian tells his readers that Heracles had not known them before finding them in India and that pearls there were worth three times their weight in pure gold.[120] Solinus later cited even more exotic minerals like diamonds, magnetic iron ore (or lodestone), and a white marble known as lycnite.[121] Isidore would add a long list of precious and semiprecious stones, including beryl, chrysoprase, diamonds, carbuncles, and a variety of coal known as lignite.[122] Needless to say, Columbus's writing displays abundant references to a marvelous mineral bounty, not just to the inexhaustible gold deposits he thought would be harvested from the mountaintops, mines, and rivers of his Indies, but also to its abundant pearls and to "countless" other precious metals and stones.

As for plants, the territories of India, according to Megasthenes, "possess huge mountains that abound in fruit-trees of very kind, and many vast plains of great fertility,"[123] very numerous plants, most of which grew spontaneously from the soil,[124] and, most importantly, two annual harvests.[125] The inhabitants had "abundant means of subsistence,"[126] so much so, that in "primitive times" they had subsisted "on such fruits as the earth yielded spontaneously."[127] Diodorus Siculus offers perhaps the most vivid portrayal of nature's nurture of peoples who would have had no need to worry or toil:

"India has many lofty mountains that abound in fruit trees of every variety, and many large and fertile plains, which are remarkable for their beauty and are supplied with water by a multitude of rivers," all of which yielded vast amounts of millet, rice, and so many sorts of fruit that, "to write about them would be a long task." Thanks to all this, "a famine has never visited India or, in general, any scarcity of what is suitable for gentle fare." And by reason of the fact that the land enjoyed every year two summers and two harvests, Indians never lost anything, "since the fruit of one or the other sowing comes to maturity." In many cases it was not even necessary to till the ground, since nature automatically produced enough for everyone: "The fruits also which flourish wild and the roots which grow in the marshy places, by reason of their remarkable sweetness, provide the people with a great abundance of food."[128] Nature's overweening care not only supplied the vegetable basis for a thriving food chain, but it also created all sorts of monstrous vegetation.

Strabo, citing Onesicritus, reports "numerous strange trees," including gigantic ones "whose branches have first grown to the height of twelve cubits, and then, after such growth, have grown downwards, as though bent down, till they have touched the earth."[129] Apart from producing coveted spices like "cinnamon, nard, and other aromatic products," India was a country "abounding in herbs and roots both curative and poisonous."[130] According to Pomponius Mela, India was so rich that "honey drips from the leaves, trees bear wool, and rafts of split bamboo even convey, like ships, two persons at a time, some even conveying three at a time."[131] And Pliny reported trees "so lofty that it is not possible to shoot an arrow over them," and the soil was so rich that "if one is willing to believe it, squadrons of cavalry are able to shelter beneath a single fig-tree."[132] Isidore, for his part, marvels at the "perennial" nature of tree leaves on the Indian island of Tile.[133]

Columbus's Indies were themselves, as one reads in his 15 February 1493 letter to Santángel announcing the discovery, "fertile to an unthinkable degree" (*fertilissimas en demasiado grado*).[134] Like the early Indographers, he marveled at its biannual harvests; at the fact that its trees and shrubs never lost their foliage; and at the overwhelming scale of its mountains, fields, rivers, and basins—all of which amounted to an overindulgent nature that spontaneously and continuously generated the greatest sizes, quantities, varieties, and qualities of plants imaginable. And the natural products to be had from these plants ranged from goods Columbus thought he recognized—such as aloe, cinnamon, cotton, ginger, honey, incense, mastic, pepper, sandal, timber, and wax—to entirely alien goods that prompted Columbus to lament his speechless ignorance, even as he wildly speculated that they could be put to the broadest range of uses—from shipbuilding to dying textiles, cooking, and curing disease.[135] Like the early Indographers, Columbus also marveled at the vegetable monstrosity of his Indies—from wild grass that grew "taller than the saddles on our horses," to skyscraping or wide-spanning trees "as different from ours as the day is from the night" (*tan disformes de los nuestros como el dia de la noche*), and to enormous "fruit of a thousand kinds, and all different from ours and different in flavor [*diversas de las nuestras y del savor*], but no less precious."[136]

Nature's profligacy and gigantism extended even to those vegetable products that were soon introduced to the island of Hispaniola on the second voyage. Columbus's accounts of the first efforts to colonize the newly discovered territories attest to the carefulness with which he monitored the testing of known species of edibles on foreign ground. In the same letter where Columbus triumphantly informed the Catholic Monarchs that his Indies yielded two harvests annually, he explained that

> the orchard seeds that we brought with us all germinated within three days, and we were able to eat vegetables within fifteen days. And any other seeds that were to be planted would all do the same. . . . The fruit pits we brought were all born within seven days, and so are the vine shoots born that were brought from Castile. They were planted and, within a month, they grew . . . clusters all over. The same with the sugar cane. Melons and pepins and cucumbers bore fruit within forty days of being planted, and they ripened, and we now have them every day—and the best melons that anyone has ever seen! They were planted in January, and by the beginning of March, we were already eating them. And I understand that we will have them all year long, as well as calabashes. I ordered very little wheat to be planted, because we lacked the right tools and it was winter [i.e., December] when we came, but for one *fanegada* of land planted, a farmer can expect fifty times the yield. The said wheat germinated very quickly, and on Passover, a great big bundle of it was brought over to the church, all spiked out and seeding. And the same goes for chickpeas and lima beans.[137]

Indeed, the chickpeas and other legumes imported on the second voyage for the sustenance of a colonial population that could hardly stomach "Indian" staples were "far larger than in Castile."[138]

argument, Columbus was rehearsing an indelible link between the fertility of tropical soil and the astounding proliferation of domestic beasts *and* humans in the Indies:

> The chickens born here, grow large enough to eat in eight to twelve days, and very many of them are born. Pigs are multiplied in marvelous numbers. The goats and sheep are few, and so are the mares. The only thing missing here are farmers and beasts to do the plowing, although the latter must be saved [for other purposes], because a horse is worth here more than a fortress, for even though these people are cowardly, they are innumerable, and I believe that there must be millions of millions of them [*cuento de cuentos*]. And when it comes to horses, they cannot bear to wait for them, or even to look at them, for even if there are three thousand of them, one can confidently go at them with just one horse, because they will not dare to wait for it. They believe that horses fly, and speak, and understand [as humans do], and when they sometimes find that they cannot run from a horse, they will then speak to it as if to a man, and, for this reason, I hold [the horses] I have here in great esteem, and I order them to be tended to as much as I possibly can.[183]

In yet another intriguing passage of an earlier letter to Fernando and Isabel (20 January 1494), recounting the exploration of the Lesser Antilles on the same voyage, Columbus accused shipment of the first slaves taken from islands believed to have been plagued by cannibals. And here too Columbus was associating the fertility of the soil with a limitless supply of slave labor: "May Your Highnesses judge whether they [i.e., the inhabitants of the Lesser Antilles] ought to be captured. For I believe that, in this case, every year, infinite numbers [*ynfinitos*] can be had of them and of the women."[184] Columbus was not just promising limitless payloads of Indian slaves. He was promising that these slaves would be even better than any slaves currently imported to Europe from sub-Saharan Africa: "May you also believe that one of them would be worth more than three black slaves from Guinea in strength and ingenuity, as you will gather from those I am now shipping out."

Columbus was certainly never all of one mind concerning the temperature of his Indies. At times he appears to have experienced the infernal heat that was traditionally supposed to desolate tropical places. And it was no doubt in connection with such heat that, like the early Indographers, Columbus would have "seen" gold everywhere his gaze rested, or that signs of gold or other treasure, as with the early Indographers, should have been associated in his writing with the presence of physical and cultural monstrosity. Thus in the recently discovered letter of the second voyage recounting the exploration of the Lesser Antilles (20 January 1494), the southeastern quarter of the Caribbean where he had expected to find the man-eating Caribes, Columbus recalls what he had been told by one of his frightened Indian informants—that, "in these parts of the cannibals, there was a small island, and that three-fourths of it were gold, and now it all makes sense, for I see that the land is suited for [generating gold]."[185] And on the third voyage, when Columbus asked the locals on the Venezuelan mainland where they gathered the gold for the beautiful ornaments they exhibited on their bodies, "they all pointed to a land neighboring theirs, to the west, which was supposed to be high up but not very far from there. But all of them told me not to go there, because they ate men over there, and I then understood that they were cannibals, and that they would be just like the others [i.e., like those allegedly found on the second voyage in the Lesser Antilles]."[186] Indeed, cannibals, whom Columbus first visualized in the manner of Ctesias's cynocephali, and whom he later portrayed as physically "deformed" or "disfigured," were the depraved and unsavory guardians of the gold treasure harbored by an allegedly hot Indies. It goes without saying, that it was also in connection with Indian "heat" that Columbus influentially portrayed the inhabitants of the Bahamas and Caribbean basin as "ingenious" and "cowardly" or downright "cruel," thereby, paving the way to justify their subjection or enslavement.

But for obvious reasons (i.e., the need to sell the idea of a benign and welcoming Indies to those back in Europe), Columbus preferred to attribute to the lands he had discovered a temperateness that in every way alluded to the generous perfection of Eden. We may never know whether Columbus conceived of the temperateness of his Indies as *absolute* in relation to Mediterranean Europe's alleged temperateness, or whether, as is more likely, he considered his Indies to be distinctly hotter than Mediterranean Europe but, simultaneously, relatively temperate compared to the overheated complexion traditionally ascribed to the tropics. Like some of the earliest Indographers, Columbus may also have believed that what should have been the lethal heat of his Indies tended to be counteracted, indeed *tempered,* by the presence of large bodies of water that cooled things down and irrigated the soil. Thus in his account of the exploration and colonization of Hispaniola on the second voyage, Columbus insisted on tying the temperateness and fertility of the island to the proliferation of "great rivers," whose presence suggested that Hispaniola was significantly larger than Spain itself—including "one river that is far greater than any other in Spain."[187]

Whatever value Columbus assigned to the temperateness of his Indies, this temperateness is everywhere directly associated in his writings with uninterrupted and high-pitched fertility and inhabitability—and sometimes also with the physical or psychological traits of the inhabitants. For instance, in the course of the second voyage, as he marveled at the unspeakable beauty of the newly discovered island of Jamaica (26 February 1495), Columbus claimed that "the temperance of the heavens here and in the other islands is such, and so great, that no one would lend credit to his eyes except at spring time. A winter does exist here, but [it is] not very strong. It begins at the same time as in Castile, with similar rainfall and weather. It lasts until January, but there is no snow. And then comes the summer, which is not very hot, just as the winter is not very cold."[188] This temperateness accounted for the perennial activity and accelerated life cycles of plants and beasts in a region of the world that behaved exactly like the place described by the earliest Indographers:

> The trees never shed their leaves at one time or another. The greens and fruit are always bearing fruit; and the birds always have nests, and eggs, and chicks. All of the orchard seeds are always booming; and even other vegetables, if they are planted, will be harvested twice a year. And I can say this about every planted and wild fruit, so good is the aspect of the heavens and the complexion of the soil. It is a marvel to see how fast livestock and poultry multiply and grow: chickens bear chicks every two months, and they are already edible within ten to twelve days. And pigs, of which I brought only thirteen females, have proliferated so much that they now run wild through the mountains.[189]

Columbus also cited this marvelous temperateness in connection with the physical or psychological traits of the Indians. In the letter recounting the exploration of the Lesser Antilles on the second voyage (20 January 1494), he observed that the island of Hispaniola was "the most temperate, both in terms of cold and heat. And today [i.e., 20 January] we have the same cold as in December, which is very mild, nor do I think we should expect greater heat."[190] Then, in a passage that attests to the strong tie in his mind between temperature, latitude, and the nature of places, Columbus reminded the Catholic Monarchs that he had always insisted "that the fact that the hair of the Indians was not curly but lank led me to believe that this land was most temperate." This curious explanation may well have carried a silent apology for the fact that Columbus had failed to come across the dark-skinned, woolly-haired "Ethiopians" that had long been associated with the hotter latitudes of the globe. Undoubtedly, the absence of physiognomic traits that could have *automatically* equated the newly discovered peoples with the slaves already harvested by the Portuguese in sub-Saharan Africa was a stumbling block for Columbus's plan to import slaves from the Indies—most likely, one of the reasons why King Fernando and, in particular, Queen Isabel were hesitant to authorize an indiscriminate Indian slave trade. On yet another remarkable occasion, Columbus may have also been attempting to explain why, across from Guinea, on the same latitude as Sierra Leone, he had failed to find dark-skinned peoples. Having endured infernally hot weather across the Atlantic on his third voyage, Columbus unexpectedly found that the island of Trinidad and the "Land of Grace" in today's Venezuela harbored "the softest temperance."[191] The land and trees were unspeakably green, "as beautiful as those in April in the orchards of Valencia." And the locals, for their part, were "of very handsome stature, and whiter than others I have seen in the Yndies; and their hair very long and straight. And [these were] people more astute and of greater ingenuity, and not [as] cowardly." Indeed, in the connection between temperateness and the skin color, hair quality, and psychological traits of the Indians found in Venezuela, Columbus may have once again been trying to excuse his monumental failure to find the most coveted tropical cargo of all.

In sum, Columbus had one foot in a tradition that had long tended to construe the tropics as the hot, infertile, and uninhabitable fringes of a world whose geographical and political center was Mediterranean Europe; and the other foot in a previously less successful tradition that had tended to construe the tropics as a vast, temperate, fertile, and populous region of a world whose true geographical and political center did not necessarily reside with Mediterranean Europe. His writings, productively or paradoxically, alternated between the perception that life in the tropics was the accidental offspring of a fickle nature; and the perception that life in the tropics was part of a far more general design in nature. Whatever we make of these contradictions in Columbus's writings, Columbus proved to be no less feverish than the early Indographers in his account of a place that he mindfully situated to the west and to the south of El Hierro Island—across the Atlantic, yes, but within the tantalizing reaches of the torrid zone. Indeed, Columbus never ceased to wonder at the marvels and monsters of a place that he stubbornly defined as a part of legendary India.[192] And it is no coincidence that the terms "marvel" and "diversity" or "disfigurement" (*maravilla, diversidad, desformidad*) should have proliferated in his writing as favorite code words for signifying the highly generative tropicality of his Indies. One needs only consider the instantly famous description of Cuba and Hispaniola in the letter to Luis de Santángel announcing the discovery to come across the phraseology of wonder that would tend to punctuate Columbus's admittedly "disoriented" Indophilia. Cuba's lands were

> all beautiful, *of a thousand shapes* [*de mill fechuras*], and all are easily accessible, full of trees *of a thousand kinds* [*de mill maneras*] and tall, and they seem like they reach the sky. And I was told they never shed their foliage, from what I understand, for I saw them as green and beautiful as they are in Spain in May, some of them flowering, others bearing fruit, and yet others at another stage, each according to their nature. And the nightingale was singing and other little birds *in a thousand manners* [*de mill maneras*] in the month of November. There where I visited, there are six or eight kinds of palm trees, *which are a wonder to behold on account of their beautiful deformity* [*es admiración verlas por la diformidad hermosa dellas*], except that so are the other trees and fruit and greenery. In it are *marvelous pine groves* [*pinares a maravilla*], and there are enormous fields for planting, and there is honey, and many kinds of birds, and *very diverse sorts of fruit* [*frutas muy diversas*]. In its lands are many metal mines and there are *people without number* [*gente yn stimabile numero*]. Hispaniola is a *marvel* [*maravilla*]—its sierras and mountains, and the basins and fields, and the soils so rich for planting and sowing, for breeding livestock of all kinds, for town and village buildings. The sea harbors are such as one cannot believe them to exist unless one has seen them, and as far as rivers are concerned, there are many and big, with good waters, most of which carry gold. In the trees and fruit and greenery, there are huge differences with respect to those of Juana [Cuba]. On this island, there are many spices, and huge mines of gold and other metals.[193]

Columbus's urgent appeal to Indographic wonder did not subside with increased familiarity toward the lands and peoples he had discovered in the high Atlantic. As his earliest chronicler Peter Martyr reminds us, Columbus's victorious return to Europe was instantly clouded by doubt in court circles as to whether he had traveled far enough to the west to have reached the promised Indies.[194] (Martyr himself seemed to believe that

Columbus had only managed to reach the legendary mid-Atlantic region of Antilia.) And in the face of these early signs of trouble, it is only to be expected that Columbus should have insistently continued to indulge the description of a nature whose overwhelming profligacy and gigantism he read as confirmation that he had reached the easternmost suburbs of the legendary India. Indeed, if by dint of longitude, Columbus could not prove that he had reached the East "by way of the West," certainly by dint of latitude, and thereby of nature, he would always argue that he had reached the right place across the Atlantic.

From Place to Colonialism in the Aristotelian Tradition

Not only are the heavens the cause in things correctly generated,
but also in the faults of nature and in monstrosities.

Roger Bacon, *Opus maius* IV, 4

Bartolomé de las Casas had compelling reasons for counting Albertus Magnus among Columbus's forebears and for employing Albertus's remarkable *De natura loci* (about 1251–1254) to explain Columbus's geography and its ancient sources. Long before the discovery, Albertus had issued one of the earliest claims by a Christian author that the torrid and southern temperate zones were, contrary to conventional wisdom, eminently suited for life. And this claim was part of one of the most authoritative and thorough disquisitions ever written on the nature of places. In *De natura loci,* the Discoverer would have certainly found schooled corroboration of his experience with the Portuguese in sub-Saharan Africa—experience that had led Columbus to believe that the torrid zone might be generally temperate, fertile, and, therefore, inhabitable. Albertus's prefatory contribution to the Age of Exploration—and specifically to the discovery—has often been cited in relation to this and other "exceptions" to the established geographical tradition that portrayed the *orbis terrarum* as an unrepeatable island besieged by extreme arctic and tropical temperatures. But the precise nature of Albertus's contribution bears further scrutiny.[1]

In the late nineteenth century, historian Pierre Mandonnet reconsidered Columbus's well-known friendship with the Dominican friar Diego de Deza in order to argue that Albertus and his disciple Thomas Aquinas—the Dominicans' two most influential thinkers—had directly informed Columbus's plan to navigate to the Indies.[2] We know that Columbus had met the erudite Deza in Alcalá de Henares in 1485 as he prepared to present the plan for his undertaking to the Catholic Monarchs for the first time. Deza, who had held the principal chair in theology at the University of Salamanca, had joined Fernando and Isabel's itinerant court as Prince Don Juan's tutor. When

Columbus and Deza followed the court to Salamanca in 1486, Columbus's friendship with Deza enabled him to take up residence in the college monastery of San Esteban, the Dominicans' center of learning in the Iberian peninsula.[3]

Deza became Columbus's powerful protector in court until the Discoverer's death in 1506. He also played a key role in overturning the royal council's final rejection of Columbus's proposal in early January of 1492.[4] At the encampment of Santa Fe outside the city of Granada, where the Spanish court celebrated the fall of the last Muslim stronghold in the Iberian peninsula, the task of persuading Fernando to reconsider Columbus's proposal one last time fell to Deza and to Fernando's chamberlain Juan Cabrero.[5] Years after the discovery, in a letter to his son Diego following Isabel's death in 1504, Columbus acknowledged his lifelong debt to Deza by referring to him as "the reason why Their Highnesses came to possess the Indies and I remained in Castile."[6]

According to Mandonnet, Deza and other Dominicans introduced Columbus to Albertus's and Aquinas's commentaries on Aristotle's *De caelo* (in which Aristotle speculated that only a short distance separated the Pillars of Hercules from the end of the Orient) as well as to Albertus's views in *De natura loci* regarding the torrid and southern temperate zones.[7]

Regrettably, we have no detailed documentation of the scientific and technical sources presented for and against Columbus's project during the years it was discussed in the royal council. Mandonnet—who, like Las Casas, was a Dominican—echoed Las Casas's and Ferdinand's biases in pitting the "sound" arguments of Columbus and his few courtly supporters against the "short-sighted" objections of the members of Fernando and Isabel's council.[8] For Mandonnet, the Dominican order had been a bastion of the scientific movement inaugurated by Albertus, Aquinas, and Aristotle's other followers in the early decades of the high scholastic tradition, while Columbus's opponents in court represented the "vulgar and antiscientific" views promoted by church fathers such as Lactantius and Saint Augustine.[9] Later historians have rightly argued that this opposition is not altogether fair: the Dominicans were not the sole religious order to support Columbus, and the assemblies that evaluated his plan included thoroughly schooled individuals who must have reasoned forcefully against such a risky venture.[10] Indeed, what we do know about the official debate that preceded the discovery strongly suggests that it was a schooled one, carried out on both sides with utmost concern for theological and philosophical correctness.

Mandonnet's reference to Albertus and Thomas in relation to the discovery was probably dictated as much by loyalty to the Dominican order as by the intellectual affinity established by Las Casas in *Historia de las Indias* between Albertus's geographical theories and Columbus's plan to venture into the tropics. One could have conceivably argued that it was Columbus's Franciscan supporters from the monastery of Santa María de la Rábida in Huelva—particularly the "able astrologer" Fray Antonio de Marchena, whom the Catholic Monarchs would order to accompany Columbus on his second voyage—who might have introduced Columbus to similar claims about the distance between Spain and the Indies and the habitability of the torrid and southern temperate zones. One of the principal sources probably available by then to Franciscans of the Iberian Peninsula was the geographical section of Roger Bacon's monumental *Opus maius* (about 1266–1267).[11] The Oxford schoolman (about 1214/1220–about 1292) had theorized place in terms almost identical to Albertus's a decade or so after the composition of *De natura loci,* and, as we know thanks to Alexander von Humboldt, Bacon's geography also ghosted extensive passages of Pierre d'Ailly's *Ymago mundi* (1410).[12]

In fact, the "schooled" claim that the torrid zone was universally temperate, fertile, and inhabitable had been proliferating among Christian scholars since at least the thirteenth century, thanks to the recent arrival in the Latin West of Greek and Arabic sources that included objections to the theory of the five zones. The most important among these newly translated sources was the *Introduction to the Phenomena* by Geminos of Rhodes (80–10 BCE), often known in the Latin West as *De dispositio spherae* and thought at the time to have been written by Ptolemy himself as an introduction to his astronomical *Almagest.*[13] Other key sources cited by Christian scholars were the *Almagest* itself (2nd century CE) as well as Avicenna's *Canon of Medicine* and his commentary to Aristotle's zoology, *De animalibus* (11th century).[14] These new sources soon lent authority to arguments wielded by a variety of schoolmen against the claim that the torrid zone was a generally desolate belt of the globe—among them, for instance, the early commentators of Sacrobosco's widely read *De sphaera,* composed before 1220, and also the Oxford schoolman Robert Grosseteste, whose optical treatises *De lineis, angulis, et figuris* and *De natura locorum* closely anticipated the theories of place developed by Albertus's *De natura loci* and Bacon's *Opus maius* IV.[15] Other vital sources containing refutations of Parmenides' traditional claim about the torrid zone were introduced to the Latin West later, chief among them Strabo's *Geography* (1st century), which was known only fragmentarily until the mid-fifteenth century. It is thanks to Strabo that we know the names of the first theoretical geographies in the West to have argued that Parmenides' theory of the five zones was wrong with regard to the torrid zone, though all of these works are now lost: Eratosthenes' *Geography* (3rd century BCE), Polybius's *The Inhabited World below the Equator* (2nd century BCE), and Posidonius's *The Ocean* (1st century BCE).[16]

Among the numerous postils in Columbus's library declaring the temperateness of tropical places, we do have some traces of Columbus's contact with the traditions imported into the Latin West since the twelfth century.[17] Pierre d'Ailly and Jean Gerson's *Tractatus* twice cites the tradition of Pseudo-Ptolemy and Avicenna. In the margins of chapter 7 of d'Ailly's *Ymago mundi*, "De varietate opinionum circa habitationem terre," Columbus or his brother Bartholomew, naming Avicenna "and others," noted that "they say that under the equinoctial line is a *most temperate place [locus temperantissimus]*."[18] Significantly, Columbus adds to this postil the following: "Earthly paradise. It is there."[19] This was a reference to the hexameral tradition that had long described God's "paradise of pleasure" as the most temperate, bountiful, and amenable of all places on earth. Jerome's version of Genesis 2:8, which stated that God had planted paradise "from the beginning," was read by some hexameral writers not as a temporal locator referring to the beginning of time before God created man but rather as a geographical one, indicating that God had created paradise in a place now inaccessible to man somewhere "in the east." The indelible connection in Columbus's mind between the alleged temperateness of the torrid zone and that "most temperate place" where God had planted Adam explains why, in the *Diario* and other writings, Columbus often invoked Edenic imagery to marvel at the relative temperateness he generally experienced in the Bahamas and the Caribbean basin. This connection is of equal importance for explaining why, upon discovering a new southern continent on his third voyage, Columbus would come to fathom that he had reached the suburbs of the garden forbidden to a fallen humanity.[20] Thus in a later postil to d'Ailly's *Compendium cosmographie* I, Columbus again conjoins the classical view of the torrid zone as temperate with Christian traditions regarding the location of terrestrial paradise: "Ptolemy maintains [i.e., in the *Geography*] that under the equinoctial line are very black people. And later, in the book *On the Disposition of the Sphere* [i.e., Geminos of Rhode's *Introduction*], [Ptolemy] maintains that it is temperate. Avicenna teaches that the place under the equinoctial line is extremely temperate, because the earthly paradise is located there in the east."[21]

Columbus also left traces of contact with the tradition earliest launched by Eratosthenes, Polybius, and Posidonius in the copy now preserved at the Biblioteca Colombina of *Historia rerum ubique gestarum* by Aeneas Sylvius Piccolomini (Pope Pius II). Piccolomini had been one of the first humanists in Europe to own a manuscript copy of Guarinus Veronensis's 1458 translation of Strabo's *Geography*.[22] On the margins of Piccolomini's famous history, Columbus would note: "Eratosthenes says that under the equinoctial circle is a most temperate place. And so does Avicenna." Anxious to connect written authority with lived experience, Columbus concludes: "Directly underneath the equinoctial circle stands the Most Serene King of Portugal's fort of [São Jorge da] Mina, which we saw."[23]

By the end of the fifteenth century, numerous sources in the Latin West claimed that the torrid zone might not be the desolate expanse described by Parmenides, and Columbus could certainly have drawn from any number of them. Unfortunately, in the postils to d'Ailly's and Piccolomini's works we have the only direct evidence of Columbus's contact with this geographical tradition. We may never know the extent of Columbus's acquaintance with the schooled arguments developed by Sacrobosco's early commentators or by theorists of place such as Grosseteste, Albertus, and Bacon. It certainly makes sense to think that Columbus should have come across Albertus's *De natura loci* through a learned mentor like Diego de Deza or through Columbus's other acquaintances at San Esteban. And it makes even more sense that someone formally educated, like Deza or another reputable member of the Dominican order, would have wielded Albertus's *De natura loci* against the traditional claim that the torrid zone was desolate. It should also be added that one of the few incunabula in the Biblioteca Colombina identified as Columbus's is Pseudo-Albertus's *Philosophia naturalis,* or *Philosophia pauperum* (Venice, 1496), an epitome of Albertus's commentaries on Aristotle's key cosmological works—*Physics, On the Heavens, Meteorologica, On Generation and Corruption,* and *On the Soul*. Columbus purchased this volume after the discovery, probably seeking to defend the intellectual merits of his discoveries from his detractors, and although it contains no postils by Columbus, its presence in his library could well represent an attempt to reclaim an older acquaintance with Albertus's thought.[24]

All this does not amount to saying that Columbus actually read Albertus's *De natura loci*. Mandonnet's attempt to indebt Columbus to Albertus and Thomas is but one example of the partisanship and proprietorship that have often accompanied claims concerning the discovery—just as Americanists eager to counter the Black Legend's vision of Spain as a backward and brutal empire have protested Ferdinand's and Las Casas's negative portrayals of Columbus's opponents in the royal council. The problem with linking the intellectual genesis of the discovery too closely with one or another source is that the rules we often apply to modern authorship were not the same for the Aristotelian commentary tradition. Because we are dealing with an intellectual culture that thrived on commentary, and because sources were not always acknowledged, it is often the case that claims that at first appear to be original to one author have a long and diverse genealogy. In fact, the authority writers granted to individual claims in this tradition did not lie with their novelty or uniqueness but rather with a given author's aptitude at articulating them anew within a set of generally recognized parameters.[25]

This is precisely the role that Albertus and many other authors played in Las Casas's intellectual biography of Columbus. Las Casas does not claim that Columbus had read *De natura loci,* which attests to the great restraint Las Casas tended to exercise in the use of his sources. Instead, taking the license allowed every historian to weave in the plausible with the factual, Las Casas only ventures to hypothesize that in Albertus and other authorities Columbus could very well have found support for his geographical ideas concerning the torrid and temperate zones. And at this juncture, it is crucial to bear in mind that, in the eyes of Las Casas and other historiographers of the period, one of the purposes for writing history (apart from its potential to serve as legal testimony) was precisely to comment on the existing historical record and thus to constantly evaluate the validity of its claims.[26]

Las Casas's intellectual portrait of Columbus in the opening chapters of *Historia de las Indias* (2–14) happens to be such an exercise in commentary—in this case, a commentary of the account that Ferdinand gives for the reasons that had moved his father to discover the Indies. Immediately following Ferdinand's rendering of Columbus's views about the torrid and southern temperate zones, Las Casas wrote three chapters (6–8) explicitly intended to "digress" from the storyline of Ferdinand's *Historie.* At the opening of the sixth chapter, Las Casas carefully states that, *in addition* to the reasons cited by Ferdinand as having persuaded Columbus of the feasibility of an ocean crossing, Columbus "could have well been swayed [to believe that he could discover the Indies] by the opinions of many and notable ancient philosophers that the three parts of the world [the torrid and the northern and southern temperate zones] were inhabitable."[27] In the conclusion to this chapter, which discusses all the sources from which Columbus could have gathered evidence for his supposition that the torrid zone was habitable, Las Casas scrupulously asserts: "It seems very clear how much reason Columbus could have had in judging it likely—indeed very likely, *given the testimonies of such authorized writers*—that there were lands and peoples where he went to search for them; and in being compelled to go and find them."[28] It is in this series of chapters that Albertus's *De natura loci* takes center stage over all other sources cited by Las Casas.

The purpose of his digression was not to tell his readers what Columbus *had* read; rather, it was to establish the learned arguments for why Columbus or anyone else would have been right to think that the torrid zone was universally temperate, fertile, and inhabitable. Indeed, this may be the most urgent claim governing the composition of both *Historia de las Indias* and *Apologética historia*—Las Casas's natural and moral history of the Americas. By way of schooled argumentation and with recourse to testimony about the nature and culture of the New World accumulated over decades of colonial experience, Las Casas sought to prove this claim in an effort to discredit apologists of empire who had invoked place as the basis for considering Amerindians to be slaves by nature. And, as Las Casas well understood, no one among Aristotle's Christian commentators could claim higher authority on the subjects of nature and place than Albertus Magnus, "whom God most singularly perfected in the secrets of nature and in all natural philosophy."[29]

What follows, then, is not intended to establish that Columbus had firsthand knowledge of Albertus's *De natura loci*. Instead, I aim to describe the logic that governed Albertus's attempt to relocate ancient and medieval geography within a philosophical and technical knowledge system that explicitly connected concepts of place with political theory. Geography was a *techne* profoundly implicated in the quest for a philosophical explanation of the behavior of all physical creatures that occupied a natural place in the world-machine. And without an understanding of the nature of places, as Albertus insists in his opening statements to *De natura loci,* one could not hope to be perfectly versed in the natural sciences.[30] It is this aspect of geography—largely omitted from the historiography of the discovery—that Las Casas would record in his anticolonialist *Historia de las Indias* and *Apologética*.

In Albertus's claim that the torrid zone might enjoy temperate habitation, Las Casas read far more than an authoritative exception to the geographical canon that had stood in the way of Columbus's plan to sail to the west and to the south in the direction of the Indies. The claim that the torrid and temperate zones were not the universally hot and uninhabitable wasteland once imagined by Parmenides had gradually been proved true by the exploits of the Portuguese in Atlantic Africa (from 1435), the extended basin of the Indian Ocean (from 1498), and Brazil (from 1500), and by those of the Spanish in the Bahamas and Caribbean basin (from 1492), Mexico (from 1519), and Peru (from 1532). (These accomplishments may partially explain why the first printed editions of Albertus's *De natura loci* were issued in 1514, 1515, and 1517, as exploration on the rims of the Caribbean was yielding incontrovertible evidence of huge continental populations.)[31] Even if, in the mid-sixteeenth century, it might still be somewhat contentious to claim that the torrid zone was universally temperate, no one in his or her right mind in Spain could claim any longer that this vast belt was universally barren and inhospitable. Albertus and those authors who had followed in the steps of Eratosthenes were once again, so to speak, on the cutting edge of geographical theory, and Las Casas rightly viewed Albertus's *De natura loci* as an insuperable intellectual weapon to win a harrowing legal debate that had largely construed the question of the Indian in terms of Aristotle's ideas about nature. It did not matter to Las Casas that *De natura loci* itself also espoused the tripartite geopolitics by which Greek, Roman, and Christian writers had long sought to rationalize a temperate Europe's aspirations to empire—in fact, this helped Las Casas's case against the legality of the conquest. For the point was *not* to dispense altogether with the epistemic system underlying this geopolitical model but rather to invoke one of its founding figures in favor of the claim that, like Mediterranean Europe, the American tropics were universally temperate. And if the American tropics could be construed in this manner, then the arguments wielded by such schooled figures as John Mair, Bernardo Mesa, and Juan Ginés de Sepúlveda that Amerindians were by nature slaves would be rendered groundless. It was a matter of depriving a legal system of one of the most precious titles Spain might have claimed to its occupation of the Americas.

Las Casas read Albertus's *De natura loci* as a philosophical geography, that is, a description of the inhabited world that examined the causes acting on all physical creatures that had been accorded a place by nature. And it is in this light that one can best understand Albertus's legacy to the cosmological tradition that witnessed Europe's discovery of dense populations beyond the known inhabited world.

Albertus played a crucial role in the reception and institutionalization of Aristotle's philosophical works in the Latin West.[32] He and his disciple Thomas Aquinas (about

of the cosmos. But Aristotle's discussion in these two works was still far too general to account for the great diversity of places and things in nature.

In Aristotle's *Physics,* nature (*phusis*) is "a principle or cause of being moved and of being at rest in that [thing] to which it belongs primarily, in virtue of itself and not accidentally."[59] Things that are by nature possess an intrinsic power to be moved, in contrast with things brought about by art (like beds and other artifacts), which possess no such innate impulse except insofar as they are made from other natural things (like the wood used to fabricate beds).[60] Defining cause as "that out of which a thing comes to be and which persists," Aristotle identifies the following causes of things that are by nature: matter and form—matter being separable in statement from form but never existing apart from it; mover, or moving, cause—which usually involves an extrinsic agent and would play a central role in Albertus's own understanding of the nature of places; and end, or final, cause, "that for the sake of which" a thing is moved or comes to rest.[61] Of these four causes, it is the relation of matter to form that Aristotle regularly associates with nature, that is, with the innate and active ability of natural things to be moved or to be at rest.[62]

In Aristotle, the relation of matter to form is the relation of potency to actuality: matter in one particular form, having the potential to take on a different form, cannot be said to have its new nature—does not exist *by nature*—until that inherent potential becomes actual.[63] Therefore, "form indeed is the nature rather than matter: for a thing is more properly said to be what it is when it exists in actuality than when it exists potentially."[64] But while form, when it acts as an end, or final, cause, can be said to cause matter to be moved, the ability to be moved resides with matter itself. Hence the most fundamental tenet of Aristotle's physics of motion: "motion is in the movable."[65] This means that matter, not inert at all, actively seeks form, indeed matter *runs* after form: "what desires the form is matter, as the female desires the male and the ugly the beautiful."[66] And the "being moved" by which matter-as-potentiality achieves form-as-actuality does not require active formative intervention by an outside agent. Furthermore, the relation between matter and form follows the same orientation for Aristotle as that between body (matter/form) and soul. Unlike Plato, who conceives of the soul as "descending" upon matter and informing or "colonizing," it, Aristotle conceptualizes the soul as the form or actuality of those bodies that have a potential to be alive.[67] Such bodies naturally and immediately desire a soul. While for Plato, the soul is a self-moving mover and shaper of motionless and lifeless matter, for Aristotle potentially live bodies naturally desire a soul.[68]

Aristotle's concept of place (*topos*) is meant to be understood in direct relation to the *telos* that governs the relation of matter to form and body to soul. What defines all natural bodies (as opposed to a theoretically infinite body) is that they possess interval in all directions—length, breadth, and depth—and are bounded by a surface.[69] And the concept of being bounded by surface, of being limited, as all bodies are, remains inseparable in Aristotle's cosmology from the concept of being placed: "It is the nature of every kind of sensible body to be somewhere, and there is a place appropriate to each, the same for the part and for the whole, e.g., for the whole of the earth and for a single clod, and for fire and for a spark."[70] If natural things innately and actively possess a principle or cause of being moved or being at rest, then for a body to be moved at all is to be moved *in, from,* or *to* place. Hence the general explanation Aristotle provides at the opening of his discussion of place in the *Physics* for why students of nature ought to cultivate knowledge of place: "because all suppose that things which exist are somewhere (the non-existent is nowhere—where is the goat-stag or the sphinx?), and because motion in its most general and proper sense is change of place, which we call 'locomotion.'"[71] This is no doubt the ultimate source for Albertus's judgment in *De natura loci* that philosophers erred who failed to understand the importance of investigating the nature of place in the natural sciences.

For Aristotle, motion is the actualization of some potential.[72] In the process of being moved, natural things realize an inherent potential—whether to become other things, to alter their magnitude (i.e., from small to large or from one to many), to acquire new properties (i.e., from light to heavy), or merely to move to another location.[73] Aristotle assigns local motion (change of place) priority with respect to changes in substance, magnitude, or quality. The concept of priority itself has three distinct meanings: "A thing is said to be prior to other things when, if it does not exist, the others will not exist, whereas it can exist without the others; and there is also priority in time and priority in being [i.e., in perfection of nature]."[74] Local motion (locomotion) is prior to all other types of change in all three senses of priority. First, it can occur without other types of change (a fruit may fall from a tree without fundamentally ceasing to be itself); in contrast, changes in quality, substance, or number usually imply some sort of locomotion (a growing fruit is, by virtue of occupying an increasingly larger space, shifting location). Second, locomotion can occur either before all other changes happen in a thing or in the absence of any other type of change in complete beings (beings that are eternal and unalterable, like celestial bodies) or in beings that have already achieved their actuality and can therefore change no further. Third, of all the types of change, locomotion is the most perfect because it "does not involve a change of being in the sense in which there is a change in quality when a thing is altered and a change in quantity when a thing is increased or decreased."[75] Following Aristotle's reasoning, celestial bodies change place but do not alter their being, and a ripe fruit falling from a tree might have finished ripening but is still changing place as it falls.[76] This is why, for Aristotle, locomotion, or change of place, is motion in its most general and proper sense.

That natural place *is* something (meaning not a thing but a principle), and that it has some sort of power, is shown by the fact that the primary bodies, or four elements (provided they are not subject to an external force), are moved to and come to rest in their proper places—in the case of fire up and in that of earth down.[77] (The differences between places are, for Aristotle, up or down, before or behind, and right or left.)[78] And in nature, up or down are absolutes: up is where fire and light things are carried (i.e., away from the center, or toward the extremity, of the cosmos), whereas down is where earth and weighty things are carried (i.e., toward the center, or away from the extremity).[79] Therefore, all natural bodies have a place that is proper to them, that is, place is the *where* things come to rest as they realize their inherent potential to be moved toward form-as-actuality: place is the actually up or actually down of things.[80] Before elaborating on this particular point, it is useful to consider what place is not for Aristotle, since it illuminates Albertus's conception of place.

Aristotle flatly rejects the idea that the influence or power of place resides in its being something prior in time to placed body. Reading Hesiod's cosmogonic *Theogony* (8th/7th century BCE)—"'First of all things came chaos to being, then broadbreasted earth'"—Aristotle asks whether "things need to have space first." From the terms he uses and from his subsequent references to the *Timaeus,* it is clear that Aristotle distinguishes place from space (*chôra*), a concept that in Plato *does* entail priority in the fullest sense with respect to things.[81] As one reads in the *Timaeus,* space "exists always and cannot be destroyed. It provides a fixed state for all things that come to be. It is itself apprehended by a kind of bastard reasoning that does not involve sense perception, and it is hardly even an object of conviction. We look at it as in a dream when we say that everything that exists must of necessity be somewhere, in some place and occupying some space, and that that which doesn't exist somewhere, whether on earth or in heaven, doesn't exist at all."[82] For Aristotle, on the contrary, place is not temporally prior to body: "If this is its nature," he exclaims, "the power of place must be a marvellous thing, and be prior to all other things. For that without which nothing else can exist, while it can exist without the others, must needs be first."[83] In other words, while Plato posits absolute space as existing without and before body, as well as being more perfect than body, Aristotle conceptualizes place as concurrent in time with body insofar as body is movable.

According to Aristotle, place is also not a body, for the simple reason that no two bodies can ever be in the same place—a statement of enormous relevance for geography, a discipline that, according to Albertus, concerned itself with the similarities and differences between places.[84] Furthermore, place cannot be body's matter or form, since these are not separable from body, whereas body can be removed from its place.[85] Also, place cannot be smaller than body; otherwise there would be bodies whose nature it is to be nowhere. Nor can place be greater than body, for there can be no interval between placed body and its place.[86] Finally, place cannot be all of the body of a thing that contains another, for this would make place greater than placed body.[87]

Since place is none of these things, there is only one more thing it can be. Because place contains body, it is some sort of limit or bounding surface with respect to body. Just as form is the limit of body, place is the innermost limit of the containing body.[88] Hence Aristotle's first definition of place as "the boundary of the containing body at which it is in contact with the contained body."[89] An immediate distinction is in order between containing bodies that can be moved (vessels) and those that remain fixed (places): a boat floating on a river's running water can be said to be contained by a vessel (moving water) or by a place (the river bed itself). In this manner Aristotle reaches a second definition of place as "the innermost motionless boundary of what contains [a thing]."[90]

Aristotle continues his treatment of place in *On the Heavens,* where he discusses the finite motion of the elements in contrast with the eternal motion of the indestructible heavens. In attempting to prove that motion in things is eternal, Aristotle has in the *Physics* already established categories of motion for all things that are by nature. Of the three types of locomotion (circular, linear, and a combination of both), circular locomotion is prior in degree of perfection to rectilinear locomotion.[91] Circular locomotion, by which Aristotle means uninterrupted and uniform rotation around a center or point, can continue indefinitely, repeating itself without end.[92] Every part of a rotating body can return to its point of departure without ever having to stop and reverse course.

With rectilinear locomotion, a body or one of its parts returns to its point of departure only after stopping and reversing its direction. [93] Rectilinear locomotion is, in this sense, not as perfect as circular locomotion. In *On the Heavens,* Aristotle attributes circular locomotion to the divine bodies of the heavens and rectilinear locomotion to the four elements.[94] Things that are absolutely light (having no heaviness) are moved upward, and things that are absolutely heavy (having no lightness) are moved downward.[95] Just as matter possesses an inherent ability to be moved toward form, so does each of the elements (body) possess an innate inclination or tendency (*rhopē*) for motion toward proper place.[96] Fire, being absolutely light, has an active orientation upward and is moved up; earth, being absolutely heavy, has an active orientation downward and is moved down; whereas air and water, which combine different measures of lightness and heaviness, tend to be moved up to the surface or down to the bottom of other elements: air tends to be moved up toward the surface of earth and of water but down toward the bottom of fire; water, down toward the bottom of fire and of air but up toward the surface of earth.[97] Thus each outer element in the series is, in a sense, the proper place, or form, of its antecedent: water of earth, air of water, and fire of air.[98] Since each element can be generated out of another, every element can be said to be potentially another and therefore potentially lighter or heavier: as air is generated out of water, for example, it becomes lighter and is moved to rest in its proper place as air. As one element becomes another, it is moved "into that place and quantity and quality which belong to its actuality."[99]

In Aristotle's account of place, motion explicitly resides solely within the movable. A movable body alone has the active inclination and the power to be moved to its proper place. The power of place with respect to a natural body, like that of form with respect to matter, resides not with its having the power to move natural body but with its being *where* a natural body, upon the realization of some inherent potential, is inclined to be moved and to rest. Given the opportunity, a natural body always runs after its proper place. Thus Aristotle posits place as a determinative cause, or principle, of the cosmos.

We must still consider the role Aristotle assigns to movers in relation to movable things, since Albertus would come to associate nature and place almost exclusively with movers rather than with the innate and active ability of natural things to be moved. Aristotle states that all things in motion are moved by something.[100] Recall that for Aristotle motion is the realization of an innate potential.[101] Like the relation of matter to form, and of natural body to place, the relation of the naturally movable body to its mover is the relation of potency to actuality. Insofar as motion is natural, the mover-as-already-actual "brings to actuality the proper activities that [movable things] potentially possess."[102] A natural body is moved to actualize its potential on immediate physical contact with its mover, or else it can be moved indirectly by a given mover through intermediate touching bodies.[103] According to Aristotle, the series of movables and their movers in the cosmos has to end with a first mover and a first moved.[104] In opposition to Plato's mover of body, which Plato regards as self-moving motion, or soul, Aristotle's first mover is an unmoved mover.[105]

This unmoved mover in Aristotle's *Physics,* historically identified as the timeless and boundless divinity of *Metaphysics* IX, is accountable for bringing to actuality the particular activity potentially owned by the first moved body—the rotating body accountable for the motion of every other being in the physical world. Motion in natural things is eternal because, insofar as nature everywhere dispenses order, things that have a potential to be moved naturally never fail to be moved in contact with their proper actuality.[106] As Aristotle states, "If anything is of a certain character naturally, it either is so invariably and is not sometimes of this and sometimes of another character."[107] In contact with the first mover-as-eternal, the first moved body, never failing to realize its potential to be moved, is moved without beginning or end in time. Because the unmoved mover is eternal, the first moved is uniformly and eternally being moved. Since only circular locomotion can go on forever without ever having to stop and change direction, this is the motion proper to this first moved body.[108] On Aristotle's account, this first moved body occupies the extremity of the cosmos, itself bringing to actuality the activities potentially possessed by all other natural things.[109]

Movers play a crucial role in one other respect in Aristotle's natural philosophy. Consider the celebrated passage in *On Generation and Corruption* where Aristotle posits the sun as the main generator of contraries in the elements and their compounds—one of the key passages in Aristotle's *libri naturales* that would serve generations of commentators as a "charter" of astrology.[110] Aristotle specifies that matter and form alone cannot account for the continuous generation of natural things.[111] A third party also intervenes in the generation and corruption of elemental bodies. (We can certainly assume that matter and form still accounts for the nature of things in the manner laid out in the *Physics,* for what is at stake in this passage is not Aristotle's explanation of things that are by nature, but rather his explanation of their coming-to-be and passing-away.) As Aristotle explains generation, the single, continuous motion of the first moved on the periphery of the cosmos can be considered the cause only of one single, continuous effect, namely, the eternity of motion in natural things. We might say that this first moved is immediately accountable solely for the daily, uniform rotation of the entire vault of the heavens around the elements.

But what causes natural things to come to be and to pass away is the motion of the primary, or celestial, bodies along the inclined circle of the ecliptic.[112] Because the ecliptic is slanted, one always sees that primary bodies in the sky alternately approach and retreat, generating by growing near and destroying by growing remote. (In astronomical terms, primary bodies were thought to be the cause of generation as they approached any given zenith in the sky relative to the observer and the cause of destruction as they receded toward any given horizon.) Proof that motion along the ecliptic is the cause of generation in elemental bodies is that "coming-to-be occurs as the sun approaches and decay as it retreats."[113] In line with Aristotle's view of the role of movers in relation to natural things, we ought to say that the sun, by its dual motion along the ecliptic, brings to actuality the activities potentially possessed by elemental bodies.

In sum, movers play a crucial role in Aristotle's philosophy, and they do so by providing the opportunity for movable body to realize a given potential. But in Aristotle's account of nature, the power of moving to place remains with the movable. And such self-referentiality in the motion of natural things did not easily accommodate the idea of the creative and provident divine dear to Albertus and his contemporaries.

From Albertus's viewpoint, an additional problem with Aristotle's theory of place was that it failed to account for anything other than what place was or for the inclination of the four elements to be moved to and rest in their proper places. Albertus thus saw the need to extend Aristotle's theory of place in order to explain the evident diversity of places and of things placed in the cosmos. To explain this diversity himself, Albertus would focus on the role of movers in the natural motion of things, significantly altering Aristotle's concepts of nature and place to meet criteria of Christian doctrine.

Aristotle's definition of place as the innermost motionless boundary of containing body is certainly to be found in recognizable form in Albertus's *De natura loci,* which posits that place is the concave part of the surface toward which a given body tends to be moved.[114] To this extent, Albertus might have agreed with Aristotle, say, that air's innermost surface was water's place. But their accounts of the physics that governed this placing would have differed radically. Unlike Aristotle, Albertus characterized place as "an active principle of generation in the manner of a father" (*generationis principium activum quemadmodum pater*).[115] And it was the *activity* of place that from the outset differentiated Albertus's physics from Aristotle's. In this sense, Albertus's work bears closer affinity with late Neoplatonists like Porphyry's pupil Iamblichus, for whom place was "a corporeal power sustaining and supporting bodies, raising up the falling ones and gathering together the scattered ones, filling them up and encompassing them from every side."[116]

Albertus owed this memorable definition to Porphyry's introduction to Aristotle's logical *Categories,* the *Isagoge* translated into Latin and glossed by Boethius (about 470–524).[117] Porphyry had used the following terms to explain one of the acceptations for the category genus: "The principle of generation for each man, whether from he who generates him or from that place where he has been generated. Thus, we say that Orestes had his *genus* from Tantalus, and Tantalus from Hercules, and, on the other hand, that Pindar is a Theban by *genus* but Plato an Athenian; and, therefore, one's native country [*patria*] is the principle of generation for each man, just as a father."[118] Porphyry's analogy between fatherland and father as principles, or causes, of generation could hardly be more appropriate for understanding Albertus's departure from Aristotle's ideas about the place of natural things, especially when one takes into account—as Albertus consciously did—the role that Aristotle himself ascribes to the father in the generation of offspring and to movers in the physical world.

What fatherhood means for Aristotle can be readily found in his controversial distinction between male and female in his *Generation of Animals.*[119] Aristotle associates the former ("that which generates in another") with the "effective" and "active," and the latter ("that which generates in itself") with the "passive," although he does not mean by that term something lacking in itself a principle of motion and rest (matter *always* has an inherent and active ability to be moved and be at rest).[120] In those species of animals in which the male produces semen, the seed that the female contributes to the embryo is her menses, a spermatic residue akin to semen, which Aristotle sees as "material for the semen to work upon."[121] What semen contributes to the embryo is its power and motion, and this power communicated to the new embryo is "that which acts and makes [i.e., forms]," while, in relation to the embryo, the female's "seed" in the womb is "that which is made and receives the form."[122] Nature, in Aristotle's account of the embryo's generation, uses semen the way an artist would a tool, that is, as something "possessing motion in actuality, just as tools are used in the products of any art, for in them lies capable (Aristotle) but rather that which masters matter (Plato and Plotinus). A thing's nature *is* a thing's soul.

While for Aristotle, the first moved on the edge of the cosmos brings to actuality those activities potentially possessed by all other bodies, for Albertus, the *motor primum* (or the intelligence that moved it) would play the active formative and motive role that soul had played toward matter for thinkers like Plato and Plotinus. While for Aristotle, the periphery and the center of the cosmos are, respectively, the actually-up and the actually-down of the cosmos, for Albertus, the periphery of the cosmos would function as God's supreme agent of form and motion in the physical world. For this reason, once he has enumerated the reasons in *De natura loci* why place ought to be considered an active principle of generation, Albertus proposes to consider the nature of places in terms of their location under the heavens.[149]

According to Albertus, there are two ways to conceptualize place—the principal one has to do with its distance from the periphery of the cosmos; the other has to do with its location relative to planetary orbits.[150] The first mover operates on all lower things.[151] And it is the acolytes of this first mover—the stars, the sun, the moon, and the rest of the planets—that run in the opposite direction of this outer sphere along the inclined plane of the ecliptic, stirring things up in the elemental region and, thereby, generating huge diversity. Albertus was in this manner laying out the groundwork for using technical disciplines like mathematics, astrology, astronomy, geometry, geography, and optics as tools for prognosticating the nature of places and of things placed.

According to Albertus, the first mover is directly accountable for the formation and placement of the four elements: a given distance from the orb generates fire, another air, another water, and another earth, along with their respective qualities—the hot, the cold, the wet, and the dry, which are the natural virtues of the elements.[152] This notion was certainly inspired by Aristotle. In *On the Heavens,* Aristotle claims that distance from the outer sphere of the cosmos affects the rate at which each planet completes its own cycle. While the outer sphere revolves swiftly in one direction, dragging along the entire vault of the heavens every day, each planet moves at its own rate in the opposite direction—the sun along the slanted ecliptic, and the other planets close to the plane of the ecliptic. The closer a planet stands to the outer sphere of the cosmos, the longer it takes to complete its cycle in the opposite direction, and the farther a body stands from the outer sphere, the faster it completes its cycle: "For it is the nearest body which is most strongly influenced, and the most remote, by reason of its distance, which is least affected, the influence on the intermediate bodies varying, as the mathematicians show, with their distance."[153] But the notion in *De natura loci* that the outer sphere induces a particular form into matter through a particular place and at a particular distance from that matter—indeed, the notion of *flux*—constitutes a departure from Aristotle inspired by the place terminology Neoplatonists had used to describe the relation of successively lower emanant entities to the One.

Consider one of the principal sources of Neoplatonic doctrine in Albertus's time, the Pseudo-Aristotelian *Liber de causis* (9th century), which asserts that an emanant's share in the first cause is a function both of its distance from the first cause and of its own capacity as a "thing" for receiving the first cause in itself—a metaphysical claim that carries clear implications for causality in the physical world.[154] Indeed, what characterizes Albertus's rewriting of Aristotle's theory of place is the application of such metaphysical principles to the domain of physics: if, within the domain of Neoplatonic metaphysics, distance from the first cause referred to the order that a particular level of reality as emanant held in relation to the One, then, in the field of physics, distance from the first mover—indeed, place—referred to the measurable interval between a given physical body and the edge of the cosmos as well as to the order of that body in the downward sequence of movers and moved, of places and things placed.

In Albertus's account, distance from this first mover also denotes the order and function of a given physical body within a hierarchy of being. Bodies are located with respect to the outer sphere of the cosmos in a descending order of nobility, and in this order, they are also greater or lesser causes of those things that happen in nature.[155] Aristotle certainly thinks about place in terms of priority and the perfection of nature. Indeed, the idea of priority permeates nearly every aspect of Aristotle's thought.[156] He organizes the chain of movers and moved according to perfection of motion. On the low end of this chain are those bodies potentially moved by other bodies but not themselves moving any others. On the high end is a mover that moves everything else but is not itself moved by anything else. This unmoved mover is perfect, pure actuality eternally actualizing the activities potentially possessed by all other things in the cosmos. And the next best thing to being eternal and unmoved in nature is for a thing to be eternally moved as is Aristotle's first moved on the periphery of the cosmos. In fact, every movable body in nature comes as close to achieving this end as is possible according to its individual potential. Thus for Aristotle, "earth moves not at all and the bodies near it with few movements. For they do not attain the final end [i.e., being moved eternally] but only come as near it as their share in the divine principle permits."[157] Unlike elemental bodies, celestial bodies are made of a divine (incorruptible) substance Aristotle and others before him had called *aither,* and they are moved eternally, each in the manner and place that is proper to it.[158] The first moved on the edge of the cosmos—that being most immediate in the chain to the unmoved mover—attains the end of being moved eternally by means of one single, swift motion that repeats itself without beginning or end. Whereas, the planets under the first moved attain the end of being moved eternally "at the cost of multiplicity of movement."[159] Different priorities of motion are at play in this particular claim of the *Physics:* potential mobility is less perfect than actual mobility; slow motion, less perfect than swift motion; the rectilinear motion of elemental bodies, less perfect than the rotatory motion of celestial bodies; and the composite motion of the planets, less perfect than the uniform motion of the first moved. In theory at least, the more perfect the natural motion of a thing, the higher its place in the chain of movers and moved. With Aristotle, every degree of potentiality implies a certain motion and a certain place in the cosmos. But the notion that form and motion to place are induced on lower things by higher ones in the chain of movers and movables is entirely alien to a philosophy of nature that insists on the active potentiality of matter. Indeed, the doctrine of emanation would provide Albertus good insurance against Aristotle's apparent refusal to grant the unmoved mover a creative or provident role in the cosmos.

Readers familiar with the concept of the *scala naturae* documented in Arthur Lovejoy's *The Great Chain of Being* (1936) may recognize how readily someone attempting to harmonize Aristotle's theory of place with the idea of a creative and provident divine might have literalized the place-based metaphors commonly used to describe the graded relation of all emanant creatures to God. Consider the parallels between Albertus's notion of hierarchical emplacement in the cosmos and the terms originally used by Plotinus in the *Enneads* to describe the "descending" emanation and ordination of reality out of the Good or the One: "There is from the first principle to ultimate an outgoing in which unfailingly each principle retains its own seat while its off-shoot takes another rank, a lower, though on the other hand every being is in identity with its prior as long as it holds that contact."[160] Even a pure metaphysician like Plotinus, concerned with little else than characterizing the divine, had readily laid at the door of physics the idea that emanants have a place in the hierarchy of being as a function of their share in the One. In a passage of the treatises on providence concerned with explaining the nature of evil, or privation of the Good, Plotinus asserts: "There is, then, a Providence, which permeates the Cosmos from first to last, not everywhere equal, as in a numerical distribution, but proportioned, differing, according to the grades of place—just as in some one animal, linked from first to last, each member has its own function, the nobler organ the higher activity while others successively concern the lower degrees of the life, each part acting of itself, and experiencing what belongs to its own nature and what comes from its relation with every other."[161]

Spatial terminology to describe the emanation of subordinate levels of reality from the One were equally compelling to those authors who early on transmitted Plotinus's thought to the Latin West. Macrobius's fifth-century *Commentarium in somnium Scipionis* explains that "since Mind emanates from the Supreme God and Soul from Mind, and [Soul], indeed, forms and suffuses all below with life, and since this is the one splendor lighting up everything and visible in all, like a countenance reflected in many mirrors arranged in a row, and since all follow on in continuous succession, degenerating step by step in their downward course, the close observer will find that from the Supreme God even to the bottommost dregs of the universe there is one tie, binding at every link and never broken."[162] The idea that *up* is closer to the Good and *down* farther from it finds its physical correlate in Macrobius's subsequent account of how chaotic matter was once molded to create the visible cosmos. The physical world "copied"—albeit in degraded form—the hierarchical placement of metaphysical entities:

> That which was the purest and clearest took the highest position and was called ether [i.e., a fiery substance different from Aristotle's quintessence]; the part that was less pure and had some slight weight became air and held second place; next came that part which was indeed still clear but which the sense of touch demonstrates to be corporeal, that which formed the bodies of water; lastly, as a result of the downward rush of matter, there was that vast, impenetrable solid, the dregs and off-scourings of the purified elements, which had settled to the bottom, plunged in continual and oppressing chill, relegated to the last position in the universe, far from the sun. Because this became so hardened it received the name *terra*.[163]

Macrobius's portrayal of earth's indecorous plunge toward the center of the cosmos indeed echoes the rhetoric of "privation" that characterizes Plotinus's portrayal of matter

as evil: "For in Matter we have no mere absence of means or of strength; it is utter destitution—of sense, of virtue, of beauty, of pattern, of Ideal-principle, of quality. This is surely ugliness, utter disgracefulness, unredeemed evil."[164] Thus to think of the center of the cosmos as earth's proper place by nature was not merely to think that the center was where earth-as-absolutely-heavy tended to be moved and come to rest, as Aristotle might have it. For Macrobius and other Neoplatonists, earth ought to occupy the lowest, farthest place from the first cause on the periphery of the cosmos because earth was the most ignoble among all creatures in the ladder of being flowing down from the divine.[165]

Early church doctors also provided important models for extending the metaphors used in metaphysics for describing the hierarchy of emanants issuing from God to the field of physics. The most important among them may well have been the fifth-century Syrian monk who wrote under the pseudonym Dionysius the Areopagite (the figure in Acts of the Apostles allegedly converted by Saint Paul to Christianity in the Areopagus of Athens). Pseudo-Dionysius's mystical treatises bequeathed to the Latin West some of its most enduring categories of spiritual and temporal hierarchy. In a section of *De divinibus nominibus* indebted to Plotinus's discussion of providence and evil in the *Enneads,* Pseudo-Dionysius portrays the place of beings in relation to the "Most Perfect Goodness," by explaining that this Goodness extends not just to the most perfect substances, those closest to it, but to all substances, being totally present to some, less so to others, and barely present to others, so that each substance participates of this Goodness to its own degree.[166] Another key figure was the Greek monk John of Damascus (about 675–about 749), whose familiarity with Aristotle's terminology would prompt Albertus to cite him in his *Physica* and *De natura loci* as an authority on the subject of place. In his theological *De fide orthodoxa,* John of Damascus readily recognizes that spatial terminology is utterly inadequate to refer to metaphysical entities but perfectly adequate to describe the manner in which God's providence operates in the visible cosmos. Having defined place in terms reminiscent of Aristotle, as the inner limit of any given container, John of Damascus enumerates the various ways in which a metaphysical entity like God could be thought of as being in place:

> There is also an intellectual place where the intellectual and incorporeal nature is thought of as being and where it actually is. There it is present and acts; and it is not physically contained, but spiritually, because it has no form to permit it to be physically contained. Now, God, being immaterial and uncircumscribed, is not in

a place. For he who fills all things and is over all things and Himself encompasses all things, is His own place. However, God is also said to be in a place; and this place where God is said to be is there where His operation is plainly visible. Now, He does pervade all things without becoming mixed with them, and to all things He communicates His operation in accordance with the fitness and receptivity of each—in accordance with their purity of nature and will, I mean to say.[167]

In sum, the metaphysical notion that the rank of an emanant in the hierarchy of being is a function of its share in the One easily translated in this tradition to the physical notion that bodily creatures had a place in relation to the first mover, God's first physical effect in the visible cosmos. In Albertus's *De natura loci,* place denoted order of nobility in the downward flow of form and motion from the outer sphere of the cosmos. And, for thinkers like Albertus, the idea that creatures had a place in the cosmos according to their rank in the scale of perfection stood only a step away from the idea that places and peoples *also* were distributed hierarchically across the globe—if only because both ideas were predicated on the compelling principle that, where *nature* was concerned, as Plato plainly states in *Laws,* "Soul is the master, and matter its natural subject."[168] The enduring claim that temperate nations were naturally predisposed to rule hot and cold ones rested precisely on the notion that in temperate places nature worked in an orderly manner, whereas in extreme places nature handled itself in a disorderly, even monstrous, fashion. Among those peoples who inhabited "temperate" places, the soul tended to master the body; among those peoples who inhabited "extreme" places, the body tended to master the soul. This is the true and ominous meaning, for example, of Averroës's memorable claim in his work on Aristotle's *Meteorologica* that the life of Ethiopians and other creatures outside the temperate bounds of the inhabited world were "not natural" and "beyond nature."[169]

Having reoriented Aristotle's theory of place to accommodate the idea of a creative and provident divine, Albertus was prepared to explain the great diversity of places and things placed beyond the constrained parameters observed by Aristotle in the *Physics* and *On the Heavens.* His explanation for diversity would hinge on a concept that is entirely absent from Aristotle's natural philosophy but central to Neoplatonic metaphysics: the radiation of light.[170] Indeed, it is Albertus's particular use of this concept that brings *De natura loci* closest to the doctrine of emanation espoused in Plotinus's *Enneads.*

As Albertus has already established in his treatise, place is the active means through which the heavens induce form, and thereby, motion to place. The divine power flowing down from heaven and inducing form and motion through place is light, which is why, according to Albertus, astrologers had been justified in thinking of it as the very "firmament of place" or "foundation of place."[171] The idea that light is prior to place indubitably found support in a hexameral tradition that had long attempted to explain Genesis 1:3–5: "Be light made. And light was made. And God saw the light that it was good; and he divided the light from the darkness." In *De genesi ad litteram,* for instance, Saint Augustine thought that these versicles described the creation of spiritual form, which had come after the creation of both the spiritual realm and inchoate matter ("heaven and earth") but which had preceded the actual diversification of this unformed matter into all the things that composed the physical universe.[172] Within the Aristotelian tradition, Albertus's conception of light as, in a sense, the place of place, or the place before place, bears particularly strong affinities with Proclus's own rewriting of Aristotle's theory of place, which plainly defined place as light and light as the most immaterial of all bodies—a divine substratum holding the universe together.[173]

Albertus was not the first Christian author to introduce light into the newly emerging domain of Aristotelian physics. A compatible view was already under way in the spatialized optics developed earlier in the thirteenth century by Albertus's contemporary Robert Grosseteste. In his seminal treatise *De luce,* Grosseteste defines light as the "first corporeal form" (*prima forma corporalis*), which by its instantaneous diffusion is supposed to have dragged matter along, extending it in all three dimensions.[174] Grosseteste's version of Creation describes a flash of light that extended matter outward in ever more rarified form to the periphery of the cosmos; matter then radiated back toward the center, successively forming the various celestial and elemental spheres.[175] Like Albertus, Grosseteste thought of light as the "form" (*species*) and "perfection" of all bodies, a notion that should instantly recall the active and motive role that Plato, Plotinus, and their followers had assigned to soul relative to matter.[176] (Plotinus had in fact stated that Soul "appears to be present [in animate bodies] by the fact that it *shines* into them: it makes them living beings not by merging into body but by giving forth, without any change in itself, images or likenesses of itself like one face caught by many mirrors.")[177]

Neither Grosseteste nor Albertus thought of this light, however, as only visible light.[178] Albertus explains that the divine power pouring down from heaven could

conceivably be called light, provided that such a term denoted the complex of different powers that flowed down from the heavens to things below. After all, the hot, the cold, the dry, and the wet were also communicated by the heavens to things below, and yet these other powers could not be called visible light.[179] (These and other invisible powers may be what at the time justified grouping arts like astrology and magic under the rubric of the "occult"—that which was hidden from the senses.)[180] On the other hand, Albertus reasons, some authors did refer to form and to different sorts of formative power as the "radiance of intelligence" (*splendor intelligentiae*), so that, metaphorically speaking, one could concede that light was that power by means of which the heavens conferred on place the power to form things.[181] Albertus thus meant to establish light as a central component of his natural philosophy, whereas Aristotle's own philosophy of nature theorizes place largely in terms of motion. Albertus's reference to this power as radiance of intelligence reminds us that he considered light of whatever sort in the physical world to be an extension of the divine.

Albertus's silent partner in the elaboration of a theory of diversity based on light radiation was the ninth-century philosopher al-Kindī, whose *De radiis* had profitably extended to the realm of physics the metaphor Plotinus had used in the *Enneads* to describe the emanation of all reality from the One. In fact, al-Kindī's explanation for diversity in the natural world was most likely inspired by a passage in the *Enneads* IV where Plotinus himself talks about light radiation as the cause of diversity in the material world.[182] Al-Kindī and his contemporary Albumasar (author of the astrological *Liber introductorium*) were both Persian, and their readiness to deploy the concept of "light radiation" to explain cause and effect in the natural world may well have originated with Zoroastrian cosmogony, which told how the god Ôhr-mazd created out of "Infinite Light" (*A-sar Rôsnîh*) a luminous ball of white fire (*Âsrô*) from which all things were then to be born.[183] Of course, the sun and its light had inspired no dearth of cults among the ancients, distinct from the cult inspired by Zoroaster (about 628–about 551 BCE). Greek poets and thinkers who had deployed sun and light images to various ends were probably mindful of the sun's symbolic role in Eastern religions as well as of sun worship in Egypt, Persia, and other areas of the Mediterranean and the Near East.[184] The concept of light radiation itself, or "emission of rays" (*aktinobolia*), had been present in Greek astrology, although even the great Ptolemy had not particularly emphasized light radiation in his *Tetrabiblos*.[185]

But the framework that lent authority to the concept of light radiation in al-Kindī's *De radiis* was metaphysics itself. No philosophical work in the West had used metaphors of sun and light as fruitfully or as influentially as Plato's *Republic*. Plato was responsible for most deeply impressing upon the West the notion that light was Truth.[186] And it was mainly from Plato's teachings about the Good-as-Sun in the *Republic* that Plotinus would see himself to be drawing the comparison between emanation from the One and the radiation of light.[187] Plato's comparison of the Good with the sun was consciously fashioned as a compromise born of humanity's inability to apprehend the metaphysical realm of eternal Being, at least initially, without reference to images drawn from changeable realm of Becoming—that is, through those things that are apprehended by the five human senses.[188] In order to discuss the Good-as-Sun, Plato first considers in the *Republic* the hierarchy of the human senses, beginning with touch (the lowest) and ending with sight, which Socrates characterizes for Glaucon as "the most sunlike of the organs of the senses." As Socrates explains it, sight receives from the sun "the power it has [to see] as a sort of overflow from the sun's treasury. . . ."[189] (The concept of overflow from a copious source was to have an echo in Plotinus's claim that emanation was the result of a superabundance of vitality in the One.)[190] Socrates goes on to establish that "as the good is in the intelligible region with respect to intelligence and what is intellected, so the sun is in the visible region with respect to sight and what is seen."[191] The good causes the mind's eye to see, just as the sun does with respect to sight—a concept that would prove of crucial importance to Augustine's famous doctrine of illumination.[192] For Plato, the analogy did not end here, for "the sun not only provides what is seen with the power of being seen, but also with generation, growth, and nourishment although it itself isn't generation [i.e., is not perishable]."[193] And such a view about the sun's generative role in nature invited other metaphysical writers in the West who metaphorized God as light to conceive of light itself as a link between the divine and the visible cosmos, or, in Plotinian terms, as that efflux of lower Soul that conferred form to lifeless, motionless matter. As Plotinus believed, this divine light permeated everything, from brightest first to darkest last, and with this light, Soul then *saw*, and in seeing, brought about the things of the material cosmos.[194] Light was for Plotinus that divine efflux by virtue of which Soul-as-Nature accomplished its work in the material cosmos.

Like Plato, Plotinus recognized the inadequacy of the metaphors he had chosen, not only for discussing something beyond all description like the One or the Good, but also for explaining the diversity that existed beyond it—Intellect, Soul, and, of course, Nature.[195] As he memorably explains in the *Enneads,* what accounts for this diversity

> must be a *circumradiation*—produced from the Supreme but from the Supreme unaltering—and may be compared to the brilliant light encircling the sun and ceaselessly generated from that unchanging substance.
>
> All existences, as long as they retain their character, produce—about themselves, from their essence, in virtue of the power which must be in them— some necessary, outward-facing hypostasis continuously attached to them and representing in image the engendering archetypes: thus fire gives out its heat; snow is cold not merely for itself; fragrant substances are a notable instance; for, as long as they last, something is diffused from them and perceived wherever they are present.[196]

In other instances in the *Enneads,* Plotinus certainly attempted to void this metaphor of its patent physicality by asserting that the light of an omnipresent and indeterminate One could have neither a center (meaning, a source) nor a circumference—indeed, by negating the very notion of radiation to describe its metaphysical being.[197]

But if Plotinus deemed his light metaphor—or for that matter any metaphor—to be inadequate for describing the manner in which lower realities originated from the One, he was certainly willing to construe light as the divine power by virtue of which "lower" Soul, that is Nature, gave of itself to all things material. Of course, celestial bodies played a crucial role as "instruments" of Soul. Each configuration of the celestial vault was supposed to be accompanied by the appropriate changes in the elemental region: "The Circuit [orb] does not go by chance but under the Reason-Principle of the living whole [the cosmos]; therefore there must be a harmony between cause and caused; there must be some order ranging things to each other's purpose, or in due relation to each other: every several configuration within the Circuit must be accompanied by a change in the position and condition of things subordinate to it, which thus by their varied rhythmic movement make up one total dance-play [i.e., Plato's harmony of the spheres]."[198] In a subsequent passage that indubitably served as the seed for the theory of diversity formulated in al-Kindī's *De radiis,* Plotinus, using the sun as his prime example, describes the role of celestial bodies in conveying Soul's light to the elemental bodies:

"In all the efficacy of the sun and other stars upon earthly matters we can but believe that though the heavenly body is intent upon the Supreme, yet—to keep to the sun—its warming of terrestrial things, and every service following upon that, all springs from itself, its own act transmitted in virtue of soul, the vastly efficacious soul of Nature."[199] If all celestial bodies were the tools by which lower Soul, in a sense, permeated the entire material cosmos, each individual planet or star radiated a particular power dispensed by Nature. Thus the individual powers radiating from each celestial body added up to a single complex of powers. And as the sky's configuration changed from moment to moment, so this complex of powers changed, bringing about changes below: "Each of the heavenly bodies, similarly, gives forth a power, involuntary, by its mere radiation: all things become one entity, grouped by this diffusion of power, and so bring about wide changes of condition; thus the very groupings have power since their diversity produces diverse conditions; that the grouped beings themselves have also their efficiency is clear since they produce differently according to the different membership of the groups."[200] Although Plotinus barely concerned himself with the material world (only insofar as it denoted privation of the Good), he paved the way for others to develop his doctrine of emanation into a fully articulated theory of nature. Of course, the astrological views expressed in these passages predate those of the *Enneads,* but it was Plotinus who, by associating Nature with Soul and the light radiating from Soul with divinity, provided a strong metaphysical foundation for the use of technical disciplines like astrology by Aristotelians such as Grosseteste, Albertus, and Bacon—all of whom hoped for a science that would one day accurately specify and predict the nature of places and of things placed.

Other influential metaphysical writers would feel compelled to metaphorize divinity as the radiation of light and to construe light in the physical world as divine. The mystical works of Pseudo-Dionysius, for instance, bequeathed to the Latin West what may be the richest store of light metaphors to describe divinity. Echoing Plato's *Republic,* Pseudo-Dionysius explains in *De divinibus nominibus* that just as the sun, by the mere fact of being, illuminates all things to the extent of their ability to share in its light, so the Good, which is the archetype of the sun, by its mere presence in all existents, "pours down the rays of all goodness" on them.[201] In *De caelesti hierarchia,* which specifies nine categories of angelic intelligences, Pseudo-Dionysius also explains that human intellect cannot really rise to apprehend metaphysical hierarchies without first understanding, for instance, that material lights are visible images of the giving forth of immaterial lights.[202]

In *De fide orthodoxa,* John of Damascus explains the multiplicity that is supposed to issue from God by stating that "the divine irradiation and operation is one, simple, and undivided; and . . . while it is apparently diversely manifested in divisible things, dispensing to all of them the components of their proper nature, it remains simple. Indivisibly, it is multiplied in divisible things, and, gathering them together, it reverts them to its own simplicity."[203] Discussing the account of the creation of the sun and moon in Genesis, but indeed referring to all celestial bodies alike, John states: "It was into these luminaries that the Creator put the primordial light."[204] The readiness both to construe God as light and to define light itself as extension of the divine is also to be found in the Pseudo-Aristotelian *Liber de causis:* "The First Cause is above all description. And tongues fail to describe it only because they are unable to describe its being, since the First Cause is above every cause and is described only through the second causes that are illuminated by the light of the First Cause."[205]

It is in al-Kindī's *De radiis* that we have, however, the most likely source of inspiration for the theories of natural diversity developed by noted thirteenth-century authors like Grosseteste, Albertus, and Bacon.[206] Al-Kindī's treatise espouses the notion most probably borrowed directly from Plotinus that every metaphysical and physical being radiates forth some sort of power, a likeness or form of itself communicated to other things.[207] This explains the role in the practice of natural magic not only of such objects like gems and stones but also of incantations and prayer for changing the outcome of things. What specifically concerns us here is his explanation for celestial radiation. According to al-Kindī, every star (and planet) possesses its own individual "nature and condition" and therefore emits rays that are peculiar to it—not shared with any other celestial body.[208]

On al-Kindī's authority, each star has its own place in the *mundana machina* and therefore a unique "gaze" on a given place or thing in the cosmos—meaning that both its distance from a given point and the angles at which its rays reach that point are different from those of every other star in the heavens. The rays from one and the same star have different effects on different places and things, no matter how close those places and things might stand to one another. Furthermore, the effect of the sum total of rays emitted by one configuration of celestial bodies differs from the effect of those rays emitted by any other configuration. By the same token, one and the same configuration of the heavens has different effects on different places and things. The Plotinian resonances in al-Kindī's reasoning are quite easily recognizable in *De radiis:*

"For every star pours its rays into every place, so that the diversity of rays, as though melded into one, varies the contents of all places, for in every different place the rays have a different tenor which is derived from that total harmony of the stars."[209] Having established the unrepeatable character of individual and collective forces radiating down on each and every place and thing, al-Kindī also introduces the element of time to explain transformation in the natural world. As the heavens move, one configuration of celestial bodies gives way to the next, and the complex of rays bearing down on each and every place below also changes, causing things to mutate constantly and thereby to move in different ways.[210] Thus every place at every point in time generates a thing that is both unique to that place and in constant flux—changing in some way or on its way to becoming something else altogether.

Al-Kindī also made two claims that would also be of great importance to the spatialized optics developed in the early thirteenth century by Grosseteste in seminal treatises such as *De lineis, angulis, et figuris* and *De natura locorum,* though al-Kindī's *De radiis* was by no means the most important source used by him or by Albertus and Bacon in the field of *perspectiva*.[211] According to al-Kindī, rays flowing from the center of a celestial body to the center of the earth—meaning rays falling perpendicular to a given point on the globe's surface—are the strongest of all rays. Whereas, rays falling obliquely with respect to the earth's center—at a slant with respect to a given point on the globe's surface—grow weaker in proportion to the obliquity of the angle of incidence.[212] The second concept concerns the ability of "prejacent matter" to receive the form communicated by stellar rays—a point that closely echoed the metaphysical claim in Plotinus and his followers that, while the Good permeated the entire cosmos, each and every creature received from the Good in accordance with its own capacity to receive. The term *materia preiacens* means for al-Kindī nothing other than matter that, having one form, serves as the raw material for stellar rays to generate a different form.[213] The new form generated by the action of stellar rays varies greatly, depending on the particular composition of prejacent matter.[214] In the case of rays acting on an opaque object like human skin, for example, light might be reflected while heat itself penetrates and "vivifies" the body.[215] But the same rays might act very differently on another object. Whence "the diversity of things in the world of the elements at any given time proceeds from two chief causes, namely, the diversity of matters, and the operation of the various stellar rays."[216]

Such concepts were important to the spatialized optics developed in the thirteenth century by Grosseteste, who claims in his own *De natura locorum* that by using geometry's lines, angles, and figures to represent the emission of rays, "the diligent inspector of natural things can determine the causes of all natural effects."[217] In the treatise that logically precedes this argument, *De lineis, angulis, et figuris,* Grosseteste enumerates those factors that determine the effects of rays on things. First is the distance between any given radiating body and its object: the shorter the ray between them, the greater its power; the longer the ray between them, the lesser its power.[218] Second is the angle at which a given ray strikes a surface: the more perpendicular the ray with respect to this surface, the stronger its power; the more oblique the ray, the weaker its power.[219] Third is the reflection, absorption, or refraction of rays by different surfaces.[220] This last factor concerns not only rays themselves but also the composition of the objects that receive them, which affects the ability of those objects to accept the forms conveyed by those rays.

Simple optical principles such as these would play a key role in the explanations forwarded in such works as Grosseteste's *De natura locorum,* Albertus's *De natura loci,* and Bacon's *Opus maius* IV concerning the inhabitability and uninhabitability of places across the globe. And these same optical principles would come to govern Albertus's explanation for why the belt between the tropics, contrary to the traditional theory of the five zones, could be said to be universally temperate, fertile, and habitable.

Al-Kindī concludes his doctrine of rays by stating that knowledge of the configuration of the stars at any given point in time is knowledge of the nature of things past, present, and future. Since all things that come to be or to pass in the elemental world do so by virtue of the sum total of stellar rays bearing down on them, all things, whatever they have been, are, or will be, are precisely encoded in that "celestial harmony."[221] This is, so to speak, al-Kindī's "charter" of astrology and its most immediate inspiration may have been the concept of universal sympathy epitomized by Plotinus in his statement that the stars were akin to "letters perpetually being inscribed on the heavens."[222] Predicated on the gulf that was supposed to separate the changeable realm of Becoming from that of eternal Being in Plato's thought, Plotinus's notion that celestial bodies—as emanants of lower Soul—were, in some sense, mirrors, copies, or traces of higher being, once again supplied the metaphysical foundation for al-Kindī's astrological doctrine of rays.

Plotinus's simile was to find enormous resonance with Christian writers who regarded nature as a book that encrypted a divine message.[223] As one reads in a postil on the margins of Columbus's copy of d'Ailly and Gerson's *Tractatus,* "The form of the heavens is a kind of natural book written by God's hands, in which he created the luminaries like letters or, so to speak, legible writings."[224] Columbus himself, who in the years following the discovery came to demonstrate thorough acquaintance with the astrological theories espoused by d'Ailly and Gerson, had contact with al-Kindī's doctrine of rays through Gerson's *Trigilogium astrologie theologisate* (1419), a treatise that pointed out some of the serious shortcomings in the astrological *perspectiva* proposed by works like *De radiis.* In his "thirty propositions of theologized astrology," Gerson echoes some of the serious misgivings that critics had long voiced concerning the viability and accuracy of astrology as a prognostic tool. And in passages bearing the ink underlines of a most attentive reader, perhaps Columbus himself, Gerson complains not only that the heavens contain seemingly infinite combinations of "numbers and figures" but also that the power of any given light radiating down from each of the heavenly bodies is intercepted and distorted by the lights of other heavenly bodies, making it quite impossible to ascertain what the true "aspects" of the stars are in relation to the earth.[225]

Al-Kindī's doctrine of rays played a central role in Albertus's rewriting and expansion of Aristotle. By Albertus's account, anyone seeking to understand all natures and properties of particular places in the regions of air, water, and earth would have had to understand that each and every point in these elements received a special property from the stars gazing down on it.[226] Any point one might take as the center of a given habitat for humans, beasts, plants, and minerals was the center of a unique horizon, so that, from one point to the next, the horizon changed, as did the entire gaze of the heavens bearing down on that horizon's center.[227] For this reason, no place was supposed to be like any other, and the "nature, properties, habits, acts, and abilities" of each thing belonged to it alone. This was true even for different parts of the same thing, even for those things that one took to be in the same place and even for seemingly identical things like twins—be they twins in plants, beasts, or humans.[228] Albertus reminds us that heaven imparted "formative powers" on every creature in existence.[229] And since it did so by means of light from the stars, the unique configuration of rays falling on the center of each horizon was accountable for the unrepeatable form that each and every creature in its place received from heaven.[230]

Albertus concludes his meditation on the uniqueness of places by calling his reader's attention back to Porphyry's discussion of place as an active principle of generation: "This is, properly, place," he writes, "of which Porphyry says that it is single with respect to individual things; because, as Boethius [i.e., Porphyry's commentator] explains, it cannot be comprehended or even imagined that two things could occupy exactly the same place."[231] Places closer together tended to share more properties than places farther apart, and therefore those things that were closer together also tended to share more properties than things farther apart.[232] But every formative power radiating from heaven, and thus every single place, and every single thing that had a place by nature, was absolutely unrepeatable. As proof of this claim, Albertus invokes the case of the lodestone, which from one side repels iron and from the opposite side attracts it.[233] This "contrariety" in one and the same object could not be attributed to matter itself, for matter was not the cause of power or form in things, but rather to place itself: each end of the lodestone displayed a different property because it was in a different place informed by a different configuration of stellar rays.[234] Place, for Albertus, was thus unique, as was the nature of things in their places.

Having established the unrepeatable nature of places, Albertus accounts for the unceasing mutability of things that had a place in the region of the elements: naturally it was the daily east-to-west motion of the entire celestial vault and the individual countermotions of the planets under the inclined belt of the zodiac that were supposed to determine this constant flux. Not only did any given place have a nature that it shared with no other, but the nature of one and the same place constantly changed with the rising and setting of celestial bodies.[235] With this claim, Albertus's theory of natural diversity was complete, at least insofar as universal causes were concerned. For, like al-Kindī and Grosseteste, Albertus also took into account those particular factors that were supposed to modulate or even counteract the celestial powers radiating down on elemental bodies. Once again, elemental bodies were construed as receptive to stellar radiation in accordance with their composition—indeed, they might have been said to "resist" celestial powers in accordance with the internal properties they already possessed.[236] This notion was profoundly connected, of course, to the concept of receptivity to form that so pervades Neoplatonic thought. Also, factors like the presence of mountains or coastal waters could also alter "accidentally" (*per accidens*) the natures of places and things induced by stellar rays. (Recall, for instance, the role that the Nile and the Ganges rivers played, according to Mediterranean geographers, in counteracting the lethal heat of the tropics.) In addition, the natures induced by the heavens could always be counteracted artificially (*per artificium*) by experts cognizant of the powers communicated by the stars.[237] This is, of course, Albertus's own charter of astrology, directly lifted from the famous overture to the influential *Tetrabiblos,* in which Ptolemy extols the many benefits that came from the practice of this technical discipline.[238]

In sum, Albertus and like-minded thinkers believed that to know the place of a thing was to know its nature, and this knowledge also promised to serve as an antidote for nature. Hence, geography's instrumentality to Albertus's philosophy of nature. As Albertus clearly recognized long before the induction of Ptolemy's *Geography* to the Latin West, without the technical ability to locate places by latitude and longitude, philosophy's quest was bound to remain imperfect.[239] And for Albertus, as for other theoretical geographers since antiquity, differences in terrestrial latitude had greater bearing on the diversification of habitats than differences in longitude.[240] Indeed, latitude played a more critical role than longitude in the habitability or uninhabitability of places.

The next step toward specifying the nature of places and things placed was to establish the proper causal correlations between the celestial and elemental regions of the cosmos. This task, as Gerson's critique of al-Kindī's doctrine of rays has shown, was daunting, and it had long doomed astrology to remaining a highly speculative and contentious field forever in its infancy. Indeed, the problem for astrologers had always been how to factor in all the powers conveyed by the stellar rays converging at any given time on the center of any given horizon, not to mention how to factor in all the accidents—of body or of place—that were supposed to modulate or counteract those universal powers. The only immediate solution to this problem was to proceed, as Ptolemy and others had done, from the most universal divisions of the elemental region according to the heavens to the most particular. In *De natura loci,* Albertus did not set out to specify the very numerous correlations between the heavens and the region of the elements; his task had been only to provide a philosophical and technical model for other naturalists to approach the problem of specifying and predicting the nature of places and of things that had a place by nature. His model was to serve as a starting point for all the natural sciences—from those concerned with the psychology and/or physiology of humans, beasts, and plants to those that sought to study presumably soulless substances like metals and stones. And to the extent that humans followed the natures they received from places, this model was also important for moral philosophy, that is, for those domains of knowledge concerned with understanding uniquely human conduct. For Albertus and other Aristotelians, moral philosophy would come to be largely defined by Aristotle's *Nicomachean Ethics,* which was already familiar to Albertus when he wrote *De natura loci,* and by Aristotle's *Economics* and *Politics,* which were translated soon thereafter.[241]

Fortunately for us, the causal correlation between heaven and earth that immediately concerns our discussion of the early transatlantic encounter had long been invited by Parmenides.[242] Albertus invokes two major ways of relating the known inhabited world to the heavens: the more universal one involves dividing the entire globe into five horizontal zones (Parmenides' method); the less universal one involves dividing the *orbis terrarum* itself into seven *climata* (the method devised by Eratosthenes).[243]

With recourse to the doctrine of rays, Albertus would reframe the theory of the five zones. But equally mindful of the optical principles that the doctrine of rays provided, Albertus would also offer an alternative to the traditional paradigm that was to come in very handy to Las Casas nearly three hundred years later. In the sixteenth century, Albertus remained an unrivaled authority among Aristotelians on the subject of nature, and his *De natura loci* was perhaps the most thorough philosophical geography ever written. Because of this, Albertus's theory that the torrid zone might be vastly temperate, fertile, and inhabitable was destined to provide Las Casas with a weapon against the schooled apologists of empire who had argued since the turn of the sixteenth century that the peoples discovered by Columbus, because they occupied the hot fringes of the inhabited world, were slaves by nature.

Albertus first enumerates the reasons why, as the theory of the five zones claimed, it was reasonable to think that the tropical and arctic regions of the globe were universally inhospitable. First, on any given point between the tropics of Cancer and Capricorn, the sun's rays fall perpendicularly on the surface of the globe twice a year at noon—once as the sun transits along the slanted ecliptic on its way north and a second time on its way south. Authors who had claimed that the torrid zone was scorched argued that sunrays falling perpendicularly on the oceanic waters of this region grew "combustive" upon being reflected on themselves.[244] The combustive action of these concentrated rays would have rendered the ocean between the tropics unfordable and its shores uninhabitable, especially because waters together with shorelines were supposed to act in the manner of a concave mirror that concentrated the sun's rays, making them even more lethal.[245] With regard to the cold regions near the poles, Albertus once again invokes optical principles to explain why they too might have been thought to be uninhabitable: polar regions were "too far away" from the sun's path—meaning that the sun's rays reached them too obliquely, falling on the globe's surface at excessively dull and obtuse angles.[246] Extending Albertus's reasoning, we might explain the difference in temperatures between the equatorial and polar regions as follows. A given amount of light radiation falling perpendicularly or nearly so on the plane of a given horizon within the tropics—that is, approaching or reaching an angle of ninety degrees—covers an area approaching a^2 or equal to a^2 on the globe's surface. The same amount of light radiation falling ever more obliquely on the plane of a given horizon within the arctic or antarctic regions—that is, approaching an angle of zero degrees—would cover an area ever greater than a^2 and approaching infinity. In other words, a given quantity of heat energy falling on a given area near the equator would, near the poles, be dispersed over a significantly larger area, hence the differences in temperature between the hot and cold zones of the globe.

Having provided this and other reasons why the theory of the five zones made sense, Albertus explains why this theory might also prove inadequate to describe the nature of the tropical and polar regions. It is important to note that Albertus, like the pagan geographers of antiquity and like the hexameral writers who preceded Augustine, espoused an open geographical model for the terraqueous globe ultimately based on Aristotle's claim concerning the natural places of the elements at the center of the cosmos: earth's place was below water's. As Albertus insists, hypothesizing the habitability of the southern hemisphere, the ancient writers who used to think that the earth was not round—those writers who believed that dry land was restricted to a northern quarter of the globe and that the rest of the globe was composed of nothing other than water, air, and fire—were wrong.[247] For Albertus, the spheres of earth and water were *concentric*, not eccentric, as these authors had claimed, for, as he had already proved in his own *De caelo et mundo*, earth's place was beneath all the other elements at the center of the world.[248] Not surprisingly, the sources cited by Albertus in favor of his open geography are Homer's mention in the *Odyssey* of "a people split in two" and the model that Crates equivocally developed as an illustration of Homer's geography, positing inhabited landmasses in the temperate zones of the remaining three quarters of the globe.[249] However, Albertus pushes his argument even farther, objecting to the Cratesian view that the inhabited world in the northern temperate zone was incommunicated from that in the southern one by a vast Ocean River running through a hot equatorial region. And he just as adamantly objects to the established view that the inhabited world ended toward the south with the vast, sandy deserts that were seen to stretch along the Tropic of Capricorn in northern Africa.[250] The source for his arguments against the theory of the five zones and in favor of a temperate, fertile, and inhabitable torrid zone appears to have been a geographical work, or part of a work, titled *De divisione locorum habitabilium,* which, according to Albertus, recorded the reasoning of Ptolemy and Avicenna.[251] Whether or not this work was the main conduit through which Albertus and his contemporaries came to know this tradition, we do not know, but it must have been the translation of an Arabic manuscript composed after Avicenna wrote his works in the early part of the eleventh century.

The highly abstract character of *De natura loci* did not prevent Albertus from citing existing geographical testimony, indirect as it might be, in support of his theories on the torrid zone. As Albertus notes, experience suggested that the inhabited world extended well within the reaches of the torrid zone: Ptolemy and Avicenna had seen "with their own eyes" men from the region between the Tropic of Cancer and the equator and had read the books on the stars composed by the philosophers of that region.[252] Both Ethiopia and India were known to harbor numerous and famous cities all the way to the equator, and many of their inhabitants had even ventured north, proving in the flesh that the equatorial region was hospitable. Well over two centuries before Columbus would present his plan to Fernando and Isabel, Albertus was more than willing to do what Columbus's learned detractors in Castile refused to do when figures like Geraldini pointed out that the Portuguese had already found a vastly inhabited world in the tropical Atlantic: he was willing to use bits and pieces of experiential evidence, outdated though they might be, as grounds for revising an established cosmological paradigm such as the theory of the five zones.

Albertus's theoretical argumentation against the theory of the five zones ultimately hinged on the optical principles he had brought to bear on Aristotle's theory of motion. He first reminds his reader that the sun is the main generator of contraries in the region of the elements: with each approach and retreat along the ecliptic, to and from any given zenith in the sky relative to the observer, the sun causes things to come into being and to pass away. With this in mind, Albertus reasons that the cycle of generation and corruption occurs especially in those places "where the sun *equally* advances and retreats," and since this is supposed to happen on the equator, it follows that the most productive habitats have to be equatorial.[253] Albertus's logic can be summarized as follows: in places along the equator the sun passes directly overhead twice a year, once every six months. By approaching and retreating from the equator twice a year, the sun generates two cycles of growth and decay—and in the case of plants that yield crops, two crops a year. The sun's retreat northbound from any given zenith along the equator to the Tropic of Cancer and its return southbound from the Tropic of Cancer to that zenith takes exactly the same length of time as its retreat southbound from any given zenith along the equator to the Tropic of Capricorn and its return northbound from the Tropic of Capricorn to that zenith. Places on the equator experience two crops a year not just because the sun approaches any given zenith there twice a year but also because each interval in between is sufficiently long for plants to experience full cycles of growth and decay—nature at its most efficient. By the same token, in places between the equator and the tropics, the sun also passes directly overhead twice a year, but at unequal intervals. For those places approaching the equator, each interval may be sufficiently long for plants to experience growth and decay and thus to yield two crops a year. But for places approaching one or the other tropic, one of those intervals grows shorter and shorter, making it harder and harder for plants to experience full cycles of growth and decay more than once a year. Finally, in places on the two tropics, the sun passes overhead only once a year, with plants consequently producing only one crop a year— tropical nature at its least efficient. Albertus's point about nature's great efficiency in equatorial places does not just concern plants: it concerns all creatures that undergo cycles of growth and decay—whether humans, beasts, plants, or, indeed, minerals.

The second point in Albertus's argument concerns the temperature of places in the belt of the tropics. (The theory of the five zones easily misled one to believe that the torrid zone was everywhere hot at all times.) Albertus reasons that the temperature of any given place is mainly a function of the sun's approach and retreat along the slanted ecliptic to and from the zenith in the sky relative to that place. The sun generates heat as it approaches that zenith and leaves behind cold as it recedes away from it. Since the intermediate point between heat and cold is the temperate, tropical places can also be regarded as (relatively) temperate: the heat caused by the sun's approach to any given zenith within the belt of the tropics is always tempered by the sun's retreat away from that zenith.[254] This would include any given place along the tropics of Cancer and Capricorn, each of which experiences heat around the times of the solstice in its hemisphere and cold around the times of the solstice in the opposite hemisphere. For Albertus, tropical nature was not, therefore, the unrelenting mistress that so many had claimed her to be.

The third point in Albertus's argument concerns the power of planetary rays within the belt of the tropics. He reasons that celestial bodies are most effective on the elements and their compounds in a place in which their rays are "maximally multiplied."[255] This he supposes to occur "in the paths of the planets." Since this path falls between the tropics, their power is strongest within the belt of the tropics. And since the power of celestial bodies is the power to generate things, generation is especially strong in tropical places. In other words, it is not only the sun but also the moon and the other planets that generate contraries in the elemental world. Their approach and retreat along their respective orbits causes things to come into being and to pass away. Moreover, the angle at which planetary rays fall to the ground determine their intensity: the more perpendicularly they fall to the ground, the more intense; inversely, the more obliquely they fall, the less intense. The sun's rays always fall perpendicularly to the ground somewhere in the belt of the tropics, therefore its rays are supposed to be most intense in tropical places. By the same token, the moon and the other planets never stray far from the plane of the sun's ecliptic, always transiting under the slanted belt of the zodiac. Therefore their rays almost always fall perpendicularly to the ground somewhere in the belt of the tropics. So their rays also tend to be most intense in tropical places. Thus for Albertus the most powerful cycles of growth and decay were to be found in a region that had long been deemed by many to be generally sterile.

The fourth point in Albertus's argument concerns the relative perfection of things generated within the belt of the tropics. According to Albertus, some authors had addressed this question by considering what was known "about images," that is, what was known concerning the projection of physical light onto surfaces.[256] Images were supposed to be most perfect in those places where planetary rays fell to the ground perpendicularly. The strong Neoplatonic inflection of this reasoning merits some explanation. In Albertus's *De natura loci,* place is the active medium through which form and thereby motion to place are induced on things placed. This form, along the lines of Plotinus's concept of emanation, is a kind of *logos*—that is, a copy or image—conferred unto every lower emanant by its antecedent. In Albertus's doctrine of rays, since light is that divine "power" in nature that induces form on bodies, the angle at which stellar rays fall on the surface of the globe affects how they convey form. Light falling perpendicularly on any given point within the tropics remains "undistorted," thus conveying form perfectly; however, light falling obliquely is "distorted," thus conveying form imperfectly. For all these reasons, Albertus continues, it seemed to great minds that the region that the ancients had considered to be torrid was not burned everywhere but was instead hospitable, not only on the continental shores of the Indian Ocean, whose floor was supposed to be a carpet of diamonds (the most perfect of all stones), but also on its numerous islands.[257]

The last proof in Albertus's argument concerns the temperateness of equatorial latitudes relative to latitudes near each tropic. On Strabo's authority, the earliest variant of this argument would have appeared in Eratosthenes' lost *Geography*. According to Albertus, life on the Tropic of Cancer is "laborious and unpleasant," whereas life on the equator is "continuous and delightful."[258] He explains that while the sun passes overhead twice a year on the equator, its "ray" does not linger there. The sun also does not return to the equator until it has passed "at least four signs of the zodiac," meaning at least four months. For these two reasons, the heat caused by the sun's approach to the equator does not set fire to anything or tend to accumulate over time. In other words, because the ecliptic is slanted and the sun presumably travels at a constant speed around it, the rate at which the sun's declination changes relative to the equator around the times of the equinoxes is significantly faster than the rate at which the sun approaches either tropic near the times of the solstices. The sun's rays do not have enough time to scorch the equator, though they do have time to scorch the tropics. In astronomical terms, in the torrid zone the number of days during which a gnomon has no or little shadow at noon is greater for latitudes near the tropics around the times of the solstices than for latitudes near the equator around the times of the equinoxes. Eratosthenes certainly had elaborated this argument against the theory of the five zones in order to explain why there should have been vastly fertile and inhabited regions such as Ethiopia and India beyond the arid belt that stretched across northern Africa and Asia Minor. The theory of the five zones had long committed its advocates to construing any and all biological activity in sub-Saharan Africa and the extended basin of the Indian Ocean as a result of nature's exceptions and immoderacies—as an accident that produced marvels and monsters. Albertus instead was asking his readers to imagine not just that the hyperproductivity of places long reported by travelers to and from Ethiopia and India obeyed universal causes, but also that the belt of the tropics had itself been *privileged* by nature above all other places on earth. This represents a significant departure from the view of Averroës and others that life in the tropics was beyond nature and a step toward the realization that Mediterranean Europe was little more than the poor suburb to a vastly more temperate, fertile, and populated globe than the followers of Augustine had dared imagine. On this very crucial count, it makes perfect sense that, centuries later, Albertus's inaugural treatise should have played such a central role in Las Casas's works. Albertus's theories would help Las Casas to explain why Columbus had been right to suspect that the torrid zone was temperate, fertile, and inhabitable; why Columbus had indeed proceeded to find such temperate places in the Bahamas and Caribbean basin; and why Columbus and his ideological heirs in the Spanish empire had been wrong to continue to construe the Indians as Europe's natural subordinates on the allegedly hot fringes of the inhabited world.

Let us now consider the logical connection Albertus establishes between the theory of the five zones and the nature of things thought to be generated in the hot, cold, and temperate regions of the globe, for by means of this paradigm Albertus meant to establish a basis for the study of humans, beasts, plants, and minerals. Albertus's most immediate source appears to have been Avicenna's medical *Canon,* though the source of the ideas presented by Albertus in this part of *De natura loci* is ultimately the Hippocratic *Airs, Waters, and Places* (4th century BCE). In this part of *De natura loci* Albertus espouses the geopolitical model that would later serve as the target of Las Casas's attack on the reasons of empire.

Albertus's account of the effect of place on human physiology and psychology focuses specifically on the effect of temperature on the body's "complexion," that is, on the balance of the four qualities (hot, cold, dry, and wet) in the body, which—paired up just as in the case of the elements—were supposed to form the body's "humors": yellow bile (hot and dry), blood (hot and wet), phlegm (wet and cold), and black bile (cold and dry).[259] Just as places had a complexion, so did bodies, and in Albertus's discussion of the effect of place on the body's complexion the effect of temperature on the blood and related organs is of crucial importance for explaining the nature of peoples. For Albertus this nature concerned the body's degree of interference with the operations of the soul.

According to Albertus, the extreme heat induced by the sun caused things generated in the hottest parts of the world to grow hot, dry, and wrinkled "like peppercorns," and just as black as Ethiopians.[260] In the case of Ethiopians themselves, this heat caused women's wombs to be hot and dry, and it burned the already hot seed of the fathers, so that the bodies of their children were "nigrified" by the scorching of the embryo's blood in the womb.[261] Albertus's description of heat's effect on Ethiopian physiology conjures up not only the very image of monstrosity long associated in Mediterranean Europe with the darker peoples of the world, but also the very image of evil associated by Christian lore with the consumptive fires of hell: the heat of tropical places was supposed to vaporize the fine moisture out of the bodies of Ethiopians and scorch the remaining earthy residue, resulting in their "negritude."[262] Heat and dryness not only caused the earthy components in them, like bones and teeth, to be inordinately white, but also the hair on their bodies to be sparse and crisp.[263] Heat, moreover, caused the flesh of Ethiopians to swell with blood, as one was supposed to see when they opened their mouths to expose their tongues and jaws; and it made their eyes and eyelids scarlet red, all in the manner of "glowing coals."[264]

At this point in his discussion, Albertus introduces one of the two main psychological traits that were supposed to distinguish Ethiopians from other peoples. The overheated air in that region constantly drained moisture from the bodies of Ethiopians, making their bodies not only porous and dry but also light and agile. And because the spirit was also drained from the blood, "their vitals are rendered cold and timid."[265] The *spiritus* was supposed to be the very noblest, most rarified substance in the physical body, acting as a link between soul and body.[266] It was in some sense the means by which soul breathed life into the body. Thus Albertus leaves us to suppose that the rise of overheated blood to the surface of the body caused a cooling down of the heart along with the blood and other humors. Along with the eduction of heat from the heart and of the spirit from the blood came the loss of the body's natural vitality, resulting in short life spans. Just as Arrian noted the great celerity with which people in India "ripened" and "spoiled," so does Albertus state that due to the loss of vitality from the body, Ethiopians lived to be thirty years old and then grew old and frail.[267] Albertus's source must have been Avicenna's *Canon of Medicine,* which states the following about the effects of hot countries on human physiology and psychology: "The hair becomes dark or black and frizzly, and becomes gathered into tight clumps like pepper-flowers; the digestion is weakened. Old age comes on early, owing to the great dissipation of breath [i.e., *spiritus*], and the draining away of the bodily moisture. This is seen in the land of the blacks [i.e., Ethiopia]. Persons who reside in such countries become aged at thirty, are timid (as the breath is so much dispersed), and the body becomes soft and dark."[268] The most abundant humor in the bodies of Ethiopians was, according to Albertus, yellow bile (hot and dry), which caused their complexions to be "choleric" in nature and, no doubt, also affected their character.[269]

The second psychological trait that Albertus attributes to Ethiopians is ingenuity, or inventiveness, which of course presupposed intelligence. Following the tradition that linked Ethiopians to Indians, Albertus explains that the inhabitants of the equator thrived on account, it seems, of the subtlety of the *spiritus* that was left in their blood; and that the acting heat and the "keenness" of their spirits caused them to excel "in ingenuity."[270] This was supposed to have been indicated by the fact that India produced great philosophers, especially those versed in astrology and magic, all because the planets cast their rays on those latitudes perpendicularly. In other words, while the heat in Ethiopia and India drained the *spiritus* from the blood, and along with this breath of life from the soul a significant degree of vitality, the constant evaporation that took place through the body's pores also purified the blood and other humors—all of which had a refining effect on that spirit that remained in the blood. Presumably, the soul present to body was, by this means, relieved to a certain degree of the burdens of the body, whence the ingenuity (and intelligence) of equatorial peoples. This inventiveness, however, came at the price of the heart's courage. Matters were supposed to be even worse for those peoples who lived closer to the Tropic of Cancer, for heat was even greater in those latitudes around the times of the summer solstices, and therefore the eduction of the spirit from their blood was even greater. For this reason, Albertus concludes, among the Ethiopians, "the blackest are indeed slight of body and frivolous of mind."[271] In sum, Albertus considered the black inhabitants of the belt of the tropics intelligent and ingenious but cowardly and in some cases shallow-minded.

Having completed his discussion of the effect of hot places on Ethiopians, Albertus next considers the cold places—beyond the seventh clime—inhabited by the peoples along the northern frontiers of the Roman Empire, namely, the ancient Dacians, Goths, Slavs, and Parthians. Unlike Ethiopians, these peoples had very white skins and the cold air caused their pores to close down, enclosing the humidity of their bodies and making their complexions "phlegmatic" in nature.[272] The constriction of the body in these peoples also prevented the eduction of heat from the heart and of *spiritus* from the blood, resulting in their bodies' retaining their natural vitality.[273] Because their hearts remained extremely hot and well supplied with blood and *spiritus,* the inhabitants of cold places were "audacious."[274] But this audacity came at a price, because the constriction of their bodies also sealed in the impurities of their humors, making their blood "tardy" and "thick," slow to be moved, and "unreceptive" to what Albertus calls "animal forms."[275] In other words, their blood resisted the proper induction of form, and thereby, of motion, by soul. For this reason, northern peoples were supposed to be "dull" and "stupid."

This particular passage in *De natura loci* shows us what Albertus and other Neoplatonists meant by nature. For them a thing's nature was not its inherent and active potential to be moved but rather that which formed and moved that thing, namely, soul. Thus one can infer what it meant for every type of body to be within its nature. In the case of the elements and inanimate compounds, their nature was to be moved, not immediately but mediately, by whatever intelligence moved the prime mover on the edge of the cosmos. (Matter itself was supposed to be motionless, lifeless.) And this "being moved" by soul was shared by all physical creatures. In the case of plants, their nature was to be moved immediately by that soul that communicated such "forms" or powers as were necessary for the subsistence and perpetuation of the genus, such as nutrition and reproduction. And this nature was shared by other besouled creatures, that is, beasts and humans. In the case of animals, their nature was to be moved immediately by that soul that *in addition* communicated those "forms" or powers necessary for locomotion, namely, sensation. This nature was shared only by humans. And in the case of humans, their nature was to be moved immediately by that soul that *in addition* communicated such "forms" or powers as were necessary for exercising free will—mainly, reason.

For Albertus and other Neoplatonists, then, to be human was of course to be endowed with the power of reasoning that was immediately communicated by soul, but as physical creatures humans were receptive to the forms or powers communicated by soul to the extent allowed by those physical properties communicated by place. In Albertus's account of the peoples who inhabit the globe's cold regions, the greater slowness and viscosity of the blood, caused by the constriction of their bodies, tended to interfere with the proper reception of the forms or powers communicated by soul, mainly, reason. Whereas, the vital heat retained by the heart and blood was a measure of great vitality. In sum, boreal peoples were supposed to be by nature audacious but dull and stupid. These qualities were, so to speak, affections of the soul insofar as soul was present to body. And it is in this uneasy interface between soul and body that we come to witness the transition in Albertus's argument from the idea that creatures had a place in the cosmos according to their rank in the scale of perfection to the idea that peoples also were hierarchically distributed across the globe—indeed, that place implied position in a moral order.

The next step for Albertus was to outline the geopolitical model that accorded peoples in the temperate middle a privileged position on the global stage. In this section of *De natura loci* Albertus recalls the version of this model offered by Vitruvius in *De architectura* (1st century BCE). According to Albertus, the inhabitants of the fourth and fifth *climata* (i.e., temperate latitudes) displayed the virtues that pertained to those who lived in the middle.[276] We are left to infer that the temperate air caused their pores not to open or to close too much; that their bodies retained an intermediate amount of moisture, their hearts an intermediate degree of heat, their blood of *spiritus,* and their bodies of vitality; and therefore that they displayed moderate virtues. Indeed, Albertus states that middle peoples enjoyed long life spans, the healthiest biological functions, the best customs, and pursuits worthy of praise. They were just, devoted, peaceful, and sociable. For these reasons, the rule of the Romans had lasted longer than other rules: against the wolfish nations of the north, who, falling prey to their own ferocity had often sprung heedlessly to action, the Romans were supposed to have wielded true audacity. And against the hopelessly frivolous nations of the south, who, by means of their great ingenuity and reasoning abilities had crafted many a ploy against them, Romans had wielded true wisdom. In sum, the inhabitants of the temperate middle were supposed to possess the wisdom and audacity that eluded their nordic and tropical neighbors. And these natural predispositions explained why Rome had extended and preserved its rule across northern Europe and North Africa. Albertus's use of the terms "wisdom" and "audacity" to characterize the inhabitants of middle places instantly puts his ideas on the nature of place in the service of moral philosophy, specifically ethics and politics.

The version of the tripartite geopolitics Albertus offers as an immediate sequitur to his discussion of the psychological and physiological effects of place on humans does not yet include the notion that nordic and tropical peoples were by nature slaves. The geopolitical model offered by Vitruvius specifically refers to the Roman concept of *dominium* and accounts for those virtues that were supposed to have enabled Romans to conquer, and continue to lord over, peoples Vitruvius considered to be their subjects. The work that specifically established the idea of the natural slave in the philosophical discourse of the Latin West, Aristotle's *Politics,* had not yet been translated into Latin when Albertus wrote *De natura loci.*[277] So it is in the commentary Albertus wrote years later on the complete Latin translation of the *Politics* by William of Moerbeke (about 1260), that Albertus would come to establish a direct connection between nature, place, and the condition of slavery.

Albertus's commentary on Aristotle's discussion of peoples in the hot, cold, and temperate regions of the *oikoumenē* (*Politics* VII), opens with a question concerning nature's bearing on polity: "Who ought to be citizens *by nature*, for which the Greeks are extolled, and who the custodians of the city?"[278] Albertus tells his readers that the problem of who ought to be citizens by nature could readily be solved by looking at those Greek city-states that had been approved of as such and at the entire *orbis terrae*, to the extent that it had been known to be inhabited:

> For, the peoples in cold places, and those around Europe, are full of spiritedness, but they are rather deficient in intellect and skill. For this reason, they generally continue in their freedom, but they cannot live in cities and rule over their neighbors. On the other hand, those who live around Asia are intelligent and inventive, with respect to their soul [*secundum animam*], but they lack spiritedness. Therefore, they remain subject and enslaved.
>
> However, the Greek people, because it is intermediate, with respect to place [*secundum loca*], participates in both [virtues]. It is both spirited and intelligent. Therefore, it remains free, it lives very much in cities, and, having received a single form of government, it can rule over all peoples.[279]

In Albertus's assertion that Asians were intelligent and inventive *secundum animam*, we have an important reminder of the extent to which Albertus and other Neoplatonists associated nature with soul—in the case of human nature, with that immortal part of the soul which, present to body, was supposed to endow human beings with reasoning power and thereby with the ability to make choices and to act justly or not. The problem with the inhabitants of a hot Asia in this tripartite scheme was, in some sense, an excess of intelligence, or inventiveness, and a defect of spiritedness, or courage. This imbalance deprived them of the requisite will power to carry out what the mind saw and invented. The problem with the inhabitants of a cold Europe was in some sense an excess of spiritedness and a defect of intelligence and inventiveness. This imbalance deprived them of the necessary reasoning ability to direct their will toward proper action. The Greek nation, on the other hand, was "optimally civil" in relation to Asians and Europeans, having just the right degree of intelligence, inventiveness, and spiritedness. This balance endowed them with both the reasoning power to make choices and the will power to take proper action.

By emphasizing the fact that Greeks mediated between Europeans and Asians *secundum loca,* Albertus is explicitly linking his commentary to the theory of place he had formulated years before in *De natura loci.* More to the point, by explaining that this geographical "meddling" caused Greeks to participate in the virtues of both the Europeans and Asians, Albertus was expressing a fundamental principle concerning the relationship between places and peoples, between the physical and the moral, and between nature and culture. Middle places were supposed to generate moderate peoples; extreme places, immoderate ones. In his later discussion of Eratosthenes' seven *climata,* Albertus explains that any given point in the middle of each of the *climata* was temperate *relative* to any given point toward its extremes. The notion of middle in matters of place was like the notion of middle in matters of moral virtue, "for in personal habits what is too little for one person is too much for another, and what is moderate for one is extreme for another."[280] Albertus's comparison was aimed at illustrating the ever more subtle differences in temperature, and therefore in nature, between places whose differences in latitudes were reckoned to be smaller and smaller.

But what immediately concerns us in Albertus's comparison is the steadfast connection between place meddling and moral moderation. As Aristotle explains in the *Nicomachean Ethics,* excellence in moral virtue was "a state concerned with choice, lying in a mean relative to us, this [mean] being determined by reason and in the way in which the man of practical wisdom would determine it."[281] Moral virtue was so, not simply on account of standing opposite moral vice, but rather on account of mediating between vicious moral extremes. One moral extreme concerned the vice of excess, while the other concerned the vice of defect:

> There are three kinds of dispositions, then, two of them vices, involving excess and deficiency and one an excellence, viz. the mean, and all are in a sense opposed to all; for the extreme states are contrary both to the intermediate state and to each other, and the intermediate to the extremes; as the equal is greater relatively to the less, less relatively to the greater, so the middle states are excessive relatively to the deficiences, deficient relatively to the excess, both in passions and in actions. For the brave man appears rash relatively to the coward, and cowardly relatively to the rash man; and similarly the temperate man appears self-indulgent relatively to the insensible man, insensible relatively to the self-indulgent, and the liberal man prodigal relatively to the mean man, mean relatively to the prodigal. Hence

also the people at the extremes push the intermediate man each over to the other, and the brave man is called rash by the coward, cowardly by the rash man, and correspondingly in the other cases.[282]

Virtue, then, concerned for Aristotle moderation relative to defect and excess—a formula that continues to hold sway in ethical discourse today. And it is precisely this moral formula that governed Aristotle's geopolitical distinction between the Greeks and the "barbarians" who inhabited a cold Europe and a hot Asia. What Albertus means in his commentary on Aristotle by asserting that the Greeks "participated" in the qualities of those who inhabited a cold Europe and a hot Asia is that the Greeks displayed true wisdom relative to their neighbors, not by virtue of being more intelligent or inventive than they, but by virtue of middling between the sheer stupidity of those to the north and the frivolous shrewdness of those to the south. Greeks displayed true courage relative to their neighbors, not by virtue of being more spirited than they, but by virtue of middling between the misdirected boldness of those to the north and the hopeless cowardice of those to the south. And this scheme also implies that the Greeks displayed true temperance in their customs, middling between the tyrannical repressiveness of those to the north and the consumptive self-indulgence of those to the south.

The enduring obsession underlying this tripartition of the inhabited world was nothing less than the relationship between soul and body. In the eyes of Albertus and other Aristotelians, the human body's *interference* with the immediate operations of the human soul tended to prevent the inhabitants of extreme places from cultivating the moral virtues necessary for building a proper polity. And to the extent that their bodies interfered with their souls, such peoples could be considered to be outside their nature: their bodies mastered their souls. On the other hand, in the case of the inhabitants of temperate places, the body did not interfere with the immediate operations of the soul. And for this reason, the Greeks could be considered to be inside their nature: their souls mastered their bodies. Aristotle himself had invited this distinction between barbarians and Greeks in the very opening of his *Politics,* where he concerns himself with the basic components of the state. According to Aristotle, the basic hierarchical relations without which a state could not exist were, first, that between male and female, which ensured the continuation of the human race, and, second, that between natural lord and subject, which ensured the preservation of both the ruler and the ruled.[283] Lord and subject were hierarchically bound to each other by reason of fulfilling complementary functions, as were, by extension, masters and slaves: "For that which can foresee by the exercise of mind is by nature lord and master, and that which can with its body give effect to such foresight is a subject, and by nature a slave; hence the master and slave have the same interest."[284] Among the Greeks, among whom there were supposed to be natural rulers, nature had made females subordinate to males but also different from slaves.[285] Whereas, among the barbarians, among whom there were no natural rulers, nature had made no distinction between males and females, so that to speak of all barbarians, male or female, was to speak of slaves by nature.[286]

Against those who maintained that natural slavery did not exist, Aristotle argued that in all things made up of parts, be those parts continuous or discrete, there was a distinction between the ruling and the ruled elements.[287] In all things animate or inanimate, there was a ruling principle.[288] And in animate beings, which were composed of soul and body, "the one is by nature the ruler and the other the subject."[289] Aristotle was profoundly indebted, here as in the *Nichomachean Ethics,* to the terms in which Plato described the relationship between soul and body, though it is unlikely that Aristotle saw himself as moving away from the notion that soul was the form or actuality of those bodies that have a potential to be alive and toward the metaphysical notion that immortal soul descended upon, or colonized, the body. Whatever the case may be, Aristotle clarifies that soul's rule over body was to be found "in things which retain their nature, and not in things which are corrupted. And therefore we must study the man who is in the most perfect state both of body and soul, for in him we shall see the true relation of the two; although in bad or corrupted natures the body will often appear to rule over the soul, because they are in an evil and unnatural condition."[290] Those whose souls ruled their bodies were, therefore, within their nature, whereas those whose bodies ruled their souls were outside their nature. And wherever those whose souls ruled their bodies came in contact with those whose bodies ruled their souls, the ones were masters, and the others slaves by nature: "For he who can be, and therefore is, another's, and *he who participates in reason enough to apprehend, but not to have, [reason] is a slave by nature.* Whereas the lower animals cannot even apprehend reason; they obey their passions. And indeed the use made of slaves and of tame animals is not very different; for both with their bodies minister to the needs of life."[291] This handy definition of the natural slave automatically applied to most barbarians, who belonged to the human race insofar as they possessed an inherent ability to reason, but who, due to a disorder of soul and body, failed to heed reason's call and were therefore relegated to the same condition as that of lower animals.[292]

This is precisely what many centuries later would run through the minds of schooled Aristotelians who pointed to the "brutishness" of the Indians in order to justify the conquest. Recall John Mair's momentous assertion that the inhabitants of the Indies lived "like beasts" (*bestialiter*) in the equatorial region and were thus by nature slaves.[293] Or the "opinion" written by Bernardo Mesa on occasion of the *junta* called by King Fernando of Aragon in 1512 to examine Castile's titles to the Indies, which ventured that the Indians' "lack of understanding and capacity" might owe to the fact that "there are certain lands that the aspect of the heavens renders subject to others."[294] Or consider Juan Ginés de Sepúlveda's meticulously wrought *Democrates secundus,* which used every available strategy to describe the inversion of the soul-body compact in the Indians. Sepúlveda deemed the peoples of the New World and adjacent islands to be "barbarous, inhuman peoples, shunning civil life and the milder customs and virtues."[295] And the labor of empire was like the labor of doctors tending to the evil and corrupted humors of diseased patients.[296] Even the best among the Indians could not have dreamed of possessing the innate prudence and ingenuity of Spaniards, the courage that had once made Spaniards famous against the Roman legions, or the frugality and sobriety that now distinguished Spaniards from all other Europeans.[297] Indians were no more than little humans (*homunculi*) who, prior to the arrival of the Spaniards, had engaged in every conceivable immoderacy and pursued every nefarious pleasure, not least of all that of eating human flesh.[298] They had been so ferocious in their wars that they did not feel they were victorious until they had satisfied their monstrous gluttony with the flesh of their enemies. Indians were "spiritless and timid," so much so that they could hardly bear the sight of Spanish soldiers and many thousands of them had often fled "like women," dispersed by Spanish armies barely a hundred strong.[299] Worse yet, the fact that Indians were "ingenious" enough to craft things could not be considered an indication that they had human prudence: "For we see that certain little beasts, like bees and spiders, fabricate things by their labor that no human industry can adequately imitate."[300] In sum, the case against the new barbarians discovered by Columbus "to the west and to the south" would come to hinge precisely on the invocation of a perverted nature dangerously gnawing away at the outer fringes of geography and civility.

While the Aristotle of *On the Soul* had formulated his psychology in direct opposition to Plato's metaphysics of soul, the Aristotle of the *Politics* would seem to have yielded significantly to the terms in which Plato described the relation between soul and body. To be sure, Aristotle's distinction between Europeans, Asians, and Greeks was directly indebted to Plato's discussion in the *Republic* of the attributes of the well-ordered city and the well-ordered human soul.[301] The dialogue between Socrates and Glaucon in the *Republic* describes the human soul as constituted by three hierarchically related parts: "calculation" (*logismos*), "spiritedness" (*thumos*), and "appetite" (*epithumia*).[302] The well-ordered soul—that in which calculation (or reason), assisted by spiritedness (or will power), rules over appetite (or instinct)—manifests wisdom, courage, and temperance. By implication, the disorderly soul manifests folly, cowardice, or intemperance. Socrates even metaphorizes the three parts of the soul as man (reason), a lion (courage), and a many-headed monster (Chimera). Should the man fail to summon the lion in taming this monster, he will become prey to both lion and monster.[303] Without wisdom, courage, or temperance, man cannot hope to act justly, nor the city dispense justice to its citizens. Aristotle's geopolitical model would accord Greeks the ability to carry out reason's works by summoning will power against the predatory claims of unrestrained instinct. Barbarians, on the other hand, either failed to reason properly or to summon the requisite will power, thereby, in Plato's terms, falling prey to the lion, or to the Chimera, or to both. Such a model, despite its apparent simplicity, has provided an enduring rationale for Western colonialism: colonizers invariably justify their misdeeds by persuading themselves that those they are out to control or exterminate lack either the intelligence or the will power to overcome instinct. And in the case of Europe's great territorial expansion, this rationale would not just be wielded by schoolmen as an afterthought to empire's machinery. The notion that the Indians suffered from a disorder of soul and body that justified subjecting them or enslaving them had already been alive and well in the testimonies of Europeans who had traveled to, or had heard about, the New World, beginning with Columbus himself. Indeed, the projection of this moral model onto the world map had proved to be of crucial importance to Columbus's invention of the American tropics.

A brief review is in order of the tripartite geographical model known to Columbus through Pierre d'Ailly and Jean Gerson's *Tractatus*. In a section bearing the traces of Columbus's and his brother's diligent readings, d'Ailly offers an explanation for the effects place on the natures of nations that is in every fundamental respect identical with that contained in Albertus's *De natura loci*. And it is this section of the annotated

Tractatus that most eloquently illustrates the deep assumptions concerning the nature of place that Columbus shared, no matter how imperfectly, with many a schooled Aristotelian.

Columbus annotated the version of Aristotle's geopolitical model contained in d'Ailly's *Ymago mundi:* "The inhabitants toward the south are greater in intellect and prudence, but they are less strong, audacious, and spirited; and those who inhabit the north are more audacious and of lesser prudence and fortitude. The Greeks were the ones in the middle, and they possess sufficient fortitude and prudence."[304] But the treatise that now concerns us is d'Ailly's *Tractatus eiusdem de concordia discordantium astronomorum* (1414), one of many works besides *Ymago mundi* that d'Ailly composed in answer to his colleagues' worry in the church that the recent division of the papacy between Rome and Avignon signaled the imminent arrival of the Antichrist. One of d'Ailly's preoccupations as an astrologer looking into the role that the great schism played in apocalyptic history was precisely how to establish the proper causal correlations between the celestial and elemental regions of the cosmos. With this problem in mind, d'Ailly wrote a difficult treatise intended to reconcile those differences among astrologers that he saw as having direct bearing on the inquiry at hand. Because apocalyptic history was, for d'Ailly and other natural theologians, the history of the rise and fall of religious sects since the beginning of time, the ultimate purpose of this treatise "on the agreement of discordant astronomers" was to elucidate the most decisive effects of celestial bodies on the psychology and physiology of large numbers of peoples—particularly those effects that predisposed nations to rise to power or to fall under the yoke of others. Naturally, the astrological correlation that astronomers univocally held as the most universal concerned the division of the known inhabited world according to the general temper and distemper induced by the heavens.

It is at this juncture in *De concordia discordantium astronomorum,* that d'Ailly recapitulates the geopolitical model offered by Aristotle in *Politics* VII. As d'Ailly explains, changing somewhat the axis followed by Aristotle (Europe, Asia, and Greece), the inhabitants of the north were intellectually deficient but courageous. On the other hand, the inhabitants of the south were inventive, "as befits [their] soul," but they lacked spiritedness, and as a consequence they had been subjected and remained slaves.[305] Like Albertus before him, d'Ailly emphasizes the fact that tropical peoples possessed reason *secundum animam,* that is as humans, in preparation to tell us that something interfered with the normal operations of their souls. In the corresponding postil, Columbus or his brother Bartholomew note that "the inhabitants of the north are deficient in intellect but full of spiritedness. In the inhabitants of the south everything is the opposite."[306]

According to d'Ailly, these differences between nordic and tropical peoples were a function of the different qualities of their bloods: thicker blood was hotter than finer and more fluid blood; therefore, northerners had a hot complexion while southerners had a cold one.[307] D'Ailly borrowed this explanation directly from Aristotelian zoology, specifically, from the Pseudo-Aristotelian *Problems* and from Aristotle's *Parts of Animals.* In *Problems,* Pseudo-Aristotle explains the cowardice of those in hot countries and the courage of those in cold countries as a result of natural compensation for the heat and cold of their respective places and seasons: "Why are the inhabitants of warm regions cowardly, and those who dwell in cold districts courageous? Is it because there is a natural tendency which counteracts the effects of locality and season, since if both had the same effect mankind would inevitably be soon destroyed by heat or cold? Now those who are hot by nature are courageous, and those who are cold are cowardly. But the effect of hot regions upon those who dwell in them is that they are cooled, while cold regions engender a natural state of heat in their inhabitants."[308] In other words, people in hot countries countered the heat by cooling down, which made them cowardly, and people in cold countries countered the cold by heating up, which made them courageous. In *Parts of Animals,* Aristotle explains the correlation between courage and cowardice, intelligence and dullness, in terms of the characteristics of blood: "Different bloods differ in their degrees of thinness or thickness, of clearness or turbidity, of coldness or heat; and this whether we compare the bloods from different parts of the same individual or the bloods of different animals. . . . The thicker and the hotter blood is, the more conducive is it to strength, while in proportion to its thinness and its coldness is its suitability for sensation and intelligence. The best of all [animals] are those whose blood is hot, and at the same time thin and clear. For such are suited alike for the development of courage and of intelligence."[309] In other words, inhabitants of cold climates had thicker and hotter blood, which made them courageous and strong; those in warm climates had cooler and thinner blood, which made them timid and intelligent; but the inhabitants of temperate climes had more equable complexions and thus had blood both relatively hot and relatively thin, which made them both courageous and intelligent—and therefore better suited for ruling. The postil corresponding to this part of d'Ailly's explanation simply reads: "Northerners have a hot complexion, [and] southerners a cold one."[310]

D'Ailly then focuses on the effects of heat on tropical peoples, this time by citing a familiar passage in Avicenna's *Canon*.[311] The postil paraphrasing d'Ailly's reading of Avicenna should suffice to remind us of Albertus's description of the effect of tropical heat on Ethiopians: "Hot places turn the hair black and curly, and make the digestion weak. Men grow old there in thirty years. And their vitals are timid, because their spirit is very relaxed."[312] In yet another reference to the cowardice of tropical peoples, d'Ailly this time paraphrases a passage in the popular version of Ptolemy's *Tetrabiblos* annotated by the Egyptian physician and astrologer Haly ('Ali ibn Ridwān).[313] As d'Ailly explains it, the very timidity of tropical peoples often caused them to exercise great cruelty and ferocity, as a way of preventing others at all costs from visiting any harm upon them.[314] D'Ailly's references to the preemptive cruelty and ferociousness of tropical peoples is significant in view of Columbus's sudden idea in the course of his first voyage that by sailing farther to the east and to the south through the Caribbean he was bound to stumble upon peoples who ate human flesh. The postil corresponding to this part of d'Ailly's argument notes that "southern peoples [are] ferocious and cruel or savage on account of [their] timidity."[315] The last postil in this passage of d'Ailly's *De concordia discordantium astronomorum* concerns the political lesson to be drawn from this tripartition of the inhabited world. Thus Columbus writes, "The inhabitants of the north and of the south are unfit for exercising power. In this respect, this [middle] region possesses both [i.e., spiritedness and intellect]."[316]

What Las Casas may have understood more clearly than any of us in five hundred years is that the Discoverer had fully intended to bring this compelling political lesson to fruition in his beloved Indies—even as he confirmed that land and life extended well beyond the traditional limits of the known inhabited world, and even as he marveled at the temperance, fertility, and inhabitability of the Bahamas and Caribbean. Such was the twisted logic of empire. Such were the contradictions of a brave new Europe intent upon remaining the moral center of a landscape that suddenly appeared to have misplaced its borders.

En la Parte del Sol

IBERIA'S INVENTION OF THE
AFRO-INDIAN TROPICS, 1434–1494

Columbus conceived of reaching the East "by way of the West" in the midst of a rivalry between Castile and Portugal for control of Atlantic Africa's waters and shores. Las Casas aptly called this earlier chapter in the history of Christian Europe's expansion in the Atlantic a "prelude" to the "destruction of the Indies."[1] Historians have long recognized that Iberia's bid for Africa's side of the Atlantic was itself a natural extension of the arduous southward push of Christian forces through the peninsular territories that had been lost by the Visigoths to Umayyad invaders in 711.[2] Since the latter half of the eleventh century (even before the First Crusade to the Holy Land was launched in 1095), papal bulls had promised the remission of sins to Christians waging war on Muslim enemies in the Iberian al-Andalus.[3] These and other types of pontifical concessions came with time to be regarded by both Crowns as affording them special legal protection against each other's claims to the Atlantic.[4]

The concept of an expanse located "to the west and to the south" in Alexander VI's controversial concessions of 1493 found its most immediate ground in the jargon of papal bulls expedited by Alexander's predecessors for Africa's side of the Atlantic. This legal jargon shifted in the course of the fifteenth century to reflect expanding claims to territories occupied by peoples other than traditional Muslim enemies in the Mediterranean basin. Apart from targeting so-called pagan peoples like the Canarians and Islamicized "infidels" just beyond the enemy sultanate of Fez (in today's Morocco), papal documents also came to endorse crusades within the densely populated territories newly found by the Portuguese beyond the southernmost reaches of Atlantic Africa recently known to Europeans. This suddenly available expanse extended south beyond the Canaries and the coastal reaches of the Sahara Desert into a previously dreaded torrid

zone that gradually began to yield its wealth of natural and human resources directly to Europeans.

The Portuguese empire owed its discovery of the African tropics to Henry the Navigator (1394–1460), the crusading scholar-prince who had distinguished himself in the conquest of the African port of Ceuta. Henry's intense desire to find an anti-Muslim ally in the legendary Prester John of "the Indies" led Portuguese vessels to the upper banks of the Gambia River (13° 28′ N) and to the vicinity of today's Liberian capital, Monrovia (6° 18′ N).[5] Henry, by the way, believed that this priest-king dwelled in the part of sub-Saharan Africa facing the Indian Ocean to the east of the Nile River, that is, in what today would be the Ethiopian highlands.[6]

Castile, too, had wished from the start to tap into Atlantic Africa's tropical resources, hoping to bypass the costly arbitration of the trans-Saharan trade into the Mediterranean. As one historian of the early Atlantic has indicated, "When Spaniards establish[ed] contact with Atlantic Africa in the fifteenth century, one of their clearest objectives was traffic with the Sudan [sub-Saharan Africa]. They sought unmediated access to the caravan routes so that from their coastal posts they might profit from the important traffic in gold, slaves, spices, ivory, indigo, shellac, etcetera, that came to these routes from remote areas like Nigeria and Senegal."[7] After 1434, the year when Prince Henry's vessels first crossed the threshold between the Canaries and Cape Bojador, a number of papal bulls specified and reserved this new crusading domain for Portugal. Every legal and diplomatic move Fernando and Isabel were to make upon Columbus's return in 1493 to reserve for themselves the new discoveries in the high Atlantic were to be made in direct relation to Portugal's claims to the tropical expanse beyond the Canaries and Bojador. Indeed, Castile's invention of a tropical domain it called the Indies was predicated on Portugal's invention of the tropical domain of Guinea.

Las Casas would include a searing "prelude" on the destruction of Africa in his anticolonialist *Historia de las Indias* precisely because he understood that the emergence of the allegedly uninhabitable torrid zone as a profligate and vastly populated target of imperial expansion on Africa's side of the Atlantic was a requisite framework for understanding Columbus's enterprise—from Columbus's methodical southing, to the frequent allusions to Guinea in his *Diario* and letters, and to the geopolitics he came to practice in the Bahamas and the Caribbean basin.[8]

Castile had tagged northern Africa as a target of expansion as early as 1291.[9] Looking forward to a future invasion of the Muslim territories across the Strait of Gibraltar, Castile reached an accord with the kingdom of Aragon designating the territories east of the Mediterranean river Moulouya, near modern-day Morocco's eastern border, to Aragon (Mauretania Caesarensis), and the territories west of Moulouya, that is, modern-day Morocco, to Castile (Mauretania Tingitana). This agreement, known as the Accord of Monteagudo, rested on the claim that both the late Roman diocese of Hispania and the fallen Visigothic kingdom later seated in Toledo had extended into Mauretania. (Hence d'Ailly insisted in the famously annotated chapter of *Ymago mundi,* where he argues for a small distance between Spain and India, that Spain in this case meant the northwest African territory previously known as Hispania Ulterior.)[10] As one might expect, Aragon's and Castile's agreement concerning northwest Africa set the stage for future conflict between Castile and Portugal over the Marinid sultanate of Fez as well as over the Canary Islands, which Castile came to regard as an extension of the old Mauretania Tingitana.

The Castilian and Portuguese Crowns would stake out their claims to Atlantic Africa several decades after the drafting of the Accord of Monteagudo, in the aftermath of the battle of the Salado River (30 October 1340).[11] In this decisive battle, Alfonso XI of Castile and Afonso IV of Portugal jointly crushed the coalition troops of the sultans of Granada and Fez, bringing an end to Morocco's presence in the Iberian peninsula. Months after this victory, Afonso IV obviously calculated that Castile was now bound to focus on further isolating Muslim Granada from its allies across Gibraltar, so the Portuguese king secured an endorsement for future expansion across the Strait of Gibraltar from Benedict XII, the third antipope in Avignon.[12] Benedict's papal bull *Gaudemus et exultamus* (30 April 1341) granted Afonso IV crusader's privileges and promised him a tenth of the church's revenues in Portugal for a two-year period in exchange for what this papal bull hailed as a "defensive" and "offensive" war against the sultanates of Granada and Benamarim (Fez).[13] Not surprisingly, the period following the collaborative victory of the Salado River in 1341 also saw the emergence of explicit competition between Castile and Portugal over the Canary Islands.

The Isles of the Blest, or Fortunate Isles, had been rediscovered in 1312 by the Venetian Lancellotto Malocello.[14] Strabo and other ancient geographers call them so for the accidental mildness and generosity of a habitat that ought to have been as unforgiving as the neighboring fringes of the Sahara Desert.[15] (The Canaries are tempered by the northeast trade winds, which turn south from the Atlantic waters off of the coasts of Portugal and Spain.) Lancellotto built a fort that was soon abandoned on the island now bearing his name (Lanzarote), but his feat did reinscribe the Canaries onto European cartography and inspired sporadic expeditions by Mediterranean ships throughout the fourteenth century.[16] Among these was a fully armed expedition chartered out of Lisbon in 1341 that carried a small outfit of Florentines, Genoese, and Castilians.[17] Captained by the Florentine Angiolino del Tegghia de Corbizzi and the Genoese Niccoloso da Recco, the fleet raided the archipelago and hauled back to Portugal several native captives and various samples of local goods.[18] But in 1344, much to the dismay of both Afonso IV and Alfonso XI, Benedict's successor in Avignon, Clement VI, granted crown and scepter of the Fortunate Isles—distinctly located "between the south and the west" (*inter meridiem et occidentem*)—to the Admiral of France Don Luis de la Cerda, great-grandson of King Louis IX of France (Saint Louis) and great-great-grandson of King Fernando of León and Castile (*Tue devotionis sinceritas,* 15 November 1344).[19] The purpose of this investiture, conferred by Clement VI in exchange for an annual revenue of 400 florins for the papal see, was to spread the orthodox faith in the Canaries—or, as Clement explained in another bull informing Portugal, Castile, and Aragon of Don Luis's investiture as "prince of fortune," to eradicate the "filth of pagan errors" from the Canaries.[20] In two subsequent bulls (both named *Prouenit ex tue* and dated 13 January 1345), Clement VI granted plenary indulgences—like those granted to help the Holy Land, as the second bull explains—to the new prince Don Luis and to all participants in the conquest and conversion of the Canaries.[21] These bulls obliquely prefigured the possibility of extending crusaders' privileges to those willing to fight *any* non-Christians other than Muslims (in this case, "pagans") by labeling the newly donated territories in the Atlantic "islands alien to Christ's faith and Christian rule"—that is, islands that appeared to have no prior knowledge, or at least no memory, of Christianity.[22]

Although Clement's donation was wasted on the inept Admiral of France, Portugal and Castile did feel compelled for the first time to proclaim their respective titles to Atlantic Africa.[23] Afonso IV of Portugal protested the donation of the Canaries to Don Luis, alleging that Portugal had already sent its own people to explore and to forcefully occupy the Canaries (this may be have been a reference to the raiding expedition launched from Lisbon in 1341). Portugal, argued Afonso, stood geographically closer to the Canaries and was therefore better disposed than other kingdoms to subjugate these pagans.[24] For his part, Alfonso XI of Castile registered his protest against Clement's donation by citing his ancestral right to the African territories that the Visigoths had fought to preserve.[25] But these protests were of no avail, and the remainder of the fourteenth century was marked only by sporadic raiding expeditions to the Canaries, largely outfitted from Catalonia, Mallorca, and Andalusia.[26]

Iberia's goal of expanding across Gibraltar began to be realized on African soil in the opening years of the fifteenth century—with the military campaign that Jean de Béthencourt and Gadifer de La Salle waged under the Castilian banner against the inhabitants of the Canaries in 1402 and with Portugal's 1415 siege of the Mediterranean port of Ceuta in the Marinid sultanate of Fez.[27] Following the 1402 assault on the Canary Islands, the antipope in Avignon, Benedict XIII, issued two bulls by the same title, *Apostolatus officium* (22 January 1403), granting spiritual graces to soldiers and prelates willing to assist Béthencourt and La Salle. These two devout and zealous conquerors had already subdued Lanzarote and were now prepared to subdue the other islands in order to convert their "ignorant" peoples (*ignorantes*)—meaning, once again, peoples who had no prior knowledge, or memory, of Christianity.[28] Those willing to enlist in this exemplary enterprise would be contributing to the exaltation of God and his faith "to the ends of the earth." This geographical terminology—*in fines orbis terrae*—mindfully echoed the final command that the resurrected Christ had issued to his apostles, "Go ye into the whole world, and preach the gospel to every creature" (Mark 16:15). At the turn of the fifteenth century, "the ends of the earth" aptly described the Canarian archipelago in relation to Christian Europe. Benedict's bulls explicitly granted such privileges over people who, unlike Muslims, had apparently never had any contact with Christianity. It goes without saying that Las Casas, who considered any and all material donations of territories whose inhabitants had been ignorant of the faith to be illegal, harshly impugns Béthencourt and La Salle's misdeeds in the Canaries, characterizing Béthencourt as a mercenary who had placed himself in the service of Enrique III of Castile in order to wage "cruel war on the naturals [of these islands], following nothing other than his whim or, better said, his greed and desire to lord over those who owed him nothing at all."[29] The friar would reserve even more inflammatory terms for the raids later conducted by the Portuguese, specifically those of Henry the Navigator on the African continent beyond the Moroccan kingdom of Fez.

As for the crusading bull that Pope Martin V issued following of the fall of Ceuta (*Rex regum*, 4 April 1418), it recognized the right of King João I of Portugal to attack in

Africa not just Saracens and Agarens but also "other infidels"—an inclusion that was easily interpreted as giving the Portuguese Crown right of way to all territories on the African continent.[30]

The occupation of the Canaries in the name of Castile—more so, Portugal's victory over Ceuta—marked the beginning of an active rivalry between the two kingdoms for control over Atlantic Africa. [31] Throughout the fifteenth century, until the drafting of the Treaty of Alcáçovas (Toledo, 1479–1480), Portugal would try to wrest, purchase, or lease out some or all of the Canary Islands from Castile. Castile, for its part, would refuse to relinquish its claims to the Muslim territories in Atlantic Morocco or to the ocean sound and littoral directly east of the Canarian archipelago on the northwestern fringes of the Sahara Desert. More importantly, Castile ignored Portugal's claim that it held exclusive rights to the fishing and trade routes along the African mainland since 1434.

At the time when Prince Henry's vessels began raiding the Atlantic coast of Fez (soon after 1418), the Canary Islands and neighboring African coastline marked the farthest limits of the inhabited world recently known to Christian Europeans in the Atlantic—in the case of the Canaries, dating back to 1312, when Lancellotto built his fort, and in the case of their immediate African shores perhaps dating back to 1291, when the fall of Acre to Mamlūk forces in Jerusalem spelled the end of Christendom's hold on the Palestinian Levant. In that bitter year for Christendom, the Genoese merchant brothers Ugolino and Guido Vivaldi found themselves crossing the Strait of Gibraltar in search of an alternate lifeline to the Levantine trade, allegedly on their way to India, and reached the African coastline directly across from the Canaries.[32] Portuguese historians, beginning with Jaime Cortesão in the mid-twentieth century, have duly recognized that the Vivaldi expedition is Christian Europe's first documented bid to reach directly the coveted goods of the Afro-Indian tropics. The only Christian expedition that may have trumped the Vivaldi brothers by reaching the mainland beyond the Canaries is recorded by Abraham Cresques in his famous Catalan Atlas (1375), which shows a square-rigged vessel just below the Canaries carrying the Mallorcan Jacme Ferrer and his crew (**fig. 5.1**). According to the legend for this figure, "Jacme Ferer's ship set sail on St. Laurence's Day, the 10th August 1346 bound for Río de Oro," what Arabic and Christian geographers thought might be a western branch of the Nile River that emptied out onto the Atlantic (it was in fact the Senegal River [15° 45′ N]).[33] The Catalan Atlas does depict the mouth of this river, strongly associated with the rich sub-Saharan gold trade, directly across from Ferrer's ship, but we do not know if this expedition ever reached its destination,

nor should we understand this river as marking anything more than an unconfirmed geographical accident.[34]

The African waters and coastline directly across from the Canaries—the Canarian "sound," so to speak—are bounded by two infamous capes that came to be cited prominently in the legal documents by which Portugal would attempt to assert its sovereignty over the African mainland south of Morocco—Cape Nam (Cape Drâa [28° 47′ N]) and Cape Bojador (almost certainly Cape Juby in modern-day Morocco [27° 57′ N]).[35] The Catalan Atlas provides what would become a rather standard depiction in fifteenth-century portolans of the relationship between the Canaries and these two capes: Cape Nam ("cavo de no") stood more or less to the east of the northeasternmost Lanzarote Island, or Insula de Lançaroto (modern 29° N), marking the southern

5.1   Detail of the Canaries and Cape Bojador, from the Catalan Atlas (1375). From Georges Grosjean, ed., *Mappamundi: The Catalan Atlas of the Year 1375* (Dietikon-Zurich, 1978), panel 6. Courtesy of the Bibliothèque Nationale, Paris, France; and Urs Graf Publishing Company, Dietikon-Zurich, Switzerland.

reaches of the sultanate of Fez and of the Atlas mountains as well as the beginning of Saharan Africa's sandy littoral. And Cape Bojador, or Buyetder, stood to the east of the southwestern El Hierro Island ("Insula delo Fero" [modern 27° 44′ N]), sharply marking the end of the Canarian sound and the beginning of an uncharted coastline that dropped indefinitely to the south.[36]

The Portuguese chronicler João de Barros tells us in his *Ásia* that when Prince Henry began dispatching reconnaissance vessels south of Atlantic Morocco (1418), Portuguese sailors were in the habit of describing the dangers that awaited them beyond Cape Nam by reciting an ominous refrain: "He who goes beyond Cape 'No', shall return or not."[37] Cape Nam is not, however, the *finis terrae* that appears to have posed the greater geographical obstacle to Prince Henry's exploits in Atlantic Africa. The seemingly unfordable geographical feature standing in Henry's way was Cape Bojador, which Henry and his contemporaries unequivocally saw as a prominent continental accident *directly across* from the Canaries. Prince Henry's panegyrist Gomes Eanes de Zurara writes in his *Crónica dos feitos notáveis que se passaram na conquista da Guiné por mandado do Infante D. Henrique* that Henry was very curious to know about "the land that lay *beyond the Canary Islands and a cape called Bojador,* because at that time, no memory or record indicated that any man had ever known precisely the nature of the land that lay beyond the said cape."[38] It seems that Henry had conceived of the Canaries and Bojador as forming the doorway to *terra incognita* farther to the south. Equally insistent on the geographical immediacy of Bojador to the Canaries are the works of cartographers who in the course of the fifteenth century registered Portugal's discoveries in Atlantic Africa—including the calfskin portolan chart at the Bibliothèque Nationale in Paris, which can no longer be credibly attributed to Columbus, but which was drawn on the eve of the discovery (about 1492); and Behaim's globe, which presents *cabo bossador* pointing west to a Canarian conglomerate that, curiously, oversteps the very Tropic of Cancer (**figs. 3.8**, pp. 204–205, and **5.2**).[39] Key Spanish sources on the discovery, such as Fernández de Oviedo and Las Casas, also do not fail to couple Bojador with the Canaries. Fernández de Oviedo, who specifies the location of the Canaries between the latitudes of 27° N and 29° N, claims that "the last of [the Canaries]" (El Hierro) stood "west-to-east [*del hueste al este*] with respect to Cape Bojador, and sixty-five leagues away from it."[40] Las Casas, for his part, places the southeastern island of Fuerteventura barely "fifteen leagues" from "Cape Bojador"—a rather sharp measurement for the short distance between Fuenteventura and today's Cape Juby.[41]

5.2 Detail of the Canaries and Cape Bojador, from Martin Behaim's globe, 1492. From E. G. Ravenstein, FRGS, *Martin Behaim: His Life and His Globe* (London, 1980). Courtesy of the John Carter Brown Library at Brown University, Providence, Rhode Island.

Henry's "invention" of the geographical expanse lying beyond the Canaries and Bojador must be properly regarded as the immediate antecedent to Columbus's own exploration of the Bahamas and Caribbean basin. Just as Prince Henry considered the Canaries and Bojador to be the enticing threshold to unexplored African territory to the south, so would Columbus—who insistently (and wrongly) situated San Salvador on the same parallel as El Hierro—consider the islet of the landfall his entry port to unexplored Indian territory to the south.

Both Zurara and Barros used ominous images to convey the horror with which Prince Henry's sailors had regarded the dangerous shallows and frothy currents of Cape Bojador—a geographical feature that both his sailors and those back in Portugal who were "versed in nature" had taken as a warning of the lethal wasteland that awaited anyone who would dare tread into the latitudes of the globe seared by the sun.[42] Indeed, Prince Henry had been publicly scorned for his attempts to sail past Bojador, not just by sailors in his service, Barros states, but also by other people "of higher regard" in

Portugal. In Barros's words, Henry's distinguished and/or learned critics complained in the following terms:

> We certainly do not understand what has moved the prince, nor what sort of yield he expects from this discovery, except the loss of all who embark on those ships, and the proliferation of orphans and widows in our kingdom, not to mention the erosion of their fortunes, for the danger and expense involved are all too clear, and the gain as uncertain as we all know. For there always were kings or princes in Spain eager to engage in great enterprises, and just as ambitious in their desire to seek and discover new riches as the prince, and we do not read in their chronicles that they have endeavored to discover this land, even though they deem it to lie so near them. Instead, as a venture from which they expected neither fame nor profit, they did not pursue its discovery, being content with the land we do have now, which God granted as the limit of habitation for men: and if there is any [land] where the prince claims there is, we should believe that it was reserved by God as little more than *pasture for beasts*. For, as far as the ancients who wrote about these parts of the world are concerned, all of them said that *this part where the sun dwells, which they call the torrid zone, is uninhabitable*. And, already, the place where the prince is sending his ships to explore, *lies so close to the sun's fire,* that no matter how white men might be, as some are among us, none will fail to return as black as the Guineans who neighbor this heat.[43]

The Canary Islands and Cape Bojador are certainly not directly on the Tropic of Cancer, but rather about three degrees and thirty minutes due north of it. And it would still take Henry's vessels two years after the rounding of Bojador actually to reach the tropical Bay de Río de Oro in Western Sahara (1436). But to judge from Zurara's and Barros's accounts, Henry's envoys were not to realize that they had just reached the Tropic of Cancer, nor, for that matter, would Henry's chroniclers.[44] From the standpoint of Henry, his sailors, and his critics in Portugal, it was Cape Bojador that played the limit-role that had always been assigned by geographers to the Tropic of Cancer. Bojador was the sinister toll to the deadly torrid zone. And it took Henry twelve years, fifteen abortive expeditions, and tossing his men ever more lucrative bait to persuade anyone at all to round this cape of no return.[45]

Gil Eanes's return from the voyage past Cape Bojador in 1434 incited great joy at Henry's court, as it proved that the coastline beyond was not the hellish expanse promised by Henry's critics in Portugal. According to Barros, what most had pleased Henry was Eanes's news that, although he had found no people or towns around Bojador, the area nevertheless seemed "fresh and gracious; and that as proof that the land was not as sterile as people had claimed, he had brought in a barrel full of dirt with some herbs that looked like others that bore flowers in Portugal and were known as Saint Mary's roses. When these herbs were brought to the prince, he gazed on them for a long time, showing no less joy than if they had been fruit and sign from the Promised Land and giving many thanks to God. And he begged Our Lady whose name those roses bear to lead him further on the path of this discovery for the praise and glory of God, and for the increase of His holy faith."[46] In 1435 Eanes returned with Afonso Gonçalves Baldaia to find "traces of men and camels" farther south along the coastline than they had traveled the first time, and there, two armed youths sent inland to survey the area clashed with a group of nineteen youths armed with javelins.[47] "This," as Las Casas judges in *Historia de las Indias,* "was the first scandal and injustice and bad Christian example perpetrated by the Portuguese on that coast—which was newly discovered— against peoples who had never offended them; so that the entire land justly rose in hatred of the Christians, and, from then on, in legitimate defense, they would justly kill as many Christians as they could."[48]

On finding signs of life beyond Bojador, Prince Henry, with consent from the Portuguese Crown, sought papal protection for what he now saw as indisputably theirs, but an ill-fated campaign in 1437 against the Muslim city of Tânger in Mediterranean Africa, as well as the social unrest that followed King Duarte's death in 1438, were bound to distract Henry from making much progress beyond Cape Bojador for several years.[49] Not surprisingly, it is also right after his men rounded Cape Bojador, in 1435, that Henry asked King Juan II of Castile for permission to conquer in his stead the islands that Castile had not yet occupied in the Canaries. Evidently Henry hoped to use those islands as bases from which to launch further exploration to the south and, no doubt, to begin a conquest campaign that would eventually squeeze Castilian forces out of the Canaries.[50] Permission was, of course, denied.

In 1441, after long years of largely unprofitable surveys of the coastline beyond Bojador, the first black slaves were captured by Henry's men near today's Bay de Río de Oro in Western Sahara (today 23° 45′ N).[51] Horrified by this other inaugural scene of destruction in Zurara's and Barros's chronicles, Las Casas observes: "It is something to see how highly the Portuguese historians sing the praises of such abominable misdeeds, offering them all as great sacrifices to God."[52] Las Casas condemns Prince Henry's monstrous invention in no uncertain terms, referring thus to the ill-gotten popularity that the first slave raids had earned Prince Henry in the eyes of the Portuguese:

> They say that [Prince Henry], insofar as he let show, pursued [these navigations] out of zeal for serving God and for bringing the infidel back into the fold (although he chose the wrong means to do so); and thus, I believe, that he rather offended than served God, because he defamed His faith and caused those infidels to loathe Christianity; and for every soul he thought he was incepting to the faith—souls who probably, or rather, surely received baptism out of fear or were forced to do so—[the Portuguese], more than anything else, ended up delivering many more souls to Hell. And it is clear that he alone was guilty of all this, because he sent [the Portuguese] there and was their leader; and, taking part of the profits and imparting favors to those who perpetrated such atrocities, he approved of everything.[53]

Las Casas, who methodically argues in *Historia de las Indias* why acts such as these had been illegal and sinful, did not just reserve his opprobrium for an easy target such as the Portuguese. No matter how much Las Casas would come to emphasize that Columbus was "first apostle and minister of these Indies," he equally denounced in the bitterest terms Columbus's lead in the imitation of Africa's destruction in the Indies. On the margins of the summary copy he produced of the *Diario,* Las Casas balks at the abductions Columbus had carried out on his first voyage with the intention of taking his captives to Castile so that they could be trained as translators. In an entry describing the reconnaissance of Río de Mares on Cuba's northeastern coast, Columbus smugly reported having received a father who had paddled his way to the *Santa María* in the middle of the night to beg to the Admiral to let him join three children already held captive.[54] Replying to Columbus's self-satisfied remark that father and children had now been content to be reunited, Las Casas objects: "Why instead did you not give him back his children?"[55] In the corresponding chapter of *Historia de las Indias,* Las Casas goes so far as to claim that "for this injustice alone, and this unreasonable and culpable feat, even if the Admiral had committed no other, he should have known himself to deserve from God all the tribulations and anguish that [Columbus] later suffered in the course of his life."[56] Columbus may have been an instrument of God's providence, but, to the extent that he had treated Indian lives and property as goods for his free disposal, the Discoverer would remain for Las Casas Henry's heir to the destruction of the African tropics.

It was in the wake of the first slave raids on the coastline extending beyond Cape Bojador that Prince Henry asked Pope Martin V, as João de Barros claims, for "perpetual donation to the Crown of those domains that extended through all the lands to be discovered along this our ocean sea from Cape Bojador all the way to, and including, the Indies."[57] Curiously enough, the bulls drafted to accommodate this petition did not reserve a special clause for the Atlantic space beyond Bojador.[58] But in 1443 the Portuguese regent, Dom Pedro, in the name of the young Afonso V, did issue a decree forbidding anyone in Portugal from venturing beyond Cape Bojador without express permission from Henry, and all licensed vessels were ordered to pay the appropriate portions of their revenues to Henry and to the Crown.[59] Dom Pedro's decree granted Henry these privileges on account of having sent his ships to explore "that land that lay beyond Cape Bojador, because before this, no Christian had ever known anything about it, nor had anything been known about its populations, nor had they been directly drawn on charts or *mappaemundi*, except by the whim of those who drafted them, from Cape Bojador on."[60]

Cape Bojador acquired truly urgent legal solvency for Portugal in subsequent years, as the Portuguese Crown came to realize that Castile was, if nothing else, holding an ever tighter grip on the region of the Canaries. In 1454, following Prince Henry's most recent campaign to wrest control of the archipelago from Castilians, Afonso V of Portugal tried to boycott Castile's commercial ventures along Atlantic Morocco, to assert further control over the ocean sound between the Canaries and the African mainland, and to halt altogether the transit of Andalusian vessels to the territories discovered by Henry's caravels south of Cape Bojador. Afonso V sought special shelter once again in the tradition of the papal concessions that had long lent a seal of approval to the crusades against Muslims in the Mediterranean basin.[61] To this end, the king persuaded Pope Nicholas V to grant him sole spiritual and temporal ministry over all territories already occupied and, more significantly, *to be occupied* by Portugal in Atlantic Africa in the future.[62] From Rome, which was still smarting from the fall of Constantinople to the Ottomans (1453), Nicholas V issued a most belligerent bull (*Romanus pontifex*, 8 January 1454), granting Afonso V and his successors broad and unlimited power to invade, conquer, dispossess, subjugate, and perpetually enslave "any and all Saracens, pagans, or other enemies of Christ, wherever they be established."[63] The territories that were offered to such broad Portuguese discretion included the Azores and Madeira Islands and the Muslim territories in northwest Africa. But this time they extended "from Cape Bojador and Cape Não [Nam], through all of Guinea, and beyond it toward the southern shore extending beyond them in a row."[64] What was probably understood by "southern shore" is those African shores that, assuming Africa could be rounded by sea, were thought to face the equatorial portion of the Ocean River. The geographical order in which Nam and Bojador are named in this bull is *not* casual. Even though Bojador stood farther south from Portugal and Castile than Nam, indexing Bojador first was a clever way of sheltering Nam as part of the African coastline that Prince Henry had indisputably been the first to discover. This bull also made ample room for targeting any African peoples other than Muslims and pagans by calling them "other enemies of Christ, wherever they be established."

The following year, Nicholas's successor, Calixtus III, expedited the bull *Inter cetera* (13 March 1456), confirming Nicholas's donation but specifying that its beneficiary was the military Order of Christ headed by Prince Henry and substantially expanding the reach of the territories discovered by Henry beyond capes Bojador and Nam from Africa's meridional shoreline "all the way to the Indians."[65] Portugal had now carved out for itself a geopolitical space beyond Cape Bojador that, in line with a geographical tradition dating back to the earliest Indographers, immediately associated sub-Saharan Africa with the extended basin of the Indian Ocean. It is specifically this territory (the Afro-Indian tropics) that, upon Columbus's triumphant return to Europe in 1493, João II of Portugal would try to claim as his exclusive domain.

The dispute between Castile and Portugal for control of the African side of the Atlantic found partial resolution with the drafting of the Treaty of Alcáçovas in 1479–1480. The treaty brought an end to the war that Afonso V had waged in 1464 against Fernando and Isabel to contest the latter's succession to the Castilian throne. With this treaty, Portugal was forced to recognize Castile's sovereignty in the Canaries.[66] And in exchange for the Canaries, Castile recognized Portugal's exclusive control of "all trade, lands, and ransom in Guinea, along with its gold mines and any other isles, coasts, or lands discovered or to be discovered, found or to be found; Madeira, Porto Santo, and the deserted islands; and the islands of the Azores, and the Flores Islands; as well as the Cape Verde Islands and all the islands it has now discovered, and any other islands to be found or conquered *from the Canary Islands down and toward Guinea.*"[67] Hoping now to consolidate a monopoly that would isolate the Canaries from the rest of the Atlantic, Portugal lost little time in requesting from Pope Sixtus IV yet another bull confirming the terms of the crucial documents previously expedited by Nicholas V and Calixtus III and of the peace treaty just signed with Castile. Predictably, the document *Aeterni regis clementia* (6 June 1481) defined Portugal's present *and* future domains in the Atlantic as, in effect, everything "to the far side and the near side of the Canary Islands and looking at Guinea" (*ab insulis de Canaria ultra et citra et in conspectu Guinee*).[68] Sixtus IV once again specifically indexed the territories newly discovered under Prince Henry's patronage and donated by Nicholas V and Calixtus III as standing "in islands, towns, ports, lands, and places acquired and to be acquired from the capes of Bojador and Nam along all of Guinea and beyond that southern shore all the way to the Indians."[69]

Although the Treaty of Alcáçovas did bring a period of relative ease between Castile and Portugal over the territories each now recognized officially as the other's, the ocean sound and continental shores comprehended by capes Nam and Bojador continued to be a source of diplomatic and sometimes armed conflict between the two kingdoms. In 1491, as the final siege to Muslim Granada dampened Columbus's last lobbying efforts with the Crowns of Aragon and Castile, tension ran high between the Catholic Monarchs and João II regarding the fisheries off of the coastline comprehended by capes Nam and Bojador. The Spanish Crown had repeatedly ignored Portugal's claim that the rich fishing grounds off Bojador were part of Castile's concessions to Portugal in the Treaty of Alcáçovas. In a letter written outside besieged Granada, Fernando and Isabel reminded João II that he had agreed to allow Spanish vessels to fish off capes Nam and Bojador until the question had been properly examined and settled, and they promised to charge a "person of science" with the task of determining whether the disputed area fell north or south of the imaginary boundary specified by the treaty as below the Canarian archipelago.[70] (The order in which this Castilian document refers to capes Nam and Bojador, contrary to the order used by Portuguese documents, was clearly meant to disentangle the sound comprehended by Nam and Bojador from the territories that Prince Henry had recently discovered beyond Bojador.) In the heat of this conflict over the Canarian sound, Fernando and Isabel repeatedly warned Columbus and those collaborating in the preparations for his ocean crossing, that under no circumstances should they go "to Mina or interfere with the business that the Most Serene King of

Portugal carries out there, because it is our will to keep, and to enforce the keeping of, what we have accorded with the said king of Portugal."[71]

This interdiction was particularly urgent, given that Columbus meant to launch the outward passage from the Canary Islands and that the Portuguese were likely to keep close watch on the route he had chosen. The Canaries marked Castile's westernmost and southernmost territories in the Atlantic, and as such they represented Columbus's best shot at crossing the Atlantic. The southernmost point of this archipelago—El Hierro Island—also marked the political boundary beyond which Castile now officially recognized Portugal's monopoly in Guinea. Evidently Columbus was ordered to push his luck across the ocean mindful of this boundary ("from the Canary Islands down and toward Guinea"). And for this very reason Columbus would insist in his *Diario* that San Salvador stood on the same latitude as El Hierro. Columbus was meant to sail west across the Atlantic—west, that is, until he reached land, or until such a point where he deemed it safe to steer in some other direction. Unfortunately for the Portuguese Crown, the Treaty of Alcáçovas granted Portugal sovereignty from the Canary Islands down and toward Guinea, but it inadvertently opened a legal loophole for the Spanish Crown by failing to take into account the expanse to the west and to the south of the Canaries—in the direction of Columbus's India. Upon Columbus's victorious return to Europe in 1493, this understandable omission would result in a hefty loss for the Portuguese seaborne empire.

Columbus's stormy passage back to Europe in 1493 accidentally placed him back in the hands of João II before he had a chance to appear before Fernando and Isabel. Having strayed off course toward the Azores, where local authorities tried to arrest him, Columbus later found himself seeking shelter from more inclement weather in the port villa of Cascais, at the entrance to Lisbon. There, on 4 March 1493, fearing that his precious cargo might be confiscated by local authorities or stolen, Columbus saw no choice but to write to João II, requesting permission to dock in Lisbon and impressing upon the king, as Las Casas writes, "that he did not come from Guinea but from the Indies."[72] Portuguese chroniclers report that Columbus was said to have returned from the islands of Çipango and Antilia, or just from Çipango.[73]

On 8 March 1493 Columbus received a reply from João II, who, citing the danger of shipping back out to sea before the weather had cleared, invited Columbus to meet with him in person.[74] The following day, the Discoverer found himself face-to-face with the monarch who had, not once but twice, rejected his plan to cross the ocean. [75] One can only imagine the distaste that Columbus's return to Lisbon visited upon João II and his courtiers, especially because Columbus made no effort to spare the king the public embarrassment of having rebuffed his proposal to cross the Atlantic. In his *Crónica de el-rey D. João II* (about 1504), Ruy de Pina states that Columbus proceeded to recount the events of his voyage and to gloat about the riches he had found, displaying little regard for "the terms of all truth," so much so, that João II's councilors, offended by Columbus's insolence, advised the king to have Columbus assassinated. [76]

João de Barros reports in *Ásia* that when Columbus appeared before João II, the king's expression fell "upon seeing that the natives who came with [Columbus] were not black with woolly hair nor did they bear the aspect of those from Guinea; but instead they displayed a moderate skin color, and hair as [João II] was told people had in India, which he had tired so much to reach." [77] By the physical aspect of Columbus's abductees, João II clearly hoped to detect from *where* Columbus had returned. Should Columbus have hauled back to Lisbon "black" captives with "woolly" hair (as Ethiopians had long been described), then perhaps João II might have found firmer ground to detain Columbus on a charge of crossing over into the lower latitudes of the African Atlantic now recognized by Castile as Portugal's. Columbus's abductees puzzled João II by displaying medium-colored skins and countenances that did not match those of slaves taken from sub-Saharan Africa. On this count, Columbus had probably not sailed below the latitude of the Canaries. But were these abductees Indian? Their physiognomy was deceptive, because their skin color ought have been black, just like that of our legendary Ethiopians, but it was not. Yet they did display long, lank hair, as Indians were alleged to possess, and this was a sign that Columbus might have trumped Portugal's efforts to round Africa into the extended basin of the Indian Ocean or that he had at least come very close to doing so.

In other words, what João II tried to gather from the bodies of these islanders was not simply whether Columbus had sailed far enough west to have reached the periphery of Asia but whether he had attempted to reach the lower latitudes of those Indies that João II had so fervently wished to secure for himself via Africa. Had Columbus merely sailed due west? Or had he also sailed due south? The native bodies offered for display by Columbus, however, conveyed utterly contradictory information concerning the general latitude Columbus had explored. If Columbus had only sailed to the west, or to the west and to the north, then João II simply had no grounds to contest Spanish claims to the lands discovered by Columbus—unless the Portuguese king were to have argued that all territories discovered or to be discovered *anywhere* in the Atlantic—except for the Canaries—automatically belonged to the Portuguese Crown.

But João II could not have cared less about what Castile might find to the west, or to the west and to the north of the Canaries. He wanted to block Castile from gaining access to precious Africa and India. And if Columbus had already sailed, or intended to sail in the future, below the latitude of the Canaries, then João II saw one way to stop further Castilian expansion toward the Indies dead in its tracks. As Las Casas renders the entry in the *Diario* for the interview on 9 March 1493, the Portuguese monarch

> received [Columbus] with much honor, bestowed on him much favor, asked him to be seated, and spoke very courteously, assuring [Columbus] that he would have everything that was of service to the sovereigns of Castile and to [Columbus] selflessly accomplished. And he showed great pleasure at learning that the voyage had ended safely and been carried out successfully, *but he understood from the treaty signed between him and the sovereigns that the said conquest belonged to him.* To which the Admiral replied that he neither had seen the said treaty nor knew anything else except that the sovereigns had ordered him not to go to [São Jorge da Mina] or anywhere in Guinea, and that this had been ordered to be so proclaimed in all the ports of Andalusia prior to his departure.[78]

Dom João's invocation of the Treaty of Alcáçovas implies either that he believed he had exclusive rights to everything Portugal had discovered or would discover in the Atlantic except for the Canaries or else that he now interpreted the terminology *de las yslas de Canaria para yuso contra Guinea* to mean that Portugal had exclusive rights not merely to the waters and shores below the Canaries and toward the African shores but also to everything below the latitude of the Canaries, whether to the east or to the west of the archipelago. And João II was impressing upon Columbus that Portugal was willing to break peace with Castile in order to enforce such terms. Columbus lied, for his part, about not having any knowledge of the compact between Castile and Portugal, and shrewdly avoided supplying João II with any more specific information concerning his recent whereabouts by stating no more than that he had been forbidden from sailing to the south and to the east of the Canaries.

The months following Columbus's return from the Caribbean were to witness frantic posturing and diplomacy between two kingdoms again on the brink of war.[79] According to Ruy de Pina, after Columbus's interview with João II, the king wasted little time in preparing an armada charged with tracking down the newly discovered lands under the admiralship of Francisco d'Almeida, who later became viceroy of India.[80] The noted chronicler for the kingdom of Aragon, Jerónimo de Zurita, in his *Historia del rey D. Fernando el Católico,* adds that the Portuguese armada outfitted by João II was meant to find its way to the contested territories in the high Atlantic with help from two pilots who had been forcefully removed from Columbus's caravel *Niña*.[81] On 5 April 1493, João II also dispatched his first embassy to Barcelona, entrusting another Ruy de Sande, major of Torresvedras, with informing the Crowns of Aragon and Castile of Columbus's stopover in Lisbon. According to Zurita, Sande was instructed to tell Fernando and Isabel that João II trusted the king and queen, should any of their vessels have discovered lands that belonged to him, to observe the "friendship and fraternity" between the two Crowns, and that, in turn, Dom João vowed to do the same for them. Ruy de Sande was also instructed to convey how pleased João II had been to learn that Columbus had obeyed Fernando and Isabel's instructions, *"by following his course and by discovering from the Canary Islands directly due west without treading toward the south,* as [Columbus] himself had certified. And because [João II] harbored no doubt that the king and queen would send back their vessels to continue the discovery of what they had found by this route, he begged them affectionately to be pleased to follow that order always. For, whenever he should send any ships to discover, they could rest assured that *he would order them not to trespass beyond the limit on the north."*[82] João II had clearly opted this early on in the game for interpreting the Treaty of Alcáçovas to mean that Portugal had exclusive jurisdiction over everything that had been found or might be found below the entire latitude of the Canaries. And, as we are about to see, such an interpretation of Alcáçovas now rested on the reasonable theory—rendered even more reasonable by Columbus's finds in the high Atlantic—that islands and mainlands might now be found to the west and to the south of the Canaries, and that such lands might be fabulously rich precisely because they stood within the bounds of a formerly dreaded torrid zone.

News of the discovery may have reached Fernando and Isabel in Barcelona even before Columbus had docked in Lisbon or met with João II.[83] Martín Alonso Pinzón, the unruly captain of the caravel *Pinta* who had rushed ahead of Columbus in the Caribbean to conduct exploration on his own, called port in the Galician town of Baiona during the last days of February 1493. Perhaps hoping that the *Niña* had gone down in the storm off of the Azores, which would have shoved Columbus out of the way, Pinzón sent a petition to Barcelona for an audience with Fernando and Isabel. The sovereigns swiftly declined Pinzón's advances, making it clear that the Crown would deal only with Columbus. This rejection caused Pinzón "such chagrin and contempt," writes Ferdinand in his biography of his father, "that he returned to his homeland [Palos] a sick man, where eight days later he died of grief."[84]

Fernando and Isabel, for their part, sprang to action in order to secure their newly acquired territories on the ocean sea. It appears that by the early days of March 1493, they had already taken steps to procure papal endorsement of rights that, they correctly anticipated, would be contested by the Portuguese Crown.[85] Next on their list was the arming of a return fleet to the newly discovered territories in the high Atlantic, although this would have to wait until Columbus returned to Spain, which did not happen until 15 March 1493. It remains unclear when (or by what means) Fernando and Isabel received the recently found letter that Columbus had written to them on 4 March 1493 from the entrance to Lisbon announcing the discovery.[86] On 30 March 1493, replying to this official letter by Columbus, or to another he would have written from Seville around 17 March, Fernando and Isabel summoned the Discoverer back to Barcelona to report to them in person the events of his voyage.[87] In their letter to Columbus, the Catholic Monarchs urged "our Admiral of the Ocean Sea, viceroy, and governor of the islands that have been discovered in the Indies" not to leave Seville for Barcelona without first making arrangements for a return voyage to be launched before summer's end.[88]

On that same day, Fernando and Isabel also issued a royal provision announcing that they had ordered the discovery of "certain isles and terra firma in the part of the ocean toward the part of the Indies" (*algunas yslas e tierra firme en la parte del mar oçeano a la parte de las yndias*); and they forbade anyone from shipping out to them without royal license.[89] The locator "in the part of the ocean toward the part of the Indies," identically repeated in numerous other royal documents issued in preparation for Columbus's second voyage, consciously registered the meridional inflection of Columbus's exploration by indicating not that the newly discovered lands stood generally in the high Atlantic, but rather that they stood *in that part* of the Atlantic that extended *toward the part of the Indies.*[90] It is also clear that, this early on, the Spanish Crown remained noncommittal about whether or not Columbus had sailed far enough to reach "the parts of India."

As we all know, Fernando and Isabel also made haste to publicize the discovery. Sometime in the course of the following weeks (April 1493), the first printed edition of the *carta-relación* Columbus had composed on the last leg of his voyage to the *escribano de ración* Luis de Santángel announcing the discovery (15 February 1493) appeared in the city where Fernando and Isabel's court was stationed.[91] In this letter to the keeper of the royal purse, which was probably edited by a third party on its way to the printing press, Columbus could not help but index in one form or another the tropical inclination of the lands he had discovered. The most obvious way in which the author did so was, naturally, by announcing from the outset that "in twenty days [he had] passed *to the Indies* with the armada which the Most Illustrious King and Queen Our Sovereigns [had given him]"—a geographical reference that should instantly prompt us to recall the manner in which Marco Polo's maritime Indography had come to be plotted on Behaim's globe and the few known *mappaemundi* of the period.[92] Logically, Columbus also registered the tropicality of the Bahamas and the Caribbean by ceaselessly marveling at a nature that was radically different from Europe's—indeed a nature "deformed" (*diforme*), productive to the point of defying any description and, most significantly, working its prodigal magic every day year-round. Columbus reports seeing "trees of a thousand kinds" that "I was told never shed their foliage, from what I understand, for I saw them as green and beautiful as they are in Spain in May, some of them flowering, others bearing fruit, and others at some other stage, each according to their nature."[93] The perennial nakedness of the peoples who roamed the islands naked "as their mothers bear them" (*como sus madres los paren*) also betrayed the fact that they inhabited the hotter latitudes of the globe, even as their medium-colored skin defied the canonical expectation of blackness or other manifestations of alleged monstrosity in the hot extremes of the inhabited world: Columbus carefully notes that he has failed to find "monstrous men as so many expected. On the contrary, all are people of beautiful countenances, nor are they black as in Guinea, except that they do have lank hair [as Indians were supposed to have], and they do not generate where the aspect of the solar rays is too strong; it is true that the sun is very strong there, as [those lands] stand twenty-six degrees from the equinoctial line."[94] Just as these medium-colored islanders failed to generate, or avoided living, where the sun's rays were too strong, so did they know how to temper the cold of high mountains, which Columbus observes they inhabited not by nature but "by custom.

For with the help of the viands they prepare, they eat [foods] with many and extremely hot spices." The heat these Indians induced into their diet counteracted the cold felt in the sierras. "Therefore," he concludes, "I have found no monsters, nor have I had report of any, except for [those of] an island that is second at the entrance to the Indies, which is populated by a people who are regarded in all the islands as very fierce and who consume live flesh."[95] As Columbus's *Diario* shows, the deferral of human monstrosity to the outer margins of the archipelago he thought he had found in the Indies was directly informed not only by the notion that extreme latitudes gave way to extreme natures but also by the urge to identify a somatic substitute for blackness in the newly discovered peoples—and along with this substitute (physical deformity) a negative moral trait (anthropophagy) that would serve as justification for capturing slaves.

For the time being, the peoples Columbus had found in the Bahamas and the outer shores of Cuba and Hispaniola displayed psychological traits that Mediterranean thinkers had long associated with their neighbors in the lower latitudes of the globe. In the letter to Luis de Santángel, Columbus vehemently asserts that the beautiful islanders were "marvelously timorous" (*temerosos a maravilla*), that they lacked any iron weaponry, and that upon sighting his crew for the first time they often "fled so quickly that parents did not wait for their children" (*fuian a non guardar padre a fijo*). And this was not because they had been treated badly but because they were "cowardly beyond measure" (*temerosos sin remedio*).[96] Referring to the fact that he had left a garrison with thirty-nine men in the newly built fort of Navidad, Columbus assured his distinguished interlocutor that, even if the "king" he had found in Hispaniola (referring to the unfortunate cacique Guacanagarí) were to turn against the Christian settlers, this king had no chance of hurting them, for "neither he nor his people know about weapons, and they walk around naked; as I have said before, they are the most cowardly people in the world, so the people I have left there are enough to destroy the entire land, and the island poses no danger to them as long as they know how to govern it."[97] Columbus's reservation regarding his settlers' ability to govern the island in his absence turned out to be prophetic, for upon returning to Navidad on his second voyage, Columbus found that his men's behavior had been so egregious that the islanders had finally risen against them, butchering every one of the Christians and razing the fort.

In his letter to Santángel, Columbus was equally anxious to emphasize the great intelligence displayed by these "tamest" of peoples. According to Columbus, the islanders "did not know any sect or idolatry, except that they believe that all the forces of good are in the heavens. And they believed that I myself, along with these ships and crew, had come from heaven, and with this understanding they welcomed me everywhere once they had lost their fear."⁹⁸ Columbus immediately takes pains to explain that the belief among the Indians that the Christians had come from heaven did not mean that they were "stupid" (*ignorantes*). On the contrary, the islanders displayed "very subtle ingenuity" (*muy sotil ingenio*): they had so mastered the art of navigating through the seas, "that it is a marvel to see how thoroughly they give notice of everything they have seen." And those whom Columbus had taken in San Salvador to serve as informants and interpreters had swiftly learned to communicate with the Christians "by words or by signs": "When I arrived at the Indies, in the first island, I took some of them by force so that they would learn [our language] and tell me what was to be found in those parts; and thus it was that they then began to understand us, and we them, whether by words or by signs, and these have been of great service to us."⁹⁹ Indeed, the Indians that Columbus found in the high Atlantic displayed the intelligence and cowardice that Mediterranean geographers had long ascribed to the inhabitants of the tropics in assigning them a subordinate place in the hierarchy of nations. In sum, even as Columbus (or those who edited his famous letter for the publication) attempted to erase his tracks through the Atlantic (whether by minimizing the number of days it had taken to cross the ocean or by insisting that the lands explored by him stood on the approximate latitude of the Canaries), tropicality remains the key organizing principle of the document by means of which the Spanish Crown sought to broadcast its claim to the territories "in the part of the ocean toward the part of the Indies."

By mid-April 1493, rumor had reached Barcelona that João II was preparing to send or had already sent an armada to secure the lands discovered by Columbus.¹⁰⁰ This armada returned, of course, empty-handed. On 22 April, anticipating the arrival of the Portuguese ambassador Ruy de Sande, Fernando and Isabel dispatched a member of the royal household, Lope de Herrera, to Lisbon in order to announce the discovery to João II officially, to thank him for his hospitality toward Columbus, to ask him to forbid anyone in his kingdom from sailing without consent from Aragon and Castile to the lands Columbus had discovered, and, lastly, by way of veiled threat, to beg João II to consider this request in light of the fact the Catholic Monarchs and their ancestors had always been the first to recognize Portugal's exclusive claims to Guinea and São Jorge da Mina.¹⁰¹ In addition to this, a few days later (27 April 1493), wishing to feed the newly arrived Ruy de Sande a morsel to take back to his king, Fernando and Isabel issued another royal provision forbidding all fishing in the waters off of Cape Bojador. This measure was meant not only to prevent any incident in the contested waters between the Canaries and the African mainland from giving João II an excuse to carry out his intent of delivering an armada into the high Atlantic, but also to send a clear signal that Aragon and Castile were intent on approaching any foreseeable disagreement over the newly discovered territories in the high Atlantic in light of the peace treaty that João II had mindfully cited to Columbus.[102] And just in case diplomacy with Portugal failed, the Spanish sovereigns also ordered Don Juan de Guzmán, Duke of Medina Sidonia, who had sent confirmation to them of Dom João's intentions, to arm all the available caravels in his domains, "so that we might make use of them for whatever they are needed."[103]

Columbus had taken formal possession of the newly discovered "isles and terra firma" for the kingdoms of Castile and Aragon on no other premise than that Christian rulers possessed—in the interest of the faith and without need for right of way from the papal see—automatic dominion over non-Christians.[104] From this standpoint, Castile had never before seen the need to reinforce the case for its occupation of the Canaries on the basis of any papal documents beyond those issued by Benedict XIII in 1403 to endorse Béthencourt and La Salle's assault on its inhabitants. Nor should Portugal have needed to punctuate every significant move it had made on Atlantic Africa with a document from the papal see.[105] It is true that, since the thirteenth century, key Christian figures in the development of international law had already spawned a debate in ecclesiastic and academic circles concerning the right of Christians to invade at will territories ruled by someone other than a Christian prince. Chief among such dissident thinkers had been Pope Innocent IV, who mounted the first efforts in the thirteenth century to conduct diplomacy with Mongol rulers, and his contemporary Thomas Aquinas, who insisted that "natural" law gave infidels rightful possession of their lands.[106] But the assumption behind every raid operation (*salteo*) visited on the inhabitants of the Canaries and other parts of Atlantic Africa since the fourteenth century, and behind every attempt to subdue peoples who by now included "pagans" and "any other enemies of Christ," was quite simply that infidels lacked the legal rights and privileges accorded to other Christians.

This assumption found one of its best exponents in fifteenth-century Spain in the figure of Alonso de Cartagena, bishop of Burgos. In 1435 Prince Henry the Navigator unsuccessfully sought permission from King Juan II of Castile to attempt the conquest of those islands in the Canaries that had not yet been subdued. King Duarte of Portugal

then asked Pope Eugenius IV to donate the unconquered Canaries to Portugal, noting that they were closer to Portugal than to Castile and populated by infidels not yet under the yoke of any Christian prince and therefore in urgent need of evangelization.[107]

In the *Allegationes* presented by Castile in 1435 to counter Portugal's petition to the pope, Alonso de Cartagena argued, among other things, that the Canaries were part of the Mauretania Tingitana once ruled by the Visigoths.[108] Castile was the proper heir to Mauretania Tingitana, even if it had been temporarily prevented from enjoying its domain by Muslim invaders. By requesting permission from Juan II to conquer the islands that had not yet been subdued in the Canaries, Prince Henry had tacitly acknowledged Castile's sovereignty over the entire archipelago. Moreover, when King Enrique III of Castile had ordered the occupation of the island of Lanzarote (via Béthencourt), he had done so with the intention of recuperating all the islands in the conglomerate. And, more importantly, once Castile had reappropriated this first island, Castile must be considered to be in possession of the entire archipelago. This total dominion was valid not simply by virtue of the islands' geographical proximity to one another (a claim that would have played into the arguments presented by Portugal for their right to the Canaries). Such dominion also was valid by virtue of what Alonso de Cartagena mysteriously called "the intellectual unity of some whole."[109] What the Bishop of Burgos meant by this is not entirely clear, but it extended to the notion that the Canary Islands "possess a certain unity in polity and rituals, and similar barbarity and fierceness, and all are practically one people."[110] According to Alonso de Cartagena, possession of the whole by means of the part—possession of the entire archipelago by metonymy—was particularly licit when the other parts that composed such an entity were "vacant."[111] The islands that had not been "recuperated" during the reign of Henry III had been at that time, and now still remained, "vacant." This meant, explains Alonso de Cartagena, not that these islands lacked any inhabitants, but rather, that they lacked a Christian prince to exercise "supreme dominion" over them.[112]

The notion that unconquered territories could be considered vacant—that is, lacking a proper landlord—is of crucial importance for understanding the legal language and rituals that would accompany Columbus's first voyage through the Bahamas and the Caribbean. It should be no surprise that Columbus and his men, upon landing for the first time on an unknown shore where they saw no more than naked people who appeared neither hostile nor armed, should have instantly opted for taking formal

possession of the site of the landfall. Las Casas recounts that, having sighted naked people on the island, and having paddled his way ashore in an armed launch,

> Columbus unfurled the royal banner, and [his] captains two flags with the green cross, which the Admiral carried for standards on all his ships, with an *F* and a *Y,* and above each letter its crown, one on one side of the [cross] and the other on the other. Once ashore, they saw very green trees and many waters and diverse sorts of fruit. The Admiral called his two captains and also the others, who jumped ashore, and Rodrigo de Escobedo, the notary of the whole armada, and Rodrigo Sánchez de Segovia. And he summoned them as witnesses to the fact that he was taking, as indeed he took, possession of the said island for the king and queen his lords, making all the required protestations, as fully recorded in the testimonials committed to writing on this occasion.[113]

Columbus followed this protocol everywhere he landed, as he later recounts in the letter to Santángel: "I found very many populated islands harboring peoples without number, and I have taken possession of all of them for Your Highnesses with proclamation and royal banner unfurled, *and no one contradicted me*" (*y no me fue contradicho*).[114] The legal ceremony first carried out in San Salvador had been meant, among other things, as a *provisional* measure that Columbus carried out repeatedly through the Bahamas, and along Cuba and Hispaniola—alert at one point or another to signs of Mongol armies or of sizable cities and recognizable merchandise, or else eager to determine whether the natives he met along the way were subject to local kings or to foreign governors.[115]

The premise that non-Christian territories lacked proper landlords may explain a key element of Columbus's often calculated ethnography: his insistence that Indians failed to see themselves as owners of land or resources. As we have seen, in 1495, following the massive land grab that accompanied his grand fleet's arrival in Hispaniola on the second voyage, Columbus "observed" that Indians were lazy idlers who had no use for private property because Hispaniola was so vast and productive that it could have amply sustained one hundred times its population. And this portrait of idle and unpossessive Indians, not unlike the prelapsarian creatures in Hesiod's *Works and Days* and the Mosaic account of creation, pointed to tropical nature as an overgenerous mother who had spared her children the need to toil the earth or to hoard any goods in order to survive.

The concept of possession by metonymy also appears early on in the *Diario:* upon making landing of the second island in the Bahamas, which he baptized Santa María de la Concepción (Rum Cay), Columbus declared his firm intention "not to pass by any island of which I might not take possession; although, if [possession is] taken of one, it can be said to be taken of all."[116] Columbus would not remain content to base this claim solely on the possibility that the two islands he had just discovered formed part of an archipelago. He also repeatedly insisted that the Bahamas, Cuba, and Hispaniola formed a largely univocal geopolitical entity, inhabited by peoples who displayed similar physiological and psychological traits as well as "one tongue and the same customs" (*una fabla y vnas costumbres*)—even as he carefully noted significant disparities among them and confessed his utter inability to parse their speech, presumably failing to recognize linguistic differences among groups.[117]

In any case, the legal premise attending the formal rituals by which Columbus appropriated the Bahamas, Cuba, and Hispaniola for the Spanish Crown was that Fernando and Isabel, as Christian princes, possessed automatic jurisdiction over territories not already occupied by other Christian rulers. And on this count alone, upon receiving the news that Columbus had returned safely to Europe, Fernando and Isabel would not seem to have needed the pope's permission to continue the task Columbus had already begun in the Bahamas and outer shores of the Caribbean basin.

Papal bulls did serve a few purposes, however, and the Portuguese king Afonso V had fully recognized them decades before when he asked for *Romanus pontifex* and *Inter cetera,* the two documents that had granted Portugal exclusive access to the expanse discovered by Prince Henry's vessels beyond Cape Bojador. Papal bulls provided a ready title of possession or occupation, issued by a third party presumably acting in good faith, which obviated the need for any other proof of domain: the pope is said to have played the role of notary for Christian rulers.[118] These documents were formally promulgated in public spaces, and they could be lugged around to display as titles. Thus on 4 August 1493, in preparation for Columbus's return to the Caribbean, Fernando and Isabel would send a copy of one of the bulls expedited by Alexander VI (4 May 1493) to be proclaimed in Seville, ordering Columbus to take it on his second voyage "so that, should you chance upon land, you might then present it."[119] Evidently, this document was meant to be flashed at possible Christian intruders in the territory newly claimed by Castile and Aragon—intruders who, presumably, would be bound to recognize the pope's authority, even if they might have made land before Columbus. The nature of the powers and

privileges granted by papal bulls such as these was exclusionary, that is, they proscribed other Christians from engaging in any and all traffic within the territories in question, and the penalty was automatic excommunication at the very moment of disobedience, disposing of the need for a formal trial.[120] This very threat was used in the first bull expedited by Alexander VI in favor of Fernando and Isabel (*Inter cetera* [I], 3 May 1493) forbidding anyone "of any dignity, estate, rank, order, or condition" to engage in any traffic whatsoever with the islands and lands discovered by Columbus without special permission from Castile and Aragon.[121]

Far more important, however, was the provisory nature of papal donations and concessions.[122] Christian princes might think they possessed the right to occupy infidel lands at will without need for prior papal consent, but any title of possession was valid only for territories *already* acquired and, in the case of archipelagos like the Canaries, for those islands that were thought to form a unit with islands already acquired. This title, however, did not cover territories that one intended to appropriate in the future. And this was precisely the key shelter that Nicholas V and Calixtus III had offered the Portuguese Crown through *Romanus pontifex* and *Inter cetera*. Even before Portuguese vessels had reached what was at first believed to be Africa's meridional shores (the Gulf of Guinea), and long before the Portuguese reached India, these papal documents had already guaranteed Portugal sovereignty over all territories extending beyond Cape Bojador and Cape Nam. *Romanus pontifex* and *Inter cetera* had served as promissory notes, so to speak, since the faculties they granted had been made effective immediately solely with respect to territories *already* acquired by Portugal at the time; but for territories that had not yet been acquired—namely, what *Romanus pontifex* deemed might be left of Guinea, plus Africa's "meridional shore," and what *Inter cetera* added as "all the way to the Indians"—such powers and privileges had been synchronized to become effective *ipso facto* at the moment of acquisition.[123]

The postponement of these faculties might not have been ideal from the standpoint of an embryonic imperial power attempting to preempt another, but this may not have mattered as much to Portugal, because Portugal was by the mid-fifteenth century far ahead of Castile in the exploration of Atlantic Africa. By contrast, upon Columbus's return to Europe in 1493, the Spanish Crown would feel less confident of its ability to maintain a lead over Portugal in the direction of the newly discovered territories, and so Fernando and Isabel asked Pope Alexander VI to make all concessions effective immediately, not just for the islands and land newly acquired by Columbus, but also for

all territories that might be found in that direction in the future—meaning that even if any ships belonging to Portugal or to any other Christian nation were to get there first, the territories in question would still belong to Aragon and Castile.[124]

The papal bulls expedited by Alexander VI in the months following Columbus's return to Europe were written with a very close eye to the contents and wording of the key pontifical concessions on which Portugal based its monopoly beyond Cape Bojador: first, Nicolas V's *Romanus pontifex,* which donated to the Portuguese Crown "the said . . . conquest extending from Cape Bojador and Cape Não [Nam], to and along all of Guinea, and beyond it toward the meridional shore extending beyond them in a row"; second, Calixtus III's *Inter cetera,* which expanded the geopolitical expanse in question "all the way to the Indians"; and, third, Sixtus IV's *Aeterni regis,* which amended the terms of the Treaty of Alcáçovas to confirm Portugal's rights over what stood "beyond" and "before" the Canaries and "toward Guinea," along the "meridional shore," and "all the way to the Indians."[125]

The first document expedited by Alexander VI, *Inter cetera* [I], had been requested by Fernando and Isabel in the early days of April, just before they received Columbus in Barcelona, and it arrived in court by 28 May.[126] This remarkable document opens by explaining that, of all the works Christianity could perform in the world, the highest was evangelical—to subdue and reduce barbarians to Christianity.[127] The Catholic Monarchs had, above all nations, worked toward this goal, as was proved by the recovery of Granada from the tyrannical rule of the Saracens. For this reason, the papacy was willing to make any concessions that would help the Catholic Monarchs proceed with such a sacred and praiseworthy venture. The conquest and recuperation of Granada had prevented the Catholic Monarchs for a long time from seeking out and discovering "certain remote and unknown lands and islands until now undiscovered by others" for the purpose of converting their inhabitants to Christianity.[128] But, having completed the conquest of Granada, the Catholic Monarchs had dispatched Christopher Columbus with men and ships to look for these remote and unknown territories by every means possible through parts of an ocean where no one had ventured before.[129] The pontiff indicated the meridional inflection of this novel enterprise, explaining that Columbus and his men had discovered these territories by sailing "through the western parts, as is said, *toward the Indians,* on the ocean sea."[130] Alexander also recognized that the numerous peoples found by Columbus in the high Atlantic constituted a new kind of non-Christian: these peoples lived peacefully, walked about stark naked, did not crave human flesh, believed in one god who had created heaven, and, according to Fernando and Isabel's envoys, showed sufficient aptitude for embracing Christianity and for adopting proper customs.[131] Needless to say, Alexander's characterization of the newly found peoples in the high Atlantic was directly informed by Columbus's ethnography: just as Columbus insisted on the cowardice and subtle ingenuity of the Indians in the letter announcing the discovery, so did Alexander insist on erasing any traces of belligerence or predatory instinct in them, arguing instead that they were properly endowed to assume what by Europe's standards was a rational way of life.

To reinforce the idea that Fernando and Isabel's actions in the high Atlantic were irreversible, Alexander mentioned that Columbus had already ordered the construction of a well-garrisoned fort in one of the islands (Navidad, on northern Hispaniola) and that his armada had also found gold, perfumes, and all other sorts of precious things.[132] In light of this, and above all—insisted Alexander—for the exaltation and diffusion of Christianity, the Catholic Monarchs had, in imitation of their predecessors, studied the matter of subjugating the inhabitants of the new territories and converting them to the Christian faith. In recognition of such a sacred and praiseworthy cause, the papal see not only gave permission to Fernando and Isabel but "exhorted" and "required" them to continue with the said "expedition." For this purpose, the papal see "donated," "conceded," and "assigned" to the sovereigns "each and every one of the aforesaid lands and islands, including those that remain unknown and those that have so far been discovered by your envoys and those to be discovered from now on, which are not at present gathered under the yoke of some other Christian lords."[133] This donation, concession and assignation came "with full, free, and omnimodal power, authority, and jurisdiction" over the newly discovered territories.[134]

During the months following Columbus's return to Europe, the papal curia expedited four other bulls addressing his discoveries: one of them, *Eximie devotionis,* was requested and drafted in July, but antedated to 3 May 1493, probably in order to serve as an immediate complement for *Inter cetera* [I]. *Eximie devotionis* mainly established that Alexander VI was conferring on Fernando and Isabel the very same faculties and privileges in the new overseas domains that Portuguese monarchs already enjoyed in Africa, Guinea, São Jorge da Mina, and various islands.[135] Another bull, *Piis fidelium* (dated 25 June 1493), ordered a certain Bernardo Buil—a Benedictine friar who would soon declare himself in favor of a slash-and-burn policy against Indian uprisings in Hispaniola—to accompany Columbus on his second voyage as the apostolic vicar in charge of overseeing the diffusion of the faith in the newly discovered territories.[136] From our standpoint, these documents add nothing useful to *Inter cetera* [I] concerning the orientation of Columbus's enterprise. However, the remaining two papal documents issued on occasion of the discovery, *Inter cetera* [II] (dated 4 May 1493) and *Dudum siquidem* (dated 26 September 1493), are of particular importance for the present argument.

Columbus's triumphant entrance to Barcelona in mid-April brought more concrete information to court concerning the whereabouts of the overseas domains he had discovered. And João II's ambassador Ruy de Sande, who arrived on Columbus's heels, delivered the message that as long as Fernando and Isabel kept sending reconnaissance missions to the west and to the north of the Canaries without venturing to the south, Dom João would not allow his own explorers to venture to the west and to the north of the Canaries. *Inter cetera* [I] was received in Barcelona at the end of May, and in view of what Columbus had informed them and of the message delivered by Ruy de Sande, the Catholic Monarchs saw the need to request an amended version of this bull from the pope, the purpose of which was to define the location of the new overseas domains as precisely but as broadly as possible. Recall that Columbus's *Diario* entry for 16 September explains that, having sailed somewhere between 267 and 306 leagues due west along the parallel of the Canaries, Columbus observed a drastic change in the complexion of the elements, and he found that from there onward, all the way to the Bahamas, the air was so exceedingly temperate that it felt "like the month of April in Andalusia."[137] In this very neighborhood, Columbus also grew alarmed to witness a phenomenon unknown to Mediterranean sailors before him: the compass needles on his ships "northwested a full point" instead of pointing north to Polaris, or slightly to the east of it, as happened in Europe.[138] (Compasses point toward the magnetic north and not toward the north marked by Polaris.) These perturbing phenomena in the midst of an otherwise featureless sea would later prompt Columbus, when he found himself in Barcelona, to suggest that a vertical line of demarcation be drawn from pole to pole one hundred leagues to the west of the Portuguese Azores or of the Cape Verde Islands in order to separate Spain's overseas expansion zone from Portugal's in Atlantic Africa. The proposed line of demarcation did not, however, obviate the pressing need to specify that the territories discovered by Columbus in the high Atlantic extended "to the west and to the south." By Columbus's reckoning, after all, he had sailed more or less due west along the parallel of the Canaries and then veered generally south from there.

In view of all this, during the month of June 1493, the papal curia drafted a second *Inter cetera* that arrived in Barcelona by mid-July as Columbus now hurried to ready a colonizing fleet.[139] Although *Inter cetera* [II] was drafted in June, it was antedated to 4 May 1493, no doubt with a view to forestalling any trouble Portugal might stir up concerning the time interval since the issuing of *Inter cetera* [I] on 3 May, for it was now assumed in Barcelona that a Portuguese armada was roaming the high Atlantic in search of the lands Columbus had just claimed for the Spanish Crown.[140] This new papal bull, which otherwise followed the first *Inter cetera* almost to the letter, relabeled the concessions "all islands and terrae firmae, discovered and to be discovered, found and to be found *to the west and to the south,* drawing and establishing a line from the arctic pole, that is from the north, to the antarctic pole, that is to the south; whether the terrae firmae and isles discovered and to be discovered be toward India [*versus Indiam*] or whether they be toward any other part, which line must be distant from any of the islands commonly called Azores and Cape Verde one hundred leagues to the west and to the south."[141] And just in case Almeida's armada had found lands in the direction where Columbus had sailed, this document made Alexander's concession retroactive to the moment in which Columbus, following the break-up of the caravel *Santa María,* had been "forced" to settle on Hispaniola (25 December 1493).

Based on testimony Columbus had surrendered to the Crown upon his arrival in Barcelona, *Inter cetera* [II] was probably meant to supersede its model. On 4 August 1493, the Catholic Monarchs sent a copy of *Inter cetera* [II] to be promulgated in Seville, with express orders for Columbus to take it on his second voyage in case he stumbled across intruders within the newly designated domains. In 1502 Columbus incorporated his copy of *Inter cetera* [II], not *Inter cetera* [I], to his *Libro de Privilegios* or "book of privileges," which is the version later consulted by Las Casas for *Historia de las Indias*.[142] And years later, in 1512, as a direct reply to the first protests by Dominican friars against the abuses committed by colonists against the natives of Hispaniola, the early apologists of empire called to testify at the historic *junta* of Burgos would cite *Inter cetera* [II], not *Inter cetera* [I], as proof that Fernando "the Catholic," in his capacities as regent of Castile, remained in lawful possession of the Indies.[143] For decades to come, *Inter cetera* [II] would remain the centerpiece of a schooled debate concerning Spain's titles to its occupation of the Americas. And the geographical terminology used by Alexander VI in this document to demarcate the lands he had donated to the Catholic Monarchs would not be forgotten. We need only consider the question with which Las Casas's learned nemesis, Juan

Ginés de Sepúlveda, opened his *Democrates secundus* (1544–1545), the most complete philosophical argument in favor of empire ever written in Spanish domains: "Is it by a just war, or unjustly, that the kings of Spain and our countrymen have brought and work to bring into subjection those barbarous peoples who inhabit the western and southern region and who are commonly called Indians in Spanish?"[144]

The geographical locator deployed in *Inter cetera* [II] for demarcating Fernando and Isabel's overseas domains unequivocally indicates that, even as the Catholic Monarchs made the first attempts to split the Atlantic into eastern and western halves for Portugal and Castile, the real bone of contention between the two kingdoms was the zone of expansion below the entire latitude of the Canaries. And since *Inter cetera* [II] was in part addressed to the Portuguese Crown, the point from which this document invited Portugal to reckon the sailing direction "to the west and to the south" was not just the point on the proposed vertical line due west of the Canaries but rather *any* point along that dividing line—whether the Portuguese were to make their reckoning out of the higher latitudes of the islands of the Azores (by today's measurements, 38° N) or out of the lower latitudes of the Cape Verde Islands (modern 16° N). However, what was truly becoming explicit is this: Portugal and Castile were now wrestling each other for control of a vast domain below the general latitude of the Canaries that both parties had begun to understand as highly desirable—precisely because it stood toward and inside the belt of the tropics.

Indeed, by June 1493, even before *Inter cetera* [II] had been sent to Barcelona from Rome, João II of Portugal was planning his own partition of the Atlantic. By this time, Spanish ambassador Lope de Herrera had officially announced the discovery to João II, begging the king not to dispatch any ships to the newly discovered territories and warning him that Fernando and Isabel had always labored to enforce Portugal's rights to what lay below the Canaries and toward Guinea. João II now dispatched another embassy to Barcelona in order to persuade Fernando and Isabel that the terms of the concession made to Portugal by the very treaty they were citing—*de las yslas de Canaria para yuso contra Guinea*—really meant *everything* below the latitude of the Canaries. João II's new ambassadors to Spain—Pero Diaz, who was one of Dom João's judges, and Ruy de Pina, a gentleman of the royal household who later became Dom João's chronicler—took their time to reach Barcelona, no doubt to give Almeida's armada the chance of finding lands in the direction where Columbus had found them.[145] Two months later, on 14 August 1493, João II's ambassadors finally arrived in Barcelona. Aragon's chronicler

Jerónimo de Zurita informs us that the plan presented by ambassadors Diaz and Pina consisted of drawing a straight east-to-west parallel out of the Canaries that would have given Castile and León rights to whatever it discovered to the west and to the north of the Canaries but reserved everything below the proposed parallel for Portugal.[146]

João II's proposal evidently caused some consternation in Barcelona, even though, by this time, Fernando and Isabel were in possession of the infamous papal document that would serve as the legal touchstone of a nascent empire—the "leaden bull" (*plúmbea bula*), as Las Casas grimly terms Alexander's historic concession.[147]

Suspecting that João II was onto something big, the Spanish Crown set things in motion to figure out what this might be. Columbus's discovery in the high Atlantic had now shown that dry land could surface anywhere around the globe, and the next problem was to determine how much more of it there was and where to find it. On 26 August 1493, the archbishop of Toledo, Don Pedro de Mendoza, was entrusted by the Spanish Crown to write a letter to Jaume Ferrer de Blanes, the great cosmographer who later hastened Columbus to plunge south on his third voyage in search of equatorial riches. Archbishop Mendoza's letter urged Ferrer to come to Barcelona and to "bring with you the *mappamundi* and other instruments you might have pertaining to cosmography."[148] Ten days later, on 5 September 1493, Queen Isabel wrote a letter to an already anxious Columbus in Seville, explaining that she was sending him a copy of the *libro* he had turned in for the royal chancellery (Columbus's *Diario*), coaxing him to send her the nautical chart (*carta de marear*) that he had promised in his *Diario* to draw for the Crown and urging him to "make great haste in your departure, so that, with the grace of Our Lord, it may be carried out without delay, for you know how much the good of the enterprise rides on this."[149] She added that, although talks with Portugal's ambassadors were coming along, Columbus should not for a minute assume that all was resolved and lower his guard: "I would like for you to think the very opposite, that you may not become careless or meet your duty without vigilance, so that in no way shall you be deceived."[150]

Negotiations with João II's ambassadors had in fact reached an impasse, for Diaz and Pina had been prepared to negotiate with Castile on the basis of the embassy that Lope de Herrera had delivered to Lisbon three months before. And, whereas João II had hoped to reach an agreement dividing the Atlantic vertically (north and south), Fernando and Isabel's deputies had shown up at the negotiation table wielding a papal bull that divided the Atlantic horizontally (east and west).

Between Cathay and a Hot Place

REORIENTING THE ASIA-AMERICA DEBATE

Everyone knows that in 1492 Columbus double-crossed his learned contemporaries by following a western route across the Atlantic to lands initially identified as part of legendary India. Few seem aware that Columbus was also determined to steer south into the belt of the tropics. Columbus made this a crucial and explicit goal of the project he presented to the Crowns of Aragon and Castile during the years leading up to the discovery. In the course of his four transatlantic voyages, he stubbornly aimed south for tropical latitudes. And those who in the following century recorded his deeds not only took notice of his pervasive southing but also hailed the "discovery" of the torrid zone as one of his great achievements. Yet despite the early sources' loud talk of Columbus's southing—or maybe because of it—Americanists seldom trouble themselves with Columbus's descent to the Indies, unless it is to ask whether he really intended to reach Asia.

Indeed, some Americanists, not trusting Columbus to tell the truth about his real destination, have preferred to see him as the guardian of a tightly held secret—a prior discovery that would explain why, on his first voyage, Columbus so easily appeared to relinquish the quest for the Mongols in favor of exploring, and ultimately colonizing, the Caribbean basin. For these revisionists, Columbus's shying away from his proclaimed goal of the seat of the Mongolian emperor betrays his following the cues of a previous encounter with the Americas, not someone ultimately driven, as I shall argue, by shifting and at times contradictory certainties concerning the belt of the tropics. For the revisionists, Columbus's southing can only mean that he already knew where he was going; otherwise, he should have continued his exploration due west in search of Asia. But as I will try to suggest, the choice Columbus faced was not between Asia to the west and America—or Antilia, or whatever name we give the mid-Atlantic lands he reached—to the east. The choice, at least as the Columbus of the *Diario* appears to have seen it, was between Cathay—the seat of Magnokhanic Asia—to the north and India—Marco Polo's maritime India—to the south. It was the choice between two places that were different from each other, not by reason of longitude, but by reason of latitude. And Columbus ultimately yielded to the lure of a tropical India.

Perhaps our knowledge of the Americas as a continental mass stretching from pole to pole west of Europe and Africa has made it hard to realize that, at the end of the fifteenth century, a sailing voyage from Mediterranean Europe "to the parts of India" would have implied a sharp drop in latitude to a place that was now increasingly being visualized as a vast geographical system centered on the belt of the tropics and a place that was gradually coming to be perceived as a veritable factory of riches—not in spite of the fact that it stood in the torrid zone but precisely *because* it did so. And perhaps because, in retrospect, it makes sense that Columbus should have been looking for the abundant natural and human resources that we know were ultimately found and exploited by Europeans in the tropics, it is difficult to fully appreciate how tentative, how fraught with danger, and how plagued by contradictions, this search really was for Europeans in the early phases of the Age of Exploration. Or perhaps it is our own equally strange, highly mediated, and still unresolved "familiarity" with a place that continues to evoke the marvelous and the monstrous that renders us indifferent, or even blind, to Columbus's unrelenting tropicalism. Whatever the case may be, and regardless of the position we take in the debate over Columbus's understanding of the true identity of his Indies, it seems fair to say that the certainties that pointed him to the lower latitudes of the globe remain poorly understood. For less sympathetic readers of Columbus, such certainties have been no more than the tiresome symptoms of a half-baked, idiosyncratic, and ultimately fickle mind. Nothing could be farther from the truth, and we must now consider Columbus's share, modest as it might have been, in a complex intellectual culture that had always associated latitude with the nature of places. Our task is to show that there was method in his southing. These last two chapters focus on Columbus's invention of the American tropics and its peoples in the extant summary copy of his celebrated *Diario*.

Columbus was certainly not the "schooled" individual that his son Ferdinand, and Las Casas after him, originally claimed. Ferdinand's claim that his father had studied at the University of Pavia is now understood as an attempt to redefine Columbus as the formally educated man that he was not. But Columbus's plan *was* crafted on the basis of philosophical and technical knowledge that he shared, no matter how informally, with schooled minds in Christian Europe. Testimony of the arguments wielded by his opponents in the Castilian royal council against the feasibility of an ocean crossing unmistakably points to a schooled debate carried out by both sides with greatest regard for theological and philosophical correctness and with equal concern for weighing out the "evidence" provided by old and new geographical information. Columbus and his opponents radically disagreed about the manner in which earth and water had come to be lodged at the center of the cosmos in the beginning of time and about how life had come to be allocated in the region of the four elements. No matter what sort of information, theoretical or experiential, might have initially inspired Columbus to cross the ocean, his project would come to be formulated in direct opposition to a geographical canon that saw the totality of the inhabited world as a closed and unique continental system whose northern and southern fringes were rendered hostile to life by the intolerable cold and heat of the arctic and the tropics.

Columbus and his supporters advocated an open geographical system that, at least in theory, extended all around the globe. This and no other is the meaning of Ferdinand Columbus's easily misinterpreted claim that his father had believed "that all the water and the earth in the universe constituted and formed a sphere that could be rounded from east to west, men being able to walk all around it until they came to stand feet to feet, the ones opposite the others, wherever they wished to be that stood on the opposite side."[1] This claim in the Fernandine *Historie* may have its origin in the notorious passage in Columbus's *carta-relación* of the third voyage in which the Discoverer justified the intuition of having found "infinite land that is toward the south" by explaining that the two heaviest elements were mixed together "like the bitter core of the walnut with a thick membrane girdling the whole."[2] Or perhaps this claim was lifted by Columbus's biographer from a fancy source like Mandeville's *Travels,* which claimed that anyone wishing to round the globe would always find "men, lands, and isles" all the way back to his point of departure.[3] Whatever the case may be, it is not that Columbus's detractors in the royal council that evaluated his plan had believed the earth to be flat, as numerous post-Enlightenment versions of the discovery have mistakenly claimed, but rather that the particular model of geocentricity advocated by these detractors explained the presence of dry land above water by supposing that at the time of Creation the sphere of water had been displaced toward one side of the sphere of earth to allow for the habitation of terrestrial creatures.[4] In the eyes of those intent upon derailing Columbus, this meant that any and all lands had come to be huddled together in a small quarter of an otherwise aqueous globe.

By chancing upon San Salvador in the high Atlantic, Columbus instantly proved that his learned adversaries in the royal council had been dead wrong regarding the distribution of dry land on the globe, even if Columbus's feat did not automatically persuade everyone that he had reached the periphery of Asia described by Marco Polo in *Il milione*. Earth and water could now be thought of as concentric; dry land was the result of irregularities in the earth's sphere and could, in theory, surface anywhere around the globe. This realization automatically brought the Spanish and Portuguese Crowns to the brink of war upon Columbus's return in 1493 over an oceanic expanse that they now had reason to believe might contain other islands, even a continent, awaiting to be discovered.

Columbus and his supporters in Castile also believed that the inhabited world extended well beyond the northern temperate zone into the allegedly uninhabitable cold and hot regions of the globe—for our purposes, that the belt of the tropics was far more generally productive and hospitable than had been supposed by the theory of the five zones. News of the discovery not only prompted the Spanish and Portuguese Crowns to adopt an open geographical model of the globe but also to suspect that the real and hypothetical territories they were now wrestling for were fabulously wealthy, precisely *because*—as Fernando and Isabel state in their letter to Columbus on the eve of his second voyage—these territories stood or might stand "in the part of the sun." Columbus's *Diario* is a monument to nature's overweening superlativism in the tropics. And it should be no surprise to find that, during the tense period between Columbus's return in 1493 and the signing of the Treaty of Tordesillas in 1494, the diplomatic maneuvers launched by Spain and Portugal largely focused on gaining jurisdiction to a part of the globe they now conceptualized as extending below the latitude of the Canaries—"in the part of India," or "toward the part of India," or "to the west and to the south," or "in the part of the sun."

What follows is an attempt to read the early transatlantic encounter as a "vertical" rendezvous between Mediterranean Europe and the American tropics. Columbus's distinction between Europe's higher latitudes and the lower latitudes he had come to explore fundamentally informed his understanding of the Bahamas and the Caribbean basin as a place and of its peoples as political subordinates in an incipient global order. His invention of the geopolitical extension we may properly call the American tropics obeyed two equally compelling but contradictory impulses: the impulse to construe the Bahamas and Caribbean as a vastly temperate, fertile, and populated place—a paradise of pleasure—and the impulse to accord its native peoples the abject political status that Mediterranean geographers had long accorded their neighbors in the hotter regions of the globe. Las Casas's summary copy of Columbus's *Diario* bears witness to this ambivalent legacy.

Martin Behaim's 1492 globe (**fig. I.3**, pp. 12–13) provides an eloquent visual representation of the geographical principles that guided Columbus across the Atlantic. This globe encodes the open geography of the ancients in several ways. First, it extends the known continental masses to the south well beyond the Tropic of Capricorn and to the east by approximately 225 degrees of longitude. (Both measurements far exceeded the 90 degrees of latitude and 180 degrees of longitude covered by Ptolemy's *Geography*, falling nearer those of Ptolemy's predecessor, Marinos of Tyre: if Portuguese exploration was proving that Marinos had been correct in asserting that the inhabited world extended beyond the Tropic of Capricorn, why not also adopt his longitudinal estimate over Ptolemy's?) Second, Behaim's globe depicts mythic mid-ocean islands such as Saint Brandan's Isle ("Jnsula de sant brandan"), which is drawn on the equator, and Antilia, or Isle of Seven Cities ("Insula antilia-septe ritade"), which is drawn on the Tropic of Cancer. In addition, Behaim's globe refers to the "thousands" of islands that the Venetian merchant Marco Polo had indexed on the Sea of Chin (South China Sea) and the Indian Ocean in his account of India.[5] Behaim was, so to speak, "freshly" informed by Ptolemy's *Geography*, by the works of medieval travelers like Marco Polo and by recent Portuguese discoveries in Atlantic Africa. His globe unequivocally renders Europe as little more than the northwestern neighbor to a huge inhabited world that was now heavily weighted toward the seemingly interminable littorals of the tropics.

Behaim also lays out Marco Polo's India almost exactly within the parameters of the torrid zone—from Çipango and the Chinese port of Zaiton all the way to the islands of Madagascar and Zanzibar. This is not to say that Marco Polo's India accounts for all of India on Behaim's globe. In the cartographic tradition inaugurated by Eratosthenes, the northernmost limit for Africa and India was not the Tropic of Cancer (approx. 24° N) but rather the axial parallel of Rhodes (37° N; in Ptolemy, 36° N). This parallel ran across from the Strait of Gibraltar to "the capes and most remote peaks of the mountain-chain that forms the northern boundary of India" (what Strabo calls the "Taurus Range").[6] Behaim's most immediate source, Ptolemy, observed this limit to the north for the Indian coordinates of his *Geography*—the highest Indian latitudes recorded by Ptolemy being those of the river sources that flowed south into India from the Imaos range, or Himalayas (37° N). Consequently, parts of Behaim's India extend north of the Tropic of Cancer toward the latitudes prescribed by Ptolemy.

Marco Polo's India, however, was a *maritime* India—primarily concerned with water routes and coastal regions. Therefore, it makes sense that those Indian toponyms on Behaim's globe, including Çipango, that were extracted from Marco Polo's *Il milione* should have been visually organized almost entirely around that tropical accident known to Ptolemy's followers in the Latin West as the Indian Ocean.

Columbus's India, like Marco Polo's, was a *maritime* one. This is one of the reasons why—wind patterns aside—Columbus showed no interest in either attempting a western passage out of Cádiz along the parallel of Rhodes, which passed just below Cádiz through the Strait of Gibraltar (on Ptolemy's authority, 36° N), or in returning to explore the higher latitudes from which he had sailed once he found land across the Atlantic. Instead, Columbus chose the lower latitude of the Canaries, which choice was meant to take him across the Atlantic just above the twenty-seventh parallel all the way "to the parts of India." And Columbus's India most definitely was not the same place as Cathay—the geopolitical region of northern China designated by Marco Polo and other European travelers as the seat of the Mongol empire. Indian places that served as fundamental references for Columbus—namely, the island of Çipango and the cities of Zaiton and Quinsay—stand on Behaim's globe at a notably lower latitude than the northern Chinese province of Cathay. While Çipango, Zaiton, and Quinsay are laid out along the Tropic of Cancer, Cathay stands halfway between the Tropic of Cancer and the Arctic circle, squarely in the middle of the northern temperate zone (**fig. I.4**, pp. 14–15).

Behaim plots the port of Zaiton and the "inland" city of Quinsay (on Marco Polo's authority, 25 miles distant from the coast) in the province of Mangi, the southern portion of mainland China extending from a river labeled "Kirumaru" all the way south to the Indian Ocean. The Kirumaru River, which Behaim labels at an approximate latitude of 37° N, corresponds to today's Hwang-ho, or Yellow, River; and the province of Mangi corresponds to the Southern Song empire defeated by the Mongols at the time of Marco Polo's residence in China. Marco Polo's celebrated host, Khubilai Khān, had completed the conquest of the Southern Song beyond the Yangtze River in 1279.[7] On Behaim's globe, Mangi is flanked to the north by Cathay and to the south by the "Upper Indian Ocean" ("Oceanus Indicus superiora"). Insofar as Mangi extends due south of the approximate latitude of the Kirumaru River, and insofar as it faces south on the "Upper Indian Ocean," Mangi should be considered a part of India, which explains why, in the famous prologue to the *Diario*, Columbus should have accorded his Great Khān the double title of lord of Cathay and lord of India. Indeed, the domains of the Great Khān are conceived in the *Diario* as possibly descending south toward the lands Columbus had just discovered.

A word is in order on the Indian territories that Khubilai Khān failed to win for his empire—the island of Çipango and the mainland province of Ciamba (another key place for Columbus). Behaim plots the island of Çipango as part of a huge archipelago that, on Marco Polo's authority, had remained politically independent from the mainland. The information provided by Behaim in the main legend for Çipango thus reads: "This island of Zipangu lies in the east of the world. The inhabitants worship idols. *The king is subject to no one.* In the island is found exceeding much gold and likewise precious stones and pearls. This is stated by Marco Polo of Venice in his [third] book."[8] Indeed, Marco Polo's account of India recorded the ill-fated campaign mounted by Khubilai Khān against Japan in 1274, a campaign that Khubilai was forced to abandon after massive loss of life to typhoons and after thwarted attempts to subdue its expertly trained belligerents.[9] According to Marco Polo, the Sea of Chin (South China Sea) was really an ocean that contained, by count of the few pilots and sailors who had dared venture into it, 7,378 islands. Most of these islands were populated and overflowing with aromatic plants and infinite spices—among them copious quantities of black pepper and of another kind of pepper white as snow, facts that Columbus noted in his Latin copy of *Il milione, De consuetudinibus et condicionibus orientalium regionum*.[10] (Marco Polo's description of the exuberance of this region indubitably bears some weight on Behaim's decision to plot Çipango itself on the Tropic of Cancer, the boundary between the Sea of Chin and the Indian Ocean.) To the potentially autonomous islands of the Sea of Chin we must add the 1,378 islands counted by Marco Polo on the Indian Ocean, which Behaim, probably misreading the Latin edition of Marco Polo's work at his disposal, multiplied to "more than 12,700."[11] Finally, we have the mainland province of Ciamba, which according to Marco Polo could be reached by sailing 1,500 miles due southwest of the Mangian port of Zaiton.[12] Ciamba corresponds to the kingdom of Champa (the southern coast of

Vietnam), which Khubilai tried to wrest from King Jaya Indravarman VI in 1279, in the same year that the conquest of the Southern Song was completed.[13] According to Marco Polo, Khubilai's armies had found that the fortresses and cities of Ciamba were so well designed and defended that the Mongol army was forced to withdraw, at which point the king of Ciamba offered to pay an annual tribute in exchange for retaining political autonomy.

The distinction in the *Diario* between a mainland subject to the Great Khān and territory outside of his empire—be it a mainland paying tribute or at war with him, or a vast ocean dotted by thousands of islands that might have been spared the fury of the Mongols—was to play a crucial role in Columbus's survey of the Bahamas and the outer shores of the Caribbean basin. As readers of Columbus, we have often surrendered to the temptation of reading Behaim's globe and other cartographic works of the period horizontally, that is, as a possible clue to Columbus's underestimate of the longitudinal distance between the ends of East and West. But it is in the *verticality* of Behaim's globe that we truly have a model for understanding more fully the orientation, goals, and indeed the major dilemmas of Columbus's enterprise.

The distinction between a temperate Cathay and a tropical Indies is not unique to Behaim's globe. It features clearly in other cartographic works of the period informed by Ptolemy and Marco Polo—including the pseudo-cordiform world map drafted by Henricus Martellus about 1489, in the wake of Bartholomeu Dias's rounding of the Cape of Good Hope, and Martin Waldseemüller's singularly famous *mappamundi* of 1507— the map that equivocally baptized the southern landmass discovered by Columbus in 1498 as Vespucci's *America* (**figs. 6.1** and **6.2** for Martellus; **figs. I.12**, pp. 54–55, and **6.3** for Waldseemüller).

A similar distinction had been made by works that preceded the introduction of Ptolemy's *Geography* to the Latin West. In Abraham Cresques's Catalan Atlas (1375), to cite the most elaborate portolan known today, Catayo stands on an east-west rhumb line that cuts across through the Pyrenees, whereas the coastal city of Zaiton and the city of Quinsay ("ciutat de Cansay") face south on the Indian Ocean, scraping just above an east-west rhumb line that cuts across to the south of the Atlas Mountain Range in northern Africa (**fig. 3.1**, third through sixth panels, pp. 170–173). Drawing from a portolan in the same school as Abraham Cresques's, the heraldic itinerary we know as *Libro del cognosçimiento de todos los rregnos e tierras et señorios que son por el mundo* manifestly states how someone "situated" in Castile during the late fourteenth century might have placed Cathay and India on the world map. The author emphatically teaches his readers "that Catayo is the end of the face of the Earth in the line of Spain."[14] And, echoing a geopolitical model now familiar to us, the author also establishes that the inhabitants of Tribit (Tibet), a kingdom immediately placed between Catayo and India, were "of good understanding and healthy memory," "learned," "lawful," and "pious" because they stood on the easternmost part of the inhabited world, and this kingdom was rooted "in the middle clime, where natures are temperate."[15] By contrast, the *Libro del cognosçimiento* offers the Indians, gathered around an Indian Ocean that the author literally considers to be an "accident" that tempered the otherwise intolerable heat of the tropics: "After [the people of Tribit] are those from India, who are below the equinoctial line. And their land is very hot, although the majority of their towns are on the shores of the sea and there are many islands, and for this reason the air receives moisture from the sea with which the dryness and the heat are tempered down."[16] The author of the *Libro del cognosçimiento* was here projecting the geopolitical model that assigned Mediterranean Europeans a place and a nature different from those of their neighbors in Africa's hotter regions onto the inhabitants of the Asian interior and those of the Indian Ocean. A similar geopolitical distinction between Cathay and the "parts of India" would come to inform Columbus's survey of the Bahamas and Caribbean a century later.

Columbus himself believed that Cathay was neither the same place, nor possessed the same nature, as his Indies. His capital source, Pierre d'Ailly, explains in *Ymago mundi* that modern cartographers located Cathay in the region of Scythia, having the ocean to the east, the islands of the ocean to the south (meaning, India), and the desert of Belema to the north.[17] A postil corresponding to this passage in *Ymago mundi* reads: "Those who point where Scythia is, the kingdom of Cathay, which has the ocean to the east."[18] D'Ailly's identification of Cathay as part of Scythia is significant. The toponym *Scythia* had been assigned by Greeks and Romans to the nomadic tribes on the eastern half of northern Europe and in the western and central parts of northern Asia, tribes conspicuously described by the ancients as avid consumers of mare's milk, and in some instances, like Herodotus's *History*, as ritual blood-suckers and flesh eaters.[19] Herodotus located Scythia across the Danube River and the Carpathians in the direction of today's Central Russian Uplands.[20] Later, in 329 BCE, Alexander the Great campaigned all the way to the central Asian regions of Bactria and Sogdiana, nations that extended between the Oxus (Amurdaya River) and the Jaxartes (Syrdaya River)—the region now shared

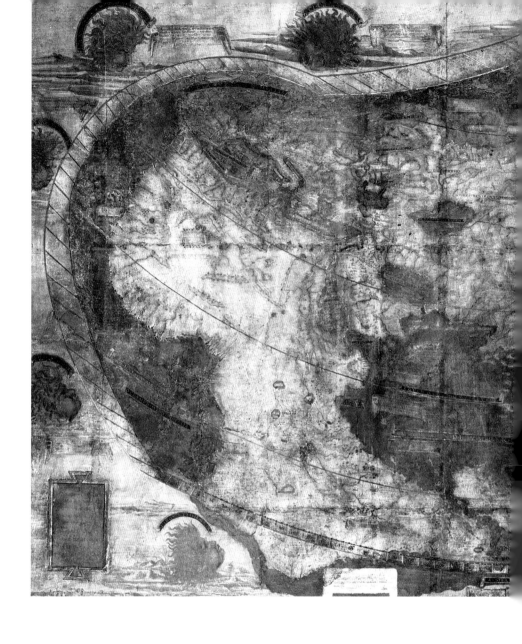

6.1 Henricus Martellus's *mappamundi*, about 1489. Courtesy of The Beinecke Rare Book and Manuscript Library, Yale University, New Haven, Connecticut.

6.2 Detail of Martellus's *mappamundi*, about 1489. Courtesy of The Beinecke Rare Book and Manuscript Library, Yale University, New Haven, Connecticut.

by Uzbekistan and Kazakhstan to the southeast of the Aral Sea. Following Alexander's foundation of Alexandria Eschate on a tributary of the Jaxartes (Khozendt, in today's Tajikistan), Greek cartographers also used the name *Scythia* for the region today extending north of the Syrdaya River, in the direction of the West Siberian Plain.[21] Strabo thus informs us in his *Geography* that the Jaxartes is the boundary between Sogdiana and the "nomads," that is, the Scythians.[22] Strabo also adopted the quadripartite division of the inhabited world drawn by his predecessor Eratosthenes, who had divided the northeastern quarter (Scythia) from southeastern quarter (India) along the parallel of Rhodes (on Eratosthenes' authority, about 37° N).

The earliest known Latin geographer, Pomponius Mela, also provided a crucial distinction between Scythia and India in a passage of his *Chorographia*: according to Mela, the farthest peoples in Asia were the Indians, the Seres—or Silk People (i.e., the inhabitants of northern China known to Europeans by way of the "Silk route" through Central Asia)—and the Scythians. "The Seres," Mela explains, "inhabit more or less the middle of the eastern part. The Indians and the Scyths inhabit the extremities [i.e., to the south and to the north], both peoples covering a broad expanse and spreading to the ocean not at this point only [that is, toward the east]. For the Indians also look south and for a long time have been occupying the shore of the Indian Ocean with continuous nations, except insofar as the heat makes it uninhabitable. The Scyths look north too, and they possess the littoral of the Scythian Ocean all the way to the Caspian Gulf."[23] Pliny, describing northern Asia, notes that the "Scythians stand all the way from the extreme Aquilon [i.e., north] to the beginning of the summer sunrise [i.e., northeast]."[24] And, finally, Ptolemy himself, establishing a certain symmetry between Scythia and India, divides central Asia between Scythia *intra* Imaum and Scythia *extra* Imaum— Imaos corresponding to a "vertical" offshoot from the Himalayas that was thought to split northern Asia in half.[25] According to Ptolemy, Scythia extra Imaum was bounded on the east by the land of the Seres, and on the south by India extra Gangem (**figs. 1.1**, pp. 62–63; **1.6**, pp. 80–81; and **2.2**, pp. 120–121).

Greco-Roman sources thus remained unequivocal concerning Scythia's boreality. And it is no coincidence that the arrival of the Mongol hordes to the margins of the Danube River well over a millennium later (1241) should have prompted Europeans to identify the "devilish" horsemen as descendants of Scythians and other nomadic tribes of central Asia. Travelers to the domains of the Great Khān soon observed, by the way, that the Tatar tribes of central Asia were inveterate wanderers fond of drinking a fermented milk—often to the point of mortal intoxication—and that they thought nothing at all about eating human flesh in times of need.[26] The connection between Mongols and Scythians appears to have been so common as to merit controversy in the pages of that other major work that Columbus may have annotated in preparation to cross the Atlantic, Aeneas Sylvius Piccolomini's *Historia rerum ubique gestarum.* A series of related postils in the copy now held at the Biblioteca Colombina not only identifies the lord of Cathay as a descendant of central Asia's ancient nomads but also indicates the place Columbus assigned to Cathay and the nature he believed would have given rise to an intellectually complex and materially powerful Mongol nation.

In a heavily annotated section of *Historia rerum,* Piccolomini labors to reconcile Strabo's and Pliny's ancient accounts of the Scythians with the testimony of Cathay freshly rendered in Rome by a certain Nicholas of Venice, whom we know as the Venetian merchant Niccolò de' Conti.[27] Although Conti remains a relatively minor figure in the testimonial literature on Magnokhanic Asia, he does play a significant supporting role in the history of the discovery. Conti has been identified as the unnamed interlocutor (*unus*) from whom the Florentine humanist Paolo dal Pozzo Toscanelli, Columbus's controverted correspondent, gathered information about Ming China for the letter he would send in 1474 to the mysterious "canon of Lisbon" Fernão Martins with the aim of coaxing King Afonso V of Portugal to cross the Atlantic to Asia.[28] Between 1414 and 1439, Conti had followed the routes of the Indian Ocean as far as the Bay of Bengal's easternmost shores and the islands of Sumatra and Java, although it seems quite certain that he never traveled north to China. He probably harvested his testimony of China as he passed through Siam, and he evidently failed to realize that the Mongol khāns no longer controlled Cathay or the rest of China. On his return to Europe through Sinai and Egypt (Mamlūk territory), Conti was forced to abjure Christianity in favor of Islam, so he then presented himself to Pope Eugenius IV in order to plead for reinception to the Catholic faith. The penitence imposed upon him for becoming a renegade was to provide a detailed account of his travels. And this account was consigned to writing by Eugenius's secretary, the Tuscan humanist Francesco Poggio Bracciolini, in a work known as *De varietate fortunae* (1447).[29] Columbus may well have known of Conti's travels from this work, for he carefully supplements Piccolomini's account of Conti's crowded Cambaleschia (Peking) and Nemptai (Nanjing), with information apparently indebted to a section in the fourth book of *De varietate fortunae* not mentioned by Piccolomini.[30] Needless to say, Columbus was not the only European

Chapter 6

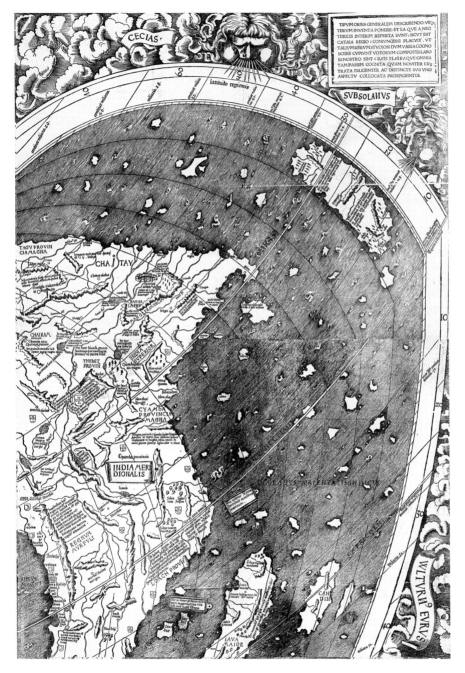

6.3 Detail of Martin Waldseemüller's *mappamundi*, 1507. Courtesy of the Map Collection at the Library of Congress, Washington, D.C. Cathay on this map is just north of the fortieth parallel, whereas India Superior is just north of the Tropic of Cancer, on the same general latitude as Zipangri (Japan).

who continued to believe in the fifteenth century that the Mongols still controlled the regions Cathay and Mangi. So too did figures like Conti, Bracciolini, Piccolomini, and Toscanelli fail to realize that the Mongols had been evicted from China a century earlier (circa 1368) or that the figure they called Great Khān was now really a member of the Ming dynasty.[31]

Piccolomini reasons out the link between the ancient Scythians and Cathay in the following manner: sources like Strabo and Pliny located the nomadic Scythians in the northerly latitudes beyond the Jaxartes River. Also, the author continues, modern cartographers placed Cathay "beyond the Jaxartes," surrounded by many subject kingdoms and colonies under the rule of an emperor called Khān.[32] Some cartographers in Piccolomini's time placed Cathay in the colder northern latitudes of the world, a choice that Piccolomini contests because he believes that nature could only have given way to a complex polity such as Cathay within the bounds of the temperate zone.[33] Columbus (or his brother Bartholomew), realizing that Piccolomini's preliminaries are about to disclose important information about his precious Cathay, wrote three celebratory postils in the margins of Piccolomini's text.[34] The first merely reads, "[about] Cathay." The second, bearing the drawing of one of Columbus's famous "hands" pointing at Piccolomini's text, reads, "Many things about Cathay. He places Cathay beyond the Jaxartes. Many provinces. Many kingdoms." The third adds: "Great Khān, emperor of Cathay, lord over a great number of provinces."

At this point, Piccolomini paraphrases Conti's description of two formidable cities: the old Cathayan capital of Cambaleschia, with its huge armored citadel, satellite forts, and all types of weapons and war machinery; and the equally spectacular city of Nemptai, which, according to Conti, had been recently founded by the emperor, stood nearly fifteen days away from Cambaleschia and was the most densely populated of all cities.[35] (Conti's Cambaleschia was clearly Peking, modern 39° 55′ N, and Nemptai may correspond to the city of Nanjing [modern 24° 25′ N], which the first Ming emperor Zhu Yuanzang had chosen in 1379 as capital for his new empire on the southern banks of the Yangtze River—that is, on the old border that Khubilai had crossed to the south in 1279 in the final phase of his conquest of Mangi.)[36] More importantly, Conti had claimed that all buildings in Cambaleschia and Nemptai were similar to those found in Italy and that there men were likewise moderate, civil, and wealthy.[37] Here Columbus supplements Piccolomini's account of Conti's Cambaleschia and Nemptai thus: "The city of Nemptai, from which certain envoys of its emperors came to Rome *in the times of this author* [*tempus auctoris istius*]."[38] Columbus appears to be have been referring to Conti, or rather to Bracciolini, who in another section of the fourth book of *De varietate fortunae* tells us that at the time he was preparing to insert Conti's account of India in his work a certain envoy had traveled north to Rome from Upper India. This envoy had been sent to Rome by a Nestorian patriarch who wanted him to gather information about those Christians who lived in the land of the western sun, "in another orb."[39] The kingdom of this Christian ruler allegedly stood a twenty-days' journey from Cathay itself. Piccolomini's mention of Nemptai thus prompted Columbus to recall an embassy from a "city" that, on Conti's authority, would have been part of Cathay and fifteen days away from Cambaleschia; or a city that, if Columbus was thinking of the Nestorian envoy who had turned up in Rome, would have been part of a neighboring kingdom in Upper India, and twenty days away from Cambaleschia.

It does not matter for our purpose whether Columbus imagined Nemptai as part of Cathay or as a city in the northernmost reaches of India bordering Cathay. What mattered to the postil writer and to his immediate source, Piccolomini, was not so much that Conti had placed both cities in Cathay, but that he had characterized them in identical terms. Columbus twice reiterates Conti's terminology in the margins of *Historia rerum*. His postil on Nemptai concludes by paraphrasing Piccolomini's account of Conti's testimony: "These cities [Cambaleschia and Nemptai] are densely populated and in all of each city the houses, palaces, temples, and other urban embellishments [are] similar to those of Italy. Moderate men and owners of many riches."[40] Another postil, in the opposite margin of Piccolomini's text, reads: "In these cities, the houses, palaces, temples and everything [are] in the manner of Italy."[41] Not surprisingly, Conti's description of these mighty cities leads Piccolomini and his celebrated annotator to infer the location of Cathay and its relation to the ancient Scythia. The ensuing discussion in *Historia rerum* of course concerns the relation between latitude and the nature of places.

Having established Conti's description of Cambaleschia and Nemptai, Piccolomini remarks that if one were to believe Conti, the inhabitants of Cathay must have radically altered their customs because the Scythians described by ancient authors were supposed to be exceedingly rough pastoral peoples.[42] Such a drastic transformation between the ancient Scythians and the modern Cathayans—from the ferile to the civil—could only mean one thing: the ancient Scythia and the modern Cathay were not the same place, for the horrifying fringes of the cold north could not possibly have harbored those customs that had given glory to ancient Greece and that now caused Italy itself to thrive.[43] Given this constraint on the geographical distribution of complex intellectual and material culture, Cathay could not stand as far north as the *mappaemundi* of the period seem to have indicated.[44] Cathay could only be, like ancient Greece and modern Italy, the fruit of a temperate place. Columbus did not fail to note the political equation drawn by Piccolomini between places like Greece and Italy and a place like Cathay. He pointed to the customs "on account of which, either Greece formerly shined, or now Italy flourishes, or certainly Cathay itself, which they praise so highly."[45] And in the following postil, Columbus adds: "Cathay [is] not to the north that the picture shows."[46] In other words, Cathay stood in the temperate zone. According to Piccolomini, any inhabited land beyond the Jaxartes River would have extended beyond the seventh clime (Borysthenes, 50° N), for it was along this parallel that modern *mappaemundi* located the Jaxartes.[47] Therefore, the only way to explain the abysmal political metamorphosis of the ancient Scythians into the Mongols now seated in Cathay was by way of geographical displacement: the Scythians had descended from the colder latitudes beyond the Jaxartes to the more temperate latitudes of Asia, where they had either adopted or developed a complex intellectual and material culture such as those cultures found in ancient Greece and modern Italy. While the Great Khān of the Mongols was now seated in a temperate Cathay, his empire extended north and south of the Jaxartes—south all the way to the mountainous boundaries that separated northern Asia from southern Asia, that is, from India. Just as the ancestors of the Great Khān had invaded most of Asia, so too now, to cite Columbus, "the empire of the Great Khān extends beyond and before the Jaxartes, including the Gordians, the Bactrians and other nations all the way to the mountains of India as well as Ariana."[48] Columbus's last postil to Piccolomini's discussion of the Scythians and the Mongols unequivocally identifies the Great Khān as a Scythian ruler: "The Scythians or the Great Khān formerly ruled over most of Asia."[49]

The tripartite distinction between a temperate, and therefore civilized, Cathay, and its intemperate, and therefore savage, neighbors in the cold north (Scythia) and in the hot south (India) would play a crucial role in Columbus's exploration of the Bahamas and Caribbean basin. Just as Mediterranean Europe had descended south into sub-Saharan Africa, so had the mighty Mongols descended south into India in the times of Marco Polo. Just as Mediterranean Europe had given rise to mighty nations naturally predisposed to rule over their barbarous neighbors in northern Europe and sub-Saharan Africa, so had Cathay bred a nation naturally predisposed to rule over both their neighbors in northern Asia and the "parts of India." This tripartite geopolitics allowed Columbus to persuade himself in the opening entries of his *Diario* that just as Guinea was for Portugal, so the India he had just discovered served as poaching ground for the armies of the great lord of Cathay. And it was also this geopolitical model that undoubtedly made it possible for Columbus to explain away the abysmal gap between the formidable cities and fleets Marco Polo had ascribed to Cathay and Mangi and the comparatively modest human settlements he found in the Bahamas and Caribbean basin.

Two other brief examples from the folios of Piccolomini's *Historia rerum* suffice to show that Columbus drew a significant latitudinal distinction between Cathay and his India. One of Columbus's most celebrated postils to *Historia rerum* concerns Piccolomini's mention of Pliny's account in *Naturalis historia* of a commercial Indian vessel that, following Julius Caesar's conquest of Gaul, was allegedly swept by a storm across the ocean all the way north to the shores of Germania.[50] According to Piccolomini, this incident proved that the "Northern Sea" was neither frozen solid nor unfordable. Columbus duly noted the arrival of this ancient vessel "from India to Germany." Then, in a separate postil in the opposite margin of Piccolomini's text, Columbus clearly felt compelled to corroborate Piccolomini's belief in the navigability of the North Atlantic by recalling something he had witnessed during an outing to Hibernia (Ireland) and Ultima Thule (Iceland) in the early years between 1476 and 1477: "Men from Cathay came toward the East. We saw many notable things, and especially in Galway, Ireland, a man and his wife adrift on two logs, admirable in their aspect."[51] We shall never know who these drifters were or whence they came—whether indeed they had been carried east across the North Atlantic to Ireland, or whether, more likely, they had been swept down from the Arctic latitudes of the Inuit peoples. Whatever the case may be, the issue of whether or not the North Atlantic was traversable prompted Columbus to tie the arrival in Galway of the two odd-looking castaways with the region of Cathay, no doubt associating their physical uncanniness with the Tatar features that had so intrigued European travelers to Mongolia since the thirteenth century—wider faces, small eyes that slanted out toward the eyebrows, flat noses, and prominent cheekbones.[52]

A few folios later, where Piccolomini follows Ptolemy in locating the Seres as Scythia's neighbors to the east, Columbus wrote another postil that specifically locates the China known by way of the Silk Road trade on the north with respect to India on the south. The region of the Seres, Columbus writes, "is toward the beginning of India, that is, across from Spain (Hispania) and Ireland toward the north."[53] Columbus was here deploying the locator "the beginning of India" as a latitudinal marker consistent with Eratosthenes' original division of Scythia and India along the parallel that also divided Europe from Africa—that is, the parallel of Rhodes (by Eratosthenes, 37° N; by Ptolemy, 36° N). If one were to cross the Atlantic from the Strait of Gibraltar along the parallel of Rhodes and then steer north, one would be entering Serica—"across from Spain and Ireland toward the north." (Modern Cathay was the ancient Serica.) But if one were to cross the Atlantic along the parallel of Rhodes and then veer south, one would have been entering India.

Columbus ultimately launched his Atlantic crossing from the Canaries, along the latitude of El Hierro Island. Once he had reached land across the Atlantic, instead of sailing back north toward Cathay, he proceeded to sail generally south in the direction of the maritime India described by Marco Polo. It is in the latitudinal opposition between Marco Polo's Cathay and Marco Polo's India—not in the longitudinal opposition between Marco Polo's Asia and "new" lands in the high Atlantic—that we should properly situate what must have arisen as a vexing dilemma for Columbus once he crossed the ocean: should he try to establish diplomatic contact with the Mongols in Mangi or Cathay? Or should he sail south in search of India's tropical bounty?

The fundamental geographical relation in the *Diario* between Marco Polo's Cathay and the place Columbus explored in the high Atlantic is not, as Americanists who have questioned whether Columbus really intended to reach Asia have tended to suggest, the east-west relation between Asia and alien lands that had already been discovered by the anonymous pilot or that were known to Columbus in some other way before crossing the Atlantic in 1492. Instead, it is the north-south relation—or if we count the topographical slant of Cuba's and Hispaniola's outer shores toward the southeast, the northwest-southeast relation—between the seat of the Mongol empire in the northern portion of continental China and the tropical landscape Marco Polo had separately treated as India. Indeed, it is the relation between a temperate Asia and a tropical Asia.

This is not to say that Americanists who have claimed that Columbus really wished to reach new lands in the high Atlantic were wrong to suspect that he was less than keen on renewing diplomacy with the Mongol empire. In works like *Toscanelli and Columbus* (1902), *Études critiques sur la vie de Colomb avant ses découvertes* (1905), and *Histoire critique de la grande entreprise de Christophe Colomb* (1911), Henry Vignaud formulated a paradox of enormous consequence for Americanism: if the intention expressed in the

of El Hierro between a Portuguese vessel returning from the *volta da Mina* and a canoe carrying armed Caribe women who had strayed over 1,800 miles from one of the islands in the Lesser Antilles inspired Columbus to launch his enterprise.[65] In his reading of the *Diario*, Pérez de Tudela y Bueso has addressed Vignaud's paradox in the following terms:

> Let us state from this very moment, and categorically so, that the Admiral's exploration of the Antilles, adequately considered, shows that it is not fundamentally subject to Toscanelli's directions, or to Cathay's pressing call. The determination to sail West [Pérez de Tudela y Bueso places the contradiction played out in the *Diario* along an east-west axis] turned out to be, from the very start, terribly weak in the Discoverer; and, ultimately, it showed itself to be a determination to do the very opposite. . . . Without much hesitation, and showing few signs of internal turmoil, once he was convinced that the search for the Great Khān, toward the West, promised more difficulties than a lucrative outcome, the Discoverer engaged the obsession—seemingly demential in the Classical Columbus—of backing away to the East, against all possible odds.[66]

In other words, Columbus would have pretended to look for the Great Khān only so that he could retrace his steps back due east in search of the land he knew existed in the high Atlantic. The *Diario* would have to be considered *en su doble faz*—a Janus-faced document relentlessly pointing to the fancied encounter between Old World sailors and stray female protonauts from the Antilles.[67]

Vignaud's legacy persists as a laceration on the pages of Americanism that never quite heals. Not just in classical works such as Manzano Manzano's and Pérez de Tudela y Bueso's, but also in more freshly minted studies—from specialized studies of Columbus's navigation to impeccable histories on Spain's role in the Age of Exploration and the works of literary scholars concerned with the structure and meaning of the documents authored by Columbus. Maritime historian Luis Miguel Coín Cuenca, for instance, has argued in *Una travesía de 20 días a dos rumbos que cambió el mundo* (2003) that Columbus carefully concealed in his *Diario* the fact that he was crossing the Atlantic along the latitude of the Cape Verde Islands (19° N), in search of high Atlantic territories that he may have intuited or even known existed. For his part, the great historian Hugh Thomas, in his monumental *Rivers of Gold: The Rise of the Spanish Empire, from Columbus to Magellan* (2003), briefly recounts the story of the unknown pilot and cites Manzano

Manzano's thesis if only to tell us that the story of the protonaut "is unnecessary to explain Columbus's frame of mind."[68] Thomas also invokes momentarily the great incognitum posed by the multiple mission goals stated in the official documents drafted between the Crown and Columbus prior to his voyage:

> What territories did Columbus expect that he might conquer for Spain? He anticipated finding various islands, but these included Cipangu [Japan] and a mainland [*tierra firme*], that is, China [Cathay]. Yet there was no mention in the *Capitulaciones* of the Indies, nor of Cathay, though Columbus would take with him letters to the Great Khān and an interpreter who knew some Eastern languages. Perhaps he expected to find a backward territory off China or Japan that he could seize without difficulty? It is unclear. Nor is it obvious what the Crown thought.[69]

This is not to say that Thomas would embrace the thesis of a pre-discovery, nor that he would challenge the traditional thesis about Columbus's destination. The question Thomas raises, however, suggests that even straitlaced Americanism has found itself obliged to tip its hat at a mystery that our early sources on the discovery—from Peter Martyr to Antonio de Herrera y Tordesillas—hardly mentioned.

Peter Hulme, in a study published on the eve of the quincentenary, *Colonial Encounters: Europe and the Native Caribbean, 1492–1797* (1986), aptly observed that the question of Columbus's destination is fatefully bound to the highly controversial question of Columbus's motivation.[70] To put it in our own terms, the problem of Columbus's geography has been, is, and will remain inextricable from the problem of his politics: as long as the issue of Columbus's politics remains a highly contentious issue, so will Americanists find it necessary to address, or at least to avoid judiciously, the issue of his geography. Literary scholars themselves have felt compelled to address the geographical paradox originally formulated by Vignaud as they tackle the textual problematics and rhetorical imperatives of documents like the *Diario*. Hulme himself, to cite a prominent example, understands the Indies enterprise as an uncertain commercial venture, the goal and destination of which was deliberately left open-ended in the *Capitulaciones de Santa Fe*. As Hulme reasonably claims, the reference to "islands and mainlands" in this legal document left open the possibility of exercising diplomacy or of colonizing, both of which, according to the author, coexisted uncomfortably during the initial stages of the first voyage but were ultimately resolved in favor of colonizing.[71]

In his reading of the *Diario,* Hulme reframes the tension between the diplomatic and the colonial dimensions of the enterprise of the Indies as an interplay between what he calls "Orientalist discourse," informed by Marco Polo's account of the Mongol empire, and the "discourse of savage gold," informed by Herodotus's description of barbarians in his *History.*[72] One discourse, Hulme explains, is identifiable in Columbus's references to processed gold, Cathay, the Great Khān, soldiers, merchant ships, and buildings; the other, in his references to source gold, savagery, monstrosity, and anthropophagy. The early entries in the *Diario* thus reenact an interplay in which these two discourses are "jockeying for position" and in which one—Orientalist discourse—is eventually defeated.[73] The fleet's change of course in Cuba due southeast, in which direction Columbus thought he would find gold and cannibals, marks, according to Hulme, the defeat of Orientalist discourse (of processed gold) by the discourse of savage gold.[74] According to Hulme, Columbus was not at all interested in meeting the Great Khān.[75] Although the author sees the diplomatic and colonizing dimensions of the enterprise of the Indies as discursively available to Columbus, he adds that "the discourse of savage gold—the discourse that articulates Castilian expansionism—is in the last analysis the controlling motor of the *Journal* despite the fact that the enterprise had been initiated and framed within the discursive parameters of Genoese commerce."[76]

Margarita Zamora, in her *Reading Columbus* (1993), which includes a compelling consideration of the corporate authorship of the *Diario,* reframes the opposition originally expressed by Vignaud between the goal of reestablishing diplomatic contact with the Mongols and that of acquiring new territories, as an opposition between the evangelical dimension of Columbus's enterprise and his own mercantilism. Failing to find any reference to the evangelical dimension of the enterprise in any of the official documents drafted between Columbus and the Crown before the first voyage, Zamora resuscitates Vignaud's theory, even if somewhat tentatively, in the form it has taken in Manzano Manzano's study:[77]

> The prediscovery documents generated by the Crown are also curiously enigmatic about Columbus's destination. Not once is it explicitly stated as Asia, which most historians believe to have been the goal of the voyage. [In a note, the author cites Manzano Manzano's work.] The characteristic phrasing in the texts—"certain islands and mainlands in the Ocean Sea"—is tantalizingly vague. Although Rumeu de Armas [1985] makes a strong case that such ambiguity was intended to

confound Portuguese spies, it is equally conceivable that the blanket terminology was intended to serve whatever eventuality might result, reflecting the degree of uncertainty at court regarding what Columbus was likely to find. In any case, Ferdinand Columbus concedes that his father expected to run into some large island in the western Ocean Sea before reaching Asia. The source of the popular conviction that the goal of the first voyage was none other than to reach the Asian mainland by sailing west is Columbus himself.[78]

Zamora is referring to the prologue of the *Diario,* which was, she argues, like Vignaud before her, nothing other than a "letter" that, supposed by Las Casas to be the *Diario*'s prologue, shamelessly rewrote the terms of a blatantly imperialistic venture.[79] While Zamora does not go as far as Rómulo D. Carbia in accusing Las Casas of misrepresentation and fraud, she does believe that the evangelical slant of the *Diario* is largely the result of Las Casas's "editorial manipulations."[80] And her case draws moral force, at least in the narrow sense in which we are considering in her study, from the groundwork provided by proponents of the thesis that Columbus did not originally mean to reach Asia.

Stephen Greenblatt, in his *Marvelous Possessions* (1991), raises a question regarding Columbus's landfall in San Salvador, once again drawing from the paradox originally formulated by Vignaud. This question arises from Greenblatt's observation that the documents drafted between Columbus and the Crown prior to the first voyage speak to irreconcilable goals: "Why did Columbus, who was carrying a passport and royal letters, think to take possession of anything, if he actually believed that he had reached the Indies?"[81] Like other readers of the *Diario,* Greenblatt is puzzled by the fact that Columbus's armada should have taken possession of Guanahaní in spite of its being inhabited.[82] Greenblatt is asking how it might be possible for Columbus to take possession of and simultaneously intend to exercise diplomacy in a territory he believes to belong to the Great Khān. But rather than address the pressing issue of Columbus's geography, Greenblatt asserts that the act of formal possession was a legalistic act not intended to be witnessed or duly noted by the Indians of San Salvador but rather by the readership of, among other documents, the widely publicized letter to Santángel (1493). Perhaps because Greenblatt is primarily concerned with what might be termed the "autism" of Columbus and his crew in the act of taking formal possession of San

Salvador, the author feels uncompelled to address the problematics of place raised by his invocation of Vignaud's paradox.

The fact remains, as Hulme puts it, that "the Columbus of the *Journal* and the *Letter* [to Santángel] 'believed' he had reached Asia"—an observation that we ought to extend to all of Columbus's known works.[83] This is not to say that Columbus himself never doubted whether he had reached Asia or that Columbus remained unperturbed by the abysmal gaps between his Indies and Marco Polo's Asia. The writings of the Discoverer do reveal a profound anxiety concerning the identity of the lands he had found, particularly as his detractors in Spain questioned more and more whether he had indeed sailed far enough to the west to have reached the Asia they knew through travelers like Marco Polo, Mandeville, and Conti. It is only to say that, at least in his writings, Columbus remained quixotically fixated on the notion that he had reached the East "by way of the West." The Columbus we know, through his own writings or through the eyes of contemporaries and near contemporaries who recorded the discovery, never once acknowledged that the lands he had discovered in mid-Atlantic were anything other than part of the Indies: the newly discovered lands—including the southern continent Columbus knew he had discovered on his third voyage—were connected to, contiguous with, or at a swiftly communicable distance from the mainland where Marco Polo had placed the territories subject to the Mongols. And the concept that would govern the distinction in Columbus's writing between the seat of the Mongols in Cathay and Marco Polo's India was terrestrial latitude. On the *Diario*'s authority, Columbus took formal possession of land always on the lookout for signs of Mongol occupation and of the complex intellectual and material culture Europeans associated with Marco Polo's Asia. And if Columbus does not seem especially anxious to present himself before the Great Khān, at least the Columbus who still believed that he had reached Asia, it is perhaps because establishing contact with this great lord of the temperate north might have led Columbus dangerously astray from the pressing goal of laying claim to the natural and human resources he expected to find in the tropics. Indeed, the *Diario* shows Columbus scouting out the boundaries of the legendary ruler's empire not to establish immediate contact with his court but to stay clear of what he believed might be the Great Khān's domains: once Columbus had situated the Mongol lord of Cathay at a safe distance due northwest of Cuba's outer shores, Columbus began to back away toward the southeastern corner of the Caribbean basin, further into what he believed to be India.

Indeed, Columbus's tropicalism ultimately exerted a far greater gravitational pull on the Discoverer than the goal of reestablishing diplomacy with the Mongols. The certainty that by sailing to the north, or to the northwest, he would reach Cathay ultimately proved less compelling for the Columbus of the *Diario* than the certainty that by sailing to the south he would find ever greater tracts of land, vast quantities of gold, precious stones, spices, and also innumerable peoples that might serve as empire's subjects or slaves. And as Columbus sailed away from the higher latitudes of Cathay toward the lower latitudes of the Indies, the certainty of having found childlike peoples who displayed the "intelligence" and "cowardice" Mediterranean Europe traditionally ascribed to its neighbors in the hot south—the Taínos—gave way to the certainty of soon finding monsters who displayed the "cunning" and "cruelty" long ascribed to those who inhabited the extreme places of the globe—Columbus's Caribes.

The official documents issued to Columbus in preparation for his first voyage speak to the open geographical model that he and his supporters had recovered from pagan antiquity—to the notion that dry land could be found all around the globe, whether because the known continental masses extended beyond the latitudinal and longitudinal limits assigned by theoretical cartographers to the known inhabited world or because there were other islands and continents unaccounted for until then (the inhabited worlds once theorized by Crates of Mallos). These official documents gave Columbus as much leeway as possible—in terms of the course he might follow (save for sailing below the Canaries and toward Guinea), his possible destinations, and, by corollary, the conduct he should adopt along the way.[84] Advocates of the pre-discovery thesis have approached these documents as if they had been drafted to conceal information regarding Columbus's true destination and goal, an interpretative stance committed to the premise that the markedly different goals suggested by these documents indicate geographically and politically irreconcilable destinations: Asia or entirely alien territories in the high Atlantic.

A leaner reading of these official documents suggests that they were drafted to grant Columbus, as Fernando and Isabel's deputy, the broadest possible range of action over the most broadly defined allowable geographical extension. And this reading should not require us to dispense with the golden rule of all exploration protocols: once you have defined a set of possible destinations and goals, *what* you do along the way is always contingent upon *where* you happen to find yourself; that is, your goal at one point or another is locally determined and time specific. In other words, the set of destinations and goals suggested by the documents drafted between the Crown and Columbus, no matter how contradictory they appear, *could be* and indeed *were* invoked or pursued by Columbus in different places and at different times during his first voyage. Let us briefly reconsider what these documents tell us about Columbus's enterprise.

The famous concession known as *Capitulaciones de Santa Fe,* issued by the Catholic Monarchs on 17 April 1492 at the royal encampment outside the newly conquered Granada, opens by announcing Fernando and Isabel's intention of rewarding *don christoual de colon* "in partial return for what he *has discovered* on the ocean seas."[85] The use of the present perfect in this statement of purpose has been the trump card played by Henry Vignaud and those who after him argued the case for a previous discovery of unknown lands in the high Atlantic.[86] Notable editors of the *Capitulaciones* were not exempt from mistaking the use of this verb tense as an error in the copy they had at their disposal. Las Casas himself, always on cue with Ferdinand's *Historie*—and after Las Casas, the prominent editor Navarrete (1825)—opted for correcting his version to read "what he will discover" (*lo que ha de descubrir*).[87] Columbus's most sober biographer in the twentieth century, Antonio Ballesteros Beretta, has offered the simplest solution to this problem, stating that "the phrase *has discovered* does not refer to something completed or preterite. Rather, it means something [Columbus] has conceived in his mind, something he has mentally discovered by means of study and speculation."[88] Legal historian Alfonso García-Gallo points out that Columbus had insisted on being designated "admiral" in the islands and mainlands he was setting out to find effective on the very date the *Capitulaciones* were to be expedited. Columbus did so because as a mere captain of his fleet he would have wielded power only over crew and vessels, but as an admiral he would have shipped out to sea already wielding jurisdiction over both waters and shorelines. The most reasonable way Fernando and Isabel could confer such a title before Columbus had even begun to outfit his armada was to assume that they already possessed the domain in question, and this mock assumption required referring to the discovery as a deed accomplished.[89] This argument acquires particular strength when we consider, as does García-Gallo, that the titles that the *Capitulaciones* then conferred upon Columbus are based only on territories "to be discovered," not on anything already discovered by him.[90] Thus "as lords that they are of the said ocean seas," Fernando and Isabel appointed Columbus, "as of this moment . . . admiral in all those islands and mainlands that by virtue of his labor or ingenuity will be discovered or won in the said ocean seas"—a title that was meant to be enjoyed by Columbus for the rest of his life and by his heirs in perpetuity.[91] It bears adding that Columbus's immediate investiture as admiral also served as a life insurance of sorts on behalf of his family, for should he have died before returning to Spain, the Crown would already have been committed to recognizing his first-born son Diego as the next admiral.

The *Capitulaciones* then name Columbus viceroy and governor general "in all the *same mainlands and isles* that, as stated, he *were to discover or win* in the said seas."[92] Columbus requested the joint titles of admiral and viceroy-governor following the model provided by a certain Don Alfonso Enríquez, who had served the Catholic Monarchs in this double capacity in the territories of Castile and León.[93] The *Capitulaciones* does not specify anything concerning the title of viceroy-governor other than that Columbus would have the right to present the candidates from which the Crown would then select a magistrate (*regidor*), "and in this way the lands that Our Lord will let him find and win in the name of Their Highnesses will be better governed."[94]

The remainder of this document enumerates the benefits that accompanied the title of admiral, a title that Columbus would be most anxious to preserve in the difficult years ahead. The admiralship entitled him to one tenth of the profits "from all and any merchandise—be it pearls, precious stones, gold, spicery and whatever other things and merchandise of whatever sort [*specie*], by whatever name, and in whatever manner— which were to be bought, bartered, found, won, or which lay within the limits of the said admiralship."[95] This title also granted Columbus full power to preside as judge, not only in all legal suits that should arise over merchandise produced *within* his admiralship, but also in all suits concerning goods bartered in from other merchants "in the place where such commerce and agreement will be conducted and reached."[96] By virtue of this admiralship, Columbus also acquired the right to invest one eighth of the costs to arm any new expeditions and in turn to perceive one eighth of the profits deriving from them. Vignaud and others who have thought that the *Capitulaciones de Santa Fe* ought to have mentioned such places as Cathay, Çipango, or India as destinations—or such goals as are made explicit elsewhere, like diplomacy and evangelization—have ultimately failed to take into account the formal constraints that governed the composition of this official document.[97]

The document was not meant to identify Columbus's routes or destinations, only to indicate them in the broadest possible terms—"isles and mainlands on the ocean seas"—and only as a function of its main purpose. It was a concession specifying the titles, prerogatives, and privileges granted to Columbus in exchange for his services. And these services included the discovery and forceful or strategic acquisition and occupation of unspecified islands and mainlands in the ocean seas, as well as the establishment of every sort of commercially profitable traffic—buying, bartering, finding, winning (i.e., looting), cultivating, or extracting every available good within the broadly defined geographical limits of the new admiralship. And the goods included in this commercial charter did not just include mineral and vegetal resources such as pearls, precious stones, gold, silver, and spices. They included not just natural goods in their raw form, processed, or manufactured, nor beasts and animal products, but also things "of whatever sort, by whatever name, and in whatever manner."[98] Thus, by Columbus's authority in the extraordinary letters he wrote announcing the discovery, the goods defined by the political and commercial charter of the *Capitulaciones* included human slaves. In the letter to Santángel, in which he promises his patrons shiploads of innumerable goods—among them gold, spices, mastic, cotton, lignum aloe, rhubarb, and cinnamon—from a fabulously wealthy Indies, Columbus also promises that Fernando and Isabel would soon have "as many slaves as [Their Highnesses] wish to order, and they will be from among the idolaters."[99] And in the original letter Columbus addressed to Fernando and Isabel, which saw print only recently in the newly discovered *Libro copiador,* Columbus would show even less inhibition concerning the categories of Indians who should be enslaved. Referring to the Caribes—the "monstrous" eaters of human flesh—Columbus assures Fernando and Isabel that "whenever Your Highnesses wish for me to send you slaves, I wish to bring or to send most of them from among these."[100]

It appears that, upon reflecting on the terms of the *Capitulaciones de Santa Fe,* Columbus pushed for an amendment that would render not just his admiralship, but also the office of viceroy-governor for life and perpetually hereditary. The unprecedented concession of such a demand came at a price to Columbus, and days later, the Catholic Monarchs issued another document known as *Carta de merced* (30 April 1492), which alone was the document later "confirmed" by the Crown upon Columbus's return to Europe in 1493, and which, for obvious reasons would acquire precedence over the *Capitulaciones* in the eyes of Columbus's heirs and of his biographer son Ferdinand.[101] (Ferdinand cites only the *Carta de merced* and not the *Capitulaciones;* for this reason Las Casas thought that the clause "what he has discovered" in the *Capitulaciones* he had at his disposal should be corrected to read "what he will discover.") The *Carta de merced* nowhere refers to the waters and shores Columbus hoped to reach as something he "hath discovered" or to the Catholic Monarchs as already "lords of the ocean seas," which may suggest that doubt lingered in the court at Santa Fe over whether the Catholic Monarchs could invest Columbus as "already" admiral of a domain of which he had not yet taken possession in their name. (In this particular regard, as with the bulls *Romanus pontifex* and *Inter cetera* and the donations later granted by Alexander VI for the discovery, popes were evidently perceived by the crowns of Portugal and Castile to enjoy greater latitude than Christian princes.)

The *Carta de merced* marked from the outset the conditional nature of Columbus's titles by announcing that he was being sent by Fernando and Isabel "to discover and win with certain vessels belonging to us and with our people certain islands and mainland on the ocean sea and it is hoped that with the help of God some of the said islands and mainland shall be discovered and won on the ocean sea by your hand and ingenuity."[102] In compensation for this service, albeit *after* he had reached all or part of "the said isles and mainland in the said ocean sea," Columbus would automatically become admiral and viceroy-governor and he would wield the honorific title of *don*.[103] This document deliberately curbed the geographical breadth of Columbus's future powers by referring this time not to "mainlands" but to only one "mainland," and not to "ocean seas" but rather to one "ocean sea." From this amendment to the *Capitulaciones,* one can surmise two contingencies aptly pointed out by Juan Manzano Manzano, a staunch defender of the pre-discovery thesis: to judge from the careful phrasing of in the *Carta de merced,* if Columbus were to reach the Asian mainland described by Marco Polo as subject to a powerful lord like the Great Khān, there was little chance that his aspiration to become viceroy-governor would ever become anything other than symbolic. If Columbus were to reach a mainland different from Asia (perhaps even the antipodal continent once theorized by Crates of Mallos), then his powers would be limited to that one mainland in that one ocean sea, and these powers would not extend to any other mainlands that might be discovered on that or any other ocean seas in the future. The Crown perhaps hoped to confine Columbus's ample administrative, juridical, and fiscal powers to the "few" islands and/or one mainland he might discover on this particular voyage. And Columbus accepted these terms in exchange for extending all conditional titles for life to him and to his sons and heirs.[104]

Finally, as Manzano Manzano also points out, while the *Capitulaciones* had served as a legal document between two parties—the Crown and Columbus—the

Carta de merced was drafted to be presented by Columbus to third parties as proof of the titles, prerogatives, and privileges that Fernando and Isabel had granted him, for this document also issued a direct order to all pertinent land and sea authorities in their domains to recognize the powers conditionally vested in Columbus. As with the *Capitulaciones,* the *Carta de merced* was not meant to identify Columbus's destination or goals except in terms that would grant him the greatest possible range of action as deputy to the crowns of Castile and Aragon. And, as even Manzano Manzano seems to recognize in his recent revival of the legend of the anonymous pilot, the fact that the "islands and mainland" specified in the *Carta de merced* could turn out to be new for Europeans in no way prevented Columbus from conceiving these as connected to, or contiguous to, or at a swiftly communicable distance from, Magnokhanic Asia. We are talking, of course, about Columbus's Indies.

The Crown had reserved the function of positively identifying the general destination and goals of Columbus's modest armada for the one official document that should serve this function by its very nature. Along with the *Capitulaciones de Santa Fe,* the Crown had issued an open letter known as *Carta comendaticia* for Columbus to carry with him as a passport (17 April 1492).[105] This document, drafted in lingua franca, was addressed to authorities and individuals of every known or foreseeable status and nationality.[106] As a document requesting free passage and offering remuneration for any assistance lent to Columbus's armada, the *Carta de merced* complied with the diplomatic obligation of stating Columbus's general route, destination, and mission: "We send by these presents the noble Christopher Columbus with three armed caravels by way of the ocean seas *to the parts of India,* for certain causes and business concerning the service of God and the increase of the orthodox faith, as well as our benefit and gain."[107] This document thus conveys that Columbus was transiting or had transited "the ocean seas" on his way "to the parts of India" and that his mission concerned both religious matters and unspecified business that was, in all likelihood, meant to be presented by Columbus as commercial in nature. (For obvious reasons, nothing is said in this letter concerning the contingency of discovering or acquiring lands mentioned in the *Capitulaciones.*) Advocates of a pre-discovery thesis have found themselves at a loss to explain the *Carta comendaticia:* the most prominent exponents of this thesis in the twentieth century, Vignaud and Manzano Manzano, simply omitted this document altogether from their arguments. Carbia, who did not advocate the story of the anonymous pilot but believed that the references to Cathay and Çipango in the primary documents referring to the discovery were the result of later forgeries effected by Las Casas, mistranslated the phrase *ad partes Indie* to mean not "to the parts of India" but rather "in the general direction of India" (*para el lado de la India*).[108] (If such had been the intended meaning of this phrase, it ought to have read instead *versus Indie*.) Emiliano Jos later contested Carbia's interpretation of the *carta comendaticia* by pointing to the terminology used in an official register now held in the Archivo General de Simancas and first published by Navarrete in his *Colección de los viages y descubrimientos* (1825).[109] This document (5 May 1492) specifies the repayment of funds loaned out to the Crown by the *escriuano de raçion* Luis de Santángel for the purpose of outfitting Columbus's armada. (Santángel, to whom Columbus later addressed his letter of discovery, belonged to a banking family and was the keeper of the Crown's privy purse.)[110] By this document, the Crown disbursed 1,140,000 *maravedíes* "to pay to the said *escrivano de raçion* in return for the same amount, which he loaned to pay for the three armed caravels that Their Highnesses ordered to go *to the Indies* [*a las yndias*] and to pay the said Christopher Columbus, who is going in the said armada."[111]

In short, the *Carta comendaticia* is unequivocal concerning the ultimate destination of Columbus's armada. Even as the authors of this document imagined Columbus tendering his passport to an authority seated somewhere other than India, it is clear that Columbus was supposed to introduce himself and his crew as travelers in transit *ad partes Indie*. And if Columbus's ultimate destination was indeed "the parts of India," the *Carta comendaticia* is the earliest known document in the Columbian corpus to signal that Columbus intended to sail not just to the west across the ocean but also to the south—whether we take "the parts of India" to mean the southwestern quarter originally assigned by Eratosthenes to the part of the inhabited world that extended to the east of the Nile and to the south of the parallel of Rhodes or—like the Columbus who chose to cross the Atlantic along the parallel of the Canaries—the vastly tropical expanse on which cartographers like Behaim had tended to plot Marco Polo's India.

On 30 April 1492 the Catholic Monarchs issued five other documents in anticipation of Columbus's voyage. Four of these were royal mandates for the purpose of supplying Columbus with a fleet: local authorities of coastal cities and villas in Andalusia and other parts of the kingdom were instructed to provide all the necessary goods for fitting out his armada; judges were to commute the sentences of criminals willing to risk their lives by shipping out with him; tax collectors in Seville were instructed to waive taxes on any victuals and food set aside for Columbus's armada; and prospective captains and crews for his armada were ordered to recognize and obey him as their captain.[112] Naturally, these mandates mentioned no more than that Columbus had been ordered to ship out as captain general of an armada "to certain parts of the ocean sea" or simply "to the part of the ocean sea" (*a çiertas partes de la mar oçeana* or *a la parte de la mar oçeana*). But along with these royal mandates Fernando and Isabel also extended Columbus a *Carta de creencia,* or letter of credence, which was to serve him to present himself across the Atlantic. This is the only other known official document issued to Columbus before the discovery that has been thought to tell us something about the destination and goals of his enterprise.

Like the passport expedited days earlier, this letter of credence was drafted in Latin, except that it was issued in triplicate and addressed to a "Most Serene Prince," whose name Columbus was meant to insert in the appropriate blank space provided. (Columbus was accompanied by an interpreter on his voyage, the *converso* Luis de Torres, who, according to the *Diario,* "knew Hebrew and Chaldaean, and even a dash of Arabic" [2 November 1492].)[113] The letter of credence was drafted in the manner of a belated reply that aimed to resume diplomatic contact that would have taken place at some point in time between the domains of this unspecified ruler and either the specific domains now ruled by Fernando and Isabel or, more generally, Roman Christendom: "From the accounts of certain of our subjects and of others who have come to us secretly from these kingdoms and parts, we have understood how much esteem and good will you harbor for us and for our standing, and how eagerly you have wished to be informed about things concerning us."[114] Vignaud and his heirs were forced to dismiss this form letter as a cynical document, or at the very least as an empty formality without a future. Vignaud believed that, Columbus's true destination being Antilia, he had requested this letter of credence from the Crown only at the insistence of Martín Alonso Pinzón (later captain of the *Pinta*), who himself was obsessed with reaching the fabulously wealthy island of Çipango.[115] Carbia asserted that this form letter was simply addressed to no one in particular.[116] And Manzano Manzano saved room for his version of the pre-discovery thesis by reasoning that, while Columbus would quickly capitulate to the illusion that he was near Cathay and Çipango, *his* Çipango (a toponym he first uses for Cuba, then for Hispaniola) was not originally Marco Polo's Çipango, but rather, the island previously discovered by the anonymous pilot in the high Atlantic.[117] Columbus would have requested the letter of credence as a cover for his tightly guarded secret.

Let us briefly review what the letter of credence can tell us when we read it, as do many Americanists today, like a document drafted to cover an honestly anticipated contingency. Reference in this letter of credence to previous diplomatic and informal contact with the domains of a ruler who had been well disposed toward Christians has enticed advocates of the traditional thesis, beginning with Emiliano Jos and the earlier Manzano Manzano, to venture a few title-holders as the possible addressees, foremost among them the successors to the legendary figure of Prester John, the Tatar emperor Timur (1336–1405), and the Mongol emperor famously portrayed by Marco Polo, Khubilai Khān (1215–1295).[118]

Since at least the first half of the twelfth century, the legend of Prester John had lent voice to the hope among Christian Europeans that Christ's last command to his apostles had by now been at least partially fulfilled (Mark 16:15), and that somewhere in Asia or Africa Christian allies, or at least sympathizers and potential converts, might be found to crush Europe's Saracen enemies in the Mediterranean basin. Forging such allies and, with their aid, bringing down the sect of Mohammed was supposed to be part of a preordained drama that would reach its climax with the reconquest of Jerusalem. Columbus was no stranger to this scheme: it had already been an explicit subject of conversation between Columbus and the Catholic Monarchs even before he had undertaken his first voyage.[119] In an entry to the *Diario* (26 December 1492), attempting to distract attention away from the disastrous marooning of the caravel *Santa María* on Hispaniola's northern coast and toward the benefits promised by the discovery, Columbus reminds Fernando and Isabel of his previous request "that all the revenues from this my enterprise should be spent in the conquest of Jerusalem, and Your Highnesses laughed and replied that this pleased you, and that even without my asking so, this was already your will."[120] Whatever other goals we might think fueled Columbus's desire to cross the Atlantic, it was the "higher" goal of increasing the ranks of the faithful against the infidels—or, as his passport declares, "for certain causes and business concerning the service of God and the increase of the orthodox faith"—that Columbus chose, and intelligently so, as the defining frame for his enterprise in the controversial prologue of his *Diario*.

Where the potentates implied by the letter of credence might be thought to dwell is a matter of significance for our understanding of Columbus's enterprise. The earliest known reference to Prester John appears in the anonymous twelfth-century *De adventu patriarchae Indorum ad urbem sub Calixto papa secundo,* which reported the visit to

Rome in 1122 of a patriarch alleged to have arrived from the capital of India, where he presided over a Christian enclave that looked after the tomb of Saint Thomas.[121] The hagiographic tradition inaugurated by the apocryphal *Acts of Saint Thomas* (3rd or 4th century) has led scholars to link the apostle's first alleged activities in India with the domains of the Partho-Indian ruler Gundaphara in the upper Indus Valley. Before its alleged transfer to the Syrian city of Edessa (3rd century), the shrine of Saint Thomas might have been in one of three rather different locations on the Indian subcontinent: the northwestern corner of the Punjab, where Gundaphara ruled; the southwestern coast of Malabar, where the sixth-century *Christian Topography* by Cosmas Indicopleustes first identified a Christian enclave; and the southeastern coast of Coromandel, where Marco Polo later situated another Christian enclave that was presumably guarding Thomas's tomb.[122] Whatever place the author of *De adventu* may have thought this patriarch of the Indians had come from, the focus and extent of Prester John's domains came to vary greatly, depending on which version of his legend one reads and on the geopolitical circumstances that prompted the invocation of his name.

The forgery that popularized the figure of Prester John—a letter "addressed" by the priest-king to Emperor Manuel of Constantinople in 1163 (composed about 1165) asserted: "Our Magnificence rules in three Indies, and our land runs from ulterior India, in which the body of Saint Thomas Apostle rests, through the desert, and it extends to the east, and returns westward to the deserted Babylon, next to the tower of Babel."[123] The reference to three Indies may have its earliest antecedent in the apocryphal *Acta apostolorum,* a sixth-century compendium on the lives of the apostles wrongly attributed to the first-century figure of Abdias, first bishop of Babylon (Luke 10:1–20).[124] According to Pseudo-Abdias, who attributes this threefold division to unnamed historians, one of these Indies, where the apostle Saint Matthew had preached, "verged" on Ethiopia. The second, where Saint Thomas had preached, faced the Medes, or India Citerior— probably associated by Pseudo-Abdias with Gundaphara's domains in the upper Indus Valley. And the third, where Saint Bartholomew had preached, marked the end of all land, facing the ocean sea to the east, or India Ulterior.[125] The author of the *Acta apostolorum* evidently thought of this tripartite India as comprising all those territories associated with the extended basin of the Indian Ocean. The *Letter of Prester John,* however, simultaneously indexes these three Indies and a seemingly more restricted territory that would appear to run from Mesopotamia to the "sunrise," or the eastern end of Asia. Whatever picture of Prester John's territory the letter's author had, this apocryphal document extolled the overwhelming natural riches, marvels, and monsters that Mediterranean geography had strongly ascribed to the Afro-Indian tropics.[126] And, as we might expect, the fact that Prester John was lord of "the three Indies" also gave readers license to locate him in those parts of sub-Saharan Africa to the east of the Nile associated with the extended basin of the Indian Ocean. This appears to be the case with the letter that Pope Alexander III addressed in real life to Prester John, *Indorum rex*, in 1177, which was dispatched to the black Negus of Ethiopia, the leader of the Monophysite heresy in sub-Saharan Africa.[127]

Another early reference to Prester John simultaneously points us north *away* from the Indies, to the other side of the steep Hindu Kush, in the area beyond the Oxus (Amurdaya) River known to the Romans as Transoxania (roughly corresponding to present-day Uzbekistan, with parts of Kazakhstan and Turkmenistan). This reference was recorded by Otto of Freising in a historical atlas that famously conceived world history since Creation as a history torn between the divine city of Jerusalem and the worldly city of Babylon, *Chronica sive historia de duabus civitatibus* (completed 1257).[128] Following the fall of Edessa to the Muslims in 1144, the chronicler had witnessed an audience between Pope Eugenius III and the Frenchman Hughes, bishop of Djebele, who had been sent from Syria to request military reinforcements from Rome. According to this envoy, a Nestorian priest-king by the name of John who ruled in the farthest reaches of the East, beyond Persia and Armenia, had recently defeated the Persians and was poised to cross the Tigris River in order to come to the rescue of the Church of Jerusalem. Hughes's description of Prester John as a direct descendant of the Persian Magi who were thought to have traveled to Bethlehem to pay homage to the newborn Jesus (Matthew 2:1–12) would appear once again to tie the figure of the priest-king to the hagiographic tradition on Thomas's early works in the Indus region shared by Parthia and India.[129] But the historical event that inspired Hughes's report to Eugenius III was the 1141 victory of Yeh-lü Ta-shih, ruler of the central Asian empire of Qara-Kitay, or Black Cathay (his empire reached to the southwest into Transoxania), over the Seljuk Sultan Sanjar of Persia.[130]

While the basic components of the Prester John legend tend to make him lord of the pliable expanse of the Indies, the geopolitical contingencies that led to the invocation of his name tended to shuffle him around to those areas that happened to be of particular interest to Christian Europeans at one time or another. Thus in 1221, nearly a century after Yeh-lü Ta-shih's victory over Sanjar, the first rumblings of the raids conducted by Chingiz Khān's Mongol cavalries on the Muslim-occupied Transoxania reached the crusading army stationed at the Egyptian port of Damietta. Rumors of this campaign prompted the Paris schoolman Jacques de Vitry, who was then bishop of Acre, to ring the voice of alarm in Europe concerning a certain King David "of India," who was supposed to be a relative of Prester John and was generally known by that name.[131] This king had risen, according to Jacques, as Christianity's protector and had just scored a great victory against Muslim infidels.[132] Decades later, Marco Polo did not hesitate to apply the label of Prester John to Toghril, khān of the central Asian Kerait tribe. With the help of his Mongol underlord Chingiz Khān, Toghril defeated the rival tribe of the Tatars at the end of the twelfth century; he in turn was overthrown and killed by the future first emperor of the Mongols.[133] Where these events are described in Marco Polo's *De consuetudinibus,* in the copy acquired by Columbus from the Bristol merchant John Day after the discovery (1497), we have Columbus's only direct reference to the legendary priest-king: "where Prester John is."[134] In his book on India, Marco Polo also pointed to a Prester John type in the east African region of Abascia, or Abyssinia, or, as he and others also call it, India Meridiana.[135] Columbus would not fail to take notice of this priest-king either. The corresponding postil reads: "Christian king."[136]

Although numerous twelfth- and thirteenth-century sources situate Prester John in central Asia, it is rather more likely that the authors of the letter of credence in Fernando and Isabel's court would have had in mind an addressee in the "parts of India" that corresponded to the Indian Ocean rather than in the continental interior. Like the ventures carried out by the Portuguese in Atlantic Africa, Columbus's enterprise was, after all, conceived and executed primarily as a navigational venture planned to require initially little more than brief inland incursions. The Indian Ocean was the unifying geographical accident for the Indies. And if travel through the Asian interior was defined by the use of caravans, armies, or cavalries, what defined travel through the "parts of India" had always been the use of sailing vessels. Indeed, by the time Columbus was preparing to cross the Atlantic, the figure of Prester John had largely been relocated back from the Asian interior to the territories associated with the extended basin of the Indian Ocean, more often than not, to the eastern part of sub-Saharan Africa known to Columbus and his contemporaries as Ethiopia.[137] The most diverse geographical sources in the fourteenth century came to associate the name of Prester John with the heretical Christian dynasties of "Indian" Africa: the Dominican missionary Jourdain de Sévérac, who in his *Mirabilia descripta* (written about 1330–1340) left an invaluable testimony of his saga through the Indian subcontinent, refers to Prester John's Ethiopian domain as India Tertia.[138] Abraham Cresques's Atlas of 1375 claims that the Muslim ruler of Nubia (a province of sub-Saharan Africa) waged constant war "against Nubian Christians, who are under the rule of the Emperor of Ethiopia and belong to the realm of Prester John" (**fig. 3.1**, lower center of the fourth panel, p. 171).[139] And the anonymous *Libro del cognosçimiento* (late 14th century), which played a crucial role in persuading Prince Henry to bid for the territories extending beyond Cape Bojador, assures us, perhaps following Marco Polo's discussion of Abyssinia, that the Christians ruled by an Ethiopian Prester John were "black as pitch" (*negros como la pez*) and they branded a cross on their foreheads as a sign that they had been baptized.[140]

Prester John's "return" to the Indies in the fourteenth century had obeyed a number of historical contingencies, including Christian Europe's failure to locate any rulers that matched his description in the Asian interior, and the Mongol occupation of the Abbasid Caliphate of Baghdad in 1258, which had displaced the epicenter of Europe's worries about its Saracen enemies toward the Mamlūk sultanate of Egypt.[141] Moreover, embassies had begun to arrive in the Mediterranean sent by sub-Saharan rulers eager to establish cordial relations with Christian Europeans. Jacopo Filippo Foresti's historical atlas, *Supplementum chronicarum* (Venice, 1483), records Giovanni di Carignano's report in a now lost treatise or map of his meeting in Genoa with thirty Ethiopian ambassadors on their way back from Avignon and Rome who had been sent in 1306 by Prester John "to the King of the Spains" to forge an alliance against their common enemies in northern Africa.[142] In a section at the end of the *Supplementum* dedicated to the figure of Prester John, Foresti significantly refers to the legendary priest-king as the "highest patriarch of the Indians and the Ethiopians."[143] Although this embassy is indeed known to have been fitted out around 1310 by the ruler of the Ethiopian highlands Wedem Ar'ad (reigned 1299–1314), we do not know whether it ever reached Iberia. Yet this was not the last attempt to establish an alliance between the heads of the Monophysite church and the papal see or the Christian kingdoms of the Iberian Peninsula. By virtue of the Accord of Monteagudo signed only a few years earlier (1291), Aragon had assigned to itself the conquest of Mauretania Caesarensis east of the Mouluya River. It appears that more than a century later, Prince Henry's obsession with involving the Negus of Ethiopia in his crusade against northern Africa was inspired by Henry's brother-in-law, Alfonso V of Aragon—the uncle of King Fernando the Catholic.[144] Alfonso's court had maintained diplomatic relations after 1428 with a "real" Prester John, Zar'a Yâkob ("Seed of Jacob"), an Ethiopian ruler who had strived for years to reconcile the Monophysite church with that of Rome.[145] Embassies of this sort would have been forced to bypass enemy Muslim territory, hence, the reference in the letter of credence issued by Fernando and Isabel to the "secrecy" with which communication had been carried out.

If this accurately represents the diplomatic history implied by the letter of credence issued to Columbus, then one of the letter's addressees could have been a successor of the Ethiopian Negus in African territory facing the Indian Ocean, and his territories could have conceivably extended to the other Indies. Relatively fresh news of Prester John would have also circulated in Iberia by way of the Cordoban traveler to North Africa and the Levant, Pero Tafur.[146] Tafur's *Andanças e viajes por diversas partes del mundo avidos* (Events and Voyages that Have Taken Place in Diverse Parts of the World; completed about 1453–1457) was based in part on the "Indian" testimony given to Tafur by our very own Venetian merchant Niccolò de' Conti. Not surprisingly, Tafur's account of Prester John's domains simultaneously pointed to the Ethiopian highlands and to the Indian subcontinent.[147] If the letter of credence was no more than a wildcard addressed to any Christian potentate who might generally match the description of Prester John, the territory implied by the letter given to Columbus would not have been, once again, the Asian interior, but rather any one or all of the "three Indies" legend associated with Prester John, and the part of India that Columbus would have expected to reach first would have been what authors variously called India Ulterior, or India Maior (the Hind of Arab geographers), or Marco Polo's India Minor, or, in Ptolemaic jargon, India extra Gangem.

The possibility of finding a Prester John type even in this farthest of Indies was not inconceivable to Columbus and his contemporaries. Martin Behaim's globe, which bears witness to the many geographies associated with the legend, locates Prester John in central Asia and in Ethiopia, but it also points to the farthest confines of the Indian Ocean. A legend in the midst of what would have been Ptolemy's Magnus Sinus (the coastline leading to the terminal equatorial port of Kattigara) tells us that "this sea, land and towns all belong to the great Emperor Prester John of India." (**fig. I.3**, p. 13, gore I, 15° N).[148] And a second legend in the southern hemisphere evidently meant to apply to the entire basin of the Indian Ocean, reads: "All this land, sea and islands, countries and kings were given by the Three Holy Kings to the Emperor Presbyter John, and formerly they were all Christians, but at present not even 72 Christians are known to be among them" (gore H, 40° S). The ultimate source for this particular legend on Behaim's globe was the forged letter to Manuel of Constantinople that had popularized the priest-king as lord "in three Indias."

Scholars have suggested that the reference to past diplomacy in the letter of credence might also point to a successor of the Tatar ruler Timur, whose seat had been the city of Samarkand, in modern-day Uzbekistan. Timur's raiding campaigns had extended through Persia all the way across the Indus River into Delhi, and beyond Delhi into the basin of the Ganges River.[149] Ruy González de Clavijo's *Embajada a Tamorlán* (1406) recounts the diplomatic exchange that had taken place since 1402 between Timur, who initiated this exchange, and Queen Isabel's grandfather, Enrique III of Castile (the monarch who in turn sponsored Béthencourt and La Salle's raids on the Canaries).[150] Although Timur failed to follow his raids on Delhi and along the Ganges River with effective annexation, it would have been reasonable for the Crown to suppose that the letter of credence was, in theory, deliverable to one of Timur's successors in "the parts of India."[151] Columbus himself had learned about Timur's exploits from the folios of Piccolomini's *Historia rerum*.[152]

But among the Asian rulers whose domains had reached into India, none had awakened as much general curiosity in Christian Europeans as the rulers of the Mongol empire, especially Marco Polo's Khubilai Khān, who conquered Mangi in 1279. It is the elusive figure of the Great Khān that threatens to corporealize in the opening entries to the *Diario,* and it would continue to haunt the margins of Columbus's geography at one time or another during his transatlantic career. The arrival of the Mongol hordes in Russian, Hungary, and Poland (1236–1241), and their almost immediate withdrawal due to the death of Chingiz Khān's successor Ögedei, had unleashed a wave of apocalyptic angst through Europe's learned circles—not unlike that later felt by Pierre d'Ailly and his close contemporaries on account of the rift between Rome and Avignon. The Mongol ruler who had ordered the invasion of Europe in the mid-thirteenth century clearly did not match the description of a pious "Prester John," but the mysterious retreat of his horsemen back into the Asian grasslands indubitably opened the door for Europeans to hope that the Great Khān might yet convert to the Christianity, or at the very least be persuaded to join forces with crusading armies against the Saracens.

The question was what role the Tatars might play in the unfolding of a world history that was often conceived by Christians eschatologists—among them Roger Bacon, Pierre d'Ailly, and Columbus—as leading to the final confrontation between the armies of Christ and those of the Antichrist, and then to the victorious gathering of Christians in a reconquered Jerusalem.[153] Roger Bacon, who learned about the Mongols from the Flemish Franciscan William of Rubruck, found in questions of this order occasion to argue in his *Opus maius* IV for the usefulness of "knowledge of place" to theology. Citing Aethicus Ister's version of a prophecy contained in Pseudo-Methodius's seventh-century *Apocalypse,* Bacon explained that a race that had been shut out by Alexander beyond the gates of the Caspian mountains was meant to break free into the world to greet the Antichrist and hail him as the god of all gods.[154] Bacon, who wrote in the aftermath the Mongol conquest of Baghdad, easily supposed that the Tatars were this accursed race. D'Ailly, who would take many of his cues from the Apocalyptic geopolitics of *Opus maius* IV, not only identified the Mongols as the northerly nomads allegedly contained by Alexander the Great in the Caucasus Mountains; in his *Tractatus de legibus et sectis contra supersticiosos Astronomos,* he also linked the Mongol invasion of the Caliphate of Baghdad in 1258 with Albumasar's prediction in *De magnis coniunctionibus* that the Muslim faith would meet its destruction 693 years after its inception by Mohammed.[155] Lamenting the fact that this destruction had not altogether come to pass within the time frame predicted by Albumasar, d'Ailly nevertheless assured his readers that the Saracens would eventually be destroyed by Tatars or Christians. This destruction clearly was under way, since the Tatars had already ransacked Baghdad and slain its Caliph, who was considered the Muslim equivalent of the pope.[156] One can easily imagine what could have crossed Columbus's mind when he later annotated these lines from *De legibus et sectis:* "Saracens will be destroyed either by Tatars or by Christians. Tatars will destroy the kingdom of Baghdad and the Caliph."[157] We do not know the dating of this postil, although Columbus eventually did use this passage from d'Ailly for the *Libro de las profecías* (dated 1504), a collection and commentary of authoritative, mostly scriptural, sources that Columbus believed prefigured the discovery and evangelization of the Indies and of all nations before the eventual reconquest of Jerusalem.[158] But to judge from the letter of credence drafted in preparation for the first voyage, Columbus had long figured out that his enterprise could come to play a crucial role in enlisting the Great Khān in a global conflict to defeat Muslim forces in the Levant and northern Africa. This strategic fantasy had flourished in Roman Christendom long before Columbus crossed the Atlantic.

In 1245 Pope Innocent IV had sent two letters to the third Mongol emperor Güyük Khān, inviting the new ruler to accept the principles of Christian doctrine, protesting his terrorizing raids on Christian nations, and begging him to inform the papal see of his next move.[159] Güyük, like his predecessors, believed that he was the divinely ordained ruler of a universal empire in the making, and in his reply to Innocent the Mongol ruler asked how the Pope could be so sure of speaking for God and ordered him to present himself at the Mongol court to pay his respects to the "emperor of all peoples."[160] This initial impasse between the Roman papacy and Güyük's court was only the first of numerous frustrated diplomatic exchanges between Christian Europeans and the Mongols in the course of the thirteenth and early fourteenth centuries, and yet the unequivocal message that the khāns saw it as their mission to subjugate all peoples was repeatedly diluted by numerous signs that the Mongols remained open to some sort of dialogue. One of Innocent's famous envoys to Güyük's court, the Franciscan friar John of Piano Carpini suggests this very possibility in the chronicle of his journey to Mongolia between 1245 and 1247. Carpini's *Ystoria mongalorum* not only portrays a wise ruler who accorded special protection to foreign ambassadors (especially Christians, it seems), but it also assures its readers that members of Güyük's court and of his family who had already converted to the Nestorian heresy "told us that they firmly believed he was about to become a Christian, and they have clear evidence of this, for he maintains Christian clerics and provides them with supplies of Christian things; in addition he always has a chapel before his chief tent and they sing openly and in public and beat the board for services after the Greek fashion like other Christians, however big a crowd of Tartars or other men be there."[161] The Mongols themselves did not fail to cultivate this hope among Christians for political advantage. In 1248, following Friar John's return to Europe, King Louis IX (Saint Louis), who was training his crusaders in Cyprus, received an embassy from Güyük's commander Eljigidei, who had crossed the Caucasus mountains in preparation to launch the first campaign on the Caliphate of Baghdad.[162] Eljigidei was well informed about Friar John's mission to Mongolia, and in his letter to King Louis, which asked King Louis to "distract" the Mamlūks in Egypt while the campaign on Baghdad was completed, Eljigidei claimed that he had been sent by Güyük to the aid of Levantine Christians. Eljigidei's envoys cunningly added that Güyük's mother was the daughter of "Prester John," that Güyük and Eljigidei themselves had just professed the faith, and that they now wished to collaborate in the reconquest of Jerusalem.[163] King Louis's return embassy to Güyük (1247–1250) found that the khān had died and that the standing regent, Güyük's widow, Oghul Qaimish, had once again taken the hard-line approach previously followed by Güyük toward the papacy.[164] (Oghul Qaimish was probably compelled to assume this hostile stance against Christians in light of the fact that her son's claim to the imperial seat was opposed by the mother of the future fourth khān Möngke, Sorghaqtani, who was indeed a Nestorian.) Despite this setback, the campaign on the Caliphate of Baghdad was later revived by the Mongols, and the early decades of Īlkhān rule in Persia witnessed many calls like Güyük's for an alliance against Saracen enemies.[165]

In the meantime, the most detailed and influential travel writers, while stopping short of claiming that the shamanistic Tatars were shopping around for a monotheist faith to bring unity to their empire, made candid reference to members of the imperial household who had already converted to Nestorianism (particularly noblewomen), and to the relative tolerance and amused curiosity that the khāns of this period displayed toward Nestorians, Muslims, and members of other sects who gravitated toward the imperial court.[166] William of Rubruck, who took leave from Louis IX's headquarters in Damietta on a self-appointed mission to Mongolia (1553–1553), tells the readers of his *Itinerarium* that both Möngke's mother, Sorghaqtani, and his favorite concubine, Oghul Tutmish, both recently deceased, had been devout Nestorians; and Rubruck offers an exquisitely detailed account of a formal theological debate summoned by Möngke Khān in which the Franciscan newcomer and Muslim and Nestorian representatives were asked to defend their beliefs against Möngke's *tuins,* or shamans.[167] Marco Polo's *De consuetudinibus* opens precisely with an account of the perilous journey through the Asian interior that had unexpectedly landed his father and uncle, Niccolò and Maffeo, in the court of Möngke Khān's successor, the fifth Mongol emperor Khubilai Khān (their first journey took place between 1254 and 1269).[168] Having consulted with his councilors, an extremely affable and inquisitive Khubilai "asked these men to do him a favor and return to the pope with one of his barons, called Cogatal, to ask the holy pope of the Christians on his behalf to send him one hundred Christian scholars who could teach him their doctrine in a reasonable and discreet manner, if it were true that the Christian faith was the best of all, and that the gods of the Tatars were demons, and that they and other Orientals were misled by the gentile cult; for he wished to hear from well-founded sources what faith should be kept and for what reasons."[169] In addition to this task, Khubilai asked his ambassadors to the pope "on their return, to bring him oil from the lamp that hung in the Sepulcher of Our Lord Jesus in Jerusalem, for he believed that Christ was among the number of good gods."[170]

From Marco Polo himself we also learn of the fate of this embassy: the death of pope Clement VI and the troubled election of a new pontiff had detained the Polo brothers in Europe for two years.[171] Having waited enough, the brothers decided to leave Venice in 1271, this time bringing along Niccolò's adolescent son Marco, and they traveled to Acre, intent on reaching Jerusalem in order to comply at least with Khubilai's petition for oil from the Holy Sepulcher. Before leaving Acre for Jerusalem, the Polos secured from "archdeacon" Tedaldo Visconti an apology letter for Khubilai citing the troubles of the curial electorate. From Jerusalem, the Polos turned back north to the Armenian port of Lajazzo (in today's southern Turkey), where an urgent letter reached them from Visconti, asking them to return to Acre, because he had just been elected pope (Gregory X). Back in Acre, the Polos must have faced yet another disappointment, for Visconti this time did hand them a pontifical letter for Khubilai Khān, but, instead of the one hundred learned men requested by the khān, he sent along only two Dominican Friars, Niccolò of Vicenza and William of Tripoli, who at the first sign of hardship in Armenia would defect from the Polos' caravan. The three Polos were to return from the Far East to Venice in 1295, having been asked by Khubilai once again to deliver another message, as Francesco Pipino's translation reads, "for the pope and certain kings of the Christians," but we do not know if the letters given to them by the Mongol ruler were ever delivered, or if so, to whom.[172] We do know that the Latin version annotated by Columbus was Pipino's own abridgment of Marco Polo's *Il milione,* which in a previous version specified that Khubilai's intended addressees included the king of France *and* the king of Spain (Hispania).[173] If the letter of credence expedited in triplicate to Columbus was drafted with a descendant of Khubilai Khān in mind, it may well be that Fernando and Isabel's chancellors had access to Marco Polo's unabridged original, which appears to have been known in Aragon and Castile for some time. It is also remotely possible that Khubilai's letter had reached the Iberian peninsula, and that record still existed of its arrival.[174]

In any case, it is Marco Polo's account of the first embassy carried out by his father and uncle on behalf of Khubilai Khān that found its way into the celebrated letter sent in 1474 by the Florentine humanist Paolo dal Pozzo Toscanelli to King Afonso V of Portugal by way of a certain Fernão Martins, canon of Lisbon, urging the Portuguese king to pursue a western route to Asia. Toscanelli later sent a now lost copy of this letter to Columbus, who transcribed it onto a blank folio in his copy of Piccolomini's *Historia rerum.*[175] In this letter to Dom Afonso, Toscanelli mentions that the populous country that harbored the wealthy port of Zaiton, in Marco Polo's Mangi, stood under the rule of a single prince, who is called the Great Khān, a name which in Latin means King of Kings. His seat and residence is for the most part in the province Katay.

His forebears, who craved intercourse with Christians, already 200 years ago sent to the pope and requested of him several men learned in the faith so that they might be enlightened. But those who were sent encountered difficulties on their journey and returned home.

Even in the time of [Pope] Eugenius [IV] a man came to Eugenius who affirmed his great good will for the Christians, and I had a long talk with him on many things,—on the vast size of the royal buildings, on the vastness of the rivers in breadth and wondrous length, on the multitude of cities on the banks of the rivers, and of how on a single river some 200 cities have been built with marble bridges of great width and length, adorned with columns on both sides.[176]

Toscanelli's interlocutor was Niccolò de' Conti himself, the Genoese informant who had supplied many of the Indiana contained in Pero Tafur's *Andanças e viajes* and whose account of the formidable cities of Cambaleschia and Nemptai informed Piccolomini's discussion about the middle location and temperate nature of Cathay in *Historia rerum*. One must bear in mind, however, that by the time Conti visited the farthest parts of India, Mongols had long been evicted from both Mangi and Cathay, and whoever was displaying "great benevolence toward Christians" (perhaps the inhabitants of the Upper Indian city of Nemptai, as Columbus claims on the margins of *Historia rerum*), the rivers, cities, and bridges Conti had mentioned to Toscanelli now formed part, if anything, of the Ming empire in mainland China.

The diplomatic contingencies anticipated by the letter of credence suggest a huge and diverse geographical expanse—central Asia, the geographical system of the Indian Ocean (including the "Indian" part of Africa), and mainland China (Cathay and Mangi). But for Columbus the "princes" implied by this curious letter all had one thing in common: the domains they might have inherited from previous Prester Johns, Timurs, or Great Khāns conceivably stood within—or extended *south* into—that tropical destination that Columbus, in his controversial prologue to the *Diario,* consistently indexes as *yndia* or *las dichas partidas de yndia* ("the said parts of India").

With the prologue, or preamble, to his *Diario,* Columbus inaugurated the lifelong habit of reminding Fernando and Isabel of those things which they had said or done and would have just as soon forgotten. Columbus would thence remain anxious to set down in writing his interpretation of things, indubitably thinking of this as a way of covering his back in case of trouble. This prologue represents Columbus's own understanding of the terms, destination, and goals of his enterprise, and not at all, as Vignaud and other authors have claimed, a third party's shameless rewriting of the political and commercial expansionism of the *Capitulaciones* as a purely diplomatic and evangelical mission to Asia.[177]

The prologue organizes for Columbus's patrons the diverse elements of his enterprise as he hoped Fernando and Isabel understood them—precisely matching terms and concepts specified in *all* the known official documents drafted between the Crown and Columbus in anticipation of his first voyage. And, not surprisingly, this prologue strictly observes the hierarchical relation that Columbus and his contemporaries assigned to the spiritual and temporal worlds. The letter of credence declares that Columbus's armada had been sent first for "certain causes and business pertaining to the service of God and the increase of the orthodox faith," and second for "our own benefit and gain." In the prologue, Columbus reasonably links the voyage he was undertaking first, though not exclusively, to the nobler goals expressed both in the passport (*Carta comendaticia*) and in the letter of credence, which alludes to a diplomatic and missionary history whose purpose had been the conversion of non-European nations to Christianity as well as the unification of all believers in the armed struggle against Muslims and, in due time, in the struggle against the newly risen sect of the Antichrist. In other words, the *Diario*'s prologue urgently links Columbus's enterprise with the militant religiosity that had lent a seal of approval to the Christian *reconquista* of Muslim Iberia since the eighth century, to the crusades that Europe had waged in the Holy Land since the eleventh century, to Castile and Portugal's expansion in Atlantic Africa during the course of the fifteenth century, and, most recently, to the conquest of Granada and the expulsion of Jews from Fernando and Isabel's domains. But, contrary to what Vignaud and others have argued, Columbus did not forget to link the voyage he was undertaking to the baser goals of his enterprise as expressed in the *Capitulaciones de Santa Fe* and its amendment, the *Carta de merced,* namely, political and commercial expansionism.

Thus Columbus begins his prologue by declaring himself an eyewitness to and beneficiary of the fall of Muslim Granada at the turn of 1492: "on the second day of the month of January, I saw the royal banners of Your Highnesses raised by force of arms to the towers of the Alhambra, which is the fortress of the said city, and I saw the Moorish king come out to the gates of the city and kiss the royal hands of Your Highnesses and of the Prince my Lord. . . ."[178] The momentous finale of the *reconquista* offered Columbus an anchor for the evangelical and diplomatic goals that are expressed in the passport and letter of credence Columbus had received prior to his voyage. Naturally, Columbus's enterprise was meant to compensate for the failures of a diplomatic and missionary history that, in the prologue's case, prominently featured the goings and comings of the three Polos to the court of Khubilai Khān. Some Americanists, beginning with Vignaud, have argued that Columbus had not read Marco Polo before embarking on his first voyage, and that he only resorted to the works today counted as part of his library in the Biblioteca Colombina *after* the discovery, as he saw himself in need of defending the claim that he had reached Asia. However, regardless of the position we take on the chronology of Columbus's readings, or on the role they played in his enterprise, we can be certain, thanks in part to the few cartographical works surviving from the period, that it was not necessary to read Marco Polo in order to know one's Marco Polo. In the course of nearly two hundred years, *De consuetudinibus* had come to define nearly everything Europeans knew regarding Magnokhanic Asia, and in the prologue to the *Diario*, Columbus was rehearsing his Marco Polo by way of the letter that Paolo Toscanelli had originally written to Fernão Martins in 1474:

> And then in that same month [of January], because of information which I had given to Your Highnesses concerning the lands of India and of a prince who is called Great Khān, which in our romance language means "king of kings"; how, many times, he and his predecessors had sent to Rome to ask for doctors versed in our holy faith in order that they might instruct him in it; and how the holy father had never provided them, and thus so many peoples were lost, falling into idolatries and converting to sects of perdition; and Your Highnesses, as Catholic Christians and princes who love the holy faith and strive for its increase, and who are enemies of the sect of Mohammed and of all idolatries and heresies, thought of sending me, Cristóbal Colón, to the said parts of India to see the said princes, and the peoples and the lands, and the disposition of the lands and of everything, and to see how their conversion to the holy faith might be undertaken. And you ordered that I not go by way of the East, by which way it is customary to go, but by way of the West, by which way we know not for certain whether anyone has gone before.[179]

This segment of the prologue is unequivocal concerning the general destination and goals of Columbus's charge to reach the East "by way of the West." Columbus tells us that, having supplied information to the Crown "concerning the lands of India and of a prince who is called Great Khān," he had been sent "to the said parts of India to see the said princes, and the peoples and the lands, and the disposition of the lands and of everything, and to see how their conversion to the holy faith might be undertaken." Vignaud did not wish to recognize the geographical and political distinctions made by Columbus between the lands of India and the seat of the Mongol empire or between those parts of India that might belong to the Great Khān or other princes and those parts of India that could conceivably be discovered and "gained" on behalf of the crowns of Castile and Aragon. And failing to regard this as a crucial geopolitical distinction, Vignaud proposed that the divide between the diplomatic and evangelical goals expressed in the prologue and the political and commercial goals expressed in the *Capitulaciones* pointed to geographically irreconcilable places: Asia and the high Atlantic island of Antilia. This is precisely the mistake that Manzano Manzano thoughtfully sought to correct later in order to save room for the thesis of a pre-discovery.

In the prologue, Columbus does not claim that he was sent to Cathay, only that he had given information to Fernando and Isabel "concerning the lands of India and of a prince who is called Great Khān." Just as he had done in the postils to d'Ailly's *Ymago mundi* and to Piccolomini's *Historia rerum,* Columbus was here establishing a geopolitical distinction that crucially dispenses with the need for the kind of geographical divorce Vignaud proposed in order to solve his paradox. Not only was Columbus drawing a distinction between those parts of India that belonged to the Great Khān and those that did not, but he was also pointing to a crucial distinction between the Great Khān as lord of India and the Great Khān as lord of Cathay. Even if we were to entertain the possibility that Columbus had never set eyes on Marco Polo, d'Ailly, or Piccolomini, Columbus could not have failed to notice that the text he was paraphrasing in this segment of the prologue, Toscanelli's letter, asserted that the populous nation where the port of Zaiton was located (Mangi) stood "under the rule of a single prince, who is called the Great Khān. . . . His seat and residence is for the most part in the province Katay." Just as Fernando could be construed as king of Aragon and of Sicily, and Isabel as queen of Castile and of Granada, so was Columbus here implicitly construing the Great Khān as lord of Cathay and of India. The Great Khān was, for Columbus, lord of India because the Mongols had *descended*, first from the colder regions of Asia to a temperate Cathay, and later from Cathay into the Indian province of Mangi in southern China. And while Columbus considered that the diplomatic and missionary imperatives of his enterprise might conceivably lead him back north to Cathay, it is as a lord whose domains might reach into "the parts of India" that the Great Khān played any role in Columbus's reiteration of the destination and goals of his enterprise: "[Your Highnesses] thought of sending me, Cristóbal Colón, *to the said parts of India to see the said princes,* and the peoples and the lands, and the disposition of the lands and of everything, and to see how their conversion to the holy faith might be undertaken."[180] The prologue explicitly shows that Columbus understood his primary destination to be "the parts of India," and that the Great Khān who would intermittently haunt his writing in years to come was both lord of Cathay and lord of India.

Columbus perceived no contradiction between the diplomatic and evangelical goals we see expressed in the passport and the letter of credence and the political and commercial expansionism expressed in the *Capitulaciones* and *Carta de merced*. In fact, in the same breath in which Columbus tells us that he has been sent to the parts of India "to see the said princes, and the peoples and the lands" he also announces the exploratory character of an enterprise that was meant to yield new territories and resources for the crowns of Castile and Aragon. This is in part the meaning of his assertion that part of his mission was to see "the peoples and the lands, and the disposition of the lands and of everything."

Indeed, Columbus does not wait to remind his royal benefactors of the baser goals expressed by the *Capitulaciones* and the *Carta de merced*. It may be no coincidence that, while Columbus had anchored the nobler goals of his enterprise to a holy war against the infidels, he would then anchor its baser goals to the infamous edict by which Fernando and Isabel had reluctantly announced the expulsion of Jews from their domains (31 March 1492). After all, even though this edict was predicated on the accusation that Jews had been causing new generations of *conversos* to relapse into so-called Judaizing practices, popular bouts of anti-Semitism on the Iberian peninsula had often fixed on the crucial role that privileged Jews had played in the fiscal administration of local government and in other economic activities in order to reinforce the damning stereotype of Jews as children of Mammon who had made their riches on the sweat and tears of Christians. It may well be this strain of anti-Semitism, added to the perception that this new exodus of Jews was bound to yield considerable economic benefit in the domains of Fernando and Isabel, that prompted Columbus to draw a connection for his addressees between the edict of 31 March 1492 and the material rewards promised by the enterprise he was now undertaking:

> So, after expelling all Jews from Your kingdoms and domains, in that very month of January, Your Highnesses commanded me to go sufficiently armed to the said parts of India. And for this, you granted me great favors and you knighted me so that from then on I would be called "Don" and would be Grand Admiral of the Ocean Sea and Viceroy and Perpetual Governor of all the isles and terra firma I might discover in the ocean sea. And likewise my eldest son would succeed me, and his son him, from one generation to another till the end of time.[181]

In sum, the prologue to the *Diario* does not represent an attempt, either by Columbus himself or by a later impostor, to redefine the blatantly materialistic venture foreseen by the *Capitulaciones* and *Carta de merced* as a spiritually transcendent diplomatic venture. On the eve of his discoveries, Columbus saw the voyage he was undertaking across the Atlantic as a spiritually and materially significant enterprise, and his prologue reminded his benefactors of the rights and privileges they had bestowed on him in exchange for the fulfillment of every goal expressed or implied by the official documents they had signed in preparation for his voyage. Columbus believed that every one of these goals could be met at different times and in different places—all within the general region that he and the Crown had designated as "the parts of India." In Columbus's India, there was room for exercising diplomacy with formidable rulers like Prester John, Timur, and the Great Khān as well as room for discovering and conquering new lands that might have escaped imperial aspirations. And, at least on parchment, Columbus was pledging to honor fully the terms of his agreement with Fernando and Isabel. Just as until now he had obeyed their orders to the letter, parting promptly from Granada for the Port of Palos, where he had proceeded to outfit an armada and recruit a crew, and from there parting for the Canaries just as he had been told to do, so now he had taken the route out of the Canaries "to the Indies" with the intention of fulfilling everything else Fernando and Isabel had commanded:

> And I parted from the city of Granada on the twelfth day of May in the same year of 1492 on a Saturday, and I came to the town of Palos, which is a seaport, where I armed three vessels very well suited for such a feat. And I parted from the said port

very well supplied with very many provisions and with many people, on the third day of the month of August of the said year on a Friday, half an hour before sunrise; and I followed the route to Your Highnesses' Canary Islands, which are in the said ocean sea, *in order from there to take my route and sail so far that I would reach the Indies and present Your Highnesses' embassy to those princes and thus carry out what you had ordered me to do.*[182]

As part of this pledge, Columbus also promised to keep track night and day of the route he was following to the Indies (his *Diario*), as well as to draw a new portolan (*carta de navegar*), and even to compose a book that would contain coordinates and maps in the guise of Ptolemy's *Geography*:

And for this purpose I thought of writing throughout this whole voyage, very diligently from day to day everything I would do and see and experience, as will be seen in what follows. Also, my Lord Princes, apart from writing down every night whatever happens during the day, and every day what I have traveled during the night, I intend to make a new sailing chart. In [it] I will place the entire sea and lands of the ocean sea in their proper places under their compass bearings [*debaxo su viento*], and moreover, [I will] compose a book and place all of the same in a map [*por pintura*], by latitude from the equinoctial line and by longitude from the west; and above all it is very important that I forget sleep and pay much attention to navigation in order thus to carry out the said purposes, which will be great labor.[183]

We may never know whether Columbus ever fulfilled the promise to draw the portolan or to compose the Ptolemaic work he announced. If he did, these precious samples of Columbian cartography, which would have spared Americanists many a headache over the identity of the lands Columbus intended to reach, never made it with the original copy of the *Diario* to the royal chancellery in 1493, for later, during the anguished months of diplomacy that followed Columbus's return to Europe, we find Fernando and Isabel urging Columbus to produce just such works.

In the curious letter they would write to Columbus expressing concern that Portugal was now intent on reaching islands and terrae firmae that might be the richest of all because they stood "in the part of the sun" (5 September 1493), Fernando and Isabel also made this request of Columbus: "And so, in order for this book of yours [the *Diario*] to be better understood, we would need to know the degrees of the isles and land that you found and the degrees of the route you followed in our service, that you may then send them to us, as well as the chart that we asked you to send us before your [second] departure: send it to us very carefully drawn, with all the place names written on it, and if you consider that we should not show it to anybody, then write to us telling us so."[184] In another letter expedited on the same date (5 September 1493), Isabel told Columbus that she was forwarding a copy of the original *Diario* previously surrendered to the Crown in Barcelona, explaining that the need to keep its production secret from Portugal's ambassador had delayed its delivery and that, in order to deliver it on time to Columbus before his departure, it had been written "in two hands" (*a dos letras*).[185] The original *Diario* was lost, and it was probably this copy, now also lost, that Las Casas would have had a chance to consult in the archives of the Columbuses decades later, as he prepared to write *Historia de las Indias.*

To say that Columbus was pledging to meet all the goals expressed in the official documents we have examined is not to say that Columbus would not be torn by the choices he faced once he had crossed the Atlantic. Indeed, the drama played out in the *Diario* is in part that of the *homo viator,* God's rational creature traveling through life torn between the noble dictates of the higher soul and the deplorable callings of the physical body, in Columbus's case, between the lofty calling to seek new converts in a cosmic struggle against God's enemies and the baser need to ride the wave of political and commercial expansionism. As Las Casas very well understood when he wrote *Historia de las Indias,* Columbus had been, on the one hand, "first apostle and minister of these Indies," and, on the other, a *colonizador* and a "populater of new land" (*poblador de lo nuevo*) whose venality had introduced the scourges of slavery, compulsory tribute, and forced peonage to the Indies.[186] In the *Diario* this conflict would find geographical expression in the distinction between Magnokhanic Asia—an Asia that would have pulled Columbus back north toward the higher latitudes, where he expected to reach Cathay—and the maritime regions of India—an Asia that lured Columbus south into the lower latitudes of the globe, where he hoped to fulfill empire's infamous dream. As we well know, it was the lure of the tropics that ultimately gained the upper hand.

The Tropics of Empire in Columbus's *Diario*

In that land where trees fail to grow roots, men must harbor little truth and show even less perseverance.

attributed to Queen Isabel of Castile by Gonzalo Fernández de Oviedo y Valdés, *La historia general y natural de las Indias* IV, 1 (1535)

Columbus could have meant that the lands he had discovered were not nearly as hot as one could expect of the globe's lower latitudes, but that they were still significantly hotter than Mediterranean Europe. Such a distinction would certainly explain why, even as he insisted that his Indies were marvelously temperate, Columbus felt no compulsion to abandon the geopolitical model that accorded temperate nations the natural right to govern themselves and others, and hot nations the natural predisposition to be subjects or slaves to others.

The distinction between relative and absolute temperateness would also carry implications for understanding the cross-purposes at work in a document that we know, on the one hand, as Columbus's *Diario,* but that, on the other, Las Casas copied and summarized as the working notes for his own *Historia de las Indias* and *Apologética historia.* If we read the extant *Diario* only as the work of the Discoverer, Columbus's insistence on the temperateness of the Indies served him, in effect, as a reply to his detractors in Castile who had foretold that his descent to the belt of the tropics was bound to turn up neither land nor life; such a reply did not necessarily constitute an attempt on his part to claim that the Indies were absolutely temperate vis-à-vis Mediterranean Europe. If, on the other hand, we read the extant *Diario* as a crucial accessory to Las Casas's fiercely anticolonialist works, there can be no doubt that the good Las Casas was bent on interpreting the sublime temperateness described by Columbus as an *absolute* temperateness vis-à-vis Europe's. Las Casas aimed at shaking the ground on which apologists of empire had argued that Spain had legitimately come to occupy the Americas and subjected or enslaved its peoples. Thus Las Casas was bent on proving that the Indies were *universally* temperate, in fact, more *properly* temperate than any other place in the previously known inhabited world! Thus Columbus's *Diario* would serve Las Casas as potent firsthand testimony to the effect that American geography presented the very same temperate conditions that Europeans had long associated with their own privileged location in the world-machine. Columbus's stubborn insistence on the temperateness of his Indies unwittingly yielded the political lesson Las Casas would deploy systematically in defense of Amerindians: if the Indies were as temperate as, or more properly temperate than, Mediterranean Europe, then the Indians were *not* "by nature" Europe's subjects or slaves. This was perhaps Las Casas's most urgent task in the writing of *Historia de las Indias* and the *Apologética.* It should not be surprising to find that those passages that Las Casas quotes verbatim from the *Diario* as Columbus's "own words" tend to deal with the sublime complexion and fecundity of the newly discovered lands, as well as with, of course, the nature that Columbus ascribed to their peoples. Significantly, Las Casas's pen would transmute the "tameness" and "cowardice" that Columbus ascribed to the Indian from the moral defects that the ancients had ascribed to barbarians to the spiritual graces that Jesus had placed at the very core of his teachings in the Sermon on the Mount (Matthew 5–7). Consider only two of its most famous versicles, to appreciate Las Casas's brilliant sleight-of-hand as a benevolent tergiversator of Columbian ethnography: "Blessed are the poor in spirit, for theirs is the kingdom of heaven. . . . Blessed are the meek, for they shall inherit the earth."[7]

Whatever value Columbus assigned to the temperateness of his Indies, it is also true that Columbus was not all of one mind about the complexion of these lands. And any reading of Columbus's *Diario* ought to make room for such contradictions without depleting our confidence in the systematic quality of Columbus's thought. Just as Columbus marveled at the temperateness of the lands he explored, at times he still experienced the scorching heat that advocates of the theory of the five zones had long ascribed to the torrid zone. Consider once again the entry in Columbus's *Diario* where he disputes the latitude of 42° N read by his quadrant for Puerto Gibara in northeastern Cuba (21 November 1492).[8] Having all along extolled the temperateness of the land he had explored on his way from the Bahamas to Cuba, Columbus suddenly argued that the great heat in Puerto Gibara indicated that he was significantly closer to the equator than his instrument read—and that this must be one of the richest gold-bearing regions of the globe. As he would explain in his *carta-relación* of the fourth voyage (7 July 1503), "Gold is generated in sterile lands and *wherever the sun is strong.*"[9] Or consider again the famous instance in Columbus's *carta-relación* of the third voyage (30 May–31 August 1498), when, hitting the mid-Atlantic Doldrums, Columbus fancied that the heat of the torrid zone was literally about to set his vessels and crew aflame.[10] The counterpoint between temperateness and heat in Columbus's characterization of the Indies does not just reflect the objective conditions he experienced as a result of changes in latitude or accidents that altered local conditions; it also reflects the imperative of explaining *something* about the location or nature of a particular place and its contents—just as Columbus does when he suddenly invokes the Puerto Gibara's heat in order to locate himself in relation to the equator, dispute his quadrant's reading, and then identify the nature of the place where he found himself. More significantly, perhaps, the counterpoint between temperateness and heat in Columbus's writing is the symptom of unresolved conflict between inimical perceptions of the belt of the tropics: on the one hand, sub-Saharan Africa and the extended basin of the Indian Ocean were construed as a gigantic, hyperproductive, hyperpopulated, and even temperate region of the globe; on the other hand, the tropics were construed as the scorched, barren, uninhabitable, and unnavigable fringes of the "island" of the earth. To be sure, while Columbus the *explorer* had contributed to proving the ancients wrong by inventing a vastly temperate, fertile, and inhabitable expanse to the west and to the south of Mediterranean Europe, Columbus the *colonizer* continued to regard this expanse as the sweltering wasteland whose peoples were nature's subjects or slaves. Las Casas fully recognized this double bind in Columbus's geopolitics when he copied Columbus's *Diario* for *Historia de las Indias* and the *Apologética*. And while Las Casas willingly admired Columbus as God's minister and apostle in the Indies, Las Casas also profoundly despised the geopolitics Columbus had practiced in the Bahamas and Caribbean basin. Indeed, it might be said that Las Casas's anticolonialist works sought to disembowel once and for all the contradictory logic that had informed Columbus's exploration and colonization of the Bahamas and the Caribbean basin.

By 19 September 1492, well into the high Atlantic, the fleet had for days come across what Columbus took to be imminent signs of nearing land—birds of various species, including a tern, two tropical birds, and an albatross; flotsam that looked like river weed carried out to sea; and even a live crab, which, Columbus explains, would never have been found more than 80 leagues from land. On the basis of these "sure signs of land," Columbus came to venture that he was sailing between islands "to the side of the north and of the south."[11] But he refused to waste time tacking back and forth in search of them, as Las Casas reports, "because his will was to push forward all the way to the Indies, and the weather [was] fair; for, God willing, it would all be seen on the way back." Columbus probably believed that these were the oceanic islands plotted in the *mappaemundi* of the period in the midst of the ocean thought to separate the ends of the East from those of the West—like Antilia, or the Island of the Seven Cities, plotted on Behaim's globe. He wisely decided to push forward in search of the Indies; unfortunately, the fleet was becalmed, and the variable winds that followed forced him to steer for several days to the north of the largely westward route the *Diario* records since leaving the Canaries (20–23 September). The ships kept encountering more and more "sure signs of land," including a bird caught by the crew that, Columbus claimed, "was a river bird and not a seabird, [because] it had feet like those of a gull," but the fleet was nowhere near any land yet, and, as Las Casas remarks on the margins of the *Diario,* the first inklings of discontent had begun to surface among Columbus's crew.[12]

On 25 September, still three weeks away from landfall, Columbus recorded in his *Diario* an exchange with Martín Alonso Pinzón, captain of the caravel *Pinta,* about a now-lost navigational chart on which Columbus had, in Las Casas's words, "painted certain isles on that sea."[13] Columbus may well have imagined that he was nearing the "Indian" mega-archipelago where Marco Polo had located the gilded island of Japan— that is, in the Sea of Chin to the east of the southern Chinese province of Mangi. In light of the fact that the fleet was encountering ever stronger clues of nearing land, Columbus concurred with Pinzón that they had reached the "province" (*comarca*) where those islands ought to be sighted. Columbus attributed the fact that they should not have yet chanced upon one of these islands to the "water currents that had constantly dragged the vessels back toward the northeast"—currents that the navigator must have also secretly hoped would hasten the return passage to Europe. Unless we are to believe Vignaud and his successors, for whom the chart Columbus carried on his first voyage would have specified lands that had been discovered already, theoretical knowledge itself must have played no little role in Columbus's surprise at not yet having sighted any land. He worried that water currents had dragged his ships to the northeast not only because this would have slowed his westward progress across the Atlantic but also because he *expected* to find land on or below the latitude of the Canaries on his way to the Indies. As we have seen, Columbus's plan to reach the East "by way of the West" involved bridging the distance between Atlantic Africa and the extended basin of the Indian Ocean. The open geographical model that Columbus and his supporters had inherited from pagan antiquity predicted that land could be found all around the globe, whether because Europe, Africa, and Asia extended farther to the east and to the south than traditionally expected or because they did not account for the totality of dry land on the globe. This open geographical model further predicted, ultimately in debt to Aristotle's *Meteorologica* and *On Generation and Corruption,* that the lands of elephants that Aristotle had called Spain and India stood at a communicable distance from each other because the sun's heat caused more water to evaporate toward the equator than toward the poles, uncovering greater tracts of land in the belt of the tropics than elsewhere. Columbus thus believed that his best chance of bridging the distance between the two, or of skipping his way from island to island across the ocean, lay in tropical latitudes;

the distribution of the "isles" he appears to have painted on the lost chart may well have obeyed this rather simple cosmological principle.

These islands failed to materialize. On the very day that Columbus concurred with Pinzón that they had reached the province of islands Columbus had drawn on his chart, a false alarm of land lured the fleet away once again from its westerly course. For three days, the caravels steered in vain to the southwest, then to the west, again to the southwest, and finally back to the west, in search of an island that never appeared (25–27 September). But this deception did not seem to dishearten Columbus, who proceeded to find ever-greater signs of land everywhere he looked around him. On 29 September, Columbus would register the first of many comparisons in years to come between the tropical latitudes he had visited with the Portuguese in Atlantic Africa and the latitudes of his Indies. These were the sorts of observations that later prompted the cosmologist and explorer Alexander von Humboldt in the nineteenth century to admire the systematic mind at work in Columbus's writings. Having sighted a frigate bird, Columbus explains that "this bird makes albatrosses vomit what they eat in order to eat it itself, and it does not nourish on anything else. It is a seabird, but it does not rest at sea nor venture more than twenty leagues from land. There are many of these [birds] in the Cape Verde Islands."[14]

By 3 October, calculating that he had sailed nearly 800 leagues to the west of El Hierro and having sighted none of the land whose symptoms he had read everywhere in nature around him, Columbus began to fear that he might have overshot "the islands that he had drawn on his chart."[15] Once again, Columbus explained in his *Diario* that "even though he had notice of certain islands in that province," he dared not waste time tacking back and forth in search of them, "because his goal," writes Las Casas, "was to pass to the Indies, and if he were to delay himself, he says, it would not [have made] good sense." On 6 October, Pinzón suggested that they abandon their westerly course once again, and steer to the southwest in search of the great island of Çipango. Evidently fearful that his ships might continue to miss the islands he had expected to find on his way to the Indies, Columbus refused to follow Pinzón's recommendation. He argued, and reasonably so, that a diagonal course to the southwest would, if they continued failing to chance upon land, further delay the surer prospect of making terra firma. (Columbus seemingly construed this terra firma as Marco Polo's Mangi.) As Las Casas reports, Columbus had reasoned "that if they missed [Çipango], they would not be able to make land so quickly, and that it was better to aim at once for terra firma and then for the islands."[16] This is precisely the protocol Columbus followed a month later, when having identified northeastern Cuba as terra firma (Mangi), he chose to steer definitively to the southeast, *away* from the "colder" latitudes where he situated the mainland seat of the Mongols, Cathay, aiming instead for the islands of his Indies.

At last, on 7 October, Pinzón once again raised a false alarm of land; by the end of the day Columbus must have been under great pressure to do *something* that would distract his men. He ordered the caravels to abandon a westerly course and to steer due southwest, because, as Las Casas reports, "a great multitude of birds was passing from the part of the north to the southwest, which made it seem that they were off to sleep on land, or perhaps that they were fleeing from the winter that, in the lands from which they were coming, must have been pushing to set in."[17] This decision was "providential," to use Las Casas's term for the saga of the discovery, since days later, as Columbus's crew readied for mutiny, the fleet came within sight of the Bahamian island that the Indians supposedly called Guanahaní. Columbus, probably mindful that he had been saved by the bell, renamed the site San Salvador—perhaps today's Watling Island (24° N). The Discoverer now stood at the threshold of the American tropics, and the landfall would mark the beginning of an interminable quarrel with language for failing to capture the superlative temperateness and fecundity of his precious Indies.[18]

The geopolitical paradox that Las Casas saw at work in Columbus's exploration and colonization of the Indies, and in the later efforts of Columbus's ideological heirs in Spain to legalize the misdeeds of empire, makes itself felt from the very beginning, in the earliest words on record about the Americas by a European. The celebrated entry in the *Diario* for 11 October 1492, which also recounts the momentous events of 12 October, articulates the very terms of this paradox: even as Columbus set foot on San Salvador to marvel at a superlatively temperate landscape overflowing with "very green trees, and many waters, and fruits of diverse kinds," he was to ascribe to the naked people he encountered on the beach the nature that Mediterranean Europe had long associated with its neighbors in the lower, and traditionally hotter, latitudes of the globe.[19] One could easily read Columbus's testimony of this first encounter between Europeans and the native peoples of the Americas as a rather matter-of-fact account of the events of that very consequential day and as a candid, even laudatory, first snapshot of Amerindians. Yet Columbus disembarked on the shores of San Salvador in the company of Aristotle, poised to construe "Indians" as the "ingenious" but fatefully "dispirited" *barbaroi* whom Aristotle and his commentators had long considered nature's slaves. Indeed, Columbus's account of the landfall redundantly indexes the "defect" of "spiritedness"—meaning, ultimately, the absence of will power—that Aristotle and his commentators attributed to the inhabitants of hot nations. And this case against the Amerindian hinged on the perceived correlation between latitude, temperature, and the nature of places.

Having recounted the formal planting of the royal banner and the ceremony by which Columbus took possession of Guanahaní, Las Casas cites Columbus's own testimony of the encounter:

> I, he says, so that they would be very friendly to us, because I recognized that they were peoples who would better be freed and converted to our Holy Faith by love than by force, gave to some of them certain red caps and glass beads which they hung around their necks, and many other things of little value, in which they took much pleasure and became so much our friends, that it was a marvel. They came swimming later to the ships' launches where we were, and they brought us parrots and cotton thread in balls and javelins and many other things, and they traded them with us for other things we gave them, like small glass beads and [hawk's] bells. In sum, they took everything and gave of what they had very willingly, although it seemed to me that they were a people very poor in everything.

One can scarcely help sharing Columbus's genuine wonder at this scene. But in his "recognition" that these were people who were unlikely to display resistance to evangelization, who so easily lent themselves to the friendly reciprocity of Columbus and his crew, who surrendered whatever they had *de buena voluntad* (literally, "with good will"), and who appeared to lack a very complex material or abstract culture, we have the tacit workings of colonialist argumentation—the reasoning, in this particular case, that a certain "defect" in the Indians, namely, the malleability of their will power, rendered them empire's potential subjects.

Significantly, Columbus immediately corroborates this first impression of Indian psychology in the *Diario* with a physical portrait of the peoples he had met earlier that day. And this portrait itself can be said to have encoded information concerning the latitude and temperature of San Salvador. Having described the bartering scene on the shores of San Salvador, Columbus observes that "all of [the Indians] go around naked as their mothers bore them, and even the women, although I did not see more than one who was very young." As we have seen in Columbus's own letter to Luis de Santángel announcing the discovery, perhaps even more clearly in the bull *Inter cetera* [I], expedited by Alexander VI to Aragon and Castile, Europeans were simply awestruck by the nudity of the peoples encountered by Columbus in the high Atlantic. Indian nudity was an instant reminder of the "innocence" that humanity would have experienced prior to its expulsion from earthly paradise; and in Columbus's writing, this trace of Eden on the bodies of the natives is insistently tied to the sublime temperateness, fertility, and inhabitability of the newly found India. Again, one must bear in mind that Columbus either assigned a *relative* value to the temperateness of his Indies (that is, compared to the unbearable heat that had long been expected of the torrid zone) or was not of one mind about the temperature of the Indies. Thus his references to temperature throughout the *Diario* obeyed different imperatives, depending on where he happened to find himself and what he wished to prove for his intended readers, Fernando and Isabel. Columbus, who would later insist that the Indians went about naked "year-round," must have reasoned, when he saw their naked bodies for the first time on San Salvador's beach, that the natives wore no clothes because, like the Canarians, they inhabited a place that stood at a significantly lower and hotter latitude than Mediterranean Europe, or to use Martyr's terms, "outside every European climate, to the south."

In short, even as Columbus marveled at the sublime temperateness of San Salvador, he also located the landfall site on a distinctly warmer latitude than Mediterranean Europe. Indeed, in his description of San Salvador's islanders, Columbus explains that "all those that I saw were all young, for I saw none older than thirty years of age." We need only recall the words of Arrian's *Indica* or the words of Columbus and his contemporaries' most immediate source, Avicenna's *Canon of Medicine,* to realize that such specific information about the age span of San Salvador's inhabitants could only have been tied in Columbus's mind to the effect—accelerated "ripening"—that heat was supposed to visit on the black and timid inhabitants of sub-Saharan Africa and the extended basin of the Indian Ocean.

But if the islanders of San Salvador initially appeared to live the short lives of tropical peoples, Columbus carefully distinguishes between these Indians and the "Ethiopians" he had read about and encountered during his travel to Guinea. Columbus's Indians displayed neither the physical monstrosity nor the scorched, curly hair nor the "burnt" black color that geographical lore had long attributed to Ethiopians; indeed, the newly found people were "very well formed, with handsome bodies and very good faces, their hair coarse, almost like the threads on horses' tails, and short. They wear their hair just above the eyebrows, save for a little in the back [of their heads] which they wear long and never trim. Some of them paint themselves with black, and they are of the color of the Canarians, neither white nor black." By invoking the Indians' shapely bodies, lank hair, and complexioned skin color, Columbus was qualifying the tropicality of the place he had just discovered. Columbus was wary of the possibility that Dom João of Portugal might come to invoke the terms of the Treaty of Alcáçovas in order to usurp Columbus's Indies. Perhaps he also feared that his royal patrons might judge him ill for having disobeyed their interdiction. One or both of these fears must have played some role in the equation he drew between the skin color of the Indians and that of the Canarians. Thus San Salvador was not, in his view, as tropical as Guinea, but semitropical like the Canary Islands—not tropical enough to have scorched the skin and frizzed the hair of *these* Indians, but tropical enough that the Indians had in fact "invented" for themselves the lightest form of clothing one could possibly have worn in a hot place for the purpose of protecting oneself from the elements. As Columbus explains a few months later (24 December 1492), this time describing the body paint used by locals on Hispaniola's northern coast, Indians painted themselves "on account of the sun, so that it will not cause them so much harm."[20]

In the momentous entry for the landfall, having turned his attention from physical traits to the art of body painting, which he barely recognizes at this point as a form of *techne* or as in some way symbolic, Columbus proceeds to describe other skills, or rather, the absence of certain skills, which further builds the case for the defect of "spiritedness" in the peoples he has just encountered: "They do not carry arms," he writes, "nor are they acquainted with them, because I showed them swords and they grabbed them by the edge and ignorantly cut themselves. They have no iron. Their javelins are shafts without iron, and some of them bear on the end a fish tooth, and others [bear] other things." In noting the absence of their weaponry, which Columbus instantly qualifies by explaining that the Indians *did* possess ironless tools presumably "only" for hunting game or fish, Columbus was establishing the psychological trait for which long would be known the Taínos or, by Columbus's later translation of the qualifier *taino,* "tame" peoples he had encountered during his first outing to the Indies. Not only were the peoples of San Salvador rather prematurely perceived by Columbus as nonbelligerent, but they were also supposed to be victims of a predator that at this point in the *Diario* remains nameless: "They are all equally of good-size stature, and of good, well-formed countenances. I saw some who had signs of wounds on their bodies, and I asked them by signs what that was. And they showed me how people came here from other islands that were near, and how they tried to take them, and how they defended themselves. And I believe that they come here from terra firma to take them captive."[21] In the deeply projective attempt to identify a third party from the mainland that raided the islands just discovered by Columbus, we have the initial outline of the geopolitical "map" that Columbus would come to complete of the Bahamas and Caribbean basin in the early stages of his momentous voyage. From this point forward, the *Diario* registers Columbus's attempts to situate—geographically *and* politically—the peoples he encounters on his way to Hispaniola's Bay of Samaná in relation to *other* places and peoples, in this early instance, in relation to a predatory enemy that treated the territory just discovered by Columbus as a slaving backyard.

Having "shown" his royal addressees the nature of the San Salvadorans, Columbus was ready in the *Diario* to draw the political lesson with which we are now familiar: "They must be good servants and of great ingenuity, because I see that they instantly repeat everything that is said to them; and I believe they would readily become Christians, for it seemed to me that they were not part of a sect. I, God willing, will take from here at the time of my departure six of them to Your Highnesses, so that they will learn to speak. . . . All these are," as Las Casas interjects, "the Admiral's words." Columbus's claim that the "ingenious" and "servile" inhabitants of San Salvador "instantly repeat everything that is said to them" redundantly signaled their status as natural subordinates, for this is what children naturally do. Indeed, in the recently discovered *carta-relación* dated 20 April 1494, recounting for Isabel and Fernando the events of the second voyage, Columbus would offer a portrait of the Indians that suggests that their "childlike" behavior was a "natural" trait that made it impossible for them to govern themselves on their own:

> For these people of this land are the most docile and timorous and of good disposition to be found in the world [*la más mansa y temerosa y de buena condición que ay en el mundo*]. And thus I repeat again and again that I am lacking nothing in order to turn them to our Faith, save for knowing how to speak and to preach to them in their tongue. For they truly have no sect or idolatry, nor do they concern themselves with anything but their bread, which they call *caçavi*, and their women. And, as for their acts, words, and thoughts, they are those which nature gave to them in particular. *All [their] acts are like those of children, except for the fact that they*

are men, and nature prevents them from being such. And any act they witness, they do as they see others do; because if someone steals or does wrong, it is just as happens with children. They are [mentally] subtle [*sotiles*], for they then go and do what they have seen done.[22]

Without question, in Columbus's insistence on the ingenuity, mental subtlety, servility, docility, and timorousness of the islanders found in the Bahamas and the outer shores of the Caribbean basin we have not simply the observations of a keen ethnographer—which Columbus unmistakably was. We also have the beginning of a colonization program for a bourgeoning overseas empire that was soon to be mired in a schooled debate on the legality of the conquest. It was the deep and resilient *logic* that had let Mediterranean thinkers long view their neighbors in the hotter latitudes of the globe as natural subordinates. The newly discovered peoples in the high Atlantic were recognizable to Columbus as human, but *nature* had prevented them from acting as anything but "children"—"ingenious" but ultimately lacking in the "spiritedness" of fully realized men. And these peoples owed their childlike nature to their place in the world-machine.

We have suggested that Columbus's landfall testimony speaks to a tradition that had long associated latitude with temperature, temperature with the nature of places, place with the physiology and psychology of peoples, and human nature with the "place" that polities ought to occupy in a global world order. It remains for us to trace the manner in which Columbus came to complete the charting of what was to prove an influential "map" of the Bahamas and Caribbean basin. As noted from the outset, Columbus—at least the "Columbus" of the *Diario*—having struck land on 12 October 1492, thought that the island he was naming San Salvador stood in the uppermost, easternmost reaches of legendary India. And India was a vast geographical system that Columbus and his contemporaries imagined to be organized around that distinctly "tropical" accident we know today as the Indian Ocean. Columbus believed, or wanted to believe, that San Salvador formed part of the Indian mega-archipelago that Marco Polo had located to the east of the mainland province of Mangi (**fig. I.4**, pp. 14–15). And in his deeply projective reading of the "wounds" on the bodies of San Salvador's islanders, Columbus was inscribing the idea that the islands of his India already served as poaching ground for the seaborne armies of the great lord of Cathay. Such is the meaning behind Columbus's attempt to "correct" what his Indian informants seemed to be communicating by signs (perhaps, that they had been wounded by the natives of other islands) in order to assert his conviction that San Salvador's islanders were in fact victims of slave raids conducted from terra firma. Needless to say, the opening entries of the *Diario,* from 11 October to 6 November 1492, reenact Columbus's attempts not just to identify any traces of the complex intellectual and material culture Marco Polo and other travelers had associated with the confines of Asia but also to establish whether or not the legendary empire of a temperate Asia had already won the bid for the Indian tropics. In this process of verification, Columbus would come to persuade himself that, if he continued to south away from the latitude where he had found the ingenious but cowardly peoples of Guanahaní toward the equator, eventually he would come across a "shrewd" and "cruel" race of monsters who raided the islands of the Indies in order to feed on the flesh of their captives. In other words, Columbus would come to construe the peoples he had found in the Bahamas and the outer shores of the Caribbean, namely, the Indians we know today as the Taínos, as victims twice in need of "protection"—both from political predators who descended from the temperate latitudes of the globe in order to harness free labor for a "civilized" north, namely, the Mongols, and from natural predators who rose from the hottest latitudes of the globe in order to harvest a horrifying food staple for the "ferocious" south, namely, the Indians we know today as the Caribes. And this geopolitical invention directly reflected an established tradition in the West concerned with the problematic interface between body and soul.

On 13 October 1493, Columbus observed again that San Salvador's islanders were "all young, and all of good stature, very beautiful people; their hair not crisp but lanky and coarse like horse hair. . . . And none of them [were] black, but rather of the color of Canarians, nor should one expect anything else, since [this island] stands east to west on the same line with El Hierro in the Canaries."[23] Columbus also reiterates that the inhabitants of San Salvador were "a people greatly docile" (*gente farto mansa*). By Columbus's latitudinal equation, his fleet would have been dragged slightly off course to the north across the Atlantic, only to fall back on the 27th parallel where Columbus seemed to locate El Hierro (modern 27° 44′ N). Columbus himself must have known that San Salvador was already slightly below El Hierro, for Peter Martyr was soon to report that Columbus had navigated westward from the Canaries, "always following the sun, though slightly to the left." But just as Columbus registered two sets of distances traveled for the purpose of feeding his anxious crew the lower figures, so he may have been afraid to admit how much he believed he had dropped from the twenty-seventh

parallel. Whatever the case may be, the equation between San Salvador and El Hierro, in effect, "located" the landfall site at the very threshold of the tropics, and indeed, weeks later, Columbus would implicitly signal that he had reached the Tropic of Cancer when he identified Cape Maisi on Cuba's eastern tip as the very end of mainland Asia, for he explains that Alpha et Omega was within a stone's throw of the Indian port of Zaiton, in Marco Polo's mainland province of Mangi.

The assumption that San Salvador stood on the fringes of the torrid zone goes a long way toward explaining what Columbus thought and did following landfall. While bartering with the Indians of San Salvador on 13 October, Columbus looked around for gold and spotted a few gold nosepieces. By means of signs, Columbus presumably learned from the Indians that "by going south or by rounding the island on the south" he would find a "king" who stashed "great vessels" full of precious gold.[24] Or, as he later explains, "gold is born on this island."[25] Realizing that the Indians did not seem to know exactly how to get to the place where this local king was supposed to rule, Columbus declares that he wanted "to ship out for the southwest, for according to what many of them indicated to me, they were saying that there was land to the south and to the southwest and to the northwest; and that these [peoples] from the northwest had come many times to wage war on them."[26] This was, in Columbus's mind, a sign of possible trouble, perhaps already an indication that Mongol armadas or other hostile vessels from the mainland were in the habit of descending on San Salvador and other Indian islands for the purpose of rounding up slaves; and so Columbus quite naturally concluded that it was best "to go *to the southwest* in search of gold and precious stones," a goal unequivocally tied at this point in the *Diario* with that of "going to see if I will run across the island of Çipango."[27] In his distinction between a "northwest" inhabited by slaving warriors and a "southwest" where he expected to find the precious goods of the tropics, Columbus was articulating the very paradox that has so puzzled readers of the *Diario*: why, if Columbus intended to reach Asia, would he so easily relinquish the search for Mongol China? For now, one may say that, on the *Diario*'s authority, faced with the prospect of encountering slaving warriors to the northwest and with that of finding gold and precious stones to the southwest, Columbus chose to search for the booty of the Indies, hoping that he might soon come across the tropical island of Çipango.

By 14 October 1492, Columbus, stationed in San Salvador, had begun to spin the dreams of empire that become other peoples' nightmares. Between a stone reef and San Salvador's shore, he had found "depth and harbor for as many ships as there are in the

whole of Christendom."[28] He also explained to Fernando and Isabel that he had scouted out the island in search of a suitable spot to build a fortress and that he had come upon a tiny peninsula that he thought could be dug out on the side of the shore in only two days for the purpose of rendering it impregnable, "although I do not see this to be necessary, for these people are very innocent about weapons, as Your Highnesses will see from seven that I ordered to be captured in order to take them [to Castile] and have them learn our language and return them [to the Indies]. Except that Your Highnesses may, whenever you order so, take them all to Castile or hold them captive in the same island; because with [only] fifty men, all of them could be held in subjection, and could be made to do whatever one may wish."[29]

Back onboard the *Santa María* that day, Columbus stated that he had sighted so many islands that he knew not where to turn, and that the captives he had already taken from San Salvador made signs to Columbus that "there were so very many that they could not be counted." At this point he aimed for the largest one he spotted, explaining to the Catholic Monarchs that "they are all very plain, without mountains, and very fertile, and all are inhabited and they make war on one another, even though these men are very simple and very handsome in body." This time Columbus claimed, not that the islanders were prey to slave raiders from terra firma, but rather that they preyed upon one another—an assertion that blatantly contradicts his insistence on Indian docility. This assertion also paved the way for Columbus to fathom eventually that the peoples he had found in the Bahamas and the outer shores of the Caribbean basin were at war with, or rather, that they were preyed upon by man-eating raiders who came from other islands to the southeast. As Columbus, in his mind, was to move away from the slave raiders who were supposed to come from the terra firma due northwest, namely, the men of the Great Khān, the conviction would gradually take hold of him that he was moving in the direction of the dog-headed men of *caniba* or *caribe,* eventually located by Columbus due southeast.[30]

On 15 October 1492, Columbus headed southwest from San Salvador to an island he christened Santa María de la Concepción (perhaps Rum Cay) (**fig. I.2**, pp. 8–9). He sailed by way of the west to the southern end of this island, calling port for a night before he ventured west toward an island where his Indian captives had presumably indicated that people wore gold bracelets on their arms and legs, ears, noses, and necks. Having found no gold as yet in Santa María de la Concepción, Columbus voiced his suspicion that what the Indians had told him was no more than "a ruse in order to escape."[31]

One of these Indian captives did manage to flee on a canoe that had approached one of the caravels for the purpose of bartering, and once the canoe returned to shore, its occupants disbanded instantly, "like chickens."[32] But Columbus meant to compensate for the disheartening thought that his Indian informants were lying to him and that he might not find the gold he expected by declaring that no matter *what* he found, his intention was still "not to pass by any island of which I might not take possession; although, if [possession is] taken of one, it can be said to be taken of all."[33] As we know, the legal concept cited by Columbus—possession by metonymy—was predicated on the notion that the portion of that which one was taking possession shared something fundamental in common with the whole one aspired to possess. Indeed, Columbus does not fail to inform his royal patrons in this *Diario* entry that the natives of Santa María de la Concepción were "of the same condition as those of the other island of San Salvador," and that *all* surrounding islands were "very green and fertile of very sweet airs; and there must be many things that I do not know because I do not wish to delay myself lowering sails, in order to visit many islands in search of gold."[34] Consequently, Columbus set eyes on an island to the west that he would name Fernandina (most likely Long Island).

On 16 October 1492 Columbus headed west for Fernandina. Its coastline ran "from north-northwest to south-southeast," and Columbus called port on its north-northwestern end.[35] Following a lengthy and busy bartering session with canoes from this island, Columbus declared his intention to follow the sloping coast of Fernandina clockwise around to its southern shores, "until I find Samoat, which is the isle or city where the gold is; for this is what those who are coming to the ship are saying, and the same was said by those of San Salvador and Santa María." Significantly, Columbus added to his contention that all the islands around him shared a similar nature and similar peoples by remarking that the islanders of Fernandina, who had poured out to the ships in hordes to lay eyes on the newcomers, were "a people similar to those of the said islands, and [they have] one language and one set of customs, except that [the people of Fernandina]," whom Columbus located due southwest of San Salvador and east of Santa María de la Concepción, "already seem to me to be more civil and given to commerce and more subtle of mind; for I see that they have brought cotton here to the ship and other little things for which they know better how to bargain payment than the others did." In support of this contention, Columbus adds that, unlike the women of Santa María de la Concepción and San Salvador, the ones in Fernandina appeared to wear a cotton piece on their pudenda "that barely cover[ed] their nature." In other words,

these people seemed to be more "aware" of their nakedness than the people Columbus had found previously. While Columbus, for legal reasons, resisted the notion of political heterogeneity in this vast archipelago, his use of the adverbial "already" (*ya*) appears to denote the conviction, repeated elsewhere in the *Diario*, that the more he headed *west* toward the hypothetical mainland, or south into the tropics, the "shrewder," and perhaps the more "civilized," the people he might find would be. It is unclear what exactly informed this conviction—whether his belief that he was approaching the mainland territories of legendary India described by Marco Polo (Mangi or Ciamba); his belief that one would find increasingly more civil people as one moved from any of the four extremes of the inhabitable world toward its center, as one reads in the folios of d'Ailly's *Ymago mundi;* or his belief that by sailing south, one would find increasingly more "ingenious" people capable of "inventing" more than others (although, by implication, also increasingly less "spirited"). Whatever the case may be, Columbus was anxious to find any signs of intellectual or material culture that would match available descriptions of the Far East. And he failed miserably at this task.

On 17 October 1492, Columbus intended to head down directly for the south-southeastern tip of Fernandina, where he expected to find the alleged gold mine of Samaot. His goal was "to pursue the route of the south and of the southeast."[36] But Pinzón momentarily persuaded him to survey Fernandina counterclockwise, by rounding the north-northwestern end where the fleet was now stationed, because an Indian informant had "insisted" that this would be a faster route around the island. As Columbus began to survey Fernandina in the direction suggested by the *Pinta*'s captain, he soon found himself marveling at "as much greenery and to such a degree as in the month of May in Andalusia. And the trees are all as different [*disformes*] from ours as day from night; and so it is with the fruits and pasture and stones and all other things. It is true that there were some trees of the same nature as those of Castile; nevertheless, there was a great difference. And the other trees of other kinds were so many that there is no one who can tell it or compare them with others of Castile." On Columbus's authority, the people of Fernandina were "of the same condition" as the other Indians he had already found. Inland exploration turned up small hamlets with houses "well-swept and clean," and Columbus reprimanded the men he had sent to probe the interior, because they came back to the ships reporting a golden nosepiece half the size of a *castellano* "on which they saw letters," but they failed to deliver it to Columbus. Continuing its survey, the fleet quickly came upon shallows to the west of Fernandina, so Columbus retraced

his steps, and then made for the southeastern tip of the island as he had originally planned.

On 19 October, having reached Fernandina's southern shores, and having found neither a gold mine nor a city, Columbus decided to sail *to the southeast,* toward an island that he now thought was the "gilded" Samaot, or Samoete, but that he renamed Yslabela or Isabela (probably Crooked Island). Columbus remarks that this island was even more beautiful and fertile than the rest, so much so that "my eyes [do not] tire of regarding such beautiful greenery and so different from our own. And I even believe that in it there are many herbs and many trees that are worth a lot in Spain for the purpose of making dyes, and for medicines made from spices. But I do not know them, which gives me great sorrow."[37] On this island of Samoete he expected to find a "king" who wore "clothes and much gold." But Columbus, who now saw the need to call his sovereigns' attention away from the fabulous quantities of gold he had not yet found, and toward the countless and nameless riches promised by the greenery, explains that he did not lend much credit to what his informants had "told" him about this "king," "both because I do not understand them well, and because I recognize that they are so poor in gold, that any amount that this king might carry on him must seem like much to them."[38] So Columbus vowed to continue his exploration until he came across a place where there would be "gold and spices in large quantity."

On 21 October 1492, Columbus attempted to reach the southern flank of Isabela from the west but found so much shoal that he was unable to proceed. Having found neither king nor gold, he returned to the northwestern tip of Isabela. There he reports having sighted large amounts of aloe (a plant that was not introduced to the Americas until the following century).[39] He once again describes in superlative terms a greenery and bounty that surpassed what he had seen so far, so much so that "it seems that man should never want to leave this place."[40] Significantly, this also was the place where his men caught an iguana that they mistook for a "serpent"; it would seem that the more Columbus failed to find the gold of the Indies, the more he was prone to exalting the temperateness and fertility of a land that truly felt as if it must stand near Paradise, or as if it had only just recently fallen. On this island, Columbus once again declared his intention of sailing toward a large island, which the Indians appeared to call Colba (Cuba), but which, for the moment, he believed to be the gilded Çipango, "in which they say there are many and very large ships as well as many merchants." Columbus also wanted to reach another great island, which his informants called *bosio,* or *bohio*

(Hispaniola). Columbus now seemed to believe that he might be closing in on the tropical Çipango, and he must have felt compelled to fully express the dilemma that defines his first exploration of the Bahamas and Caribbean basin. Columbus explains that once he reached Cuba, Bohío, and any other islands in between, he would determine the quantity of gold and spices to be found there and, depending on this, would decide "what I ought to do. Although, I still am determined to go to terra firma, and to the city of Quinsay," which he most likely associated with the slave raiders to the northwest, "in order to give Your Highnesses' letters to the Great Khān, and ask for a reply, and return with it [to Castile]."[41] In other words, the impulse of fulfilling the diplomatic goals implied by the letter of credence, stood in inverse relation to the impulse of finding gold and spices; and, as we are beginning to see, the conflict between these two options was beginning to find geographical expression in the *Diario* between the impulse to head northwest—where Columbus would have expected eventually to find the city of Quinsay, in the northern part of Mangi, or Cathay itself, which was supposed to stand directly north of Mangi—and the impulse to head southeast, toward the islands of India.

On 22 October 1492, while he was still stationed on Isabela, Columbus awaited in vain for the gold-laden king to appear. The people on Isabela, he writes, were "like the others of the other islands, also naked and their bodies painted, some in white, others in red, others in black, and so on, in different ways." And only some of these Indians carried gold nosepieces, which the crewmen, like everywhere else they had gone, bartered for with glass beads and hawk's bells. The following day, on 23 October, realizing that there was no gold mine on Isabela, Columbus decided to wait no longer for the island "king or lord" to appear and declared his intention of sailing for Cuba, which he believed was Çipango. He explains that, although he suspected Isabela to be very rich in spices, he was unable to recognize any of them, and so he thought it was best to continue his voyage until such a time as he struck "very profitable land." Thus on 24 October 1492 Columbus headed "to the west by southwest" (*al gues sudueste*) for what he supposed to be the "island of Cuba," explaining that he had "heard" from the islanders of Isabela that Cuba was rich in "gold and spices and great ships and merchants." He believed this to be "the isle of Çipango, of which marvelous things are told. And in the spheres that I saw, and in the drawings of *mappaemundi,* it lies in this region." By 27 October, Columbus had skirted around the sandy cays that form the Great

Bahama Bank and from there steered "to the south by southwest" (*al sursudueste*) toward Cuba.

On 28 October 1492, Las Casas, now paraphrasing the *Diario,* reports that the fleet had sailed into a deep, gorgeous river on the northeastern coast of Cuba (near today's Bay of Bariay). Columbus called this land Juana in honor of the Infante Don Juan. According to Las Casas, Columbus found himself once again at a loss to describe a greenery that he found to be ever more beautiful and fertile than the one he had seen in the other islands: "The Admiral says that he never saw anything so beautiful, the river full of trees all around, beautiful and green and different from ours, with flowers and with their fruit, each in its own kind; many birds, and small birds that sang very sweetly. There were a great many palm trees different from those of Guinea and from ours, of medium height, with no cover at the stem, and with great leaves that are used to roof the houses."⁴² Inside an abandoned house full of fishing gear (Indians often fled at the very sight of the fleet), Columbus found little more than a curious "dog that never barked." The Indians Columbus had brought with him from the Bahamas told him by signs that this island had "gold mines and pearls, and the Admiral saw that the place was suited for this and for clams, which are an indication of [pearls], and the Admiral understood that ships of the Great Khān came there, and [that they were] very large, and that from there to the terra firma was a ten-day's journey."⁴³ If Polian geography in any way influenced this calculation, "a ten-day's journey" would have certainly been compatible with Marco Polo's claim that Çipango stood 1,200 miles due east of Mangi. Whatever the origin for this calculation, Columbus was for the moment assuming that Cuba was the tropical island of Japan.

On the following day, 29 October 1492, from this river he had called San Salvador, Columbus coasted west along Cuba in the direction of the city where the Indians appeared to locate "that king"— perhaps, in Columbus's mind, the Great Khān. As he sailed in that direction, he noticed that he was gradually following along a coastline that appeared to be increasingly slanting to the north. Near a harbor he named Río de Mares (Puerto Gibara), Columbus found a hamlet "whose men and women and children fled, leaving behind their houses with all that they contained." As Las Casas reports, "the houses . . . were now more beautiful than those which they had seen, and he believed that the more they approached terra firma the better they would be." Here in Río de Mares, Columbus made an observation that indicates that he had still not made up his mind about the temperature of his Indies. Even though Río de Mares clearly stood farther south than the islands of the Bahamas, Columbus found, in Las Casas words, that "the airs [were] delightful and sweet all night long, neither cold nor hot. And yet on the way from the other islands [to] that one, he says that it [had been] very hot; [but] not here, where it was temperate like in May. He attributes the heat of the previous islands to the fact that they were very plain, and to the fact that the wind [the fleet] had ridden until then came from the east and for this reason [was] hot."[44] The sea appeared always to be calm "like the river of Seville, and the water suitable for cultivating pearls." From Río de Mares, a Columbus eager to read the legendary Orient in his Indies, also sighted a low mountain shaped like a "mosque."

On 30 October 1492 the fleet sailed "to the northwest" (*al norueste*) along the Cuban coastline. Pinzón had understood from the Indians he stocked in his caravel that they were four days away from Cuba, and "that this Cuba was a city, and that this land was a very great terra firma that extended greatly to the north, and that the king of this land waged war with the Great Khān whom they called *Cami,* and his city *Faba,* and many other names."[45] On the basis of this information, Columbus decided on that day that he would dispatch an embassy inland, not to the Great Khān himself, as is often easily misunderstood, but to a local king who appeared to be at war with the lord of the Mongols. Columbus thought of "sending a present to the king of the land and sending him the letter from the sovereigns," that is, of course, the letter of credence that addressed a "Most Serene Prince," whose name Columbus was supposed to write down in the appropriate blank. The notion of a king at war with the Great Khān may have originated from the pages of Marco Polo, either from Marco Polo's account of Khubilai's conquest of Mangi or from his account of the bordering province of Ciamba, where Marco Polo located a ruler who had spared his kingdom the ravages of the Mongol armies by agreeing to pay an exorbitant tribute to the Great Khān. Whatever the origin of this geopolitical conceit, Columbus's references to Magnokhanic Asia in this entry suggest that he wanted to believe not that he was in Cathay but that he was in a land that continued to the north all the way to Cathay. Columbus's idea of sending an embassy to the local king was not necessarily aimed at establishing contact with the Great Khān; rather, it was most likely intended as a means to identify the geographical and political boundaries of his empire. In *Historia de las Indias,* Las Casas would comment on Columbus's famous blunder in the following terms: "It is a marvel to see how, once man desires something and firmly impresses it upon his own imagination, then at every step he comes to fancy that everything he sees or hears argues in its favor. For the said Martín

Alonso [Pinzón] had seen the chart or picture that the said Florentine physician Paolo [Toscanelli] had sent to the Admiral . . . and he located these islands on that region. . . . The Admiral had also persuaded himself of this; and thus everything the Indians communicated to him by signs, being as different [from what he understood] as the sky is from the earth, he corrected and interpreted in favor of what he wished [to believe]: that this land was, either one of the kingdoms of the Great Khān [i.e., the conquered Mangi or the tributary Ciamba], *or land that verged on them.*"[46]

It is also on this day that the *Diario* registers Columbus's infamous latitudinal figure of 42° N for Puerto Gibara. Much ink has been spilled over the question of Columbus's latitudes. Morison believed that Columbus had "mistakenly" set his quadrant on Alfirk instead of on the North Star.[47] Others have seen a deliberate attempt to "disorient" any unwanted perusers of the *Diario* by displacing the lands Columbus had explored far to the north of the Canary Islands. Rolando Laguardia Trías, for instance, persuasively argues that Columbus could have culled this figure from the table of solar declinations by the Andalusian astronomer Ibn al-Kammad, which Columbus had copied onto a blank opening folio of d'Ailly and Gerson's *Tractatus.*[48] Whatever the immediate source for this egregious figure, it displaced the figures for the lands Columbus had just explored all the way north to the very middle of the "temperate" zone, where one would have expected to find Cathay. This figure aside, by now Columbus would have seemed to abandon the idea that Cuba might be the tropical Çipango, thinking instead that it was part of the mainland where Marco Polo had located the domains of the Great Khān. By imagining that Juana's coastline "greatly extended to the north," Columbus had drawn a *vertical* relation between Río de Mares and Cathay itself, and this vertical relation could only have been the relation between a tropical Asia and a temperate Asia. Columbus concludes his entry for this day by mentioning, in the words of Las Casas, who himself understood that 42° N was an outrageous figure for the latitude of Río de Mares, "that he would work to go to the Great Khān, whom he thought might be around there, or to the city of Cathay, which is very big, according to what he had been told before leaving Spain." Columbus would never have made the mistake of mistaking Cathay for a city, which elsewhere he calls a province, and we should assume that what he meant by "the city of Cathay" was Cambalich, or Peking, where the Mongol dynasty had been known to have kept one of its seats. Had Columbus continued to push his way along this slanting coastline, he would have eventually found that Juana was only another island of the Indies.

On 31 October 1492, the caravels wasted all night fruitlessly tacking against a "cold" wind that prevented Columbus from overtaking the next cape he had sighted on Cuba's coastline. Observing that this wind "was now blowing directly from the north, and that the entire coast ran from the north by northwest to the southeast, and that yet another cape now showed further ahead, and because the sky showed signs of powerful wind, [Columbus] decided to turn back toward Río de Mares," where the fleet was to remain anchored for several days. This was Columbus's only explicit attempt to sail in the direction where he believed Cathay to be, and such a feeble gesture on his part has naturally invited readers of the *Diario* to ask whether Columbus really meant to reach Asia or whether he just meant to find new lands in the mid-Atlantic that he knew or suspected were there. We may never know the answer to this question, but what does remain crystal clear is this: the *Diario* expresses Columbus's political dilemma—should he try to establish diplomatic contact with Magnokhanic Asia, or should he try to lay claim to gold, spices, and other precious resources while looking for any connection between the seat of the Mongols (Cathay) and the Indies? And this dilemma would come to be drawn more and more clearly—and *projectively*—as the oppositional dynamics between an imperial power from the cooler latitudes of the globe (i.e., the Mongols, *or their counterparts,* the Christians) and a tropical population (i.e., the Indians) possibly subject to depredation from the north.

On 1 November 1492, upon returning to Río de Mares, the fleet found that all the locals had fled the river hamlet. Columbus sent one of his abductees to tell the apprehensive Indians that he and his crewmen were not there to harm them, that they were *not* people "of the Great Khān," and that the Christians were there in fact planning to give out of the things they had brought with them.[49] Columbus tried to convey to the Indians who dared return that day to trade with the ships that he was only looking for gold, but no gold turned up. Instead, Columbus saw a nosepiece that he thought was made of the lesser metal silver, and, lowering his expectations accordingly, he took this for a sign that the land was rich in silver. Columbus once again noted that the people on this terra firma were "of the same quality and customs as the others encountered; they are without any sect that I know of, for until now I have not seen these that I bring with me say any prayers. On the contrary, they repeat the *Salve* and the *Ave Maria* with their hands pointing toward heaven, as they are shown, and they make the sign of the cross. They all speak the same language and all are friends, and I believe [that this is true] of all the islands, and that they wage war with the Great Khān, whom they call *Cavila* and the province itself *Bafan*. And so they also go about naked like the others."[50] Columbus had now become convinced "that this is terra firma, and that I stand before Zaiton and Quinsay, one hundred leagues more or less from one and from the other. And this is very clear from the sea, which looks different from what it has been until now, and yesterday, as I sailed due northwest, I found the air to be cold." If we go by the Polian geography depicted on Behaim's globe, Columbus wished to believe that he stood on a coastline that soon turned northward in the direction of the Mangian city of Quinsay, where it would have been colder than in Río de Mares and that in the opposite direction this coastline extended due southeast toward Asia's easternmost end, where Columbus would have expected to find the tropical port city of Zaiton, on the Indian fringes of Mangi (**fig. I.4**, pp. 14–15).

On 2 November 1492, Las Casas reports that Columbus decided to deliver on his promise to send an embassy to the local king. Columbus gave his envoys, who included the "translator" Luis de Torres, beads to barter out for food, as well as spice samples, so that they might be able to recognize anything of value in the course of their mission. He then waved them off, warning them that they had six days to come back and instructing them to inform this king that the Crown had sent Columbus with letters and a royal gift in order to learn about him and to establish friendship with him. Columbus also ordered these envoys to ask around about the location of those provinces, ports, and rivers that were supposed to be found in this region. A perplexed Las Casas reports that, again, Columbus had used a quadrant that evening to find his location and found himself to be 42° N of the equinoctial circle. Columbus also seemed to think that he was at a distance of 1,142 leagues from El Hierro in the Canaries.

For the next few days, Columbus scouted out the area surrounding Río de Mares. In Las Casas's words (3 November), Columbus climbed "a hill from which he hoped to gather something about the land, but he could see nothing on account of the great tree groves, which [were] very fresh, and odoriferous; for which reason he says he had no doubt that the land yielded aromatic herbs. He says that everything he saw was so beautiful, that his eyes did not tire of regarding such beauty, [nor his ears] the singing of the great and little birds."[51]

On 4 November 1492, as Columbus waited anxiously for the embassy's return, some of his men claimed to have found "cinnamon trees," so Columbus proceeded to show samples of cinnamon and pepper to the local Indians who, appearing to recognize them, pointed *to the southeast*. Columbus then showed them gold and pearls, and the elderly men presumably informed him that in a place called Bohío he would find people wearing plenty on their necks, ears, arms, and legs. Columbus further understood "that there were great ships and merchandise, and [that] all this was *toward the southeast* [*al sueste*]."[52] Significantly, it was on that day that the Indians also "informed" Columbus that, "far from there, dwelled one-eyed men, and others with dogs' snouts who ate men, and who, upon capturing someone, would disembowel him and drink his blood and slice off his genitals."[53] In all likelihood, Columbus gleaned his version of Ctesias's legendary cynocephali from the pages of John Mandeville, who claimed that in the islands of the ocean sea toward the farthest confines of India, lived a race of dog-headed men and women who were "fully reasonable and of good understanding," except for the fact that they worshipped a god with the head of an ox.[54] According to Mandeville, these dog-headed people were supposed to be tall, strong, great warriors who, upon capturing their enemies in battle, proceeded to feast on their flesh. Whatever the bookish origin for Columbus's dog-headed anthropophagi, having "received" such disquieting information from the locals in Río de Mares, Columbus returned to the caravel *Santa María* to wait for his envoys' return, and he was now determined to sail due southeast in search of the lands pointed out by the Indians. Although Columbus was not yet fully convinced of the existence of the monsters indicated by his informants, the prospect of coming across them must have prompted him to reassure the Catholic Monarchs at this point in his *Diario* that the people he had found so far were still the "childish" Indians he had first met in San Salvador: "These people are very gentle and very timid, naked, as has been said before, without weapons and without law."

On 5 November 1492, Las Casas writes that an apprehensive Columbus ordered the ships to be pulled ashore separately from each other rather than huddled together—as Columbus was quick to explain, *not* because he mistrusted the Indians, whom he considered to be "very trustworthy people." As he awaited the return of his embassy to the local king on the shores of Puerto Gibara, the thought crossed Columbus's mind that the fleet might be ambushed, if not by the locals who had already shown signs of apprehension, by the army of that king. But Columbus's attention was diverted from this worry by a crewman who claimed to have found mastic nearby. It was not the right time to collect it, Columbus claims in the *Diario,* but the land seemed to yield enough to harvest each year a thousand *quintales,* and he adds that he also had come across aloe in the area. Significantly, Columbus concludes in this entry that Río de Mares "is among the best in the world, [with] the best airs *and the tamest people;* and, because it has a cape with a rather low cliff, a fort can be built, in order that, if all this turned out to be a rich and great thing, merchants would find safe harbor there from any other nations."[55]

At last, on 6 November 1492, Columbus's envoys returned to Puerto Gibara accompanied by two "principal" Indians from a larger town that they had found some twelve leagues inland. The envoys recounted how they had been received with awe by the townspeople and treated as though they had been sent from heaven. Columbus considered taking the two Indians to the Catholic Monarchs, but aware of how vulnerable the ships were to retaliation as they surged on dry land, he released them. The envoys had shown the Indians from that inland town "the cinnamon and pepper and other spices that the Admiral had given them: and [the Indians] told [them] by signs that there was much nearby *to the southeast,* but that they did not know if there was any here."[56] Upon realizing that there were no signs of manufactured goods that might have betrayed their origin in a city, the envoys had decided to make their way back to Río de Mares. In other words, the envoys had failed to find any signs of the material culture that had long been associated with the urban centers of the Far East. Columbus's envoys are reported to have found a bountiful land full of strange plants and birds but devoid of four-legged beasts, except for "dogs" that failed to bark.[57] It is tempting to read in the recurring image in the *Diario* of the "mute" dogs owned by the "tame" Indians Columbus had found so far, a trace of the literary and pictorial tradition in Europe that had often portrayed infidels as predatory "dogs"—not surprisingly, as cynocephali—who, by means of their incomprehensible speech, were supposed to "bark" at the true religion.[58] Columbus's mute dogs now stood in stark opposition to the ferocious and cruel dog-headed monsters allegedly located by his informants somewhere to the southeast—as the very negation of the resistance to colonial occupation that had already begun to rear its ugly head in the entries of the *Diario*. Indeed, in these curious dogs that failed to bark, Columbus may well have been reinforcing his willful portrayal of a place and a people to be easily domesticated and exploited because such was their nature. Accordingly, Columbus insists in this entry that the land was both "fertile" *and* "tilled" and that, by his calculations, it promised to yield over four thousand cotton *quintales* each year to Castile. Allegedly, there was so much of this cotton around that it grew wild all year long. To this promise of bounty, Columbus adds that the tame natives he had found in Cuba willingly traded everything they had "for a paltry price, and that they would give a large basket of cotton for the tip of a lacing or anything else given to them." And again he insists that these people were "very much without evil or war, all nude, the women and the men, as their mothers bore them. It is true that the women bring a cotton cloth large enough to cover their natures, but that is all. And they all are of beautiful countenance, and they are not very black, only perhaps a little less so than those of the Canaries." Significantly, Columbus closes the entry for 6 November 1492 by declaring that he hoped the Catholic Monarchs would undertake the conversion of the people he had discovered, and that his intention now was "to go to the southeast [*al sueste*] to seek gold and spices and to explore land." From this point on in the first voyage, the Discoverer tried to aim for the southeast, and the presence of the Great Khān, merchant ships, gilded kings, and Mongol armies would remain, as one distinguished Caribbeanist has noted, only "vestigial" in the *Diario*.[59]

This pivotal entry in the *Diario* is by no means the last time we hear about the empire of Cathay in the documentary corpus of Columbus's voyages. On the second voyage, for instance, as Columbus saw himself tracing the Tropic of Cancer along Cuba's inner shores, he was willing to entertain the idea, even if for a fleeting moment, that Cuba was not the mainland province of Mangi but just an island, as his Indian informants seemed to be telling him. Columbus reasoned that, if this were the case, he could reach the end of Cuba, "and from there I would navigate *to the north and to the west* until I found Catayo."[60] Michele Cuneo, who accompanied his friend Columbus on this exploration of Cuba, later reported in a famous letter to Girolamo Annari (Savona, 15 and 28 October 1495) that the Discoverer had also entrusted his brother Bartholomew with the mission of exploring the waters *to the north* of Hispaniola, being utterly convinced that "five hundred leagues" in that direction Bartholomew was bound to strike Cathay.[61] Indeed, even in the course of the disastrous fourth voyage, as a feverish and broken Columbus came to realize that the Central American coast nowhere seemed to open out onto the Indian Ocean, he continued to insist that the seat of the legendary Mongol lord still hovered somewhere to the north of the lands he had explored in the Bahamas and Caribbean basin. Whether or not he suspected by now that he had not reached Asia, Columbus claimed by the end of his voyage that Cuba was nothing less than "the province of Mangi, which verges on that of Catayo."[62]

In the course of the first voyage, though, as Columbus turned his attention toward a southeastern horizon where he expected to come across great quantities of gold and spices, the predatory warrior Mongols from the cold northwest suddenly gave way in his mind to the predatory anthropophagi from the hot southeast, even if at first to express incredulity at the news his informants appeared to be telling him. From this point forward, Columbus would follow a route *away* from the higher and cooler latitudes where he had situated Magnokhanic Asia and toward the lower and hotter latitudes of his precious India. It was in pursuit of a tropical expanse that he fancied to be overflowing with gold and spices that Columbus eventually grew convinced that he was also on the trail of a "monstrous" race that preyed upon the "childish" peoples of the Bahamas and Caribbean. The "horror" felt by those reporting face-to-face encounters with alleged anthropophagi invariably alludes to a curiously indescribable physical deformity that was supposed to express the distasteful inclinations of those who craved human flesh.[63] Thus months later, having reached Cabo de las Flechas, or the Bay of Samaná, the last stopping point on Hispaniola before heading back for Europe, the armada spotted on the shore a small troop of Indian men armed with bows and arrows who then began to barter with Columbus's men on the shore (13 January 1493). About one of these men, who was asked to come aboard the *Niña* in order to talk to the Admiral, Columbus would write, in Las Casas's words, that "he was *very deformed in his aspect* [*muy disforme en el acatadura*], more than any other [Columbus] had seen. His face was all sooted up with charcoal, even though, in all places, they tend to dye themselves with different colors. The Admiral judged that he must be one of the Caribes who eat human flesh."[64] Years later, in the course of the fateful fourth voyage, when he failed to find a passage along the Central American coast into what he believed was the Indian Ocean, Columbus would again assert the connection between extreme places and extreme physiologies and mores in the form of a most memorable tautology. Vexed by a landscape that refused to "conform" to the image he had forged for himself of the Indies and by a hostile tropical nature that had visited every possible hardship on his ships, his crew, and himself, Columbus would describe a people he had found on the coast of Cariay, in today's Nicaragua, in the following terms: "I came across another people who ate human flesh: the deformity of their facial expression revealed this" (*Otra gente hallé que comían hombres: la desformidad de su gesto lo dize*).[65] Without any room for doubt, in the deformity that Columbus and other Europeans perceived in the rictus of alleged man-eaters was inscribed the millenarian notion that things tropical, whether marvelous or monstrous, remained outside or beyond nature.

In Cabo de las Flechas Columbus would not fail to establish a connection between the extreme physical appearance of the Indian "monster" who had been brought aboard for questioning and the particular psychology of the peoples he now expected to find in the southeasternmost reaches of the Indies. "The Admiral says more," writes Las Casas, "that in the previous islands, [the Indians] showed great fear of the Caribes—and in other islands they called them *caniba,* but in Hispaniola *caribes*—and that they must be *a bold people* [*gente arriscada*], for they patrol all these islands and eat the people they can find."[66] When the "monstrous" informant was returned to shore, his partners in crime, realizing that the Christians intended to barter them out of all their weapons, quickly made for their bows and arrows, and after a loosing scuffle with Columbus's men, ultimately fled for their lives into the lush greenery of the tropics. Informed of what had happened ashore, Columbus contemplated the first slave raid of Caribes, explaining that, "if these people are not Caribes, they must at least be their neighbors and of the same customs—a people *without fear* [*sin miedo*], not like the others of the other islands, who are cowards and are ignorant of weapons beyond the bounds of reason."[67] This did not mean, of course, that the man-eating Caribes were actually "courageous." We need only read the recently discovered *carta-relación* that Columbus wrote to Fernando and Isabel on his return passage to Europe (4 March 1493) to realize that the "boldness" and "cruelty" that Columbus ascribed to the Caribes were no more than the desperate corollaries to an extreme form of cowardice:

> These [Caribes] eat human flesh; they are great archers; they possess many canoes, almost as large as rowing galleys, with which they raid all the islands of India; and they are so feared, that they have no equals among them. They go about naked like the others, except that they wear their hair very long, like women. I reckon that it is the great cowardice [of the] peoples of the other islands, which is hopeless, that makes them say that these people of *caribe* are *daring* [*osados*]; but I have the same opinion about [the Caribes] as about the others, and whenever Your Highnesses should wish for me to send them slaves, I hope to bring them, or send them, from amongst these, for the most part.[68]

Columbus's understanding of the geopolitical model he gleaned from d'Ailly's *Ymago mundi* are summed up in his marginal comments on that famous work: "The inhabitants toward the south [*versus meridiem*] are greater in intellect and prudence, but they are less strong, audacious, and spirited; and those who inhabit the north [*versus septentrionem*] are more audacious and of lesser prudence and fortitude. The Greeks were the ones in the middle, and they possess sufficient fortitude and prudence."[69] Consider also Columbus's postils to d'Ailly's account of the tripartite model provided by the Egyptian physician and astrologer Haly in his popular commentary to Ptolemy's *Tetrabiblos*. This model asserted that the peoples in the arctic and tropical extremes of the world were physically and morally turpid creatures capable of the greatest acts of cruelty *precisely* because they were so cowardly. To cite Columbus's annotations to d'Ailly, "Southern peoples [are] aggressive and cruel or savage on account of their cowardice."[70]

Columbus never missed an opportunity for arguing that the inhabitants of the Bahamas and Caribbean basin were "ingenious" and "tame" or downright "cowardly." A month after landfall, on 12 November 1493, he reached a river inlet barely southeast of Puerto Gibara that he named Río del Sol, or River of the Sun, perhaps because it was Sunday or because he saw himself approaching the Tropic of Cancer as he sailed along Cuba's outer shores. Here, Columbus proceeded to make good on the initial promise to bring to Castile a handful of Indian captives who could then be taught Spanish. His purpose was, he claims, to use these captives later as translators for the purpose of indoctrinating and acculturating local Indians, "because I saw, and I recognize . . . that these people have no sect, and are not idolaters; on the contrary, [they are] very tame, and they know not what evil is, nor how to kill others or capture them, and [they are] without weapons, and so cowardly [*temerosos*], that hundreds of them will flee from one of [our men], even when they are only being taunted. And [they are] credulous and they know that there is a God in Heaven, and they firmly believe that we have come from Heaven; and [they are] very attentive to any prayer we tell them to pray, and they make the sign of the cross."[71] A few weeks later, still in Cuba (5 December 1492), having reached the cape he named Alpha et Omega because he thought it was the very end of the East (Cape Maisi), Columbus described the anguish with which locals had pointed due farther southeast to the island of Bohío (Hispaniola). Columbus's informants at this cape, which he already associated with the literally tropical port of Zaiton on the Tropic of Cancer, seemed to communicate that everyone in the lands Columbus had explored down to this point was terrified of the people of Hispaniola and of other islands in the southeastern direction, because those peoples were supposed to eat human flesh. As Las Casas reports, "The Admiral says that he did not believe them, but rather [he believed] that those of the island of Bohío must be more clever and possess greater ingenuity to capture them than they themselves possessed, because they were very faint of heart [*flacos de corazón*]"—meaning, of course, "timid" or "cowardly."[72] Underlying Columbus's temporary incredulity was the notion that as one traveled farther south, one was bound to find ever more "ingenious" peoples, in the case of the alleged man-eaters, "shrewder"—but also ever more "cowardly" peoples, whose greater cowardice compelled them to perpetrate acts of abject cruelty, in this case, feeding on the flesh of those they captured in their raids.

Two weeks later, now tugging along Hispaniola's northern coast, Columbus was ready to plainly articulate the geopolitical paradox of empire (16 December 1492):

> May Your Highnesses believe that these lands are so greatly good and fertile, and especially those of this island of Hispaniola, that no one can put it into words, and no one will believe it who has not witnessed it. And may You believe that this island and all the others are just as yours as is Castile, for nothing is lacking except settling in, and ordering [the Indians] to do whatever You wish. For I, with these people I bring with me, who are not very many, could make run of all these islands without resistance, because I have already seen three of these mariners step ashore to find a multitude of Indians who all fled, without [our] wanting to harm them. They have no weapons, and they are all naked, and possess no knowledge of weaponry, and they are so very cowardly, that a thousand would not stand to three [of us]. And so, they are fit to be ordered about and to make them work, plant, and do everything else that may be needed, and build towns and be taught to go about clothed and follow our customs.[73]

While Columbus did not cease to marvel at the fact that Hispaniola seemed even cooler than the Bahamas and Cuba, in part because of geographical accidents like mountains that counteracted the heat, the islanders of Hispaniola appeared to him to be more ingenious and more docile than those he had encountered before—an impression that was clearly linked in his mind to his southing farther and farther into the hotter latitudes of the globe. Describing an Indian's talent at bartering with Columbus's crew, Columbus is supposed to have remarked, in Las Casas's paraphrase, that "all these things and the way they carry themselves and their customs and tameness and counsel show them to be more alert and shrewd than others he had found until then."[74] Indeed, in Columbus's mind, while this place exhibited a temperateness, fertility, and habitability that contradicted what the theory of the five zones had claimed about the belt of the tropics, the Indians seemed to exhibit the ingenuity and cowardice that had long been ascribed to the naturally inferior peoples of the tropics.

Examples abound in Columbus's writing—from the *Diario* itself to the letters on the second voyage recently discovered as part of the so-called *Libro copiador* and Columbus's well-known accounts of the third and fourth voyages—of the great "ingenuity" and "cowardice" of Indians. And such ethnographic testimony did not obey the idiosyncrasies of a fickle or delusional mind, as scholars sometimes like to claim about the Discoverer. Rather, this testimony obeyed a complex knowledge system that had for nearly two millennia drawn an indelible connection between latitude, temperature, and the nature of places. So steadfast was the association in Columbus's mind between place and the nature of peoples that it misled him eventually to spawn a most peculiar conception about the shape of the globe, as we read in the memorable *carta-relación* of the third voyage (30 May–31 August 1498) (**fig. I.8**, pp. 30–31). On this voyage Columbus aimed for the equator in search of the hypothetical lands and a continent that Fernando and Isabel had previously urged him to seek "in the part of the sun." Columbus no doubt expected to travel so far to the south into the torrid zone that, if he were to strike land in the Atlantic, he might come across "great and valuable things like precious stones and gold and spices and medicines," those coveted commodities that the cosmographer and gemologist Jaume Ferrer de Blanes had promised Columbus would find in "the very hot regions whose inhabitants [were] black."[75] From the Cape Verde Islands, Columbus dipped to a latitude he read at 5° N, which he thought was also the latitude of Sierra Leone in Guinea. He could not have hoped for greater heat toward the equator, for once he reached what he thought was the proper latitude, the dreadfully calm furnace of the Doldrums in mid-Atlantic visited such heat on the armada that Columbus came to think that his vessel and crew were about to "burst into flames, for it came all at once, so unpredictable, that there was no one who dared go below deck to tend to the water and provisions."[76] Thankfully for the fleet, the winds picked up again a week later, and Columbus proceeded to sail along the same parallel, not daring to test his fortune by sailing farther south, "because I found very great change in the heaven and stars, but I found no change in the temperature."

Continuing to suffer braising temperatures, Columbus now hoped against hope that once he reached the approximate longitude he had crossed on his first voyage 100 leagues due west of the Azores, the fleet might once again strike the same sublime temperateness he had tended to experience throughout the Indies. Indeed the heat soon did subside for no apparent reason, and Columbus continued along what he thought was the parallel of Sierra Leone until, realizing that they were running short of drinking water, he decided to make for the islands of the Caníbales, the equivocal name he had by now coined for the alleged man-eaters of the Caribbean. Columbus's armada almost immediately came within sight of the island he named Trinidad, at the mouth of today's Orinoco River delta.

On Trinidad, just across from the mainland he first called Tierra de Graçia, or Land of Grace, Columbus found not just a temperate and exuberant landscape, but also a squadron of young men "of beautiful disposition, and *not black, but rather whiter than others I have seen in the Indies,* and of very handsome countenance and beautiful bodies, and their hair long and lank, cut in the manner of Castile" (**fig. I.9**, pp. 32–33).[77] In fact, Columbus was bound to find that all the people he had come across in the course of his exploration of the Gulf of Paria were "of beautiful stature, of tall bodies and of very beautiful countenances, their hair very long and plain. . . . The color of these people is whiter than others I have seen in the Indies."[78] Indeed, Columbus seemed rather shocked—most likely, he was dismayed—not to have found "Ethiopians" in the southernmost reaches of his Indies. Even though he had southed his way across the Atlantic almost to the very equator, and even though he had found "infinite land that is to the south," the Discoverer had failed to find either the heat or the blackness of skin that Jaume Ferrer had urged him to seek for the purpose of harvesting the trove of goods that places like India, Arabia, and Ethiopia were supposed to generate. Ferrer had written his exhortation to Columbus at Fernando and Isabel's insistence three years earlier, in 1495, as Columbus fought to maintain control of Hispaniola's increasingly discontent colonists and as he struggled in vain to make good on the promise to deliver the fabulous booty of the Indies to Castile. Now, an increasingly discredited Columbus, who feared that he might never find the precious booty that was turning Portugal into a powerful seaborne empire—black slaves, gold, ivory, and spices—must have felt under considerable pressure to explain why he had failed to find heat or blackness near the equator. As we saw before when we discussed Columbus's remarkable postils and commentary to d'Ailly's "De quantitate terre habitabilis," it is in the very *carta-relación* of the third voyage that Columbus found himself attempting to justify his intuition that the waters of the Orinoco River flowed from "infinite land that is to the south." Now, the very same Columbus who had once staked out his enterprise on the claim that the torrid zone was not the hot, infertile, and uninhabitable place predicted by the theory of the five zones, was also poised to argue—in the interest of excusing his failure to find heat, blackness, and the "precious" bounty of torrid latitudes—that the temperateness,

Notes

Introduction: Why Columbus Sailed South to the Indies

1. Thus reads the controversial prologue to Columbus's *Diario* (some scholars have called it a cover letter), which reminds Fernando of Aragon and Isabel of Castile that they had ordered Columbus not to travel "by land to the East, by which way it is customary to go, but by way of the West, by which way we know not for certain that anyone has passed." See Pérez de Tudela y Bueso et al. 1994, 1:109. All translations from this collection of Columbiana are mine. In the case of Columbus's *Diario* (ibid., 1:108–245), I have frequently relied on the superb English translation by Dunn and Kelley 1989. For Columbus's most famous letters, including the letter to Luis de Santángel announcing the discovery (15 February 1493), I have consulted the translations by Cecil Jane (1930–1933/1988).

2. In the words of one eminent twentieth-century scholar, Emiliano Jos, the Discoverer bolstered his conviction that the ocean could be forded "by supposing the length of the earth's circumference to be smaller than it was, and by according the solid mass a greater number of degrees along the globe's parallels than it had" (1979–1980, 37). All translations from Jos are my own.

3. Anghiera, *De orbe nouo* 1.1, 1.2, and 1.6 (1530, iiir, vr, and xxiir, resp.). All translations from this work are my own.

4. Bernáldez 1870; Pérez de Oliva 1965; Fernández de Oviedo y Valdés 1535; F. Columbus 1571/1992; López de Gómara 1552/1992; Las Casas 1994; and Herrera y Tordesillas 1600–1615/1991. An invaluable assessment of these sources on the discovery appears in Ballesteros Beretta's erudite biography of Columbus (1945, 1:1–88).

5. Fernández de Enciso 1519, aiiiiv; Cortés y Albacar 1551/1998, xxv–xxiir; García de Palacio 1587/1998, 11v; Syria 1602/1998, 18–21; and Nájera 1628/1998, 4v.

6. For Columbus's sailing directions from Cádiz to the Canaries, see entry for 3 August 1492 in Pérez de Tudela y Bueso et al. 1994, 1:110. The account by Samuel Eliot Morison and the maps provided by Erwin Raisz for Morison's book, *Admiral of the Ocean Sea: A Life of Christopher Columbus* (1942), are still often considered the best approximations we have of Columbus's routes. I rely on this standard work in my use of modern nomenclature and in my reference to Columbus's routes by modern standards. For a recent reconstruction of Columbus's itineraries on land and on water, see Varela Marcos and León Guerrero 2002 and 2003. For recent attempts to revise standard accounts of Columbus's routes, see, for instance, Coín Cuenca 2003. A most lucid analysis of Columbus real and imagined routes appears in Cerezo Martínez 1994, 71–79 and 120–126.

7. Anghiera, *De orbe nouo* 1.1 (1530, iiir).

8. All modern-day latitudes in the present book are taken from the *Oxford Atlas of the World*, 11th ed., 2003.

9. Taviani 1985a, 69; 1996, 1:104.

10. For this royal prohibition to Columbus, see Pérez de Tudela y Bueso et al. 1994, 1:87–88.

11. Morison 1945, 1:207.

12. Coín Cuenca's study of Columbus's transatlantic route on the first voyage goes so far as to contend that Columbus concealed in his *Diario* the fact that he was descending to the approximate latitude of the Cape Verde Islands (19° N) in search of lands about whose existence he had previous intuition or information (2003, 69–79). This study, however, should be treated with extreme caution, in view of its misrepresentation of crucial sources like Anghiera 1530, Bernáldez 1870, and particularly Fernández de Oviedo y Valdés 1535.

13. Pérez de Tudela y Bueso et al. 1994, 1:119–120. Wry disagreement exists concerning the site of the landfall originally identified as Watling Island by the eighteenth-century official historian Juan Bautista Muñoz in his unfinished *Historia del Nuevo Mundo* (1793/1973). A general account of this long-standing debate can be found in Taviani, who subscribes to the thesis that San Salvador is Watling Island (1996, 2:175–215). A skeptical but intelligent treatment of this and other theses that all too readily rely on the extant summary copy of the *Diario* for identifying the modern site of the

landfall appears in Henige 1992, 157–286. For a guide to the literature published on this subject until just before the last quincentenary celebration of the discovery, see Provost 1991.

14. Entry for 13 October 1492 in Pérez de Tudela y Bueso et al. 1994, 1:123.

15. This point has been kindly urged on me by Felipe Fernández-Armesto.

16. Pérez de Oliva 1965, 41 and López de Gómara 1552/1979, 28–29.

17. Columbus measured the latitude for Puerto Gibara twice, on 30 October and 2 November 1492. Another measurement off the coast of Cuba resulted in the same figure of 42° N in the *Diario*'s entry for 21 November. Columbus also measured the latitude of Moustique Bay on 13 December of that year. For these four entries, see Pérez de Tudela y Bueso et al. 1994, 1:138, 141, 152, and 174, resp. That the *Diario* might have been altered in court to keep possible spies in the dark, is suggested by Queen Isabel's letter to Columbus of 5 September 1493, on the eve of his second voyage, mentioning the delivery of a transcript of the original *Diario* to its author that had been drafted in secret and, as the queen explains, "in two handwritings" (*de dos letras*). See Pérez de Tudela y Bueso et al. 1994, 1:483–484. The most compelling technical explanation to date for the erroneous latitudes registered by the *Diario* has been forwarded by Laguardia Trías 1963 and 1974.

18. Pérez de Tudela y Bueso et al. 1994, 1:254–255.

19. Ibid., 1:523–538.

20. For an attentive analysis of the map attributed to Juan de la Cosa, see Cerezo Martínez 1994, 88–118.

21. Pérez de Tudela y Bueso et al. 1994, 1:489.

22. Fernández de Oviedo y Valdés, *La historia general y natural de las Indias* 2.9 (1535, 12v–13v).

23. Ibid. 2.8 (11v). All translations from this work are my own.

24. Pérez de Tudela y Bueso et al. 1994, 1:619–625.

25. Ibid., 2:721–746; this quote, 730.

26. Ibid., 1:726.

27. See his *carta-relación* of the third voyage in ibid., 2:1093–1119; this quote, 1096.

28. Ibid., 2:1097.

29. Ibid., 2:1097–1098. For the course he steered at this point, "north by northwest" (*al norte, cuarta del nordeste*), see Las Casas *Historia de las Indias* 1.5.4.131 (1994, 2:1040).

30. Ibid., 1.5.4.131 (2:1041). All translations from Las Casas's *Historia* are my own.

31. Columbus assigned 24° to the distances of the tropics of Cancer and Capricorn from the equator. For instance, in his *carta-relación* of the fourth voyage (7 July 1503), he reminds us that during his exploration of southwestern Cuba on the second voyage he had followed the twenty-fourth parallel to the west. (As we have seen, the *carta-relación* of the second voyage has already referred to the parallel he was tracing as that of *Cancro*.) In his letter of the fourth voyage, Columbus also refers to

Marinos of Tyre's estimate in Ptolemy's second-century *Geography* that the inhabited world extended south all the way to the Tropic of Capricorn, explaining that Marinos had placed the southern limit of Ethiopia in sub-Saharan Africa "at more than twenty-four degrees" south of the equator (*más de 24 grados*). See Pérez de Tudela y Bueso et al. 1994, 3:1519–1545; this quote, 1524. This is also the figure assigned to either tropic in the geographical sketches drawn by Alessandro Zorzi in his *Informazione di Bartolomeo Columbus della Navegazione di ponente et di garbin di Beragua nel Mondo Novo* [about 1506], apparently following Columbus and his brother Bartholomew's own view of the lands explored by Columbus since 1492.

32. Colón 1992, 382; my translation. I here follow Varela's paleographic interpretation of *[. . .]es* as *q'es*, meaning, "that is": *tierra infinita q'es al austro*. Pérez de Tudela y Bueso et al. 1994, 2:1116 interprets *[. . .]es* as *pues*, which would render instead "infinite land, because to the south of it no one has ever taken notice" (*tierra infinita: pues al austro dela qual / fasta agora no se a avido notiçia*). This rendition incorrectly implies that this "infinite land" had been previously discovered by Europeans, and that no one knew what lay south of it, which, given that Columbus is the first European known to have surveyed the coast of South America, is simply not what he means. Varela's interpretation, on the other hand, correctly interprets Columbus's "infinite land" as a continent extending toward the southern hemisphere. For Ferdinand's and Las Casas's versions of this entry in Columbus's log for the third voyage, see F. Columbus, *Historie del S. D. Fernando Colombo* 71 (1571/1992, 161v–163r); and Las Casas, *Historia* 1.5.4.138 (1994, 2:1068–1072). A crucial qualification of Columbus's claim that he had reached the outskirts of Eden on his third voyage appears in Scafi's long-awaited history of the cartography of Paradise in the Western tradition (2006, 240–242).

33. Pérez de Tudela y Bueso et al. 1994, 2:1229–1239; this quote, 1230.

34. Ibid., 3:1438–1440; this quote, 1438.

35. Morison 1942, 2:380; Taviani 1991, 1:251.

36. Pérez de Tudela y Bueso et al. 1994, 3:1519–1545; this quote, 1523.

37. López de Gómara 1552/1979, 19. All translations from this work are my own.

38. See Pérez de Tudela y Bueso et al. 1994, 3:1391, a declaration Columbus wrote some time between 1501–1502, reasserting the rights and privileges that he was trying to persuade the Crown to restore to him.

39. For syntheses of these factors, see the nautical biography of Columbus by Morison 1945, 1:203–219 and 264–267; see also Taviani 1991, 1:12–18 and 2:36–38.

40. Taviani 1990, 139–144.

41. Morison 1942, 1:207. As we shall see, early testimony of the plan Columbus had presented to King Dom João II during his years in Portugal, speaks about "Çipango and other terrae incognitae" as Columbus's targets.

42. Pérez de Tudela y Bueso et al. 1994, 1:152.

43. Las Casas, *Historia* 1.5.4.131 (1994, 2:1038).

44. Pérez de Tudela y Bueso et al. 1994, 3:1527; emphasis added.

45. Fernández de Navarrete 1825, 2:103–105.

46. Pérez de Tudela y Bueso et al. 1994, 2:835.

47. Ferrer's treatise was part of a commentary on Dante's *Divina commedia* which was later included in a compilation of his works (Ferrer de Blanes 1545/1922–1925, Dr ff.).

48. Pérez de Tudela y Bueso et al. 1994, 2:832.

49. Ibid., 2:1096. Oddly enough, Harrisse 1871 and Lollis 1892/1969, both of whom emphasize the influence of Toscanelli on Columbus and the object of reaching Magnokhanic Asia, pay little attention to Columbus's southing and do not mention Ferrer at all.

50. See Irving 1828, 2:151–153; and Taviani 1991, 1:180–192 and 2:218–236. Taviani's account of the origins of the discovery, *Cristoforo Colombo: La genesi della grande scoperta* (1974; English trans. 1985a), along with *I viaggi di Colombo: La grande scoperta* (1984; English trans. 1991), have been most recently revised to appear as a single work titled *Cristoforo Colombo* (1996). However, except for information expressly excerpted from this latest Italian edition, I use the available English translations of the earlier two works (1985a and 1991, resp.).

51. See note to Doc. 311 Pérez de Tudela y Bueso et al. 1994, 2:833.

52. Jos 1979–1980, 70.

53. An indispensable guide to the vast bibliography on Columbus is Provost 1991. I followed Provost's lead in consulting the following works on Columbus's navigation and, more specifically, on his measurement of latitudes: Bertelli 1892; D'Albertis 1893; Desimoni 1894; Young 1906; Dunraven 1912; Charcot 1928; Magnaghi 1928 and 1930; Williamson 1930; Fontoura da Costa 1934/1960; Nunn 1937; McElroy 1941; Morison 1942; Rey Pastor 1945; Laguardia Trías 1963, 1974, and 1992; García Frías 1974; Rogers 1976; 1985a, 1991, and 1996; Kelley 1987 and 1998; Charlier 1988; Cerezo Martínez 1994; Varela Marcos and León Guerrero 2002; and Coín Cuenca 2003, among others.

54. Fernández de Oviedo y Valdés, *La historia general y natural de las Indias* 2.4 (1535, iiiiv); Morison 1942, 1:240–263.

55. Humboldt 1836–1839, 3:20–25; my translation.

56. See Vignaud 1902, 1905, and 1911; Ulloa 1928; Carbia 1930/1936; Jane 1930–1933/1988; Manzano Manzano 1976; and Pérez de Tudela y Bueso 1983 and 1994.

57. Fernández de Oviedo y Valdés, *La historia general y natural de las Indias* 2.2 (1535, iiv–iiir).

58. Vignaud 1911, 1:176 and 2:174–175. All translations from Vignaud are my own.

59. Jane 1930–1933/1988, 1:xcix–cxxii.

60. As Jane asserts, "The more the real nature of his opinions is considered, indeed, the less probable does it appear to be that they can have had any scientific basis, the less probable does it appear to be that Columbus was possessed of even a tithe of the scientific knowledge with which he is credited by his son and to the possession of which he himself laid claim" (Jane 1930–1933/1988, 1:lxix).

61. Pérez de Tudela y Bueso et al. 1994, 2:1281–1285; this quote, 1282.

62. Strabo, *Geography* 2.1.35 (1917–1932).

63. Averroës 1562/1962, 435v L. All translations from Averroës are my own. Averroës owes this claim in part to Aristotle's horizontal division of the globe into hot, cold, and temperate zones in *Meteorologica* II, 5 (1995c).

64. Ptolemy's *Geography* 1.9 (Berggren and Jones 2000, 69).

65. See Las Casas's *Brevissima relaçion dela destruyçion delas yndias* (1552b).

66. Taviani 1991, 1:59–67 and 2:89–93.

67. Ailly and Gerson 1480–1483/1990, 13v. All translations from this work are my own, in consultation with the Spanish translation by Antonio Ramírez de Verger. In the particular case of d'Ailly's *Ymago mundi* (1410), I have also consulted the French translation by Edmond Buron (1930).

68. See Virgil, *Georgics* 1.321–329 (1981); Ovid, *Metamorphoses* 1.45–51 (1991); Mela, *Description of the World* 1.3 (1998); Pliny, *Natural History* 2.68 (1938–1963); and Lucan, *La guerre civile* 9.852–874 (1998). But perhaps the most detailed and influential source in this regard would be Macrobius, *Commentary on the Dream of Scipio* 2.5–9 (1990).

69. Pérez de Tudela y Bueso 1994, 2:853–869; this quote, 863.

70. Waldseemüller 1507/1907, 47.

71. Translation by Robert Mac Donald. For a superb analysis of this map, and of the process by which Waldseemüller and his colleagues came to introduce the name America, see Johnson 2006.

72. Fernández de Enciso 1519, aiiiiv. All translations from this work are my own.

73. Anghiera, *De orbe nouo* 8.10 (1530, cxviir).

74. López de Gómara 1552/1979, 14.

75. Herrera y Tordesillas 1600–1615/1991, 1:264; my translation.

76. For indispensable treatments of the concept of invention in connection with the discovery, see O'Gorman's classical work 1958/1977; Rabasa 1993; and Padrón 2004, 1–44.

77. See, for instance, crucial works like Arnold 1996 and Stepan 2001.

78. Las Casas 1992; Acosta 1590/1998; and Vega 1609.

79. Cañizares Esguerra 1999.

80. Bolívar 1815/1976; Bello 1826.

1 *Machina Mundi*

1. For a provisional definition of colonialism, see Osterhammel 1997, 16–17: "A relationship of domination between an indigenous (or forcibly imported) majority and a minority of foreign invaders. The fundamental decisions affecting the lives of the colonized people are made and implemented by the colonial rulers in pursuit of interests that are often defined in a distant metropolis. Rejecting cultural compromises with the colonized population, the colonizers are convinced of their own superiority and of their ordained mandate to rule." Colonialism, as Osterhammel explains, "is not only a relationship that can be described in structural terms, but also a particular *interpretation* of this relationship" (16). The present book considers the broad intellectual framework that gave shape to this modality of empire in the earliest years of Spain's occupation of the Americas.

2. Wagner and Parish 1967 remains a reliable biography of Las Casas. See also the synthetic biography by Parish 1992 and her collaborative work on Las Casas's residency in Mexico, Parish and Weidman 1992. Extensive and painstaking documentation on Las Casas's life and works is to be found in Pérez Fernández 1981, 1984, and 1994. An indispensable assessment of the range of Las Casas's activities and learning can be found in Adorno 1992.

3. Las Casas's status as Columbus's "editor" must be qualified: only a handful of originals by Columbus is preserved (Varela 1992, 80–83). A significant share of Columbus's writings is known to us only through Las Casas, who fully or partially cited or paraphrased them along with a vast array of other sources (Varela 1988, 29–30). The summary copy of the *Diario* was made in preparation for the writing of *Historia de las Indias,* along with a copy of a *carta-relación* of the third voyage (1498–1500), which, until the discovery in 1985 of a collection of letters known as Columbus's *Libro copiador,* remained the only extant version of this letter (Gil 1992a, 76–79; see Doc. 6 in Rumeu de Armas 1989, 1:343–373). Independent versions of Columbus's letters attest to Las Casas's accuracy as an amanuensis (Varela 1988, 29–37). The extent to which Las Casas may have altered the original contents of the *Diario* itself, however, has been fiercely debated by Americanists: one influential thesis maintains that Las Casas merely copied, corrected, and added interpolations to an already altered copy rendered by a Crown amanuensis (Rumeu de Armas 1976; 1973, 127–133). Against this view, another thesis contends that while Las Casas handled his sources meticulously he himself copied and summarized a complete copy of the original. The passages Las Casas transcribed literally would have been those he considered fundamental to his own arguments in *Historia de las Indias* (Pérez Fernández 1994, 203–213). Other theses deem Las Casas's mediation of the *Diario* far more intrusive: while Columbus might be considered the author

of the quoted passages, the alterations suffered by the original, particularly in the hands of Las Casas, warrant treating the *Diario* as a composite document and Las Casas as one of its "authors" (Henige and Zamora 1989; Henige 1991, 11–30 and 54–64). On the far end of this debate, it has been argued that Las Casas intentionally altered the contents of the original log to reflect his own views of the discovery as an event of primarily theological significance (Zamora 1993, 21–94). An important critique of Henige's and Henige and Zamora's views appears in Hulme 1993. The present book assumes a double perspective of the *Diario*—both in line with other documents more directly attributable to Columbus and in line with the argument of Las Casas's *Historia de las Indias*. On the subject of Las Casas as a source on Columbus's life, see Ballesteros Beretta, whose richly documented biography of Columbus considers Las Casas's *Historia de las Indias* "the most abundant and detailed source on the Columbian era" (1945, 1:34–55; this quote, 50; all translations from Ballesteros Beretta are my own); as well as Wagner and Parish's indispensable biography of Las Casas (1967, 195–208). On the subject of Las Casas's extensive documentation in *Historia de las Indias*, the fullest treatment to date is Pérez Fernández 1994, 3:185–269.

4. Las Casas's summary copy of the *Diario* and the manuscript of *Historia de las Indias* are preserved at the Biblioteca Nacional de Madrid (MS Vitrina 6–7 and MS res. 21, 22, 23, resp.). D'Ailly's *Ymago mundi* (1410) survives as part of d'Ailly's and Gerson's annotated *Tractatus* in the Biblioteca Capitular y Colombina de la Catedral de Sevilla (GG-178-21).

5. For an extensive catalogue of authors and works directly or indirectly known to Columbus, see West and Kling 1991, 7–40. For indispensable treatments of Columbus's scientific and technical sources, including succinct descriptions of the works Columbus owned or knew most directly, see Contreras 1979 and 1992. See also Flint's synthesis of Columbus's intellectual formation, which includes a rich consideration of Columbus's marginalia to the works he owned (1992, 42–77); and Gil 1989, 21–223, although the author insists—against a rather broad consensus—that d'Ailly's and Gerson's *Tractatus* and other works annotated by Columbus were not purchased until 1497, when Columbus saw the need to arm himself with authoritative works to fend off his project's detractors.

6. The Biblioteca Capitular y Colombina holds two other works heavily annotated by Columbus: the geography by Aeneas Sylvius Piccolomini (Pope Pius II), *Historia rerum ubique gestarum* (Cologne, 1477), which along with *Tractatus de ymagine mundi* appears to contain the earliest postils (Contreras 1992, 166); and Francesco Pipino's abridged Latin translation of Marco Polo's *Il milione: De consuetudinibus et condicionibus orientalium regionum* (Antwerp, 1485), which Columbus did not purchase until 1497 (Vigneras 1957). Other incunabula in this library that Simón de la Rosa y López 1891 identified as Columbus's are the following: Christophoro Landino's Italian translation of Pliny the Elder's major work, *Historia naturale* (Venice, 1489); Abraham Zacutus's 1473 *Almanach perpetuum* (Leiria, 1496); Alfonso de Palencia's Spanish translation of Plutarch's *Parallel Lives* (*Vidas*

de los ilustres varones, Seville, 1491); a manuscript of the anonymous fifteenth-century *Concordiae Bibliae Cardinalis;* a work dubiously attributed to Albertus Magnus, *Philosophia naturalis* or *Philosophia pauperum* (Venice, 1496); St. Anthony of Florence's *Sumula confessionis* (Venice, 1476); and a fifteenth-century palimpsest of Seneca's *Tragedies.* Both Pliny's *Historia* and Plutarch's *Vidas* contain scant marginalia by Columbus. The works held at the Biblioteca Capitular y Colombina also include the celebrated manuscript of his *Libro de las profecías* (dated 1504), which is a compilation of scriptural passages that Columbus believed to prefigure his discovery. Finally, Columbus's "library" includes an annotated copy of Claudius Ptolemy's *Cosmographia* (Rome, 1478), which is held at the Biblioteca de la Real Academia de la Historia. For the description and history of this incunabulum, see Contreras 1992, 139–145.

7. The claim that d'Ailly and other authors played no part in the genesis of the discovery was championed by Vignaud 1905, 297–299, who revived the legend of the anonymous pilot printed in 1535 by Gonzalo Fernández de Oviedo in *La historia general y natural de las Indias* 2.2 (1535, iiv–iiir). According to this legend, the pilot from a ship carried across the ocean by a storm had confided to Columbus that he had found inhabited lands to the West. Vignaud's claim about d'Ailly was subsidiary to Vignaud's general thesis that Columbus's goal was not Asia, but the lands discovered by his pilot friend. For an outline of this famous thesis, see Vignaud 1911, 2:483–485. For an early reply to Vignaud, see Salembier 1914. Much of the ensuing debate over d'Ailly's role has concerned the dating of Columbus's postils. A forceful refutation of Vignaud's claim was issued by d'Ailly's most distinguished modern editor, Buron 1930, 1:16–37, though his own dating of Columbus's postils to as early as 1481 was later shown to be hasty. Caraci 1971 assigns 1491 as the latest possible date for Columbus's reading of d'Ailly on the basis of postil 621 to *De correctione kalendarii,* which reads "in this year 1491" (*hoc anno 1491*) (see also Watts 1985, 85–86). Manzano Manzano—a recent advocate of the thesis of the "anonymous pilot"—nonetheless assigns d'Ailly a significant role in the planning stages of the discovery (1976, 177–178), while Pérez de Tudela y Bueso, whose peculiar formulation of a pre-discovery traces Columbus's project to a fancied encounter between a Portuguese ship and a canoe carrying a party of Antillean women, denies Columbus's readings any significant role in the conception of his enterprise (1983, 11–14; 1994, lxxx–lxxxiii). (A shrewd assessment of Manzano Manzano's and Pérez de Tudela y Bueso's theses appears in Larner 1988, 9–19.) The rather standard view that Columbus resorted to d'Ailly and other authors during his years in Castile (1485–1492), after he had first envisioned finding land in the high Atlantic but before he launched his first voyage, appears in Morison 1942, 1:120–125; Manzano Manzano 1964, 84–87; and Taviani 1985a, 174–179, 1985b, and 1985c. However, dust never settles for long on any matter concerning Columbus. See, for instance, Gil's claim that Columbus remained unfamiliar with d'Ailly until 1497 (1989, 123–126; restated in 1992b, ix). Gil's claim is based on a letter

from Bristol merchant John Day to Columbus accusing shipment of a copy of Marco Polo's work (Vigneras 1957, 226–228). Gil takes this letter to be compelling evidence that the extant copy of d'Ailly's work was included in this shipment. Gil's thesis is reiterated in Comellas's version of the genesis of the discovery (1991, 102–117).

8. See Mandonnet 1893a and 1893b. Years after the discovery, Columbus acquired a copy of Albertus's *Philosophia naturalis* (Venice, 1496)—an epitome, probably spurious, of Albertus's commentaries to Aristotle's *Physica, De caelo, De generatione et corruptione, Meteorologica,* and *De anima* (Rosa y López 1891, 20). Columbus's copy of the *Philosophia,* which Albertus scholars have in the past misidentified as *De natura loci* (Bergevin 1992, 92; Tilmann 1971, 8; and Schneider 1932, 65–67), is barely mentioned in key studies of Columbus's sources (West and Kling 1991, 25; Contreras 1992, 136–137; and Flint 1992, 199).

9. For Ferdinand's and Las Casas's versions of the intellectual origins of the discovery, see F. Columbus, *Historie del S. D. Fernando Colombo* 1–15 (1571/1992, 1r–38v), and chaps. 1–14 of Las Casas, *Historia* 1.1.1.1–1.1.5.14 (1994, 1:353–410), resp. For Benjamin Keen's English translation of Ferdinand's biography of his father, see F. Columbus 1992.

10. F. Columbus claimed, for instance, that his father had studied at the University of Pavia (*Historie* 3 [1571/1992, 7v]). Regarding this famous blunder, see Morison 1942, 1:17–18. For more detailed considerations of this aspect of Columbus's life, see Ballesteros Beretta 1945, 1:207–215; and Taviani 1985a, 45 and 268–270. The earliest Columbus scholar to have shed doubt on the authorship of the Fernandine *Historie* was Henry Harrisse, who argued (mistakenly) that the *Historie* had been ghostwritten by one of Fernando's close acquaintances, Hernán Pérez de Oliva (Harrisse 1871, 91). Later scholars have variously claimed that the *Historie* was a total or partial forgery by Ulloa, Las Casas, or others. Rumeu de Armas, for instance, attributes Ferdinand's *Historie* 1–15 (except chapter 6) to an "anonymous biographer" whom Las Casas would have failed to recognize as the true author of these chapters on Columbus's early years (1970; in expanded form, 1973, 67–118 and 237–317). For a consideration of Rumeu's claim, as it concerns Las Casas's documentation for his own account of Columbus's early years, see Pérez Fernández 1994, 194–199. On the general history of this debate, see Ballesteros Beretta 1945, 1:65–74; the useful discussion by Taviani and Caraci 1990, 2:23–64, in the Italian edition of Ferdinand's *Historie* recently printed as part of the Nuova Raccolta Colombiana; and the recent synthesis by Marín Martínez 1993, 1:223–238, who suscribes to the moderate thesis that considers Ferdinand's *Historie* to be authentic, despite inaccuracies attributable to him or to intermediaries of the version we know. The best synthesis of the scholarship on this problem is provided by Taviani and Caraci 1990, 2:23–64.

11. On the origins of the misconception that Columbus's belief in the globe's sphericity went against the views of his contemporaries, see Russell 1991; Cormack 1995.

12. A useful recent synthesis of the intellectual genesis of the discovery can be found in West 1992. For the standard treatments of the traditional thesis initiated by Ferdinand, see Morison 1942, 1:76–129; Ballesteros Beretta 1945, 1:307–358, 365–373, and 493–503; Taviani 1985a, 127–185 and 383–455; and Heers 1981, 129–168. Ballesteros Beretta and Taviani contain rich bibliographies and consider central debates regarding Columbus's formulation of his project. Other eminent treatments include Jos 1942 and 1979–1980, 33–50; Manzano Manzano 1976, 177–238, and 1964, 82–96; Cioranescu 1967, 11–57. Though he assigned a minimal role to d'Ailly in the genesis of the discovery, Nunn (1924 and 1937) still offers a useful study of the technical aspects of Columbus's geography. A helpful account of the worldview that anticipated these aspects of Columbus's geography can be found in Simek 1996.

13. D'Ailly is usually cited in strict relation to these fundamentals: see, for instance, Kravath 1987, 160–164; Phillips and Phillips 1992, 79 and 109; Simek 1996, 35–37, 49–51, and 93; Buisseret 1998; and West 1998.

14. See the monumental work on Columbus's messianic thought by Milhou 1983; and the study of Columbus's *Libro de las profecías* by West and Kling 1991. Flint (1992, 3–41 and 149–214) and Zamora (1993, 95–151), building in part on Woodward's indispensable work on medieval *mappaemundi* (1987, 286–370), offer valuable insights into Columbus's sacred cartography. In this connection, see also Sweet 1986; Kadir 1992, 40–61; Rabasa 1993, 49–82; and most recently Watts, who points to the eschatological content of Columbus's geography as part of her argument that religious ideology strongly persisted in Renaissance cartography well beyond the introduction of Ptolemy's *Geography* (Watts 2007, 385–387). While all of these works usefully mention d'Ailly, the works that have most significantly changed our understanding of d'Ailly's legacy to Columbus are Watts 1985, which examines Columbus's prophetic ideology, and Smoller 1994, which has done more to explain the full scope of d'Ailly's thought than any other study since Buron's pioneering work on the subject (1930, 1:91–113).

15. López de Gómara 1552/1979, 28–29.

16. I follow Lang's use of the term Neoplatonism as a set of widely diverse philosophical arguments whose ultimate premise was Plato's concept of the Good or the One (1992, 250n2). In the present book, the term Neoplatonism applies more distinctly to those arguments that posited nature as *efficient* with respect to things that were "by nature" and as second cause or instrument of God (see chapter 4). For a discussion of the varieties of Platonic thought and of its early derivations, see Gersh 1986, 1:1–50. An indispensable source on the reception of Aristotle by his early commentators is the collection of essays edited by Sorajbi 1990. On the varieties of Platonism that preceded the rise of Aristotelianism in the Latin West, see Chenu 1997, 49–98.

17. See Aristotle's definition of nature in the *Physics* 2.1.192b9–23 (1995i). Aristotle provided scholastic writers with the blueprints for discussing place in connection with the nature of existents. I am,

provisionally, following Aristotle's assertion that every physical body "is naturally carried to its appropriate place and rests there, [which] makes the place up or down" (*Physics* 4.4.211a4–5); and his treatment in *On the Heavens* 4.3–5 (1995f) of the tendency of the four elements—earth, water, air, and fire—to be moved by virtue of their heaviness or lightness to their proper places toward or away from the center of the spherical cosmos.

18. See Albertus Magnus, *De natura loci* 1.1 (1980b, 2, lines 71–74): "Every productive and operative power comes from heaven." All translations from *De natura loci* are my own, in consultation with Tilmann 1971. This power did not come directly from the periphery of the cosmos but through intermediate bodies that successively acted as locating bodies, or places, for others. Necessary treatments of the contradictions between Aristotle's physics and the views of the Neoplatonists can be found in Lemay's study of Albumasar's astrological *Introductorium in astronomiam* (1962, esp. 41–132) and in Lang's analysis of the manner in which medieval writers altered crucial aspects of Aristotle's physics (1992, esp. 97–160). The paradoxes incurred by Albertus in *De natura loci* have been kindly suggested to me by Lang.

19. The pervasive emplacement of physical creatures in the spherical cosmos was by no means new to early Christian commentators of Aristotle's natural works such as Albertus. The medieval concept of the *scala naturae*—principally rooted in Plato, Aristotle, and Plotinus—had already reached the Christian West in the works of church authors like Saint Augustine or the fifth-century Pseudo-Dionysius the Areopagite as well as in Macrobius's influential synthesis of Neoplatonic doctrine, the fifth-century *Commentarium in somnium Scipionis*. For a general understanding of the concept of the Great Chain of Being as a spatial concept, see Lovejoy 1964, 52–66, 99–103, who offers an implicit discussion of the subject; and Kuntz 1987. For an informative treatment of the concepts of "place" that preceded Aristotle's introduction into the Latin West during the twelfth and thirteenth centuries, see Casey 1997, 3–115, even though the author emphasizes the emergence of the concept of "absolute space" in Western philosophy.

20. This point is strongly illustrated by Lamb in her studies of Spanish cosmography and navigation (1969a, 1985, and 1995b; collected in 1995a); and by Cosgrove 2001, 102–138, in his discussion of the Neoplatonic reception of Ptolemy's *Geography* in the Renaissance. Cognate views are held by Brotton, in his study of the connection between cartographic production and commercial expansion in early modern Europe (1998, 17–45, esp. 19); and by Grafton, Shelford, and Siraisi, who maintain not only that the empirical knowledge facilitated by geographical exploration during the fifteenth century neither immediately nor cleanly displaced the learned context in which geography had long been practiced in Europe, but also that the practical culture of explorers and merchants remained intimately connected with learned (that is, scientific and technical) culture well into the mid-sixteenth century: "Merchants and navigators on the one hand, scholars and philosophers on the

other inhabited much the same cosmos, imagined much the same history, and saw no necessary conflict between the lessons of experience and those of books" (1992, 68). A demonstration of the overlap between geography's "learned" and "practical" contexts in the Renaissance appears in Lamb 1969b, 1974, 1976, 1985, and 1995b (collected in 1995a); as well as in Cormack's case study of the teaching of geography in English universities (1997, 25–26 and 48–89) and in her more recent study of the pedagogical use of maps in the Renaissance (2007). For a study relevant to the question of geography's ties to other disciplines, see Livingstone 1992, which argues forcefully for a geographical historiography attentive to the complex reciprocity between geography and its intellectual and social contexts (see esp. 1–23). With the recently published third volume of the History of Cartography, *Cartography in the European Renaissance* (Woodward 2007b), a loud call is being issued to consider the network of disciplines that reflected the harmony and internal workings of the Aristotelian cosmos as a fundamental link in the development of geographic, more specifically cartographic, knowledge from the later Middle Ages to the Renaissance. Making a case for the need to understand "the social and intellectual frameworks in which maps were produced and used" in the later Middle Ages, Morse underscores that world maps from this period conceptualized the earth itself as part of the system of the world (2007, 30–34; this quote, 30). As Morse argues, "part of the curiosity about the physical world that characterized the twelfth-century Renaissance was the desire to understand the earth as part of a system. The concern among philosophers for the *machina uniuersitatis* or the *machina mundi* led them to focus on the system underlying the universe and the laws that governed it. The details of the earth itself . . . were of less interest to them than the grand mechanism of the world" (31). For his part, Cosgrove shows the persistence of such a connection for the study of geography in Renaissance cosmography's representation of the world-machine (2007, 82–87). For a new and fundamental discussion of the continuities and discontinuities in the transition between late medieval and early modern cartography, see Woodward 2007a.

21. Ferrer Maldonado 1626, 49.

22. My translations.

23. Glacken 1990, 270.

24. Alexander von Humboldt observed that crucial aspects of Columbus's geography were indirectly derived through d'Ailly from Roger Bacon. See Watts 1985, 82; and Humboldt 1836–1839, 1:63–64. Scholars in recent years have shown that d'Ailly's borrowings from Bacon extended well beyond geography and include Bacon's astrology and apocalypticism. See Watts 1985, 86–92; and Smoller 1994, 30–31 and 53–57.

25. For an explanation of Ptolemy's contribution to the field, see Dilke 1987; Berggren and Jones 2000, 3–54.

26. In his dedication to Pope Alexander V, Jacopo insisted on this mistranslation of the Greek original, because the word *cosmos* meant the earth and sky together, and this, argued Jacopo, was the very subject of Ptolemy's *Geography* (see the Bologna edition, 1477). On the multiple uses of the term "cosmography" in the Renaissance, see Cosgrove 2007, 56–61. On the reintroduction of Ptolemy's *Geography* at the turn of the fifteenth century, see Aujac 1998 and Gautier Dalché 2007, esp. 287–295. For a classic account of the *Geography*'s impact in Europe, see Edgerton 1987, though one should treat with caution the author's implicit view that the mathematical spatiality introduced by Ptolemy's *Geography* stood in competition with medieval cartography's highly ideological spatiality. The related view that Ptolemy's *Geography* revolutionized medieval space by turning it into a "neutral space" mapped by a grid system can be found in works like Crosby 1997, 97–98. These traditional views of the impact and meaning of Ptolemy's *Geography* have been strongly contested by Biddick 1998 and, most particularly, by Gautier Dalché 1999 and 2007. In a finely nuanced discussion of the multiple fates of Ptolemy's *Geography* in the Renaissance, Gautier Dalché most recently argues that the reintroduction of this work to the Latin West should no longer be seen as a single, revolutionary event that would have rescued cartography from the allegedly "non-scientific" ideas of the Middle Ages, or that would have automatically invited Ptolemy's readers to discard the authority of received knowledge in favor of the authority of experience. The author argues instead that Europe's assimilation of the *Geography* was only very gradual; that it "took place in an intellectual and cultural context within which complex and varied motivations were at play" (2007, 285); and that, rather than continue to engage in a discussion of the technical "progress" presumably represented by the "rediscovery" of the *Geography*, we would do better "to describe what was going through the minds of [Renaissance] scholars as they read the work of the Alexandrine geographer; to articulate what they saw as the purpose behind the study of such texts and maps; and finally, to judge whether the results measured up to their expectations" (286). Gautier Dalché amply shows that the multifarious context in which Ptolemy's work was assimilated not only included modes of representing space that were hardly seen as incompatible with Ptolemy's, but also included the reading of his work in relation to multiple areas of knowledge that today might seem irrelevant for the study of cartography. Cosgrove, for his part, has argued that Ptolemy's *Geography* continued for a long time to be placed "at the heart of all learning" (2001, 109). And, pointing to geography's pervasive interdisciplinarity in the early modern period, the author most recently cautions that only by "softening disciplinary boundaries today" can we arrive at "a sympathetic understanding of the achievements and failures of Renaissance cosmography" (2007, 56). Cosgrove has also noted that Jacopo d'Angelo's "linguistic fusion of geographical mapping and cosmography introduced a continuing tension within Renaissance cosmography, apparent in its graphic presentation" (55). Cosgrove would ultimately seem to suggest that it is precisely the

multidisciplinary comprehensiveness admitted to the genre by Jacopo's deliberate mistranslation of Ptolemy's title as *Cosmographia* that helped to bring about a crisis of identity in Renaissance cosmography, especially as more and more information kept being assimilated to the corpus. For stimulating refutations of the alleged "neutrality" of Ptolemaic spatiality, see Mignolo 1995, 219–258; and Padrón 2004, 35–41.

27. A similar view has been put forward recently by Gautier Dalché (2007, 299–301), who shows that d'Ailly meticulously read Ptolemy's *Geography*, comparing its data with information provided by long-established Latin sources. Incidentally, d'Ailly's astrological use of terrestrial coordinates had been common currency among his Arabic and Latin predecessors. On the uses of latitude and longitude in the Middle Ages, see Wright 1923. Cartography's connections to astrology in the late medieval and early modern periods deserve far more attention than they have received. The subject is typically acknowledged but treated gingerly in important studies such as Harley and Woodward 1987, 502–509 ("Concluding Remarks"), esp. 507; and Livingstone 1992, 66–83. A requisite study in this regard is Aujac 1993, 7–191, which argues for the need to understand Ptolemy's *Geography* as part of a cosmological system that ties it to both his astronomical *Almagest* and his astrological *Tetrabiblos*. It should be added that Christian writers had been treated to Ptolemaic geography long before Jacopo d'Angelo's 1406 translation of the *Geography*, both in the *Almagest*—first translated into Latin by Gerard of Cremona in 1175—and, significantly, in the astrological *Tetrabiblos* (or *Quadripartitum*)—translated by Plato of Tivoli in 1138. For the dates of these translations, see Haskins 1924, 15 and 68, resp.). For the explicitly geographical segments in these works, see Ptolemy, *Almagest* 2.6 (1998) and *Tetrabiblos* 2.2–3 (1980).

28. On d'Ailly's life and his role in the schism, see Guenée 1991. On d'Ailly's and his contemporaries' preoccupation with the Antichrist, see Guenée 1991, 130–132; Smoller 1994, 85–101.

29. The immediate source for D'Ailly's historical astrology was Abū Ma'shar's *De magnis coniuntionibus* (Albumasar 1515); see Smoller 1994, 61–84. On the dissemination of conjunctionist explanations for religious and political change in Christian Europe, see Garin 1990, 1–28; and North 1989. Of related interest are Parel's recent work on Machiavelli's philosophy of history (1992, 26–62), and Grafton's study of Cardano's astrology (1999, 38–55 and 127–155).

30. For an excellent survey of environmentalist theories in the Spanish colonial Americas, see Cañizares Esguerra 1999. The author contends that race theory has its prehistory, not in nineteenth-century Europe, but in seventeenth-century Spanish America, with the revision by local elites of European astrology and humoral physiology. For a recent assessment of Las Casas's geopolitics in the *Apologética*, see Padrón 2004, 173–181.

31. Among Las Casas's most controversial moves during his long career as an advocate of Indian rights was the drafting for his bishopric in Mexico of a *confesionario* that instructed priests to deny dying

Spanish colonists final absolution lest they return all property expropriated from Indians under their care. This confessional guide, which was instantly read by Las Casas's enemies in Spain as a challenge to Charles V's titles to his possessions in the Americas, earned Las Casas the charge of "high treason" before the Council of Castile shortly after his last return to Spain in 1547. On this episode in Las Casas's life, see Wagner and Parish 1967, 166–174; Parish 1992, 45–46; and, especially, Parish and Weidman 1992, 57–70. A later version of this confessional guide which Las Casas published without license as *Aqui se contienen unos avisos y reglas para los confessores que oyeren confessiones delos españoles que son o han sido en cargo a los Indios delas Indias del mar Oceano* succinctly illustrates Las Casas's most radical indictment of the conquest: "All deeds performed throughout these Indies—from the arrival of Spaniards in each of its provinces, to the subjection and enslavement of its peoples, along with all means adopted and goals pursued within or near its confines—stand against all natural and civil law, and also against divine law. Consequently, everything done here is unjust, iniquitous, tyrannical, and deserving of all infernal fires." (Las Casas 1552a, avir; my translation). Las Casas was familiar with the different branches of law, especially canon law, which explains the impassioned legalistic jargon of this passage. On Las Casas's knowledge of canon law, see Pennington 1970.

32. Las Casas, *Historia* 1.1.2.2 (1994, 1:358).

33. Las Casas's highly critical accounts of Columbus's role in the introduction of mass slave raids, compulsory tribute, and, ultimately, *repartimientos* or *encomiendas* in the Caribbean, appear in Las Casas, *Historia* 1.4.5.102–105 and 1.5.7.155–161 (1994, 2:918–934 and 2:1136–1165, resp.). On the early history of the *encomienda* in the Caribbean, see Zavala 1973, 13–40.

34. My reading of Columbus's *Diario* coincides with Henige and Zamora 1989, Henige 1991, and Zamora 1993 *only* to the extent that any statement one makes of Columbus's views in the *Diario* must take into account Las Casas's hand in the production of the extant copy of this document. However, in the absence of other recensions of the *Diario*—and given the demonstrated care Las Casas took elsewhere in the handling of his sources—one would be hard-pressed to accept Zamora's contention that Las Casas intentionally altered the contents of the *Diario* (even invented parts of it) to reflect religious views that, Zamora argues, were glaringly absent from Columbus's original plan to navigate west to the Indies (see esp. Zamora 1993, 57).

35. The Latin term *mos,* in its plural form (*mores*), meant "custom" or "set of customs"; that is, the rule or rules of conduct that applied specifically to humans as animals endowed with intellect. The scholastics largely treated the concept of the moral in relation to Aristotle's *Nicomachean Ethics, Economics,* and *Politics.* Partly indebted to this commentary tradition, the "natural" and "moral" histories of the Americas such as Las Casas's own *Apologética*—or the Franciscan Fray Bernardino de Sahagún's *Historia de las cosas de la Nueva España* (completed about 1577) and the Jesuit cleric

Joseph de Acosta's *Historia natural y moral de las Indias* (1590)—deployed the concept comparatively, to refer to those customs by which a given nation was to be distinguished from others. See the prologues to Las Casas (1992, 1:285–286) and Sahagún (1979–1980, 1:1r–3r); and, most particularly, Acosta (1590/1998, 9–12, 300–302), which offers an explicit reflection on the connections between natural and moral philosophy in the context of Acosta's ethnography.

36. It is during the early sixteenth century, and primarily in Spain, that scholasticism came to grapple directly with the questions posed by European colonialism, as is argued by Pagden 1982. Las Casas, who claimed that Columbus had chosen his Spanish surname (Colón) in connection with the Latin term *colonus* (*Historia* 1.1.2.2 [1994, 1:359]), fully and self-consciously articulated in *Historia de las Indias* and the *Apologética* the system of knowledge connecting geography and political theory in the scholastic tradition in order to refute the titles on which Crown apologists had justified Spain's occupation of the Americas. Although we tend to associate "colonialism" with the rise of global capitalism during the fifteenth and sixteenth centuries (see, for instance, Abernethy 2000, 3–63), the preoccupation with extra-territorial rule or occupation was very present in medieval political thought and practice. See, for instance, Phillips's treatment of European expansionism between the eleventh and fifteenth centuries (1998). See also Muldoon 1999 and Pagden 1995, both of whom emphasize the continuities between medieval and modern theorizations of empire. Medieval geography's connections with religious and political expansionism are fruitfully explored in recent essay collections, such as Tomasch and Gilles 1998 and Cohen 2000.

37. See Glacken's classical treatment of nature/culture concepts in the West, although the author tends to draw a distinction between climatic and astrological explanations of polity which the early authors presently considered do not (1990, esp. 254–287 and 429–460).

38. The seed for this model was St. Augustine's account in *De civitate Dei contra paganos* of a single humanity's gradual dispersion following the Great Flood and Babel's destruction. See *City of God* 16.1–11 (1957–1972). On the Noachid tradition in the Middle Ages, see Friedman 1981, 87–107 *passim*. The classic account of this tradition for the sixteenth and seventeenth centuries, particularly as it was brought to bear on European ethnography in the Americas, is Hodgen 1964, 207–294. See also Allen 1963, 113–137, whose work refers to the seventeenth century. A most illuminating analysis of the extension of biblical genealogies to the Americas as a part of the machinery of colonialism can be found most recently in Gliozzi 2000.

39. Parel 1992 offers an instructive case study of this cosmological correlation (26–44).

40. Pliny, *Natural History* 2.80 (1938–1963). On the circulation of Pliny's work in the medieval and early modern periods, see Healy 1999, 380–392. As mentioned above, Columbus himself owned and annotated a copy of Pliny's work (Rosa y López 1891, 15–16). For a description of this copy, see Contreras 1992, 118–120.

41. Pliny, *Natural History* 2.80: "For it is beyond question that the Ethiopians are burnt by the heat of the heavenly body near them, and are born with a scorched appearance, with curly beard and hair, and that in the opposite region of the world the races have white frosty skins, with yellow hair that hangs straight; while the latter are fierce owing to the rigidity of their climate but the former wise because of the mobility of theirs; and their legs themselves prove that with the former the juice is called away into the upper portions of the body by the nature of heat, while with the latter it is driven down to the lower parts by falling moisture; in the latter country dangerous wild beasts are found, in the former a great variety of animals and especially of birds; but in both regions men's stature is high, owing in the former to the pressure of the fires and in the latter to the nourishing effect of the damp; whereas in the middle of the earth, owing to a healthy blending of both elements, there are tracts that are fertile for all sorts of produce, and men are of medium bodily stature, with a marked blending even in the matter of complexion; customs are gentle, senses clear, intellects fertile and able to grasp the whole of nature; and they also have governments which the outer races never have possessed, any more than they have ever been subject to the central races, being quite detached and solitary on account of the savagery of the nature that broods over those regions."

42. Aristotle, *Politics* 7.7.1327b24–34 (1995j): "Those who live in a cold climate and in Europe are full of spirit, but wanting in intelligence and skill; and therefore they retain comparative freedom, but have no political organization, and are incapable of ruling over others. Whereas the natives of Asia are intelligent and inventive, but they are wanting in spirit, and therefore they are always in a state of subjection and slavery. But the Hellenic race, which is situated between them, is likewise intermediate in character, being high-spirited and also intelligent. Hence it continues free, and is the best-governed of any nation, and, if it could be formed into one state, would be able to rule the world."

43. Pagden 1995, 11–28 and 98. An indispensable study of the manner in which Greeks, Romans, and Christians constructed a Eurocentric perspective of the globe can be found in Cosgrove 2001, 29–78.

44. Vitruvius, *On Architecture* 6.1.9–11 (1931–1934).

45. Albertus Magnus, *De natura loci* 2.4 (1980b, 27, lines 70–83). For relevant treatments of this tripartite geography see Tooley 1953, who focuses on the case of Jean Bodin; Friedman 1981, 51–52; Floyd-Wilson 2003, who offers a lucid discussion of its sources and circulation in the Renaissance; and more recently, Isaac 2004, 56–74 and 82–109, who provides a useful account of the classical, Hellenistic, and Roman authors who espoused these or similar views. This tripartite geography enjoyed such wide circulation in Christian Europe that in some works it acquired parodic overtones. Take, for instance, Peter Heylyn's late *Cosmographie* (1657). Heylyn's version imported a popular

translation of Guillaume de Salluste du Bartas's *La sepmaine* (1578), a didactic poem inspired by Moses' account of the Creation:

> O see how full of wonders strange is Nature,
> Sith in each Climate, not alone in stature,
> Strength, colour, hair; but that men differ do
> Both in their humour, and their manners too.
> The Northern man is fair, the Southern foul;
> That's white, this black, that smiles, and / this doth scowl;
> Th' one's blithe and frolick, th' other dull / and froward;
> Th' one's full of courage, th' other a / fearfull coward, &c.

(Heylyn 1657, 17)

46. For my account of this hermeneutic tradition, I am fully indebted to Goldenberg's recent erudite study (2003, esp. 168–177). For another useful discussion of the interface between the curse of Ham and medieval geography, see Friedman 1981, esp. 87–107. An illuminating analysis of the colonialist argument that rendered Amerindians as descendants of Ham can be found in Gliozzi 2000, 101–129.

47. Augustine himself believed, contrary to the pagans, that there was no such thing as natural slavery, but rather that God had, by way of Noah's curse on Ham's progeny, instituted slavery as one of sin's wages. See *City of God* 19.15. All English quotes from the Bible are taken from the Douay-Rheims Version (*Holy Bible* 1971). I have also consulted the Latin Vulgate (*Biblia sacra* 1969).

48. Goldenberg 2003, 131–138.

49. Ibid., 141–177.

50. Ibid., 141–156. On Philo's interpretation for the name Ham, see *Questions and Answers on Genesis, II* 65 (1993, 836).

51. Goldenberg 2003, 47–51. See Philo's *Questions and Answers on Genesis, II* 82 (1993, 840).

52. Goldenberg 2003, 46–47. See Philo's *Allegorical Interpretation, I* 68 (1993, 32).

53. Goldenberg cites this as the first recorded instance in which the curse of Ham was invoked in a Christian West that had just rediscovered "black" Africans, in this instance to justify the Portuguese slave trade (2003, 175). Also, see Sweet's concise account of the development of Iberian attitudes toward sub-Saharan Africans (1997, 159).

54. See Zurara, *Crónica dos feitos notáveis* 12–16 (1978–1981, 1:61–80). See also Las Casas, *Historia* 1.2.2.24 (1994, 1:468); and Las Casas's main Portuguese source, the first "decade" of *Ásia* 1.6 (1552/1932, 25–29), by Crown historian João de Barros. For a general account of the justification

of the slave trade in Portugal, see Saunders 1982, 35–86. Of related interest is Fernández-Armesto 1987, 223–245, which compares European perceptions of blacks, Canarians, and Amerindians.

55. Zurara, *Crónica dos feitos notáveis* 16 (1978–1981, 1:77). All translations from this work are my own. Zurara uses "Caym" (Cain) instead of "Cham" (Ham), a mistake that refers us to what was by then the common practice of associating Ham with the progeny of Cain. See Goldenberg 2003, 178–182, and Friedman 1981, 87–107.

56. Scholastic writers like Albertus and d'Ailly attributed the "theory of the five zones" to Pythagoras (6th century BCE), and to Homer before him. It is the geographer Strabo, our primary source on earlier Greek cartographic developments, who reports that the Stoic Posidonius (about 135–51/50 BCE) ascribed this theory to Parmenides (Strabo, *Geography* 2.2.2 [1917–1932]; for Strabo's crucial exposition of this theory, see *Geography* 2.2.2–2.3.3). Today the theory of the five zones is traced to Parmenides, though some doubt remains as to its origins. See Aujac 1987a, 145 and note 83.

57. Woodward 1987, 299–300. For Macrobius's treatment of this theory, see *Commentary on the Dream of Scipio* 2.5–9 (1990, 200–216). On Macrobius's role in the transmission of Neoplatonism to the Latin West, see Gersh 1986, 2:493–595.

58. This idea is traced to Homer's description of Achilles' shield in the *Iliad* 18.478–608 (1990, 483–487): "And he [Hephaestus] forged the Ocean River's mighty power girdling / round the outmost rim of the welded indestructible shield" (*Iliad* 18.708–709 [1990, 487]). See Aujac 1987a, 131. The most useful early source on this and other aspects of Homeric geography is Strabo, *Geography*, esp. 1.1.3–10.

59. On Eudoxus, see Aujac 1987a, 140; on Eratosthenes, see Aujac 1987c, 155–156; and on Crates, see Aujac 1987b, 162–163.

60. Ailly and Gerson 1480–1483/1990, 11v–12r.

61. Woodward 1987, 353–354. D'Ailly's *mappamundi* combines the division of the globe into five zones with the further division of the known inhabited world in the northern quadrant into seven *climata*. This division dates back to the Hellenistic period (4th to 3rd centuries BCE), and it is implicitly assumed in Ptolemy's treatment of parallels in the *Almagest* (Toomer, introduction to Ptolemy 1998, 1–26, esp. 19; Dilke 1987, 182–183; Ptolemy, *Almagest* 2.6 and 2.12 [1998]). Ptolemy exercised direct influence on the Arab iconography of the seven *climata*, which, significantly, would locate the administrative center of Islam in the central fourth clime (Karamustafa 1992, 76–80). On the characteristics and dating of extant Arab versions of the seven *climata*, see Tibbetts 1992, 146–148.

62. For the representation of Ethiopians during the Greco-Roman period, the classical source is Snowden 1970. See also Romm 1992, 49–60. On the tendency to equate Ethiopians and Indians in Greek and Latin geography, see McCrindle 1926, 1–4; André 1949; Dihle 1962; Friedman 1981, 8;

and Schneider 1997. Two useful sources on ancient and medieval Indography are Wittkower 1942 and Gil 1995.

63. See Homer, *Odyssey* 1.23–24 (1996, 78). This claim is made by Strabo in his critique of Posidonius's interpretation of these Homeric verses (*Geography* 2.3.7–8).

64. Herodotus, *History* 4.44 (1987).

65. Ibid., 3.101.

66. See Strabo, *Geography* 15.1.13 and 15.1.24–26.

67. See Pliny, *Natural History* 6.22: "In the regions south of the Ganges the tribes are browned by the heat of the sun to the extent of being coloured, though not as yet burnt black like the Ethiopians; the nearer they get to the Indus the more colour they display." For Pliny's source, see Mela, *Description of the World* 3.67 (1998). For the Latin version, see Mela 1971, 58.

68. See Arrian, *Anabasis of Alexander* 5.4.4 and *Indica* 6.9 (1973–1983).

69. For Ptolemy's enclosure of the Indian Ocean, see *Cosmographia* 7 (1478, unfoliated, col. 236). For all citations from this edition, I have consulted the original at the John Carter Brown Library, Providence, Rhode Island.

70. See Ptolemy, *Cosmographia* 7 (1478, unfoliated, col. 233).

71. Isidore, *Etimologías* 7.6.17 (1983). All translations from this work are my own.

72. Ibid., 9.2.128.

73. Ailly and Gerson 1480–1483/1990, 17r.

74. See postil 58 in Ailly and Gerson 1480–1483/1990, 17r.

75. See chapter 3 for a consideration of the terms "India" and "Indies" and chapter 7 for a discussion of Columbus's expectation of finding "black" peoples in the Caribbean basin.

76. Pliny, *Natural History* 2.80.189: "We must deal next with the results connected with these heavenly causes." The theory of the five zones precedes this geopolitical division (*Natural History* 2.68.172 ff.).

77. On this point, d'Ailly is following Māshā'allāh's discussion of the division of heavens and earth according to the temperate and the intemperate. See chaps. 3 and 31 of Messahallah 1549 (Biir–v and Diiir–v, resp.).

78. Ailly and Gerson 1480–1483/1990, 16r–v. D'Ailly's partition also appears in *Tractatus eiusdem de concordia discordantium astronomorum,* a treatise included in the Louvain edition of d'Ailly's and Gerson's works. Overlooked by Columbus scholars, this other treatise is of great importance for understanding not only Columbus's (and his brother Bartholomew's) geopolitics, but the workings of the knowledge system behind this geopolitics. See Ailly and Gerson 1480–1483/1990, 151r–151v. For Aristotle's version of this geopolitical model, see note 42 above.

79. On this subject, we can be thankful to Pagden's related studies on the concepts of "natural slavery" and "empire" in sixteenth-century Spain. See Pagden 1982, 27–118; 1995, 29–102. See also Hanke's inaugural work on this subject (1959).

80. See Ailly and Gerson 1480–1483/1990, 16r. The geopolitical model in Ptolemy's *Tetrabiblos* 2.2 (1980) reads thus:

> The demarcation of national characteristics is established in part by entire parallels and angles, through their position relative to the ecliptic and the sun. For while the region which we inhabit is in one of the northern quarters, the people who live under the more southern parallels, that is, those from the equator to the summer tropic [i.e., Tropic of Capricorn], since they have the sun over their heads and are burned by it, have black skins and thick, woolly hair, are contracted in form and shrunken in stature, are sanguine of nature, and in habits are for the most part savage [Gr. *agrioi;* Lat. *siluestres*] because their homes are continually oppressed by heat; we call them by the general name Ethiopians. Not only do we see them in this condition, but we likewise observe that their climate and the animals and plants of their region plainly give evidence of this baking by the sun.
>
> Those who live under the more northern parallels, those, I mean, who have the Bears over their heads, since they are far removed from the zodiac and the heat of the sun, are therefore cooled; but because they have a richer share of moisture, which is most nourishing and is not there exhausted by heat, they are white in complexion, straight-haired, tall and well-nourished, and somewhat cold by nature; these too are savage in their habits because their dwelling-places are continually cold. The wintry character of their climate, the size of their plants, and the wildness of their animals are in accord with these qualities. We call these men, too, by a general name, Scythians.
>
> The inhabitants of the region between the summer tropic and the Bears, however, since the sun is neither directly over their heads nor far distant at its noon-day transits, share in the equable temperature of the air, which varies, to be sure, but has no violent changes from heat to cold. They are therefore medium in colouring, of moderate stature, in nature equable, live close together, and are civilized in their habits. The southernmost of them are in general more shrewd and inventive, and better versed in the knowledge of things divine because their zenith is close to the zodiac and to the planets revolving about it.

For Haly's commentary to Ptolemy's model, see Ptolemy's *Liber quadripartiti Ptholemei,* 1493, 31r.

81. Pliny, *Natural History* 7.2.21.

82. Ibid., 7.2.32.

83. Ptolemy 1493, 31r.

84. Averroës 1562/1962, 438v H–I.

85. Ibid., 440v G–H.

86. See Ailly and Gerson 1480–1483/1990, 13r–v. D'Ailly mentions Aristotle; his commentator Averroës; Seneca (1st century CE); Pliny the Elder; and the apocryphal *4 Esdras* (*Fourth Ezra,* 2nd century BCE). See also Columbus's postils to Ailly and Gerson (23b–g), which cite other authors, including Marinos of Tyre (about 100 CE), known only through Ptolemy's *Geography.* It was from this chapter that the Fernandine *Historie* partly culled a list of authors who would have armed Columbus with the arguments for an oceanic crossing. See F. Columbus, *Historie* 7 (1571/1992, 14r–15v).

87. On this episode in Columbus's life, see Morison 1942, 52–55; Ballesteros Beretta 1945, 1:362–373; Taviani 1985a, 110–120 and 367–374; and Enseñat de Villalonga 1999, 219–228. On the founding of São Jorge da Mina, see Hair 1994. As Gil notes (1992a, 43–51), Columbus's experience in Guinea served as an important reference point for his own descriptions of the Bahamas and Caribbean.

88. The standard definition for "Guinea" provided by the *Encyclopaedia Britannica* 2007 preserves even today the connection between latitude and the complexion of sub-Saharan peoples: "The forest and coastal areas of western Africa between the tropic of Cancer and the equator. Derived from the Berber word *aguinaw,* or *gnawa,* meaning 'black man,' . . . the term was first adopted by the Portuguese and, in forms such as Guinuia, Ginya, Gheneoa, and Ghinea, appears on European maps from the 14th century onward." See *Encyclopaedia Britannica Online,* http://search.eb.com/eb/article-9038432.

89. Pérez de Tudela y Bueso et al. 1994, 1:254–255.

90. F. Columbus, *Historie* 4 (1571/1992, 7v–9v). All translations from this work are my own, in consultation with Ginevra Crosignani and Kristine Haugen.

91. The actual latitude of São Jorge da Mina is 5° 5′ 25″ N (Ballesteros Beretta 1945, 1:372).

92. Postils 16a and b to Ailly and Gerson 1480–1483/1990, 12r. Significantly, these annotations are set apart from most other annotations in *Ymago mundi* by the drawing of a double-frame around them.

93. Postil 234 to Ailly and Gerson 1480–1483/1990, 25r–25v. This postil is also one of the few in *Ymago mundi* singled out by means of a double-frame around it.

94. For explicit references to the inhabitability of the tropics or to places within the tropics, see the following postils in d'Ailly and Gerson's *Tractatus* (1480–1483/1990): **16a (12r)**; **16b (12r)**; 18 (12r); **19 (12r)**; *23b (13r)*; 33 (15r); 34 (15r); *44 (15v)*; 73 (18r); 75 (18r); 79 (18r); 234 (25r); 266 (27r); 267 (27r); 320 (29r); 322 (29r); 482 (41v); 483 (41v); 484 (41v); 485 (41v); 489 (42r); 490 (42r); 660 (73v)?; *663 (75v)*; 670 (78r); 673 (78v); 691 (89v)?. See also Aeneas Sylvius Piccolomini's *Historia rerum ubique gestarum* (1477/1991): 2 (2r)?; **4 (2r)**; 6 (2r)?; 20 (3r)?; **22 (3v)**; **23 (3v)**; 24 (3v); **25 (3v)**; 26

(3v); 27 (3v); *29 (4r);* 36 (4v); 86o (unnumbered folio [?110v]); and Marco Polo's *De consuetudinibus et condicionibus orientalium regionum* (1485/1986): *278 (60r); 281 (61r); 321 (67r); 322 (67r).* For the authorship of the postils, I am following Contreras (1992, 157–170). Italicized postils in the preceding list were originally identified by Don Simón de la Rosa y López as Columbus's. Those in plain font were attributed by him to both Columbus and his brother Bartholomew. Postils in boldface have been added by Contreras to those already identified by Rosa y López as only Columbus's. Postils with question marks are of unknown authorship. Many more postils in these works implicitly refer to habitation in the tropics, especially in Marco Polo, whose account of India was interpreted by cartographers like Behaim as spanning the entire breadth of the torrid zone.

95. On Castile's recognition of Portugal's monopoly beyond the Canaries, see my discussion of the Treaty of Alcáçovas below, and chapter 5. Significantly, the Canary Islands first appears as a latitudinal reference point in Columbus's description of the skin "complexion" of the inhabitants of San Salvador, which he later compared to that of the Canarians. See entry for 13 October 1492 in Pérez de Tudela y Bueso et al. 1994, 1:123 and my discussion of Columbus's *Diario* in chapter 7. Of course, the Canaries had been a target of the Mediterranean slave trade and of colonial incursion following their rediscovery in the opening years of the fourteenth century (Verlinden 1955, 546–567). On the history of Christian presence in the Canaries, see Pérez-Embid's key study on the rivalry between Spain and Portugal for control of the Atlantic (1948, 58–220); Rumeu de Armas 1996, 61–168; and Fernández-Armesto 1987, 151–168.

96. For a discussion of the Canaries and Bojador as the entrance to the tropics, see chapters 2, 5, and 7.

97. Las Casas, *Historia* 1.2.1.17 (1994, 3:429–493). Rich historical corroboration for this connection can be found, for example, in Russell-Wood 1995, which argues that Spain's actions in the Americas were the corollary to a wide range of beliefs and practices patent for many decades in Portugal's slave trade along western Africa. Las Casas's principal (and despised) sources on this "prelude" were the already mentioned chronicler of Henry the Navigator, Gomes Eanes de Zurara, author of *Crónica dos feitos notáveis* (1978–1981); and Crown historian João de Barros, author of *Ásia* (1552/1932). Las Casas's grim epithet for Spain's actions in the Americas was widely disseminated through his *Brevíssima relaçion dela destruyçion delas yndias* (1552), an inflammatory treatise he printed without license, in light of Charles V's wavering commitment to the terms of the so-called New Laws (1542), which had abolished Indian slavery and severely stunted the future of the hereditary *encomienda* system (Las Casas 1552b).

98. See Fernández de Enciso 1519, aiiiiv; Cortés y Albacar 1551/1998, xxv–xxiir; García de Palacio 1587/1998, 11v; and Nájera 1628/1998, 4v.

99. Postil 49 to Ailly and Gerson 1480–1483/1990, 16r.

100. Postil 866 to ibid., 151v.

101. Postil 870 to ibid., 152r. On the basis of Simón de la Rosa y López's original examination of the postils in Columbus's library, Contreras 1992, 167, states that postils 866–869 on fol. 151v of *Tractatus eiusdem de concordia discordantium astronomorum* are equally attributable to Columbus and to his brother Bartholomew, while the postil that completes this set on fol. 152r (No. 870) is Columbus's. Given the thematic complementarity of the postils in these folios and their relative isolation from other postils, it seems arbitrary to attribute some to any of the two brothers and the last one to Columbus. One or the other brother would have written them. However, I assume that these are Columbus's postils, because they express the exact same paradigm as postil 49 in d'Ailly's *Ymago mundi*, which is unequivocally attributed to Columbus, and because they are absolutely consistent with the manner in which the Discoverer came to conceive of the psychological traits of Bahamian and Caribbean peoples. In any case, Bartholomew was Columbus's "right hand," and there is no reason to believe that the views expressed by postils 866–870 were not shared by the Columbus brothers. Even if this particular set of postils had been written by Bartholomew, we must think of them as consistent with Columbus's thought.

102. See postil 48 to Ailly and Gerson 1480–1483/1990, 16r.

103. Pérez de Tudela y Bueso et al. 1994, 1:123.

104. Ibid., 1:142.

105. Falero 1535/1998, ciiiir; all translations from this work are my own.

106. Ibid., ciiiir–v.

107. For an informative discussion of the crusading mindset in Spain until the late sixteenth century, see Housley 1992, 267–321; an excellent survey of relevant scholarship appears on pp. 483–488. Of related interest are Phelan 1970, 5–28, and Graziano 1999, 15–56, considering the issue of Christian eschatology in the context of Spain's conquest and colonization of the Americas.

108. Fernández de Oviedo y Valdés, *La historia natural y moral de las Indias* 3.6 (1535, xxviir).

109. Tornamira 1585/1998, 2–3; all translations from this work are mine.

110. The explicit connection between the practice of geography and the acquisition of empire was a commonplace in the geographical works of the period. See, for instance, Fernández de Enciso 1519, aiir–v; Cortés y Albacar 1551/1998, iiir–v and viv–viir); and García de Palacio 1587/1998, 5r. On the study of this question in recent years, see Godlewska and Smith 1994.

111. Syria 1602/1998, 18–19; all translations from this work are my own. Syria's source is Strabo, *Geography* 2.5.26. Praise for the cultural achievements of a temperate Europe that had—throughout history—reduced other peoples to civility was not unique to the geographies produced in Spanish. Works imported into Spain from elsewhere in Europe made similar claims for the superiority of

the inhabitants of the temperate zone. Notable examples are Peter Apianus's widely published and translated *Cosmographicus liber* (about 1524), which, in an expanded version by Gemma Frisius, was rendered by Gregorio Bontio as *"Libro de la Cosmographia" de Pedro Apiano* (1548, 32); and Johann Boemus's equally popular *Omnium gentium mores* (1520), which was rendered in expanded form by Francisco Thamara as *El libro de las costumbres de todas las gentes del mundo, y de las Indias* (1556, 11r–12r).

112. This point is brilliantly demonstrated in Carroll's seminal paper on the physics of Platonic psychology (1975, 18–22a). See also Lang 1992, 111–112.

113. In his study of the theory of natural slavery among the sixteenth-century schoolmen who discussed the titles Spain might have to its colonies, Pagden rightly observes that this Aristotelian doctrine "was seen as part of a wide network of beliefs, not only about the structure and function of the human mind, but also about the organising principles of the universe itself, of which man is only one small part" (1982, 49).

114. For explicit treatments of the theory of celestial influence in Spanish geographies, see Falero 1535/1998, aivv; Fernández de Enciso 1519, aiiiiv–avr; Chaves 1548, xxxv–xxxiiir; cccviiiv–xlv; lxxvr–lxxxvir; clxvir–clxviiv; Medina 1538/1972, 6r–v; Zamorano 1581/1998, 1v; Tornamira 1585/1998, 12–17 and 49; Syria 1602/1998, 13; and Nájera 1628/1998, A2. A memorable exposition of the theory of celestial influence appears in Velázquez Minaya 1618, 68v: "The region of the elements . . . [is] . . . without a doubt inferior to the celestial region, because the elemental region is generable, corruptible, changeable, inconstant, and of itself timorous. The celestial region is incorruptible, firm, eternal, beautiful, resplendent. The elementary region is [its] slave and subject. The celestial region is the mistress and queen, and, as such, it sits on a nobler throne; it reigns and rules over the elemental region, and it gives it nourishment and sustenance" (my translation). For indispensable assessments of astrological thought in medieval philosophy, see Thorndike 1955 and Lemay 1987.

115. The revival of interest in "nature" in the Latin West during the twelfth and thirteenth centuries had brought new attention to the status of humans as complex creatures at the intersection of metaphysics and physics, endowed with both an intelligent soul and a physical body (Chenu 1997, 4–24). The geographers of the Spanish Empire followed a long line of scholastic writers who condemned astrological practices that—like the casting of horoscopes—contradicted the doctrine of "free will." They were careful to state that celestial bodies influenced human behavior insofar as humans freely abandoned reason in pursuit of satisfying the impulses of their physical bodies. See Falero 1535/1998, aiiv–aiiir; biir); Tornamira 1585/1998, Aiiir–v, 62; and García de Palacio 1587/1998, 1r.

116. Albertus was one of the defining voices of high scholasticism (1250–1350), which saw to the establishment of Aristotle's *libri naturales* and those works by his Greco-Latin and Arabic commentators as the core of natural philosophy in the Latin West (Wallace 1978).

117. North 1986.

118. Lucretius, *De rerum natura* 5.91–96 (1924): "observe first of all sea and earth and sky; this threefold nature, these three masses . . . these three forms so different, these three textures so interwoven, one day shall consign to destruction; the mighty and complex system of the world [*machina mundi*], upheld through many years, shall crash into ruins."

119. Chalcidius 1872, 32c–d. Rich treatments of this term can be found in Delp 1995, especially 248–252; and Mittelstrass 1995. This concept is mentioned by a number of other contemporary scholars, including White 1962, 125n5; and Nelson 1981, 160–198. The classic treatment on the subject of mechanistic concepts of the cosmos in the Western scientific tradition is Dijksterhuis 1959, although the author maintains, to the detriment of the qualitative models preceding the Scientific Revolution, that only the development of a mathematical model of nature that offered a systematic view of the workings of the cosmos could be properly called mechanistic (1986, 495–99). On Chalcidius's contribution to Neoplatonism in the Latin West, see Gersh 1986, 2:421–492.

120. Chantraine 1968, 699.

121. White 1962, 103–129; Chenu 1997, 1–48; and Gimpel 1988, esp. 147–170. As Grant 1996, 21, explains regarding the emergence of this among Aristotelians, "The idea that God was the direct and immediate cause of everything yielded to an interpretation of the world that assumed that natural objects were capable of acting upon each other directly. God had conferred on nature the power and ability to cause things. He had made of it a self-operating entity. Nature, or the cosmos, was thus objectified and conceived as a harmonious, lawful, well-ordered, self-sufficient whole, which could be investigated by the human intellect. The world was transformed conceptually from an unpredictable, fortuitous entitiy to a smoothly operating machine, *machina*, as it was frequently called in the twelfth century."

122. Alverny and Hudry 1974, 219.

123. Delp 1995, 26; my translation.

124. Pseudo-Aristotle, *On the Universe* 6.398b7–16 (1995a). Greek sources use the terms *mēchanopoioi*, *mēchanotechnai*, and *megalotechnoi* for machine operators or technicians (Furley 1955, 390–391, notes a and 1). For the analogies contained in the anonymous thirteenth-century translation of *De mundo* and in Nicholas of Sicily's translation, see Lorimer 1924, 78 and 79, resp.

125. Thorndike 1949, 78–79.

126. The illustration used by Sacrobosco for this crucial property of the world-machine was the miracle of a solar eclipse during a full moon on the day of the Crucifixion. Of this miraculous event,

Dionysius the Areopagite (probably Pseudo-Dionysius) is quoted as having written thus: "Either the god of nature suffers, or the world-machine is dissolved" (Thorndike 1949, 117).

127. Ailly and Gerson 1480–1483/1990, 158r.

128. See Falero 1535/1998, aiiiir; Chaves 1548, iiii; Pérez de Moya 1567, 317; Zamorano 1581/1998, iv; Tornamira 1585/1998, 23; Velázquez Minaya 1618, 3r; Ferrer Maldonado 1626, 49; and Syria 1602/1998, 4. Other Spanish geographies in which the term is used are Cortés y Albacar 1551/1998, xr; Escalante de Mendoza 1998, 80v and 83r [unpublished manuscript, 1575]; and García de Céspedes 1606/1998, 2r.

129. Syria 1602/1998, 4.

130. Las Casas, prologue to *Historia* (1994, 1:346).

131. For a thorough analysis of the process of drafting *Historia de las Indias,* see Pérez Fernández 1994, 109–186.

132. On the extraordinary scope of Las Casas's documentation, see Pérez Fernández 1994, 185–269.

133. The 1552 prologue to *Historia de las Indias* announces the treatment of "the qualities, nature, and properties of these regions, kingdoms, and lands, as well as what they contain, along with the customs, religion, rites, ceremonies and condition of their indigenous peoples, comparing them with those of many other nations, and touching upon the pertinent matters in cosmography and geography" (Las Casas 1994, 1:349). But in 1555, Las Casas would extract chapters 68–165 from *Historia de las Indias* to form chapters 1–120 of the *Apologética.* In a marginal note to chapter 67 of *Historia de las Indias,* which concludes his account of Columbus's exploration of the Caribbean, Las Casas explains that he has decided to compose a new volume with these chapters, due to the complexity and extension of their subject matter (Las Casas, *Historia* 1.3.3.68 [1994, 3:670 and note 57]). On Las Casas's decision to write the *Apologética* as a companion volume to *Historia de las Indias,* see Pérez Fernández 1994, 165–170 and 182–183.

134. Las Casas 1992, 1:283; emphasis added; all translations from the *Apologética* are my own.

135. On the dating of *De unico vocationis modo,* see Pérez Fernández 1981, 200–206.

136. Pérez Fernández 1994, 57. For Las Casas's reference to chapters 1–4 in *De unico vocationis modo,* see Las Casas 1990, 13. For the contents of these four chapters, see García del Moral 1990, lvi–lvii.

137. Las Casas was granted access to these archives by Doña María de Toledo, the wife of Columbus's other son and legitimate heir Don Diego (Pérez Fernández 1994, 213–218).

138. Las Casas would have begun using the summary copy of Columbus's *Diario* on the island of Hispaniola as early as 1527 (Pérez Fernández 1994, 218–219).

139. As Pérez Fernández 1994, 206–207, has observed, the passages in the summary copy of the *Diario* that tend to cite Columbus word by word are those concerning the Christian significance of the

discovery, the natural conditions of the Bahamas and Caribbean basin, and the behavior of the Indians in their interactions with Columbus's crew.

140. Pérez Fernández 1994, 218–219.

141. On this final stage in the drafting of *Historia de las Indias* (1552–1561), see Pérez Fernández 1994, 111–184, esp. 111–112.

142. Pérez Fernández 1994, 145 and 136–140.

143. On the significance of Las Casas's activities on this visit to Seville, see Pérez Fernández 1984, 831–839. For a useful account of the contents and fate of Ferdinand's library, see Rumeu de Armas 1973, 4–20.

144. Ferdinand purchased a copy of the *princeps* edition of Albertus's *De natura loci* in 1521. It is registered as No. 1718 in F. Columbus 1963a, 1963b, and 1963c, but this copy has been lost along with thousands of other volumes once part of the Biblioteca Colombina. At least 43 manuscripts of *De natura loci,* including Albertus's holograph, survive today in libraries across Europe (Fauser 1982, 38–45). This work was printed in Vienna (1514) and Strassburg (1515). It also appeared with other *opuscula* by Albertus in *Tabula tractatuum paruorum naturalium* (Venice, 1517).

145. Anthony Grafton has kindly suggested that Las Casas's penchant for out-documenting his sources may in part obey the heated controversy in learned circles caused by a predecessor of Las Casas in the Dominican order, the erudite forger Annius of Viterbo. In his influential *Commentaries on Various Authors Discussing Antiquities* (Rome, 1498), Annius had endeavored to fill out the Bible's "lacunae" and to redefine pagan history and mythology as outcrops of Biblical antiquity and historiography (Grafton 1991). Annius was very important for the historiography of the sixteenth century, for he "created not only texts but rules for the choice of texts as well, general and plausible ones. These rules in turn formed the basis of all later systematic reflection on the choice and evaluation of sources" (Grafton 1991, 80). Among Annius's most controversial moves was the inclusion in his *Commentaries* of a "complete" version of Berosus's *Antiquities* (3rd century BCE), a collection of Babyloniaca that had survived only in fragments known largely through Flavius Josephus's first-century *Jewish Antiquities* (Grafton 1991, 80–82). Annius's imaginative forgery had evidently tainted, in the eyes of many of Las Casas's contemporaries, even those supposedly "authentic" fragments of Berosus's Babyloniaca that had survived in the works of Josephus and other ancient writers. And among Annius's numerous critics was another member of the Dominican order, the distinguished humanist Juan Luis Vives, who in his own commentary on Saint Augustine's *City of God* had fiercely set out to discredit Annius's version of Berosus (Grafton 1991, 93). Las Casas, like other historians of his generation, relied on a good number of the ancient sources included in Annius's *Commentaries.* And, in the *Apologética* 107–108 (1992, 2:813–824)

we find Las Casas in the somewhat awkward position of defending Annius's version of Berosus. Sixteenth- and seventeenth-century ethnographers (this includes cosmographers and chroniclers of the Indies) tended to believe that Amerindians were part of Noah's progeny dispersed after the Flood and the failed building of the Tower of Babel. This genealogy not only argued in favor of the humanity of the Indians (against apologists of empire who deemed them to live like "beasts"), but it also allowed Las Casas and other sympathetic writers to establish parallels between ancient pagans and Amerindians that worked in favor of the latter. In many of their achievements and mistakes, Amerindians were no less laudable and no more culpable than their pagan counterparts, from whose ashes and monuments, after all, Christendom had risen (see Pagden's useful discussion of the *Apologética* [1982, 119–145, esp. 134–135]). Largely following Augustine's cues in *De civitate Dei* 16, writers like Las Casas ultimately conceptualized cultural differences as the result of distortions of one single language spoken—and a single set of customs practiced—by Noah and his sons prior to the dispersals that followed the Flood and the fall of Babel. Removed in space and time from their origins, pagans had been as susceptible, if not in some respects *more* susceptible, than Amerindians, to distorting this primeval language and set of customs. The various cultural traits to be found from one people to another distantly, or not so distantly, echoed everything from the modes of worship and sacrifice to the sciences and to the arts that Noah had allegedly taught humanity after the Flood. With this in mind, it is not difficult to see why Las Casas would have attempted to defend Annius's Berosus against Vives's commentary on Augustine: Pseudo-Berosus claimed that Janus, the "porter" god who, Romans supposed, had constructed the first temples and instituted the first pagan rites, was really none other than Noah, who, having taught Armenians and other peoples all things divine and human, had proceeded to do the same with the peoples of the Italic peninsula (Las Casas, *Apológética* 107 [1992, 2:814–815]). The implication for Las Casas's argument was that, just as the cult of Janus among the Romans reflected its origins in Noah's works, so did the modes of worship and sacrifice in the Indies have their roots in Biblical antiquity. To this effect, Las Casas found himself in a predicament that writers of the period probably had difficulty avoiding: he felt he had no choice but to rely on Annius's *Commentaries;* he took what he probably knew was an indefensible position in the debate over the authenticity and authority of the sources this work included. At the same time, he was extremely careful to lay bare the process of proof by which he arrived at his claims. Following a painstaking discussion of sources that directly or indirectly supported Berosus's contention about Janus's true identity, some of which came directly from Annius's *Commentaries,* Las Casas concluded: "From among the modern writers, it would be sufficient here to cite Johannes Annius of Viterbo, who wrote commentaries on those five books of Berosus. In many parts of these books, and in those of Methastenes, and in those about Fabius Pictor, and in Xenophon's *De aequivocis,* and in other ancient treatises collected and commented by him, [Johannes Annius] asserts that the said book [*Antiquities*] is by Berosus, and that Noah came to be called Janus, and his wife Esta and Vesta, along with all the other things which we have mentioned above. And, truly, on account of all the things that Johannes Annius mentions in the said places, aside from the fact that he is a master and doctor of theology, he should not be held in any less esteem on the subject of ancient world histories than the well-read and learned Luis Vives" (Las Casas, *Apologética* 108 [1992, 2:820]). Indeed, the anxiety that Las Casas must have experienced concerning the use of such a deeply influential and controversial work as Annius's *Commentaries* could easily have extended to his use of sources elsewhere in *Historia de las Indias* and *Apologética historia,* especially given that Las Casas was arguing a case in favor of—to cite imperial ideologues like Juan Ginés de Sepúlveda—"barbarians" who "not only lack any culture, but also do not even use or know letters, and do not preserve the monuments of their memory, save for a certain dark and vague memory of some events recorded on certain drawings" (Sepúlveda 1984, 34; all translations from Sepúlveda's *Democrates secundus* are my own, in consultation with the Spanish translation by Angel Losada).

146. Compare F. Columbus, *Historie* 6 (1571/1992, 12v–14r) to Las Casas, *Historia* 1.1.2.5 (1994, 1:368–370); as well as F. Columbus, *Historie* 7 (1571/1992, 14r–15v) to Las Casas, *Historia* 1.1.4.11 (1994, 1:396–398). Whether or not these chapters ought to be attributed to Ferdinand or to an "anonymous biographer," Las Casas appears to have believed that he was following Ferdinand.

147. Las Casas, *Historia* 1.1.4.11 (1994, 1:396).

148. For a list of Las Casas's sources, see Pérez Fernández 1994, 259–269.

149. F. Columbus, *Historie* 5 (1571/1992, 12r).

150. Las Casas, *Historia* 1.1.3.5 (1994, 3:369).

151. For Albertus's arguments regarding this matter, see Albertus Magnus, *De natura loci* 1.6 (1980b, 9–12).

152. Vignaud 1911, 1:60. For someone like Vignaud, who showed an interest in Columbus's southing as a sign of Columbus's secret plan to reach Antilia, Albertus's presence in Las Casas's intellectual biography of Columbus stood to bolster Vignaud's refutation of the traditional thesis about Columbus's destination. On one instance of Las Casas's out-documenting his sources, see Pérez Fernández 1984, 791.

153. Las Casas, *Historia* 1.1.3.6–7 (1994, 1:371–383).

154. See Hanke 1959 and Pagden 1982. I am closely following Pagden's lead in this part of my argument, 27–108.

155. Pagden 1982, 28–29.

156. Ibid., 29.

157. Pérez de Tudela y Bueso et al. 1994, 3:1673–1674.

158. Ibid., 3:1673.

159. Ibid., 3:1673–1674.

160. See chapter 5.

161. For an extremely useful account of this debate, see Muldoon 1979.

162. Pagden 1982, 28–29.

163. On John Mair's role in the development of the "theory of natural slavery" among Crown apologists in Spain, I have consulted Pagden 1982, 38–41. For additional information about Mair's life, thought, and influence, see Beuchot 1976 and Carro 1951, 261–334.

164. For Aristotle's theory of slavery, see *Politics* 1. For his discussion of slaves "by nature," see *Politics* 1.5–6. A succinct explanation of Aristotle's concept of natural slavery appears in Pagden 1982, 41–47.

165. For the Latin original, see Carro 1951, 292n45; my translation, in consultation with Pagden's translation (1982, 38–39).

166. Pagden 1982, 30–37. As Pagden notes, our only source on these momentous protests by the Dominicans is none other than Las Casas, *Historia* 3.1.2.3–6 (1994, 3:1757–1774).

167. Las Casas, *Historia* 3.1.2.4 (1994, 3:1762).

168. Ibid., 3.1.3.5 (1994, 3:1767).

169. See Doc. 96 in *Cedulario cubano* 1929, 427–431; this quote, 431; my translation. In this *cédula real,* Fernando repeatedly alludes to official deliberations that would have taken place before Isabel's death, perhaps as early as 1495 or 1496, and most likely in answer to the first massive slave raids conducted by Columbus in the Indies. As Pagden has noted, "The Castilian Crown had never, in fact, been certain that it had the right to enslave Indians" (1982, 31–33). For Fernando's concern with the proceeds from gold mining in Hispaniola, we need only read a missive that the king had sent to Diego Colón only a month earlier (23 February 1512). Addressing his officials in Hispaniola, Fernando complained: "And in [the message] I write to you alone—my officials, not the Admiral—I say that I greatly marvel at the fact that in this [recently arrived] ship, you should not have sent any gold. And, verily, the more one thinks about it, the more it seems to me that you have erred greatly, considering what I have written to you before, for this was an adequate ship for this purpose. And so that this error be corrected, I say to you that for no reason in the world should there be any gold of mine lying idle over there. On the contrary, it should all come to me as fast as you can manage, even at the risk of loss, as I have commanded you on other occasions" (Doc. 94 in *Cedulario cubano* 1929, 417–424; my translation).

Indeed, in an early letter to a member of their Council, the Bishop of Seville Don Juan de Fonseca (16 April 1495), Fernando and Isabel had ordered him not yet to bill the buyers of the first massive round of Indian slaves just sent by Columbus to the market of Seville, "because we would like to be informed by *letrados,* theologians, and canonists whether, in good conscience, they can be sold as slaves or not. And this cannot be done until we see the letters that the Admiral has written to us in order to know the cause he has for sending them over here as captives" (Pérez de Tudela y Bueso et al. 1994, 2:789–790). For Las Casas's vivid account of the rounding up of the slaves Columbus then sent to Seville, see Las Casas, *Historia* 1.4.1.104 (1994, 2:928–931).

Columbus's "letters" did arrive in court, and they included the famous "Memorial" entrusted to his envoy Antonio Torres in which Columbus proposed an all-out trade in slaves from among a group of belligerent Indians he had identified on his first voyage as Caribes. Columbus justified the proposed trade alleging that the Caribes were anthropophagous, and that abstracting them from their native soil and sending them as slaves over to Europe, would serve to purge them, literally and spiritually, of "that monstrous custom they have of eating men" (*aquella inhumana costunbre que tienen de comer onbres*). See Pérez de Tudela y Bueso et al. 1994, 1:543–545; this quote, 544. Fernando and Isabel approved Columbus's proposal to enslave "man-eating" Caribes, and for decades to come the convenient excuse of delivering humanity from monstrous predators would serve to justify many slave raids on the Indies. Isabel herself, who did not like the idea of enslaving Indians, would confirm the status of Caribes as slaves for the taking in 1503 (Pérez de Tudela y Bueso et al. 1994, 3:1579–1581).

But the round of Indian slaves held in Seville was ordered returned to Hispaniola only a year later (Pagden 1982, 31), no doubt because they were identified as Taínos from Hispaniola, not Caribes. And since the great majority of Indians captured, dispossessed, and forced to pay tribute or to work in *repartimientos* could not be categorized as man-eaters either, the question would remain open as to whether or not they could be subjected to what critics like the Dominicans were beginning to regard as a form of virtual slavery. We should emphasize, against Pagden's view (1982, 33), that the fact that Indians did not bear the "natural" mark of slaves—that is, "blackness"—must have played no little part in complicating the issue of their enslavement. See my discussion of the Indians' skin complexion in chapters 5 and 7.

170. Las Casas, *Historia* 3.1.3.6 (1994, 3:1769–1770).
171. Pagden 1982, 37. Indeed the *real cédula* sent by Fernando to silence the protesting friars was accompanied by copies of Alexander's infamous concessions.
172. For Las Casas's account of the Burgos *junta,* see Las Casas, *Historia* 3.2.1.7–12 (1994, 3:1775–1803).
173. Ibid., 3.2.1.8 (1994, 3:1781–1782).

174. Ibid., 3.2.1.9 (1994, 3:1784). See also Pagden's analysis of Mesa's "opinion" (1982, 47–50).

175. Las Casas, *Historia* 3.2.1.9 (1994, 3:1785; emphasis added).

176. Compare Pagden 1982, 47.

177. For the development of this debate, see Pagden 1982, 50–108.

178. On Sepúlveda, see Pagden 1982, 109–118.

179. On this episode in Las Casas's efforts against Sepúlveda, see Wagner and Parish 1967, 170–182. Extensive documentation of the confrontation between Las Casas and Sepúlveda, including their participation in the Juntas de Valladolid, can be found in Pérez Fernández 1984, 721–807.

180. The contents of the future *Apologética* were announced in Las Casas's Latin *Apologia*, a point-by-point refutation of Crown jurist Juan Ginés de Sepúlveda's own *Apologia pro libro de iustis belli* (1550/1997). See Las Casas 1552/1988, 83. On the *Apologética* in relation to the debates between Las Casas and Sepúlveda, see Pagden 1982, 119–145.

181. See Argument 4 in Sepúlveda (1550/1997, [197]; my translation, in consultation with the translation by Angel Losada). For Thomas Aquinas's argument, see *In libros Politicorum Aristotelis expositio* I.1.i.23 (1951, 23). Sepúlveda's preferred witness to the "barbarism" of the Indians was, not surprisingly, one of the works Las Casas knew and despised most: Fernández de Oviedo's *La historia general y natural de las Indias* 13.6 (1535, xxviir). Sepúlveda's version of the tripartite geography of nations also derived from Thomas Aquinas's *In libros Politicorum Aristotelis expositio* 7.1.5. 968–1127 (1951, 361–364); and from the influential *De regimine principum* 3.4, a "mirror of princes" early on attributed to Aquinas but largely authored by his disciple Ptolemy of Lucca. For Ptolemy of Lucca's reference to hot, cold, and temperate nations, see *On the Government of Rulers* 2.1.5 (1997, 105).

182. On Sepúlveda's attempts to obtain license to publish *Democrates secundus,* and on Las Casas's role in blocking its publication, see Pérez Fernández 1984, 722–729. On the basis of Las Casas's own assertions in *Apologia* (1552/1988, 67), Pagden believes that Las Casas never read Sepúlveda's *Democrates secundus,* only a Spanish translation of the 1550 *Apologia pro libro de iustis belli* published in Rome (1982, 119).

183. Sepúlveda 1984, 1.

184. See for instance Albertus's and d'Ailly's discussions of the five zones: *De natura loci* 1.6 specifically refers to the zones as *plagae sive zonae* (Albertus Magnus 1980b, 9, lines 51–52); and *Ymago mundi* as *plagae seu regiones* (Ailly and Gerson 1480–1483/1990, 12r).

185. Docs. 77 and 91 in Adão da Fonseca and Ruiz Asencio 1995, 125–130 and 137–139, resp.; all translations from this work are my own. A most meticulous analysis of these papal bulls can be found in García-Gallo 1987. See chapter 5.

186. See Doc. 29 in Adão da Fonseca and Ruiz Asencio 1995, 68–92 and 158–167. The clauses regarding Castile's and Portugal's possessions in the Atlantic were added to the treaty dated 4 October 1479,

and the final document was ratified by the Catholic Monarchs on 6 March 1480. See also Doc. 12, dated 6 May 1480, in Pérez de Tudela y Bueso et al. 1994, 1:41–46. The Treaty of Alcáçovas constituted a defining framework in future legal disputes between Castile and Portugal for control of the Atlantic, not to mention in the drafting of the legal documents that preceded the famous Treaty of Tordesillas (7 June 1494), the treaty that would divide the Atlantic between Spain and Portugal along a meridian that was located "three hundred and seventy leagues to the west of the Cape Verde Islands." See Doc. 98 in Adão da Fonseca and Ruiz Asencio 1995, 158–167; my translation. On the Spanish interpretation of the Treaty of Alcáçovas until the signing of the Treaty of Tordesillas, see Castañeda 1973. An indispensable analysis of the effects of the Treaty of Alcáçovas on the documents that led to the Treaty of Tordesillas appears in Adão da Fonseca 1993, 271–294. See also Pérez Embid 1948, 214–220; García-Gallo 1987, 331–350; and Rumeu de Armas 1992, 73–85.

2 Columbus and the Open Geography of the Ancients

1. On the royal council appointed in 1486 to evaluate Columbus's plan, see Ballesteros Beretta 1945, 1:446–455 and 487–493; Manzano Manzano 1964, 65–111; and Taviani 1985a, 172–173 and 441–443. On the royal council's final assembly in Santa Fe, see Ballesteros Beretta 1945, 1:513–515; Manzano Manzano 1964, 251–260; and Taviani 1985a, 196–197.
2. Pérez de Tudela y Bueso et al. 1994, 2:1281–1285; this quote, 1284.
3. Ibid., 1:236.
4. For a succinct account of this disagreement, see O'Gorman 1958/1977, 55–76.
5. F. Columbus, *Historie del S. D. Fernando Colombo* 5 (1571/1992, 12v).
6. Las Casas, *Historia de las Indias* 1.3.1.29 (1994, 1:504).
7. Ibid. See also F. Columbus, *Historie* 12 (1571/1992, 32r–34r).
8. A well-documented survey of Geraldini's activities in the Spanish court can be found in Oliva 1993, 176–185. As Pérez Fernández argues, it seems that it was Charles V and not his grandfather, Fernando of Aragon, who presented Geraldini for the bishopric of Santo Domingo. See note 1 to Las Casas, *Historia* 3.2.1.9 (1994, 3:2524).
9. For Geraldini's account of Columbus, and of the events in the encampment of Santa Fe, see *Itinerarium* 12 and 14 (1631/1995, 185–191 and 202–209, resp.).
10. On the *Itinerarium* and its circulation until 1631, see Oliva 1993, 189–202. On the circumstances that led to its publication, see 206–209.
11. Geraldini, *Itinerarium* 11 (1631/1995, 183), declares that the inhabitants of the lower latitudes were not entirely sound of judgment, lacked a noble soul, did not believe in God, had no knowledge of letters, engaged in no commercial activities, lacked inherited laws, or rights, or institutions,

dissolved marriage at the slightest disagreement, and possessed no government—all this because the land close to the equator was extremely fertile, which meant that its peoples did not have to exercise their minds or their bodies in order to survive. Therefore, equatorial peoples were slow-witted and lazy.

12. Geraldini, *Itinerarium* 14 (1631/1995, 204–205; my translation).

13. Henry Harrisse, one of Columbus's most meticulous biographers in the nineteenth century, duly cautioned that Geraldini's status as a witness of the events that preceded the discovery should be carefully weighed against the fact that the *Itinerarium* itself is not a consistently reliable historical source: "Being an eyewitness and an active participant of the deeds that he recounts, his testimony will have great power, though the book to which he consigns them reveals a certain frivolity of spirit, a lack of critical sense, and such flights of imagination, that one should not approach it except with great care" (1871, 1:368; my translation). Henry Vignaud, who earned a reputation for attempting to discredit every crucial written source on Columbus's life, additionally speculated that the 1631 edition of the *Itinerarium* might present interpolations effected on the lost original to make them appear as Geraldini's own (1911, 2:7–8). This said, even Harrisse (1871, 1:380–381) and Vignaud (1911, 2:57–58) cite Geraldini as an impeccable source on the Santa Fe assembly. While we must not read Geraldini's testimony as "disinterested," we certainly have no credible evidence to believe that this testimony is not his own: Ballesteros Beretta, for instance, momentarily wondered whether the Fernandine *Historie* published by Alfonso Ulloa in 1571 could itself be the source of an adulteration to Geraldini's original testimony of the Santa Fe assembly (1945, 1:514–515). According to Ballesteros Beretta, the anonymous author of this forgery in Italy would have intended to replicate Ferdinand's unsympathetic—and presumably Hispanophobic—portrayal of Columbus's opponents in the royal council. But recent comparison of the extant Latin codices of Geraldini's *Itinerarium* reveals no discrepancies to support Ballesteros Beretta's speculation (Oliva 1993, 202–206). The same can be said of the only codices known to have survived in Pompeo Mongallo da Leonessa's Italian translation, one held by the British Library (MS Harley 3566) and the other by Lisbon's Biblioteca Nacional (Fundo Geral 11169). The codex in Lisbon may be by Mongallo himself, who claimed he had worked from Geraldini's much deteriorated original (Oliva 1993, 190–191).

Less persuasive is Ballesteros Beretta's explanation for the fact that Geraldini—not Ferdinand or Las Casas—should mention Nicholas of Lyra among the authorities cited by Columbus's opponents in the royal council. Ballesteros Beretta suggests that the Italian author of the forgery in Geraldini's work would have included Nicholas of Lyra because this forger knew that Lyra was "one of Columbus's preferred authors when it came to the interpretation of Sacred Scripture" (1945, 1:514). As an example, Ballesteros Beretta cites Columbus's famous postil 166 in Pierre d'Ailly's *Ymago mundi*, which would most certainly not have been available to an impostor in Italy. The same is true of the other texts where Columbus cites Lyra: Columbus's *Diario* of the third voyage and his famous compilation of scriptural passages, *Libro de las profecías* (dated 1504). Geraldini's mention of Lyra in fact contradicts Ballesteros Beretta's claim that Geraldini's testimony of the Santa Fe assembly was forged to replicate Ferdinand's derogatory portrayal of Columbus's opponents in the royal council: Lyra unequivocally points to the *learned* nature of the objections raised against Columbus's plan. It is certainly possible for a forgery to be more elaborate than its source. But as Ballesteros Beretta himself admits, his case is built from silence. The historian finds himself in the indefensible position of relying on the testimony of the Santa Fe assembly contained in the *Itinerarium* while simultaneously suggesting that part of this testimony may not be Geraldini's own. See Ballesteros Beretta's use of Geraldini (1945, 1:151, 489–490, and 513). Other authors who have relied on Geraldini's testimony are Morison 1942, 1:133–134; Manzano Manzano 1964, 102, 255, and 257–258, who hails Geraldini as an "exceptional witness" (my translation); and Taviani 1985a, 197 and 485, and 1996, 1:371–377, who considers Geraldini's intervention to have been of great importance if not crucial to the Santa Fe assembly.

It should be noted that Ferdinand could have been aware of Geraldini's role in the Santa Fe assembly, given that Columbus and Geraldini were friends, but we know nothing about Ferdinand's sources to suggest that his own account of the royal council's objections to Columbus's plan is indebted to Geraldini. Since Ferdinand visited Hispaniola in 1509 to return definitively to Europe shortly thereafter, he never saw Geraldini's *Itinerarium* in Hispaniola. Las Casas, for his part, remains unfamiliar with Geraldini's version of the royal council's proceedings. His only source regarding the debate in the royal council appears to have been the Fernandine *Historie*. Las Casas may have met Geraldini, since his stays in Hispaniola between 1521 and 1526 overlapped with Geraldini's tenure as bishop (1519–1524). But if the two did meet, and if Las Casas was aware of Geraldini's participation in the Santa Fe assembly, Geraldini is nowhere mentioned or cited as a source in *Historia de las Indias*. For the time being, Geraldini should continue to be considered an independent source.

14. Randles 1990, 51.
15. See *Holy Bible* 1989; and *Biblia sacra* 1983.
16. For a comprehensive and highly illuminating treatment of this cosmological problem in the West, including writers like Albertus and d'Ailly, see Duhem's "L'équilibre de la terre et des mers" 1 and 2, 1958, 9:16–235. See also Grant 1994, 622–637. For Archimedes' proof of earth and water's concentricity, see his *On Floating Bodies* 1.2 (1912): "The surface of any fluid at rest is the surface of a sphere whose centre is the same as that of the earth."
17. Thorndike 1949, 78.
18. For a discussion of T-O maps, which tend to be seen mostly in copies of Isidore of Seville's *Etymologiae* and *De natura rerum*, see Woodward 1987, 296–297, 301–302, and 343–347.

19. On Herodotus's challenge to Homeric geography, see Aujac 1987a, 136–37; and, particularly, Romm 1992, 32–41, which discusses the connection between Herodotus's inconsistent "empiricism" and his characterization of unknown peripheries as "empty spaces" or *erēmoi*. The relevant passages discussed by Romm are Herodotus, *History* 2.23, 4.8, and 4.36 (1987), where the author dismisses the concept of the Ocean River; and *History* 3.98, 4.17, 4.185, and 5.9, where he variously deploys this concept to describe territories about which there is no reliable information.

20. See Homer, *Iliad* 21.196–197 (1990; 526); and Hesiod, *Theogony*, lines 366–367 (1993).

21. Plato, *Phaedo* 109a–113c (1997c).

22. Seneca, *Natural Questions* 3.15.1 (1971–1972).

23. Pliny, *Natural History* 2.66 (1938–1963).

24. Ibid., 2.66.

25. Colón 1992, 382.

26. Pérez de Tudela y Bueso et al. 1994, 2:1114: "como el amago dela nuez con vna tela gorda que va abraçado en ello."

27. Aristotle, *Meteorologica* 1.13.349b17–19 (1995c).

28. Aristotle, *On Generation and Corruption* 2.2.329b6–330a29 (1995e). A most useful account of the origins and development of this theory can be found in Lloyd 1964.

29. Aristotle, *On Generation and Corruption* 2.3.330a30–331a6.

30. Ibid., 2.4.331a7–333a15.

31. Ibid., 2.4.331a13–20.

32. Ibid., 2.10, esp. 2.10.336a32–336b1–15.

33. Aristotle, *Meteorologica* 1.9–2.2, esp. 2.2.354b25–30.

34. Ibid., 1.9.346b35–347a9.

35. It was, incidentally, Aristotle's theory of water circulation that largely stood behind Pierre d'Ailly's famous corroboration of Aristotle's claim in *On the Heavens* that only a short distance lay between the Pillars of Hercules and the end of the Orient. For according to d'Ailly, the absence of the sun's heat caused greater accumulation of water in the poles than in the equator, where one could conversely expect to find a much greater proportion of land. See d'Ailly's *Epilogus mappemundi*, in Ailly and Gerson, 1480–1483/1990, 42r–v; and Columbus's postils 494, 495, 496, and 497. Columbus explicitly ties this passage in d'Ailly (postil 496) to the widely cited chapter 8 in *Ymago mundi*, where d'Ailly discusses the extension of inhabited land (d'Ailly and Gerson 1480–1483/1990, 13r–v). It should be added that on this and many other counts, d'Ailly's geography was heavily dependent on Roger Bacon's *Opus maius* IV (about 1266–1267). See Bacon 1897, 1:290–292.

36. See Aujac 1987b, 163.

37. Homer, *Odyssey* 1.23–24 (1996, 78).

38. Strabo, *Geography* 1.2.24–28 and 2.5.10–13 (1917–1932).

39. Ptolemy, *Geography* 1.6–20 (Berggren and Jones 2000, 63–83).

40. Ptolemy, *Almagest* 2.1 H88 (1998), specifies the northern horizontal quadrant as being bound "by the equator and a circle drawn through the poles of the equator"; and his *Geography* 7.5 (Berggren and Jones 2000, 110) specifically places the southernmost and northernmost limits of the known world at 16° 25′ S and 63° N of the equator (approximately 80 degrees in latitude), and its easternmost and westernmost limits at 119° 30′ E and 60° 30′ W of the meridian of Alexandria (approximately 180 degrees in longitude).

41. See Ptolemy, *Almagest* 2.1 H88 (see also 1998, 75 and n. 1); and 6.6 H498, 294. Ptolemy's astrological *Tetrabiblos* 2.2 (1980) also uses the phrase "our portion of the inhabited world" to describe the quadrant occupying half of the northern hemisphere. (I have not yet been able to ascertain whether this phrase is also used in the Greek original of the *Geography*.)

42. Ptolemy, *Geography* 1.8–9 (Berggren and Jones 2000, 67–70).

43. See under "Unknown Land" in Beggren and Jones 2000, 180–181; and, in particular, Ptolemy's *Geography* 7.5 (Beggren and Jones 2000, 107–111). Ptolemy's endorsement of an "open" geography was not as exceptional in Antiquity as the annotators of this translation claim (Beggren and Jones 2000, 22 and n. 22).

44. Macrobius, *Commentary on the Dream of Scipio* 2.5.16, 203 (1990).

45. For a discussion of quadripartite maps, see Woodward 1987, 296–297, 302–304, and 357. Such maps tend to be identified with Isidore's works, as well as with the eighth-century *Commentarium in Apocalypsim* by the Benedictine abbot Beatus of Liebana.

46. For Acosta's influential thesis that humans, beasts, and plants had come to populate the Americas by way of a land bridge, see *Historia natural y moral de las Indias* 1 (1590/1998,13–84).

47. Consider Hesiod's influential account of the ages of man in *Works and Days* (1993), which recounts the successive creations of five different races of humans by different deities, or Ovid's later version of the ages of man in the *Metamorphoses* 1.76–150 (1999), completed in 7 CE, which simultaneously claims that it was the trickster god Prometheus who modeled man from earth and water and recounts the Hesiodic myth of the ages of man. The contrast between Greco-Roman mythology and Christian theology (which tolerated only one creation of man in one place at one time) is best illustrated by myths describing autochthonous generation, or generation from the soil. Perhaps the best-known example is the birth of Erichthonius, son of Hephaestus and Gaia (earth). When Hephaestus attempted to rape the chaste Athena, she flung his semen to the ground and Erichthonius sprang from the earth. Erichthonius's birth is retold in the Apollodorian *Library* 3.14.6 (1997) (1st or 2nd century CE), but the earliest reference to him may appear in Homer's *Iliad* 2.545–549 (1990, 117), which describes Erichthonius (Erechtheus) as the son of "the grain-giving

fields" (Gantz 1993, 233–237). This myth may stand behind Plato's funeral oration *Menexenus,* in which Pericles' mistress Aspasia eulogizes Athenians as being literally "children of the soil" (237b–238a [1997b]). Another important instance of autochthonous generation appears in Pausanias's *Description of Greece* (2nd century CE), which refers to Pelasgus (father of the Peloponnesians) in similar terms (8.1.4–5 [1898]). The Apollodorian *Library* 2.1.1 and 3.7.7 attributes the telling of the Pelasgian creation to Hesiod. Finally, Greco-Roman mythology did not rule out the possibility that humankind had populated by preternatural means otherwise inaccessible lands. The example mentioned here appears in Homer, who tells us in the *Odyssey* V and VI that Odysseus was carried off by Poseidon's fury to the land of Scheria (believed to correspond to the island of Corfu), whose inhabitants the Phaeacians had been led by their god-king Nausithous "in a vast migration . . . far from the men who toil on this earth" (6.7–8 [1996, 174]). Hence the words of Nausicaa (King Alcinous's daughter) to Odysseus: "'We live too far apart, out in the surging sea, / off at the world's end— / no other mortals come to mingle with us" (6.204–205 [1996, 174]). Another early example comes from Hesiod, who tells us in *Works and Days,* lines 189–192, that Zeus granted "the divine race of Heroes" (the fourth generation of men), "life apart from other men, / Settling them at the ends of the Earth./And there they live, free from all care, / In the Isles of the Blest [Canary Islands], by Ocean's deep stream" (1993).

48. Strabo, *Geography* 2.5.13.

49. Augustine, *The Literal Meaning of Genesis* 1.12 (1982). For the Latin text, see Augustine 1970, 19. Augustine's commentary of these verses is lamentably brief, especially compared to those of his immediate predecessors Saint Basil (about 329–379) and Saint Ambrose (died 397). See Basil's *Homily* 4 in *Exegetic Homilies* (1963); and Ambrose's *Homily* 4 in *"Hexameron," "Paradise," and "Cain and Abel"* (1961).

50. Augustine, *The City of God against the Pagans* 16.9 (1957–1972).

51. Ibid., 16.1–11.

52. Ibid., 16.9.

53. See Woodward's discussion of the content and meaning of medieval *mappaemundi* (1987, 326–342).

54. For the manner in which Albertus and Bacon worked their way around the question of the antipodes, see *De natura loci* 1.7 (1980b, 12–14) and *Opus majus* IV (1897, 1:290–308).

55. Bernáldez, *Historia de los Reyes Católicos* 118 (1870, 1:358).

56. Mandeville, *El libro de las maravillas del mundo* 22 (2002, 197); all translations from this work are my own.

57. For a discussion of Prester John, see chapter 6.

58. Aristotle, *Physics* 4.1 (1995i).

59. Ibid., 4.4.211.a4–5.

60. Aristotle, *On the Heavens* 4.3–5 (1995f); and Aristotle, *On Generation and Corruption* 2.3 (1995e). See also chapter 4.

61. Paul of Burgos 1485, 1:iiiv; all translations from this work are my own.

62. Ibid., 1:iiiv–iiiir.

63. See Duhem 1958, 9:87–93. My discussion of the antecedents for Burgos's views on the proportion between earth and water largely follows Duhem 1958, 9:87–103.

64. Paul of Burgos 1485, 1:iiiir.

65. See Duhem 1958, 9:91–93; and Aristotle, *On Generation and Corruption* 2.6.333a16–34. Aristotle is here replying to Empedocles' assertion that the elements were "all equal" (2.6.333a20).

66. Duhem 1958, 9:92.

67. Aristotle, *Meteorologica* 1.3.340a11–13.

68. Aristotle, *Physics* 4.6–9, esp. 4.9.

69. See Duhem 1958 9:95–96; and Plato, *Timaeus* 32b–c (1997e).

70. See Duhem, 1958 9:95; and Macrobius, *Commentary on the Dream of Scipio* 1.6.32 (1990). For the Latin text, see Macrobius 2003, 31–32.

71. Paul of Burgos 1485, 1:iiiir.

72. Ibid., 1:iiiir. For this reason, Burgos explains, "philosophers" had claimed that the proportion between earth and water was also one to ten. It is unclear which of Aristotle's commentators Burgos has in mind. According to Duhem 1958, 9:96, Aristotle's late ancient commentators did not quite spell out the conclusion that the volume ratio between the spheres of earth and water was one to ten, but many certainly assumed that water's total volume was significantly greater than earth's.

73. Ptolemy, *Almagest* 2.1 H88.

74. Paul of Burgos 1485, 1:iiiir. Burgos is here making a distinction between the "wrong" term *condensentur* and the "right" term, *congregentur*.

75. Basil, *Exegetic Homilies* 4.3. Basil's example refers us to the early attempt by Egypt's King Sesostris II (19th century BCE), imitated by subsequent rulers, to build a canal between the Nile River and the Red Sea. This attempt is documented in, among other works, Aristotle's *Meteorologica* 1.14.352b1–353a14, though Basil's source is more likely to be Pliny (*Natural History* 6.33).

76. See Duhem's discussion of Philoponus (1958, 9:93–97); and Olympiodorus et al. 1551, ?105r and ?108r.

77. See Duhem's discussion of Olympiodorus (1958, 9:97–98); and Olympiodorus et al. 1551, 5r.

78. Duhem 1958, 2:283–284 and 9:97–98. Pliny presents an important exposition of this Posidonian theory (*Natural History* 2.65). This theory of water's eccentricity with respect to earth developed

in Posidonius's lost treatise *On the Ocean* was not new among the high scholastics. It was already strongly implied, for instance, in Sacrobosco's discussion of water's sphericity in his popular *De sphaera* 1 (Thorndike 1949, 83).

79. Paul of Burgos 1485, 1:vr. The Christian tradition that explained the presence of land on the globe by citing God's suspension of physical principles has been traced as far back as the teachings of the *Mutakallimun*, the Muslim scholars of the ninth century. See Duhem 1958, 9:102–103, citing Maimonides' assertion that it was the *Mutakallimun* who claimed that the presence of land "above" water was determined by God. For Maimonides' mention of this claim, see his *Guide for the Perplexed* 1.74 (1963, 218).

80. Paul of Burgos 1485, 1:iiiir. Burgos uses the verb form *inclinentur*. For the explanation corresponding to the figure that illustrates Burgos's theory, see ibid., vr.

81. Ptolemy, *Almagest* 4.

82. Paul of Burgos 1485, 1:iiiiv.

83. Ibid., 1:vr.

84. Randles 1990, 13–15.

85. It should be noted that Geraldini's testimony wrongly situated the extent of Portugal's exploration near the Antarctic circle (approximately 66° 30′ S); Bartolomeu Dias's historic rounding of the Cape of Good Hope in 1488—a feat that Columbus would surely have made known to Geraldini and other members of the Santa Fe assembly—had extended Portugal's exploration to little more than 35° S.

86. Las Casas, *Historia* 1.3.1.39 (1994, 1:504), who saw the enterprise of the Indies as a duplication of Portugal's imperial exploits on the western coast of sub-Saharan Africa, takes license to add to Ferdinand's account what he believes was implicit in the minds of Columbus's opponents when they argued that only littoral navigation was possible: "It was impossible to navigate, were it not along the *rivieras* or coasts, *as the Portuguese did in* Guinea" (emphasis added).

87. Cape Bojador is, actually, Cape Juby, 27° 57′ N, in modern-day Morocco. The best source on this initial period of Portuguese Atlantic exploration is Russell's recent biography of Henry the Navigator (2000). This biography should be read in conjunction with Adão da Fonseca's brilliant analysis of Portugal's territorial expansion during the fifteenth century (1993). On the rounding of Cape Bojador, see Russell 2000, 109–134; Zurara, *Crónica dos feitos notáveis* 7–9 (1978–1981, 1:43–53); and Barros, *Ásia* 1.2–5 (1552/1932, 11–25).

88. Zurara, *Crónica dos feitos notáveis* 8 (1978–1981, 1:47).

89. Ibid., 8 (1978–1981, 1:48).

90. Barros, *Ásia* 1.2 (1552/1932, 13–14); all translations from this work are my own.

91. Ibid.

92. For Columbus's claim that São Jorge da Mina was "temperate" and densely populated see postils 16a–b, and 234 in Ailly and Gerson 1480–1483/1990, 12r and 25r, resp. For the claim that Columbus or Bartholomew had witnessed Dias's report to Dom João, see postil 23b to Ailly and Gerson 1480–1483/1990, 13r.

93. On the rounding of Africa, see Pliny, *Natural History* 2.67 and 6.34.175–176, who reported the voyage by the Carthaginian sailor Hanno (5th century BCE) from Cádiz to "Arabia"; and Strabo, *Geography* 2.3.4–5, who reproved Posidonius for believing the story of Eudoxus of Cyzicus, a Greek sailor who presumably had served King Euergetes II of Egypt (reigned 145–116 BCE) and later headed a doomed expedition from Cádiz to India. The earliest expedition recorded by Pliny and Strabo came from Herodotus, *History* 4.42–43, who stated that King Necho II of Egypt (reigned 610 and 595 BCE) had sent a fleet of Phoenicians from the Red Sea back to Egypt. On Taprobane, see Pliny, *Natural History* 6.24.89; and Mela, *Description of the World* 122 (1998): "Taprobane [Sri Lanka] is said to be either a very large island or the first part of the second world [i. e., Crates' *antoikoi*]." For the Latin version of Mela, see *De chorographia* 3.70 (1971). For a scrupulous study of the textual tradition on Taprobane, see Weerakkody 1997. Key sources on Taprobane are Pliny, *Natural History* 6.24; and Strabo, *Geography* 1.4.2, 2.1.14, 2.5.14, 2.5.32, 2.5.35, and 15.1.14–15. According to Pliny, Taprobane had been considered part of the "Antichthones" (actually, Crates of Mallos's *antoikoi*) until Alexander the Great's military campaign in India (about 326 BCE) revealed it to be an island (*Natural History* 6.24.81). Onesicritus, a member of Alexander's Indus flotilla (326–325 BCE), located it "twenty days' voyage distant from the mainland" (Strabo, *Geography* 15.1.15; Megasthenes called its inhabitants "Palaeogoni" and claimed that it was even richer in gold and pearls than India (Pliny, *Natural History* 6.24.81); Eratosthenes situated it "seven days' sail from India," and claimed that it harbored elephants like the Ethiopia to which it extended (Strabo, *Geography* 15.1.14); Strabo himself referred to its location in different manners, supposing it, among other things, to be inhabited despite standing "far south of India" within the torrid zone (*Geography* 2.5.14). Ptolemy would provide latitudes for Taprobane that situated it barely north of the equator (*Cosmographia* 7 [1478, unfoliated, columns 233–236]).

94. See for instance, the letters that Anghiera 1992, 41 and 43, wrote to Cardinal Ascanio Sforza and to Archbishop Diego de Souza in the late summer of 1493, as Columbus headed back for the Caribbean basin.

95. Barros, *Ásia* 3.11 (1552/1932, 112). On Columbus's years in Portugal, see Morison 1942, 1:39–60; Ballesteros Beretta 1945, 1:251–392; and Taviani 1985a, 63–167 and 296–432.

96. Thus in the 1930s Jane, one of Columbus's most influential modern editors in the English world, wrote that "the Indies" was an extremely vague term that included Cathay (1930–1933/1988, lv–lvi).

97. See chapters 3 and 6.

98. Barros was extremely mindful of the connection between the territories discovered by Prince Henry beyond Bojador and the extension granted by Alcáçovas to Portugal to the south and to the east of the Canaries.

99. I am following Lovejoy's useful coinage of this terminology (1964, 52).

100. Marco Polo returned to Europe around 1294, and he found himself captured by the Genoese and imprisoned in Genoa in 1298, where he dictated his book to another prisoner, Rustichello da Pisa. This version, rendered by Rustichello in Old French, was known as *Le divisament dou monde* and soon translated in other languages. Back in Venice, sometime between 1310 and 1320, Marco Polo would compose a new version in Italian known as *Il milione,* now lost, which served as the basis for Francesco Pipino's abridgment in Latin, *De consuetudinibus et condicionibus orientalium regionum* (Larner 1999). It is an annotated copy of Pipino's Latin abridgment that is now held in the Biblioteca Colombina as part of Columbus's "library."

101. Ballesteros Beretta 1945, 1:330–331.

102. See chapter 6.

103. Marco Polo, *De consuetudinibus* 3.8 (1485/1986, 57r–59v).

104. An informative summary of cartographic knowledge in Europe circa 1492 appears in Wallis 1992. On the navigational techniques that Columbus would have learned from the Portuguese, see Waters 1992.

105. Las Casas, *Historia* 1.3.1.28 (1994, 1:495; emphasis added).

106. Ferdinand and Las Casas made this claim for Dom João's betrayal of Columbus's confidence, though there is no independent documentation to confirm it. See F. Columbus, *Historie* 11–12 (1571/1992, 30r–34r); and Las Casas, *Historia* 1.3.1.28 (1994, 1:494–499). For useful considerations of this episode in Columbus's life, see Morison 1942, 1:92–98; Ballesteros Beretta 1945, 1:373–392; and Taviani 1985a, 164–167 and 428–432.

107. For Dom João's charter of this expedition out of the Cape Verde Islands (4 August 1486), see Pérez de Tudela y Bueso et al. 1994, 1:52–53. For Dom João's reply to Columbus's request (20 March 1488), see Pérez de Tudela y Bueso et al. 1994, 1:56–57.

108. See Morison, 1942, 1:118; Ballesteros Beretta 1945, 1:471–478; and Taviani 1985a, 190–191 and 476–477.

109. On Columbus's negotiations with England, see Morison 1942, 1:118–119; Ballesteros Beretta 1945, 1:478–482; and Taviani 1985a, 474–475.

110. F. Columbus, *Historie* 11 (1571/1992, 31v; emphasis added).

111. On Columbus's negotiations with France, see Ballesteros Beretta 1945, 1:482; and Taviani 1985a, 475–476. Morison claims that Bartholomew had already left Castile for France no later than 1490 (1942, 1:119).

37. Pérez de Tudela y Bueso et al. 1994, 1:565–573; this quote, 571.

38. Ibid., 2:721–746; this quote, 722.

39. Strabo, *Geography* 2.5.7.

40. Ibid., 17.1.48.

41. See Herodotus, *History* 2.29; and Strabo, *Geography* 2.5.7. Eratosthenes famously calculated the earth's circumference to be 252,000 stades and divided this circumference into 60 intervals. According to Eratosthenes, the distance from the equator to the Tropic of Cancer was four-sixtieths of the earth's circumference, meaning that the Tropic of Cancer stood 16,800 stades north of the equator, the equivalent of approximately 24° N latitude. Eratosthenes further assumed that Syene and Meroë lay along the same meridian, and that Meroë was 5,000 stadia to the south of Syene, or the equivalent of about 17° N (modern 16° 52′ N) latitude. The stade originally designated "the distance covered by a plow in a single draft," but authors disagree on its exact modern equivalents; see Aujac 1987a, 148n3. For a discussion of Eratosthenes' measurement of the earth's circumference, see Aujac 1987a, 154–155.

42. Arrian, *Indica* 25.4.8 (1973–1983).

43. Strabo, *Geography* 15.1.13. Indographers after Onesicritus would long continue to stress Taprobane's meridional remoteness. According to Strabo, Eratosthenes (about 275–174) had situated Taprobane "seven days' sail towards the south from the most southerly parts of India, the land of the Coniaci," and supposed that it extended "eight thousand stadia in the direction of Ethiopia" (Strabo, *Geography* 15.1.14). Strabo himself referred to Taprobane's location in different manners, supposing it to be inhabited despite standing "far south of India" (Strabo, *Geography* 2.5.14). And Ptolemy would later provide latitudes for Taprobane that situated it barely north of the equator (*Cosmographia* 7 [1478, unfoliated, cols. 233–236]).

44. Pliny, *Natural History* 6.24.81. The idea that Taprobane was part of the "antichthones" was in fact held by Pliny's predecessor, Pomponius Mela, in his *Chorographia*. See *Description of the World* 3.70.

45. Pliny, *Natural History* 6.34.89. Key sources on Taprobane are Strabo, *Geography* 1.4.2, 2.1.14, 2.5.14, 2.5.32, 2.5.35, and 15.1.14–15; and Pliny, *Natural History* 6.24. For a scrupulous study of the textual tradition on Taprobane, see Weerakkody 1997.

46. Strabo, *Geography* 2.1.2.

47. Since the measure of the stade is unclear, I provide instead measurements in degrees, which can easily be deduced from Eratosthenes' measurement in stades. See note 41, above.

48. Aujac 1987a, 153–157.

49. Strabo, *Geography* 2.5.6. Needless to say, this projection of the inhabited world—which clearly took into account the fact that horizontal distances on the globe's surface decreased as points on either side of the meridian in question approached the poles—automatically assigned greater width or

"longitude" to those inhabited latitudes approaching the equator, that is, to the Afro-Indian tropics, than to those approaching the north pole.

50. Strabo, *Geography* 2.5.7; see also 1.4.6.

51. Ibid., 1.4.2.

52. Ibid., 2.1.1.

53. Eratosthenes added the "lengths" in stades that joined India's easternmost point to the Indus River (16,000), to the Caspian Gates (14,000), to the Euphrates River (10,000), to the Nile (5,000), to the "Canobic" mouth of the Nile (in Alexandria, 1,300), to Carthage (13,500), and to the Pillars of Hercules (at least 8,000). According to Strabo, he also added about 2,000 on either side "to keep the breadth from being more than half the length." Strabo, *Geography* 1.4.5.

54. Strabo, *Geography* 1.4.6.

55. Aujac 1987a, 156.

56. For Strabo's discussion of Eratosthenes' seals, I follow *Geography* 2.1.

57. Strabo, *Geography* 2.1.22.

58. As Strabo explains (*Geography* 2.1.22), Eratosthenes did not specify whether the western boundary of the second seal was parallel or not to the Indus River, nor whether its southern boundary was parallel to the parallel of Rhodes, so that these boundaries can be represented as diagonals.

59. The third seal presents particular difficulties for Strabo because of its irregular shape: its northern side is diagonal to the axial parallel, because it runs to where the Euphrates River begins; the Euphrates itself snakes to the south, then to the east, and finally to the south toward the Persian Gulf; the Persian Gulf itself undercuts the "southern" side of this seal diagonally. See Strabo, *Geography* 2.1.23–26.

60. Ibid., 2.1.32.

61. Ibid., 2.1.3–13, for Strabo's evaluation of Eratosthenes' calculation.

62. Ibid., 16.4.2.

63. Ibid., 2.5.15. Later (2.5.33) Strabo describes Lybia as a "trapezium," since the diagonal line that runs toward the Pillars of Hercules from Ethiopia is approximately parallel to Libya's Mediterranean shores, and then turns northward to form a "sharp" promontory, before turning back into the Mediterranean Sea. Elsewhere (17.3.1) Strabo describes Lybia as a right triangle formed by the Mediterranean coast, the Nile, and the Atlantic coastline joining Ethiopia with Maurusia, or Mauretania. He accords Lybia about 13,000 or 14,000 stades in breadth and no more than twice that measure in length (26,000 to 28,000 stades).

64. Strabo, *Geography* 15.1.13 and 15.24–26.

65. Pérez de Tudela y Bueso et al. 1994, 2:832.

66. Strabo, *Geography* 2.5.16.

67. See Aujac's discussion of Hipparchus (1987b, 164–167); and Strabo, *Geography* 1.1.12.

68. Strabo, *Geography* 2.5.34.

69. It appears that Ptolemy, like Strabo, owed his own table of latitudes to Hipparchus's calculations. See Dilke 1987, 182–183. On the division of the world according to seven *climata*, see also chapter 1, note 61.

70. Equinoctial hours were units of time measured during the equinox, when day and night were of equal length to each other.

71. Laguardia Trías 1964 and 1973.

72. Strabo, *Geography* 2.5.36–42.

73. Ibid., 2.5.38. Coelesyria, Upper Syria, and Babylonia would have roughly crossed the Syrian Desert, from the Mediterranean Sea and the Tigris River. Susiana and Persia presumably stood east of the Tigris and north/northeast of the Persian Gulf (part of Eratostheneses' third sphragis). And Carmania and Upper Gedrosia presumably belonged to Ariana (Eratosthenes' second sphragis).

74. Strabo, *Geography* 2.5.36.

75. Ibid.

76. Ibid., 2.5.35.

77. Postil 56 to Piccolomini 1477/1991, 6v. All translations from this work are my own, in consultation with the Spanish translation by Antonio Ramírez de Verger.

78. Strabo, *Geography* 1.2.24–1.2.30.

79. Ibid., 2.5.10.

80. Ibid., 2.5.13. See my discussion of this issue in chapter 2.

81. Woodward 1987, 353.

82. Two Latin translations from different Greek codices were produced in the early fifteenth century, one by Jacopo d'Angelo (about 1406), containing no maps; and another, with maps, in 1415 by Francesco Lapacino and Domenico Buoninsegni. It seems that the maps contained in all known manuscripts and printed editions of the *Geography* were constructed by Maximus Planudes about 1300 on the basis of the instructions contained in Ptolemy's work. See Berggren and Jones 2000, 45–52; and Diller 1940.

83. Woodward 1987, 354.

84. Postil 79 in Ailly and Gerson 1480–1483/1990, 18r.

85. Postil 75 in ibid., 18r.

86. Ptolemy, *Geography* 7.5 (Berggren and Jones 2000, 108–111).

87. Ibid., 1.6–20 (Berggren and Jones 2000, 63–83).

88. Ibid., 1.23 (Berggren and Jones 2000, 85).

89. See Berggren and Jones 2000, 168; and Ptolemy, *Geography* 1.8 (ibid., 67–68) and *Cosmographia* 4 (1478, unfoliated, col. 152).

90. Ptolemy, *Cosmographia* 4 (1478, unfoliated, col. 144).

91. See Ptolemy, *Cosmographia* 4 and 7, resp. (1478, unfoliated, cols. 149 and 233, resp.). See also the entry for "Unknown Land" in Berggren and Jones 2000, 180–181; and, in particular, *Geography* 7.5 (Berggren and Jones 2000, 108–111). Ptolemy's endorsement of an open geography was not as exceptional in antiquity as the editors claim (see Berggren and Jones 2000, 22n22).

92. Ptolemy, *Cosmographia* (1477, 1478, and 1482).

93. Ravenstein 1908, 32–34.

94. Ibid., 62–64.

95. Pérez de Tudela y Bueso et al. 1994, 1:116.

96. The first one of these works, seemingly a Ptolemaic map, was promised by Columbus in the prologue to the *Diario*. See ibid., 1:109. Another, he appears to have sent to the Crown from the recently founded town of La Ysabela during the second voyage (20 January 1494), showing parallels and meridians, as well as a red vertical meridian that divided the discoveries he had just realized in the Lesser Antilles from those realized in the Bahamas and outer shores of the Caribbean in the course of the first voyage. See ibid., 2:526–527.

97. For a recent example, see Comellas 1995, 66–76.

98. Pérez de Tudela y Bueso et al. 1994, 1:1281–1285; emphasis added.

99. Ibid., 2:835; emphasis added.

100. Bernáldez 1870, 1:357; my translation.

101. Pérez de Oliva 1965, 41; my translation.

102. Fernández de Oviedo y Valdés, *La historia general y natural de las Indias* 1.2.1 and 1.2.2 (1535, iir and iiv, resp.).

103. F. Columbus, *Historie* 3 (1571/1992, 7r–v).

104. López de Gómara 1552/1979, 28–29.

105. Las Casas, *Historia* 1.3.1.30 (1994, 1:509).

106. For an analysis of these sketches, see Baldacci 1997, 23–32.

107. The map was controversially attributed to Columbus by Charles de la Roncière in 1924. For a recent discussion of the so-called "Columbus Chart," see Comellas 1995.

108. For the section of Zorzi's *Informazione* concerned with Bartholomew Columbus's account of his brother's fourth voyage, see Pérez de Tudela y Bueso et al. 1994, 3:2084–2087. For a list of the places named in the geographical sketches attributed to Bartholomew, see ibid., 3:2088–2089,

2090–2091, and 2092–2093. A superb analysis of the geographical notions contained in these sketches can be found in Cerezo Martínez 1994, 119–128. All translations from Zorzi are my own.

109. See Colón 1992, 382; and Pérez de Tudela y Bueso et al. 1994, 2:1230.

110. For a brief discussion of the debate surrounding these sketches, see Cerezo Martínez 1994, 127.

111. Herodotus, *History* 3.98–100.

112. Ibid., 3.106.

113. Freese 1920, 111.

114. Ibid., 114.

115. Ibid., 120.

116. Isidore, *Etymologías* 14.3.7.

117. Diodorus Siculus, *Bibliotheca historica* 2.36.

118. Strabo, *Geography* 15.1.37.

119. Pliny, *Natural History* 6.24.89.

120. Arrian, *Indica* 8.8–12.

121. Solinus 1958, 193–195.

122. Isidore, *Etymologías* 14.3.7.

123. McCrindle 1960, 29.

124. Ibid., 31.

125. Ibid.

126. Ibid., 30.

127. Ibid., 34.

128. Diodorus Siculus, *Bibliotheca historica* 2.36.

129. Strabo, *Geography* 15.1.21.

130. Ibid., 15.1.22.

131. Mela, *Description of the World* 3.62.

132. Pliny, *Natural History* 7.2.21.

133. Isidore, *Etymologías* 14.3.5.

134. Pérez de Tudela y Bueso et al. 1994, 1:240.

135. For a classical study of Columbus's confrontation with American nature, see Gerbi 1975/1985, 3–22. A useful reflection on Columbus's role as a "witness" in the invention of American exotica can be found in Campbell 1988.

136. Pérez de Tudela y Bueso et al. 1994, 2:724, 1:129, and 1:571.

137. Ibid., 1:572.

138. Ibid., 2:722.

139. Ibid., 2:724.

140. Ibid., 2:738.

141. Ibid., 2:1148; emphasis added.

142. Herodotus, *History* 3.106.

143. Freese 1920, 111.

144. Ibid., 112.

145. Ibid., 114.

146. McCrindle 1960, 30.

147. Strabo, *Geography* 15.1.15.

148. Ibid., 15.1.37.

149. Isidore, *Etymologías* 12.4.5.

150. Pérez de Tudela y Bueso et al. 1994, 1:128–129. Dunn and Kelley 1989, 89 interpret the term *gallos* as "small, edible saltwater fish with a golden color."

151. Pérez de Tudela y Bueso et al. 1994, 1:133.

152. Ibid., 1:206.

153. Ibid., 3:1519.

154. Herodotus, *History* 3.101.

155. Freese 1920, 110.

156. Ibid., 115–116,

157. Ibid., 117.

158. Friedman 1980, 61.

159. For Megasthenes' and Strabo's contributions to Western teratology, see Strabo, *Geography* 15.1.57–59, and 15.2.1–2.

160. Pliny, *Natural History* 6.21.58: "Its races and cities are beyond counting, if one wished to enumerate all of them."

161. Ibid., 7.2.32.

162. Ibid., 6.35.187.

163. Solinus 1958, 186; all translations from this work are my own.

164. Mandeville 2002, 23, 205.

165. Pérez de Tudela y Bueso et al. 1994, 1:142.

166. Ibid., 1:209.

167. Ibid., 3:1535.

168. Arrian, *Indica* 15.12.

169. Solinus 1958, 183.

170. Diodorus Siculus, *Bibliotheca historica* 2.36.

171. Ibid., 2.37.

172. Ibid.

173. Strabo, *Geography* 15.1.13.

174. Ibid., 15.1.20.

175. Ibid.

176. Ibid., 15.1.22.

177. Mela, *Description of the World* 1.11: "We are told that the first humans in Asia, starting from the east, are the Indians, the Seres [Silk People], and the Scyths. The Seres inhabit more or less the middle of the eastern part. The Indians and the Scyths inhabit the extremities, both peoples covering a broad expanse and spreading to the ocean not at this point only. For the Indians also look south and for a long time have been occupying the shore of the Indian Ocean with continuous nations, *except insofar as the heat makes it uninhabitable*" (emphasis added).

178. Mela, *Description of the World* 3.67: "From the Ganges to Point Colis, except where it is too hot to be inhabited, are found black peoples, Aethiopians so to speak."

179. Ibid., 1.52.

180. Diodorus Siculus, *Bibliotheca historica* 2:88–91.

181. Arrian, *Indica* 9.7–8.

182. See Herodotus, *History* 3.94; and Columbus's letter to Luis de Santángel (15 February 1493), in Pérez de Tudela y Bueso et al. 1994, 1:249.

183. Pérez de Tudela y Bueso et al. 1994, 1:572.

184. Ibid., 1:535–536.

185. Ibid., 1:523–538.

186. Ibid., 2:1104.

187. Ibid., 1:565.

188. Ibid., 2:744–745.

189. Ibid., 2:745.

190. Ibid., 1:571.

191. Ibid., 2:1109–1110.

192. In my use of the term "wonder," I am gratefully indebted to Daston and Park 1998.

193. Pérez de Tudela y Bueso et al. 1994, 1:250–251; emphasis added.

194. Anghiera 1992, 41 and 43.

4 From Place to Colonialism in the Aristotelian Tradition

1. Beazley 1879–1906, 3:500–504; Gérard 1904, 153; Mandonnet 1893a, 39–82, and 1893b; and Kimble 1938, 69–99, esp. 82–85.

2. Mandonnet 1893a and 1893b.

3. On Columbus's connection with Deza and the monastery of San Esteban, see Ballesteros Beretta 1945 1:451–458; Manzano Manzano 1964, 42–43 and 79; and Taviani 1985a, 192, 442, and 481–482. Surprisingly, Las Casas cites Deza's role as Columbus's protector but says nothing about Columbus's stay in the monastery of San Esteban (*Historia de las Indias* 1.3.1.29 and 1.3.1.30 [1994, 1:503 and 510, resp.]).

4. On the royal council appointed in 1486 to evaluate Columbus's plan, see Ballesteros Beretta 1945, 1:446–455 and 487–493; Manzano Manzano 1964, 65–111; and Taviani 1985a, 172–173 and 441–443. On the royal council's final assembly in Santa Fe, see Ballesteros Beretta 1945, 1:513–515; Manzano Manzano 1964, 251–260; and Taviani 1985a, 196–197.

5. It has been claimed that the cautious Hernando de Talavera, the learned Jeromite friar who had presided over the assemblies that rejected the enterprise of the Indies, also joined ranks at this time with Deza and Cabrero. See Manzano Manzano 1964, 261–77; and Taviani 1985a, 199–201.

6. For this letter, dated 21 December 1504, see Colón 1992, 518–519.

7. Mandonnet 1893a, 99–152; 1893b. The passages discussed by Mandonnet are Albertus's *De caelo et mundo* 2.4.11 (1980a), Aquinas's *De caelo et mundo* 2.28 (1963–1964), and Albertus's *De natura loci* 1.12. For Aristotle's assertion, see *On the Heavens* 2.14.298a7–15 (1995f).

8. For Ferdinand's and Las Casas's views of the royal council, see, respectively, *Historie del S. D. Fernando Colombo* 12 (1571/1992, 32r–34r), and *Historia* 1.3.1.29 (1994, 1.3.1.29, 1:503–507).

9. Mandonnet 1893a, 131–132; my translation. The reference is to the refutation of the pagan theory of the antipodes in Lactantius, *The Divine Institutes* 3.24 (1964), and Augustine, *The City of God against the Pagans* 16.9 (1957–1972). Mandonnet's mention of Lactantius is somewhat misplaced, since Lactantius himself had difficulty accepting the notion that the inhabited world was located on a spherical surface at the center of the cosmos.

10. Ballesteros Beretta 1945, 1:446–455 and 487–493, tends to impugn Las Casas (rather than Ferdinand) with the invention of this opposition between a "learned" Columbus and the "short-sighted" members of the royal council. Ballesteros Beretta attributes the early diffusion of this opposition (this time as an opposition between the Dominican order and the members of the royal council) to the Dominican friar Antonio de Remesal's *Historia general de las Indias y particular de la gobernación de Chiapa y Guatemala* (1619). Remesal claimed that when Columbus stayed in

Salamanca, he found support for his theories only with the members of the monastery of San Esteban. According to Remesal, Columbus "came to Salamanca to communicate his arguments with the teachers of astrology and cosmography, who lectured on these subjects at the University. He began to outline his arguments, and only the friars of San Esteban paid attention and welcomed him. Because at that time, not only theology and the arts were cultivated in that convent, but every other subject taught in the various schools [of the University]" (1619/1964, 1:134; my translation). As Ballesteros Beretta points out, Remesal's claim that "the assemblies of astrologers and mathematicians" gathered in San Esteban and that "there Columbus presented his conclusions and defended them" (1619/1964, 1:134), should not be interpreted to mean that the first official meetings of the royal council appointed by Fernando and Isabel gathered in the University of Salamanca to pronounce judgment on Columbus's proposal (a myth found in some scholarly and many popular accounts of Columbus's interactions with the Crown). Remesal's assertion quite clearly refers to the gatherings of scholars that regularly took place in the various schools of the university, not to the official *junta* later presided over by the Jeromite Hernando de Talavera (Ballesteros Beretta 1945, 1:452–455). While Ballesteros Beretta sees no reason to deny that Columbus might have met informally with the members of San Esteban, he rejects the exclusive role assigned by Remesal to the Dominican order in persuading the Crown to finance Columbus's project. See also Manzano Manzano 1964, 70–72, 78–79, and 96–106, which correctly attributes the invention of the opposition between a "learned" Columbus and the "short-sighted" members of the royal council to Columbus's son Ferdinand. For an invaluable study of the learned arguments wielded by the members of the royal council against Columbus's plan, see Randles 1990.

11. The descriptor *buen estrologo* was used by the Catholic Monarchs in a letter dated 5 September 1493, which ordered Columbus to bring Fray Antonio de Marchena with him on the second voyage in order to assist him with determining "the degrees on which stand the islands and land you have found" (Pérez de Tudela y Bueso et al. 1994, 1:488–490). On the role that Fray Antonio de Marchena and the monastery of La Rábida played during Columbus's years in Spain, see Morison 1942 1:108–110; Ballesteros Beretta 1945, 1:400–413; Manzano Manzano 1964, 26–33, 60–63, and 228–240; and Taviani 1985a, 168–173 and 433–440.

12. Crucial discussions on the subject of Roger Bacon's treatment of place, especially as concerns his geography, are Hackett 1997; and Woodward and Howe 1997. Unfortunately, I have scant information about the diffusion of Roger Bacon's geography in Spain. We know thanks to Little 1914, 382, that a thirteenth-century manuscript of *Opus maius* IV does survives in the library of the Monasterio de El Escorial in Madrid (Escorial, g.iii.17).

13. Geminos, *Introduction aux phénomènes* 16.21–38 (1975). This work was translated into Latin by Gerard of Cremona in the twelfth century.

14. See Ptolemy, *Almagest* 2.6 (1998), and Avicenna, *Canon of Medicine* 1.1.3.34 (1930). Schoolmen variously attribute this view to Avicenna's *De animalibus* I, IV, or X. I have found it, elsewhere, in *De animalibus* XII, "Capitulum I, De complexione et humiditatibus" (Avicenna 1508/1961a, 44v–45r; this quote, 45r), which states that the inhabitants of the equator enjoyed a more temperate climate than those toward the tropics, except in those places that were covered by "the mighty sea." The translations of these works came from the school of Toledo: the *Almagest* was translated by Gerard of Cremona in 1175 (Haskins 1924, 95n83); the *Canon,* also by Gerard of Cremona in the late twelfth century (Haskins 1927, 324); and *De animalibus* by Dominic Gondisalvi and John of Seville in the late twelfth century (Haskins 1924, 13).

15. See lecture 13 in Robertus Anglicus's 1271 commentary to *De sphaera* (Thorndike 1949, 236–242); and lectures 11 and 16 in the commentary attributed to Michael Scot, which was written about 1231 (Thorndike 1949, 317–322 and 331–336, resp.). Grosseteste's critique of the theory of the five zones appears specifically in *De natura locorum* (1912c, 66–68), which logically presupposes *De lineis, figuris, et angulis.* See my discussion of *De lineis* below.

16. See Strabo's discussion of Posidonius's *The Ocean* in his *Geography* 2.1.1–2.3.8, esp. 2.3.2 (1917–1932).

17. See chapter 1.

18. Postil 18 to Ailly and Gerson 1480–1483/1990, 12r.

19. Postil 19 to ibid.

20. For an excellent synthesis of the exegetical tradition that located paradise in a temperate place, we have Las Casas's own explanation for why Columbus, upon reaching the waters of the Orinoco delta, believed he was near Eden. See Las Casas, *Historia* 1.5.5.141–145 (1994, 4:1082–1106).

21. Postil 673 to Ailly and Gerson 1480–1483/1990, 78v.

22. Diller 1975, 126–129.

23. Postils 22a and b to Piccolomini 1477/1991, 3v.

24. If Columbus was looking to find Albertus's geographical ideas in this newly printed work, he most surely was disappointed. See Albertus 1890. The mistaken claim that the Albertine volume preserved in the Colombina is *De natura loci* was disseminated by Schneider 1932 on the basis of Gillet 1932.

25. On the relationship between authorship and originality in scholastic thought, see Minnis 1988.

26. On Las Casas's view about the writing of history, see his prologue to *Historia* (1994, 3:327–337).

27. Ibid., 1.1.3.6 (3:371).

28. Ibid., 1.1.3.7 (3:379; emphasis added).

29. Ibid., 1.1.3.6 (3:372).

30. Albertus Magnus, *De natura loci* 1.1 (1980b, 1, lines 6–8).

31. On the circulation of *De natura loci,* see chapter 1, n. 143.

32. Albertus was praised in his time for the scope of his learning as *doctor universalis.* His fame as a natural philosopher among Aristotelians also earned him the title conferred by the Vatican in our own time as "celestial patron saint of those who study the natural sciences" (Weisheipl 1980b, 46–47).

33. Wallace 1978, 96.

34. An indispensable account on translation activity in the twelfth and thirteenth centuries continues to be Haskins (1924 and 1927, 278–302). More recently, see Lindberg 1978a, and 1992, 215–244; and Grant 1996, 18–32. For a list of translations and translators of Aristotle, Pseudo-Aristotle, and commentators of the *corpus aristotelicum,* see Dodd 1982.

35. On the incorporation of Aristotle's *libri naturales* into the arts curriculum at Paris, see Kibre and Siraisi 1978, 130. On the history of the initial prohibition and later acceptance of Aristotle's works at Paris, see Rashdall 1936, 1:354–358; and Leff 1992, 319–325. For the documents concerning the prohibition, expurgation and later inception of Aristotle's works in Paris, see Grant 1974, 42–43.

36. Robert Grosseteste, for instance, had written substantially on Aristotle at Oxford, and Roger Bacon had recently lectured on him at Paris in the 1240s.

37. Wallace 1978, 96 and note. See also Albertus Magnus, *In II Sententiarum* 13.C.a.2 (1894, 27:247).

38. Wallace 1978, 96 and note; and Albertus Magnus, *In II Sententiarum* 13.C.a.2 (1894, 27:247a).

39. In 1255, following decades of opposition from those who considered Aristotle's teachings to pose a threat to orthodoxy, the "three philosophies" were formally incorporated into the new faculty of the arts curriculum at Paris: students were now required to follow a course of study leading from the most basic to the highest domains of knowledge—first, the logical arts (*trivium*), then the mathematical arts (*quadrivium*), and finally the three branches of philosophy (sequentially, natural, moral, and first philosophy)—before they could aspire to degrees in theology, medicine, or law. On the curricula at Paris and Oxford, see Weisheipl 1964 and 1978; on the curricula at Oxford, Paris, Bologna, and Padua, see Kibre and Siraisi 1978.

40. Weisheipl 1980b, 30. See Albertus Magnus, *Physica* 1.1 (1987–1993, 1:1, lines 9–14).

41. Weisheipl 1980b, 30.

42. Among Albertus's paraphrases that do not correspond by title to Aristotle's authentic natural works, one should include the ninth-century astro-geological treatise *De causis proprietatum elementorum,* which Albertus considered a complement to *De natura loci;* some of the *parva naturalia* or minor works—including *De nutrimento et nutribili, De intellectu et intelligibili, De somno et vigilia,* and *De spiritu et respiratione;* and the first-century botanical *De vegetabilibus,* now commonly attributed to Nicholas of Damascus (Weisheipl 1980a). See also Albertus Magnus, *Tabula tractatuum parvorum naturalium* (1517).

43. Albertus Magnus, *Physica* 1.1 (1987–1993, 1:1, lines 38–42).

44. Wyckoff 1967, xxviii.

45. Albertus Magnus, *De natura loci* 1.1 (1980b, 2, lines 56–60). The only such fragment Albertus mentions by either Aristotle or Plato is one he later attributes to Aristotle, presumably titled *De natura latitudinis et longitudinis locorum et locatorum* (ibid., 3.1 [1980b, 29]). No such work by Aristotle or spuriously attributed to him is known to exist. On the circulation and influence of Pseudo-Aristotle in the Latin West, see Thorndike 1923, 2:246–278; and Schmitt 1986.

46. Aristotle's God was a thinking divine whose "thinking is a thinking on thinking." See Aristotle, *Metaphysics* 12.9.1074b34 (1995b).

47. Lang 1992, 128–134. These distinctions are established in Albertus Magnus, *Physica* 8.1 (1987–1993, 2:549–581). See particularly ibid., 8.1 (2:575, line 13).

48. Lang 1992, 134. See also Albertus Magnus, *Physica* 8.1 (1987–1993, 2:575, lines 74–81). Albertus's distinction between God's eternity and the perpetuity of motion, as well as his distinction between matter created by God in its first form and matter given second form by nature drew inspiration from hexameral readings of Genesis 1:1, "In the beginning God created earth and heaven," and Genesis 1:2, "And the earth was void and empty, and darkness was upon the face of the deep," resp. See Augustine, *The Literal Meaning of Genesis*, 1.1, 1.4, 1.5, and especially 1.17 (1982): "unformed creation is marked off from formed creation in order that it may not find its end in an unformed state but rather be set aside to be formed later by other created beings of the corporeal world." For the Latin text, see Augustine 1970, 3–5, 7–8, 21–22, and 23–26, resp.; this quote, 25–26. See also *City of God,* 11.4–6. Albertus may have drawn his concept of "first form" from Augustine's "seminal reasons," a term that denoted God's creation of certain things in a state of potentiality that, as nature ran its course, developed into full actuality (Markus 1967, 398–399).

49. One finds this idea clearly stated in Augustine, for instance, in *City of God* 5.11: "The supreme and true God with his Word and Holy Spirit, which three are one, is the one almighty God, the creator and maker of every soul and every body. It is by participation in him that happiness is found by all who are happy in verity and not in vanity. He made man a rational animal, combining soul and body. When man sinned, God did not permit him to go unpunished, nor yet did he abandon him without mercy. To the good and to the evil he gave being, possessed also by stones; germinative life, possessed also by trees; conscious life, possessed also by animals; and intellectual life, possessed also by angels alone. From him comes all limit, all form, all order; from him comes measure, number and weight; from him comes whatever exists in nature, whatever its kind and whatever its worth; from him come seeds of forms and forms of seeds and movements in seeds and forms. He gave also to flesh a source, beauty, health, fruitfulness in propagation, arrangement of limbs and the saving grace of harmony. To the irrational soul also he gave memory, sensation and appetite; to the rational soul he gave in addition mind, intelligence and will. Neither heaven nor earth, neither

angel nor man, not even the inner organs of a tiny and despised animal, not the pinfeather of a bird nor the tiny flower in the meadow nor the leaf on the tree did God leave unprovided with a suitable harmony of parts, a peace, so to speak, between its members. It is impossible to suppose that he would have excluded from the laws of his providence the kingdoms of men and their dominations and servitudes." On nature's role in carrying out divine providence, see also *City of God* 12.5: "Those things in nature that were not granted everlasting being suffer changes for better or for worse as they serve the course of events to which they are subject by the law of the Creator, thereby moving through divine providence toward the end marked out for them on the guiding chart of the universe. Thus not even such decay as brings destruction of changeable and mortal things can make what was cease to be in the sense that what was ordained to be is not in due sequence created out of it." And in *On the Literal Meaning of Genesis* 4.12, Augustine writes: "But the universe will pass away in the twinkling of an eye if God withdraws His ruling hand." For the Latin text, see Augustine 1970, 109.

On the concept of providence in Christian thought, see Gilson 1940, 148–167. For echoes of Plato's thought in Augustine, see Plato, *Laws* 10.903b–c (1997a): "'The supervisor of the universe has arranged everything with an eye to its preservation and excellence, and its individual parts play appropriate active or passive roles according to their various capacities. These parts, down to the smallest details of their active and passive functions, have each been put under the control of ruling powers that have perfected the minutest constituents of the universe.'" See also Plotinus's treatises on "providence," especially Plotinus, *Enneads* 3.2.13 (1962): "We cannot but recognize from what we observe in this universe that some such principle of order prevails throughout the entire of existence—the minutest of things a tributary to the vast total; the marvellous art shown not merely in the mightiest works and sublimest members of the All, but even amid such littleness as one would think Providence must disdain: the varied workmanship of wonder in any and every animal form; the world of vegetation, too; the grace of fruits and even of leaves, the lavishness, the delicacy, the diversity of exquisite bloom: and all this not issuing once, and then to die out, but made ever and ever anew as the Transcendent Beings move variously over this earth."

50. As Lang argues in her study of Albertus's *Physica*, "A conception of physics that treats the physical world as an effect that, when considered properly, reveals its 'higher' cause, is just the conception of physics central to Neoplatonism" (1992, 130). Perhaps the best treatment of this subject is to be found in Deck 1967.

51. Albertus wrote highly influential paraphrases of the famous works now believed to have been written by a Syrian monk in the fifth century who wrote under the name of Dionysius the Areopagite (Pelikan 1987, 21–22). On Pseudo-Dionysius's influence in the Latin West, see Leclerq 1987. Albertus also wrote a paraphrase of the Pseudo-Aristotelian *Liber de causis* (9th century), a

work probably composed by al-Kindī's circle of translators on the basis of Proclus's fifth-century *Elements of Theology*. Albertus closely associated the *Liber de causis* with the Aristotelian corpus even though he knew it was not by Aristotle (Bonin 2001, 3–4). On the method and influence of the *Liber de causis* in the Arabic and Latin philosophical milieus, see Taylor 1986 and Lohr 1986.

52. My account of the sources that directly or indirectly informed Albertus's *De natura loci* is far from exhaustive. For an account of the sources explicitly acknowledged by Albertus or else noted by the editors of the *Editio colonniensis*, see the indices to *De natura loci* (1980b, 219–223), though the list provided in this edition does not itself cover all of Albertus's sources.

53. On the influence of Avicennian Neoplatonism in Europe, see Afnan 1958, 258–290; and Goichon 1969, 73–110.

54. Al-Kindī knew Plotinus directly or through the collection of extracts known to Arabs as the *Theology of Aristotle* (Lindberg 1998, xliv). On the origins and manuscript tradition of the *Theology*, see Zimmermann 1986; and Fenton 1986.

55. I am deeply indebted to Helen S. Lang, who in her reading of the original version of this chapter carefully pointed out the Neoplatonic inflexions in Albertus's theorization of place. In my discussion of the distinctions to be drawn between Aristotle's and Albertus's concepts of nature and place, I am closely following her lead (1992, 97–160).

56. On the subject of Albertus's Neoplatonism, particularly as it concerns Albertus's rewriting of Aristotle's *Physics*, see Lang 1992, 125–160. Lang has argued that Albertus inherited his brand of Neoplatonism in part from Augustine and in part from Avicenna, whose work offered Latin Aristotelians a compromise between Augustinian Neoplatonism and Aristotle's philosophy (1992, 251, note 2). Her argument on Avicenna's influence in the Latin West follows the contribution made by Goichon 1969. For a helpful discussion of Albertus's relation to Neoplatonism, see also Sweeney 1983.

57. Weisheipl 1980a, 565–567; and 1980b, 30–31. On the origin and dating of *De causis proprietatum elementorum*, see Vodraska's bilingual edition, 1969, 58–66.

58. Weisheipl 1980a, 564–569.

59. Aristotle, *Physics* 2.1.192b21–22 (1995i). The following discussion concerning those things that are "by nature" in Aristotle closely follows Lang's explanation on this subject 1992, 23–34 and 98–106.

60. On the distinction between those things that are by nature and those that are brought forth artificially, see Aristotle *Physics* 2.1.192b9–34.

61. Aristotle, *Physics* 2.3.194b16–195a3.

62. Lang 1992, 100; and Aristotle, *Physics* 2.2.194a12.

63. Lang 1992, 100; and Aristotle, *Physics* 2.1.193a30–193b18 and 3.3.202b10–23.

64. Lang 1992, 100; and Aristotle, *Physics* 2.1.193b7–8.

65. Lang 1992, 100; and Aristotle, *Physics* 3.3.202a.

66. Aristotle, *Physics*, 1.9.192a20–25. Lang remarks, "Here we reach the crux of Aristotle's definition of nature as a "source of being moved." In things that are by nature, to be moved means to be caused by another; but it does not mean to be passive. The passive (or middle) infinitive indicates a causal relation in which matter is caused, that is, as potential matter is moved immediately by form as actual; but matter is moved not because it is passive but because it is actively oriented toward proper form as actuality" (1992, 100). See also Aristotle, *Physics* 2.8.199b15–18: "Those things are natural which, by a continuous movement originated from an internal principle, arrive at some end."

67. Lang 1992, 111–112. For Plato's account of the descent of soul into body, see *Phaedrus* 246b–c (1997d), which specifies that body does not "move itself" until it is "taken on" by soul; and *Laws* 10.896a–897c, which reads: "So soul, by virtue of its motions, stirs into movement everything in the heavens and on earth and in the sea. The names of the motions of soul are: wish, reflection, diligence, counsel, opinion true and false, joy and grief, cheerfulness and fear, love and hate. Soul also uses all related or initiating motions which take over the secondary movements of matter and stimulate everything to increase or diminish, separate or combine, with the accompanying heat and cold, heaviness and lightness, roughness and smoothness, white and black, bitter and sweet." For Aristotle's account of the soul, see *On the Soul* 2.1.412a27–29 (1995g): "Soul is an actuality of the first kind of a natural body having life potentially in it"; and, for his explanation, see *On the Soul* 2.1412b10–413a8.

68. See Plato, *Phaedrus* 245a: "Every soul is immortal. That is because whatever is always in motion is immortal, while what moves, and is moved by, something else stops living when it stops moving. So it is only what moves itself that never desists from motion, since it does not leave off being itself. In fact, this self-mover is also the source and spring of motion in everything else that moves; and a source has no beginning." See also Plato, *Laws* 10.896a–c (1997a), where soul is "identical with the original source of the generation and motion of all past, present and future things and their contraries. . . . It has been shown to be the cause of all change and motion in everything." Things moved by others "are never endowed with the power of independent self-movement. . . . Such derived motion will therefore come second . . . being a mere change in matter that quite literally 'has no soul.'"

69. Aristotle, *Physics* 3.5.204b5–21.

70. Ibid., 3.5.205b10–11.

71. Aristotle, *Physics* 4.1.208a27–31. Lang here prefers Edward Hussey's translation of *Physics* III and IV: "because everyone supposes that things that are are somewhere" (1983).

72. Aristotle, *Physics* 3.1.201a10–201b6.

73. Ibid., 2.8.200b12–201a3.

74. Ibid., 8.7.260b17–19.

75. Ibid., 8.7.261a21–23.

76. For Aristotle's explanation of the priority of local motion, see ibid., 8.7.260a20–261a26.

77. Ibid., 4.1.208b9–11.

78. Ibid., 3.5.205b32–35.

79. Ibid., 4.1.208b11–22. The fact that up or down are in relation to center and circumference is later made explicit (ibid., 4.4.212a22–28). In *On the Heavens* 4.4.308a12–17, he will refer to up or down as "away from the centre" or "toward the centre."

80. Lang 1992, 102–103. Lang has pointed out to me that Aristotle's account of place in the *Physics* can be read as a further elaboration of the predicate "where" (Greek *pou;* Latin *ubi*) in his *Categories*.

81. For Hesiod's statement, see *Theogony*, line 116 (1993).

82. Plato, *Timaeus* 52a–b (1997e).

83. Aristotle, *Physics* 4.1.208b26–209a2.

84. Ibid., 4.1.209a6–7: "But the place cannot be body: for if it were there would be two bodies in the same place. / Further, if body has a place and space, clearly so too have surface and the other limits of body; for the same argument will apply to them: where the bounding planes of the water were, there in turn will be those of the air. But when we come to a point we cannot make a distinction between it and its place. Hence if the place of a point is not different from the point, no more will that of any of the others be different, and place will not be something different from each of them." The antecedents for this assertion appear to be in 3.5.205a10–22, where Aristotle finds himself proving why there is no such thing as "infinite body."

85. Place could not be identified with any of the four causes of natural things: matter, form, moving cause, or final cause ("that for the sake of which") (ibid., 4.1.209a20–23). Aristotle does not care to explain why place is neither the moving cause nor the final cause, but he does explain why it is neither matter nor form: since place "contains" body, it is some sort of limit. This raises the question of whether place can be the limit of the containing body—that is, whether this limit is form, or whether as the maximal interval of body it is matter (ibid., 4.2.209b1–10). His answer is that "in so far then as [place] is separable from the thing, it is not the form; and in so far as it contains it, it is different from the matter" (ibid., 4.2.209b22–31).

86. Previously in his argument, on his way to proving that there can be no such thing as an infinite body, Aristotle has stated: "Neither is the whole place larger than what can be filled by the body (and then the body would no longer be infinite), nor is the body larger than the place; for either there would be an empty space or a body whose nature it is to be nowhere" (*Physics* 3.5.205a27–30). On Aristotle's controversial theory of the void, or "place deprived of body," see *Physics*, 4.6–9.

87. Later in his argument, Aristotle states: "when we say that [a thing] is in the air, we do not mean it is in every part of the air, but that it is in the air because of the surface of the air which surrounds it; for if all the air were its place, the place of a thing would not be equal to the thing—which it is supposed to be, and which the primary place in which a thing is actually is" (ibid., 4.4.211a24–28).

88. Ibid., 4.4.211b12–13.

89. Ibid., 4.4.212a3–8.

90. Ibid., 4.4.212a20–21.

91. On the types of motion, see ibid., 8.8.261b29–31. On the "priority" of "circular" motion over "rectilinear" motion, see ibid., 8.8–9.

92. Ibid., 8.8.264b9–19.

93. Ibid., 8.8.261b31–263a3.

94. Aristotle, *On the Heavens* 1.1–3.

95. Ibid., 4.1.308a12–17. On the "absolute" lightness and heaviness of things, see ibid., 4.1.308a29–31 and 4.4.311b14–312a21.

96. Lang 1992, 103–104. For Aristotle's use of the term "inclination" or "tendency to movement," see Aristotle, *On the Heavens* 3.6.305a24–25.

97. Aristotle, *On the Heavens* 4.4.311a16–30. See also Aristotle, *On Generation and Corruption* 2.3.330b31–331a6 (1995e).

98. Aristotle, *On the Heavens* 4.3.310b8–15.

99. Ibid., 4.3.311a1–8.

100. Aristotle, *Physics* 7.1.241b34. For the development of this particular argument, see ibid., 7.1 and particularly 8.4.

101. Ibid., 3.1.201a10–201b6.

102. Ibid., 8.4.255a28–30.

103. Ibid., 7.1.243a32–245b1; and 8.5.256a.

104. Ibid., 7.1.

105. Ibid., 8.5.

106. As Lang explains, "Motion must be eternal, because potency is never neutral to actuality, and actuality never fails to be efficacious; on contact with proper actuality, potency is always moved by that actuality as its definition, end, or perfection" (1992, 131).

107. Aristotle, *Physics* 8.1.252a10–19: "But that which holds by nature and is natural can never be anything disorderly; for nature is everywhere the cause of order. Moreover, there is no ratio in the relation of the infinite to the infinite, whereas order always means ratio. But if we say that there is first a state of rest for an infinite time, and then motion is started at some moment, and that the

fact that it is this rather than a previous moment is of no importance, and that it involves no order, then we can no longer say that it is nature's work; for if anything is of a certain character naturally, it either is so invariably and is not sometimes of this and sometimes of another character (e.g., fire, which travels upwards naturally, does not sometimes do so and sometimes not) or there is a ratio in the variation."

108. Ibid., 8.10. Following Lang, "The identification of potency able to be eternal (i.e. circular motion) and its proper actuality, a first unmoved mover without magnitude, parts, or location, explains why motion in things must be eternal" (1992, 131).

109. Aristotle, *Physics* 8.10.267a21–267b8. See also Aristotle, *On the Heavens* 2.12.292b25–293a11.

110. On the "astrologization" of Aristotle's natural philosophy in the twelfth and thirteenth centuries, see Thorndike 1923, 2:246–278. On the theory of celestial influence among Christian commentators of key passages in Aristotle's *On the Heavens, On Generation and Corruption,* and *Meteorologica,* see North 1986, 45–46; and especially Grant 1994, 569–617. Lemay 1962, 52–63 forcefully argues that it was through Albumasar's influential astrological *Introductorium maius in astronomiam* (translated 1133), which cites this and other key passages in Aristotle's *On the Heavens* and *Meteorologica* as the foundation for astrology, that Latin scholars witnessed for the first time a systematic articulation of Aristotle's natural philosophy. See also North 1986, 52–63. For Albumasar's arguments in favor of astrology, see John of Seville's translation of Albumasar, *Liber introductorii maioris ad scientiam judiciorum astrorum,* Qwal III, Fasl. 1–8 (1995–1996). Albumasar's influence on writers who wished to cite Aristotle in favor of astrology can still be strongly felt, for example, in Francisco Vicente Tornamira's late-sixteenth-century *Chronographia, y Repertorio de los tiempos:* "Albumasar in his *Introductorium maius* states that the science of the stars is the very foundation of medicine, because, according to Aristotle, all superior bodies exert their influence on inferior bodies by means of motion and light. And in *Meteorologica* 1.2, he confirms this by saying that this world is well advised to be mindful of celestial motions and influences, that its virtue may be guided by them" (1585/1998, 14).

111. Aristotle, *On Generation and Corruption* 2.9.335a24–31.

112. Ibid., 2.10.336a13–336b15.

113. Ibid., 2.10.336b16–18.

114. Albertus Magnus, *De natura loci* 1.2 (1980b, 3, lines 22–23).

115. Ibid., 1.1, 1, lines 12–13.

116. This passage is taken from Simplicius's sixth-century commentary on Aristotle's *Physics,* which quotes Iamblichus's otherwise lost commentary to Plato's *Timaeus* (Samburksy 1982, [43]).

117. Roger Bacon would define place in exactly the same terms (*Opus majus* 4.4.5 [1897, 1:138]).

118. Porphyry, *Isagoge* 1.25–2.10 (1966; my translation). In the Latin West, Porphyry's treatise remained closely associated with its commentary by Boethius. For Boethius's commentaries to this passage, see *In Isagogen Porphyrii commenta*, "Editionis primae" 1.13 and "Editionis secundae" 2.3 (1966/1980, 35–37 and 174–178, resp.).

119. For a recent treatment of this debate, see Mayhew 2004. On the roles that Aristotle assigns to "male" and "female" in embryo formation, see Mayhew 2004, chapter 3; Morsink 1979; and Preus 1975, esp. chapter 2.

120. Mayhew 2004, 37–43.

121. Proof of this was the fact that menstrual blood was "akin" to primitive matter. See Aristotle, *Generation of Animals* 1.20.729a29–32 (1995a). On the female's menses as seed, see Mayhew 2004, 30–37.

122. For Aristotle's seminal discussion of the role of male and female in the generation of the embryo, see Aristotle, *Generation of Animals* 1.21.729a29–729b21.

123. Ibid., 1.22.730b20–23.

124. Ibid., 4.1.765b9–15: "But the male and female are distinguished by a certain capacity and incapacity. (For the male is that which can concoct and form and discharge a semen carrying with it the principle of form—by 'principle' I do not mean a material principle out of which comes into being an offspring resembling the parent, but I mean the first moving cause, whether it have power to act as such in the thing itself or in something else—but the female is that which receives semen, but cannot form it or discharge it.)"

125. In his paraphrase to Aristotle's *Physics*, Albertus had already used Aristotle's biological concept of the male's contribution to embryo development in order to describe the role played by movers as causes of natural things (*Physica* 2.2.3 [1987–1993, 1:101, line 86–1:102, line 19]).

126. Aristotle, *Physics* 2.3.194b30–32.

127. Lang 1992, 245. See Albertus Magnus, *Physica* 8.2.4 (1987–1993, 2:593, lines 12–14). This strongly differentiated Albertus's from Bacon's view of the relation of agent to recipient. For the latter, the generation of "species" or power involved bringing forth an active potentiality in passive matter (Bacon, *De multiplicatione specierum* 1.3 [1998a, 46]).

128. As Albertus has previously defined it in his commentary to Aristotle's *Physics*, "Nature is the principle of any [thing] and the cause of motion and rest, in which [thing] it is first *per se* and not by accident" (*Physica* 2.1.3 [1987–1993, 1:79, lines 57–58]). Or, as Albertus later states, simplifying his definition, "nature is a principle and cause" (ibid., 2.1.3 [1:79, line 68]). Nature, for Albertus, is certainly *in* the thing, but because he associates nature primarily with movers, nature is *in* the thing in the sense that it operates *on* the thing.

129. Albertus Magnus, *De natura loci* 1.1 (1980b, 1, lines 13–18).

130. Ibid., 1.1 (1, lines 18–20; emphasis added).

131. On Albertus's concept of emanation, see Bonin 2001, 15–21. In his *Liber de causis et processu universitatis a prima causa* (the paraphrase he wrote to the Proclian *Liber de causis* sometime between 1264 and 1271), Albertus refers to this flow as something that leaves the source of the flow undiminished, just as the sun remains undiminished by its radiation (Bonin 2001, 16). See also McCullough 1980, esp. 147. For Albertus's discussion, see *De causis et processu universitatis a prima causa* 1.4 (1993, 42–58). As he writes, "Flux is, simply speaking, an emanation of form from the first source" (ibid., 1.4.1 [43, lines 1–3]).

132. Albertus Magnus, *De natura loci* 1.1 (1980b, 1, lines 21–22).

133. Ibid., 1.1 (1, lines 24–26).

134. Ibid., 1.2 (4, lines 10–19).

135. Ibid., 1.1 (1, lines 29–32).

136. On Albertus's discussion of this finite chain of movers and moved in his commentary to Aristotle's *Physics,* see Lang 1992, 125–160.

137. Albertus Magnus, *De natura loci* 1.1 (1980b, 1, lines 47–52).

138. Ibid., 1.1 (2, lines 71–76).

139. In his paraphrase to the *Physics,* Albertus had already established a distinction between first matter and form (created by God), and second matter and form, imparted to a body by its primary or immediate mover (Lang 1992, 128–139). By his account, it would appear that a body that was potentially transformed and moved by its mover was in some sense the inchoate matter of what it was about to become.

140. Albertus Magnus, *Physica* 8.2.5 (1987–1993, 2:596, lines 45–46). For his argument concerning the self-moving motion of the first mover, see 8.2.5–8.2.9 (2:596–610). See also Lang 1992, 140.

141. Albertus Magnus, *Physica* 8.2.10–11 (1987–1993, 2:610–618).

142. Albertus Magnus, *De natura loci* 1.2 (1980b, 7, lines 13–17).

143. I am largely following Armstrong 1967. For invaluable accounts of Plotinian thought, see Armstrong 1940; and Deck 1967. A useful recent discussion on the ordering of reality in Plotinus can also be found in O'Meara 1999.

144. Armstrong 1967, 236–249. See also Armstrong 1940, 49–64; and Deck 1967, 22–30.

145. Armstrong 1967, 250–258. See also Armstrong 1940, 83–108; and Deck 1967, 64–72. On the question of physical reality, I have also consulted Wagner 1999.

146. Plotinus, *Enneads* 4.4.13 (1962, 297–298).

147. For Plotinus's reference to lower Soul as "the vastly efficacious soul of Nature," see ibid., 4.4.35 (1962, 319). Plotinus refers to the immobility and lifelessness of matter as follows: "For in Matter

we have no mere absence of means or of strength; it is utter destitution—of sense, of virtue, of beauty, of pattern, of Ideal principle, of quality. This is surely ugliness, utter disgracefulness, unredeemed evil" (ibid., 2.4.13 [1962, 117–118]). On the problem of Matter in Plotinus, see Armstrong 1940, 83–97; and Decker 1967, 64–80.

148. Plotinus, *Enneads* 4.3.9 (1962, 268).

149. Albertus Magnus, *De natura loci* 1.1 (1980b, 1, lines 9–10).

150. Ibid., 1.3 (4, lines 26–29).

151. Ibid., 1.4 (4, lines 33–35).

152. Ibid., 1.4 (6, lines 38–44). According to Hossfeld's edition of *De natura loci* (1980b, 6, note to line 38), this statement is drawn from Avicenna's *Sufficientia* 1.2, though I have failed to locate the indicated passage. For relevant passages, see Avicenna, *De celo et mundo* 16 (1508/1961b, 16, 42r–v); and his *Philosophia prima* 9.4–5 (1508/1961c, 104v–105v). Later, Albertus also cites Averroës and Maimonides in support of a similar claim (*De natura loci* 1.4 [1980b, 7, lines 9–13]). According to Hossfeld, Albertus is drawing in these lines from Avicenna's *Sufficientia* I.1 c.2, Averroës's *De generatione et corruptione* 1.2, comm. 50, and Maimonides' *Dux neutrorum* I.1 c.71. I have not yet studied the passages indicated by Hossfeld. But for present purposes, I suggest the following examples from Averroës and Maimonides: Averroës's epitome of the *Metaphysics* (*Compendio de metafisica* 4, comm. 53–54 [1919, 245–257]); and Maimonides' *Guide to the Perplexed* 1.70 and 1.72 (1963, 171–175 and 184–194, resp.).

153. "It is established that the outermost revolution of the heavens is a simple movement and the swiftest of all, and that the movement of all other bodies is composite and relatively slow, for the reason that each is moving on its own circle with the reverse motion to that of the heavens. This at once makes it reasonable that the body which is nearest to that first simple revolution should take the longest time to complete its circle, and that which is farthest from it the shortest, the others taking a longer time the nearer they are and a shorter time the farther away they are. For it is the nearest body which is most strongly influenced, and the most remote, by reason of its distance, which is least affected, the influence on the intermediate bodies varying, as the mathematicians show, with their distance" (Aristotle, *On the Heavens* 2.10.291a33–291b10). For Aristotle's explanation why in practice planetary cycles were not distributed in this way, see ibid., 2.12.

154. *Liber de causis* 23[24].180 (2003, 48).

155. Albertus Magnus, *De natura loci* 1.2 (1980b, 3, lines 48–52; this quote, 3, lines 49–52).

156. Nowhere is this clearer, perhaps, than in Aristotle's discussion in *On the Soul* II and III regarding the increasingly higher potentialities of besouled bodies; or than in his celebrated system for classifying animals in *Generation of Animals* II.

157. Aristotle, *On the Heavens* 2.12.292b17–21.

158. As Aristotle explains it, *aither* was so called for the fact that "it "runs always" for an eternity of time" (ibid., 1.3.270b20–24).

159. Ibid., 2.12.292b21–24.

160. Plotinus, *Enneads* 5.2.2 (1962, 381).

161. Ibid., 3.3.5 (182).

162. Macrobius, *Commentary on the Dream of Scipio* 1.14.15 (1990, 145). For the Latin text, see Macrobius 2003, 1:80. On Macrobius's use of this imagery, see Lovejoy 1964, 63. Macrobius may owe this image to a passage in Plotinus describing the Soul's relation to animate bodies: "In so far as any bodies are Animates, the Soul has given itself to each of the separate material masses; or rather it appears to be present in the bodies by the fact that it shines into them: it makes them living beings not by merging into body but by giving forth, without any change in itself, images or likenesses of itself like one face caught by many mirrors" (*Enneads* 1.1.8 [1962, 26]).

163. Macrobius, *Commentary* 1.22.5–6 (1990, 182). For the Latin text, see Macrobius 2003, 1:131–132.

164. Plotinus, *Enneads* 2.4.16 (1962, 117–118).

165. Lovejoy 1964, 101.

166. I have consulted Robert Grosseteste's translation of Pseudo-Dionysius, *De divinibus nominibus* (1937b, 1:247–248); all translations from this work are my own.

167. John of Damascus, *On the Orthodox Faith* 1.13 (1958, 197). For Burgundio's twelfth-century translation, see John of Damascus 1955, 56–57.

168. Plato, *Laws* 10.896c.

169. See chapter 1.

170. For my discussion of the metaphysics of light, I am largely indebted to Lindberg's treatment of the subject in his explanation of Bacon's theory of the "multiplication of species" (1998, xxxv–liii). For other useful treatments of this subject, see Bruyne 1998, 2:16–29; Crombie 1953, 128–134; and Hamilton 1974, 8–45. Baeumker 1908, 357–379, is often cited as a seminal treatment of this subject. On Albertus's metaphysics of light, see Sweeney 1983, 193–201.

171. Albertus Magnus, *De natura loci* 1.4 (1980b, 7, lines 24–25).

172. Augustine, *The Literal Meaning of Genesis* 1.17.32–35 (1982). For the Latin text, see Augustine 1970, 23–26.

173. Proclus asks us to conceive of the relation between light and the material cosmos as "'two spheres, one made of light and the other of many bodies, both equal in volume. One of them is placed at the center of the world and the other is immersed in the first sphere. The whole universe will thus be seen moving in its place in the immobile light" (Sambursky 1982, [67]).

174. Grosseteste 1912b, 51–52; all translations from this work are my own. For a useful discussion of Grosseteste's argument in this treatise, see Crombie 1953, 104–109.

175. Grosseteste 1912b, 55–56.

176. Ibid., 56. On the soul as form and perfection of the body, Lang (1992) points to the following sources: Plotinus, *Enneads* 4.4.20 (1962, 302–303); Augustine, *The Literal Meaning of Genesis* 7.15, 7.19, 7.21 (1982; for Latin text, 1970, 213, 214–215, and 217–219, resp.); and Avicenna's *Sufficientia* 2. 4 (1508/1961d, 27r, e).

177. Plotinus, *Enneads* 1.1.8 (1962, 26; emphasis added).

178. Crombie 1953, 109.

179. Albertus Magnus, *De natura loci* 1.4 (1980b, 7, lines 32–39).

180. See al-Kindī's *De radiis* 1 in Alverny and Hudry 1974, 215–218.

181. Albertus Magnus, *De natura loci* 1.4 (1980b, 7, lines 44–49).

182. On the subject of al-Kindī's sources, see Alverny and Hudry 1974, 155–167. The authors believe that this treatise may be an adaptation of a Greek treatise on "universal sympathy," and they identify the following sources: the ninth-century *Theology of Aristotle* (largely based on Plotinus's *Enneads* IV–VI); the *Letter to Annebo* attributed to Porphyry; Iamblichus's *On the Mysteries of the Egyptians;* and Proclus's *Elements of Theology.* Only the twelfth-century Latin translation of *De radiis* is known, not the Arabic original. According to Pingree 1987, 73, the oldest known copy in England was produced about 1240, and its presence cannot be established in Paris until several decades later. Its visible influence on Albertus's *De natura loci* may mean that Albertus had become acquainted with this treatise in Paris before founding his *studium* in Cologne.

183. I owe this insight to Richard Lemay. For the account of creation attributed to Zoroaster (about 628–about 551 BCE), I have consulted the Iranian version of the cosmogonic *Bundahišn.* See *Zand-Ākāsīh* 1.50 (1956, 17).

184. Notopoulos 1944a, 165. On the uses of light metaphors in Greece, see also Tarrant 1960.

185. Bouché-Leclercq 1899, 247–251.

186. Notopoulos 1944b, 223.

187. Armstrong 1940, 54.

188. For a useful explanation of the use of symbolism in Plato, see Notopoulos 1944a, 163–164. This conscious strategy in Plato is what one of Notopoulos's sources calls, with reference to the function of myth in the *Timaeus,* "a treatment of the eternal things by the symbolism of the passing" (Demos 1936, 538).

189. Plato, *Republic* 6.508b (1991).

190. Armstrong 1940, 52 also relates Plotinus's concept of emanation to the Stoic tradition attributed to Posidonius, which gave the name of *pneuma* or *hēgemonikon* to a fiery breath coming from and returning to the sun. Posidonius was cited in Antiquity as having stated that God was "intelligent pneuma" (Kidd 1999, 159–160).

191. Plato, *Republic* 6.508b–c.

192. Lindberg 1998, xli. Lang cites the following instance from Augustine's theological *De trinitate* 12.15 (*The Trinity* 1963, 366): "The nature of the intellectual mind is so formed as to see those things which, according to the disposition of the Creator, are subjoined to intelligible things in the natural order, in a sort of incorporeal light of its own kind, as the eye of the flesh sees the things that lie about it in this corporeal light, of which light it is made to be receptive and to which it is adapted." For the Latin text, see Augustine, *De trinitate libri XV* 12.[15 24].12–17 (1968, 1:378). A helpful discussion of Augustine's doctrine appears in Markus 1967, 362–373.

193. Plato, *Republic* 6.509b.

194. Plotinus, *Enneads* 4.3.9 (1962, 268): "While the Soul (as an eternal, a Divine Being) is at rest—in rest firmly based on Repose, the Absolute—yet, as we may put it, that huge illumination of the Supreme pouring outwards comes at last to the extreme bourne of its light and dwindles to darkness; this darkness now lying there beneath, the Soul sees and by seeing brings to shape; for in the law of things this ultimate depth, neighbouring with soul, may not go void of whatsoever degree of the Reason-Principle it can absorb, the dimmed reason of reality at its faintest."

195. On Plotinus's recognition of the inadequacy of such a metaphor, and on his attempts to correct himself, see Armstrong 1940, 59–61.

196. Plotinus, *Enneads* 5.1.6 (1962, 374).

197. Ibid., 6.4.7 (524): "Imagine a small luminous mass serving as centre to a transparent sphere, so that the light from within shows upon the entire outer surface, otherwise unlit: we surely agree that the inner core of light, intact and immobile, reaches over the entire outer extension; the single light of that small centre illuminates the whole field. The diffused light is not due to any bodily magnitude of that central point which illuminates not as body but as body lit, that is by another kind of power than corporeal quality: let us then abstract the corporeal mass, retaining the light as power: we can no longer speak of the light in any particular spot; it is equally diffused within and throughout the entire sphere."

198. Ibid., 4.4.33 (316).

199. Ibid., 4.4.35 (319).

200. Ibid., 4.4.35 (319).

201. Pseudo-Dionysius, *De divinibus nominibus* 4 (1937b, 1:146–147).

202. Pseudo-Dionysius, *De caelesti hierarchia* 1 (1937a, 2:736).

203. John of Damascus, *On the Orthodox Faith* 1.14 (1958, 202). For Burgundio's translation, see John of Damascus 1955, 64–65.

204. John of Damascus, *On the Orthodox Faith* 2.7 (1958, 216). For Burgundio's translation, see John of Damascus 1955, 85.

205. *Book of Causes* 5[6].57 (1984, 24). For the Latin text, see *Liber de causis* 2003, 14.

206. For al-Kindī's bearing on Grosseteste and Bacon, see Lindberg 1998, xliv–liii. One of the earliest references to al-Kindī's connection with the theories of diversity espoused by Grosseteste and Bacon may be Thorndike 1923, 1:646 and 2:443.

207. An early treatment of al-Kindī's *De radiis* can be found in Thorndike 1923, 1:643–646. For useful studies, see Alverny and Hudry 1974, and, more recently, Travaglia 1999. Thorndike rightly traces this magical thought to Plotinus's *Enneads* (Thorndike 1923, 2:443). See, in particular, the following tractates in the *Enneads* IV 4 and IV 5: "Problems of the Soul (II)" and Problems of the Soul (III)" (1962, 288–388).

208. Al-Kindī, *De radiis* 2, in Alverny and Hudry 1974, 219. All translations from this work are by Robert Mac Donald.

209. Ibid., 219–220.

210. Ibid., 220.

211. For Grosseteste, Lindberg (1998, xxxiii–xxxiv) cites such works as Euclid's *Optica* and *Catoptrica*, Aristotle's *Meteorologica*, al-Kindī's *De aspectibus*, and, possibly, Ptolemy's *Optica* (see also Grant 1974, 385). For Bacon, whose spatialized optics is by far the most elaborate, Lindberg cites such sources as Ptolemy's *Optica*, Alhazen's *Perspectiva* and *De speculis comburentibus*, al-Kindī's *De aspectibus*, Euclid's *Elements*, *De speculis*, and *De aspectibus*, an anonymous *De speculis*, and Theodosius's *De speris*, among others.

212. Al-Kindī, *De radiis* 2, in Alverny and Hudry 1974, 219.

213. Ibid., 220–221.

214. Ibid., 221.

215. Ibid., 220.

216. Ibid., 221.

217. Grosseteste 1912c, 65, lines 27–29; my translation.

218. Grosseteste 1912a, 61, lines 11–27. For an English version and study of *De natura locorum* and *De lineis,* see Eastwood 1964.

219. Grosseteste 1912a, 61, line 28 through 62, line 21.

220. Ibid., 62, line 22 through 63, line 29. Grosseteste also described the complex of rays radiating from a single body to its object as pyramidal in shape: any given point on an object's surface was the apex of a pyramid whose base was the surface of the radiating body—a concept that would also play an important role in Bacon's philosophy of nature. See ibid., 64, lines 13–31.

221. Al-Kindī, *De radiis* 2, in Alverny and Hudry 1974, 223.

222. Plotinus, *Enneads* 2.3.7 (1962, 96).

223. This tradition was founded on a passage in Saint Paul's epistle, Romans 1:20: "the invisible things of Him, from the Creation of the World, are clearly seen, being understood by the things that are made." On the basis of this passage, the church fathers (Saints Basil, Ambrose, and Augustine) inaugurated a tradition that considered the natural world to be a legible text: the literal meaning of this text was evinced by means of natural philosophy, and its spiritual meaning by that of Christian theology. See, for instance, Curtius 1953, 319–326; Gilson 1940, 364–382; and Glacken 1990, 202–208.

224. See Postil 561 to d'Ailly's *Tractatus de legibus et sectis contra superstitiosos astronomos* (1410), in Ailly and Gerson 1480–1483/1990, 51r.

225. See Gerson's eighth proposition in ibid., 159v; and his tenth proposition in ibid., 160r.

226. Albertus Magnus, *De natura loci* 1.5 (1980b, 8, lines 46–48).

227. Ibid., 1.5 (8, lines 48–51).

228. Ibid., 1.5 (8, lines 51–56).

229. Ibid., 1.5 (8, lines 56–58).

230. Ibid., 1.5 (8, lines 60–62).

231. Ibid., 1.5 (8, lines 71–75). This passage may derive from Boethius's commentary to the passage in the *Isagoge* where Porphyry calls place a principle of generation *quemadmodum pater*. See Boethius, *In Isagogen Porphyrii commenta*, "Editionis primae" 1.3 and "Editionis secundae" 2.3 (1966, 35–37 and 174–178, resp.).

232. Albertus Magnus, *De natura loci* 1.5 (1980b, 8, lines 78–82).

233. Ibid., 1.5 (8, lines 82–86).

234. Ibid., 1.5 (9, lines 4–7).

235. Ibid., 1.5 (9, lines 12–17).

236. Ibid., 1.5 (9, lines 31–33).

237. Ibid., 1.5 (9, lines 38–40).

238. Ptolemy, *Tetrabiblos* 1.3 (1980).

239. For Albertus's discussion of latitude and longitude, see *De natura loci* 1.9–10 (1980b, 15–18).

240. Ibid., 1.9 (16, lines 86–89).

241. The *Nicomachean Ethics* had seen two partial translations since the twelfth century, being translated in full by Grosseteste between 1246 and 1247 (Dodd 1982, 77). The *Economics* saw an anonymous translation in the late thirteenth century, and the *Politics* was translated by William of Moerbeke about 1260 (Dodd 1982, 78).

242. See my discussion of the theory of the five zones in chapter 1.

243. Albertus Magnus, *De natura loci* 1.6 (1980b, 9, lines 49–54; this quote, lines 50–54).

244. Ibid., 1.6 (9, lines 70–73).

245. Ibid., 1.6 (9, lines 77–81). This claim may be based on Proposition 32 of Pseudo-Euclid's *Catoptrica*, which discusses the combustive effect of sunrays converging on the focus of concave mirrors: "Fire is kindled by concave mirrors that face the sun" (Takahashi 1992, 194–199). Bacon examines precisely this problem in *De speculis comburentibus* (1998b).

246. Albertus Magnus, *De natura loci* 1.6 (1980b, 9, line 81 through 10, line 1). For Albertus's full discussion of the theory of the five zones, see ibid., 1.6 (9, line 49 through 11, line 22).

247. Ibid., 1.7 (13, lines 19–51). See also Albertus Magnus, *De caelo et mundo* 1.2.4.8 (1980a, 193, lines 19 ff).

248. Albertus Magnus, *De natura loci* 1.7 (1980b, 13, lines 48–50).

249. Ibid., 1.7 (13, lines 52–67). Albertus's immediate source was Geminos, *Introduction* 16.26–30 (1975, 81–83). See also my discussion of closed and open geographical models in chapter 2.

250. Albertus Magnus, *De natura loci* 1.7 (1980b, 13, line 68 through 14, line 75).

251. Ibid., 1.6 (12, lines 28–31).

252. Ibid., 1.6 (11, lines 24–37).

253. Ibid., 1.6 (11, lines 38–44; emphasis added).

254. Ibid., 1.6 (11, lines 45–50).

255. Ibid., 1.6 (11, lines 51–56).

256. Ibid., 1.6 (11, lines 60–62).

257. Ibid., 1.6 (11, lines 66–74).

258. Ibid., 1.6 (11, lines 81–84, and 12, line 7, resp.).

259. Avicenna's popular *Canon* refers to complexion, or temperament, thus: "Temperament is that quality which results from the mutual interaction and interpassion of the four contrary primary qualities residing within the (imponderable) elements. . . . These elements are so minutely intermingled as each to lie in a very intimate relationship to one another. Their opposite powers alternately conquer and become conquered until a state of equilibrium is reached which is uniform throughout the whole. It is this outcome which is called "the temperament"" (1930, 57). On the early history of this idea, see Leicester 1974, 4–24; Lloyd 1964; Siraisi 1990, 101–104; and Grmek 1998.

260. Albertus Magnus, *De natura loci* 2.3 (1980b, 26, lines 48–49).

261. Ibid., 2.3 (26, lines 49–53).

262. Ibid.

263. Ibid., 2.3 (26, lines 56–57, and 27, lines 5–6).

264. Ibid., 2.3 (26, lines 57–60).

265. Ibid., 2.3 (26, lines 62–68).

266. I owe this explanation to Professor Kristine Haugen.

267. Albertus Magnus, *De natura loci* 2.3 (1980b, 26, lines 71–74).

268. Avicenna, *Canon* 2.11.319 (1930, 205).

269. Albertus Magnus, *De natura loci* 2.3 (1980b, 26, lines 74–78).

270. Ibid., 2.3 (26, lines 85–92).

271. Ibid., 2.3 (27, lines 2–3).

272. Ibid., 2.3 (27, lines 15–17).

273. Ibid., 2.3 (27, lines 40–41).

274. Ibid., 2.3 (27, lines 44–47).

275. Ibid., 2.3 (27, lines 52–56).

276. Ibid., 2.3 (27, lines 62–74).

277. Albertus would later be acquainted with the version of Aristotle's *Politics* first rendered into Latin by William of Moerbeke in about 1260 (Dodd 1982, 78).

278. Albertus Magnus, *Politicorum libri VIII* 7.5 (1891, 661; emphasis added). Both translations from this work are by Robert Mac Donald.

279. Ibid., 7.5 (1891, 661–662).

280. Albertus Magnus, *De natura loci* 1.11 (1980b, 19, lines 61–68).

281. Aristotle, *Nichomachean Ethics* 2.6.1106b35–1107a1 (1995d).

282. Ibid., 2.8.1108b10–25.

283. Aristotle, *Politics* 1.2.1252a24–31 (1995j).

284. Ibid., 1.2.1252a31–1252b1.

285. On Aristotle's authority, the male was in general "by nature fitter for command than the female" (ibid., 1.12.1259b3).

286. Ibid., 1.2.1252b1–9.

287. Ibid., 1.5.1254a29–31.

288. Ibid., 1.5.1254a31–33.

289. Ibid., 1.5.1254a33–35.

290. Ibid., 1.5.1254a35–1254b2.

291. Ibid., 1254b21–25; emphasis added.

292. As Aristotle has explained in the *Nicomachean Ethics* 7.5.1149a5–12, "Every excessive state of folly, of cowardice, of self-indulgence, or of bad temper, is either brutish or morbid; the man who is by nature apt to fear everything, even the squeak of the mouse, is cowardly with a brutish cowardice, while the man who feared a weasel did so in consequence of a disease; and of foolish people those who by nature are thoughtless and live by their senses alone are brutish, like some races of the distant foreigners, while those who are so as a result of disease (e.g. of epilepsy) or of madness are morbid."

293. Carro 1951, 292n45.

294. Las Casas, *Historia* 3.2.1.9 (1994, 3:1785).

295. Sepúlveda 1984, 22.

296. Ibid., 24.

297. Ibid., 33–34.

298. Ibid., 35.

299. Ibid., 35.

300. Ibid., 36.

301. Aristotle's debt in this passage of the *Politics* to Plato's discussion of the soul in the *Republic* was kindly pointed out to me by Professor Alfonso Gómez-Lobo.

302. Plato, *Republic* 4.427c–445e. The terms *logismos, thumos,* and *epithumia* are usefully discussed by Howland 1993, 40. On the subject of Plato's partition of the soul, I have consulted Irwin 1995, 203–222; van Peursen 1966, 34–49; and Murphy 1951, 24–44.

303. Plato, *Republic* 9.588b–592b. See Howland 1993, 152–155; and van Peursen 1966, 40–41.

304. Postil 49 to Ailly and Gerson 1480–1483/1990, 16r.

305. Ailly and Gerson 1480–1483/1990, 151v.

306. Postil 866 to ibid.

307. Ailly and Gerson 1480–1483/1990, 151v.

308. Problem 8 in Pseudo-Aristotle, *Problems* 14.8.909b9–15 (1995b).

309. Aristotle, *Parts of Animals* 2.2.647b31–648a11 (1995h).

310. Postil 867 to Ailly and Gerson 1480–1483/1990, 151v.

311. Ailly and Gerson 1480–1483/1990, 151v.

312. Postil 868 to ibid.

313. For Haly's commentary to the geopolitical model in Ptolemy's *Tetrabiblos* 2.2, see Ptolemy, *Liber quadripartiti Ptholemei* (1493, 31r).

314. Ailly and Gerson 1480–1483/1990, 150v.

315. See Postil 869 to ibid.

316. Postil 870 to Ailly and Gerson 1480–1483/1990, 151r.

5 *En la Parte del Sol:* Iberia's Invention of the Afro-Indian Tropics, 1434–1494

1. For Las Casas's account of the "destruction" of Africa, see *Historia de las Indias* 1.2.1.17–1.2.2.27 (1994, 1:429–493).

2. Pérez Embid 1948, 39–41.

3. Goñi Gastambide 1958, 49–52. The "verticality" of this process has been most fruitfully analyzed in recent years by Adão da Fonseca 1993 and 1999. Literature on Europe's shift from the

Mediterranean to the Atlantic is vast, but I have found a highly useful comparative analysis of this process in Fernández-Armesto 1987, which should be read in conjunction with the historian's biography of the Discoverer (1991) and his most recent history of exploration (2006, esp. 109–152).

4. For instance, Weckmann, in his classical study on Alexander's donations to Fernando and Isabela of the territories newly discovered by Columbus, underscores the long-standing tradition that assigned to the papacy jurisdiction over all western islands (Weckmann 1949).

5. As Russell notes (2000, 113–118), Henry's inspiration to round Cape Bojador to the elusive Guinea may have come from earlier sources like the anonymous late-thirteenth-century heraldic itinerary *Libro del cognosçimiento de todos los rregnos e tierras et señorios que son por el mundo* and *Le Canarien*, the earliest account of Béthencourt and La Salle's expedition to the Canaries, composed shortly after 1402 by Béthencourt's chaplains, Pierre Bontier and Jean Le Verrier. See *Libro del cognosçimiento* 1999, 48–57; and Béthencourt, *Le Canarien* 58, 66, 84 (1874, 101–103, 118–120, and 165–169, resp.).

6. Russell 2000, 120–127, argues that the link between Henry and India does not mean that Henry wished to break into the Indian Ocean, only that he wished to reach this Ethiopian ruler in order to strike an alliance to crush the Muslims.

7. Rumeu de Armas 1996, 60.

8. On Columbus's references to Guinea, see Gil 1992a, 43–51.

9. See Pérez Embid 1948, 41–46; and Rumeu de Armas 1992, 16–20; 1996, 81–82.

10. See chapter 2.

11. Pérez Embid 1948, 46–48.

12. Cortesão 1975–1978, 1:275–277.

13. *Monumenta henricina* 1960–1974, 1:178–186; all translations from this collection are my own.

14. Pérez Embid 1948, 58–59.

15. On the Isles of the Blest, see Strabo, *Geography* 1.1.5 and 3.2.13 (1917–1932). Pliny, *Natural History* 6.37 (1938–1963) calls them *Fortunatae* and provides an account of each of them.

16. Pérez Embid 1948, 65–68.

17. Ibid., 69–72.

18. *Monumenta henricina* 1960–1974, 1:201–206.

19. Pérez Embid 1948, 73–81. See *Monumenta henricina* 1960–1974, 1:207–214.

20. See *Vinee Domini Sabahot* (11 December 1344), in *Monumenta henricina* 1960–1974, 1:214–216. In a bull written only a month later (*Desiderabiliter affectantes*, 11 December 1344), Clement VI further asked the sovereigns of Portugal, Castile, and Aragon to provide logistical support for Don Luis's projected campaign in the Canaries (ibid., 1:216–217). Evidently anticipating Portugal's negative reaction to his donation of the Canaries, Clement also expedited three other bulls renewing for

another two years the commitment of a tenth of the church's revenues in Portugal to the crusade against Benamarim or Fez (ibid., 1960–1974, 1:217–221, 221–225, and 225–228, resp.).

21. Ibid., 1:228–229 and 229–230, resp.

22. Ibid., 1:229 and 230: *insula[e] a Christi fide et christianorum dominio aliena[e].*

23. Pérez Embid 1948, 79.

24. *Monumenta henricina* 1960–1974, 1:230–234, esp. 232.

25. Ibid., 1:234–235.

26. Pérez Embid 1948, 81–101.

27. On the military campaign waged in the Canaries, see ibid., 101–104. On the takeover of Ceuta, see Russell's biography of Henry the Navigator, whose leading role in Ceuta should be read as an immediate precedent to his later exploration of Atlantic Africa (2000, 29–58).

28. *Monumenta henricina* 1960–1974, 1:293–296 and 296–298, resp. I am here following Doc. 123 (1:294).

29. Las Casas, *Historia* 1.2.1.17 (1994, 1:431).

30. *Monumenta henricina* 1960–1974, 2:282–286 and 287–289, resp.

31. See Pérez Embid 1948, 11–214.

32. On Malocello's presence in Lanzarote, see ibid., 58–59; and on the Vivaldi brothers, ibid., 51–58.

33. Grosjean 1978, 53; and Russell 2000, 118.

34. Pérez Embid 1948, 105–107.

35. As Russell 2000, 111–113 insists, the "Cape Bojador" that Henry thought his men had rounded in 1434 was probably not the farther cape by that name now standing at a lower latitude on the African mainland in Western Sahara (26° N), but rather Cape Juby in modern-day Morocco (27° 57′ N), which does stand east of Hierro and Gran Canaria (27° 44′ N and 27° 55′ N, resp.) and which matches the features described by early sources.

36. Beneath the Canaries, the Catalan Atlas does depict the 1346 voyage of Jacme Ferrer to *riu dlor* (Río de Oro), which would have taken Ferrer much farther south than Bojador, but the site of this river is not charted on the map. On Ferrer's voyage, see Pérez Embid 1948, 105–107.

37. Barros, *Ásia* 1.4 (1552/1932, 20).

38. Zurara, *Crónica dos feitos notáveis* 7 (1978–1981, 1:43; emphasis added).

39. The image we have at our disposal for the portolan on the so-called Columbus Chart (fig. 3.8) is not sufficiently detailed to show a close-up of the Canaries and Bojador. For useful examples, see Pedro Reinel's portolan (about 1490), the fragment of a Portuguese portolan from the fifteenth century, and Grazioso Benincasa's portolan (1462), reproduced by Russell 2000 (illustrations 1, 5, and 7, respectively, between pp. 224 and 225).

40. Fernández de Oviedo y Valdés, *La historia general y natural de las Indias* 2.5 (1535, viv).

41. Las Casas, *Historia de las Indias* 1.2.1.20 (1994, 1:452).

42. Zurara, *Crónica dos feitos notáveis* 8 (1978–1981, 1:47–49); Barros, *Ásia* 1.2 (1552/1932, 14).

43. Barros, *Ásia* 1.4 (1552/1932, 20–21; emphasis added).

44. Henry's envoys thought they had chanced upon Río de Oro (Gold River), what had long been thought by Mediterranean and Arab geographers to be a western leg of the Nile River emptying out onto the Atlantic (Russell 2000, 131–132).

45. Zurara, *Crónica dos feitos notáveis* 9 (1978–1981); and Barros, *Ásia* 1.4 (1552/1932, 20–23). A document expedited by the Portuguese regent Dom Pedro in the name of his young nephew Afonso V in 1443 specifies the number of expeditions sent by Prince Henry to round Cape Bojador as fifteen in total (*Monumenta henricina* 1960–1974, 8:107–108).

46. Barros, *Ásia* 1.4 (1552/1932, 22). See also Zurara, *Crónica dos feitos notáveis* 9 (1978–1981, 1:52–53).

47. Zurara, *Crónica dos feitos notáveis* 10 (1978–1981, 1:55–58); and Barros, *Ásia* 1.5 (1552/1932, 23–24).

48. Las Casas, *Historia* 1.2.1.23 (1994, 1:467).

49. Zurara, *Crónica dos feitos notáveis* 11 (1978–1981, 1:59). On the events that distracted Prince Henry from resuming his exploration of the Saharan coastline, see Russell 2000, 135–194. On occasion of the rounding of Cape Bojador, King Duarte requested a papal bull at the Council of Florence (1436), which was issued by Pope Eugenius IV as *Rex regum* in Bologna (8 September 1436). See *Monumenta henricina* 1960–1974, 5:270–275. This bull largely reiterated the terms of the bulls expedited on occasion of the takeover of Ceuta. See Las Casas, note 1 to *Historia* 1.2.2.24 (1994, 1:745).

50. García-Gallo 1987, 335–336.

51. Zurara, *Crónica dos feitos notáveis* 12 (1978–1981, 62–64); and Barros, *Ásia* 1.6 (1552/1932, 1.6, 25–29). On Prince Henry and the slave trade, see Russell 2000, 239–263.

52. Las Casas, *Historia* 1.2.2.23 (1994, 1:468).

53. Ibid., 1.2.2.24 (1994, 1:470).

54. Pérez de Tudela y Bueso et al. 1994, 1:146–147.

55. Ibid., 1:147.

56. Las Casas, *Historia* 1.3.2.46 (1994, 1:589).

57. Barros, *Ásia* 1.7 (1932, 29).

58. See *Illius qui se pro diuini* (Florence, 19 December 1442), in *Monumenta henricina* 1960–1974, 7:336–337; and *Rex regum* (Florence, 5 January 1443), in ibid., 7:344–350. See note 1 to Las Casas, *Historia* 1.2.2.24 (1994, 1:745).

59. *Monumenta henricina* 1960–1974, 8:107–108.

60. Ibid., 8:107.

61. On Prince Henry's attempts to wrest the Canaries from Castile, see Russell 2000, 264–290.

62. Pérez Embid 1948, 158–165; and Rumeu de Armas 1996, 1:128–131.

63. Adão da Fonseca and Ruiz Asencio 1995, 53–57; this quote, 55.

64. Ibid., 56.

65. Ibid., 63–66; this quote, 64.

66. Castile did not succeed in wresting full control of the archipelago from its native peoples until 1496, when it finally subdued Tenerife.

67. See Adão da Fonseca and Ruiz Asencio, 68–92; this quote, 88; emphasis added.

68. Ibid., 101–113; this quote, 105.

69. Ibid., 105.

70. Pérez de Tudela y Bueso et al. 1994, 1:62–63.

71. Ibid., 1:78–81.

72. See the entry for 4 March 1493 in Columbus's *Diario*, in ibid., 1:231–232.

73. See Pina 1950, 184; Resende 1973, 241; and Barros, *Ásia* 3.11 (1552/1932, 111).

74. See the entry for 8 March 1493 in *Diario* (Pérez de Tudela y Bueso et al. 1994, 1:233).

75. João II had rejected Columbus's plan twice before: once in 1483 or 1484, during Columbus's years in Portugal; and another in 1488, when Columbus, considering that negotiations with Fernando and Isabel were heading nowhere, once again approached João II, who invited him once again to Lisbon. The renewed negotiations evidently came to a crash with the return of Bartholomeu Dias from the Cape of Good Hope, which meant that circumnavigating Africa to reach India now seemed assured.

76. See Pina 1950, 184–185; and Barros, *Ásia* 3.11 (1932, 111–112); all translations from Pina 1950 are my own.

77. Ibid., 3.11 (111).

78. Pérez de Tudela y Bueso et al. 1994, 1:234; emphasis added.

79. On the chronology of the events that followed Columbus's return to Spain and that concerned the drafting of Alexander VI's bulls of donation, I am closely following the noted legal historian García-Gallo (1987, 381–389). García-Gallo not only provides a brilliant interpretation of the diplomatic transactions and documents related to the drafting of these papal bulls, but he has also insisted that the meridian eventually specified in the Treaty of Tordesillas, running pole to pole, was meant not to divide the globe but rather to demarcate the Indies as a geopolitical space claimed by Castile directly *across from*—that is, in the very same general latitudes—as the geopolitical space claimed by Portugal in Guinea (1987, 525–550).

80. Pina 1950, 185.

81. Zurita, *Historia* I, 29, in García-Gallo 1987, 619.

82. Ibid., 615; emphasis added; all translations from García-Gallo 1987 are mine.

83. García-Gallo 1987, 426–427.

84. F. Columbus, *Historie del S. D. Fernando Colombo* 41 (1571/1992, 84v).

85. García-Gallo 1987, 360–362.

86. Pérez de Tudela y Bueso et al. 1994, 1:273–279. This letter to the Catholic Monarchs, which is very similar to the one Columbus addressed to Luis de Santángel announcing the discovery (15 February 1493), was known for a long time to have existed, but it only saw public light for the first time as part of a collection of newly found letters known as *Libro copiador de Cristóbal Colón* (Rumeu de Armas 1989).

87. García-Gallo 1987, 357–359.

88. Pérez de Tudela y Bueso et al. 1994, 1:284–285. The title reserved for Columbus at this point was *nuestro Almirante del mar oceano bisorey e gouernador de las yslas que se han descubierto en las yndias.*

89. Ibid., 1:285–286; this quote, 285.

90. Ibid., 1:312–313, 318, 353–354, 356–357, 358–359, 363, 366–368, 369–372, 378, 380, 381, and 383–384.

91. Ibid., 1:249–267. For an informative account of the diffusion of the letter to Luis de Santángel and of the Latin translation of the similar letter to Gabriel Sánchez (15 February–14 March 1493), see esp. 1:258–267.

92. Ibid., 1:249; emphasis added.

93. Ibid., 1:250.

94. Ibid., 1:254–255.

95. Ibid., 1:255.

96. Ibid., 1:251.

97. Ibid., 1:254.

98. Ibid., 1:252.

99. Ibid.

100. García-Gallo 1987, 381.

101. Zurita, *Historia* I, 25, in García-Gallo 1987, 616.

102. Pérez de Tudela y Bueso et al. 1994, 1:287–288.

103. Ibid., 1:289–290.

104. See García-Gallo's discussion of the right that Christian princes were supposed to have to the subjection of "infidels" (1987, 453–475).

105. Ibid., 455.

106. Ibid., 445–475. The classic treatment of this debate is Muldoon 1979.

107. See Alonso de Cartagena's *Allegationes* in García-Gallo 1987, 566–567.

108. Ibid., 567–572.

109. Ibid., 571.

110. Ibid.

111. Ibid.

112. Ibid.

113. Pérez de Tudela y Bueso et al. 1994, 1:121–122.

114. Ibid., 1:249; emphasis added. The protocol followed by Columbus on this occasion probably included such symbolic acts as treading through the beach on which he had landed, throwing handfuls of sand in the air, and cutting branches from the greenery (García-Gallo 1987, 472–474). On the various protocols followed by European nations to take formal possession of new territories, see Seed 1995.

115. In the entry for 23 December 1492, Columbus records his attempts on Hispaniola's northern coast to decipher what the Indians meant by term *cacique* (chieftain). As Las Casas writes, "the Admiral had been unable until then to understand whether they take it to mean *king* or *governor*" (Pérez de Tudela y Bueso et al. 1994, 1:191–196; emphasis added).

116. Ibid., 1:125.

117. In the entry for 16 October 1492, which describes his arrival on the third island in the Bahamas, Fernandina (probably today's Long Island), Columbus significantly adds to his claim regarding the unity of speech and customs in the islands he has visited so far that the inhabitants of Fernandina "already seem to me to be more docile and affable and more subtle" (*ya me pareçen algun tanto mas domestica gente y de tracto y mas sotiles*) (ibid., 1:128). In the entry for 27 November, he explains that he does not wish to detain himself in every "port" he finds, in part because "I do not know the language, and the people from these lands do not understand me, nor do I, or anyone with me, understand them; and many times I understand the opposite of what I am told by these Indians I bring with me" (ibid., 1:159).

118. García-Gallo 1987, 500. On the pope as notary public, see García-Gallo's citation of Silvio Zavala's *Las instituciones jurídicas del descubrimiento y conquista* (1987, 500n391).

119. García-Gallo 1987, 370–372. See also Pérez de Tudela y Bueso et al. 1994, 1:465–466; this quote, 465.

120. García-Gallo 1987, 501.

121. Ibid., 623–633; this quote, 629.

122. Ibid., 498–500.

123. Ibid., 499 and 499n387. See also *Romanus pontifex* (Adão da Fonseca and Ruiz Asencio 1995, 55–56).

124. García-Gallo 1987, 499.

125. On the points of coincidence between Alexander's donations to Fernando and Isabel and this earlier body of donations to Portugal, see ibid., 431–435; for a classic study of this connection, see Weckmann 1949, 229–262.

126. García-Gallo 1987, 367–369.

127. Ibid., 624.

128. Ibid.

129. Ibid., 625.

130. Ibid.; emphasis added.

131. Ibid.

132. Ibid., 625–626.

133. Ibid., 627.

134. Ibid., 628.

135. Ibid., 372–374 and 633–636; this quote, 374.

136. Ibid., 274–275.

137. Pérez de Tudela y Bueso et al. 1994, 1:113.

138. The compass needles were still pointing toward magnetic north, which is slightly displaced with respect to the geographical pole. While pilots had noticed easterly variation on their compasses in Europe, westerly variation was unprecedented and disconcerting for Columbus. See Morison 1942, 1:271–272. For a useful explanation of this phenomenon, and of its effect on the drawing of charts in the Mediterranean, see Cerezo Martínez 1994, 25–43.

139. García-Gallo 1987, 369–370.

140. Ibid., 409–410.

141. Ibid., 627–628; this quote, 627.

142. Pérez de Tudela y Bueso et al. 1994, 1:308.

143. Ibid.

144. Sepúlveda 1984, 1.

145. García-Gallo 1987, 383

146. See Zurita's *Historia* I, 25, in ibid., 617.

147. Las Casas, *Historia* 1.4.1.79 (1994, 2:835).

148. Pérez de Tudela y Bueso et al. 1994, 1:482–484; this quote, 483.

149. Ibid.

150. Ibid., 1:483–484.

151. Ibid., 1:488–491; this quote, 489.

152. Ibid.

153. Ibid.

154. Ibid, 1:489–490.

155. This bull is dated 25 September 1493 in García-Gallo 1987, 641–644.

156. Ibid., 641–642.

157. Ibid., 642.

158. Ibid.

159. Pérez de Tudela y Bueso et al. 1994, 1:498–499.

160. Ibid., 1:579–607.

6 Between Cathay and a Hot Place: Reorienting the Asia-America Debate

1. F. Columbus, *Historie del S. D. Fernando Colombo* 6 (1571/1992, 12v).

2. Colón 1992, 382; and Pérez de Tudela y Bueso et al. 1994, 2:1114, resp.

3. Mandeville, *El libro de las maravillas del mundo* 22 (2002, 197).

4. Russell 1991, 27–50.

5. According to Irish legend, the abbot St. Brendan was supposed to have embarked on an ocean journey that landed him on the island named after him. Behaim's map reads: "In the year 565 after Christ, St. Brandon in his ship came to this island where he witnessed many marvels, and seven years afterwards he returned to his country" (Ravenstein 1908, 77). Antilia, or the Isle of Seven Cities was where, according to Portuguese legend, the archbishop of Oporto, was supposed to have fled with his six bishops following the Umayyad invasion of the Iberian Peninsula in 711. Behaim's map reads: "In the year 734 of Christ, when the whole of Spain had been won by the heathen [Moors] of Africa, the above island Antilia, called Septe citade [Seven Cities], was inhabited by an archbishop from Porto in Portugal, with six other bishops, and other Christians, men and women, who had fled thither from Spain, by ship, together with their cattle, belongings, and goods. [In] 1414 a ship from Spain got nighest it without being endangered" (Ravenstein 1908, 77). The thousands of islands identified by Marco Polo on the Sea of Chin and on the Indian Ocean are indexed by dozens of beige and colored shapes. On the Indian Ocean (gore M, 7° N), a legend reads: "Marco Polo in the 39th chapter of the 3rd book states that the mariners had verily found in this Indian Ocean more than 12,700 inhabited islands, many of which yield precious stones, pearls and mountains of gold, whilst others abound in twelve kinds of spices and curious peoples, concerning whom much might be written." And it adds: "Here are found sea-monsters, such as Sirens and other fish. And if anyone desire to know more of these curious people, and peculiar fish in the sea or animals upon the land, let him read the books of Pliny, Isidore [of Seville], Aristotle, Strabo,

the *Specula* of Vincent [of Beauvais] and many others. There he shall find accounts of curious inhabitants, of the islands, the monsters of the ocean, peculiar animals on the land and the islands yielding spices and precious stones" (Ravenstein 1980, 1908).

6. Strabo, *Geography* 2.1.1 (1917–1932). See my discussion of Eratosthenes' world map in chapter 3.

7. On Khubilai Khān's conquest of southern China, see Mote 1999, 444–466; and Rossabi 1988, 77–99.

8. Ravenstein 1908, 89; emphasis added.

9. Marco Polo, *De consuetudinibus et condicionibus orientalium regionum* 3.1–8 (1485/1986, 57r–59v). On Khubilai's attempts to invade Japan, see Rossabi 1988, 99–103.

10. Marco Polo, *De consuetudinibus* 3.89 (1485/1986, 59r). See also postils 271a and 272, which read: "infinite spices" (*aromata infinita*) and "very white pepper" (*piper albissimum*).

11. Ibid., 2.42 (70v).

12. Ibid., 3.9 (59v).

13. On Khubilai's campaigns against Southeast Asia, see Rossabi 1988, 213–220.

14. *Libro del conoscimiento* (1999, 76–77).

15. Ibid., 82–83.

16. Ibid.

17. D'Ailly, *Ymago mundi* 24, in Ailly and Gerson 1480–1483/1990, 21v.

18. Postil 159 in ibid.

19. See the entry for "Scythia" in Smith 1854–[1857]. For Herodotus's description of anthropophagy among the Scythians, see *History* 4.60–65 (1987).

20. Ibid., 4.48.

21. See "Scythia" in Smith 1854–[1857].

22. See Strabo, *Geography* 11.11.2.

23. Mela, *Description of the World* 1.11 (1998). For Latin text see Mela 1971, 5.

24. Pliny, *Natural History* 6.14 (1974).

25. Ptolemy, *Cosmographia* 6 (1478, unfoliated, cols. 209–210).

26. For an account of milk drinking and flesh eating among the Mongols, see the first known European chronicler of the Tatars, the Franciscan friar John of Piano Carpini, who traveled to Mongolia as a papal envoy between 1245 and 1247. Admiring their lactophilia, Carpini asserts in his *Ystoria mongalorum* 4.8 that the Mongols drank huge quantities of mare's milk whenever they could, as well as milk from sheep, cows, goats, and camels (Wyngaert 1928, 49). Horrified by their anthropophagy, Carpini also explains that they ate dogs, wolves, foxes, horses, and, whenever it became necessary, even human flesh. He then proceeds to recount an occasion on which Chingiz

Khān, during his campaign against Cathay, ordered his men to eat every soldier in ten (ibid., 4.7 [47–48]). Marco Polo appears to have relished the mare's milk drunk by Mongols, which they allegedly fermented to the point that it looked like wine (Marco Polo, *De consuetudinibus* 1.57 [1485/1986, 21r]). And in his discussion of the northern city of "Ciandu" (Shandu, or Xanadu), where the Great Khān had his summer residence, Marco Polo maintains that it was customary to eat the flesh of criminals who had been put to death, but not of those who had been killed by disease (ibid., 1.66 [25v]).

27. Piccolomini 1477/1991, 10r–11r. Piccolomini was one of the first readers in Europe to have owned a complete Latin translation of Strabo's *Geography*. On the early diffusion of Strabo's work, see Diller 1975.

28. Ballesteros Beretta 1945, 1:330–331.

29. For the Latin original, see Grossato 1994, 79–94. For the English translation, see Major 1992.

30. It may well be that Conti's account of Cathay in book 4 of Bracciolini's *De varietate fortunae* was inserted by Bracciolini as an aside to Conti's narration. Bracciolini does not claim that Conti reached Cathay, and he does on a number of occasions supplement Conti with information he has gathered on his own.

31. On the expulsion of the Mongols from China, see Mote 1999, 517–563.

32. Piccolomini 1477/1991, 10v.

33. Perhaps the best known example of the maps mentioned by Piccolomini is the circular *mappamundi* completed in 1459 by the Venetian cartographers Fra Mauro and Andrea Bianco, which is now held in the Biblioteca Nazionale Marciana in Venice. This map, which is oriented toward the south, displays Cathay in its lower left corner, well below (i.e., to the north of) continental Europe, along the very latitudes of Scandinavia. See Nebenzahl 1990, 13.

34. Postils 110, 111, and 112 to Piccolomini 1477/1991, 10v.

35. Piccolomini 1477/1991, 10v.

36. Yule 1866, cxxxvi–cxxxvii. For Conti's account in Bracciolini, see Grossato 1994, 84–85. On Zhu Yuanzang's choice of Nanjing as his new capital, see Mote 1999, 566–568.

37. Piccolomini 1477/1991, 10v.

38. Postil 113 to ibid.; emphasis added.

39. Grossato 1994, 92; my translation.

40. Postil 114 to Piccolomini 1477/1991, 10v.

41. Postil 115 to ibid.

42. Piccolomini 1477/1991, 10v.

43. Ibid.

44. Ibid.

45. Postil 116 to ibid.

46. Postil 117 to ibid.

47. Piccolomini 1477/1991, 10v–11r.

48. Postil 118 to Piccolomini 1477/1991, 10v. The "Ariana" mentioned by Piccolomini and Columbus roughly corresponds to the territory occupied by ancient Persia, to the west of the Indus River. This is the second "sphragis" drawn by Eratosthenes to the south of the parallel of Rhodes and to the west of India. See chapter 3. See also Strabo, *Geography* 15.1.73–78; and Pliny, *Natural History* 6.25.

49. Postil 119 to Piccolomini 1477/1991, 11r.

50. Piccolomini 1477/1991, 4v; and Pliny, *Natural History* 2.67. According to Pliny, Cornelius Nepos had written before him that the proconsul of Gaul (France), Quintus Metellus Celer, had "received from the King of the Swabians a present of some Indians, who on a trade voyage had been carried off their course by storms to Germany." Piccolomini adds that he has also read about this ancient incident in "Oton," perhaps the thirteenth-century Otto of Freising, author of *Chronica sive de duabus civitatibus,* though I have not found this reference in Otto's chronicle.

51. Postil 10 to Piccolomini 1477/1991, 4v. On the debate regarding Columbus's travel to England and Iceland, see Ballesteros Beretta 1945, 1:290–301.

52. For a European account of Mongol "physiognomy," we need go no further than Carpini's *Ystoria mongalorum* 2.2: according to Carpini, their bodies were shaped nothing like other peoples'. Their eyes and their cheeks stood farther apart from each other than other peoples'. They had very prominent cheekbones, and their noses were flat and small. Finally, they had small eyes, with eyelids slanting up all the way to their eyebrows. (Wyngaert 1929, 32–33).

53. Postil 56 to Piccolomini 1477/1991, 6v.

54. For the paradox observed by Vignaud, see his *Histoire critique,* the work that completes Vignaud's controversial thesis (1911, 1:1–13).

55. Ibid., 2:135–209 and 280–286.

56. The thesis that Las Casas single-handedly was the forger behind every relevant reference to the goal of reaching Asia in the Columbian corpus was forwarded by Carbia 1930/1936.

57. It is on the basis of its putatively unorthodox and speculative nature that Columbus's learned detractors in Castile would reject the plan he had presented to the Crown. Only last-minute intervention by Fernando and Isabel's intimates moved the Crown to take a chance on Columbus, against the better judgment of the members of the royal *junta* that evaluated his plan.

58. Vignaud 1911, 1:4.

59. Ibid., 1:305–338.

60. Ibid., 2:485. Vignaud considered Columbus's postils to these works to postdate the discovery (1911, 2:338–344).

61. A tendency to underestimate Columbus's participation in an intellectual and material culture that was gradually inventing the belt of the tropics also runs through prominent revisionist works, such as Ulloa 1928; Jane, 1930–1933/1988; Carbia 1930/1936; Manzano Manzano 1976; and Pérez de Tudela y Bueso 1983 and 1994.

62. Manzano Manzano 1976, 155–165.

63. Ibid., 239–381.

64. As John Larner succinctly observed in a very useful survey published in 1988 of major scholarship produced in the decades preceding the recent quincentenary, Pérez de Tudela's argumentation in *Mirabilis in altis* stems "from the absolute necessity of 'preknowledge' to explain Columbus's certainty" (Larner 1988, 15).

65. Pérez de Tudela y Bueso 1983. In the introduction to *Mirabilis in altis,* the author admits that he had initially forwarded this idea in jest to his friends, but that he had gradually been persuaded of its merit.

66. Pérez de Tudela y Bueso 1994, clxiv.

67. Ibid., clvii–clxxiv.

68. Thomas 2003, 57.

69. Ibid., 77. See also Thomas's discussion of Columbus's return to Europe in 1493 (2003, 106–107).

70. Hulme 1986, 37.

71. Ibid., 38.

72. Ibid., 19–22.

73. Ibid., 21.

74. Ibid., 22–41.

75. Ibid., 30.

76. Ibid., 38.

77. The author shows herself unimpressed by the full wording of the "passport," which actually announces "business pertaining to the service of God and the increase of the orthodox faith." See Zamora 1993, 28n17.

78. Ibid., 28–29.

79. Ibid., 29–38, 57–62.

80. Ibid., 42 and 62.

81. Greenblatt 1991, 53.

82. See my discussion of Alonso de Cartagena's treatment of this problem in chapter 5.

83. Hulme 1986, 37.

84. For standard accounts of the drafting and meaning of these official documents, see Morison 1942, 1:138–142; Ballesteros Beretta 1945, 1:522–525 and 537–542; and Taviani 1985a, 494–502. Manzano Manzano 1964, 279–314 presents a useful analysis of these documents and of the possible models behind the titles Columbus requested from the Crown. Manzano Manzano 1976, 9–57, alters this interpretation in order to accommodate the idea that Columbus had set out to reach mid-Atlantic lands whose existence had been secretly revealed to him by the legendary anonymous pilot.

85. Pérez de Tudela y Bueso et al. 1994, 1:64–65; this quote, 64; emphasis added.

86. A few notable examples are Vignaud, who first claimed that the documents making reference to Magnokhanic Asia were a sham (1911, 2:97–103 and 211–233); Colomer Montset, who maintains that Columbus himself had already visited the New World (1952); and Manzano Manzano, who presents perhaps the most elaborate rewriting of Columbus's enterprise based on the legend of the anonymous pilot (1976, 9–17). I am here following the useful synthesis of the debate over the expression "has discovered" provided by Rumeu de Armas 1985, 153–166.

87. Rumeu de Armas 1985, 158–159. Las Casas was swayed in his choice by the phrasing of the *Carta de merced* (30 April 1492), the official document that came to supersede the *Capitulaciones* as Columbus's charter. The codex consulted by Las Casas belonged to the Columbus family, and it contained notarized copies of both documents, but only the *Carta de merced*, not the *Capitulaciones*, was confirmed by the Crown upon Columbus's return in 1493 (Manzano Manzano 1976, 10–12). The *Carta de merced*, not the *Capitulaciones*, is the document cited by Las Casas's principal source, Ferdinand, as the charter issued to Columbus. See F. Columbus, *Historie del S. D. Fernando Colombo* 43 (1571/1992, 86r–91r). As even Manzano Manzano, an adamant supporter of the pre-discovery thesis has observed, this correction on the part of Las Casas unfairly and wrongly compelled Carbia 1930/1936, one of Las Casas's most ferocious detractors among twentieth-century scholars, to accuse the Dominican friar of having forged everything that in any way indicated Asia as Columbus's destination—from the opening chapters of Ferdinand's *Historie* to the official documents drafted between the Crown and Columbus as well as the prologue that Columbus appended to his *Diario*.

88. Ballesteros Beretta 1945, 1:543.

89. García-Gallo 1987, 536–538.

90. Ibid., 537. It should be noted that elsewhere García-Gallo (1989, 669–671) does lend credit to the possibility of a pre-discovery, even as the historian admits that the concession of titles is made only for territories to be discovered in the future, not for anything Columbus might have previously discovered.

91. Pérez de Tudela y Bueso et al. 1994, 1:64. By securing the admiralship for his heirs in perpetuity "as of this moment," Columbus was in effect purchasing a life insurance policy, meaning that should

he die in the attempt to reach his destination any further exploration attempts endeavored by the Crown would have to take into account his son Diego. See Manzano Manzano 1976, 40–41. This observation was made by another advocate of a pre-discovery, Ulloa 1928.

92. Pérez de Tudela y Bueso et al. 1994, 1:64.

93. Manzano Manzano 1964, 290.

94. Pérez de Tudela y Bueso et al. 1994, 1:64.

95. Ibid.

96. Ibid., 1:65.

97. Vignaud 1911, 2:98.

98. Pérez de Tudela y Bueso et al. 1994, 1:65.

99. Ibid., 1:249–267; this quote, 256.

100. Ibid., 1:273–279; this quote, 276.

101. See Manzano Manzano 1964, 299–308, and 1976, 11–12.

102. Pérez de Tudela y Bueso et al. 1994, 1:74–77; this quote, 74.

103. Ibid. "It is Our grace and will that you, the said Christopher Columbus, after you have discovered and won the said islands and terra firma in the said ocean sea or any of them, become our admiral of the said isles and terra firma that you should in this manner discover and win, and that you become our admiral and viceroy and governor in them, and that you be able from then on to be called and titled Don Cristóbal Colón."

104. Ibid., 1:74. See Manzano Manzano 1976, 32–34.

105. Pérez de Tudela y Bueso et al. 1994, 1:71–73.

106. Ibid., 1:71.

107. Ibid., emphasis added.

108. Carbia 1930/1936, 117–118; my translation of Carbia.

109. See Jos 1979–1980, 20. This document was originally published by Navarrete 1825.

110. On Santángel's role in the discovery, see Ballesteros Beretta 1945, 1:515–522.

111. Pérez de Tudela y Bueso et al. 1994, 1:89–91; this quote, 90.

112. Ibid., 1:81–83, 83–85, 86–87, and 87–88, resp.

113. Ibid., 1:140–141.

114. Ibid., 1:89.

115. Vignaud 1911, 2:139–143.

116. Carbia 1930/1936.

117. Manzano Manzano 1976, 155–165.

118. See Jos 1979–1980; and Manzano Manzano 1964, 311–314.

119. Milhou 1983, 145–168.

120. Pérez de Tudela y Bueso et al. 1994, 1:196.

121. Slessarev 1959, 9–25. For a broader historical perspective, see Silverberg 1972, 16–35. I have consulted the version of the apocryphal *Acts of Saint Thomas* in the *Other Bible* (1984). For an English translation of the passage in question from *De adventu*, see Hosten 1923, 66–72. For the Latin text, see Zarncke 1879–1883, 1:837–843.

122. Slessarev 1959, 16–17. According to this author, the legend of Prester John may have its origin in the Thomasine tradition cultivated by the Nestorian communities that extended all the way from Syrian Edessa to the coast of Coromandel. For the earliest identification of Christian communities on the Malabar Coast, see Cosmas Indicopleustes 1909. For the identification of Christian communities on the coast of Coromandel, see Marco Polo, *De consuetudinibus* 3.24 (1485/1986, 63v–64r).

123. Zarncke 1996a, 78.

124. Hamilton 1996, 239.

125. Pseudo-Abdias 1719, 669.

126. Zarncke 1996a, 78–83.

127. Zarncke 1996b, 109. On Alexander's letter, see Silverberg 1972, 58–63.

128. Slessarev 1959, 25–36. See Otto of Freising 1912, 7.33, 365. For an English translation, see Otto of Freising 2002, 443–444.

129. Slessarev (1959, 29–30) points out that one of many legends about the three Magi, contained in the apocryphal Book of Seth, claims that, following the Pentecost, Saint Thomas had arrived in Persia, where he baptized the three kings and took them under his wing.

130. Slessarev 1959, 28; and Silverberg 1972, 16.

131. On Chingiz Khān's campaigns, see Morgan 1986, 55–83, specifically 68–69. For an indispensable treatment of the conqueror's life, see Roux's recent history of the Mongol empire 1993, 29–253.

132. Slessarev 1959, 81–82; and Silverberg 1972, 70–73.

133. Morgan 1986, 59–60; 1996; and Roux 1993, 115–127. Marco Polo uses the term Ong-Khān for Toghril, a title that had been conferred on him by the emperor of Chin for his victory over the Tatars. See Marco Polo, *De consuetudinibus* 1.51–53 (1485/1986, 19r–20r).

134. Postil 100 to Marco Polo, *De consuetudinibus* 1.51 (1986, 19r). On Prester John's "wanderings" through the Asian interior, see Silverberg 1972, 74–139.

135. Marco Polo, *De consuetudinibus* 3.43 (1485/1986, 70v–71r). Marco Polo's reference to the eastern part of sub-Saharan Africa as India Meridiana may ultimately derive from the tripartite division provided by Pseudo-Abdias's *Acta apostolorum*. The same nomenclature is used by an earlier thirteenth-century author who saw himself as following Abdias, Gervase of Tilbury. In his famous "mirror of princes," *Otia imperialia* (completed about 1218), Gervase stated that there were three Indias: an

Upper India where Bartholomew had preached; a Lower India where Thomas had preached, which led to Media and harbored the city of Edessa; and a Southern India, where Matthew had preached, which touched on Ethiopia. See Gervase of Tilbury *Otia imperialia* 2.3 (2002, 182–185).

136. Postil 346 to Marco Polo, *De consuetudinibus* 3.43 (1485/1986, 71r).

137. Slessarev 1959, 84–85; and Silverberg 1972, 163–192.

138. See Sévérac, *Mirabilia descripta* 4–6 (1863, 11–45): India Tertia appears to correspond to the eastern part of sub-Saharan Africa known to Arab geographers as the Zindj; India Minor, roughly corresponds to the Indian subcontinent beyond the Indus Valley through the Coast of Malabar, known to Arab geographers as the Sind. And India Maior appears to have extended beyond the Coast of Malabar indefinitely, that is from the coast of Coromandel and the Ganges on (for the Arabs, the Hind). It should be noted that Marco Polo borrows from two different sets of nomenclature for the three parts of India: on the one hand, he calls the Ethiopian India "India Meridionalis," which is consistent with the nomenclature used by Gervase of Tilbury, and, it seems, consistent with Pseudo-Abdias's *Acta apostolorum*. On the other hand, Marco Polo uses the terms "India Maior" and "India Minor" for the other two parts, except that, for him, the former refers to the Indian subcontinent extending from Moabar (on the Coast of Coromandel), past Malabar (on the southwestern Coast of Malabar), to Resmacoron (west of the Indus, along the Mekrān mountain range, in today's Pakistan). Marco Polo's India Minor, on the other hand, extends from the province of Ciamba all the way to the kingdom of Murfili (one of the regions of India Maior that he describes along southeastern coast of the Indian subcontinent). See Marco Polo, *De consuetudinibus* 3.42 (1485/1986, 70v).

139. Grosjean 1978, 78.

140. *Libro del conoscimiento de todos los reinos* 1999, 60–65; this quote, 60–61.

141. Hamilton 1996.

142. This passage in Foresti is quoted by Beckingham, who identifies the year for this embassy around 1310 (1996, 197–198). For the summary of Carignano's account, see the entry for the year 80 CE in Foresti 1483/1486; this quote, 148r; my translation.

143. Beckingham 1996, 198; and Foresti 1483/1486, 293v–295r; this quote, 293v; my translation.

144. Russell 2000, 121.

145. Silverberg 1972.

146. Manzano Manzano 1964, 313.

147. Tafur 1874, 1:95–109.

148. Ravenstein 1908, 96.

149. Manzano Manzano 1964, 313. On Timur's campaigns, see Manz 1989, 67–73.

150. On the diplomatic exchanges between Timur "the Lame" and Enrique III of Castile, see López Estrada 1999, 23–34.

151. For Ruy González de Clavijo's account of Timur's campaign against India, see *Embajada a Tamorlán* 8.12 (1406/1999, 287).

152. Postils 333 through 342 in Piccolomini 1477/1991, 31r–v.

153. See McGinn 1979, 149–157; and Woodward and Howe 1997. Roger Bacon, like many other Franciscans, was profoundly influenced by the eschatology of the Calabrian abbot Joachim of Fiore (1132–1202)—as d'Ailly and Columbus themselves would be. On Roger Bacon's Joachimism, see Randolph 1969a, 462–467; and Reeves 1969, 46–48. Relevant to Bacon's apocalyptics, particularly as concerns the conversion of infidel nations, are Randolph 1969b, 127–154; and Bigalli 1971. The literature on Joachim of Fiore is vast, and many studies of his life, works, and influence, continue to appear, especially in Italy; but good places to start are the newly revised edition of Reeves 1976/1999; and Bloomfield 1980. A classic discussion of Joachimism in the Franciscan order can be found in Lambert 1961. For Roger Bacon's influence on d'Ailly's apocalypticism, see Smoller 1994, 103–104; and Watts 1985, 81–92. The most thorough study of Columbus's Messianism continues to be Milhou 1983.

154. Bacon, *Opus maius* IV (1897, 1:268). For Bacon's sources, see Aethicus Ister 1993, 4:121; and the prophecy in Pseudo-Methodius, *Die Apokalypse* [13] (1998, 19).

155. Albumasar 1515.

156. Ailly and Gerson 1480–1483/1990, 47v.

157. Postil 545 to ibid. On the role that the Mongols played in Columbus's militant religiosity, see Milhou 1983, 145–168.

158. The book's purpose, as announced by its incipit, is as follows: "Here begins the book or manual of authorities, sayings, opinions, and prophecies concerning the matter of the recuperation of the Holy City and God's Mount Syon, as well as of the invention and conversion of the Isles of the Indies and of all the peoples of the nations" (West and Kling 1990, 100). For Columbus's use of the segment from *De legibus et sectis* referring to the destruction of Muslims at the hand of Mongols or Christians, see Milhou 1983, 55–56; and *Libro de las profecías* 4, in West and Kling 1991, 156–157.

159. On Innocent's early attempts to contact the Mongols, see the indispensable studies by de Rachewiltz 1971, 76–119, whose focus is the missions to the khāns; and Richard 1977, 69–78, whose work more broadly encompasses the missions to Asian rulers between the thirteenth and fifteenth centuries. More recently, see Gil's edition of travel writing to Mongolia in the thirteenth century (1993, 21–158); and the concise treatment of thirteenth-century contact provided by Larner in his recent work on Marco Polo (1999, 15–30). On the place of Innocent IV as both a theorist and a practitioner in the history of the relation between Christians and infidels, see Muldoon 1979, 5–15 and 29–48.

160. See Pelliot's study of this early phase of missionary activity to the Mongols, which includes Güyük's letter in the Persian version found in the Vatican Library and its translation to French (1922–1923).

For an indispensable study of the contents and meaning of this letter, including the translation to Latin of the Mongol original, see Voegelin 1940–1941; this quote, 388.

161. Dawson 1980, 68. For the Latin text, see Wyngaert 1929, 125.

162. Rachewiltz 1971, 119–124.

163. Ibid., 120–121.

164. Ibid., 122–123.

165. Ibid., 144–159. The Īlkhāns of Persia converted to Islam in 1295 and ended all cooperation with Christians after the signing of a peace treaty with the Mamlūks in 1322 (Morgan 1980, 183–187).

166. On Mongol shamanism and religious tolerance, see Morgan 1986, 40–44.

167. Dawson 1980, 187–194. See also Rubruck's *Itinerarium* 33, in Wyngaert 1929, 289–297. On Rubruck's mission to Mongolia, see de Rachewiltz 1971, 125–143.

168. See Marco Polo, *De consuetudinibus* 1.1–6 (1485/1986, 3r–5r). A brief biography of the Polo's can be found in Larner 1999, 31–45.

169. Marco Polo, *De consuetudinibus* 1.4 (1485/1986, 4r).

170. Ibid., 4r–v.

171. I am here following Larner's chronology (1999, 39–43).

172. Marco Polo, *De consuetudinibus* 1.10 (1485/1986, 6r).

173. Jos 1979–1980.

174. Ibid.

175. Piccolomini 1477/1991, [106r].

176. Morison 1963, 13. For the Latin text, see Pérez de Tudela y Bueso et al. 1994, 1:13–15; this quote, 14.

177. Vignaud's case against Asia as Columbus's true destination was made at the expense of such essential documents as the passport and the letter of credence. Vignaud tended to ignore these documents in favor of the *Capitulaciones,* which he argued ought to have mentioned Cathay, Çipango, and India. His case against the traditional thesis also required a skewed reading of the prologue to the *Diario,* which he mistakenly read as suppressing the venal interests expressed in the *Capitulaciones* in order to feign an evangelical and diplomatic mission to Asia. Vignaud believed that perhaps Columbus's dissolute grandson Luis Colón was the author of this imposture and that the body of the *Diario* had also been retouched to make it appear as though Columbus's objective was Asia (1911, 2:255–259). For his part, Carbia 1930/1936 went so far as to claim that Las Casas authored this and other adulterations to the corpus with the aim of redefining an imperialist venture as an evangelical one. A cognate view about Las Casas's role in the redefinition of Columbus's enterprise has been held more recently by Zamora 1993.

178. Pérez de Tudela y Bueso et al. 1994, 1:108–109.

179. Ibid., 1:109.

180. Ibid.

181. Ibid. Columbus deliberately conflates the fall of Granada, the expulsion of the Jews, and the approval of his plan as part of one and the same time and space dimension. Vignaud and others saw this conflation as proof of a careless forgery, but in recent years Milhou has brilliantly explained why Columbus incurred this "error" (1983, 169–188).

182. Pérez de Tudela y Bueso et al. 1994, 1:109; emphasis added.

183. Ibid.

184. Ibid., 1:488–491; this quote, 490–491.

185. Ibid., 1:483–484.

186. I am grateful to Chad Leahy for a meticulous explanation of Las Casas's portrayal of Columbus as a Christian pilgrim (2004). For Las Casas's etymology of the surname *Colón*, see Las Casas, *Historia de las Indias* 1.1.2.2 (1994, 3:357).

7 The Tropics of Empire in Columbus's *Diario*

1. For *Diario* entries corresponding to 3–9 August 1492, see Pérez de Tudela y Bueso et al. 1994, 108–111.

2. Anghiera, *De orbe novo* 1.1 (1530, iiir).

3. Pérez de Tudela y Bueso et al. 1994, 1:112.

4. Ibid., 1:133; emphasis added.

5. Ibid., 1:228–229; emphasis added.

6. Colón 1992, 382.

7. Matthew 5:3 and 5:5, resp.

8. Pérez de Tudela y Bueso et al. 1994, 1:152.

9. Ibid., 3:1519; emphasis added.

10. Ibid., 2:1096.

11. Ibid., 1:114.

12. *Diario* entry for 20 September 1492 in ibid., 1:115.

13. Ibid., 1:116.

14. *Diario* entry for 29 September 1492 in ibid., 1:117.

15. Ibid., 1:119.

16. Ibid.

17. Ibid.

18. As Daston and Park have noted (1998, 146–147), this quarrel with language belongs to the history of "wonder."

19. Pérez de Tudela y Bueso et al. 1994, 1:122.

20. Ibid., 1:191.

21. Ibid., 1:122–123.

22. Ibid., 1:563–573; this quote, 567; emphasis added.

23. Ibid., 1:123.

24. Ibid.

25. Ibid., 1:124.

26. Ibid., 1:123.

27. Ibid., 1:124; emphasis added.

28. Ibid.

29. Ibid., 1:124–125.

30. An elegant treatment of the cognitive process by which Columbus came to coin the term "cannibal" can be found in Lestringant 1997.

31. Pérez de Tudela y Bueso et al. 1994, 1:125.

32. Ibid., 1:126.

33. Ibid., 1:125.

34. Ibid., 1:125 and 127, resp.

35. Ibid., 1:128.

36. Ibid., 1:129.

37. Ibid., 1:131.

38. Ibid., 1:132.

39. Morison 1942, 1:326.

40. Pérez de Tudela y Bueso et al. 1994, 1:133.

41. Ibid., 1:133–134.

42. Ibid., 1:136.

43. Ibid., 1:137.

44. Ibid., 1:138.

45. Ibid., 1:139.

46. Las Casas, *Historia de las Indias* 1.3.2.44 (1994, 3:578; emphasis added).

47. Morison 1942, 1:339.

48. Laguardia Trías 1974, 52–57.

49. Pérez de Tudela y Bueso et al. 1994, 1:139–140.

50. Ibid., 1:140.

51. Ibid., 1:141.

52. Emphasis added.

53. Ibid., 1:142.

54. Mandeville, *El libro de las maravillas del mundo* 23 (2002, 205).

55. Pérez de Tudela y Bueso et al. 1994, 1:143; emphasis added.

56. Ibid.; emphasis added.

57. Ibid., 1:144.

58. Friedman 1981, 67–86.

59. Hulme 1986, 33.

60. Pérez de Tudela y Bueso et al. 1994, 2:721–746; this quote, 725; emphasis added.

61. Ibid., 2:853–869; this quote, 868.

62. Ibid., 3:1519–1545, esp. 1530–1531.

63. For specific recollections of the "physical" monstrosity that Columbus and other Europeans are said to have witnessed in the bodies of a "morally" depraved people they presumed to eat human flesh, see Wey Gómez 1992 and 2007.

64. Pérez de Tudela y Bueso et al. 1994, 1:209; emphasis added.

65. Ibid., 3:1535.

66. Ibid., 1:210.

67. Ibid., 1:211.

68. Ibid., 1:278.

69. Postil 49 to Ailly and Gerson 1480–1483/1990, 16r.

70. This postil also made reference to Ptolemy's opinion that tropical peoples had hot natures rather than cold, and Nordic peoples cold natures rather than hot. See Postil 869 to Ailly and Gerson 1480–1483/1990, 150v.

71. Pérez de Tudela y Bueso et al. 1994, 1:145.

72. Ibid., 1:165.

73. Ibid., 1:177–178.

74. Ibid., 1:178.

75. Ibid., 1:832.

76. Ibid., 2:1097.

77. Ibid., 2:1099; emphasis added.

78. Ibid., 2:1103.

79. Ibid., 2:1105.

80. Ibid., 2:1106.

81. Ibid., 2:1107.

82. Ibid., 2:1107–1108.

83. Ibid., 2:1108.

84. Ibid., 2:1109.

85. Ibid., 2:1109–1110; emphasis added.

86. Ibid., 2:1111–1113.

87. Ibid., 2:1112.

88. Ibid., 2:1113.

89. The pre-Oedipal impulse behind Columbus's imagery is usefully noted in Levin 1969, 83–84.

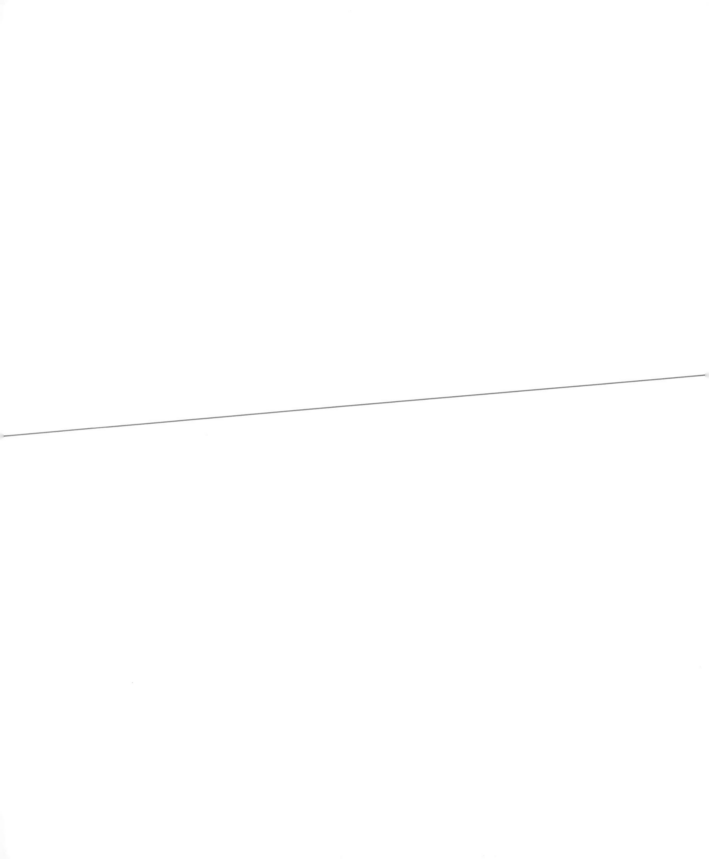

Bibliography

Manuscripts

Bacon, Roger. *Opus maius* IV. Escorial, g.iii.17 [13th century], Real Biblioteca de El Escorial, Madrid.

Geraldini, Alessandro. *Itinerarium ad regiones sub aequinoctiali plaga constitutas.* Fundo Geral 11169 [16th century], Biblioteca Nacional, Lisbon.

———. *Itinerarium ad regiones sub aequinoctiali plaga constitutas.* MS Harley 3566 [?16th century], 69v–70r, British Library, London.

Zorzi, Alessandro. *Informazione di Bartolomeo Colombo della Navegazione di ponente et garbin di Beragua nel Mondo Novo.* Collezione Alberico, no. 81 [about 1506], Biblioteca Nazionale Centrale, Florence.

Printed Sources

Abernethy, David B. 2000. *The Dynamics of Global Dominance: European Overseas Empires 1415–1980.* New Haven: Yale University Press.

Acosta, Joseph de. 1590/1998. *Historia natural y moral de las Indias*. Facsimile No. 970. Ed. Antonio
  Quilis. Madrid: Ediciones de Cultura Hispánica.

Adão da Fonseca, Luis. 1993. *Portugal entre dos mares*. Madrid: MAPFRE.

———. 1999. *The Discoveries and the Formation of the Atlantic Ocean: 14th Century–16th Century*.
  Lisbon: Commissão Nacional para as Comemorações dos Descobrimentos Portugueses.

Adão da Fonseca, Luis, and José Manuel Ruiz Asencio, eds. 1995. *Corpus documental del Tratado
  de Tordesillas*. Valladolid: Sociedad V Centenario del Tratado de Tordesillas; [Lisbon]: Comissão
  Nacional para as Comemorações dos Descobrimentos Portugueses.

Adorno, Rolena. 1992. *The Intellectual Life of Bartolomé de las Casas*. Andrew W. Mellon Lectures.
  New Orleans, La.: Graduate School of Tulane University.

Aethicus Ister. 1993. *Die "Kosmographie" des Aethicus*. Ed. and trans. Otto Prinz. Monumenta
  Germaniae Historica: Quellen zur Geistesgeschichte des Mittelalters 14. Munich: Monumenta
  Germania Historica.

Afnan, Soheil M. 1958. *Avicenna: His Life and Works*. London: George Allen and Unwin.

Ailly, Pierre d', and Jean Gerson. 1480–1483/1990. *Imago mundi* [*Tractatus de ymagine mundi*].
  Louvain. Ed. and trans. Antonio Ramírez de Verger. Tabula Americae. Facsimile No. 852.
  Madrid: Quinto Centenario and Testimonio Compañía Editorial.

Albertus Magnus, Saint. 1514. *De natura locorum*. Vienna. Microform. Watertown, Mass.: General
  Microfilm Co.

———. 1517. *Tabula tractatuum paruorum naturalium*. Venice.

———. 1890. *Philosophia pauperum*. Vol. 5 of Borgnet 1890–1899.

———. 1891. *Politicorum libri VIII*. Vol. 8 of Borgnet 1890–1899.

———. 1894. *In II Sententiarum*. Vols. 25–30 of Borgnet 1890–1899.

———. 1980a. *De caelo et mundo*. Ed. Paul Hossfeld. Vol. 5, part 1 of Geyer 1951–.

———. 1980b. *De natura loci*. Ed. Paul Hossfeld. Vol. 5, part 2, pp. 1–46, of Geyer 1951–.

———. 1987–1993. *Physica*. Ed. Paul Hossfeld. 2 vols. Tome 4, parts 1 and 2, of Geyer 1951–.

———. 1993. *De causis et processu universitatis a prima causa*. Ed. Winfred Fauser. Vol. 17, part 2 of
  Geyer 1951–.

Albumasar [Abū Ma'shar]. 1515. *De magnis coniunctionibus*. Venice.

———. 1995–1996. *Liber introductorii maioris ad scientiam judiciorum astrorum*. 9 vols. Ed. Richard
  Lemay. Naples: Istituto Universitario Orientale.

Allen, Don Cameron. 1963. *The Legend of Noah: Renaissance Rationalism in the Art, Science, and
  Letters*. Urbana: University of Illinois Press.

Alverny, M. T. d', and F. Hudry, eds. 1974. Al-Kindī: *De radiis*. Archives d'histoire doctrinale et littéraire
  du moyen age 49:139–260.

Ambrose, Saint. 1961. *"Hexameron," "Paradise," and "Cain and Abel."* Trans. John J. Savage. The Fathers of the Church 42. New York: Fathers of the Church.

André, J. 1949. Virgile et les Indiens. *Revue des Études Latines.* 27:157–163.

Anghiera, Peter Martyr d'. 1530. *De orbe novo.* Alcalá de Henares.

———. 1992. *The Discovery of the New World in the Writings of Peter Martyr of Anghiera.* Ed. Ernesto Lunardi et al. Trans. Felix Azzola. Rev. Luciano F. Farina. Nuova Raccolta Colombiana: English Edition 2. Rome: Istituto Poligrafico e Zecca dello Stato; Libreria dello Stato.

Apianus, Peter. 1548. *"Libro de la Cosmographia" de Pedro Apiano.* Antwerp.

Apollodorus. 1997. *The Library of Greek Mythology.* New York: Oxford University Press.

Archimedes. 1912. *The Works of Archimedes.* Ed. T. L. Heath, with a supplement discovered by Heiberg. New York: Dover Publications.

Aristotle. 1983. *Physics: Books III and IV.* Trans. and ed. Edward Hussey. Clarendon Aristotle Series. Oxford: Clarendon Press.

———. 1995a. *Generation of Animals.* Trans. A. Platt. In Barnes 1995, 1:1111–1218.

———. 1995b. *Metaphysics.* Trans. W. D. Ross. In Barnes 1995, 2:1552–1728.

———. 1995c. *Meteorologica.* Trans. E. W. Webster. In Barnes 1995, 1:555–625.

———. 1995d. *Nichomachean Ethics.* Trans. W. D. Ross. Rev. J. O. Urmson. In Barnes 1995, 2:1729–1867.

———. 1995e. *On Generation and Corruption.* Trans. H. H. Joachim. In Barnes 1995, 1:512–625.

———. 1995f. *On the Heavens.* Trans. J. L. Stocks. In Barnes 1995, 1:447–511.

———. 1995g. *On the Soul.* Trans. J. A. Smith. In Barnes 1995, 1:641–692.

———. 1995h. *Parts of Animals.* Trans. G. Ogle. In Barnes 1995, 1:994–1086.

———. 1995i. *Physics.* Trans. R. P. Hardie and R. K. Gaye. In Barnes 1995, 1:315–446.

———. 1995j. *Politics.* Trans. B. Jowett. In Barnes 1995, 2:1986–2129.

Armstrong, A. H. 1940. *The Architecture of the Intelligible Universe in the Philosophy of Plotinus: An Analytical and Historical Study.* Cambridge: Cambridge University Press.

———. 1967. *Plotinus.* Part 3 of *The Cambridge History of Later Greek and Early Medieval Philosophy,* ed. A. H. Armstrong, 193–282. Cambridge: Cambridge University Press.

Arnold, David. 1996 *The Problem of Nature: Environment, Culture, and European Expansion.* New Perspectives on the Past. Ed. Constantin Fasolt. Cambridge, Mass.: Blackwell.

Arrian. 1973–1983. *"History of Alexander" and "Indica."* Ed. P. Brunt. 2 vols. Loeb Classical Library 236, 269. Cambridge, Mass.: Harvard University Press.

Augustine, Saint. 1963. *The Trinity.* Trans. Stephen McKenna. The Fathers of the Church: A New Translation 45. Washington, D.C.: Catholic University of America Press.

———. 1957–1972. *The City of God against the Pagans*. Trans. W. M. Green. Loeb Classical Library 411–417. 7 vols. Cambridge, Mass.: Harvard University Press.

———. 1968. *De trinitate libri XV*. Part 16, 1–2 of *Aurelii Augustini opera*. 2 vols. Corpus christianorum, series latina 50A. Turnholt: Brepols.

———. 1970. *Sancti Aureli Augustini De genesi ad litteram libri duodecim*. Ed. J. Zycha. Corpus scriptorum ecclesiasticorum latinorum 23.1. Repr., New York: Johnson Reprint Corporation.

———. 1982. *The Literal Meaning of Genesis*. Trans. and ed. John Hammond Taylor. 2 vols. Ancient Christian Writers 41, 42. Ed. Johannes Quasten et al. New York: Newman Press.

Aujac, Germaine. 1987a. The Foundations of Theoretical Geography in Archaic and Classical Greece. In Harley and Woodward 1987, 130–147.

———. 1987b. Greek Cartography in the Early Roman World. In Harley and Woodward 1987, 161–176.

———. 1987c. The Growth of an Empirical Cartography in Hellenistic Greece. In Harley and Woodward 1987, 148–160.

———. 1993. *Claude Ptolémee astronome, astrologue, géographe: Connaissance et représentation du monde habité*. Paris: CTHS.

———. 1998. La redécouverte de Ptolémée et de la géographie grecque au XVe siècle. In *Terre à découvrir/Terres à parcourir: Exploration et connaissance du monde XIIe–XIXe siècles,* ed. Danielle Lecoq and Antoine Chambard, 55–73. Paris: L'Harmattan.

Averroës [Ibn Rushd]. 1562/1962. *Meteorologicorum*. In vol. 5 of *Aristotelis opera cum Averrois commentariis*, 400r–487v. Venice. Facsimile reproduction. 12 vols. in 14. Frankfurt am Main: Minerva.

———. 1919. *Compendio de Metafísica*. Trans. and ed. Carlos Quirós Rodríguez. Real Academia de Ciencias Morales y Políticas. Madrid: Estanislao Maestre.

Avicenna [Ibn Sīnā. 1508/1961a. *De animalibus*. In Fabrianensis 1508/1961, 29r–64r.

———. 1508/1961b. *De celo et mundo*. In Fabrianensis 1508/1961, 37r–42v.

———. 1508/1961c. *Philosophia prima*. In Fabrianensis 1508/1961, 70r–109v.

———. 1508/1961d. *Sufficientia*. In Fabrianensis 1508/1961, 13r–36v.

———. 1930. *A Treatise on the Canon of Medicine of Avicenna*. Trans. and ed. O. Cameron Gruner. London: Luzac.

Bacon, Roger. 1897. *The "Opus Majus" of Roger Bacon*. Ed. John Henry Bridges. 2 vols. Oxford: Clarendon Press.

———. 1928. *The "Opus Majus" of Roger Bacon*. Trans. Robert Belle Burke. 2 vols. Philadelphia: University of Pennsylvania Press.

———. 1998a. *De multiplicatione specierum*. In Lindberg 1998, 1–269.

———. 1998b. *De speculis comburentibus*. In Lindberg 1998, 271–341.

Baeumker, Clemens. 1908. *Witelo, ein Philosoph und Naturforscher des XIII. Jahrhunderts*. Beiträge zur Geschichte der Philosophie und Theologie des Mittelalters 3.2. Münster: Aschendorff.

Baldacci, Osvaldo. 1997. *Columbian Atlas of the Great Discovery*. Trans. Lucio Bertolazzi and Luciano F. Farina. Nuova Raccolta Colombiana 9. Rome: Istituto Poligrafico e Zecca dello Stato.

Ballesteros Beretta, Antonio. 1945. *Cristóbal Colón y el descubrimiento de América*. Historia de América 4, 5. Ed. Antonio Ballesteros Beretta. Barcelona: Salvat Editores.

Barros, João de. 1552/1932. *Ásia de Joam de Barros: Dos feitos que os portugueses fizeram no descobrimento e conquista dos mares e terras do Oriente; Primeira Decada*. Ed. António Baião. Scriptores rerum lusitanarum, Série A. Coimbra: Imprensa da Universidade.

Barnes, Jonathan, ed. 1995. *The Complete Works of Aristotle: The Revised Oxford Translation*. 2 vols. Bollingen Series 71.2. Repr., Princeton, N.J.: Princeton University Press.

Basil, Saint. 1963. *Exegetic Homilies*. Trans. Agnes Clare Way. The Fathers of the Church 46. Washington, D.C.: Catholic University of America Press.

Baur, Ludwig, ed. 1912. *Die philosophischen Werke des Robert Grosseteste*. Beiträge zur Geschichte der Philosophie und Theologie des Mittelalters 9. Münster in Westfalen: Aschendorffsche Verlagsbuchhandlung.

Beazley, C. Raymond. 1897–1906. *The Dawn of Modern Geography*. 3 vols. London: J. Murray.

Beckingham, C. F. 1996. An Eth[i]opian Embassy to Europe c. 1310. In Beckingham and Hamilton 1996, 197–211.

Beckingham, Charles F., and Bernard Hamilton, eds. 1996. *Prester John, the Mongols, and the Ten Lost Tribes*. Aldershot, Hampshire, U.K.; Brookfield, Vt.: Variorum.

Bello, Andrés. 1826. Silva a la agricultura en la zona tórrida. *El Repertorio americano* 1:1–17.

Bergevin, Jean. 1992. *Déterminisme et géographie: Hérodote, Strabon, Albert le Grand et Sebastian Münster*. Travaux du Département de géographie de l'Université Laval 8. Sainte-Foy: Les Presses de l'Université Laval.

Berggren, J. Lennart, and Alexander Jones, trans. and eds. 2000. *Ptolemy's "Geography": An Annotated Translation of the Theoretical Chapters*. Princeton, N.J.: Princeton University Press.

Bernáldez, Andrés. 1870. *Historia de los Reyes Católicos D[on] Fernando y D[oña] Isabel*. 2 vols. Seville: José María Geofrin.

Bertelli, Timoteo. 1892. La declinazione magnetica e la sua variazione nello spazio scoperto da Cristoforo Colombo. In *Raccolta* 1892–1896, part 4, vol. 2, 7–99.

Béthencourt, Jean de. 1874. *"Le Canarien": Livre de la conquète et conversion des Canaries (1402–1422)*. Ed. Gabriel Gravier. Société de l'histoire de Normandie. Publications 5. Rouen.

Beuchot, Maurice. 1976. El primer planteamiento teológico-jurídico sobre la conquista de América: John Mair. *Ciencia Tomista* 103:213–230.

Biblia Sacra [Vulgate]. 1969. Ed. Boniface Fischer et al. Stuttgart: Deutsche Bibelgesellschaft.

Biddick, Kathleen. 1998. The ABC of Ptolemy: Mapping the World with the Alphabet. In Sylvia Tomasch and Sealy Gilles, eds. *Text and Territory: Geographical Imagination in the European Middle Ages.* Philadelphia: University of Pennsylvania Press.

Bigalli, Davide. 1971. *I tartari e l'Apocalisse: Ricerche sull'escatologi in Adamo Marsh e Ruggero Bacone.* Florence: La Nuova Italia.

Bloomfield, Morton W. 1980. Recent Scholarship on Joachim of Fiore and His Influence. In *Prophecy and Millenarianism: Essays in Honour of Marjorie Reeves,* ed. Ann Williams, 21–52. Burnt Hill, U.K.: Longman House.

Boemus, Johann. 1556. *"El libro de las costumbres de todas las gentes del mundo, y de las Indias":* *Traduzido y copilado por el Bachiller Francisco Thamara cathedratico de Cadiz.* Antwerp.

Boethius, Anicius Manlius Severinus. 1966/1980. *Anicii Manlii Severini Boethii in Isagogen Porphyrii commenta.* Ed. Georg Schepss. Corpus Scriptorum Latinorum 48. Vienna. Repr., New York: Johnson Reprint Corporation.

Bolívar, Simón. 1815/1976. *Carta de Jamaica.* In *Doctrina del Libertador.* Biblioteca Ayacucho 1. Caracas: Biblioteca Ayacucho.

Bonin, Thérèse. 2001. *Creation as Emanation: The Origin of Diversity in Albert the Great's "On the Causes" and the "Procession of the Universe."* Notre Dame, Ind.: University of Notre Dame Press.

Book of Causes. 1984. Ed. and trans. Dennis J. Brand. Milwaukee, Wis.: Marquette University Press.

Borgnet, Auguste, ed. 1890–1899. *B. Alberti Magni Ratisbonensis episcopi, ordinis Praedicatorum, Opera omnia.* 38 vols. Paris: Ludovicum Vivés.

Bouché-Leclercq, A. 1899. *L'astrologie grecque.* Paris: Culture et Civilisation.

Brotton, Jerry. 1998. *Trading Territories: Mapping the Early Modern World.* Ithaca, N.Y.: Cornell University Press.

Bruyne, Edgar de. 1998. L'esthétique de la lumière. In vol. 2 of his *Études d'esthétique médiévale,* 3–29. Paris: Albin Michel.

Buisseret, David. 1998. The Cartographic Background to the Voyages of Columbus. In Schnaubelt and Van Fleteren 1998, 67–74.

Bunbury, E. H. 1883/1959. *A History of Ancient Geography among the Greeks and Romans from the Earliest Ages till the Fall of the Roman Empire.* 2 vols. 2nd ed. Republished with a new introduction by W. H. Stahl. New York: Dover Publications.

Buron, Edmond. 1930. Introduction to *Ymago Mundi,* by Pierre d'Ailly, 3 vols., 1:5–124. Paris: Maisonneuve Frères.

Campbell, Mary B. 1988. *The Witness and the Other World: Exotic European Travel Writing, 400–1600.* Ithaca, N.Y.: Cornell University Press.

Cañizares Esguerra, Jorge. 1999. New World, New Stars: Patriotic Astrology and the Invention of Indian and Creole Bodies in Colonial Spanish America, 1600–1650. *American Historical Review* 104 (1): 33–68.

Caraci, Giuseppe. 1971. A proposito delle "postille" colombiane. *Pubblicazioni dell'Istituto di Scienze Geografiche* 18:3–15.

Carbia, Rómulo D. 1930/1936. *La nueva historia del descubrimiento de América*. Buenos Aires: Imprenta y Casa Editora.

Carro, P. Venancio D. 1951. *La teología y los teólogos-juristas españoles ante la conquista de América*. 2nd ed. Biblioteca de teólogos españoles 18. Salamanca: Juan Bravo.

Carroll, William. 1975. Plato's Concept of the Soul as Self-Moving Motion. Unpublished paper.

Casey, Edward S. 1997. *The Fate of Place: A Philosophical History*. Berkeley: University of California Press.

Castañeda, F. Paulino. 1973. El Tratado de Alcaçobas y su interpretación hasta la negociación del Tratado de Tordesillas. In *El Tratado de Tordesillas y su proyección: Primer coloquio luso-español de historia de ultramar; Segundas jornadas americanistas de la Universidad de Valladolid*, 1:103–115. Valladolid: Seminario de Historia de América.

Castañeda Delgado, Paulino, ed. 1988–1998. *Obras completas: Bartolomé de las Casas*. 14 vols. Madrid: Alianza Editorial.

Cedulario Cubano (Los orígenes de la Colonización): I (1493–1512). 1929. Colección de Documentos Inéditos para la Historia de Hispano-América 6. Madrid: Compañía Ibero-Americana de Publicaciones.

Cerezo Martínez, Ricardo. 1994. *La Cartografía Náutica Española en los siglos XIV, XV, y XVI*. Madrid: Consejo Superior de Investigaciones Científicas.

Chalcidius. 1876. *Platonis Timaeus: Interprete Chalcidio cum eiusdem commentario*. Ed. J. Wrobel. Leipzig: B. G. Teubner.

Chantraine, Pierre. 1968. *Dictionnaire ètymologique de la langue grecque*. Paris: Klincksieck.

Charcot, Jean Baptiste. 1928. *Christophe Colomb vu par un marin*. Paris: Flammarion.

Charlier, Georges A. 1988. *Étude complète de la navigation et de l'itinérarire de Cristóbal Colón lors de son voyage de découverte de l'Amerique*. Liége: Charlier.

Chenu, Marie-Dominique. 1997. *Nature, Man, and Society: Essays on New Theological Perspectives in the Latin West*. Ed. and trans. Jerome Taylor and Lester K. Little. Repr., Toronto: University of Toronto Press; Medieval Academy of America.

Chaves, Jerónimo de. 1548. *Chronographia o Repertorio delos tiempos*. Seville.

Cioranescu, Alejandro. 1967. *Colón, humanista: Estudios de humanismo atlántico*. Madrid: Editorial Prensa Española.

Cohen, Jerome Jeffrey, ed. 2000. *The Postcolonial Middle Ages*. New York: St. Martin's Press.

Coín Cuenca, Luis M. 2003. *Una travesía de 20 días a dos rumbos que cambió el mundo*. Cádiz: Universidad de Cádiz, 2003.

Colomer Montset, Jaime. 1952. Las *Capitulaciones de Santa Fe* registradas en el Archivo de la Corona de Aragón, en Barcelona. In *Studi Colombiani,* ed. Paolo Revelli and Giuseppe Rosso, 2:391–403. Genoa: SAGA.

Colón, Cristóbal. 1992. *Textos y documentos completos*. Ed. Consuelo Varela and Juan Gil. 2nd ed. Madrid: Alianza Universidad.

Columbus, Ferdinand. 1963a. *Registrum "A" o Primum: Un volumen en 4to, autógrafo de D. Fernando*. Microfilm. Seville: Biblioteca Colombina.

———. 1963b. *Abecedarium "A," o primum: Un volumen en 4°, al que llamó, D. Fernando "tabla para los libros . . . ."* Microfilm. Seville: Biblioteca Colombina.

———. 1963c. *Abecedarium "B," es un volumen en fol. ordenado alfabeticamente por autores*. Microfilm. Seville: Biblioteca Colombina.

———. 1990. *Le historie della vita e dei fatti dell'ammiraglio Don Cristoforo Colombo*. Ed. Paolo Emilio Taviani and Ilaria Luzzana Caraci. 2 vols. Nuova Raccolta Colombiana 8/1–2. Rome: Istituto Poligrafico e Zecca dello Stato.

———. 1992. *The Life of the Admiral Christopher Columbus by His Son Ferdinand*. Ed. and trans. Benjamin Keen. 2nd ed. New Brunswick, N.J.: Rutgers University Press.

———. 1571/1992. *Historie del S. D. Fernando Colombo*. Venice. Facsimile. Rome: Bulzoni Editore.

Comellas, José Luis. 1991. *El cielo de Colón: Técnicas navales y astronómicas en el Viaje del Descubrimiento*. Madrid: Ediciones Tabapress.

———. 1995. *La Carta de Cristóbal Colón, Mapamundi, circa 1492*. Barcelona: M. Moleiro.

Comestor, Petrus. 1473. *Historia scholastica*. Augsburg.

Contreras, Remedios. 1979. Conocimientos técnicos y científicos del descubridor del Nuevo Mundo. *Revista de Indias* 39:89–104.

———. 1992. *La información colombina y el Descubrimiento de América*. Madrid: Josmar.

Cooper, John M., and D. S. Hutchinson, eds. 1997. *Plato: Complete Works*. Indianapolis, Ill.: Hackett Publishing Company.

Cormack, Lesley B. 1995. Flat Earth or Round Sphere: Misconceptions of the Earth and the Fifteenth-Century Transformation of the World. *Ecumene* 1:363–385.

———. 1997. *Charting an Empire: Geography at the English Universities, 1580–1620*. Chicago: University of Chicago Press.

———. 2007. Maps as Educational Tools in the Renaissance. In Woodward 2007b, 1:622–636.

Cortesão, Jaime. 1975–1978. *Os descobrimentos portugueses*. 6 vols. Lisbon: Livros Horizonte.

Cortés y Albacar, Martín. 1551/1998. *Breve compendio de la sphera y de la arte de nauegar.* Seville. In González-Aller Hierro 1998.

Cosgrove, Denis E. 2001. *Apollo's Eye: A Cartographic Genealogy of the Earth in the Western Imagination.* Baltimore, Md.: Johns Hopkins University Press.

———. 2007. Images of Renaissance Cosmography, 1450–1650. In Woodward 2007b, 1:55–98.

Cosmas, Indicopleustes. 1909. *The "Christian Topography" of Cosmas Indicopleustes.* Ed. Eric Otto Winstedt. Cambridge: University Press.

Crombie, A. C. 1953. *Robert Grosseteste and the Origins of Experimental Science, 1100–1700.* Oxford: Clarendon Press.

Crosby, Alfred W. 1997. *The Measure of Reality: Quantification and Western Society, 1250–1600.* Cambridge: Cambridge University Press.

Cross, Frank Moore, ed. 1990. *"Fourth Ezra": A Commentary on the Book of Fourth Ezra by Michael Edward Stone.* Intro. Michael E. Stone. Minneapolis, Minn.: Fortress Press.

Curtius, Ernst R. 1953. *European Literature and the Latin Middle Ages.* Trans. Willard Trask. Princeton, N.J.: Princeton University Press.

D'Albertis, Enrico Alberto. 1893. *Le costruzioni navali e l'arte della navigazione al tempo di Cristoforo Colombo.* Part 4, vol. 1 of *Raccolta* 1892–1896.

Daston, Lorraine, and Katharine Park. 1998. *Wonders and the Order of Nature, 1150–1750.* New York: Zone Books.

Dawson, Christopher, ed. 1980. *Mission to Asia.* Toronto: University of Toronto Press; Medieval Academy of America.

Deck, John N. 1967. *Nature, Contemplation, and the One: A Study in the Philosophy of Plotinus.* Toronto: University of Toronto Press.

Delp, Mark Damien. 1995. *De sex rerum principiis:* A Translation and Study of a Twelfth-Century Cosmology. PhD dissertation, University of Notre Dame.

Demos, Raphael. 1936. The Receptacle. *Philosophical Review* 45 (6): 535–557.

Desimoni, Cornelio. 1894. Questioni colombiane. In *Raccolta* 1892–1896, part 2, vol. 3, 7–116.

Dihle, Albrecht. 1962. Der fruchtbare Osten. *Rheinisches Museum für Philologie* 105:97–110.

Dijksterhuis, E. J. 1986. *The Mechanization of the World Picture: Pythagoras to Newton.* Trans. C. Dikshoorn. Repr., Princeton, N.J.: Princeton University Press.

Dilke, O. A. W. 1987. The Culmination of Greek Cartography in Ptolemy. In Harley and Woodward 1987, 177–200.

Diller, Aubrey. 1940. The Oldest Manuscripts of Ptolemaic Maps. *Transactions of the American Philological Association* 71:62–67.

———. 1975. *The Textual Tradition of Strabo's "Geography."* Amsterdam: Adolf M. Hakkert.

Diodorus Siculus. 1933–1967. *Diodorus of Sicily*. Trans. C. H. Oldfather et al. 12 vols. Loeb Classical Library 279, 303, 340, 375, 377, 384, 389, 390, 399, 409, 422, 423. Cambridge, Mass.: Harvard University Press.

Dodd, Bernard G. 1982. Aristoteles Latinus. Chapter 4 in *The Cambridge History of Later Medieval Philosophy: From the Rediscovery of Aristotle to the Disintegration of Scholasticism 1100–1600*, ed. Norman Kretzmann, Anthony Kenny, and Jan Pinborg, 45–79. Cambridge: Cambridge University Press.

Duhem, Pierre. 1958. *Le système du monde: Histoire des doctrines cosmologiques de Platon a Copernic*. 10 vols. Paris: Hermann.

Dunn, Oliver, and James E. Kelley, Jr., eds. 1989. *The "Diario" of Christopher Columbus's First Voyage to America, 1492–1493*. Norman: University of Oklahoma Press.

Dunraven, Earl of. 1912. Note on the Navigation of Columbus's First Voyage. In *Christopher Columbus and the New World of His Discovery*, by Filson Young, 399–422. 3rd ed. New York: Henry Holt.

Eastwood, Bruce Stanfield. 1964. The Geometrical Optics of Robert Grosseteste. PhD diss., University of Wisconsin.

Edgerton, Samuel Y., Jr. 1987. From Mental Matrix to *Mappaemundi* to Christian Empire: The Heritage of Ptolemaic Cartography in the Renaissance. In *Art and Cartography: Six Historical Essays*, ed. David Woodward, 10–50. Chicago: University of Chicago Press.

Enseñat de Villalonga, Alfonso. 1999. *La vida de Cristoforo Colonne: Una biografía documentada*. Cuadernos colombinos 22. Valladolid: Casa-Museo de Colón y Seminario Americanista de la Universidad.

Escalante de Mendoza, Juan de. 1998. Ytinerario de navegación de los mares y tierras occidentales. In González-Aller Hierro 1998.

Fabrianensis, Caecilius, ed. 1508/1961. *Avicenne perhypatetici philosophi: ac medicorum facile primi opera*. Venice. Repr., Frankfurt am Main: Minerva.

Falero, Francisco. 1535/1998. *Tratado del Esphera y del arte del marear*. Seville. In González-Aller Hierro 1998.

Fauser, Winfried. 1982. *Die Werke des Albertus Magnus in ihrer handschriftlichen Überlieferung*. Münster in Westfalen: Aschendorff.

Fenton, Paul B. 1986. The Arabic and Hebrew Versions of the Theology of Aristotle. In Kraye, Ryan, and Schmitt 1986, 241–264.

Fernández-Armesto, Felipe. 1987. *Before Columbus: Exploration and Colonisation from the Mediterranean to the Atlantic, 1229–1492*. New Studies in Medieval History. London: Macmillan Education.

———. 1991. *Columbus*. Oxford: Oxford University Press.

———. 2006. *Pathfinders: A Global History of Exploration*. Oxford: Oxford University Press.

Fernández de Enciso, Martín. 1519. *Suma de geographia*. Seville.

Fernández de Navarrete, Martín. 1825. *Colección de los viages y descubrimientos, que hicieron por mar los españoles desde fines del siglo XV, con varios documentos inéditos concernientes à la historia de la marina castellana y de los establecimientos españoles en Indias*. 5 vols. Madrid: Imprenta Real, 1825.

Fernández de Oviedo y Valdés, Gonzalo. 1535. *La historia general y natural de las Indias*. Seville.

Ferrer de Blanes, Jaume. 1545/1922–1925. *Sentencias catholicas del divi poeta Dante florenti*. Americana Series; Photostat Reproductions 77.152. Boston.

Ferrer Maldonado, Lorenzo. 1626. *Imagen del mundo sobre la esfera, cosmografía y geografía, teorica de planetas y arte de navegar*. Alcalá de Henares.

Flint, Valerie. 1992. *The Imaginative Landscape of Christopher Columbus*. Princeton, N.J.: Princeton University Press.

Floyd-Wilson, Mary. 2003. *English Ethnicity and Race in Early Modern Drama*. Cambridge: Cambridge University Press.

Fontoura da Costa, A. 1934/1960. *A marinharia dos descobrimentos*. 3rd ed. Lisbon: Agência Geral do Ultramar.

Foresti, Jacopo Filippo, da Bergamo. 1483/1486. [*Supplementum chronicarum*]. Venice.

Freese, J. H., ed. 1920. *The "Library" of Photius*. Translations of Christian Literature, 1st ser., Greek Texts 2. London: SPCK; New York: Macmillan.

Friedman, John Block. 1981. *The Monstrous Races in Medieval Art and Thought*. Cambridge, Mass.: Harvard University Press.

Furley, D. J., trans. and ed. 1955. *On the Cosmos*. In *Aristotle, "On Sophistical Refutations"; "On Coming-to-Be and Passing-Away"; "On the Cosmos,"* trans. and ed. E. S. Forster and D. J. Furley, 331–409. Loeb Classical Library 400. Cambridge, Mass.: Harvard University Press.

Gantz, Timothy. 1993. Vol. 1 of *Early Greek Myth: A Guide to Literary and Artistic Sources*. Baltimore, Md.: Johns Hopkins University Press.

García de Céspedes, Andrés. 1606/1998. *Regimiento de Navegación*. Madrid. In González-Aller Hierro 1998.

García de Palacio, Diego. 1587/1998. *Instrucion nauthica*. Mexico City. In González-Aller Hierro 1998.

García del Moral, Antonio. 1990. Estructura y significación teológicas. In Las Casas 1990, xliii–lxxv.

García Frías, Juan. 1974. Colón y la náutica en el siglo XVI. *Revista General de Marina* 187:297–313.

García-Gallo, Alfonso. 1987. Las bulas de Alejandro VI y el ordenamiento jurídico de la expansión portuguesa y castellana en Africa e Indias. In *Los orígenes españoles de las instituciones americanas: Estudios de derecho indiano,* 313–659. Madrid: Real Academia de Jurisprudencia y Legislación.

———. 1989. El título jurídico de los reyes de España sobre las Indias en los pleitos colombinos. In *Los orígenes de las instituciones americanas: Estudios de derecho indiano,* 667–698. Madrid: Real Academia de Jurisprudencia y Legislación.

Garin, Eugenio. 1990. *Astrology in the Renaissance: The Zodiac of Life.* New York: Arkana.

Gautier Dalché, Patrick. 1999. Le souvenir de la *Géographie* de Ptolémée dans le monde latin médiéval (VIe–XIVe siècles). *Euphrosyne: Revista de filologia clássica,* n.s., 27:79–106.

———. 2007. The Reception of Ptolemy's *Geography* (End of the Fourteenth to Beginning of the Sixteenth Century). In Woodward 2007b, 1:285–364.

Geminos, of Rhodes. 1975. *Géminos: "Introduction aux phénomènes."* Ed. and trans. Germaine Aujac. Paris: Société d'Édition "Les Belles Lettres."

Geraldini, Alessandro. 1631/1995. *Itinerarium ad regiones sub aequinoctiali plaga constitutas.* Rome. Microfiche. Woodbridge, Conn.: Research Publications International.

Gérard, Pierre. 1904. La cosmographie d'Albert le Grand d'après l'observation et l'expérience du moyen âge. *Revue Thomiste* 12: n.p.

Gerbi, Antonello. 1985. *Nature in the New World: From Christopher Columbus to Gonzalo Fernández de Oviedo.* Trans. Jeremy Moyle. Pittsburgh, Penn.: University of Pittsburgh Press.

Gersh, Stephen. 1986. *Middle Platonism and Neoplatonism: The Latin Tradition.* 2 vols. Publications in Medieval Studies, ed. Ralph McInerny. Notre Dame, Ind.: University of Notre Dame Press.

Gervase of Tilbury. 2002. *"Otia imperialia": Recreation for an Emperor.* Ed. and trans. S. E. Banks and J. W. Binns. Oxford: Clarendon Press.

Geyer, Bernhard, ed. 1951–. *Alberti Magni opera omnia.* Münster in Westfalen: Aschendorff.

Gil, Juan. 1989. *Colón y su tiempo.* Vol. 1 of *Mitos y utopías del descubrimiento.* 3 vols. Madrid: Alianza Editorial.

———. 1992a. Introducción. In Colón 1992, 15–79.

———. 1992b. Presentación: Aventuras y desventuras de la Biblioteca Colombina. In Marco Polo, *El Libro de Marco Polo: Las apostillas a la Historia natural de Plinio el Viejo,* ed. Juan Gil, ix–lxvii. Madrid: Alianza Editorial.

———. 1993. *En demanda del Gran Kan: Viajes a Mongolia en el siglo XIII.* Madrid: Alianza Editorial.

———. 1995. *La India y el Catay: Textos de la Antigüedad clásica y del Medioevo occidental.* Madrid: Alianza Editorial.

Gillet, M. S. 1932. Albert le Grand, Saint et Docteur de l'Eglise. *L'Illustrazione Vaticana* 2 (January): 67–69.

Gilson, Etienne. 1940. *The Spirit of Medieval Philosophy*. Trans. A. H. C. Downes. New York: Charles Scribner's Sons.

Gimpel, Jean. 1988. *The Medieval Machine: The Industrial Revolution of the Middle Ages*. Rev. ed. Aldershot, Hampshire, U.K.: Wildwood House.

Glacken, Clarence J. 1990. *Traces on the Rhodian Shore: Nature and Culture in Western Thought from Ancient Times to the End of the Eighteenth Century*. 1967. Berkeley: University of California Press.

Gliozzi, Giuliano. 2000. *Adam et le Nouveau Monde: La naissance de l'anthropologie comme idéologie coloniale: Des généalogies bibliques aux théories raciales (1500–1700)*. Trans. Arlette Estève and Pascal Gabellone. Lecques: Théétète Editions.

Godlewska, Anne, and Neil Smith. 1994. Critical Histories of Geography. Introduction to *Geography and Empire*, ed. Anne Godlewska and Neil Smith, 1–8. Cambridge, Mass.: Blackwell Publishers.

Goichon, A. M. 1969. *The Philosophy of Avicenna and Its Influence on Medieval Europe*. Trans. and ed. M. S. Khan. Delhi: Motilal Banarsidass.

Goldenberg, David M. 2003. *The Curse of Ham: Race and Slavery in Early Judaism, Christianity, and Islam*. Princeton, N.J.: Princeton University Press.

González de Clavijo, Ruy. 1406/1999. *Embajada a Tamorlán*. Ed. Francisco López Estrada. Madrid: Clásicos Castalia.

González-Aller Hierro, José Ignacio, eds. 1998. *Obras clásicas de náutica y navegación*. CD-ROM. Colección Clásicos Tavera, 2nd ser., Temáticas para la historia de Iberoamérica 17. Madrid: Fundación Histórica Tavera.

Goñi Gaztambide, José. 1958. *Historia de la bula de la cruzada en España*. Vitoria: Editorial del Seminario.

Grafton, Anthony. 1991. Traditions of Invention and Inventions of Tradition in Renaissance Italy: Annius of Viterbo. Chapter 3 in *Defenders of the Text: The Traditions of Scholarship in an Age of Science, 1450–1800*, 76–103. Cambridge, Mass.: Harvard University Press.

———. 1999. *Cardano's Cosmos: The Worlds and Works of a Renaissance Astrologer*. Cambridge, Mass.: Harvard University Press.

Grafton, Anthony, with April Shelford and Nancy Siraisi. 1992. *New Worlds, Ancient Texts: The Power of Tradition and the Shock of Discovery*. Cambridge, Mass.: Belknap Press of Harvard University Press.

Grant, Edward, ed. 1974. *A Source Book in Medieval Science*. Cambridge, Mass.: Harvard University Press.

———. 1994. *Planets, Stars, and Orbs: The Medieval Cosmos, 1200–1687*. New York: Cambridge University Press.

———. 1996. *The Foundations of Modern Science in the Middle Ages: Their Religious, Institutional, and Intellectual Contexts.* Cambridge History of Science. Cambridge: Cambridge University Press.

Graziano, Frank. 1999. *The Millennial New World.* New York: Oxford University Press.

Greenblatt, Stephen. *Marvelous Possessions: The Wonder of the New World.* Chicago: University of Chicago Press, 1991.

Grmek, Mirko D. 1998. *Western Medical Thought from Antiquity to the Middle Ages.* Cambridge, Mass.: Harvard University Press.

Grosjean, Georges, ed. *Mapamundi: The Catalan Atlas of the Year 1375.* Dietikon-Zurich: Urs Graf Publishing Company, 1978.

Grossato, Alessandro, trans. and ed. 1994. *L'India di Nicolò de' Conti: Un manoscritto del Libro IV del "De varietate Fortunae" di Francesco Poggio Bracciolini da Terranova (Marc. 2560).* Helios 4. Padua: Editoriale Programma.

Grosseteste, Robert. 1912a. *De lineis, angulis, et figuris seu de fractionibus et reflexionibus radiorum,* Doc. 9 in Baur 1912, 9–65.

———. 1912b. *De luce seu de inchoatione formarum.* Doc. 7 in Baur 1912, 1–59.

———. 1912c. *De natura locorum.* Doc. 10 in Baur 1912, 65–72.

Guenée, Bernard. 1991. Pierre d'Ailly (1351–1420). In *Between Church and State: The Lives of Four French Prelates in the Late Middle Ages,* trans. Arthur Goldhammer, 102–258. Chicago: University of Chicago Press.

Hackett, Jeremiah. 1997. Roger Bacon on Astronomy-Astrology: The Sources of the *Scientia experimentalis.* Chapter 8 in *Roger Bacon and the Sciences: Commemorative Essays,* ed. Jeremiah Hackett, 175–198. Leiden: Brill.

Hair, P. E. H. 1994. *The Founding of the Castelo de São Jorge da Mina: An Analysis of Sources.* Madison: African Studies Program, University of Wisconsin Press.

Hamilton, Bernard. 1996. Continental Drift: Prester John's Progress through the Indies. In Beckingham and Hamilton 1996, 237–269.

Hamilton, Gertrude Kelly. 1974. Three Worlds of Light: The Philosophy of Light in Marsilio Ficino, Thomas Vaughan and Henry Vaughan. PhD diss., University of Rochester.

Hanke, Lewis. 1959. *Aristotle and the American Indians: A Study in Race Prejudice in the Modern World.* London: Hollis and Carter.

Harley, J. B., and David Woodward, eds. 1987. *Cartography in Prehistoric, Ancient, and Medieval Europe and the Mediterranean.* The History of Cartography 1. Chicago: University of Chicago Press.

Harrisse, Henry. 1871. *D. Fernando Colón, historiador de su padre.* Seville: Sociedad de Bibliófilos de Sevilla.

Haskins, Charles Homer. 1924. *Studies in the History of Mediaeval Science*. Cambridge, Mass.: Harvard University Press.

———. 1927. *The Renaissance of the Twelfth Century*. Cambridge, Mass.: Harvard University Press.

Healy, John F. 1999. *Pliny the Elder on Science and Technology*. Oxford: Oxford University Press.

Heers, Jacques. 1981. *Christophe Colomb*. Paris: Hachette.

Henige, David. 1991. *In Search of Columbus: The Sources for the First Voyage*. Tucson: University of Arizona Press.

Henige, David, and Margarita Zamora. 1989. Text, Context, Intertext: Columbus's *Diario de abordo* as Palimpsest. *Americas* 46:17–40.

Herodotus. 1987. *The History*. Trans. David Grene. Chicago: University of Chicago Press.

Herrera y Tordesillas, Antonio. 1600–1615/1991. *Historia general de los hechos de los castellanos en las islas y tierrafirme del mar océano*. Ed. Mariano Cuesta Domingo. 4 vols. Madrid: Universidad Complutense de Madrid.

Hesiod. 1983. *"Theogony"; "Works and Days"; "Shield."* Trans. and ed. Apostolos N. Athanassakis. Baltimore, Md.: Johns Hopkins University Press.

———. 1993. *"Works and Days"; "Theogony."* Trans. Stanley Lombardo. Ed. Robert Lamberton. Indianapolis: Hackett Publishing Co.

Heylyn, Peter. 1657. *Cosmographie in Four Books: Containing the Chorographie and Historie of the Whole World, and All the Principal Kingdomes, Provinces, Seas, and Isles Thereof*. 2nd ed. London.

Hodgen, Margaret. 1971. *Early Anthropology in the 16th and 17th Centuries*. Philadelphia: University of Pennsylvania Press.

Holy Bible. 1971. Douay-Rheims Version. Revised by Bishop Richard Challoner. Rockford, Ill.: Tan Books and Publishers.

Homer. 1990. *The Iliad*. Trans. Robert Fagles. New York: Viking.

———. 1996. *Odyssey*. Trans. Robert Fagles. New York: Penguin Books.

Hosten, H. 1923. St. Thomas and San Thomé, Mylapore. *Journal of the Proceedings of the Asiatic Society of Bengal* 19:153–235.

Housley, Norman. 1992. *The Later Crusades: From Lyons to Alcazar 1274–1580*. Oxford: Oxford University Press.

Howland, Jacob. 1993. *The Republic: The Odyssey of Philosophy*. New York: Twayne Publishers.

Hulme, Peter. 1986. *Colonial Encounters: Europe and the Native Caribbean, 1492–1797*. London: Methuen.

———. 1993. Making Sense of the Native Caribbean. *New West Indian Guide/Nieuwe West-Indische Gids* 67 (3–4): 189–220.

Humboldt, Alexander von. 1836–1839. *Examen critique de l'histoire de la géographie du nouveau continent et des progrès de l'astronomie nautique aux quinzième et seizième siècles.* 5 vols. Paris: Gide.

Irving, Washington. 1828. *A History of the Life and Voyages of Christopher Columbus.* 3 vols. New York: G. and C. Carvill, 1828.

Irwin, Terence. 1995. *Plato's Ethics.* New York: Oxford University Press.

Isaac, Benjamin. 2004. *The Invention of Racism in Classical Antiquity.* Princeton, N.J.: Princeton University Press.

Isidore of Seville, Saint. 1983. *"Etimologías": Edición bilingüe.* Ed. and trans José Oroz Reta and Manuel-A. Marcos Casquero. 2 vols. 2nd ed. Madrid: Biblioteca de Autores Cristianos.

Jane, Cecil, ed. 1930–1933/1988. *The Four Voyages of Columbus: A History in Eight Documents, Including Five by Christopher Columbus, in the Original Spanish, with English Translations.* 2 vols. in 1. Repr., New York: Dover Publications.

John of Damascus, Saint. 1955. *De fide orthodoxa* Ed. Eligius M. Buytaert Franciscan Institute Publications 8. St. Bonaventure, N.Y.: Franciscan Institute.

———. 1958. *On the Orthodox Faith.* Trans. Frederic H. Chase, Jr. The Fathers of the Church 37. New York: Fathers of the Church.

Johnson, Christine R. 2006. Renaissance German Cosmographers and the Naming of America. *Past and Present* 191:3–43.

Jos, Emiliano. 1942. La génesis colombina del descubrimiento. *Revista de historia de América* 14:1–48.

———. 1979–1980. *El plan y la génesis del descubrimiento colombino.* Ed. Demetrio Ramos. Madrid: Casa-Museo Colón.

Kadir, Djelal. 1992. *Columbus and the Ends of the Earth: Europe's Prophetic Rhetoric as Conquering Ideology.* Berkeley: University of California Press.

Karamustafa, Ahmet T. 1992. Cosmographical Diagrams. In *Cartography in the Traditional Islamic and South Asian Societies,* ed. J. B. Harley and David Woodward, 71–89. The History of Cartography 2/1. Chicago: University of Chicago Press.

Kelley, James E., Jr. 1987. The Navigation of Columbus on His First Voyage to America. In *Columbus and His World: Proceedings of the First San Salvador Conference,* ed. Donald T. Gerace, 121–140. Ft. Lauderdale, Fla.: College Center of the Finger Lakes, Bahamian Field Station.

———. 1998. Fifteenth-Century Technology in Search of Contemporary Understanding. In Schnaubelt and Van Fleteren 1998, 117–164.

Kibre, Pearl, and Nancy G. Siraisi. 1978. The Institutional Setting: The Universities. In Lindberg 1978b, 120–144.

Kidd, I. G., ed. 1999. *The Translation of the Fragments.* Vol. 3 of *Posidonius,* ed. L. Edelstein and I. G. Kidd. Cambridge Classical Texts and Commentaries 36. Ed. J. Diggle et al. Cambridge: Cambridge University Press.

Kimble, George H. T. 1938. *Geography in the Middle Ages.* London: Methuen.

Kravath, Fred F. 1987. *Christopher Columbus Cosmographer: A History of Metrology, Geodesy, Geography, and Exploration from Antiquity to the Columbian Era.* Rancho Cordova, Calif.: Landmark Enterprises.

Kraye, Jill, W. F. Ryan, and C. B. Schmitt, eds. 1986. *Pseudo-Aristotle in the Middle Ages: The Theology and Other Texts.* London: Warburg Institute; University of London.

Kuntz, Paul G. 1987. From the Angel to the Worm: Augustine's Hierarchical Vision. In *Jacob's Ladder and the Tree of Life: Concepts of Hierarchy and the Great Chain of Being,* ed. Marion Leathers Kuntz and Paul Grimley Kuntz, 41–53. American University Studies, Series 5, Philosophy 14. New York: Peter Lang.

Lactantius. 1964. *The Divine Institutes.* Trans. Mary Francis McDonald. Washington, D.C.: Catholic University of America Press.

Laguardia Trías, Rolando. 1963. *Las más antiguas determinaciones de latitud en el Atlántico y el Indico.* Madrid: Consejo Superior de Investigaciones Científicas.

———. 1974. *El enigma de las latitudes de Colón.* Valladolid: Casa-Museo de Colón.

———. 1992. *Aclaratorio colombino.* Montevideo: Imprenta Militar.

Lamb, Ursula. 1969a. *The "Quarti Partitu en Cosmographia" by Alonso de Chaves: An Interpretation.* Agrupamento de estudos de história e cartografia antiga, série separatas 28. Coimbra: Junta de Investigações do Ultramar. Reprinted in Lamb 1995a, 3–9.

———. 1969b. Science by Litigation: A Cosmographic Feud. *Terrae Incognitae* 1:40–57. Reprinted with original pagination in Lamb 1995a.

———. 1974. The Spanish Cosmographic Juntas of the Sixteenth Century. *Terrae Incognitae* 6:51–64. Reprinted with original pagination in Lamb 1995a.

———. 1976. Cosmographers of Seville: Nautical Science and Social Experience. In *First Images of America: The Impact of the New World on the Old,* ed. Fredi Chiapelli, 2:675–686. Berkeley: University of California Press. Reprinted with original pagination in Lamb 1995a.

———. 1985. *Nautical Scientists and Their Clients in Iberia (1508–1624): Science from an Imperial Perspective.* Centro de Estudos de História e Cartografia Antiga, Série Separatas 154. Lisbon: Instituto de Investigação Científica Tropical. Reprinted in Lamb 1995a, 49–61.

———. 1995a. *Cosmographers and Pilots of the Spanish Maritime Empire.* Variorum Collected Studies Series 499. Aldershot, Hampshire, U.K.; Brookfield, Vt.: Variorum.

———. 1995b. The Teaching of Pilots and the *Chronographía o Repertorio de los Tiempos*. In Lamb
1995a, 1–17.

Lambert, M. D. 1961. *Franciscan Poverty, the Doctrine of the Absolute Poverty of Christ and the Apostles
in the Franciscan Order 1210–1323*. London: SPCK.

Lang, Helen S. 1992. *Aristotle's "Physics" and Its Medieval Varieties*. Albany: State University of New
York Press.

Larner, John. 1988. The Certainty of Columbus: Some Recent Studies. *History* 73 (237): 3–23.

———. 1999. *Marco Polo and the Discovery of the World*. New Haven: Yale University Press.

Las Casas, Bartolomé de. 1552/1988. *Apología*. Ed. Angel Losada. Vol. 9 of Castañeda Delgado
1988–1998.

———. 1552a. *Aqui se contienen unos avisos y reglas para los confessores que oyeren confessiones delos
españoles que son o han sido en cargo a los Indios delas Indias del mar Oceano*. Seville.

———. 1552b. *Brevissima relaçion dela destruyçion delas yndias*. Seville.

———. 1990. *De unico vocationis modo*. Ed. Jesús Angel Barreda. Vol. 2 of Castañeda Delgado
1988–1998.

———. 1992. *Apólogética historia sumaria*. 3 vols. Ed. Vidal Abril Castelló et al. Vols. 6–8 of
Castañeda Delgado 1988–1998.

———. 1994. *Historia de las Indias*. Ed. Miguel Angel Medina et al. Vols. 3, 4, and 5 of Castañeda
Delgado 1988–1998.

Leahy, Chad. 2004. Las peregrinaciones de Colón en su primer viaje (según fray Bartolomé).
Unpublished paper.

Leclerq, Jean. 1987. Influence and Noninfluence of Dionysius in the Western Middle Ages. In
Pseudo-Dionysius: The Complete Works, trans. Colm Luibheid in collaboration with Paul Rorem,
ed. Paul Rorem, 25–32. New York: Paulist Press.

Leff, Gordon. 1992. The Trivium and the Three Philosophies. Chapter 10.1 in *A History of the
University in Europe*, ed. Hilde de Ridder-Symoens, 1:307–336. A History of the University in
Europe. Ed. Walter Rüegg. Cambridge: Cambridge University Press.

Leicester, Henry M. 1974. *Development of Biochemical Concepts from Ancient to Modern Times*.
Cambridge, Mass.: Harvard University Press.

Lemay, Richard. 1962. *Abu Ma 'Shar and Latin Aristotelianism in the Twelfth Century: The Recovery
of Aristotle's Natural Philosophy through Arabic Astrology*. Oriental Series 38. Beirut: American
University of Beirut.

———. 1987. The True Place of Astrology in Medieval Science and Philosophy: Towards a
Definition. *Astrology, Science, and Society: Historical Essays*, ed. Patrick Curry, 57–73. Suffolk:
Boydell Press.

Lestringant, Frank. 1997. *Cannibals: The Discovery and Representation of the Cannibal from Columbus to Jules Verne*. Trans. Rosemary Morris. Berkeley: University of California Press, 1997.

Levin, Harry. *The Myth of the Golden Age in the Renaissance*. Bloomington: Indiana University Press, 1969.

Liber de causis. 2003. Ed. Randolf Schönberger. Trans. Andreas Schönfeld. Hamburg: Felix Meiner.

Libro del conoscimiento de todos los reinos. 1999. Ed. Nancy F. Marino. Medieval and Renaissance Texts and Studies 198. Tempe, Ariz.: Arizona Center for Medieval and Renaissance Studies.

Lindberg, David C. 1978a. The Transmission of Greek and Arabic Learning to the West. In Lindberg 1978b, 52–90.

———, ed. 1978b. *Science in the Middle Ages*. Chicago History of Science and Medicine. Chicago: University of Chicago Press.

———. 1992. *The Beginnings of Western Science: The European Scientific Tradition in Philosophical, Religious, and Institutional Context, 600 B.C. to A.D. 1450*. Chicago: University of Chicago Press.

———, ed. 1998. *Roger Bacon's Philosophy of Nature: A Critical Edition, with English Translation, Introduction, and Notes, of "De multiplicatione specierum" and "De speculis comburentibus."* South Bend, Ind.: St. Augustine's Press.

Little, A. G. 1914. Roger Bacon's Works with References to the Mss. and Printed Editions. Appendix to *Roger Bacon: Essays Contributed by Various Writers on the Occasion of the Commemoration of the Seventh Centenary of His Birth*, ed. A. G. Little, 373–425. Oxford: Clarendon Press.

Livingstone, David N. 1992. *The Geographical Tradition: Episodes in the History of a Contested Enterprise*. Oxford: Blackwell.

Lloyd, G. E. 1964. The Hot and the Cold, the Dry and the Wet in Greek Philosophy. *Journal of Hellenic Studies*. 84:92–106.

Lohr, Charles H. 1986. The Pseudo-Aristotelian *Liber de causis* and Latin Theories of Science in the Twelfth and Thirteenth Centuries. In Kraye, Ryan, and Schmitt 1986, 53–62.

Lollis, Cesare de. 1892/1969. *Cristoforo Colombo nella leggenda e nella storia*. Ed. E. Migliorini. Preface by R. Almagià. Florence: Sansoni.

López de Gómara, Francisco. 1552/1979. *Historia general de las Indias*. Caracas: Biblioteca Ayacucho.

López Estrada, Francisco. 1999. Introduction to *Embajada a Tamorlán*, by Ruy González de Clavijo, 9–74. Madrid: Clásicos Castalia.

Lorimer, W. L. 1924. *The Text Tradition of Pseudo-Aristotle "De mundo."* St. Andrews University Publications 18. London: Humphrey Milford, Oxford University Press.

Lovejoy, Arthur. 1964. *The Great Chain of Being: A Study of the History of an Idea*. Cambridge, Mass.: Harvard University Press.

Lucan. 1998. *La guerre civile (VI 333–X 546)*. Ed. and trans. Jean Soubiran. Toulouse: Editions Universitaires du Sud.

Lucretius, Titus Carus. 1924. *De rerum natura*. Trans. W. H. D. Rouse. Loeb Classical Library 181. Cambridge, Mass.: Harvard University.

Macrobius, Ambrosius Aurelius Theodosius. 1990. *Commentary on the Dream of Scipio*. Trans. and ed. William Harris Stahl. Records of Western Civilization. New York: Columbia University Press.

———. 2003. *Macrobe: "Commentaire au songe de Scipion."* Ed. and trans. Mireille Armisen-Marchetti. Paris: Les Belles Lettres.

Magnaghi, Alberto. 1928. I presunti errori che vengono attribuiti a Colombo nella determinazione delle latitudini. *Bollettino della Società Geografica Italiana*, ser. 6, no. 5: 459–494 and 553–582.

———. 1930. Ancora dei pretesi errori di Colombo nella determinazione delle latitudini. *Bolletino della Reale Società Geografica Italiana*, ser. 6, nos. 7–8: 497–515.

Maimonides, Moses. 1963. *The Guide of the Perplexed*. Trans. Shlomo Pines. Chicago: University of Chicago Press.

Major, R. H., ed. 1992. *India in the Fifteenth Century: Being a Collection of Narratives of Voyages to India, in the Century Preceding the Portuguese Discovery of the Cape of Good Hope*. Repr., New Delhi: Asian Educational Services.

Mandeville, Jehan de. 2002. *El libro de las maravillas del mundo*. In *Libros de Maravillas*, ed. Marie-José Lemarchand, 75–268. Madrid: Siruela.

Mandonnet, Pierre F. 1893a. *Les dominicains et la découverte de l'Amérique*. Paris: P. Lethielleux.

———. 1893b. Les idées cosmographiques d'Albert le Grand et la découverte de l'Amerique. *Revue Thomiste* 46–64:200–221.

Manz, Beatrice Forbes. 1989. *The Rise and Rule of Tamerlane*. Cambridge: Cambridge University Press.

Manzano Manzano, Juan. 1964. *Cristóbal Colón: Siete años decisivos de su vida 1485–1492*. Madrid: Ediciones Cultura Hispánica.

———. 1976. *Colón y su secreto*. Madrid: Ediciones Cultura Hispánica.

Marín Martínez, Tomás. 1993. Estudio introductorio. In *Catálogo concordado de la Biblioteca de Hernando Colón*, 1:17–352. Seville: Fundación MAPFRE América.

Markus, R. A. 1967. Marius Victorinus and Augustine. Part 5 of *The Cambridge History of Later Greek and Early Medieval Philosophy*, ed. A. H. Armstrong, 327–419. Cambridge: Cambridge University Press.

Martín-Merás, María Luisa. 1993. *Cartografía marítima hispana: La imagen de América*. Colección Ciencia y Mar. Barcelona: Lunwerg.

Mayhew, Robert. 2004. *The Female in Aristotle's Biology: Reason or Rationalization*. Chicago: University of Chicago Press.

Messahallah [Māshā'allāh]. 1549. *Messahalae libri tres*. Nuremberg.

McCrindle, J. W. ed. 1960. *Ancient India As Described by Megasthenês and Arrian*. Revised 2nd ed. Calcutta: Cuckervertty, Chatterjee.

McCullough, Ernest J. 1980. St. Albert on Motion as *Forma fluens* and *Fluxus formae*. Chapter 5 in Weisheipl 1980c, 129–153.

McElroy, John W. 1941. The Ocean Navigation of Columbus on His First Voyage. *American Neptune* 1:209–240.

McGinn, Bernard. 1979. *Visions of the End: Apocalyptic Traditions in the Middle Ages*. New York: Columbia University Press.

Medina, Pedro. 1972. *A Navigator's Universe: The "Libro de Cosmographia" of 1538 by Pedro de Medina*. Trans. and ed. Ursula Lamb. Chicago: University of Chicago Press.

Mela, Pomponius. 1971. *De chorographia*. Ed. Gunnar Ranstrand. Studia Graeca et Latina Gothoburgensia 28. Acta Universitatis Gothoburgensis. Stockholm: Almqvist and Wiskell.

———. 1998. *Description of the World*. Ann Arbor: University of Michigan Press.

Mignolo, Walter. 1995. *The Darker Side of the Renaissance: Literacy, Territoriality, and Colonization*. Ann Arbor: University of Michigan Press.

Milhou, Alain. 1983. *Colón y su mentalidad mesiánica en el ambiente franciscanista español*. Valladolid: Casa-Museo de Colón.

Minnis, Alastair J. 1988. *Medieval Theory of Authorship: Scholastic Literary Attitudes in the Later Middle Ages*. Ed. Edward Peters. 2nd ed. Philadelphia: University of Pennsylvania Press.

Mittelstrass, Jürgen. 1995. *Machina mundi—zum astronomischen Weltbild der Renaissance*. Basel: Heldbing und Lichtenhahn.

Monumenta henricina. 1960–1974. 15 vols. Coimbra: Comissão Executiva das Comemorações do V Centenário da Morte do Infante D. Henrique.

Morgan, David. 1986. *The Mongols*. Cambridge, Mass.: Blackwell.

———. 1996. Prester John and the Mongols. In Beckingham and Hamilton 1996, 159–170.

Morison, Samuel Eliot. 1942. *Admiral of the Ocean Sea: A Life of Christopher Columbus*. 2 vols. Boston: Little, Brown.

———, trans. and ed. 1963. *Journals and Other Documents on the Life and Voyages of Christopher Columbus*. New York: Heritage Press.

Morse, Victoria. 2007. The Role of Maps in Later Medieval Society: Twelfth to Fourteenth Century. In Woodward 2007b, 1:25–52.

Morsink, J. 1979. Was Aristotle's Biology Sexist? *Journal of the History of Biology* 12:83–112.

Mote, F. W. 1999. *Imperial China 900–1800.* Cambridge, Mass.: Harvard University Press.

Muldoon, James. 1979. *Popes, Lawyers, and Infidels: The Church and the Non-Christian World 1250–1550.* Philadelphia: University of Pennsylvania Press.

———. 1999. *Empire and Order: The Concept of Empire, 800–1800.* Studies in Modern History. New York: St. Martin's Press.

Müller, Karl, of Paris, ed. 1841–1938/1975. *Fragmenta historicorum graecorum.* 5 vols. Paris. Repr., Frankfurt: Minerva.

Muñoz, Juan Bautista. 1793/1973. Vol. 1 of *Historia del Nuevo Mundo.* Madrid.

Murphy, N. R. 1951. *The Interpretation of Plato's "Republic."* Oxford: Clarendon Press.

Nájera, Antonio de. 1628/1998. *Navegacion especulativa, y pratica.* Lisbon. In González-Aller Hierro 1998.

Nebenzahl, Kenneth. 1990. *Atlas of Columbus and the Great Discoveries.* Chicago: Rand McNally.

Nelson, Benjamin. 1981. *On the Roads to Modernity: Conscience, Science, and Civilizations.* Totowa, N.J.: Rowman and Littlefield.

North, John D. 1986. Celestial Influence—the Major Premiss of Astrology. In *Astrologi hallucinati: Stars and the End of the World in Luther's Time,* ed. Paola Zambelli, 45–100. New York: Walter de Gruyter.

———. 1980. Astrology and the Fortunes of Churches. *Centaurus* 24:181–211. Repr. in *Stars, Minds and Fate: Essays in Ancient and Medieval Cosmology,* 59–89. London: Hambledon Press, 1989.

Notopoulos, James A. 1944a. The Symbolism of the Sun and Light in the *Republic* of Plato. I. *Classical Philology* 39 (3): 163–172.

———. 1944b. The Symbolism of the Sun and Light in the *Republic* of Plato. II. *Classical Philology* 39 (4): 223–224.

Nunn, George E. 1924. *The Geographical Conceptions of Columbus: A Critical Consideration of Four Problems.* New York: American Geographical Society.

———. 1937. Marinus of Tyre's Place in the Columbus Concepts. *Imago Mundi* 2:27–35.

O'Gorman, Edmundo. 1958/1977. *La invención de América: Investigación acerca de la estructura histórica del Nuevo Mundo y del sentido de su devenir.* 2nd ed. Mexico City: Fondo de Cultura Económica.

Oliva, Annamaria. 1993. Alessandro Geraldini e la tradizione manoscritta dell' *Itinerarium ad regiones sub aequinoctiali plaga constitutas.* In *Alessandro Geraldini e il suo tempo: Atti del Convegno storico internazionale, Amelia, 19–20–21 November 1992,* ed. Enrico Menestò, 175–209. Spoleto: Centro italiano di Studi sull'Alto Medioevo.

Olympiodorus the Younger, et al. 1551. *Olympiodori philosophi Alexandrini in Meteora Aristotelis comentarii. Ioannis grammatici philoponi scholia in I. Meteorum Aristotelis. Ioanne Baptista Camotio philosopho interprete.* Venice.

O'Meara, Dominic J. 1999. The Hierarchical Ordering of Reality in Plotinus. Chapter 3 in *The Cambridge Companion to Plotinus,* ed. Lloyd P. Gerson, 66–81. Reprinted with corrections. Cambridge: Cambridge University Press.

Osterhammel, Jürgen. 1997. *Colonialism: A Theoretical Overview.* Trans. Shelley L. Frisch. Princeton, N.J.: Markus Wiener Publishers.

Other Bible. 1984. Ed. Willis Barnstone. New York: Harper Collins.

Otto of Freising. 1912. *Ottonis episcopi Frisigensis chronica sive historia de duabus civitatibus.* Ed. Adolfus Hofmeister. 2nd ed. Scriptores rerum germanicarum in usum scholarum ex monumentis germaniae historicis separatim editi. Hannover: Hahn.

———. 2002. *The Two Cities: A Chronicle of Universal History to the year 1146 A.D.* Trans. Charles C. Mierow. New foreword and bibliography by Karl F. Morrison. Ed. Austin P. Evans and Charles Knapp. New ed. New York: Columbia University Press.

Ovid. 1999. *Metamorphoses.* 2 vols. Trans. Frank Justus Miller. Loeb Classical Library 42, 43. Repr., Cambridge, Mass.: Harvard University Press.

Oxford Atlas of the World. 2003. 11th ed. New York: Oxford University Press.

Padrón, Ricardo. 2004. *The Spacious Word: Cartography, Literature, and Empire in Early Modern Spain.* Chicago: University of Chicago Press.

Pagden, Anthony. 1982. *The Fall of Natural Man: The American Indian and the Origins of Comparative Ethnology.* Cambridge: Cambridge University Press.

———. 1995. *Lords of All the Worlds: Ideologies of Empire in Spain, Britain and France c. 1500–c. 1800.* New Haven: Yale University Press.

Parel, Anthony J. 1992. *The Machiavellian Cosmos.* New Haven: Yale University Press.

Parish, Helen Rand. 1992. Las Casas' Spirituality—The Three Crises. Introduction to *Bartolomé de las Casas: The Only Way,* trans. Francis Patrick Sullivan, ed. Helen Rand Parish, 9–58. New York: Paulist Press.

Parish, Helen Rand, and Harold E. Weidman. 1992. *Las Casas en México: Historia y obra desconocidas.* Mexico City: Fondo de Cultura Económica.

Paul of Burgos. [1485?]. Additio. In *Postilla super totam Bibliam,* by Nicholas of Lyra, 1:iiiv–vr. Cologne.

Pausanias. 1898. *Pausanias's Description of Greece.* Trans. and ed. James G. Frazer. London: Macmillan.

Pelikan, Jaroslav. 1987. The Odyssey of Dionysian Spirituality. In *Pseudo-Dionysius: The Complete Works,* trans. Colm Luibheid and Paul Rorem, ed. Paul Rorem, 11–24. New York: Paulist Press.

Pelliot, Paul. 1922–1923. Les Mongols et la papauté. *Revue de l'Orient Chrétien,* 3rd ser., 3, nos. 1–2: 3–30.

Pennington, Kenneth. 1970. Bartolomé de las Casas and the Tradition of Medieval Law. *Church History* 39:149–161.

Pérez de Moya, Juan. 1567. *[Fragmentos matemáticos]: Libro Segundo, Trata de cosas de Astronomia, y Geographia, y Philosophia natural, y Sphera, y Astrolabio, y Nauegación, y Relojes.* Salamanca.

Pérez de Oliva, Hernán. 1965. *Historia de la inuencion de las yndias.* Ed. José Juan Arrom. Bogotá: Instituto Caro y Cuervo.

Pérez de Tudela y Bueso, Juan. 1983. *Mirabilis in Altis: Estudio crítico sobre el origen y significado del proyecto descubridor de Cristóbal Colón.* Madrid: Consejo Superior de Investigaciones Científicas.

———. 1994. El Descubrimiento, entre nebulosas y luz documental. In Pérez de Tudela y Bueso et al. 1994, 1:xlv–ccxlii.

Pérez de Tudela y Bueso, Juan, et al., eds. 1994. *Colección documental del Descubrimiento (1470– 1506).* 3 vols. Madrid: Fundación MAPFRE América.

Pérez Embid, Florentino. 1948. *Los descubrimientos en el Atlántico y la rivalidad castellano-portuguesa hasta el tratado de Tordesillas.* Seville: Escuela de Estudios Hispano-Americanos de Sevilla.

Pérez Fernández, Isacio. 1981. *Inventario documentado de los escritos de Fray Bartolomé de las Casas.* Estudios monográficos 1. Bayamón, Puerto Rico: CEDOC.

———. 1984. *Cronología documentada de los viajes, estancias y actuaciones de Fray Bartolomé de las Casas.* Estudios monográficos 2. Bayamón, Puerto Rico: CEDOC.

———. 1994. Estudio crítico preliminar. In Las Casas 1994, 1:11–322.

Phelan, John Leddy. 1970. *The Millennial Kingdom of the Franciscans in the New World.* 2nd ed. Berkeley: University of California Press.

Phillips, J. R. S. 1998. *The Medieval Expansion of Europe.* 2nd ed. Oxford: Clarendon Press.

Phillips, William D., Jr., and Carla Rahn Phillips. 1992. *The Worlds of Christopher Columbus.* Cambridge: Cambridge University Press.

Philo of Alexandria. 1993. *The Works of Philo: Complete and Unabridged.* Trans. C. D. Yonge. New updated ed. Peabody, Mass.: Hendrickson Publishers.

Piccolomini, Aeneas Sylvius [Pope Pius II]. 1477/1991. *"Historia rerum": Cuyo original se encuentra en la Biblioteca Colombina de Sevilla.* Cologne. Trans. Antonio Ramírez de Verger. Tabula Americae. Facsimile No. 186. Madrid: Quinto Centenario; Testimonio Compañía Editorial.

Pina, Ruy de. 1950. *Crónica de el-rey D. João II*. Ed. Alberto Martins de Carvalho. Coimbra: Atlântida.

Pingree, David. 1987. The Diffusion of Arabic Magical Texts in Western Europe. In *La diffusione delle scienze islamiche nel Medio Evo europeo (Roma, 2–4 ottobre 1984): Convegno internazionale promosso dall'Accademia nazionale dei Lincei, Fondazione Leone Caetani e dall'Università di Roma La Sapienza*, 57–102. Rome: Accademia nazionale dei Lincei.

Plato. 1991. *The Republic of Plato*. Trans. and ed. Alan Bloom. 2nd ed. New York: Basic Books.

———. 1997a. *Laws*. Trans. Trevor J. Saunders. In Cooper and Hutchinson 1997, 1318–1616.

———. 1997b. *Menexenus*. Trans. Paul Ryan. In Cooper and Hutchinson 1997, 950–970.

———. 1997c. *Phaedo*. Trans. G. M. A. Grube. In Cooper and Hutchinson 1997, 49–100.

———. 1997d. *Phaedrus*. Trans. A. Nehamas and P. Woodruff. In Cooper and Hutchinson 1997, 506–556.

———. 1997e. *Timaeus*. Trans. Donald J. Zeyl. In Cooper and Hutchinson 1997, 1224–1291.

Pliny the Elder. 1938–1963. *Natural History*. Trans. H. Rackham et al. Loeb Classical Library 330, 352, 353, 370, 371, 392–394, 418, 419. 10 vols. Cambridge, Mass.: Harvard University Press.

Plotinus. 1962. *The Enneads*. Trans. Stephen MacKenna. Foreword by E. R. Dodds. 3rd ed. Rev. B. S. Page. London: Faber and Faber.

Polo, Marco. 1485/1986. *"Libro de las maravillas del mundo"* [*De consuetudinibus et condicionibus orientalium regionum*]: *Facsímil del que, usado por Cristóbal Colón, se encuentra depositado en la Biblioteca Capitular y Colombina del Cabildo Catedral de Sevilla*. Trans. and ed. Juan Gil. Antwerp. Tabula Americae. Facsimile. Madrid: Quinto Cententario and Testimonio Compañía Editorial.

Porphyry. 1966. *Porphyrii Isagoge: Translatio Boethii*. In *Aristoteles latinus I 6–7: Categoriarum supplementa*, 1–31, ed. Laurentius Minio-Paluello. Bruges-Paris: Desclée de Brouwer.

Preus, Anthony. 1975. *Science and Philosophy in Aristotle's Biological Works*. Studien und Materialen zur Geschichte der Philosophie 1. Hildesheim: G. Olms.

Provost, Foster. 1991. *Columbus: An Annotated Guide to the Scholarship on His Life and Writings, 1750–1988*. Providence, R.I.: John Carter Brown Library.

Pseudo-Abdias. 1719. *Acta apostolorum apocrypha, Sive Historia Certaminis Apostolici, adscripta Abdiae*. In *Codex Apocryphus Novi Testamenti*, ed. Johann Albert Fabricius, 3 vols., 2:387–742. Hamburg.

Pseudo-Aristotle. 1995a. *On the Universe*. Trans. E. S. Foster. In Barnes 1995, 1:626–640.

———. 1995b. *Problems*. Trans. E. S. Foster. In Barnes 1995, 2:1319–1527.

Pseudo-Dionysius the Areopagite. 1937a. *De caelesti hierarchia* [Version (R)]. Trans. Robert Grosseteste [ca. 1235]. In *Dionysiaca: Recueil donnant l'ensemble des traductions latines des ouvrages attribués au Denys de l'Aréopage*, 2:725–1039. Bruges: Desclé de Brouwer.

———. 1937b. *De divinibus nominibus.* [Version (R)]. Trans. Robert Grosseteste [ca. 1235]. In *Dionysiaca: recueil donnant l'ensemble des traductions latines des ouvrages attribués au Denys de l'Aréopage,* 1:3–663.

Pseudo-Methodius. 1998. *Die Apokalypse des Pseudo-Methodius die Ältesten griechischen und lateinischen Übersetzungen.* Ed. W. J. Aerts and G.A.A. Kortekaas. 2 vols. Corpus scriptorum christianorum orientalium 569, 570. Louvain: Peeters.

Ptolemy, Claudius. 1477. *Cosmographia.* Bologna.

———. 1478. *Cosmographia.* Rome.

———. 1482. *Cosmographia.* Ulm.

———. 1493. *Liber quadripartiti Ptholomei.* Venice.

———. 1980. *Tetrabiblos.* Ed. and trans. F. E. Robbins. Loeb Classical Library 435. Repr., Cambridge, Mass.: Harvard University Press.

———. 1998. *Ptolemy's "Almagest."* Trans. and ed. G. J. Toomer. Princeton, N.J.: Princeton University Press.

Ptolemy of Lucca. 1997. *On the Government of Rulers: "De regimine principum."* Philadelphia: University of Pennsylvania Press.

Rabasa, José. 1993. *Inventing America: Spanish Historiography and the Formation of Eurocentrism.* Norman: University of Oklahoma Press.

Raccolta di documenti e studi pubblicati dalla R. Commissione Colombiana pel Quarto Centenario dalla Scoperta dell'America. 1892–1896. 6 parts in 14 vols. Rome: Ministero della Pubblica Istruzione.

Rachewiltz, Igor de. 1971. *Papal Envoys to the Great Khan.* Stanford, Calif.: Stanford University Press.

Randles, W. G. L. 1990. The Evaluation of Columbus's India Project by Portuguese and Spanish Cosmographers in Light of the Geographical Science of the Period. *Imago mundi* 42:50–64.

Randolph, Daniel E. 1969a. Roger Bacon and the *De seminibus Scripturarum. Mediaeval Studies* 24:462–467.

———. 1969b. Apocalyptic Conversion: The Joachite Alternative to the Crusades. *Traditio* 25 (1969): 127–154.

Rashdall, Hastings. 1936. *The Universities of Europe in the Middle Ages.* 2 vols. Oxford: Clarendon Press.

Ravenstein, E. G. 1908. *Martin Behaim: His Life and His Globe.* London: George Philip and Son.

Reeves, Marjorie. 1969. *The Influence of Prophecy in the Later Middle Ages: A Study in Joachimism.* Oxford: Clarendon Press.

———. 1976/1999. *Joachim of Fiore & the Prophetic Future: A Medieval Study in Historical Thinking.* New rev. ed. Stroud, U.K.: Sutton.

Remesal, Antonio de. 1619/1964. *Historia general de las Indias y particular de la gobernación de Chiapa y Guatemala*. Ed. Carmelo Saenz de Santa María. Biblioteca de Autores Españoles. 2 vols. Madrid: Ediciones Atlas.

Resende, Garcia de. 1973. *Crónica de D. João II e miscelânea*. Lisbon: Imprensa Nacional—Casa da Moeda.

Rey Pastor, J. 1945. *La ciencia y la técnica en el descubrimiento de América*. Buenos Aires: Espasa-Calpe Argentina.

Richard, Jean. 1977. *La papauté et les missions d'Orient au Moyen Age (XIIIe–XVe siècles)*. Collection de l'École Française de Rome 33. Paris; Rome: École Française de Rome; Palais Farnèse.

Rogers, Francis M. 1976. Celestial Navigation: From Local Systems to a Global Conception. In *First Images of America*, ed. Fredi Chiappelli, 2:687–704. Berkeley: University of California Press.

Romm, James S. 1992. *The Edges of the Earth in Ancient Thought: Geography, Exploration, and Fiction*. Princeton, N.J.: Princeton University Press.

Rosa y López, Simón de la. 1891. Discurso del Doctor D. Simón de la Rosa y López. *Libros y autógrafos de D. Cristóbal Colón: Discursos leídos ante la Real Academia Sevillana de Buenas Letras en la recepción pública del Dr. D. Simón de la Rosa y López el 29 de junio de 1891*, 1–39. Seville: E. Rasco.

Rossabi, Morris. 1988. *Khubilai Khan: His Life and Times*. Berkeley: University of California Press.

Roux, Jean-Paul. 1993. *Histoire de l'empire mongol*. France: Librairie Arthème Fayard.

Rumeu de Armas, Antonio. 1970. *Hernando Colón, historiador de América*. Madrid: Diana.

———. 1973. *Hernando Colón, historiador del descubrimiento de América*. Madrid: Instituto de Cultura Hispánica.

———. 1976. El *Diario de a bordo* de Cristóbal Colón: El problema de la paternidad del extracto. *Revista de Indias* 143–144:7–17.

———. 1985. *Nueva luz sobre las Capitulaciones de Santa Fe de 1492 concertadas entre los Reyes Católicos y Cristóbal Colón: Estudio institucional y diplomático*. Madrid: Consejo Superior de Investigaciones Científicas.

———, ed. 1989. *Libro copiador de Cristóbal Colón: Correspondencia inédita con los Reyes Católicos sobre los viajes a América*. 2 vols. Madrid: Testimonio Compañía Editorial.

———. 1992. *El Tratado de Tordesillas*. Madrid: MAPFRE.

———. 1996. *España en el Africa atlántica*. 2 vols. Las Palmas de Gran Canaria: Cabildo Insular de Gran Canaria.

Russell, Jeffrey Burton. 1991. *Inventing the Flat Earth: Columbus and Modern Historians*. New York: Praeger.

Russell, Peter. 2000. *Prince Henry "The Navigator": A Life*. New Haven: Yale University Press.

Russell-Wood, A. J. R. 1995. Before Columbus: Portugal's African Prelude to the Middle Passage and Contribution to Discourse on Race and Slavery. In *Race, Discourse, and the Origin of the Americas: A New World View*, ed. Vera Lawrence Hyatt and Rex Nettleford. Washington, D.C.: Smithsonian Institution Press.

Sahagún, Bernardino de. 1979–1980. *Códice florentino [Historia de las cosas de la Nueva España]*. Facsimile No. 574. 3 vols. Mexico City: Archivo General de la Nación; Florence: Biblioteca Medicea Laurenziana.

Sale, Kirkpatrick. 1990. *The Conquest of Paradise: Christopher Columbus and the Columbian Legacy*. New York: Alfred A. Knopf.

Salembier, Louis. 1914. Pierre d'Ailly and the Discovery of America. *Historical Records and Studies of the U.S. Catholic Society* 7:90–131.

Sambursky, Shmuel, ed. and trans. 1982. *The Concept of Place in Late Neoplatonism*. Jerusalem: Israel Academy of Sciences and Humanities.

Saunders, A. C. de C. M. 1982. *A Social History of Black Slaves and Freedmen in Portugal 1441–1555*. Cambridge: Cambridge University Press.

Scafi, Alessandro. 2006. *Mapping Paradise: A History of Heaven on Earth*. Chicago: University of Chicago Press.

Schmitt, Charles B. 1986 Pseudo-Aristotle in the Middle Ages. In Kraye, Ryan, and Schmitt 1986, 3–14.

Schnaubelt, Joseph C., and Frederick Van Fleteren. 1998. *Columbus and the New World*. New York: Peter Lang.

Schneider, Jakob M. 1932. Aus Astronomie und Geologie des hl. Albert des Grossen. *Divus Thomas* 10:41–67.

Schneider, Pierre. 1997. La confusion entre l'Inde et l'Ethiopie (VIIIème s. av. J.-C.–VIème s. ap. J.-C). PhD diss., ANRT, Université de Lille.

Seed, Patricia. *Ceremonies of Possession in Europe's Conquest of the New World 1492–1640*. New York: Cambridge University Press, 1995.

Seneca, Lucius Annaeus. 1971–1972. *Natural Questions*. Trans. Thomas H. Corcoran. 2 vols. Loeb Classical Library 7, 10. Cambridge, Mass.: Harvard University Press.

Sepúlveda, Juan Ginés de. 1550/1997. *Apología en favor del libro sobre las justas causas de la guerra*. Ed. A. Moreno Hernández. Trans. Angel Losada. Obras completas 3. Pozoblanco: Exmo. Ayuntamiento de Pozoblanco.

———. 1984. *Demócrates segundo o de las justas causas de la guerra contra los indios*. Ed. and trans. Angel Losada. 2nd ed. Madrid: Consejo Superior de Investigaciones Científicas; Instituto Francisco de Vitoria.

Sévérac, Jourdain de. 1863. *"Mirabilia descripta": The Wonders of the East*. Hakluyt Society, 1st ser., no. 31. London: Hakluyt society.

Silverberg, Robert. 1972. *The Realm of Prester John*. Athens: Ohio University Press.

Simek, Rudolf. 1996. *Heaven and Earth in the Middle Ages: The Physical World before Columbus*. Trans. Angela Hall. Woodbridge, U.K.: Boydell Press.

Siraisi, Nancy G. 1990. *Medieval and Early Renaissance Medicine: An Introduction to Knowledge and Practice*. Chicago: University of Chicago Press.

Slessarev, Vsevolod. 1959. *Prester John: The Letter and the Legend*. Minneapolis: University of Minnesota Press.

Smith, William, ed. 1854–[1857]. *Dictionary of Greek and Roman Geography*. 2 vols. Boston: Little, Brown.

Smoller, Laura Ackerman. 1994. *History, Prophecy, and the Stars: The Christian Astrology of Pierre d'Ailly, 1350–1420*. Princeton, N.J.: Princeton University Press.

Snowden, Frank M., Jr. 1970. *Blacks in Antiquity: Ethiopians in the Greco-Roman Experience*. Cambridge, Mass.: Belknap Press of Harvard University Press.

Solinus, Caius Julius. 1958. *C. Iulii Solini Collectanea rerum memorabilium*. Ed. Th. Mommsen. Berlin: Weidmannsche Verlagsbuchhandlung.

Sorajbi, Richard, ed. 1990. *Aristotle Transformed: The Ancient Commentators and Their Influence*. Ithaca, N.Y.: Cornell University Press.

Stahl, William Harris, Richard Johnson, and E. L. Burge, eds. 1971–1977. *Martianus Capella and the Seven Liberal Arts*. 2 vols. Records of Civilization: Sources and Studies 84. New York: Columbia University Press.

Stepan, Nancy Leys. 2001. *Picturing Tropical Nature*. London: Reaktion Books.

Strabo. 1917–1932. *Geography*. Trans. Horace Leonard Jones. 8 vols. Loeb Classical Library 49, 50, 182, 192, 211, 223, 241, 267. Cambridge, Mass.: Harvard University Press.

Sweeney, Leo. 1983. Are Plotinus and Albertus Magnus Neoplatonists? In *Graceful Reason: Essays in Ancient and Medieval Philosophy Presented to Joseph Owens, on the Occasion of His Seventy-Fifth Birthday and Fiftieth Anniversary of His Ordination*, ed. Lloyd P. Gerson, 177–202. Toronto: Pontifical Institute of Medieval Studies.

Sweet, James H. 1997. The Iberian Roots of American Racist Thought. *William and Mary Quarterly*, 3rd ser., 54 (1): 143–166.

Sweet, Leonard I. 1986 Christopher Columbus and the Millennial Vision of the New World. *Catholic Historical Review* 72:369–382, 715–716.

Syria, Pedro de. 1602/1998. *Arte de la verdadera navegación*. Valencia. In González-Aller Hierro 1998.

Tafur, Pero. 1874. *Andanças é viajes de Pero Tafur por diversas partes del mundo avidos (1435–1439)*. 2
vols. Colección de libros españoles raros ó curiosos 8. 24 vols. in 25. Madrid: Miguel Ginesta.

Takahashi, Ken'ichi, trans. and ed. 1992. *The Medieval Translations of Euclid's "Catoptrica."* Japan:
Kyushu University Press.

Tarrant, Dorothy. 1960. Greek Metaphors of Light. *Classical Quarterly*, n.s., 10 (2): 181–187.

Taviani, Paolo Emilio. 1985a. *Christopher Columbus: The Grand Design*. Trans. J. Gilbert and
W. Weaver. London: Orbis.

———. 1985b. Ancora sulle vicende di Colombo in Castiglia. *Presencia italiana en Andalucía: Siglos
XIV–XVII*, 221–248. Seville: Escuela de Estudios Hispanoamericanos.

———. 1985c. Si perfeziona in Castiglia il grande disegno di Colombo. *Presencia italiana en
Andalucía: Siglos XIV–XVII*, 1–19. Seville: Escuela de Estudios Hispanoamericanos.

———. 1990. Notes for the Historicogeographical Reconstruction of the First Voyage and
Discovery of the Indies. In *The Journal: Account of the First Voyage and Discovery of the Indies*, by
Christopher Columbus, ed. Paolo Emilio Taviani and Consuelo Varela, trans. Mark A. Beckwith
and Luciano F. Farina, 67–423. Nuova Raccolta Colombiana 1/2. Rome: Istituto Poligrafico e
Zecca dello Stato; Libreria dello Stato.

———. 1991. *The Voyages of Columbus: The Great Discovery*. Trans. Marc A. Beckwith and Luciano F.
Farina. 2 vols. Novara: Istituto Geografico De Agostini.

———. 1996. *Cristoforo Colombo*. 3 vols. Rome: Società Geografica Italiana.

Taviani, Paolo Emilio, and Ilaria Luzzana Caraci. 1990. Schede di commento alle *Historie*. In
Fernando Colombo, *Le Historie della Vita e dei Fatti dell'Ammiraglio don Cristoforo Colombo*, ed.
Paolo Emilio Taviani and Ilaria Luzzana Caraci, 1:7–92. Rome: Istituto Poligrafico e Zecca dello
Stato.

Taylor, Richard C. 1986. The *Kalam Fi Mahd al-Khair* (*Liber de causis*) in the Islamic Philosophical
Milieu. In Kraye, Ryan, and Schmitt 1986, 37–52.

Thomas Aquinas, Saint. 1951. *In libros Politicorum Aristotelis expositio*. Taurini (Rome): Marietti.

———. 1963–1964. *Exposition of Aristotle's Treatise "On the Heavens."* Trans. R. F. Larcher and
Pierre H. Conway. 2 vols. Columbus, Ohio: College of St. Mary of the Springs.

Thomas, Hugh. 2003. *Rivers of Gold: The Rise of the Spanish Empire, from Columbus to Magellan*. New
York: Random House.

Thorndike, Lynn. 1923. *A History of Magic and Experimental Science*. 8 vols. New York: Columbia
University Press.

———. 1949. *The "Sphere" of Sacrobosco and Its Commentators*. Chicago: University of Chicago
Press.

———. 1955. The True Place of Astrology in the History of Science. *Isis* 46:273–278.

Tibbetts, Gerald R. 1992. Later Cartographic Developments. In *Cartography in the Traditional Islamic and South Asian Societies,* ed. J. B. Harley and David Woodward, 137–155. The History of Cartography 2/1. Chicago: University of Chicago Press.

Tilmann, Jean Paul. 1971. *An Appraisal of the Geographical Works of Albertus Magnus and His Contributions to Geographical Thought.* Ann Arbor, Mich.: Department of Geography.

Tomasch, Sylvia, and Sealy Gilles, eds. 1998. *Text and Territory: Geographical Imagination in the European Middle Ages.* Philadelphia: University of Pennsylvania Press.

Tooley, Marian J. 1953. Bodin and the Mediaeval Theory of Climate. *Speculum* 28.1:64–83.

Tornamira, Francisco Vicente. 1585/1998. *Chronographia, y Repertorio de los tiempos.* Pamplona. In González-Aller Hierro 1998.

Travaglia, Pinella. 1999. *Magic, Causality, and Intentionality: The Doctrine of Rays in al-Kindi.* Florence: SISMEL, Edizioni del Galluzzo.

Ulloa, Luis. 1928. *El pre-descubrimiento hispano-catalán de América en 1477: Xristo-ferens Colom, Fernando el Católico, y la Cataluña española.* Paris: Maissonneuve Frères.

Van Peursen, C. A. 1966. *Body, Soul, Spirit: A Survey of the Body-Mind Problem.* London: Oxford University Press.

Varela, Consuelo. 1988. Introduction to *Diario del primer y tercer viaje de Cristóbal Colón,* by Bartolomé de las Casas, ed. Miguel Angel Medina et al., 11–40. Vol. 14 of Castañeda Delgado 1988–1998.

———. 1992. Introduction. In Colón 1992, 80–87.

Varela Marcos, Jesús, and María Montserrat León Guerrero. 2002. *Colón, su tesis "pezonoidal" del globo terráqueo y el itinerario del tercer viaje: La fantasía del Paraiso Terrenal.* Valladolid: Universidad de Valladolid.

———. 2003. *El itinerario de Cristóbal Colón (1451–1506).* Valladolid: Diputación de Valladolid; Cabildo de Gran Canaria; Instituto Interuniversitario de Estudios de Iberoamérica y Portugal, Casa de Colón.

Vega, Garcilaso de la, [el Inca]. 1609. *Primera parte de los "Commentarios reales."* Lisbon.

Velázquez Minaya, Francisco. 1618. *Esfera, forma del mundo, con una breue descripcion del Mapa.* Madrid.

Verlinden, Charles. 1955. *L'esclavage dans l'Europe médiévale.* Bruges: De Tempel.

Vignaud, Henry. 1902. *Toscanelli and Columbus.* London: Sands.

———. 1905. *Études critiques sur la vie de Colomb avant ses découvertes.* Paris: Welter.

———. 1911. *Histoire critique de la grande entreprise de Christophe Colomb.* 2 vols. Paris: Welter.

Vigneras, Louis-André. 1957. The Cape Breton Landfall: 1494 or 1497: Note on a Letter from John Day. *Canadian Historical Review* 38:219–229.

Virgil. 1981. *The Georgics*. Ed. Alistair Elliot. Trans. John Dryden. Ashington, Northumberland: Mid Northumberland Arts Group.

Vitruvius Pollio, Marcus. 1931–1934. *On Architecture*. Ed. Paul Granger. 2 vols. Loeb Classical Library 251, 280. Cambridge, Mass.: Harvard University Press.

Vodraska, Stanley Luis. 1969. Pseudo-Aristotle: *De causis propietatum et elementorum*. PhD diss., University of London.

Voegelin, Eric. 1940–1941. The Mongol Orders of Submission to European Powers, 1245–1255. *Byzantion* 15:378–412.

Wagner, Henry Raup, and Helen Rand Parish. 1967. *The Life and Writings of Bartolomé de las Casas*. Albuquerque: University of New Mexico Press.

Wagner, Michael. 1999. Plotinus on the Nature of Physical Reality. Chapter 6 in *The Cambridge Companion to Plotinus*, ed. Lloyd P. Gerson, 130–170. Reprinted with corrections. Cambridge: Cambridge University Press.

Waldseemüller, Martin. 1507/1907. *The "Cosmographiae introductio" of Martin Waldseemüller in Facsimile*. Trans. and intro Joseph Fischer and Franz von Vieser. Ed. Charles George Herbermann. New York: United States Catholic Historical Society.

Wallace, William A. 1978. The Philosophical Setting of Medieval Science. In Lindberg 1978b, 91–119.

Wallis, Helen. 1992. Cartographic Knowledge of the World in 1492. *Mariner's Mirror* 78 (4): 407–418.

Waters, David. 1992. Columbus's Portuguese Inheritance. *Mariner's Mirror* 78 (4):385–405.

Watts, Pauline Moffitt. 1985. Prophecy and Discovery: On the Spiritual Origins of Christopher Columbus's "Enterprise of the Indies." *American Historical Review* 90:73–102.

———. 2007. The European Religious Worldview and Its Influence on Mapping. In Woodward 2007b, 1:382–400.

Weckmann, Luis. 1949. *Las bulas alejandrinas de 1493 y la teoría política del papado medieval: Estudio de la supremacía papal sobre las islas 1091–1493*. Mexico City: Editorial Jus.

Weerakkody, D. P. M. 1997. *Taprobanê: Ancient Sri Lanka as Known to the Greeks and Romans*. Turnhout: Brepols.

Weisheipl, James A. 1964. Curriculum of the Faculty of Arts at Oxford in the Early Fourteenth Century. *Mediaeval Studies* 28:151–175.

———. 1978. The Nature, Scope, and Classification of the Sciences. In Lindberg 1978b, 461–482.

———. 1980a. Albert's Works on Natural Science (*libri naturales*) in Probably Chronological Order. Appendix to Weisheipl 1980c, 565–577.

———. 1980b. The Life and Works of St. Albert the Great. In Weisheipl 1980c, 1–51.

———, ed. 1980c. *Albertus Magnus and the Sciences: Commemorative Essays, 1980.* Toronto: Pontifical Institute of Mediaeval Studies.

West, Delno C. 1992. Christopher Columbus and His Enterprise to the Indies: Scholarship of the Last Quarter Century. *William and Mary Quarterly* 49 (2): 254–277.

———. 1998. The Imagined World of Christopher Columbus. In Schnaubelt and Van Fleteren 1998, 87–116.

West, Delno C., and August Kling, eds. 1991. *The "Libro de las profecías" of Christopher Columbus: An "en face" Edition.* Gainesville: University of Florida Press.

Wey Gómez, Nicolás. 1992. Cannibalism as Defacement: Columbus's Account of the Fourth Voyage. *Journal of Hispanic Philology* 16 (2):195–208.

———. 2007. A Poetics of Dismemberment: The *Book of Job* and the Cannibals of Cariay in Columbus's Account of the Fourth Voyage. *Colonial Latin American Literary Review* 16 (1):109–123.

White, Lynn, Jr. 1962. *Medieval Technology and Social Change.* Oxford: Clarendon Press.

Williamson, J. A. 1930. The Early Falsification of West Indian Latitudes. *Geographical Journal* 75:263–265.

Wittkower, Rudolf. 1942. Marvels of the East: A Study in the History of Monsters. *Journal of the Warburg and Courtauld Institutes* 5:159–197.

Woodward, David. 1987. Medieval *Mappaemundi.* In Harley and Woodward 1987, 286–370.

———. 2007a. Cartography and the Renaissance: Continuity and Change. In Woodward 2007b, 1:3–24.

———, ed. 2007b. *Cartography in the European Renaissance.* The History of Cartography 3/1–2. Chicago: University of Chicago Press.

Woodward, David, and Herbert M. Howe. 1997. Roger Bacon on Geography and Cartography. Chapter 9 in *Roger Bacon and the Sciences: Commemorative Essays,* ed. Jeremiah Hackett, 199–222. Leiden: Brill.

Wright, John Kirtland. 1923. Notes on the Knowledge of Latitudes and Longitudes in the Middle Ages. *Isis* 5:75–98.

Wyckoff, Dorothy. 1967. Introduction to *Book of Minerals,* by Albertus Magnus, trans. and ed. Dorothy Wyckoff, xiii–xlii. Oxford: Clarendon Press.

Wyngaert, Anastasius van den. 1929. *Itinera et relationes fratrum minorum saeculi XIII et XIV.* Sinica Franciscana 1. Quaracchi (Florence): Collegium S. Bonaventurae.

Young, Filson. 1906. *Christopher Columbus and the New World of His Discovery.* 2 vols. Philadelphia: J. B. Lippincott, 1906.

Yule, Henry, ed. and trans. 1866. *Cathay and the Way Hither: Being a Collection of Medieval Notices of China*. 2 vols. Works Issued for the Hakluyt Society 36–37. London: Hakluyt Society.

Zamora, Margarita. 1993. *Reading Columbus*. Berkeley: University of California Press.

Zamorano, Rodrigo. 1581/1998. *Compendio de la arte de navegar*. Seville. In González-Aller Hierro 1998.

Zand-Ākāsīh: Iranian or Greater Bundahišn. 1956. Trans. Behramgore Tahmuras Anklesaria. Bombay: Rahnumae Mazdayasnan Sabha.

Zarncke, Friedrich. 1879–1883. *Der Priester Johannes*. Abhandlungen der Philologisch-Historischen Classe der Königlich Sächsischen Gesellschaft der Wissenschaften 7, 827–1030; 8, 1–186. Leipzig: S. Hirzel.

———. 1996a. Prester John's Letter to the Byzantine Emperor Emanuel. In Beckingham and Hamilton 1996, 40–102.

———. 1996b. Alexander III's Letter to Prester John. In Beckingham and Hamilton 1996, 103–112.

Zavala, Silvio A. 1973. *La encomienda indiana*. 2nd ed. Biblioteca Porrúa 53. Mexico City: Editorial Porrúa.

Zimmermann, F. W. 1986. The Origins of the So-Called *Theology of Aristotle*. In Kraye, Ryan, and Schmitt 1986, 110–240.

Zurara, Gomes Eanes de. 1978–1981. *Crónica dos feitos notáveis que se passaram na conquista da Guiné por mandado do Infante D. Henrique*. Ed. Torquato de Sousa Soares. 2 vols. Lisbon: Academia Portugesa da História.

Index

Page numbers in boldface type indicate illustrations.

Armstrong, A. H., 501n143, 505n190

Arrian

    Anabasis of Alexander, 78

    Indica, 78, 179, 214, 220, 406

Artaxerxes II, 176

Arym, 189, 432

astrology

    Arabic, 93–94, 262, 266–269, 270

    celestial influence, theory of, 92–95

    Greek, 262

    Indian, 280

    scholastic and late medieval, 242, 255, 262, 265, 268–269, 271, 289

Augustine, Saint, 111, 113, 115, 124, 131, 149, 153, 232, 241, 277, 446n19

    on the antipodes, 119–123

    De civitate Dei, 119, 123, 131, 451n38, 463n145, 494n48, 494n49

    De genesi ad litteram, 122–123, 127, 261, 494n48, 495n49, 505n176

    doctrine of illumination, 263

Aujac, Germaine, 449n27

Averroës, 49, 69, 85, 148, 153, 241–242, 260, 277, 457n86, 503n152

Avicenna, 69, 85, 234, 274

    Canon of Medicine, 233, 278–279, 291, 406

    De animalibus, 233

    De celo et mundo, 503n152

    Philosophia prima, 241

    Sufficientia, 503n152, 505n176

Ayala, Pedro de, 332

Ayllón, Lucas Vázquez de, 52

Azores, 19, 308, 310, 325–327, 331, 397, 398, 429, 431

Aztecs, 90

Bacon, Roger, 96, 123, 153, 235, 265, 266, 267, 380–381, 447n24, 493n36, 507n220

    De multiplicatione specierum, 501n127

    De speculis comburentibus, 509n245

    Opus maius, 67, 144, 150, 233, 235, 239, 268, 381, 472n35, 500n117

Bactria, 345, 354

Baghdad, Abbasid Caliphate of, 378, 381

Bahamas, **6, 8–9,** 18, 37, 316, 320–321, 397, 409, 418, 428. *See also* Fernandina (Long Island); Isabela (Crooked Island); San Salvador (Guanahaní, Watling Island); Santa María de la Concepción (Rum Cay)

Bahía Cortés, 23

Baldaia, Afonso Gonçalves, 305

Ballesteros Beretta, Antonio, 42, 367, 470n13, 479n117, 490n10

Barros, João de, 453n54, 458n97

    Ásia, 132–134, 136–139, 141, 302–304, 306, 307, 311

Bartholomew, Saint, 527n135

Basil, Saint

    Exegetic Homilies, 474n49

    Hexameron, 127

Beatus of Liebana, *Commentarium in Apolcalypsim,* 473n45

Beckingham, C. F., 527n138

Behaim, Martin, 11, **12–13, 14–15,** 18, 47, 140, 155, 193, 196–197, 302, **303,** 315, 341–344, 372, 379, 401, 458n94, 519n5

Bello, Andrés, "Silva a la agricultura," 57

Benedict XII, pope, 297

Benedict XIII, pope, 299, 318

Bernáldez, Andrés, *Historia de los Reyes Católicos,* 4–5, 124, 198

Crates of Mallos, 118–119, 122–123, 131, 180, 187, 273, 366, 370

Cresques, Abraham, 167, **168–173**, 300–302, **301**, 344, 378

Crosignani, Ginevra, 457n90

Ctesias of Cnidus, 214, 217–218, 422

　　Persica, 176

Cuba (Juana), 4, 10, 16–17, 18–19, 22, 29, 178, 210, 316, 320–321, 356, 363, 365, 373, 415–417, 419–420, 428

　　Alpha et Omega (Cape Maisi), 17, 23, 51, 411, 427

　　Cape Cruz, 23

　　Río de Mares (Puerto Gibara), 17, 40, 306, 400, 417–418, 420–423, 427

Cuneo, Michele, 51, 424

curse of Ham, 70–71, 78–80

Damietta, 377, 383

Darius I, king of Persia, 78

Daston, Lorraine, 530n18

David, king "of India," 377

Day, John, 377, 444n7

De adventu patriarchae Indorum ad urbem, 374–375

De divisione locorum, 274

De natura latitudinis et longitudinis, 494n45

Deseada/La Désirade, 22

De sex rerum principiis, 94

Deza, Diego de, 231–232, 235

Dias, Bartholomeu, 134, 142, 154, 155–156, 193, 344, 515n75

Diaz, Pero, 327–329, 332

Diocletian, emperor, 151

Diodorus Siculus, *Bibliotheca historica*, 165, 176–177, 214, 220, 222

dioikein (the act of managing a household), 92

Dionysius the Areopagite, 462n126. *See also* Pseudo-Dionysius

Doldrums, 28, 40

Dominica, 22

dominium, 84, 282

Duarte, king of Portugal, 305, 318–319, 514n49

Du Bartas, Guillaume de Salluste, *La sepmaine*, 453n45

Eanes, Gil, 304

Edessa, 376

Egypt, 179, 181, 183–184, 186, 262, 350, 377–378, 382

El Cano, Juan Sebastián, 36, 164

elements, four, 117, 124–126, 129, 135, 241–242, 247–249

El Hierro, 10, 11, 16, 19, 87, 161, 164, 302, 303, 310, 361, 396, 403, 410–411, 421

Eljigidei, 382

Empedocles, 117

Enrique III, king of Castile, 299, 319, 380

Enríquez, Alfonso, 368

epithumia (appetite), 288

Eratosthenes, 49, 73, 163, 179, 180–181, **182**, 183–188, 238, 272, 341, 349, 356, 372, 477n93, 522n48

　　Geography, 180, 234, 277

　　Measurement of the Earth, 180

Erichthonius, king of Athens, 119

Escalante de Mendoza, Juan de, 462n128

Escobedo, Rodrigo de, 320

180–181, 183–193, 196, 273–274, 300, 315, 329–331, 339–341

equinoctial hours, 185–186

five zones, theory of, xiii, 50–51, 53, 71–74, 79, 87, 96, 111, 115, 131, 134, 148, 162–163, 188, 233–234, 268, 272–275, 277–278, 340, 398, 428, 492n15

global circumference, 180, 483n41

Greco-Roman, 47, 49, 61, 72–74, 78, 111, 115–120, 162, 179–181, 183–188, 191–192, 237, 349

medieval and early modern, 48, 78–79, 237, 273

open systems, 111, 115–119, 123, 127, 139, 141, 147, 149, 157, 167, 187, 273, 339, 366

orbis terrarum as exception to Aristotelian principles, 114, 118–119, 123, 126, 131–132, 134–135, 152, 154, 157, 231

reflecting concept of world-machine, 67–69

relative distribution of land and water, 114, 116–117, 124–130, 135, 148–149, 155, 156–157, 339–340, 432

scholastic, 61, 66–67, 74, 92–93, 105, 246

tripartite conception of, 69–71, 74, 105, 236, 288–289

water circulation, theories of, 116–117, 127

geopolitics, Greco-Latin tripartite, 69–71, 79, 84–86, 88–92, 100, 105–106, 112, 238, 260, 282, 285–286, 288–289, 354–355, 399, 426–427

scriptural interpretation of, 70–71, 91

Geraldini, Alessandro, 112–113, 130–131, 134–135, 148, 156, 193, 274

Itinerarium ad regiones, 112–113

Geraldini, Antonio, 112

Gerard of Cremona, 96, 449n27, 492n14

Gerson, Jean, 94–95. *See also Tractatus de ymagine mundi* (d'Ailly and Gerson)

Trigilogium astrologie theologisate, 269, 271

Gervase of Tilbury, *Otia imperialia*, 526n135, 527n138

Gil, Juan, 443n7

Gillet, M. S., 492n24

gold. *See* precious metals, stones, and spices

Goldenberg, David M., 453n46, 453n53

Gomera, 396

Gómez-Lobo, Alfonso, 511n301

Gonçalvez, Antão, 71

Gondisalvi, Dominic, 492n14

Good Hope, Cape of, 134, 142, 156, 344

Grafton, Anthony, 446n20, 449n29, 463n145

Granada, 109, 297, 309, 323, 386

Grant, Edward, 461n121

Great Chain of Being, The (Lovejoy), 257

Greater Antilles, 210. *See also* Cuba (Juana); Hispaniola (Çibao, Haiti and Dominican Republic); Jamaica; San Juan Bautista (Puerto Rico)

Great Khān, 18, 137, 141, 166, 349, 352, 354, 357, 361, 363, 365, 370, 380, 381, 385, 387–389, 390, 412, 416–420

Greenblatt, Stephen, 364

Gregorio (advisor to Fernando I), 104

Gregory X, pope, 383

Grosseteste, Robert, 96, 265, 266, 270, 493n36, 508n241

De lineis, 233, 267–268

De luce, 261

De natura locorum, 233, 267–268

Guacanagarí, 316

Guinea, 86–87, 111, 144, 223, 226, 296, 308–310, 312, 315, 317, 322–324, 327, 332, 355, 366

latitude. *See also* monstrous or deformed
humans and animals; place
calculation of, 47, 176–177
correlated to animal/human natures, 49, 53,
56, 84–86, 260
and nature of place, 151, 164, 175, 225, 429
politics of, 53–54
relation to natural resources, 22, 40, 51,
185
relation of temperature to, 10, 22, 28, 40, 42,
43, 44, 47–48, 50, 225, 275–276, 429,
432–433
science of, 44
La Ysabela, 18–19, 23, 28, 51, 178, 486n96
Leeward Islands, 22
Lemay, Richard, 500n110
Leo X, pope, 112–113
Leonessa, Pompeo Mongallo da, 470n13
Lesser Antilles, 28, 89, 210, 223–225, 361. *See
also* Deseada/La Désirade; Dominica;
Leeward Islands; Trinidad; Virgin
Islands; Windward Islands
Lestringant, Frank, 531n30
letter of credence. *See Carta de creencia*
Letter of Prester John, The, 375
Levin, Harry, 533n89
Libro de las profecías, 197–198, 381, 471n13
Libro del cognosçimiento, 344–345, 378, 512n5
light, metaphysics of, 260–266. *See also* rays,
doctrine of
Lima, Peru, 89
Lindberg, David, 504n170
Livingstone, David N., 447n20
logismos (calculation), 288
Lollis, Cesare de, 45
Lombard, Peter, *Sententiae*, 102, 239

López de Gómara, Francisco, 17, 66
Historia general de las Indias, 5, 36, 52, 199
Louis IX, king of France, 298, 382
Lovejoy, Arthur, 257, 478n99
Lucan (Marcus Annaeus Lucanus), *De bello
civili*, 51
Lucretius Carus, Titus, *De rerum natura*, 93

Mac Donald, Robert, 510n278
Machiavelli, Niccolò, 449n29
machina mundi, 61, 67, 69, 93–97, 102, 399
Macrobius, Ambrosius Theodosius, 74, 119
Commentarium in somnium Scipionis, 72, 126,
188, 241, 258, 440n68, 446n19
Madagascar, 167, 196, 341
Madeira, 308
Magellan, Ferdinand, 163–164
Maimonides, 242, 503n152
Mair, John, 102–103, 238, 287
In secundum librum sententiarum, 102
Malabar Coast, 174
Maldonado, Lorenzo Ferrer, *Imagen del mundo*,
67
Malocello, Lancellotto, 297–298, 300
Mamlūk, 300, 529n165
Mandeville, John, 365
Travels, 124, 219, 339
Mandonnet, Pierre, 231–233, 235
Mangi, 11, 18, 23, 36, 37, 140, 166, 178, 196,
342–344, 352, 355–356, 380, 385, 389,
403–404, 414, 416–419. *See also* Zaiton
Manuel, Byzantine emperor, 375, 380
Manuel I, king of Portugal, 174
Manzano Manzano, Juan, 45, 360–363, 370–371,
373–374, 443n7, 471n13, 524n86, 524n87

Nearchus, 78, 179–180

Necho II, king of Egypt, 477n93

Negus of Ethiopia, 376, 378–379

Nemptai, 350, 352–353, 385

Neoplatonism, 66, 72, 93–94, 127, 241–242,
250, 256, 259–260, 270, 276, 281, 283

Nestorianism, 353, 376, 382–383

New Laws, 458n97

New World, 95, 211

Nicaragua, 36, 425

Niccolò of Vicenza, 384

Nicholas V, pope, 307–309, 323

Nicholas of Damascus, *De vegetabilibus*, 493n42

Nicholas of Lyra, 112–113, 130–131, 148–149, 154,
470n13

Nicholas of Sicily, 461n124

Nicholas of Venice, 350, 352–353, 365, 379, 385

Niña, 313–314, 395, 425

non-Christians, Christian dominion over, 318,
320–321. *See also* Christian mission

Nubia, 378

Nuremberg, 11, 140, 193

Ocean River, 72, 114–119, 127, 132, 273, 308

Odyssey (Homer), 74, 118–119, 162, 273, 474n47

Ögedei, 380

Oghul Qaimish, 382

Oghul Tutmish, 383

oikoumenē, xiii, 118–119, 180, 193. *See also*
geography: dimensions of known
inhabited world

Oliva, Hernán Pérez de, 17

Olympiodorus the Younger, 127

Onesicritus, 78, 179–180, 215, 477n93

optics, 242, 267–268

orbis terrarum. See geography: dimensions of
known inhabited world

Order of Christ, 308

Orinoco River, 4, 28–29, 116, 136, 147, 152, 154,
174, 398, 430, 433

Otto of Freising, *Chronica sive historia de duabus
civitatibus*, 376, 522n50

Ovid (Publius Ovidius Naso), *Metamorphoses*,
50–51, 473n47

Oviedo y Valdés, Gonzalo Fernández de, 43, 45
Historia general y natural de las Indias, 5, 90,
199, 302, 357, 443n7

Oxford University, 239

Pagden, Anthony, 53, 100, 103, 451n36, 456n79,
460n113, 465n154

Palacio de Liria, Madrid, 199

Palencia, Alfonso de, 442n6

Palermo, 239

Palos de la Frontera, 5

Panamá, 36

papal bulls, 19, 295–299, 307–309, 321–326,
328, 331–332
Aeterni regis clementia (6 June 1481), 309, 323,
331–332
Apostolatus officium (22 January 1403), 299,
318
Desiderabiliter affectantes (11 December 1344),
512n20
Dudum siquidem (26 September 1493), 105,
325, 331, 332
Eximie devotionis (3 May 1493), 324
Gaudemus et exultamus (30 April 1341), 297
Inter cetera (13 March 1456), 308, 321–323,
331–332, 370

San Juan Bautista (Puerto Rico), 23

San Pablo, Dominican convent of, 98

San Salvador (Guanahaní, Watling Island), 11, 16, 18, 19, 40, 53, 87, 89, 222, 303, 310, 317, 340, 357, 364–365, 404–405, 407–414, 417, 422

Santa Crose (Brazil), 203, 210, 238

Santa María, 23, 306, 326, 374, 395, 412, 422

Santa María, Pablo de. *See* Paul of Burgos

Santa María de la Concepción (Rum Cay), 16, 321, 412–413

Santa María de la Encarnación, cathedral of, 112–113

Santa María de la Rábida, monastery of, 330, 491n11

Santángel, Luis de, 17–18, 19, 86, 166, 364, 369, 372

Santo Domingo, Dominican Republic, 103, 112

São Jorge da Mina, 86–87, 134, 144, 210, 235, 312, 317–318, 324

scala naturae, 257, 446n19

"schism," Americanist, 45

Schneider, Jakob, 492n24

scholasticism, high, 239

Scoiran (Socotra), 167

Scot, Michael, 96, 492n15

Scylax of Caryanda, 78, 179

Scythia, 345, 349, 352–356

Segovia, Rodrigo Sánchez de, 320

Select Documents Illustrating the Four Voyages (Jane), 46

Seneca, Lucius Annaeus, 148, 153

  Naturales quaestiones, 116

  Tragedies, 443n6

Sepúlveda, Juan Ginés de, 5, 56, 104–105, 238, 465n145

  Apologia pro libro de iustis belli, 105, 468n180

  Democrates secundus, 105, 287, 326–327

Seres. *See* Silk People

Sermon on the Mount, 400

Sesostris II, king of Egypt, 475n75

Seville, cathedral of, 98

Sforza, Ascanio, 395, 477n94

Shelford, April, 446n20

Sierra Leone, 28, 429, 431–432

Silk People, 165–166, 210, 349, 355

silk trade, 165–166, 210, 349, 355

Simplicius of Cilicia, 500n116

Sinai, 166–167

Sind, 480n10, 527n138

Siraisi, Nancy G., 446n20

Sixtus IV, pope, 309, 323

skin color, latitude/place and, 11, 18, 40, 42, 49, 74, 78–79, 84, 86–87, 218–219, 226, 311, 315, 406–407, 430, 432. *See also* physiognomy

slavery. *See also* Amerindians: subjuation of; non-Christians, Christian dominion over

  African, 70–71, 86, 88, 206, 223, 304–306, 430, 458n97

  Canary Islands, 298

  legal status of, 102–104, 299, 306

  natural, 102, 104, 237, 238, 272, 282, 286, 399, 401, 404, 456n79, 460n113

  papal authorization for, 308

  scriptural justifications for, 70–71

Socrates, 263, 288

Sogdiana, 345

Solinus, Caius Julius, 177, 214, 219, 220

West Indies, 161–163, 175
  geographical/natural similarity to East Indies, 164, 175
  map of, **6–7, 8–9**
William of Moerbeke, 282, 508n241, 510n277
William of Rubruck, 381, 383
William of Tripoli, 384
Windward Islands, 29. *See also* Dominica
world-machine. *See machina mundi*

Xenophon, *De aequivocis,* 465n145

Yeh-lü Ta-shih, 376

Zaiton, 17, 23, 166, 341–344, 384, 388, 411, 421, 427
Zamora, Margarita, 363–364, 529n177
Zanzibar, 167, 196, 341
Zar'a Yâkob, 378–379
Zhu Yuanzang, 352
Zindj, 480n10, 527n138
Zipangu. *See* Çipango
zodiac, 73–74, 270
Zoroastrianism, 262
Zorzi, Alessandro, *Informazione di Bartolomeo Colombo,* 203, **206–209**, 210–211, **212–213**, 438n31
Zurara, Gomes Eanes de, *Crónica dos feitos notáveis,* 71, 132–133, 302–304, 306, 458n97
Zurita, Jerónimo de, 328
  Historia del rey D. Fernando el Católico, 313